Unless Recalled Earlier

Data Structures
for Personal Computers

YEDIDYAH LANGSAM
MOSHE J. AUGENSTEIN
AARON M. TENENBAUM

Department of Computer and Information Science
Brooklyn College of The City University of New York

PRENTICE-HALL, INC.
Englewood Cliffs, New Jersey 07632

Library of Congress Cataloging in Publication Data

Langsam, Yedidyah   (date)
    Data structures for personal computers.

    Bibliography: p.
    Includes index.
    1. Data structures (Computer science)   2. Microcomputers
—Programming.   3. Basic (Computer program language)
I. Augenstein, Moshe (date). II. Tenenbaum, Aaron M.
III. Title.
QA76.9.D35L36   1985   001.64′2   84-3326
ISBN 0-13-196221-3

Editorial/production supervision and interior design: Nancy Milnamow
Cover design: Lundgren Graphics, Ltd.
Manufacturing buyer: Gordon Osbourne

Apple Computer and Applesoft are trademarks of Apple Computer Company.
BASIC-80 and Softcard are trademarks of Microsoft Company.
IBM PC is a trademark of International Business Machines Corporation.
TRS-80 and Radio Shack are trademarks of Tandy Corporation.

Prentice-Hall International, Inc., *London*
Prentice-Hall of Australia Pty. Limited, *Sydney*
Editora Prentice-Hall do Brasil, Ltda., *Rio de Janeiro*
Prentice-Hall Canada Inc., *Toronto*
Prentice-Hall of India Private Limited, *New Delhi*
Prentice-Hall of Japan, Inc., *Tokyo*
Prentice-Hall of Southeast Asia Pte. Ltd., *Singapore*
Whitehall Books Limited, *Wellington, New Zealand*

To my wife, Vivienne Esther
YL

To my wife, Gail
MA

To my son, Bezalel
AT

Contents

2 PROGRAMMING IN BASIC   43

Preface

This text is designed with two audiences in mind. One group consists of programmers who have already acquired a basic level of proficiency in programming, preferably in BASIC. Such skills may have been acquired by reading an introductory text in BASIC programming complemented by some hands-on experience on a personal computer. The programming skills acquired at this level may be disorganized and the programmer may realize that in order to solve more involved and complex problems it is necessary to learn about more high-level programming techniques. The subject of data structures coupled with enhanced programming skills is the next step in the pursuit of these high level skills.

A second group consists of those who are studying computer science in an academic environment. With the proliferation of personal computers, computer science education is becoming more popular, even in schools which previously had only one or two introductory courses in programming. Although this description will typically fit two-year schools or high schools, a number of four-year colleges with small budgets for computing also fit into this category. BASIC is frequently the language used at such institutions.

The purpose of this book is to introduce the reader to the elementary concepts of data structures in conjunction with reinforcement of high-level programming skills.

For several years, we have taught a course in data structures to students who have had a semester course in high-level programming and a semester course in assembly language programming. We found that a considerable amount of time was spent in teaching programming techniques because the students had not had sufficient exposure to programming and were unable to implement abstract structures on their own. The brighter students eventually caught on to what was being done. The weaker students never did. Based on this experience, we have reached the firm conclusion that a first course in data structures must go hand in hand with a second course in programming. This text is a product of that conviction.

The text introduces abstract concepts, shows how these concepts are useful in problem solving and then shows how the abstractions can be made concrete by using a programming language. Equal emphasis is placed on both the abstract and the concrete versions of a concept, so that the student learns about the concept itself, its implementation, and its application.

The language used in this book is BASIC. Although there are several languages which support good programming techniques and are better than BASIC for implementing abstract data structures, we have selected BASIC for several reasons. BASIC is the most widely-used high-level language today because of its widespread accessibility on personal computers. Within nonacademic circles, there is a growing interest in computer science. Many people who have an interest in data structures, but without programming skills in another high level language, have few sources to which to turn. Furthermore, although BASIC has become far from universally accepted (and will probably never be) within academic circles, its use in recognized computer science programs is spreading (particularly, as we mentioned earlier, at smaller institutions). Although BASIC has been criticized as being very problem-prone, it can be used correctly. In Chapter 2 we introduce a consistent approach to BASIC and continue to emphasize that approach throughout the remainder of the book. The only prerequisite for students using this book is the equivalent of a one-semester course in programming in BASIC. Readers who are not familiar with BASIC are referred to the Bibliography for a selection of introductory texts in the language.

Chapter 1 is an introduction to data structures. Section 1.1 introduces the concept of an abstract data structure and the concept of an implementation. Section 1.2 introduces arrays—their implementation as well as their application. Section 1.3 introduces data aggregates and how they can be implemented in BASIC.

Chapter 2 introduces and discusses structured programming techniques in BASIC and their algorithmic counterparts. These techniques present a style of programming that is used throughout the remainder of the text.

Chapter 3 discusses stacks and their BASIC implementation. Because this is the first new data structure introduced, considerable discussion of the pitfalls of implementing such a structure is included. Section 3.4 introduces postfix, prefix, and infix notations.

Chapter 4 introduces queues and linked lists and their implementations using an array of available nodes.

Chapter 5 discusses recursion and its applications. Because recursion is not implemented on most versions of BASIC, methods of simulating recursion are presented as well.

Chapter 6 discusses trees and Chapter 7 introduces graphs.

Chapter 8 covers sorting and Chapter 9 covers searching.

At the end of the book, we have included a bibliography listing a selected set of texts in the areas of BASIC programming and data structures, to which the reader is referred for further reading. In a one-semester course, Chapter 7 and parts of Chapters 1, 2, 6, 8, and 9 can be omitted.

The text is suitable for course I1 of Curriculum 68 (Communications of the ACM, March 1968), courses UC1 and UC8 of the Undergraduate Programs in Information Systems (Communications of the ACM, Dec. 1973) and course CS2 and parts of courses CS7 and CS13 of Curriculum 78 (Communications of the ACM, March 1979). In particular, the text covers parts or all of topics P1, P2, P3, P4, P5, S2, D1, D2, and D6 of Curriculum 78.

Algorithms (which we introduce in Chapter 2) are presented as intermediaries between English language descriptions and BASIC programs. They are written in a style consisting of high-level constructs interspersed with English. These algorithms allow the reader to focus on the method used to solve a problem without concern about declaration of variables and the peculiarities of a real language. In transforming an algorithm into a program, we introduce these issues and point out the pitfalls which accompany them.

The indentation pattern used for BASIC programs and algorithms is based on a format introduced in Chapter 2 which we have found to be a useful tool in improving program comprehensibility. We distinguish between algorithms and programs by presenting the former in lower case italics and the latter in upper case roman.

Most of the concepts in the text are illustrated by several examples. Some of these examples are important topics in their own right (e.g., postfix notation, multi-word arithmetic, etc.) and may be treated as such. Other examples illustrate different implementation techniques (such as sequential storage of trees). When using this text for a one-semester course, the instructor is free to cover as many or as few of these examples as he or she wishes. Examples may also be assigned to students as independent reading. It is anticipated that an instructor will be unable to cover all the examples in sufficient detail within the confines of a one- or two-semester course. We feel that, at the stage of student's development for which the text is designed, it is more important to cover several examples in great detail than to cover a broad range of topics cursorily.

The exercises vary widely in type and difficulty. Some are drill exercises to insure comprehension of topics in the text. Others involve modifications of programs or algorithms presented in the text. Still others introduce new concepts and are quite challenging. Often, a group of successive exercises includes the complete development of a new topic which can be used as the basis for a term project or an additional lecture. The instructor should use caution in assigning exercises so that an assignment is suitable to the student's level. We consider it imperative for students to be assigned several (from five to twelve, depending on difficulty) programming projects per semester. The exercises contain several projects of this type. The instructor may find a great many additional exercises and projects in the *Exercise Manual* of one of our earlier texts, *Data Structures and PL/I Programming* (Prentice-Hall, 1979). Although many of the exercises in that manual are presented using PL/I, they can readily be recast in a BASIC setting. The *Exercise Manual* for *Data Structures and PL/I Programming* is available from the publisher.

One of the most difficult choices which had to be made in writing this book was the question of which BASIC dialect to use. In order to present programs which would run on a wide variety of personal computers, it is desirable to choose the "lowest common denominator" of all commonly available BASIC dialects. On the other hand, by choosing a very small proper subset of BASIC, our programs would not be able to take advantage of "standard" BASIC features provided by the vast majority of personal computers. We decided to ensure that the programs in this book would run under each of Radio Shack BASIC Level II, Microsoft BASIC-80, and BASIC for the IBM PC. Of these three, Radio Shack BASIC Level II is fairly close to being a proper subset of the other two, and yet provides all the features which we deemed essential. One of the limitations of Radio Shack BASIC Level II is that it distinguishes variables by only the first two characters of their names and forbids the use of embedded reserved words. The same restriction applies to Applesoft BASIC. We have taken great pains to use meaningful variable names and yet to abide by these limitations. Naturally, in those versions of BASIC which do not have these limitations, the programmer is free to substitute somewhat less awkward variable names. We have deliberately not taken advantage of those advanced features (e.g., the WHILE-WEND construct, the MOD built-in function, etc.) of Microsoft BASIC-80 and BASIC for the IBM PC that are not supported by the majority of BASICs currently available for personal computers. However, we do introduce these constructs in Chapter 2 and do use them in presenting algorithms.

One feature which we felt we could not omit was the ELSE clause for the IF-THEN construct. Without the availability of the IF-THEN-ELSE, programs would become unwieldy and their pedagogical value would be greatly diminished. Unfortunately, Applesoft BASIC does not support the ELSE clause. The Applesoft programmer may simulate ELSE clauses by methods presented in Chapter 2. We also use the DEF statement to declare variable types rather than relying on the special type symbols. This is also invalid in Applesoft BASIC but can easily be remedied by inserting the type symbols. All other features used throughout this book are also valid in Applesoft BASIC. Each program (or subroutine) in this book has been tested on a Radio Shack Model III using BASIC Level II, on an Apple II Plus equipped with a Softcard using Microsoft BASIC-80, and on an IBM PC using cassette BASIC. We wish to thank Imran Khan, Linda Laub, Diana Lombardi, Joel Plaut, and Chris Ungeheuer for their invaluable assistance in this task. Their zeal for the task was above and beyond the call of duty and their suggestions were always valuable. Of course, any errors that remain are the sole responsibility of the authors.

We have prepared two sets of diskettes containing the BASIC source code of programs and subroutines in the text. One set of diskettes was prepared under BASIC-80 using the Microsoft CP/M Softcard for the Apple II Plus and the second set using IBM PC BASIC. These diskettes are available from the publisher using the tear-off card bound into the book.

Linda Laub, Carl Markowitz, and Chris Ungeheuer spent many hours typing and correcting the original manuscript. Their cooperation and patience as we continually changed our minds about additions and deletions are most sincerely appreciated. We wish to single them out for their extraordinary enthusiasm and dedication in all phases of the book's production, for which we are deeply grateful.

We would like to thank Maria Argiro, Mirrel Eissenberg, Beverly Heller, Gun Kim, Amalia Kletsky, Sholom Krischer, Linda Laub, Diana Lombardi, Chaim Markowitz, Joel Plaut, Barbara Reznik, Chris Ungeheur, and Shirley Yee for their invaluable assistance.

The staff of the City University Computer Center deserves special mention. They were extremely helpful in assisting us in using the excellent facilities of the Center. The same can be said of Julio Berger and Lawrence Schweitzer and the rest of the staff of the Brooklyn College Computer Center.

We would like to thank the editors and staff at Prentice-Hall and especially the reviewers for their helpful comments and suggestions.

Finally, we thank our wives, Vivienne Langsam, Gail Augenstein, and Miriam Tenenbaum, for their advice and encouragement during the long and arduous task of producing such a book.

Yedidyah Langsam
Moshe Augenstein
Aaron Tenenbaum

1

Introduction to Data Structures

A computer is a machine that manipulates information. The study of computer science includes the study of how information is organized in a computer, how it can be manipulated, and how it can be utilized. Thus it is extremely important for a student of computer science to understand the concepts of information organization and manipulation in order to continue study of the field.

1. INFORMATION AND MEANING

If computer science is fundamentally the study of information, the first question that arises is: What is information? Unfortunately, although the concept of information is the bedrock of the entire field, this question cannot be answered precisely. In this sense, the concept of information in computer science is similar to the concepts of point, line, and plane in geometry—they are all undefined terms about which statements can be made but which cannot be explained in terms of more elementary concepts.

In geometry, it is possible to talk about the length of a line despite the fact that the concept of a line itself is undefined. The length of a line is a measure of quantity. Similarly, in computer science, we can measure quantities of information. The basic unit of information is the *bit*, whose value asserts one of two mutually exclusive possibilities. For example, if a light switch can be in one of two positions but not in both simultaneously, the fact that it is either in the "on" position or the "off" position is 1 bit of information. If a device can be in more than two possible states, the fact that it is in a particular state is more than 1 bit of

1

(a) One switch (two possibilities).

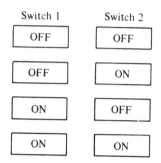

(b) Two switches (four possibilities).

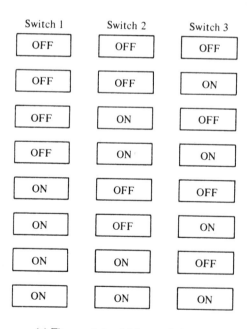

(c) Three switches (eight possibilities).   **Figure 1.1.1**

information. For example, if a dial has eight possible positions, the fact that it is in position four rules out seven other possibilities, whereas the fact that a light switch is on rules out only one other possibility.

Another way of thinking of this is as follows. Suppose that we had only two-way switches, but could use as many of them as we needed. How many such switches would be necessary to represent a dial with eight positions? Clearly, one switch can represent only two positions [see Figure 1.1.1(a)]. Two switches can represent four different positions [Figure 1.1.1(b)], and three switches are required to represent eight different positions [Figure 1.1.1(c)]. In general, n switches can represent 2^n different possibilities.

The binary digits zero and one are used to represent the two possible states of a particular bit (in fact, the word "bit" is a contraction of the words "binary digit"). Given n bits, a string of n 1s and 0s is used to represent their settings. For example, the string 101011 represents six switches, the first (starting from the left) of which is "on" (1), the second of which is "off" (0), the third on, the fourth off, and the fifth and sixth on.

We have seen that three bits are sufficient to represent eight possibilities. The eight possible configurations of these 3 bits (000, 001, 010, 011, 100, 101, 110, and 111) can be used to represent the integers 0 through 7. However, there is nothing intrinsic about these bit settings which implies that a particular setting represents a particular integer. All assignments of integer values to bit settings are equally valid as long as no two integers are assigned to the same bit setting. Once such an assignment has been made, a particular bit setting can be interpreted unambiguously as a specific integer. Let us examine several widely used methods for interpreting bit settings as integers. BASIC interpreters used on microcomputers may in fact represent integers in slightly more complicated forms, but the exact details of the representations used are not particularly important. The important point is that once a consistent method for treating bit strings as integers is specified, the details of the specification technique are irrelevant to the user.

Binary and Decimal Integers

The most widely used method for interpreting bit settings as nonnegative integers is the *binary number system.* In this system, each bit position represents a power of 2. The rightmost bit position represents 2^0, which equals 1; the next position to its left represents 2^1, which is 2; the next bit position represents 2^2, which is 4; and so on. An integer is represented as a sum of powers of 2. A string of all 0s represents the number 0. If a 1 appears in a particular bit position, the power of 2 represented by that bit position is included in the sum, but if a 0 appears, that power of 2 is not included in the sum. For example, the group of bits 00100110 has 1s in positions 1, 2, and 5 (counting from right to left with the rightmost position counted as position 0). Thus 00100110 represents the integer

$2^1 + 2^2 + 2^5 = 2 + 4 + 32 = 38$. Under this interpretation, any string of bits of length n represents a unique nonnegative integer between 0 and $2^n - 1$, and any nonnegative integer between 0 and $2^n - 1$ can be represented by a unique string of bits of length n.

There are two widely used basic methods for representing negative binary numbers. In the first method, called **ones-complement notation**, a negative number is represented by changing each bit in its absolute value to the opposite bit setting. For example, since 00100110 represents 38, 11011001 is used to represent -38. This means that the first bit of a number is no longer used to represent a power of 2, but is reserved for the sign of the number. A bit string starting with a 0 represents a positive number, while a bit string starting with a 1 represents a negative number. Given n bits, the range of numbers that can be represented is $-2^{n-1} + 1$ (a 1 followed by $n - 1$ 0s) to $2^{n-1} - 1$ (a 0 followed by $n - 1$ 1s). Note that under this representation, there are two representations for the number 0: a "positive 0" consisting of all 0s, and a "negative 0" consisting of all 1s.

A second method of representing negative binary numbers is called **twos-complement notation**. In this notation, 1 is added to the ones-complement representation of a negative number. For example, since 11011001 represents -38 in ones-complement notation, 11011010 represents -38 in twos-complement notation. Given n bits, the range of numbers that can be represented is -2^{n-1} (a 1 followed by $n - 1$ 0s) to $2^{n-1} - 1$ (a 0 followed by $n - 1$ 1s). Note that -2^{n-1} can be represented in twos-complement notation but not in ones-complement notation. However, its absolute value 2^{n-1} cannot be represented in either notation using n bits. Note also that in twos-complement notation, there is only one representation for the number 0 using n bits. To see this, consider 0 using 8 bits: 00000000. The one's complement is 11111111, which is "negative 0" in that notation. Adding one to produce the twos-complement form yields 100000000, which is 9 bits long. Since only 8 bits are allowed, the leftmost bit (or "overflow") is discarded, leaving 00000000 as minus 0.

The binary number system is by no means the only method by which bits can be used to represent integers. For example, a string of bits may be used to represent integers in the decimal number system, as follows. Four bits can be used to represent a decimal digit between 0 and 9 in the binary notation described above. A string of bits of arbitrary length may be divided into consecutive sets of 4 bits, where each set represents a decimal digit. The string then represents the number that is formed by those decimal digits in conventional decimal notation. For example, in this system, the bit string 00100110 is separated into two strings of 4 bits each: 0010 and 0110. The first of these represents the decimal digit 2 and the second represents the decimal digit 6, so that the entire string represents the integer 26. This representation is called **binary-coded decimal**.

One important feature of the binary-coded decimal representation of nonnegative integers is that not all bit strings are valid representations of a decimal integer. Four bits can be used to represent one of 16 different possibilities, since there are 16 possible states for a set of 4 bits. However, in the binary-coded decimal integer representation, only 10 of those 16 possibilities are used. That is, codes such as 1010 and 1100 whose binary values are 10 or larger are invalid in a binary-coded decimal number.

Real Numbers

The usual method used by computers to represent real numbers is *floating-point notation*. There are many variations of floating-point notation, each with its own individual characteristics. The key concept is that a real number is represented by a number, called a *mantissa*, times a *base* raised to an integer power, called an *exponent*. The base is usually fixed and the mantissa and exponent vary to represent different real numbers. For example, if the base is fixed at 10, the number 387.53 could be represented as 38,753 times 10 to the -2 power. (Recall that 10^{-2} is .01.) The mantissa is 38753 and the exponent is -2. Other possible representations are $.38753 \times 10^3$ and 387.53×10^0. We choose the representation in which the mantissa is an integer with no trailing zeros.

In the floating-point notation that we describe (which is not necessarily implemented on any particular machine), a real number is represented by a 32-bit string consisting of a 24-bit mantissa followed by an 8-bit exponent. The base is fixed at 10. Both the mantissa and the exponent are twos-complement binary integers. For example, the 24-bit binary representation of the integer 38753 is 000000001001011101100001 and the 8-bit twos-complement binary representation of -2 is 11111110, so the representation of 387.53 is 00000000100101110110000111111110.

Other real numbers and their floating-point representations are:

0	00000000000000000000000000000000
100	00000000000000000000000100000010
.5	00000000000000000000010111111111
.000005	00000000000000000000010111111010
12000	00000000000000000000011000000011
-387.53	11111111011010001001111111111110
-12000	11111111111111111111010000000011

The advantage of floating-point notation is that it can be used to represent numbers with extremely large or extremely small absolute values. For example, in the notation presented above, the largest number that can be represented is $(2^{23} - 1) \times 10^{127}$, which is a very large number indeed. The smallest positive number that can be represented is 10^{-128}, which is quite small. The limiting factor on the precision to which numbers can be represented on a particular machine is the number of significant binary digits in the mantissa. Not every number between the largest and the smallest can be represented. Our representation allows only 23 significant bits. Thus a number such as 10 million and 1, which requires 24 significant binary digits in the mantissa, would have to be approximated by 10 million (1×10^7), which requires only one significant digit.

Character Strings

As we all know, information is not always interpreted numerically. Items such as names, job titles, and addresses must also be represented in some fashion within a computer. To enable the representation of such nonnumeric objects, still another method of interpreting bit strings is necessary. Such information is usually represented in character-string form. For example, in some computers, the 8 bits 00100110 are used to represent the character "&". A different 8-bit pattern is used to represent the character "A", another to represent "B", another to represent "C", and still another for each character that has a representation in a particular machine. A Soviet machine uses bit patterns to represent Russian characters, while an Israeli machine uses bit patterns to represent Hebrew characters. (In fact, the characters being used are transparent to the machine; the character set can be changed by using a different character generator or printer.) If 8 bits are used to represent a character, up to 256 different characters can be represented since there are 256 different 8-bit patterns. If the string 01000001 is used to represent the character "A" and 01000010 is used to represent the character "B", then the character string "AB" would be represented by the bit string 0100000101000010. In general, a character string STR is represented by the concatenation of the bit strings that represent the individual characters of STR.

As in the case of integers, there is nothing intrinsic about a particular bit string that makes it suitable for representing a specific character. The assignment of bit strings to characters may be entirely arbitrary, but it must be adhered to consistently. It may be that some convenient rule is used in assigning bit strings to characters. For example, two bit strings may be assigned to two letters so that the one with a smaller binary value is assigned to the letter that comes earlier in the alphabet. However, such a rule is merely a convenience; it is not mandated by any intrinsic relation between characters and bit strings. In fact, computers even differ over the number of bits used to represent a character. Some computers use 7 bits (and therefore allow only up to 128 possible characters), some use 8 (up to 256 characters), and some use 10 (up to 1024 possible characters). The number of bits necessary to represent a character in a particular computer is called the *byte size* and a group of bits of that number is called a *byte*. The byte size of most microcomputers is 8.

Note that using 8 bits to represent a character means that 256 possible characters can be represented. It is not very often that one finds a computer that uses so many different characters (although it is conceivable for a computer to include upper- and lowercase letters, special characters, italics, boldface, and other type characters, and many personal computers use some of the 256 codes for graphics characters), so that many of the 8-bit codes are not used to represent characters.

Many codes are used not to represent displayable or printable characters, but as control codes for communications or I/O device control.

Most microcomputers represent characters internally by means of the ASCII code. ASCII (or American Standard Code for Information Interchange) is a standardized system by which manufacturers have agreed to represent various characters and symbols in order that a computer manufactured by one company can communicate with printers (and other computers) manufactured by another company.

Thus we see that information itself has no meaning. Any meaning can be assigned to a particular bit pattern, as long as it is done consistently. It is the interpretation of a bit pattern that gives it meaning. For example, the bit string 00100110 can be interpreted as the number 38 (binary), the number 26 (binary-coded decimal) or the character "&". A method of interpreting a bit pattern is often called a *data type*. We have presented several data types: binary integers, binary-coded-decimal nonnegative integers, real numbers, and character strings. The key questions are how to determine what data types are available to interpret bit patterns and which data type to use in interpreting a particular bit pattern.

Hardware and Software

The *memory* (also called *storage* or *core*) of a computer is simply a group of bits (switches). At any instant of the computer's operation, any particular bit in memory is either 0 or 1 (off or on). The setting of a bit is called its *value* or its *contents*.

The bits in a computer memory are grouped together into larger units such as bytes. In some computers, several bytes are grouped together into units called *words*. Each such unit (byte or word, depending on the machine) is assigned an *address*, which is a name identifying a particular unit among all the units in memory. This address is usually numeric, so that we may speak of byte 746 or word 937. An address is often called a *location* and the contents of a location are the values of the bits which make up the unit at that location.

Every computer has a set of "native" data types. This means that it is constructed with a mechanism for manipulating bit patterns in a way that is consistent with the objects they represent. For example, suppose that a computer contains an instruction to add two binary integers and place their sum at a given location in memory for subsequent use. Then there is a mechanism built into the computer to

1. Extract operand bit patterns from two given locations
2. Produce a third bit pattern representing the binary integer which is the sum of the two binary integers represented by the two operands
3. Store the resultant bit pattern at a given location

The computer "knows" to interpret the bit patterns at the given locations as binary integers because the hardware which executes that particular instruction is designed to do so. This is akin to a light "knowing" to be on when the switch is in a particular position.

If the same machine also has an instruction to add two real numbers, there is a separate built-in mechanism to interpret operands as real numbers. Two distinct instructions are necessary for the two operations, and each instruction carries within itself an implicit identification of the types of its operands as well as their explicit locations. Therefore, it is the programmer's responsibility to know which data type is contained in each location that is used and to select the appropriate instruction (e.g., integer or floating-point addition to obtain the sum of two numbers).

A high-level programming language aids in this task considerably. An *identifier* (or *variable name*) is used instead of a numerical address to refer to a particular memory location because of its convenience for the programmer. In BASIC, identifiers are written as a sequence of letters and digits, starting with a letter. (*Note:* Although many versions of BASIC allow variable names to be of any length, in some BASICs only the first two characters are significant. Thus SUB, SUM, and SU will all be treated as the same variable. In addition, most BASICs impose severe restrictions on the choice of variable names in that no variable may contain an embedded "reserved word." For example, the variable name BEFORE is not permitted since it contains the reserved word FOR. Other versions of BASIC limit variable names to only two characters in their entirety. We discuss this further in Section 2.1.)

If a BASIC programmer writes

    10   DEFINT X,Y
    20   DEFDBL A,B

then any variable beginning with the letter X or Y will be interpreted as an integer, while any variable beginning with the letter A or B will be interpreted as a double-precision real number (i.e., as a floating-point number with a double-length mantissa). Thus the contents of the locations reserved for XVAR and YVAR will be interpreted as integers, while the contents of AVAR and BVAR will be interpreted as real numbers. The interpreter that is responsible for translating BASIC statements into machine language will translate the " + " in the statement

    100   X = X + Y

into integer addition, and will translate the " + " in the statement

    200   A = A + B

into real addition. An operator such as " + " is really a *generic* operator because it has several different meanings, depending on its context. The interpreter relieves the programmer of specifying the type of addition that must be performed by examining the context and using the appropriate version. [*Note:* In some

BASIC dialects (e.g., Applesoft), the "type" of a variable may only be specified by means of appending a "type declaration" character to the variable name. Thus X$ represents a character-string variable, while X% would be treated as an integer variable. Many other BASICs (e.g., TRS 80 Level II) allow type specification by means of a DEF statement as well as by the use of type declaration characters. For further discussion, see Section 2.1. The reader is urged to clarify the method of type specification used in the BASIC implementation being used.]

It is important to recognize the key role played by type specification in a high-level language. It is by means of these declarations that the programmer specifies how the contents of the computer memory are to be interpreted by the program. In doing this, a declaration specifies how much memory is needed for a particular entity, how the contents of that memory are to be interpreted, and other vital details. Declarations also specify to the interpreter exactly what is meant by the operation symbols that are subsequently used.

The Concept of Implementation

Thus far, we have been viewing data types as a method of interpreting the memory contents of a computer. The set of native data types which a particular computer can support is determined by the functions that have been wired into its hardware. However, we can view the concept of "data type" from a completely different perspective: not in terms of what a computer can do, but in terms of what the user wants done. For example, if a person wishes to obtain the sum of two integers, he or she does not care very much about the detailed mechanism by which that sum will be obtained. The person is interested in manipulating the mathematical concept of an "integer"—not in manipulating hardware bits. The hardware of the computer may be used to represent an integer and is useful only insofar as the representation is successful.

Once the concept of "data type" is divorced from the hardware capabilities of the computer, there are an unlimited number of data types that can be considered. A data type is an abstract concept defined by a set of logical properties. Once such an abstract data type is defined and the legal operations involving that type are specified, we may *implement* that data type (or a close approximation to it). An implementation may be a *hardware implementation* in which the circuitry necessary to perform the required operations is designed and constructed as part of a computer. Or it may be a *software implementation* in which a program consisting of existing hardware instructions is written to interpret bit strings in the desired fashion and to perform the required operations. Thus a software implementation includes a specification of how an object of the new data type is represented by objects of previously existing data types, as well as a specification of how such an object is manipulated in conformance with the operations that have been defined for it. Throughout the remainder of this text, the term "implementation" is used to mean "software implementation."

An Example

Let us illustrate these concepts with an example. Suppose that the hardware of a computer contains an instruction

$$MOVE(SOURCE, DEST, length)$$

which copies a fixed-length character string of *length* bytes from an address specified by *SOURCE* to an address specified by *DEST*. We present hardware instructions and locations using uppercase italic letters. The length must be specified by an integer constant, and for that reason we indicate it with lowercase letters. *SOURCE* and *DEST* can be specified by identifiers that represent storage locations. An example of this instruction is *MOVE(A,B,3)*, which copies the three bytes starting at location *A* to the 3 bytes starting at location *B*.

Note the different roles played by the identifiers *A* and *B* in this operation. The first operand of the *MOVE* instruction is the contents of the location specified by the identifier *A*. The second operand, however, is not the contents of location *B*, since these contents are irrelevant to the execution of the instruction. Rather, the location itself is the operand, since the location specifies the destination of the character string. Although an identifier always stands for a location, it is common for an identifier to be used to reference the contents of that location. It is always apparent from the context whether an identifier is referencing a location or its contents. The identifier appearing as the first operand of a *MOVE* instruction refers to the contents of memory, whereas the identifier appearing as the second operand refers to a location.

We also assume the computer hardware to contain the usual arithmetic and branching instructions, which we indicate by using BASIC-like notation. For example, the instruction

$$Z = X + Y$$

interprets the contents of the bytes at locations X and Y as binary integers, calculates their sum, and inserts the binary representation of their sum into the byte at location Z. (We do not operate on integers greater than 1 byte in length and ignore the possibility of overflow.) Here again, X and Y are used to reference memory contents while Z is used to reference a memory location, but the proper interpretation is clear from the context.

Sometimes, it is desirable to add a quantity to an address to obtain another address. For example, if A is a location in memory, we might want to reference the location 4 bytes beyond A. We cannot refer to this location as $A + 4$ since that notation is reserved for the sum of the integer contents of location A and the integer 4. We therefore introduce the notation $A(4)$ to refer to this location. We also introduce the notation $A(X)$ to refer to the address given by adding the binary integer contents of the byte at X to the address A.

The *MOVE* instruction, as defined above, requires the programmer to specify the length of the string to be copied. Thus it deals with an operand that is a fixed-length character string (i.e., the length of the string must be known). A fixed-length string and a byte-sized binary integer may be considered native data types of that particular machine.

Suppose that we wish to implement varying-length character strings on this machine. That is, we want to enable programmers to use an instruction

$$MOVEVAR(SOURCE,DEST)$$

to move a character string from location *SOURCE* to location *DEST* without being required to specify any length.

To implement this new data type, we must first decide on how it is to be represented in the memory of the machine and then indicate how that representation is to be manipulated. Clearly, it is necessary to know how many bytes must be moved in order to execute this instruction. Since the *MOVEVAR* operation does not specify this number, the number must be contained within the representation of the character string itself. A varying-length character string of length l may be represented by a contiguous set of $l+1$ bytes ($l < 256$). The first byte contains the binary representation of the length l and the remaining bytes contain the representations of the characters in the string. Representations of three such strings are illustrated in Figure 1.1.2. [Note that the digits 5 and 9 in these figures do not stand for the bit patterns representing the characters "5" and "9" but rather for the patterns 00000101 and 00001001, which represent the integers five and nine. Similarly, 14 in Figure 1.1.2(c) stands for the bit pattern 00001110.]

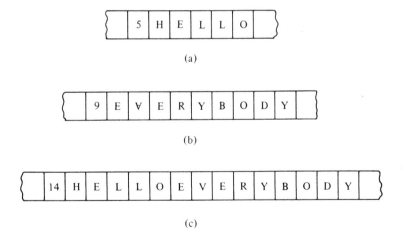

(a)

(b)

(c)

Figure 1.1.2

The program to implement the *MOVEVAR* operation can be written as follows (*I* is an auxiliary memory location):

>*for I* = 1 *to DEST*
>   *MOVE(SOURCE(I),DEST(I)*,1)
>*next I*

Similarly, we can implement an operation *CONCATVAR(C1,C2,C3)* to concatenate two character strings of varying length at locations *C1* and *C2* and place the result at *C3*. Figure 1.1.2(c) illustrates the concatenation of the two strings in Figure 1.1.2(a) and (b):

>'move the length
>*Z = C1 + C2*
>*MOVE(Z,C3*,1)
>'move the first string
>*for I* = 1 *to C1*
>   *MOVE(C1(I),C3(I)*,1)
>*next I*
>*for I* = 1 *to C2*
>   *X = C1 + I*
>   *MOVE(C2(I),C3(X)*,1)
>*next I*

However, once the operation *MOVEVAR* has been defined, *CONCATVAR* can be implemented using *MOVEVAR* as follows:

>*MOVEVAR(C2,C3(C1))*:   '   move the second string
>*MOVEVAR(C1,C3)*:   '   move the first string
>*Z = C1+C2*:   '   update the length of the result
>*MOVE(Z,C3*,1)

Figure 1.1.3 illustrates phases of this operation on the strings of Figure 1.1.2. Although this latter version is shorter, it is not really more efficient since all the instructions used in implementing *MOVEVAR* are performed each time that *MOVEVAR* is used.

The statement $Z = C1+C2$ in both of the algorithms above is of particular interest. The addition instruction operates independently of the use of its operands (in this case, parts of varying-length character strings). The instruction is designed to treat its operands as single-byte integers regardless of any other use that the programmer has for them. Similarly, the reference to $C3(C1)$ is to the location whose address is given by adding the contents of the byte at location $C1$ to the address $C3$. Thus the byte at $C1$ is treated as holding a binary integer, although it is also the start of a varying-length character string. This illustrates the fact that a data type is a method of treating the contents of memory and that those contents have no intrinsic meaning.

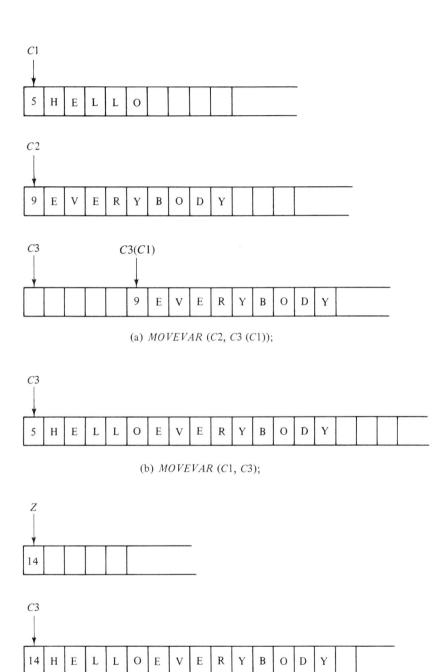

(a) *MOVEVAR (C2, C3 (C1))*;

(b) *MOVEVAR (C1, C3)*;

(c) *Z = C1 + C2; MOVE (Z, C3, 1)*;

Figure 1.1.3

Note that this representation of character strings of varying length allows only strings whose length is less than or equal to the largest binary integer that fits into a single byte. If a byte is 8 bits, this means that the largest such string is 255 (which is $2^8 - 1$) characters long. To allow for longer strings, a different representation must be chosen and a new set of programs must be written. If we use this representation of character strings of varying length, the concatenation operation is invalid if the resulting string is more than 255 characters long. Since the result of such an operation is undefined, the implementer has a wide variety of actions that can be taken if that operation is attempted. One possibility is to use only the first 255 characters of the result. Another possibility is to ignore the operation entirely and not move anything to the result field. There is also a choice of printing a warning message or of assuming that the user wants to achieve whatever result the implementer decides on.

Once a representation has been chosen for objects of a particular data type and routines have been written to operate on those representations, the programmer is free to use that data type to solve a problem. The original hardware of the machine plus the programs for implementing more complex data types than those provided by the hardware can be thought of as a "better" machine than the one consisting of the hardware alone. The programmer of the original machine need not worry about how the computer is designed and what circuitry is being used to execute each instruction. He need know only what instructions are available and how those instructions can be used. Similarly, the programmer who uses the "extended" machine (which consists of hardware and software) need not be concerned with the details of how various data types are implemented. All the programmer needs to know is how they can be manipulated.

In the next two sections of this chapter we examine a composite data structure which already exists in BASIC (the array) and its use in representing heterogeneous data aggregates. We focus on the abstract definitions of these data structures and how they can be useful in problem solving. We also examine how they are implemented in BASIC.

In the remainder of the book (except for Chapter 2, which deals with BASIC programming techniques), we develop more complex data types and show their usefulness in problem solving. We also show how to implement these data types using the data types which are already available in BASIC. Since the problems that arise in the course of attempting to implement high-level data structures are quite complex, this will also allow us to investigate the BASIC language more thoroughly and to gain valuable experience in the use of that language.

Often, no implementation, in hardware or software, can model a mathematical concept completely. For example, it is impossible to represent arbitrarily large integers on a computer since the size of such a machine's memory is finite. Thus it is not the data type "integer" which is represented by the hardware but rather the data type "integer between X and Y," where X and Y are the smallest and largest integers that can be represented by that machine.

It is important to recognize the limitations of a particular implementation. Often it will be possible to present several implementations of the same data type, each with its own strengths and weaknesses. One particular implementation may be better than another for a specific application and the programmer must be aware of the possible trade-offs that might be involved.

One important consideration in any implementation is its efficiency. In fact, the reason that the high-level data types which we discuss are not built into BASIC is because of the significant overhead that they would entail. There are languages of significantly higher level than BASIC which have many of these data types already built into them, many of which are also available on micro-computers.

Efficiency is usually measured by two factors—time and space. If a particular application is heavily dependent on manipulating high-level data structures, the speed at which those manipulations can be performed will be the major determinant of the speed of the entire application. Similarly, if a program uses a large number of such structures, an implementation that uses an inordinate amount of space to represent the data structure will be impractical. Unfortunately, there is usually a trade-off between these two efficiencies, so that an implementation which is fast uses more storage than does one which is slow. The choice of implementation in such a case involves a careful evaluation of the trade-offs among the various possibilities.

EXERCISES

1. In the text, an analogy is made between the length of a line and the number of bits of information in a bit string. In what ways is this analogy inadequate?

2. Determine what hardware data types are available on your microcomputer and what operations can be performed on them.

3. Prove that there are 2^n different settings for n two-way switches. Suppose that we wanted to have m settings. How many switches would be necessary?

4. Interpret the following bit settings as binary integers and as binary-coded decimal integers. If a setting cannot be interpreted as a binary-coded decimal integer, explain why.
   - **(a)** 10011001
   - **(b)** 1001
   - **(c)** 000100010001
   - **(d)** 01110111
   - **(e)** 01010101
   - **(f)** 100000010101

5. Microsoft BASIC, one of the most widely used implementations of BASIC, represents integers using a variant of twos-complement notation. Each integer (positive or negative) occupies 2 bytes (16 bits) of storage, with the low byte followed by the

high byte (i.e., reversed from the conventional order). Thus 38 would be represented by 0010011000000000 and -38 by 1101110011111111. How would each of the following decimal integers be represented in Microsoft BASIC?

(a) 32   (b) 258   (c) -47
(d) -32 (e) -32768 (f) 32767

6. Microsoft BASIC represents single-precision real numbers using floating-point notation. A real number is represented by a 32-bit string consisting of a 24-bit (3-byte)
mantissa followed by an 8-bit (1-byte) exponent. The real (decimal) number is first
converted into its binary equivalent with the base fixed at 2. For example, 49(ten) =
.11000100(two) $\times$ 2^6. The mantissa is chosen so that the first digit is a 1. The exponent is then added to 128 and the resulting value is represented in binary. Thus
$6 + 128 = 134$(ten) $=$ 10000110(two). Since the first digit of the mantissa is 1, it
can be dropped, and the information content of that bit can be used to represent the
sign (0 being positive and 1 being negative). In our example the mantissa is
11000100, which is represented internally by 01000100, with the first bit indicating
a positive number (-49 would be represented as 11000100). The 3 bytes representing the mantissa are ordered from low to high and thus the 24-bit representation of
the mantissa is 00000000 00000000 01000100. Combining the mantissa with the
exponent, the 32-bit representation of 49 is 00000000 00000000 01000100
10000110. How would each of the following single-precision real numbers be represented in Microsoft BASIC?

(a) 100   (b) 12000   (c) -12000
(d) 32768   (e) 32   (f) -258

7. Write three BASIC routines, each of which interprets two bit strings (a ***bit string*** is a
character string consisting of only the characters "0" and "1") of length 16 as positive binary integers and prints the bit string representing the sum, difference, and
product, respectively, of the two integers. The routines should not convert the bit
strings into integers.

8. Develop a representation of integers between 0 and 255 by bit strings of length 8 so
that only one bit changes from any integer to its successor. Write a BASIC routine
which inputs an integer and produces the bit string that represents it under this representation and another routine which inputs such a bit string and produces the integer
that it represents. Write a third BASIC routine which inputs two such bit strings and
produces the bit string that represents the sum of the two integers represented by the
two input bit strings.

9. Assume a ternary computer in which the basic unit of memory is a "trit" (ternary
digit) rather than a bit. Such a trit can have three possible settings (0, 1, and 2) rather
than just two (0 and 1). Show how nonnegative integers can be represented in ternary
notation using such trits by a method analogous to binary notation using bits. Is there
any nonnegative integer that can be represented using ternary notation and trits which
cannot be represented using binary notation and bits? Are there any that can be represented using bits which cannot be represented using trits? Why are binary computers
more common than ternary computers?

10. Write BASIC routines to convert between binary and ternary numbers (see Exercise 9). To convert from binary to ternary, the input should be a bit string and the output should be a character string consisting of the characters "0", "1", and "2". To convert in the opposite direction, the input should be a character string and the output should be a bit string.

11. Write BASIC routines that input two character strings representing ternary nonnegative integers as in Exercise 10 and output the character strings representing their sum, difference, and product, respectively.

12. What are the largest and smallest nonnegative integers that can be represented in ternary notation using n trits? How many trits are necessary to represent the nonnegative integer m? If an integer can be represented by k decimal digits, how many bits and trits are necessary to represent it?

13. In implementing the *CONCATVAR* operation in terms of *MOVEVAR* as shown in the text, why was the second string moved into the result area before the first?

2. ARRAYS IN BASIC

In this section we examine a familiar data structure, the *array*. The array is an example of a *composite structure*; that is, it is made up of simpler data types which exist in the language. The study of a composite structure involves an analysis of how simpler structures combine to form the composite and how to extract a specific component from the composite. We will see how to use the array and how it is implemented in BASIC.

The simplest form of an array is a *one-dimensional array*, which may be defined abstractly as a finite ordered set of homogeneous elements. By "finite" we mean that there are a specific number of elements in the array. This number may be large or small, but it must exist. By "ordered" we mean that the elements of the array are arranged so that there is a first, second, third, and so on. By "homogeneous" we mean that all the elements in the array must be of the same data type. For example, an array may contain all integers or all character strings but may not contain both.

There are two basic operations that can be performed on a one-dimensional array. The first is the extraction of a particular element from an array. The inputs to this operation are the array and an indication of which element of the array is to be accessed. This indication is given as an integer, called an *index*. Thus the operation

$$extract(a,5)$$

retrieves element number 5 of the array a. The second operation stores an element into an array. For example, the operation

$$store(a,5,x)$$

stores the value of the variable x into element number 5 of the array.

Thus far, we have introduced an abstract data structure and two abstract operations. BASIC includes an implementation of this data structure and these operations. To declare a one-dimensional array named A with 100 elements, all of which are integers, the programmer may write

```
10   DEFINT A
20   DIM A(100)
```

The function *extract*(a,5) is written in BASIC as A(5), which refers to element number 5 of array A. The operation *store*(a,5,x) is written as the statement

```
100   A(5) = X
```

The smallest index of the array is called the **lower bound** and the largest is the **upper bound**. You may specify the upper bound of an array in a DIM statement, but the lower bound is always fixed. Some BASIC interpreters and compilers use a lower bound of 0, while others use a lower bound of 1. Still others allow you to select either as the lower bound of all arrays in a particular program. (In order to promote program uniformity, the programs in this book will not make use of the zeroth element of the array unless otherwise specified. This enables the same program to be run regardless of the convention adopted by a particular version of BASIC.) The number of elements in a one-dimensional array, called the **range** of the array, is equal to 1 more than the difference between the upper and lower bounds. If l is the lower bound, u the upper bound, and r the range of a one-dimensional array, then $r = u - l + 1$. Thus, in a version of BASIC with a lower bound of zero, an array A established by the statement

DIM A(10)

contains 11 elements (since $10 - 0 + 1 = 11$), while in a version with a lower bound of 1, A contains 10 elements (since $10 - 1 + 1 = 10$).

One important feature of a BASIC array is that once such an array is created, it is static; that is, its upper bound (and therefore its range) cannot be changed. Attempts to reDIMension an array will result in an error. Thus a BASIC array has a fixed number of elements throughout its existence. Before any values can be stored in the array, its size must be established.

Using One-Dimensional Arrays

A one-dimensional array is used when it is necessary to keep a large number of items in memory and reference all the items in a uniform manner. Let us see how these two requirements apply to practical situations.

Suppose that we wish to read 100 numbers, find their average, and determine by how much each number deviates from that average. The following program accomplishes this. (In the BASIC programs in this book we use variable names with an arbitrary number of characters, although some versions of BASIC do not permit this. A more complete discussion of our BASIC programming conventions is deferred until Section 2.1.)

```
10   'program average
20   DIM NUM(100)
30   SUM = 0
40   'read the numbers into the array and compute their sum
50   FOR I = 1 TO 100
60       READ NUM(I)
70       SUM = SUM + NUM(I)
80   NEXT I
90   'at this point, SUM contains the sum of the numbers
100  AVG = SUM/100
110  'print headings
120  PRINT "NUMBER", "DIFFERENCE"
130  'print each number and the difference
140  FOR I = 1 TO 100
150      DEVIAT = NUM(I) - AVG
160      PRINT NUM(I), DEVIAT
170  NEXT I
180  'print average
190  PRINT: PRINT "AVERAGE IS "; AVG
200  END
500  DATA  . . .
```

This program uses two groups of 100 numbers. The first group is the set of input numbers and is represented by the array NUM, and the second group is the set of differences which are the successive values assigned to the variable DEVIAT in the loop 140–170. The question arises as to why an array is used to hold all the values of the first group simultaneously but only a single variable is used to hold the values of the second group, one at a time.

The answer is quite simple. Each difference is computed and printed and is never needed again. Thus the variable DEVIAT can be reused for the difference of the next number and the average. However, the original numbers which are the values of the array NUM must all be kept in memory. Although each number could be added to SUM as it is input, it must be retained until after the average is computed in order for the program to compute the difference between it and the average. Therefore, an array is used.

Of course, 100 separate variables could have been used to hold the numbers. The advantage of an array, however, is that it allows the programmer to declare only a single variable and yet obtain many storage locations. Furthermore, in conjunction with the FOR-NEXT loop, it also allows the programmer to reference each element of the group in a uniform manner instead of requiring a statement such as

                         60 READ N1, N2, N3, . . .

A particular element of an array may be retrieved through its index. For example, suppose that a company is using a program in which an array is declared by

10   DIM SALES(10)

The array will hold sales figures for a 10-year period. Suppose that each DATA statement in the program contains an integer from 1 to 10 representing a year as well as a sales figure for that year, and it is desired to read the sales figure into the appropriate element of the array. This can be accomplished by executing the statement

100   READ YR, SALES(YR)

within a loop. In this statement, a particular element of the array is accessed directly by using its index. Consider the situation if 10 variables S1, S2, . . . , S9, S0 had been declared. Then even after executing READ YR to set YR to the integer representing the year, the sales figure could not be read into the proper variable without coding something like

100   IF YR = 1 THEN READ S1

.

.

.

180   IF YR = 9 THEN READ S9
190   IF YR = 10 THEN READ S0

This is bad enough with 10 elements—imagine the inconvenience if there were 100 or 1000.

Implementing One-Dimensional Arrays

A one-dimensional array can be easily implemented. The BASIC declaration

10   DIM B(100)

reserves 100 successive memory locations (we are assuming a lower bound of 1), each large enough to contain a single number. The address of the first of these locations is called the **base address** of the array B and will be denoted by *base*(B). Suppose that the size of each individual element of the array is *esize*. Then a reference to the element B(1) is to the element at location *base*(B), a reference to B(2) is to the element at *base*(B) + *esize*, a reference to B(3) is to the element *base*(B) + 2*esize. In general, a reference to B(I) is to the element at location *base*(B) + (I − 1)*esize. Thus it is possible to reference any element in the array, given its index. [Naturally, if the lower bound of an array is zero, a reference to the element B(0) is to the element at location *base*(B), a reference to B(1) is to the element at *base*(B) + *esize*, and, in general, a reference to B(I) is to the element at location *base*(B) + I * *esize*.]

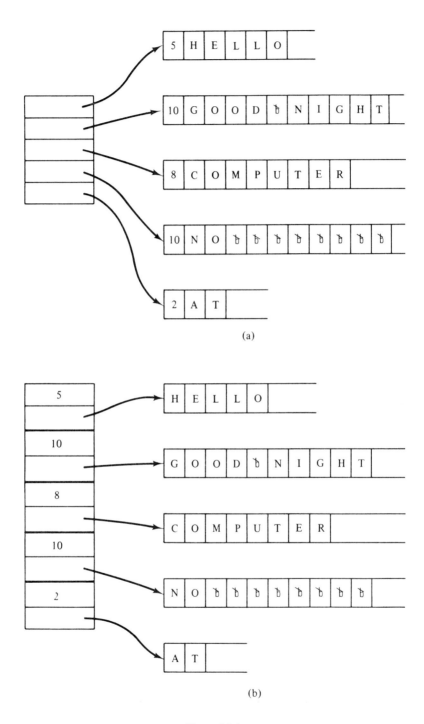

(a)

(b)

Figure 1.2.1

If the elements of an array do not have a fixed size, however, this method cannot be used to implement such an array. (An example of this is an array of character strings in which the length of each string can vary.) This is because the foregoing method of calculating the address of a specific element of the array depends upon knowing the fixed size *esize* of each preceding element. If not all the elements have the same size, a different implementation must be used.

One method of implementing an array of varying-sized elements is to reserve a contiguous set of memory locations, each of which holds an address. The contents of each such memory location is the address of the varying-length array element in some other portion of memory. For example, Figure 1.2.1(a) illustrates an array of five varying-length character strings under this implementation. The arrows in that diagram indicate addresses of other portions of memory. The character "b" indicates a blank.

Since the length of each address is fixed, the location of the address of a particular element can be computed in the same way that the location of a fixed-length element was computed in the previous examples. Once this location is known, its contents can be used to determine the location of the actual array element. This, of course, adds an extra level of indirection to referencing an array element by involving an extra memory reference, which in turn decreases efficiency. However, this is a small price to pay for the convenience of being able to maintain such an array.

A similar method for implementing an array of varying-sized elements is to keep all fixed-length portions of the elements together with the address of the varying-length portion in the contiguous area. For example, in the implementation of character strings presented in the preceding section, each such string contains a fixed-length portion (a 1-byte-length field) and a variable-length portion (the character string itself). One implementation of an array of character strings keeps the length of the string together with the address, as shown in Figure 1.2.1(b). The advantage of this method is that those parts of an element that are of fixed length can be examined without an extra memory reference. For example, the LEN function for character strings can be implemented with a single memory lookup. The fixed-length information for an array element of varying length which is stored in the contiguous memory area of the array is often called a *header*.

Two-Dimensional Arrays

An array need not be a linear set of homogeneous elements; it can also be multi-dimensional. A *two-dimensional array* is one in which each element is accessed by two indices: a row number and a column number. Figure 1.2.2 illustrates such a two-dimensional array declared by the BASIC statement

10   DIM A(3,5)

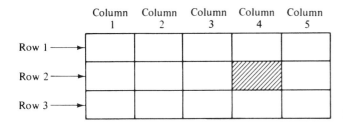

Figure 1.2.2

Assuming a lower bound of 1, the element that is darkened in Figure 1.2.2 is referred to as A(2,4), since it is in row 2 and column 4. As in the case of a one-dimensional array, the lower bound of each dimension is 1 or 0 by definition.

The number of rows or columns is equal to the upper bound minus the lower bound plus 1. This number is called the *range* of the dimension. In the array A above, the range of the first dimension is $3 - 1 + 1$ (assuming a lower bound of 1), which is 3, and the range of the second dimension is $5 - 1 + 1$, which is 5. Thus the array A has three rows and five columns. The number of elements in a two-dimensional array is equal to the product of the number of rows and the number of columns. Thus the array A contains $3 \times 5 = 15$ elements. (If the lower bound were zero, the array would have four rows, six columns, and 24 elements.)

A two-dimensional array clearly illustrates the differences between a *logical* and a *physical* view of data. A two-dimensional array is a logical data structure which is useful in programming and problem solving. For example, such an array is useful in describing an object that is physically two-dimensional, such as a map or a checkerboard. It is also useful in organizing a set of values that are dependent on two inputs. For example, a program for a department store which has 20 branches, each of which sells 30 items, might include a two-dimensional array declared by

                    10   DIM SALES(20,30)

Each element SALES(I,J) represents the amount of item J sold in branch I.

However, although it is convenient for the programmer to think of the elements of such an array as being organized in a two-dimensional table and programming languages do indeed include facilities for treating them as a two-dimensional array, the hardware of most computers have no such facilities. An array must be stored in the memory of a computer and that memory is usually linear. By this we mean that the memory of a computer is essentially a one-dimensional array. A single address (which may be viewed as a subscript for a one-dimensional array) is used to retrieve a particular item from memory. In order to implement a two-dimensional array, it is necessary to develop a method of ordering its elements in a linear array and of transforming a two-dimensional reference to the linear representation.

One method of representing a two-dimensional array in memory is the *column-major* representation. Under this representation, the first column of the array occupies the first set of memory locations reserved for the array, the second column occupies the next set, and so on. There may also be several locations at the start of the physical array which serve as a header and which contain the upper bounds of the two dimensions. (This header should not be confused with the headers discussed above. This header is for the entire array, whereas the headers mentioned earlier are headers for the individual array elements.) Figure 1.2.3 illustrates the column-major representation of the two-dimensional array A declared above (assuming a lower bound of 1) and illustrated in Figure 1.2.2. Alternatively, the header need not be contiguous to the array elements, but could instead contain the address of the first element of the array. Additionally, if the elements of the two-dimensional array are variable-length objects, the elements of the contiguous area could themselves contain the addresses of those objects in a form similar to those of Figure 1.2.1 for linear arrays.

Let us suppose that a two-dimensional array is stored in column-major sequence, as in Figure 1.2.3 and let us suppose that, for an array AR, $base$(AR) is the address of the first element of the array. That is, if AR is declared by

$$10 \quad \text{DIM AR(U1,U2)}$$

where U1 and U2 are the integer upper bounds, then (assuming a lower bound of 1) $base$(AR) is the address of AR(1,1). Let us define $r1$ as the range of the first dimension. We also assume that $esize$ is the size of each element in the array. Let us calculate the address of an arbitrary element, AR(I1,I2). Since the element is in column I2, its address can be calculated by computing the address of the first element of column I2 and adding the quantity $(I1 - 1)*esize$ (this quantity represents how far into column I2 the element at row I1 is). But in order to reach the first element of column I2 [which is the element AR(1,I1)], it is necessary to pass through $(I2 - 1)$ complete columns each of which contains $r1$ elements (since there is one element from each row in each column), so that the address of the first element of column I2 is at $base$(AR) $+ (I2 - 1)*r1*esize$. Therefore, the address of AR(I1,I2) is at

$$base(\text{AR}) + [(I2 - 1)*r1 + (I1 - 1)]*esize.$$

As an example, consider the array A of Figure 1.2.2 whose representation is illustrated in Figure 1.2.3. In this array, U1 = 3 and U2 = 5, so that $base$(A) is the address of A(1,1) and R1 equals 3. Let us also suppose that each element of the array requires a single unit of storage, so that $esize$ equals 1. (This is not necessarily true; for simplicity, however, we accept this assumption.) Then the location of A(2,3) may be computed as follows. In order to reach column 3, we must skip over columns 1 and 2. Each of those columns contains three elements consisting of one memory location each. Thus the first element of column 3 [which is A(1,3)] is six elements past the address of A(1,1), which is $base$(A).

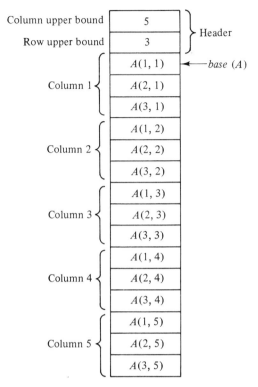

Figure 1.2.3

The element A(2,3) is one element past A(1,3). The formula above yields the address of A(2,3) as

$$base(A) + [(3-1)*3 + (2-1)]*1$$

which is

$$base(A) + 6 + 1 = base(A) + 7.$$

You may confirm the fact that A(2,3) is seven units past $base(A)$ in Figure 1.2.3.

The derivation above assumed a lower bound of 1. In those BASICs in which the lower bound is 0, the formula above for the address of AR(I1,I2) reads

$$base(AR) + [(I2*r1) + I1] * esize$$

The reader is asked, as an exercise, to derive this modification.

Multi-Dimensional Arrays

BASIC allows arrays which have more than two dimensions. For example, a three-dimensional array may be declared by

$$10 \quad DIM \ C(3,2,4)$$

and is illustrated in Figure 1.2.4(a). An element of this array is specified by three subscripts, such as C(2,1,3). The first subscript specifies a plane number, the second subscript a row number, and the third a column number. Such an array is useful when a value is determined by three inputs. For example, an array of temperatures might be indexed by latitude, longitude, and altitude.

For obvious reasons, the geometric analogy breaks down when we go beyond three dimensions. However, BASIC does allow an arbitrary number of dimensions. For example, a six-dimensional array may be declared by

$$10 \quad \text{DIM } D(2,8,5,3,15,7)$$

Referencing an element of this array would require six subscripts, such as D(2,7,1,1,14,3). The number of different subscripts which are allowed in a particular position (the range of a particular dimension) equals the upper bound of that dimension minus its lower bound plus 1. The number of elements in an array is the product of the ranges of all its dimensions. For example, the array C above contains $3 \times 2 \times 4 = 24$ elements, while the array D contains $2 \times 8 \times 5 \times 3 \times 15 \times 7 = 25{,}200$ elements (assuming lower bounds of 1).

The column-major representation of arrays can be extended to arrays of more than two-dimensions. Figure 1.2.4(b) illustrates the representation of the array C of Figure 1.2.4(a). The elements of the six-dimensional array D described above are ordered as follows:

$$D(1,1,1,1,1,1)$$
$$D(2,1,1,1,1,1)$$
$$D(1,2,1,1,1,1)$$
$$D(2,2,1,1,1,1)$$
$$D(1,3,1,1,1,1)$$
$$\cdots$$
$$\cdots$$
$$D(1,6,5,3,15,7)$$
$$D(2,6,5,3,15,7)$$
$$D(1,7,5,3,15,7)$$
$$D(2,7,5,3,15,7)$$
$$D(1,8,5,3,15,7)$$
$$D(2,8,5,3,15,7)$$

That is, the first subscript varies most rapidly and a subscript is not increased until all possible combinations of the subscripts to its left have been exhausted.

What mechanism is needed to access an element of an arbitrary multidimensional array? Suppose that AR is an n-dimensional array declared by

$$10 \quad \text{DIM } AR(U_1, U_2, \ldots, U_n)$$

which is stored in column-major order. Each element of AR is assumed to occupy *esize* storage locations and *base*(AR) is defined as the address of the first element of the array, which is AR($l,l, \ldots ,l$), where the lower bound l is either 1 or

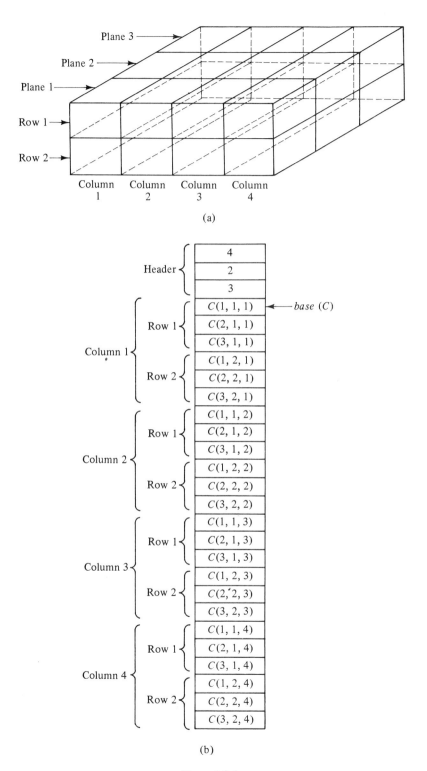

(a)

(b)

Figure 1.2.4

0, depending on the implementation. r_i is defined as $U_i - l + 1$ for all i between 1 and n. Then in order to access the element

$$AR(I_1, I_2, \ldots, I_n)$$

it is first necessary to pass through $(I_n - l)$ complete "hyperplanes," each consisting of $r_1 * r_2 * \ldots * r_{n-1}$ elements to reach the first element of AR whose last subscript is I_n. Then it is necessary to pass through an additional $(I_{n-1} - l)$ groups of $r_1 * r_2 * \ldots * r_{n-2}$ elements in order to reach the first element of AR whose last two subscripts are I_{n-1} and I_n, respectively. A similar process must be carried out through the other dimensions until the last element whose last $n - 1$ subscripts match those of the desired element is reached. Finally, it is necessary to pass through $(I_1 - l)$ additional elements to reach the element desired.

Thus the address of $AR(I_1, I_2, \ldots, I_n)$ may be written as $base(AR) + esize$ * $[(I_n - l) * r_1 * r_2 * \ldots * r_{n-1} + (I_{n-1} - l) * r_1 * r_2 * \ldots * r_{n-2} + \ldots + (I_2 - l) * r_1 + (I_1 - l)]$ which can be evaluated more efficiently by using the equivalent formula

$$base(AR) + esize * [I_1 - l + r_1 * ((I_2 - l) + r_2 * (\ldots$$
$$\ldots + r_{n-2} * (I_{n-1} - l + r_{n-1} * (I_n - l)) \ldots))]$$

This formula may be evaluated by the following algorithm (assuming a variable l to hold the lower bound, and arrays i and r of size n to hold the indices and the ranges respectively):

```
offset = 0
for j = n to 1 step −1
    offset = r(j) * offset + (i(j) − l)
next j
addr = base(AR) + esize*offset
```

Handling Subscript Errors

Suppose, as is often the case, that a programmer erroneously uses a subscript which is not within the range of the array bounds. For example, the programmer references A(I), where A is an array with subscripts 1 to 100 and where the current value of I is 101. Such mistakes are quite common when expressions are used as subscripts or inside a FOR-NEXT loop which is repeated once too often. Because the reference is illegal, the results of such a reference are unspecified by the BASIC language. Since the programmer is not programming in legal BASIC, he or she cannot expect BASIC to define what the results will be. In many BASIC implementations such a reference results in an error that causes program execution to halt.

Let us examine some of the alternative actions that might be taken when a subscript is out of bounds. The simplest alternative is to do nothing. That is, whenever a reference to an array element A(I) is made, the machine proceeds to compute the address of that element using the formula given above as though the subscript were legitimate. For example, if the size of each array element (*esize*) is one storage unit and the array was declared with bounds 1 and 100, a reference to the element with subscript 101 will result in the address which is 100 storage units past the first element of the array. That address is no longer within the array and may even be outside the area in memory set aside for the entire program. The system may take whatever action is appropriate. If the address is outside the program's memory area, this may involve printing an error message and stopping the program. However, the error message may not indicate an illegal array reference; it may state only that an attempt is being made to access a location that is nonexistent or is not allocated to the program.

It may be that the computed address is within the program area but that the information at that address is not of the proper format for an array element. When an attempt is made to interpret that information as an array element, the system will produce an error message stating that the information is in incorrect format. Again, there is no indication that the cause of the error was a subscript that was out of bounds.

Even if the programmer receives one of these imprecise messages, things could be worse. A far more distressing possibility is that the computed location is within the program area and that the information contained therein is in proper format. In that case, the system will simply use that information and will give no indication that anything is wrong. Instead, it will proceed to produce incorrect results based on that information. Often the programmer will have no indication that the results are incorrect. Or the programmer may see that they are obviously incorrect but will have no indication of where the large program went wrong.

In all of the cases noted above, the language implementation relies on the backup error-detection system of the hardware or of the operating system. It does not itself check for whether the subscript is within bounds of the specific array. Since a subscript may be a variable or an expression, there is no way to determine, without explicitly checking the subscript for validity, whether or not its value will be within bounds. A check that is made during execution must be made each time the statement is executed. Thus if a statement that appears within a loop is repeated 1000 times, an execution check would involve 1000 checks. An execution check means that every array reference involves not only an address computation but also a check for validity. This sharply decreases efficiency. Furthermore, in order to be able to check a subscript for validity, it is necessary to keep the upper bound of the array in memory during execution time.

The alternative to doing nothing is to forgo efficiency for clarity and ease of debugging. An array is not represented solely by the elements of which it is comprised. Rather, each array has a header that contains its upper bounds. This header could be located at the beginning of the contiguous area that holds the array elements, or it could be a separate entity and contain the base address of the array as well as the upper bounds. Whenever a reference to an array element is made during execution, a test is made to ensure that the subscript lies within the range before computing the element's address. If the subscript is out of bounds, a detailed error message giving the name of the array and the value of the illegal subscript can be printed.

As mentioned earlier, many BASIC implementations forgo efficiency for program reliability and perform checking throughout program execution. Should an illegal array reference occur, the ERROR condition is raised and execution halts. For those BASICs that possess an ON ERROR statement, alternative actions may be specified at the programmer's discretion.

EXERCISES

1. Write a BASIC subroutine that sorts the contents of a one-dimensional array into ascending order.

2. The *median* of an array of numbers is the element m of the array such that half the remaining numbers in the array are greater than or equal to m and half are less than or equal to m, if the number of elements in the array is odd. If the number of elements is even, the median is the average of the two elements $m1$ and $m2$ such that half the remaining elements are greater than or equal to $m1$ and $m2$, and half the elements are less than or equal to $m1$ and $m2$. Write a BASIC subroutine that computes the median of a set of numbers in an array.

3. The *mode* of an array of numbers is the number m in the array which is repeated most frequently. If more than one number is repeated with equal maximal frequency, there is no mode. Write a BASIC subroutine that either finds the mode of an array of numbers or determines that the mode does not exist.

4. Write a BASIC subroutine which reverses a one-dimensional array of numbers (so that the first element of the array becomes the element that was previously last, the second element becomes the one that was previously next to last, etc.).

5. An $n \times n$ array a is *symmetric* if the element $a(i,j)$ equals $a(j,i)$ for all i and j between 1 and n. Write a program to input the elements of a 5×5 array in column-major order, print the array in tabular format, and print a message as to whether or not the array is symmetric.

6. Write a BASIC program to read a set of temperature readings. A reading consists of two numbers: an integer between -90 and 90 representing the latitude at which the reading was taken, and the observed temperature at that latitude. Print a table consisting of each latitude and the average temperature at that latitude. If there are no readings at a particular latitude, print NO DATA instead of an average. Then print the average temperature in the northern and southern hemispheres (the northern hemisphere consists of latitudes 1 through 90 and the southern hemisphere consists of latitudes -1 through -90). (This average temperature should be computed as the average of the averages, not the average of the original readings.) Also determine which hemisphere is warmer. In making the determination, take the average temperatures in all latitudes of the hemisphere for which there are data for both that latitude and the corresponding latitude in the other hemisphere. (For example, if there are

data for latitude 57 but not for latitude -57, the average temperature for latitude 57 should be ignored in determining which hemisphere is warmer.)

7. Assume that you are writing a program for a chain of 20 department stores, each of which sells 10 different items. Every month, each store manager submits data for each item consisting of a branch number (from 1 to 20), an item number (from 1 to 10), and a sales figure (less than $100,000) representing the amount of sales for that item in that branch. However, some managers may not submit data for some items (e.g., not all items are sold in all branches). You are to write a BASIC program to read these data and print a table with 12 columns. The first column should contain the branch numbers from 1 to 20 and the word TOTAL in the last line. The next 10 columns should contain the sales figures for each of the 10 items for each of the branches, with the total sales of each item in the last line. The last column should contain the total sales of each of the 20 branches for all items, with the grand total sales figure for the chain in the lower right-hand corner. Each column should have an appropriate heading. If no sales were reported for a particular branch and item, assume zero sales. Do not assume that your input is in any particular order.

8. **(a)** Show how a checkerboard can be represented by a BASIC array. Show how to represent the state of a game of checkers at a particular instant. Write a BASIC routine which prints all possible moves that black can make from a particular checkerboard position.
   (b) Do the same as in part (a) for the game of chess.

9. Write a program to print out a method of placing eight queens on a chessboard so that no two queens are in the same row, column, or diagonal. The output of your program should be eight lines, each containing eight characters. Each character represents a position on the board which is either an asterisk (indicating an empty position) or a 1 (indicating a position occupied by a queen).

10. Assume that each element of an array A stored in column-major order occupies four units of storage. If A is declared by each of the following, and the address of the first element of A is 100, find the address of the indicated array element. (Assume a lower bound of 1 in all cases.)

    (a) DIM   A(100)   address of A(10)
    (b) DIM   A(10,20)   address of A(1,1)
    (c) DIM   A(10,20)   address of A(5,1)
    (d) DIM   A(10,20)   address of A(1,10)
    (e) DIM   A(10,20)   address of A(2,10)
    (f) DIM   A(10,20)   address of A(10,20)
    (g) DIM   A(5,6,4)   address of A(3,2,4)

11. An array can be stored in *row-major* order, in which the elements of the first row are followed by the elements of the second row, and so on.
    (a) Write a program to read the elements of a 5×5 array from data in column-major order and print them in row-major order.
    (b) Write a program to read the elements of a 5×5 array in row-major order and print them in column-major order.

12. Develop formulas and algorithms as in the text to access an array element if the array is stored in row-major order rather than column-major order (see Exercise 11).

13. A *lower triangular* array a is an $n \times n$ array in which $a(i,j) = 0$ if $i < j$. What is the maximum number of nonzero elements in such an array? How can these elements by stored sequentially in memory? Develop an algorithm for accessing $a(i,j)$ where $i \geq j$. Define an *upper triangular* array in an analogous manner and do the same as instructed above for such an array.

14. A *strictly lower triangular array* a is an $n \times n$ array in which $a(i,j) = 0$ if $i \leq j$. Answer the questions of Exercise 13 for such an array.

15. Let a and b be two $n \times n$ lower triangular arrays (see Exercises 13 and 14). Show how an $n \times (n + 1)$ array c can be used to contain the nonzero elements of the two arrays. Which elements of c represent the elements of $a(i,j)$ and $b(i,j)$, respectively?

16. A *tridiagonal* array a is an $n \times n$ array in which $a(i,j) = 0$ if the absolute value of $i - j$ is greater than 1. What is the maximum number of nonzero elements in such an array? How can these elements be stored sequentially in memory? Develop an algorithm for accessing $a(i,j)$ if the absolute value of $i - j$ is 1 or less. Do the same for an array a in which $a(i,j) = 0$ if the absolute value of $i - j$ is greater than k.

17. Develop a method of implementing a *nonhomogeneous array*; that is, implement an array whose elements are not all of the same data type. Can BASIC syntax be extended to deal with this new data structure?

3. AGGREGATING DATA IN BASIC

Very often, it is helpful to view a collection of data as a single entity. For example, suppose that we wish to retain information relating to an employee. If the employee data include a first name, middle initial, and last name, those data could be initialized as follows:

```
10   DEFSTR F, L, M
20   READ FIRST, MIDINIT, LAST

        . . .
```

Under this method, there is no relationship among the three components of the name.

An alternative organization is to group the three components of the name into a single entity (an array) as follows:

```
10   DEFSTR N
20   DIM NAME(3)
30        FIRST = 1
40        MIDINIT = 2
50        LAST = 3
60   READ NAME(FIRST), NAME(MIDINIT), NAME(LAST)
```

In this representation, NAME(FIRST) refers to the first name, NAME(MIDINIT) to the middle initial, and NAME(LAST) to the last name. The advantage of this representation is that we can refer to the complete name of the employee (by NAME) when necessary and to the individual components (by their full names) when necessary.

This representation can be extended to the case where we wish to retain information on a number of employees. For example, suppose that we wish to store the names of 50 employees. We could begin the program as follows:

```
10   DEFSTR N
20   DIM NAME(50,3)
30       FIRST = 1
40       MIDINIT = 2
50       LAST = 3
60   FOR I = 1 TO 50
70       READ NAME(I,FIRST), NAME(I,MIDINIT), NAME(I,LAST)
80   NEXT I
```

Of course, the array NAME could have been represented by three individual arrays, FIRST(50), MIDINIT(50), and LAST(50), but the relationship among the three arrays would have been lost.

Note that in both of the examples above we grouped together variables of the same data type (in this case, character strings). Variables of different data types cannot be grouped together in this manner; they must be enumerated separately. For example, if we wished to retain additional data relating to a set of 50 employees, we may group all related components explicitly into several two-dimensional arrays, as follows:

```
10   DEFSTR H, N, P, R, W
20   'employee records
30       DIM NAME(50,3)
40           FIRST = 1
50           MIDINIT = 2
60           LAST = 3
70       DIM RESIDENCE(50,4)
80           ADDR = 1
90           CITY = 2
100          STATE = 3
110          ZIP = 4
120      DIM POSITN(50,2)
130          DEPTNO = 1
140          JOBTITLE = 2
150      DIM SALARY(50)
160      DIM DEPENDENTS(50)
170      DIM HEALTHPLAN(50)
180      DIM WHENHIRED(50)
```

Using this representation we may refer to the first name of the Ith employee by NAME(I,FIRST) and to his or her job title by POSITN(I,JOBTITLE). The last names and salaries of all employees may be printed by

```
200   FOR I = 1 TO 50
210       PRINT NAME(I,LAST), SALARY(I)
220   NEXT I
```

We may print the last names and residences of all employees by simply coding

```
200   FOR I = 1 TO 50
210       PRINT NAME(I, LAST)
220       FOR J = 1 TO 4
230           PRINT RESIDENCE(I,J)
240       NEXT J
250       PRINT:                    'skip a line
260   NEXT I
```

A set of related data items grouped together into a single entity is called a *data aggregate* or a *record*. Some high-level programming languages (e.g., Pascal, PL/I, COBOL) support the aggregating of different elements into a single variable; most versions of BASIC do not (unless the elements have the same attributes, in which case they can be placed into an array). The grouping of related information into a single array contributes greatly to program clarity. However, variables with different data types, such as SALARY and HEALTHPLAN, cannot be grouped together into a single array.

Representing Other Data Structures

Throughout the remainder of this text, arrays will be used to represent the more complex data structures which are studied. Aggregating data is useful because it enables us to group objects within a single entity and to name each of these objects according to its function.

As examples of how data aggregates can be used in this fashion, let us consider the problems of representing rational numbers and multidimensional arrays.

Rational Numbers

Let us apply the concept of data aggregates to the representation of rational numbers. A *rational number* is any number that can be expressed as the quotient of two integers. Thus

$$1/2, \quad 3/4, \quad 2/3, \quad \text{and} \quad 2 \text{ (i.e., 2/1)}$$

are all rational numbers, whereas

$$\sqrt{2} \quad \text{and} \quad \pi$$

are not. A computer usually represents a rational number by means of its decimal approximation. If we instruct the computer to print 1/3, the computer responds with .333333. Although this is close enough (the difference between .333333 and one-third is only one three-millionth), it is not exact. If we were to ask for the value of 1/3 + 1/3, the result would be .666666 (which equals .333333 + .333333), while the result of printing 2/3 might be .666667. This would mean that the result of the test 1/3 + 1/3 = 2/3 would be false! In most instances, the decimal approximation is good enough, but sometimes it is not. It is therefore desirable to implement a representation of rational numbers for which exact arithmetic can be performed.

How can we represent a rational number exactly? Since a rational number consists of a numerator and a denominator, we can represent a rational number RTNL using a data aggregate as follows:

```
10   DEFINT R
20   DIM RTNL (2)
30       NMRTR = 1
40       DNMNTR = 2
```

We refer to the numerator as RTNL(NMRTR) and to the denominator as RTNL(DNMNTR).

You might think that we are now ready to define rational number arithmetic for our new representation, but there is one significant problem. Suppose that we defined two rational numbers R1 and R2 by

```
50   DIM R1(2), R2(2)
```

and we had given them values. How can we test if the two numbers are the same? Perhaps you might want to code

```
100   IF R1(NMRTR) = R2(NMRTR) AND R1(DNMNTR) = R2(DNMNTR)
          THEN . . .
```

That is, if both numerators and denominators are equal, the two rational numbers are equal. However, it is possible for both numerators and denominators to be unequal, yet the two rational numbers are the same. For example, the numbers 1/2 and 2/4 are indeed equal, although their numerators (1 and 2) as well as their denominators (2 and 4) are unequal. We therefore need a new way of testing equality under our representation.

Well, why are 1/2 and 2/4 equal? The answer is that they both represent the same ratio. One out of two and two out of four are both one-half. In order to test rational numbers for equality, we must first reduce them to lowest terms. Once both numbers have been reduced to lowest terms, we can test for equality by simple comparison of their numerators and denominators.

We define a ***reduced rational number*** as a rational number in which there is no integer greater than 1 by which both the denominator and numerator can be divided evenly. Thus

$$1/2 , \quad 2/3, \quad \text{and} \quad 10/1$$

are all reduced to lowest terms, whereas

$$4/8, \quad 12/18, \quad \text{and} \quad 15/6$$

are not. In our example, 2/4 reduced to lowest terms is 1/2, so the two numbers are equal.

A procedure known as Euclid's algorithm can be used to reduce any fraction of the form *numerator/denominator* into its lowest terms. This procedure may be outlined as follows:

1. Let *a* be the larger of the *numerator* and *denominator* and let *b* be the smaller.
2. Divide *b* into *a*, finding a quotient *q* and a remainder *r* (i.e., $a = q*b + r$).
3. Let $a = b$ and $b = r$.
4. Repeat steps 2 and 3 until *b* is zero.
5. Divide both the *numerator* and the *denominator* by the value of *a*.

As an illustration, let us reduce 1032/1976 to its lowest terms.

Step 0	numerator = 1032	denominator = 1976	
Step 1	$a = 1976$	$b = 1032$	
Step 2	$a = 1976$	$b = 1032$	$q = 1\ r = 944$
Step 3	$a = 1032$	$b = 944$	
Steps 4 and 2	$a = 1032$	$b = 944$	$q = 1\ r = 88$
Step 3	$a = 944$	$b = 88$	
Steps 4 and 2	$a = 944$	$b = 88$	$q = 10\ r = 64$
Step 3	$a = 88$	$b = 64$	
Steps 4 and 2	$a = 88$	$b = 64$	$q = 1\ r = 24$
Step 3	$a = 64$	$b = 24$	
Steps 4 and 2	$a = 64$	$b = 24$	$q = 2\ r = 16$
Step 3	$a = 24$	$b = 16$	
Steps 4 and 2	$a = 24$	$b = 16$	$q = 1\ r = 8$
Step 3	$a = 16$	$b = 8$	
Steps 4 and 2	$a = 16$	$b = 8$	$q = 2\ r = 0$
Step 3	$a = 8$	$b = 0$	
Step 5	$1032/8 = 129$		$1976/8 = 247$

Thus 1032/1976 in lowest terms is 129/247.

Let us write a subroutine to reduce a rational number RTNL. Before we call this subroutine, RTNL is not necessarily reduced, but after we return from it, RTNL is reduced.

```
2000   'subroutine reduce
2010   'step 1 – Find the larger of the numerator and denominator
2020   IF RTNL(NMRTR) > RTNL(DNMNTR)
          THEN A = RTNL(NMRTR): B = RTNL(DNMNTR): GO TO 2040
2030   B = RTNL(NMRTR): A = RTNL(DNMNTR)
2040   Q = INT(A / B):                        'step 2
2050   R = A – Q * B
2060   A = B:                                 'step 3
2070   B = R
2080   IF R > 0 THEN GO TO 2040:              'step 4
2090   RTNL(NMRTR) = RTNL(NMRTR)/A:           'step 5
2100   RTNL(DNMNTR) = RTNL(DNMNTR)/A
2110   RETURN
2120   'end subroutine reduce
```

Using the subroutine *reduce*, we can write another subroutine *equal*, which determines whether or not two rational numbers R1 and R2 are equal. If they are, the variable EQUAL is set to 1; otherwise, the variable EQUAL is set to 0.

```
1000   'subroutine equal
1010   'reduce R1 and R2 to lowest terms
1020   RTNL(NMRTR) = R1(NMRTR): RTNL(DNMNTR) =R1(DNMNTR)
1030   GOSUB 2000:      ' reduce R1
1040   R1(NMRTR) = RTNL(NMRTR): R1(DNMNTR) =RTNL(DNMNTR)
1050   RTNL(NMRTR) = R2(NMRTR): RTNL(DNMNTR) =R2(DNMNTR)
1060   GOSUB 2000:      ' reduce R2
1070   R2(NMRTR) = RTNL(NMRTR): R2(DNMNTR) =RTNL(DNMNTR)
1080   'check the reduced rationals for equality
1090   EQUAL = 0
1100   IF R1(NMRTR) =R2(NMRTR) AND R1(DNMNTR) =R2(DNMNTR)
          THEN EQUAL = 1
1110   RETURN
```

We may now write routines to perform arithmetic on rational numbers. We present a routine to multiply two rational numbers and leave as an exercise the problem of writing similar routines to add, subtract, and divide such numbers.

The input to the multiplication routine consists of two rational numbers, and our routine is to produce a third. In order to represent the three rational numbers, we choose to modify our representation slightly by defining a single data aggregate to represent all three rational numbers:

```
10    DEFINT R
20    DIM RTNL(3,2)
30        NMRTR = 1
40        DNMNTR = 2
50        FIRST = 1
60        SECND = 2
70        RESULT = 3
```

This data aggregate allows us to refer to the denominator of the first operand as RTNL(FIRST, DNMNTR) and to the numerator of the result as RTNL (RESULT, NMRTR). Recall that

$$(a/b) * (c/d) = (a*c) / (b*d)$$

However, since the numbers $a*c$ and $b*d$ may be large, we reduce the result to lowest terms before completing the multiplication routine. The following is a complete program to input two fractions repeatedly and print their product. The program is terminated when 0 is the input for the denominator of one of the fractions. Note that the subroutine *reduce* has been modified to reduce the rational number represented by RTNL(RESULT,NMRTR) over RTNL(RESULT,DNMNTR).

```
10   DEFINT R
20   DIM RTNL(3,2)
30            NMRTR = 1
40            DNMNTR = 2
50            FIRST = 1
60            SECND = 2
70            RESULT = 3
80   PRINT " ENTER THE NUMERATOR AND DENOMINATOR OF THE";
             " FIRST RATIONAL NUMBER "
90   INPUT RTNL (FIRST,NMRTR), RTNL(FIRST,DNMNTR)
100  IF RTNL(FIRST,DNMNTR) = 0 THEN GO TO 200
110  PRINT " ENTER THE NUMERATOR AND DENOMINATOR OF THE";
             " SECOND RATIONAL NUMBER "
120  INPUT RTNL(SECND,NMRTR), RTNL(SECND, DNMNTR)
130  IF RTNL(SECND,DNMNTR) = 0 THEN GO TO 200
140  'multiply the two numbers
150  GOSUB 1000
160  'print the reduced answer
170  PRINT " THE REDUCED PRODUCT IS "
180  PRINT RTNL(RESULT, NMRTR); " / "; RTNL(RESULT,DNMNTR)
190  GOTO 80
200  PRINT " A ZERO DENOMINATOR TERMINATES THE PROGRAM "
210  END

1000 'subroutine multiply
1010 'multiply the numerators
1020 RTNL(RESULT,NMRTR) = RTNL(FIRST,NMRTR) *
                                        RTNL(SECND,NMRTR)
1030 'multiply the denominators
1040 RTNL (RESULT,DNMNTR) = RTNL(FIRST,DNMNTR) *
                                        RTNL(SECND,DNMNTR)
```

```
1050   'reduce the result
1060   GOSUB 2000
1070   RETURN
1080   'end subroutine multiply

2000   'subroutine reduce
2010   'step 1
2020   IF RTNL(RESULT,NMRTR) > RTNL(RESULT,DNMNTR)
           THEN A = RTNL(RESULT,NMRTR):
               B = RTNL(RESULT,DNMNTR): GOTO 2040
2030   B = RTNL(RESULT, NMRTR): A = RTNL(RESULT, DNMNTR)
2040   Q = INT (A / B):                              'step 2
2050   R = A − Q * B
2060   A = B:                                        'step 3
2070   B = R
2080   IF R > 0 THE GOTO 2040:                       'step 4
2090   RTNL(RESULT,NMRTR) = RTNL(RESULT,NMRTR)/A:    'step 5
2100   RTNL(RESULT,DNMNTR) = RTNL(RESULT,DNMNTR)/A
2110   RETURN
2120   'end subroutine reduce
```

Multi-Dimensional Arrays

Recall from Section 2 that multidimensional arrays are actually implemented in a one-dimensional linear memory. Let us see how we can implement such arrays for ourselves in a system that permits only two-dimensional arrays. At the same time, we will also allow the lower bounds of each dimension to be specified by the user, rather than defaulting to 0 or 1. We will illustrate the implementation of three-dimensional arrays; the reader will see that the analog for any other number of dimensions is straightforward.

There are essentially two operations that must be implemented for a three-dimensional array: storing a value into the array at a specified position and extracting a value from a specified position within the array. These two operations will be denoted by

$$store(a,s1,s2,s3,v)$$

and

$$extract(a,s1,s2,s3)$$

respectively. In each of these, a is the data structure representing the array and $s1$, $s2$ and $s3$ are the three subscripts. In the *store* operation, v is the value stored at the specified position. The *extract* operation is a function that retrieves the value extracted from the specified position and assigns it to the variable *extract*.

Suppose that we wish to implement a three-dimensional array whose first dimension has lower bound 5 and upper bound 10, whose second dimension has lower bound 1 and upper bound 7, and whose third dimension has lower bound 2 and upper bound 4. Such an array would contain a total of 126 elements. This can be done by declaring a data aggregate such as

```
10   DIM BOUNDS(2,3)
20   LO = 1: 'BOUNDS(LO,I) holds the lower bound of the Ith dimension
30   HI = 2: 'BOUNDS(HI,I) holds the upper bound of the Ith dimension
40   DIM ELEMENT(126): 'the array ELEMENT holds the elements of the
                       'three-dimensional array
50   'initialization of lower and upper bounds
60   BOUNDS(LO,1) = 5
70   BOUNDS(LO,2) = 1
80   BOUNDS(LO,3) = 2
90   BOUNDS(HI,1) = 10
100  BOUNDS(HI,2) = 7
110  BOUNDS(HI,3) = 4
```

The values in the elements BOUNDS(LO,I) are the lower bounds of the three dimensions and the values in BOUNDS(HI,I) are their upper bounds. The array ELEMENT contains the actual elements of the array. The size of ELEMENT is equal to 126, which is the number of elements in the three-dimensional array $((10-5+1) * (7-1+1) * (4-2+1))$. The elements are stored in column-major order so that ELEMENT(1) represents ARRAY(5,1,2), ELEMENT(2) represents ARRAY(6,1,2), and so on. It is important to note that the array ELEMENT may not be combined with the array BOUNDS in a single array, since ELEMENT could conceivably contain characters (if we were implementing an array of character strings), whereas BOUNDS always contains integers.

The routines *store* and *extract* involve computing the offset for an array reference and using that offset as a subscript in the one-dimensional array ELEMENT. The routine *store* (which places the value V in the array position with the subscripts S1, S2, and S3) may be written as follows:

```
1000   'subroutine store
1010   'error checking
1020   IF S1 < BOUNDS(LO,1) OR S1 > BOUNDS(HI,1) OR
          S2 < BOUNDS(LO,2) OR S2 > BOUNDS(HI,2) OR
          S3 < BOUNDS(LO,3) OR S3 > BOUNDS(HI,3)
          THEN PRINT "ILLEGAL SUBSCRIPT": STOP
1030   OFFST = (S3 - BOUNDS(LO,3)) * (BOUNDS(HI,2) -
                BOUNDS(LO,2) + 1)
1040   OFFST = (OFFST + (S2 - BOUNDS(LO,2))) *
                (BOUNDS(HI,1) - BOUNDS(LO,1) + 1)
1050   OFFST = OFFST + (S1 - BOUNDS(LO,1))
```

```
1060   ELEMENT(OFFST) = V
1070   RETURN
1080   'end subroutine store
```

The routine *extract* (which sets the variable EXTRACT to the value of the array position subscripted by S1, S2, and S3) may be written as follows:

```
2000   'subroutine extract
2010   'error checking
2020   IF S1 < BOUNDS(LO,1) OR S1 > BOUNDS(HI,1) OR
           S2 < BOUNDS(LO,2) OR S2 > BOUNDS(HI,2) OR
           S3 < BOUNDS(LO,3) OR S3 > BOUNDS(HI,3)
           THEN PRINT "ILLEGAL SUBSCRIPT": STOP
2030   OFFST = (S3 - BOUNDS(LO,3)) * (BOUNDS(HI,2) -
                                   BOUNDS(LO,2) + 1)
2040   OFFST = (OFFST + (S2 - BOUNDS(LO,2))) *
                      (BOUNDS(HI,1) - BOUNDS(LO,1) + 1)
2050   OFFST = OFFST + (S1 - BOUNDS(LO,1))
2060   EXTRACT = ELEMENT(OFFST)
2070   RETURN
2080   'end subroutine extract
```

These routines use the formulas developed in Section 2 for computing the offset of a specific element in a multi-dimensional array. In the exercises, you are asked to generalize the routines above so that the number of dimensions of the array can also be input to the subroutines.

EXERCISES

1. Generalize the routines *store* and *extract* of the text so that they accept four input variables: A, N, SUB, and V, where A is a data aggregate representing a multidimensional array of N dimensions, SUB is a one-dimensional array of size N and such that SUB(I) equals the subscript of the Ith dimension in the array reference, and V is the value to be stored or extracted in the array.

2. A *complex number* is one that contains real and imaginary parts and satisfies the following properties: If $c1$ has real and imaginary parts $r1$ and $i1$, respectively, and $c2$ has real and imaginary parts $r2$ and $i2$, respectively, then
   (a) The sum of $c1$ and $c2$ has real part $(r1 + r2)$ and imaginary part $(i1 + i2)$.
   (b) The difference of $c1$ and $c2$ has real part $(r1 - r2)$ and imaginary part $(i1 - i2)$.
   (c) The product of $c1$ and $c2$ has real part $(r1*r2 - i1*i2)$ and imaginary part $(r1*i2 + r2*i1)$.

   Implement complex numbers by defining a data aggregate with real and complex parts and write routines to add, subtract, and multiply such complex numbers.

3. A *fixed-point number* is one in which the number of digits to the left and right of the decimal point remains constant. Suppose that a fixed-point number with five decimal places is represented by

```
10   DEFINT F
20   DIM FIXEDEC(2)
30       LEFT  =  1
40       RIGHT  =  2
```

where FIXEDEC(LEFT) and FIXEDEC(RIGHT) represent the digits to the left and right of the decimal point, respectively. For example, 1.00002 is represented by FIXEDEC(1) equaling 1 and FIXEDEC(2) equaling 2, while 1.2 is represented by FIXEDEC(1) equaling 1 and FIXEDEC(2) equaling 20,000.

(a) Write a routine to read a fixed-point number from a DATA statement and create a data aggregate representing that number.

(b) Write a routine that accepts such a data aggregate and prints the fixed-point number represented by it.

(c) Write three routines that accept two such data aggregates and set the value of a third data aggregate to the sum, difference, and product of the two original data aggregates.

4. Using the rational number representation given in the text, write routines to add, subtract, and divide such numbers.

5. The text presents a subroutine *equal*, which determines whether or not two rational numbers R1 and R2 are equal, by first reducing R1 and R2 to lowest terms and then testing for equality. An alternatative method would be to multiply R1(NMRTR) by R2(DNMNTR) and R2(NMRTR) by R1(DNMNTR) and testing the products for equality. Write a subroutine *equal2* to implement this algorithm. Which of the two methods is preferable?

2

Programming in BASIC

1. BASIC FOR MICROCOMPUTERS

BASIC (Beginner's All-purpose Symbolic Instruction Code) was developed at Dartmouth College in 1972 as a simple computer language to teach students how to program. BASIC has grown from a local instructional language to become one of the most widely used programming languages in the world. With the introduction of microcomputers in 1975, BASIC has matured into a powerful language that is available to almost all owners of personal computers. Although it has grown into a large and powerful language, BASIC remains simple and easy to learn.

Interpreters and Compilers

As is the case with all high-level languages, BASIC cannot be executed directly by a computer. A computer can "understand" instructions only when these instructions are presented to it in machine language. Machine language is a low-level language consisting solely of strings of 0s and 1s which represent the operations native to the machine being used. On most computers, BASIC statements are translated into machine instructions by means of an interpreter. An *interpreter* is a program that examines a line of BASIC, decodes its meaning, and instructs the computer to carry out the operations indicated. This decoding is accomplished one statement at a time. Alternatively, there are versions of BASIC which are translated into machine language by means of a *compiler*. Unlike an interpreter, a compiler first translates a complete program, known as the *source code*, into a machine language program, known as the ***object code***. Once the entire program has been translated, the object code may be executed. (We should note that most interpreters proceed in two stages as well: a ***translation phase*** in which the actual BASIC program is translated into an ***intermediate language*** representation, and an ***interpretation phase***, in which the intermediate language statements are executed, one at a time. The intermediate language resembles BASIC more closely than does machine language, so the entire process may be properly termed *interpretation* rather than *compilation*.)

There are advantages to each of the translation procedures noted above. Interpreted languages, since they translate and execute each program line, allow the user to modify a program and run it immediately without having to retranslate (or compile) the entire program. Thus interpreted BASICs are favored by students and other programmers involved in program development. It is also possible to suspend execution of the program, examine or modify any variables, and resume execution from that point. Unfortunately, a price must be paid for this flexibility. Since each line must be interpreted as it is encountered, a line that may be executed more than once, such as within a loop, would be translated more than once. For this reason, interpreted BASICs are comparatively slow. Compilation, on the other hand, translates a program statement only once, regardless of the number of times it is executed, leading to increased execution efficiency but with a concurrent loss of flexibility. In addition, there is another consideration. Compiled programs tend to be large and require more space than do corresponding interpreted programs.

As we have mentioned earlier, BASIC has evolved from its original form to a language that can be found on most personal computers. During the period of evolution, little attention was paid to keeping the language standardized, with each manufacturer enhancing the language to make the most efficient use of the specific hardware. Unfortunately, this led to a Tower of Babel of BASIC languages. It is likely that a program written in a particular dialect of BASIC will not perform properly, without some modifications, on another machine. Throughout the text we will point out some of the major incompatibilities among different versions of BASIC. In the programs that follow in the remainder of the book we have gone to great lengths to avoid using code that is heavily dependent on a specific machine or a specific version of BASIC. The reader, on the other hand, is encouraged to rewrite the programs presented here to take advantage of the full power of the version of BASIC being used.

In the following paragraphs we will outline some of the elementary BASIC concepts that will be used in forthcoming chapters. This material is not intended as an introduction to BASIC or to programming. Rather, it is an attempt to present a uniform framework from which to build expanded program constructs. It is suggested that the reader who finds these discussions unfamiliar should review the BASIC language manual accompanying the personal computer being used, as well as introductory BASIC textbooks.

Lines, Statements, and Remarks

A BASIC program consists of one or more lines. Each line begins with a number indicating the relative order in which the line (or rather the statements on that line) are to be executed. Line numbers must be integers in the range of 0 to about 64000 (depending on the version of BASIC being used). A statement may not span more than one line, but a line may contain more than one statement. When more than one statement appear on a line, a colon is used to separate the statements. A BASIC line is considered to be terminated by a carriage return (or ENTER) regardless of whether it physically occupies more than one line on the monitor or other display device. There are a maximum number of characters that may appear on a line (usually 255). For example,

> 30   PRINT 5 + 3 : PRINT "BYE"
> 10   REM *this line was typed second*
> 20   PRINT "HI"

would be processed as if it were entered as follows:

> 10   REM *this line was typed second*
> 20   PRINT "HI"
> 30   PRINT 5 + 3 : PRINT "BYE"

and result in the following output:

> HI
> 8
> BYE

In the program above, note line number 10 which begins with the keyword REM. This statement is known as a **remark** and is ignored by the translator. The purpose of a remark is to serve as documentation to the program or a portion of the program. We will have more to say about the importance of the remark later in this chapter. In many versions of BASIC, a remark may also be denoted by means of a single quote (') placed at its beginning. A remark must always be the last (or only) statement on a line, since once a remark delimiter is encountered, the remainder of the line is ignored by the computer.

Variables in BASIC

Variables in BASIC are written as a string of one or more alphabetic characters and digits, the first of which must be alphabetic. Although many versions of BASIC allow variable names to be of any length, in some implementations (e.g., Applesoft and TRS-80 Level II), only the first two characters are significant. That is, two variable names with the same first two characters both represent the same variable. Thus SUB, SUM, and SU will be treated identically in these im-

plementations. In addition, each version of BASIC has a list of "reserved"
words which are set aside for specific purposes and cannot be used as variable
names. Some versions of BASIC (e.g., Applesoft and TRS-80 Level II) impose
the additional restriction that a reserved word may not be embedded within a
variable name (e.g., STOCK may not be used as a variable since it contains the
reserved word TO). We will adhere to these restrictions in this book. That is, no
two variables appearing in the same program have the same first two characters
and no variable name includes a reserved word. For these reasons, variable
names may not be as meaningful as might be desirable.

Primitive Data Types

Every computer language supports a set of native data types. These types may be
native either to the machine on which the programs are run or to the compiler or
interpreter that is translating these programs. Most versions of BASIC, for example, support integers, reals, and strings as native data types.

Integers are whole numbers (numbers not containing decimal points) within
some range (often between -32768 and $+32767$). Positive or negative numbers
that are not integers are known as real numbers. These numbers may be represented using either fixed-point or floating-point notation. In fixed-point notation,
the decimal point is located at its proper position within the number. For example, 4.2, .003, and -452.6378 are all real numbers in fixed-point notation. For
numbers that are very large or very small, it is convenient to use floating-point
notation. A floating-point number consists of an optionally signed integer or real
number in fixed-point notation, followed by the letter E and an optionally signed
integer (representing the exponent of 10). For example, 1.86E05 represents
1.86×10^5, which is 186,000, and $-4.056E-03$ represents -4.056×10^{-3},
which is $-.004056$. On most personal computers, the exponent must be in the
range -38 to $+38$. The number of digits which the computer is capable of representing is known as the *precision* of the number. Most versions of BASIC
maintain a precision of between 7 (TRS-80, IBM BASIC, and Microsoft BASIC-
80) and 10 (Applesoft) digits. Such reals are called *single-precision reals*. Some
versions of BASIC are also capable of representing numbers of up to 16 digits.
Such numbers are known as *double-precision reals* and are indicated by the letter
D appearing in the representation instead of an E. Several versions of BASIC
(IBM BASIC and Microsoft BASIC-80) are also capable of representing numbers
in hexadecimal (base 16) and octal (base 8) notation.

Character strings are represented in BASIC by a sequence of characters enclosed in double-quotation marks and may contain up to 255 alphanumeric characters. TRS-80 BASIC requires that space be set aside explicitly for string
storage. When the TRS-80 microcomputer is first turned on, 50 bytes are set
aside for string storage. In order to set aside additional string storage space, the
statement CLEAR n (where n is a positive integer) causes the computer to reserve
n bytes for string storage. In other versions of BASIC (Applesoft and Microsoft

BASIC-80), string storage is allocated automatically. The CLEAR statement is used differently in other versions of BASIC and the reader should ascertain its exact function on any particular machine.

The type of a variable (i.e., the data type of the values that it can assume) may be indicated in one of several ways. One method is to append a *type declaration character* to the variable name. The set of declaration characters usually used are as follows:

Type	Type declaration character
Integer	%
Single-precision real	! (or by default)
Double-precision real	#
String	$

For example, in Applesoft BASIC and IBM BASIC, F# represents a double-precision real number while A$ represents a character string. Note that A$ and A! are different variables under this convention.

Some versions of BASIC allow the type of a variable to be declared by means of a DEF statement as follows:

Type	DEF statement
Integer	DEFINT
Single-precision real	DEFSNG
Double-precision real	DEFDBL
String	DEFSTR

Using DEF statements, it is possible to define and identify the type of a variable by means of its first letter. For example, if a BASIC programmer writes

$$10 \quad \text{DEFINT X,Y}$$
$$20 \quad \text{DEFDBL A,B}$$

then any variable beginning with the letter X or Y will be treated as an integer, while any variable beginning with the letter A or B will be interpreted as a double-precision real number. Thus the contents of the locations reserved for XVAR and YVAR will be interpreted as integers, while the contents of AVAR and BVAR will be interpreted as real numbers. The processor (interpreter or compiler) which is responsible for translating a BASIC program into machine language will translate the '' + '' in the statement

$$X = X + Y$$

into integer addition, and will translate the '' + '' in the statement

$$A = A + B$$

into real addition. An operator such as " + " is known as a ***generic*** operator because it has several different meanings depending on its context. The translator
relieves the programmer from specifying the type of addition that must be performed by examining the types of the operands and using the appropriate operation.

In some BASIC dialects (e.g., Applesoft), the "type" of a variable may
only be specified by means of type declaration characters. Other versions of BA-
SIC (e.g., TRS-80 Level II, IBM BASIC, and Microsoft BASIC-80) allow type
specification by either declaration characters or DEF statements. The reader is
urged to clarify the methods that can be used to specify variable types in the
BASIC implementation at hand.

Pseudocode

In Chapter 1 we discussed some of the reasons for our interest in studying the
definition and implementation of more complex data structures. One of the reasons mentioned was that it is often easy to describe the solution to a problem in
terms of more complex data structures than those available in a particular language (e.g., BASIC). Therefore, if we can present an implementation of this
complex data structure in the language being used, solutions to problems that are
stated in terms of this complex data structure can be run on the machine at hand
using the given implementation. In effect, we will have enlarged our arsenal of
available types by this data structure.

In a similiar fashion, it is possible to extend the control structures of a language beyond those supported by the semantics of the language. All high-level
languages are equipped with a set of control structures. These control structures,
as opposed to simple statements which manipulate data, govern the sequence in
which other statements are executed. For example,

```
10   READ X
20   PRINT Y
30   A = B + C
```

are examples of statements that manipulate data, while

```
40   GOTO 1000
```

is an example of a control statement.

Because of the inherent complexity of the solutions to some of the problems
in this text, it will be most helpful to have available a set of high-level control
structures with which we can express these solutions. Such solutions can often be
expressed quite simply in terms of these complex control structures. While it is
also possible to express these solutions using a more limited set of control structures, such expressions are often cumbersome and sometimes lead to problems in
detecting and isolating errors. It is therefore desirable to have such a set of high-
level control structures available.

Many newer versions of BASIC for microcomputers are equipped with sophisticated control structures found in some of the more powerful high-level languages; other versions are not so well equipped. Even in languages that do support high-level control structures, there is inconsistency in their syntactical expression and even in their semantic meaning. Therefore, in order not to depend on the form of a particular version of BASIC, yet not to be limited by the unavailability of these control structures, we choose an intermediate route. We express solutions to problems in an intermediate descriptive language which serves as a bridge between English and BASIC. We will call this intermediate language **pseudocode**. This pseudocode has the advantage that it reads like English and is at least similar to more powerful versions of BASIC and to other more powerful high-level languages. For this reason, it will be helpful as a powerful tool in stating the solutions to problems. On the other hand, since this pseudocode solution does not consist solely of BASIC statements, it cannot be entered directly into the machine for processing. The pseudocode solution must first be translated into simpler BASIC statements.

In the following paragraphs, we present several forms of control structures using pseudocode. These standard control structures will be used throughout the text in presenting solutions to problems. In some instances, we present a solution both in its pseudocode form as well as in its BASIC form; in others, we present only the pseudocode solution or the BASIC program. To distinguish typographically between pseudocode and BASIC programs, we use lowercase characters for pseudocode and uppercase characters for BASIC programs. For example, the pseudocode version of the statements

```
10   X = A + B
20   IF X > 100 THEN Z = 1
30   FOR I = 1 TO X
40       S = S + I
50   NEXT I
```

is

$x = a + b$
if $x > 100$
   then $z = 1$
endif
for $i = 1$ *to* x
   $s = s + i$
next i

Note that statement numbers are omitted from the pseudocode and that pseudocode appears slightly different from BASIC (as, for example, the *endif* and the indentation of the *then*). These differences and explanations for them will be discussed below. Solutions expressed in pseudocode are often called **algorithms;**

although they are not programs that can be directly executed on a computer, they are precise descriptions of the process to be performed in producing such a solution by a computer.

For each of the pseudocode structures discussed below, we present the structure itself, an example of its use, and a method of converting the pseudocode into BASIC. As we mentioned earlier, in order to make our programs portable from one version of BASIC to another, we have adopted a minimal standard for our conventions. Users of BASIC on specific machines are of course free to translate these control structures into less constraining forms available on their particular machine. As exercises, you are urged to explore some of these possibilities.

Flow of Control

We begin by considering several program constructs and how they appear in BASIC. Executable statements in BASIC fall into one of two major categories: simple statements that accomplish a single operation or a set of operations, and compound statements that group statements together to form an overall control structure.

The following statements are examples of simple statements:

```
10   INPUT X
20   X = X + 1
30   PRINT "X = "; X
```

Each of the statements above is "simple" in that it performs a single task. A task may consist of two parts (such as PRINT "X = "; X, which prints two items), but each such task basically represents a single operation. One such statement is executed sequentially after another in the order of the line numbers associated with the statements.

The pseudocode versions of simple statements are direct translations from BASIC. For example, the pseudocode version of the statements above are

input x
x = x + 1
print "x = "; x

The second major category of BASIC executable statements are those that control the execution of other BASIC statements:

```
10   IF A = B THEN PRINT X
```

```
10   FOR I = 1 TO X
20        PRINT I
30   NEXT I
```

These constructions determine the sequence in which the simple operations which they include are to be performed. In such constructions, the simple statements are not necessarily executed in the order in which they appear. The sequence of their execution cannot always be determined by simply looking at the code; it depends on conditions (e.g., A = B, I > X) which are tested during program execution. The sequence in which instructions are executed is called the *flow of control* of a program. We shall discuss several types of flow of control, how they can be expressed in pseudocode, and how they may be implemented in BASIC.

Sequential Flow

"Sequential flow" means that statements are executed sequentially in the order in which they appear. Sequential flow may be achieved by writing simple statements in the order in which they are to be executed (with line numbers in increasing sequence). As we shall discuss in more detail later in this chapter, the code is easier to read if each statement appears on a separate line and all the statements are indented to the same column. If the computation that is being performed is not clear from the code, remarks at key points in the code should be used to explain the purpose and the intended effects of each group of statements.

Conditional Flow

Conditional flow is "almost" sequential in that the statements, if executed, are executed in their order of appearance. However, a statement or group of statements may or may not be executed in certain cases. One example of this type of flow is achieved by an IF statement of the form

IF condition THEN statement

If *condition* is satisfied, then *statement* is executed; if *condition* fails, then *statement* is not executed. In either case, the next statement to be executed is the one that follows the IF THEN construction.

In pseudocode, we express this type of conditional flow as follows:

if condition
   then statement
endif

The reason for using the *endif* becomes clear when we consider the possibility of incorporating more than one statement in a *then* clause. In most microcomputer versions of BASIC, a colon can be used to separate the statements to be included within the THEN clause. For example, we may write

```
100   IF X > 0 THEN X = X − 1: PRINT X, X ↑ 2: COUNT = COUNT + 1
```

In pseudocode, we may include each statement on a separate line:

$$\textbf{\textit{if }} x > 0$$
$$\textbf{\textit{then }} x = x - 1$$
$$\textbf{\textit{print }} x,\ x \uparrow 2$$
$$count = count + 1$$
$$\textbf{\textit{endif}}$$

endif indicates that all of the statements between the keyword **then** and the **endif** are to be executed only if the condition ($x > 0$) is true.

Sometimes, the statements to be included in a THEN clause are too numerous and/or too long to be included within a single BASIC program line. In that case, we must "program around" the problem by writing something like the following:

```
100   IF X < = 0 THEN GOTO 150
110   'statements 120 – 140 are executed only if X > 0
120   X = X – 1
130   PRINT X, X ↑ 2
140   COUNT = COUNT + 1
150        . . .
```

This is quite awkward. In pseudocode, however, we are not limited by the length of a single line, since each component statement can be listed on a separate line, with the entire list terminated by **endif**. This leads to greater comprehensibility and neatness.

[At this point, we should say something about how BASIC programs are displayed in this book. In general, most BASICs have a limit on the number of characters in a line. We assume this limit to be 240, although it can be as low as 80. Most display devices (e.g., monitors or printers) do not permit physical lines to be so long, but rather have a line length of 80 or even 40. Thus a single BASIC line may take up more than one physical line on a particular device. For this reason, a BASIC line may be written using several textual lines, as, for example,

```
100   IF X < 0 THEN PRINT "X IS NEGATIVE":
        Y = X + A ↑ 2: A = A + 1: X = X + Y:
        PRINT "X = "; X, "A = "; A, "Y = "; Y
```

In displaying such a statement in this book, we attempt to make it as readable as possible through the use of indentation. It may be difficult to use such indentation consistently in practice, since different display devices have different physical line sizes, so that the number of blanks and the points of line division appropriate for one device are inappropriate for another. Generally, we do not use more than three text lines for a BASIC line, assuming a BASIC line length of 240 and a physical display line length of 80. In cases where more than three lines would be necessary, we split the BASIC construct into several BASIC lines using a GOTO, as above. In pseudocode, of course, there is no limit on the number of statements that can be included within a ***then*** clause—which is one of the reasons pseudocode is so convenient.]

Another conditional flow construct (which is available in some versions of BASIC) may be written in pseudocode as follows:

> ***if*** condition
>   ***then*** statement 1
>   ***else*** statement 2
> ***endif***

or, in some versions of BASIC,

> 100   IF *condition* THEN *statement* 1
>   ELSE *statement* 2

If *condition* is satisfied, *statement* 1 is executed but *statement* 2 is not. If *condition* fails, *statement* 1 is not executed but *statement* 2 is. In either case, one of the two statements (but not both) is executed. After executing either *statement* 1 or *statement* 2, the computer next executes the statement immediately following the complete IF-THEN-ELSE construction.

TRS-80 Level II BASIC, IBM BASIC, and BASIC-80 all permit an ELSE clause; Applesoft BASIC does not. Note that since the ELSE clause does not have its own line number, the limit on line length applies to the entire IF statement, including both the THEN and ELSE clauses. For this reason, in order to be able to use more space, the IF statement is sometimes indented:

> 100   IF *condition* THEN *statement* 1
>   ELSE *statement* 2

or even

> 100   IF *condition* THEN *statement* 1 ELSE *statement* 2

Of course, both the THEN and ELSE clauses can consist of multiple statements, as in

> 100   IF X > 0 THEN PRINT "X IS POSITIVE ": X = X + 1
>   ELSE PRINT "X IS NEGATIVE ": X = X - 1

In pseudocode, this would be written as

> ***if*** $x > 0$
>   ***then print*** "x is positive"
> $x = x + 1$
>   ***else print*** "x is negative"
> $x = x - 1$
> ***endif***

In those versions of BASIC that do not support the ELSE clause, or if an ELSE clause would make a line too long, the statement above can be implemented using a GOTO:

```
100   IF X > 0 THEN PRINT "X IS POSITIVE ": X = X + 1: GOTO 140
110                'else statements 120 − 130
120                PRINT "X IS NEGATIVE"
130                X = X − 1
140         . . .
```

or, if the THEN clause also becomes too long,

```
100   IF X < = 0 THEN GOTO 150
110                'then clause is statements 120 − 130
120                PRINT "X IS POSITIVE"
130                X = X + 1
140   GOTO 180: 'branch around else clause
150                'else clause is statements 160 − 170
160                PRINT "X IS NEGATIVE"
170                X = X − 1
180         . . .
```

In the remainder of this book, we will assume that ELSE clauses are permitted in BASIC. If your version of BASIC does not permit them, use the translation techniques that we have presented.

Very often in programming, it is necessary to use a *nested IF*. That is, depending on the outcome of one test, another test may have to be made. As we shall see, this is expressed quite naturally in pseudocode but awkwardly in BASIC. For example, consider the specification for an automatic teller machine.

```
input type, amount
if type = "deposit"
  then balance = balance + amount
       print "deposit accepted. amt = "; amount
       print "thank you for banking with us"
  else if type = "withdrawal"
         then if amount <= balance
                then balance = balance − amount
                     print "withdrawal = "; amount
                else print "insufficient funds"
              endif
         else print "unrecognized transaction"
       endif
endif
```

Note that this pseudocode is readable and self-explanatory due to the indentation and structuring. In many versions of BASIC, nested IFs are permitted, as in

100   IF A > 10 THEN IF B > 10 THEN X = X + 1

However, the limit on statement length in BASIC makes it impractical to use nested IFs in situations such as the algorithm above. Therefore, we usually express nested IFs using GOTOs. The BASIC version of the algorithm above is the following:

```
100   DEFSTR T
110   INPUT TYPE, AMOUNT
120   IF TYPE <> "DEPOSIT" THEN GOTO 170
130      BALANCE = BALANCE + AMOUNT
140      PRINT "DEPOSIT ACCEPTED. AMOUNT = "; AMOUNT
150      PRINT "THANK YOU FOR BANKING WITH US"
160   GOTO 250
170      'else clause
180      IF TYPE <> "WITHDRAWAL" THEN GOTO 220
190         IF AMOUNT <= BALANCE
               THEN BALANCE = BALANCE − AMOUNT:
                   PRINT "WITHDRAWAL = "; AMOUNT
               ELSE PRINT "INSUFFICIENT FUNDS"
200         'endif
210      GOTO 240
220         'else clause
230         PRINT "UNRECOGNIZED TRANSACTION"
240      'endif
250   'endif
260   END
```

Note that it is not necessary to include the remark *'endif* in the program; all that is necessary is to code the subsequent statement in the program. While the *'endif* remark is sometimes helpful as a placeholder (as in the example above), in the interest of clarity and simplicity we will usually omit it.

We should point out that nested IFs are often unnecessary in solving a particular problem. For example, suppose that it is necessary to set X to 10 if A is between 100 and 200. One version is

100   IF A >= 100 THEN IF A <= 200 THEN X = 10

Such code is overly complicated. There is no need to use a nested IF when a single (compound) test will do, as in

100   IF (A >= 100) AND (A <= 200) THEN X = 10

The second version mirrors the statement of the problem more closely than the first. In general, it is easier to read single statements involving compound tests (when those tests are connected with the same logical operators) than to read nested control structures.

There is a common pitfall in using compound tests. For example, suppose that A is an array declared by

10   DIM A(10)

and it is desired to determine whether a subscript I is within bounds of the array and whether A(I) is negative. A novice might use the following scheme:

100   IF (I >= 1) AND (I <= 10) AND (A(I) < 0) THEN . . .

However, this code is incorrect because in the case that the subscript I is out of bounds, the reference to A(I) is undefined. For example, suppose that I equals 12. Then the expression (I >= 1) is evaluated to true and the expression (I <= 10) is evaluated to false. But when the expression (A(I) < 0) is evaluated, an error results since A(I) does not exist. The code can be written correctly as

100   IF (I >= 1) AND (I <= 10) THEN IF A(I) < 0 THEN . . .

It should be noted that in some versions of BASIC and some other languages, the first statement executes correctly. In a sequence of tests connected by the "AND" operation, as soon as one operand is found to be false, no further testing of the other conditions is necessary. Similarly, when one component of a sequence of tests connected by the "OR" operation is found to be true, the entire expression is assumed to be true and no further testing is performed. When writing programs for such versions of BASIC, a judicious ordering of the tests will make statements such as the former usable. In other versions, however, such tests will result in an error.

The choice of whether to use logical operations or nested IFs should be made on the merits of each particular case. However, within the limits of a correct program, one should select the version that is clearest and most readable.

Logical Data

Note that every form of the IF statement includes a condition. This condition uses comparison operations to compare two values. For example, in

$A + B > 7$

the comparison operation " $>$ " (greater than) compares the values of A + B and 7, while in

$X <= B + 12*4$

the comparison operation " $<=$ " (less than or equal to) compares the values of X and B + 12*4. The result of the comparison operation is a *logical value*, that is, either the value of *true* or *false*. An IF statement tests a logical value; if it is *true*, the THEN clause is executed, and if it is *false*, the ELSE clause or the next statement is executed.

As we have seen in Chapter 1, every data value must be represented by some method of interpreting bit settings. This must be true of logical values as well. Most BASICs use an integer to represent a logical value. In some BASICs, the integer 0 represents *false* and the integer 1 represents *true*; in others, 0 represents *false* and -1 (which is all 1s in twos-complement notation) represents *true*; and other versions of BASIC use still other representations. (Some BASICs allow you to determine the representation used by executing statements such as PRINT 1 = 1 or PRINT 1 = 0.) However, as noted in Chapter 1, it makes very little difference what representation is used, as long as data types can be used consistently.

It is sometimes useful to allow a variable to assume a logical value. Some BASICs which represent logical values by integers allow statements such as

$$100 \quad X = A > B$$

which sets X to the integer that represents the logical value *true* if A is greater than B and to the integer that represents *false* if A is not greater than B. In most BASICs, however, such variables cannot be used as a condition in an IF statement, as in

$$110 \quad IF \ X \ THEN \ B = B + 1$$

If we knew the integer representation of *true* were 1, we could write

$$110 \quad IF \ X = 1 \ THEN \ B = B + 1$$

but this is quite enigmatic and may be incorrect in another version of BASIC which uses a different representation. For this reason, it is useful to develop a programmed implementation of logical variables, as follows.

Each program requiring logical variables would begin with

```
10   TRUE = 1
20   FALSE = 0
```

The variables TRUE and FALSE would subsequently be treated as constants (i.e., they would not appear on the left-hand side of an assignment statement or within a READ or INPUT statement). Once these "constants" have been initialized, they could be assigned to logical variables, and they could be tested against logical variables. For example,

```
50   IF A↑2 + B↑2 = C↑2 THEN RIGHT = TRUE: 'right triangle
60   ' other statements
        .
        .
        .
100   IF RIGHT = TRUE THEN . . .
```

Such a construction allows us to ask questions about whether the triangle considered was a right triangle without duplicating the test.

We can combine logical operations as follows. Suppose that we had the following code:

```
10   ABIG = FALSE
20   IF A > B THEN ABIG = TRUE
30   CBIG = FALSE
40   IF C > D THEN CBIG = TRUE
```

Then we may write:

```
50   IF (ABIG = TRUE) OR (CBIG = FALSE) THEN . . .
```

or

```
60   IF (ABIG = TRUE) AND (CBIG = FALSE) THEN . . .
```

We will make use of this simple implementation of logical variables throughout the text.

Repetitive Flow

Another major control structure is *repetitive flow*, in which a statement or group of statements is executed repeatedly until some halting condition is reached. This type of structure is called a *loop*. The computing done by most programs (whether to calculate π correct to 500 decimal places, or to calculate and print payroll checks for several thousand employees) is basically a repetitive process. Most high-level programming languages provide for some form of automatic loop control. Let us examine the basic types of loop structures that arise in programming and show how they can be implemented in BASIC.

The most basic loop construct is one that loops as long as a condition is met, as in the following pseudocode:

> **while** *condition* **do**
>   'body of loop
> *endwhile*

Whenever the **while** statement is encountered, *condition* is tested. If *condition* is satisfied, the body of the loop is executed. When the **endwhile** statement is encountered, control is returned to the **while** statement, where the process is repeated. Each execution of the body of the loop is called an **iteration**. The number of iterations through a loop may be 0, 1, 2, or 5000. The body of the loop is repeated as long as the condition in the **while** clause is true. At some point (hopefully) the condition becomes false. When this occurs, control passes to the statement immediately following the **endwhile** statement. (Of course, it is the programmer's responsibility to make sure that the loop does not execute forever.)

For example, the following loop prints all nonnegative powers of two less than *tp*:

$$power = 1$$
while *power* < *tp* **do**
    print *power*
    power = *power* * 2
endwhile

Note that the value of *power* is changed within the loop so that eventually *power* is greater than or equal to *tp* and the loop terminates. One of the requirements for the normal termination of a **while** loop is that the value of some variable appearing within the **while** condition be altered within the loop body so that the condition eventually becomes false. The condition within the **while** clause is tested before each execution of the loop body.

The **while** construct may easily be implemented in BASIC by the following

```
10    IF NOT condition THEN GOTO 110
20        'body of loop
          . . .
100   GOTO 10
110   'remainder of program
```

We can now write a BASIC program to print all powers of 2 less than TP (where TP >= 1):

```
100   POWER = 1
110   IF POWER > = TP THEN GOTO 150
120       PRINT POWER
130       POWER = POWER * 2
140   GOTO 110
150   END
```

Some versions of BASIC do support some form of the **while** statement. For example, in BASIC-80 and IBM BASIC one may code

```
10    WHILE expression
20        'body of loop
          . . .
100   WEND
```

As long as *expression* is nonzero (i.e., true), the statements between the WHILE and the WEND are executed repeatedly. Most versions of BASIC, however, do not support the **while** construct directly and therefore we will not use it in the BASIC programs in this book.

BASIC does contain another very popular and useful loop structure in which a counter is incremented (or decremented) automatically after each execution of the loop body. When the counter becomes greater than (or less than) some test value, the loop is terminated. Such a loop has the following form:

```
10   FOR I = start TO finish STEP inc
20        'body of loop
          . . .
100  NEXT I
```

In pseudocode, this becomes

> **for** i = start **to** finish **step** inc
>   'body of loop
>   . . .
> **next** i

The variable I (known as the ***index*** or the ***control variable*** of the loop) is initialized to *start* and is tested against *finish*. If the result of the test is *true*, the loop body is executed. If the result is *false*, the loop is skipped. The type of test depends on the sign of *inc*. If *inc* is positive, the test is whether I $<=$ *finish*. If *inc* is negative, the test is whether I $>=$ *finish*. When the NEXT statement is encountered, the variable I is reset to I $+$ *inc* and is again tested against the original value of *finish*. When the test fails (even if the loop body has never been executed), execution resumes with the statement immediately following the NEXT statement. If the STEP *inc* portion is omitted, the increment is set to 1.

It should be noted that the value of the loop control variable may be changed within the body of the loop (not recommended), a practice that may have an effect on the number of iterations. However, changes to the values of *inc* or *finish* have no effect on the loop iteration. (There may be some versions of BASIC for which this is not true.)

This type of loop can be used to control a simple count of the number of times a particular process is executed. It may be combined with other types of looping mechanisms to perform a significant amount of work.

For example, consider an alternative method for printing all powers of 2 less than TP:

```
100  FOR I = 0 TO 1E30 STEP 1
110       IF 2↑I >= TP THEN GOTO 140
120       PRINT 2↑I
130  NEXT I
140  END
```

The value of I is initialized to 0 and is incremented by 1. Then its power of 2 is printed, as long as that power is less than TP. Note that the TO clause contains a ridiculously large value. For all intents and purposes the value of I is increased indefinitely by 1 with no upper limit. The loop is terminated only if POWER becomes greater than TP.

The control variable of a loop is frequently used to index an array. For example, suppose that the first N elements of an array A are in increasing numerical order. It is desired to insert the value of another variable X at its proper numerical position within the array. The following code accomplishes this:

```
100   'find the proper position for X
110   FOR I = 1 TO N
120       IF X <= A(I) THEN GOTO 140
130   NEXT I
140   'at this point X <= A(I). Thus X should be inserted
      'immediately before A(I)
150   N = N+1
160   'move the remaining elements and place X in its proper position
170   FOR J = N+1 TO I+1 STEP -1: 'move each element in
180       A(J) = A(J-1)                    : 'the array larger than X
190   NEXT J
200   A(I) = X
```

Make sure that you understand how the indices are manipulated in each of the loops above. Such techniques are standard tools of programming and are used in many applications.

By now, the reader should have noticed a significant difference between a *while* and a *for-next* loop. A *while* loop is a repetitive flow control structure which is terminated when a specified condition becomes false. Such a loop may repeat zero, one, or many times, depending on the logical value of the condition at each iteration. A *for-next* loop, on the other hand, repeats a specified number of times as determined by the values of the start, step, and terminal variables in the *for* statement upon initial execution.

Some loops are not terminated by a condition in a *while* clause. Instead, the logical tests that cause loop termination are made within the loop body. In such cases, we desire a loop that is inherently infinite unless it can somehow be terminated from within. One example of such a loop is the following:

$$\textit{while } 1 = 1 \textit{ do}$$
$$\text{'body of loop}$$
$$\textit{endwhile}$$

This loop repeats indefinitely since the condition $1 = 1$ always evaluates to *true*. A simpler and more direct method is to use *true* as the condition. Such a loop is coded in pseudocode as

$$\textit{while true do}$$
$$\text{'body of loop}$$
$$\textit{endwhile}$$

This control structure may be implemented in BASIC by

    100   '*body of loop*
          .
          .
          .
    200   GOTO 100

Of course, the programmer must provide a mechanism for exiting from within the body of such a loop (usually via a GOTO).

Subroutines

The subroutine is a most helpful programming tool in reducing large unmanageable problems to reasonable size. The proper approach to designing a program of any complexity involves the separation of a complete solution into its component subtasks. This allows the programmer to focus on each individual task independently of the others. After all the tasks have been debugged, they may be combined into a single program. In the remainder of this section we present techniques that will be used to represent subroutines in pseudocode and their corresponding counterparts in BASIC. In the following section we discuss a strategy for decomposing larger programs into a set of subroutines.

In order to identify programs and subroutines, it is convenient to assign names to them. This helps in recognizing those routines that may be called more than once in a program or those routines that may be used in other programs. Because BASIC provides no syntactic method for naming programs or subroutines, we do this through a remark. Thus a program may be indicated by

    10   '*program* prog1
         . . . *balance of* prog1 . . .

and a subroutine by

    1000   '*subroutine* sub1
           . . . *balance of* sub1 . . .

For example, suppose that we wish to write a main program that will call a subroutine to print the integers and their square roots for all integers between 1 and 10. We could first write an algorithm in pseudocode as follows:

print "number", "root"
sqprint   '*subroutine* sqprint prints the numbers between 1 and 10
                   'and their corresponding square roots
print "finished"

The second line of the algorithm, *sqprnt,* is a **call** to the subroutine *sqprnt* which presumably performs the desired actions. The algorithm *sqprnt* could be written in pseudocode as follows:

> *subroutine sqprnt*
> *for* $i = 1$ *to* 10
>   *print* i , *sqr*(i)
> *next* i
> *return*

If it were desired to translate the pseudocode into a single BASIC program, it could be done as follows:

```
10   'program printroots
20   PRINT "NUMBER" , "ROOT"
30   GOSUB 100 : 'subroutine sqprnt prints the required table
40   PRINT "FINISHED"
50   END
60   '
70   '
100  'subroutine sqprnt
110  'locals: I
120  'This subroutine prints 10 lines. Each line contains an
130  'integer between 1 and 10 and its square root.
140  FOR I = 1 TO 10
150      PRINT I, SQR(I)
160  NEXT I
170  RETURN
180  'endsub
```

If the program above were run, it would achieve the desired effect.

Let us examine the notational conventions used above. In line 30 where the subroutine is called, we indicate in a remark the name of the subroutine and a brief indication of the purpose of the subroutine. When the subroutine is called, control is transferred to line 100. But before this transfer takes place, the address of the next statement is saved by the system for subsequent use by the RETURN statement. That is, the BASIC system remembers that the subroutine is being called from line 30 so that when the subroutine is completed, execution resumes at line 40. Since lines 100–130 are remarks, the first executable statement within the subroutine is at line 140. Lines 140–160 produce the appropriate table, after which control is returned to the return address (line 40) that was saved by the GOSUB statement. Whenever a subroutine is called, it returns to the statement immediately following the point of call.

Lines 100–130 are for documentation purposes only and have no effect on the execution of the program. Line 100 defines the name of the subroutine. This is helpful in identifying where the routine begins and, together with the *endsub* remark at line 180, delimits the subroutine from the remainder of the program. This is useful, for example, when it is desired to use a subroutine that already exists in a different program. The statements need only be copied if the line numbers are available, or renumbered and then copied if the line numbers are in use. In any case, it is easy to see where the subroutine begins and ends by using the name of the subroutine in an initial remark and the *endsub* delimiter in a terminating remark. In addition to delimiting the body of the subroutine itself, the name of the subroutine is also helpful in documenting the call to the subroutine. Notice the remark in the GOSUB statement at line 30, which specifies the name of the subroutine being called. This enables the reader to read the program without having to check line numbers at each point of the way. Note that beginning a subroutine with a name and terminating it with an *endsub* remark does not relieve the programmer of the responsibility of adhering to the usual rules for calling and returning from a subroutine; that is, the routine must be called by GOSUB 100 (GOSUB SQPRNT is not legal) and a return is effected by a RETURN statement (*endsub* does not effect a return). However, there are some versions of BASIC that do allow naming of subroutines and calling them by name.

Line 110 is a listing of the "local variables" of the subroutine. We say that a variable is *local* if the following three conditions hold:

1. The subroutine does not make use of a value that was assigned to the variable before the subroutine was called.
2. The variable is assigned a value within the subroutine (either in an assignment statement, a FOR statement, or in a READ or INPUT statement).
3. The value assigned to the variable within the subroutine is not used by the calling program upon return from the subroutine.

The variable I satisfies all of these conditions. The variable I is not used in the subroutine before line 140, which is its first assignment there. In fact, the variable I does not appear within the body of the main program (lines 10–50) at all. The FOR-NEXT construction within the subroutine assigns a value to I, so the second condition is satisfied. The third condition holds since no use is made of the variable I following the return from the subroutine (in lines 40–50). The primary reason for listing local variables in a remark is to help the programmer recognize potential conflicts as a result of reusing the same variable (sometimes unknowingly). If, in this example, the variable I had a value before the call to the subroutine at line 30, that value would be lost upon return from the subroutine, since the subroutine changes that value. In such cases it is therefore necessary to change the names of the variables either within the subroutine or within the main program. The use of local identifications within remarks will help the programmer identify those variable names that may have to be modified as a result of the inclusion of certain subroutines within a program.

Parameters in BASIC

The subroutine *sqprnt* in the example above consists of a self-contained set of statements that could be moved elsewhere in this or another program and accomplish the same task. In fact, if the RETURN statement is omitted, the subroutine *sqprint* could be run as a complete program. Very often, however, it is necessary that a subroutine communicate with its environment (i.e., the calling program). For example, suppose that we wish to write a subroutine that will interchange two variables. We could easily do this to interchange the two variables A and B. But if it were necessary to interchange two other variables, say C and D, the subroutine could not be used directly (without first saving A and B temporarily, moving C and D into A and B, calling the subroutine, recopying A and B into C and D, and finally restoring the values of A and B). It would therefore be helpful if we could write a general subroutine that would interchange any two numeric variables and be able to call the same subroutine to interchange A and B or C and D as necessary. Although such mechanisms are fundamental features of other high level programming languages, they are not supported in most versions of BASIC. Therefore, we present a method of accomplishing this.

In pseudocode, we can express a subroutine to do this as follows:

> **subroutine** *swap*($p1,p2$)
> *temp* $= p1$
> $p1 = p2$
> $p2 = temp$
> **return**

The variables $p1$ and $p2$ are **parameters** of the subroutine. This is indicated by their appearance in parentheses after the name of the subroutine in its first statement. When a pseudocode statement such as

> *swap*(a,b)

appears, the values of a and b (called **arguments**) are automatically substituted into $p1$ and $p2$ and the subroutine begins execution. When the subroutine returns, a receives the final value of $p1$ and b receives the final value of $p2$. Thus, interchanging the values of $p1$ and $p2$ in the subroutine will result in the interchanging of the values of a and b as well. Similarly, the statement

> *swap*(b,c)

which calls on *swap* with b and c as arguments, results in the interchange of the values of b and c.

Let us consider an example of an application of the subroutine above. Suppose that we wish to read three numbers and sort them in ascending order. Consider the following algorithm:

```
'read and sort three numbers
read a, b, c
if a > b
  then swap (a,b)
endif
if b > c
  then swap (b,c)
endif
if a > b
  then swap (a,b)
endif
print a, b, c
```

The algorithm above in pseudocode calls on the subroutine *swap* three times, with different parameters on each call. The pseudocode statement

$$swap\ (a,b)$$

causes the subroutine *swap* to be called with $p1$ having the value of a and $p2$ the value of b. Thus the values of a and b will be interchanged. The statement

$$swap(b,c)$$

causes *swap* to be called with $p1$ having the value of b and $p2$ the value of c, thus interchanging the values of b and c. Readers should convince themselves that the steps above do indeed sort the values into increasing order regardless of the original sequence.

Note that the parameters $p1$ and $p2$ serve as both inputs and outputs of the subroutine *swap*. An ***input parameter*** is one that obtains its initial value from a corresponding variable in the calling routine and whose initial value is used by the subroutine. An ***output parameter*** is one whose value is set by the subroutine for use by the calling routine after the subroutine returns. To see that $p1$ is an input parameter, note the statement

$$temp\ =\ p1$$

which utilizes the value of $p1$ without first setting it explicitly within the subroutine. Similarly, the statement

$$p1\ =\ p2$$

confirms that $p2$ is an input parameter. The same statement indicates that $p1$ is an output parameter, since its value is being set within the subroutine for use outside the subroutine. Similarly, the statement

$$p2\ =\ temp$$

indicates that $p2$ is an output parameter. The variable *temp* is neither an input nor an output parameter. Aside from the fact that it does not appear in the header of the subroutine, *temp* cannot be an input parameter because it is set by the statement

$$temp = p1$$

before its value is used. The fact that it is not an output parameter, despite its being set in the statement above, is apparent when we recognize that its value is no longer required outside the subroutine. The parameters $p1$ and $p2$ and the corresponding variables (*a* and *b* in two calls; *b* and *c* in the other) are swapped in the subroutine. *temp* is only a temporary variable used in the swapping process; once the process has been concluded, there is no need for its value. As we have already seen, *temp* is a local variable used within the subroutine.

To translate the pseudocode subroutine into BASIC, we list in opening remarks all the inputs, outputs, and local variables of the subroutine. In calling the subroutine we must explicitly assign the output values to their corresponding variables. Following is a complete BASIC version of the program to sort three numbers using the subroutine *swap*.

```
  10   'program sort
  20   'read three variables and sort them in increasing order
  30   READ A, B, C
  40   IF A > B
          THEN P1 = A: P2 = B: GOSUB 1000: A = P1: B = P2 :
          'subroutine swap interchanges P1 and P2
  50   IF B > C
          THEN P1 = B: P2 = C: GOSUB 1000: B = P1: C = P2
  60   IF A > B
          THEN P1 = A: P2 = B: GOSUB 1000: A = P1: B = P2
  70   PRINT "SORTED SEQUENCE IS "; A; B; C
  80   END
  90   DATA . . .
 100   '
 110   '
1000   'subroutine swap
1010   'inputs: P1, P2
1020   'outputs: P1, P2
1030   'locals: TEMP
1040   'swap interchanges the values P1 and P2
1050   TEMP = P1
1060   P1 = P2
1070   P2 = TEMP
1080   RETURN
1090   'endsub
```

The original algorithm contains the statement

if $a > b$
  then *swap*(*a*,*b*)
endif

Let us see how this is translated into the corresponding BASIC statements at line 40. The first step in calling a subroutine is to assign values to the inputs. This is done by the statements P1 = A and P2 = B. Once these inputs have been initalized, the subroutine can be called (GOSUB 1000) to interchange the values of P1 and P2. After the subroutine has completed its task, control is returned to the calling program (through the RETURN statement). At this point, it is necessary to assign the outputs to their corresponding variables in the calling program. This is done by the statements A = P1 and B = P2. The translations of the remaining *if* statements are similar.

Note also that, whereas the opening statement of the *swap* pseudocode algorithm is an actual pseudocode statement (not a remark) and includes the input and output parameters in parentheses, there is no corresponding BASIC statement. Rather, we indicate the beginning of the subroutine in a remark and list the input, output, and local variables in subsequent remarks.

Readers should note that we have adopted these conventions to make the use of subroutines more standard and general. Many languages (and even some versions of BASIC) support features that allow the programmer to call a subroutine directly through a statement such as SWAP(A, B) without the need to explicitly assign the values of A and B to parameters P1 and P2, and vice versa.

Functions in BASIC

A *function* is a subroutine with one output parameter; that is, it computes a single value to be returned to the calling program. In writing algorithms to perform various processes, it is often convenient to use *functional notation*. In this notation, the name of the function followed by a list of its arguments enclosed in parentheses indicates a call to the function with those arguments and represents the value of that call. For example, SQR is a function (which is available in BASIC). If the following pseudocode statements were to be translated into a BASIC program

numb = 64
root = *sqr*(*numb*)
print *numb*, *root*

the reference to SQR(NUMB) would indicate a call to the SQR (square root) function with argument 64. The result of the application of this function to the argument 64 is 8, so that the PRINT statement will print 64 and 8.

Suppose that another function, *cbr* calculated the cube root of a number. Then we could expand the algorithm above as follows:

$$numb = 64$$
$$sroot = sqr\ (numb)$$
$$croot = cbr\ (numb)$$
$$\textbf{print}\ numb,\ sroot,\ croot$$

The algorithm would now print 64, 8, 4, which are the number, its square root, and its cube root, respectively. Because SQR is a built-in function (available as part of the BASIC language itself) it is not necessary to write either an algorithm or the BASIC code for this function. However, the function *cbr* is not available within the language, so it must be implemented by the programmer. The following pseudocode implements the definition for the function *cbr*:

$$\textbf{\textit{function}}\ cbr\ (nmb)$$
$$cbr = nmb \uparrow (1/3)$$
$$\textbf{\textit{return}}$$

The function name (in this case, *cbr*) is used as an output variable within the function definition to hold the value returned by the function.

Some versions of BASIC (e.g., BASIC-80 and IBM BASIC) allow the direct definition of a function as long as it is a single formula which produces a value. For example, we can define the cube root function above by the BASIC statement

$$10 \quad \text{DEF FNCBR(NMB)} = \text{NMB} \uparrow (1/3)$$

The name of such a function must be of the form FNx, where x is any legal variable name. The variable NMB is a true input parameter which need not be given a value explicitly. Once the function has been defined, it can be used as in

$$100 \quad \text{CROOT} = \text{FNCBR (X)}$$

The variable CROOT will be set to the cube root of X regardless of any value that the variable NMB may have. The value of the variable NMB is not changed by this call.

However, some versions of BASIC (e.g., TRS-80 Level II) do not allow such functions, and it is often desirable to use functions that involve more than a simple formula of input parameters. For this reason, we often implement functions in BASIC using subroutines. For example, the *cbr* function may be coded as follows:

```
1000   'subroutine cbr
1010   'inputs: NMB
1020   'outputs: CBR
1030   'locals: none
1040   'this subroutine calculates the cube root of its input
1050   CBR = NMB ↑ (1/3)
1060   RETURN
1070   'endsub
```

We adopt the convention of using the name of the function as its output variable. If it is not possible to use the function name (e.g., if its first letter designates a different type or another variable with the same first two letters already exists in the program under some versions of BASIC), then a variable whose name is as close as possible to the function name is used as the output variable.

The following is a complete program to print a table of the numbers, square roots, and cube roots of all numbers between 1 and 10.

```
  10    'program table
  20    'This program prints a list of numbers from 1 to 10
  30    'along with their square roots and cube roots.
  40    FOR NUMB = 1 TO 10
  50        SROOT = SQR (NUMB)
  60        NMB = NUMB
  70        GOSUB 1000: 'subroutine cbr sets the variable CBR
  80        CROOT = CBR
  90        PRINT NUMB, SROOT, CROOT
 100    NEXT NUMB
 110    END
           . . .
1000    'subroutine cbr
1010    'inputs: NMB
1020    'outputs: CBR
1030    'locals: none
1040    'this subroutine calculates the cube root of its input
1050    CBR = NMB ↑ (1/3)
1060    RETURN
1070    'endsub
```

EXERCISES

1. Write code to compute the number of vacation days for an employee, NUMVAC, by the following method. Let SICK be the number of days on which the employee called in sick during the past year. The employee is ordinarily entitled to 10 vacation days. However, for each day over 10 for which the employee called in sick, his vacation is reduced by 1 day. If the employee called in sick on fewer than 5 days, he receives 2 extra vacation days. The number of vacation days may not be negative.

2. Rewrite each of the following pieces of code without using FOR-NEXT loops. Instead, use IFs and GOTO statements.

```
(a)   10   FOR I = A TO B STEP 10
      20       READ X, Y
      30       Z = Z + X * Y
      40   NEXT I
(b)   10   FOR I = A TO N STEP L
      20       READ X, Y
      30       Z = Z + X * Y
      40   NEXT I
(c)   10   FOR I = A TO N STEP 10
      20       FOR J = 1 TO 3000
      30           READ X, Y
      40           Z = Z + X + Y
      50       NEXT J
      60   NEXT I
(d)   10   FOR I = 1 TO 10
      20       FOR J = 3 TO I − 1 STEP 3
      30           SUM = SUM + J
      40           READ X
      50           IF X > 100 GOTO 80
      60           IF X > 50 GOTO 100
      70           SUM = SUM − X
      80       NEXT J
      90       SUM = SUM + I
     100   NEXT I
```

3. Determine the purpose of each of the following pieces of code and rewrite them so that they do not use any GOTO statements.

```
(a)   10   X = 1
      20   IF X > 500 THEN GOTO 60
      30   PRINT X; SQR(X); X + 500; SQR(X + 500)
      40   X = X + 1
      50   GOTO 20
      60   'remainder of program
(b)   10   I = 0
      20   IF I > 10 THEN GOTO 60
      30   PRINT I;
      40   I = I + 1
      50   GOTO 20
      60   I = 1
      70   IF I > 10 THEN GOTO 170
      80   PRINT I;
      90   J = 1
     100   IF J > 10 THEN GOTO 140
```

```
110   PRINT I*J
120   J = J + 1
130   GOTO 100
140   PRINT
150   I = I + 1
160   GOTO 70
170   END
```

4. The Royal Dromedary Corporation Ltd. has just installed a computer to assist its camel drivers in ensuring that camel caravans reach their destination safely. It has been determined by the company's Zoological Transportation Expert that a camel can safely carry the weight of 7496 straws before its back breaks. Each caravan leader keys a group of data lines for the caravan he is leading. The first data line contains the driver's name. The next data line contains the number of camels in the caravan. Then, for each camel in the caravan there is a data line that contains the number of baskets of straw which that camel is carrying followed by the number of straws in each basket. Each basket itself consists of 137 straws.

   Write a program to read a series of such data lines and, for each caravan, print the driver's name followed by a list of the camels that are carrying too heavy a load, together with the weight of those loads. If all the camels are safe, print a message to that effect. For example, typical output might be

                  BOB SMITH
                  ALL THE CAMELS ARE OK

                  JOHN JONES
                  THE FOLLOWING CAMELS ARE UNSAFE:
                  CAMEL 3 CARRYING 8467 STRAWS
                  CAMEL 6 CARRYING 7514 STRAWS

5. Assume that the data to a program consist of a number N, followed by N sets of data which are used to initialize an array declared by

                  DIM X(100,100)

   Each of the N sets of data consists of a row number R followed by an indeterminate number of integer pairs. Each integer pair consists of a column number C and a value V. The value of X(R,C) is to be set to V. Each set of row data is terminated by a pair of 0s. If a row number R is not between 1 and 100, its entire set of data is to be ignored. If a column number is not between 1 and 100, its integer pair is to be ignored (unless both C and V equal 0, in which case the end of a set of row data is signaled). All array elements that are not given values by the data must be set to 0. If an array element is given two different values, an error message is to be printed. Write a program to initialize such an array in the manner described.

6. Consider the following code, which sorts an array X of size N:

```
10    FOR TP = N TO 2 STEP −1
20        FOR I = 1 TO TP−1
30            IF X(I) > X(I+1) THEN
                  TEMP = X(I): X(I) = X(I+1): X(I+1) = TEMP
40        NEXT I
50    NEXT TP
```

   (a) Explain how the code sorts the array X.
   (b) Modify the code by using a logical flag so that if the condition $X(I) > X(I+1)$ within the FOR-NEXT loop for I is always FALSE throughout a single complete execution of that loop, the FOR-NEXT loop for TP is terminated prematurely.
   (c) Explain why the modified code also sorts the array X.

7. Write an algorithm to compute the square root of a number x (greater than 4) correct to within an error margin *err*, by the following method. Let *est* be an estimate of the square root. Initially, *est* is x/4. If the difference between *est* and *x/est* is less than *err*, then *est* is the square root. Otherwise, reset *est* to the average of *est* and *x/est*. Do not use any *goto* statements.

8. A positive integer greater than 1 is a ***prime*** if it is not divisible by any integer other than itself or 1. Examples of primes are 2, 11, 37, and 43; 4, 15, and 24 are not primes. Write a routine *prime* that returns *true* if x is a prime and *false* if it is not.

9. A ***perfect number*** is an integer greater than 1 which is the sum of all its divisors except itself. For example, 6 is a perfect number since $6 = 1 + 2 + 3$, and 28 is a perfect number since $28 = 1 + 2 + 4 + 7 + 14$. Write a program to find the smallest perfect number greater than 28.

10. Consider two arrays. Array X contains five different elements in ascending order and array Y contains six different elements in descending order. An array Z of size 11 is declared. Write a BASIC routine to set the values of Z to the values of X and Y in ascending order.

11. Write an algorithm and a BASIC program to find the smallest prime number larger than a given integer x.

12. **(a)** Write a function *fact(n)* to compute the value of the product of all the integers between 1 and n inclusive. In mathematics, *fact(n)* is written as $n!$.
   (b) Suppose that n people serve on a committee and k of them must be chosen for a subcommittee. Let *comm(n,k)* be the number of different such subcommittees that can be formed. Show that *comm(n,k)* equals $n!/(k!*(n−k)!)''$. Write a function *comm(n,k)* to compute this value.
   (c) If an urn contains p black and v white balls and $b+w$ balls are chosen at random from the urn, let *prob(p,v,b,w)* be the probability that exactly b black and w white balls are picked. Show that *prob(p,v,b,w)* can be computed by the formula $(comm(p,b)*comm(v,w))/comm(p+v,b+w)$. Write a program that reads sets of data each of which contains integers p, v, b, and w and which computes *prob(p,v,b,w)*. For each input set, the program prints the values of p, v, b, w and *prob(p, v, b, w)*.

(**d**) Modify the program of part (c) so that after all the output of that part is printed, the program prints the number of times that the function *fact* was called.

(**e**) Rewrite the program of part (c) without using any subroutines.

2. PROGRAMMING TECHNIQUES

In the preceding section we examined some of the programming constructs of BASIC and have shown how they can be extended to other control structures to produce logical, readable, and correct programs. Let us now turn our attention to specific techniques that are helpful in writing programs.

Program Development

We all have an intuitive idea of the relationship between a problem and a solution. We think of a problem as the formulation of a question that is presented and the solution as the response to that question.

For large problems, we are not the sole problem solvers. Most problem solutions that involve large amounts of data or that require a process to be performed many times are processed by a computer (so that human beings can devote their time to presumably more worthwhile endeavors). The programmer's job is essentially to formulate the solution so that a machine can be used to carry out the mechanics of that solution. Computer design has not yet reached the level where one can walk up to a computer and ask it: "What is my mortgage payment?" or "What is the value of π correct to 5000 decimal places?" It is therefore necessary to write programs to enable a machine to answer these questions. The program is a vehicle with which we may arrive at answers to these and other questions.

In the process of producing a solution from a problem, the work of the programmer must pass through several stages:

1. Problem formulation
2. Choice of algorithm and data structures
3. Coding a solution

Let us examine each of these stages in turn.

Formulating the Problem

The problem formulation phase is an extremely important one. It has been said that specifying a problem well is half its solution. As a problem is specified in more and more detail, it becomes clearer what resources are necessary for the problem's solution and how those resources are to be utilized in achieving that solution.

For example, suppose that you are hired by a college to produce a computerized system for student records. Although this may be enough of a description for specifying the requirements of a programming position, it is by no means sufficient information from which to write a program. The problem must be defined precisely so that the programmer knows exactly what inputs the program will expect and what outputs are expected from it. The inputs and outputs may be specified by company management, in which case the programmer has no choice other than to accept the specifications handed to him or her and write the program (or possibly quit his or her job). On the other hand, the programmer may have some input into the specification of the program. In that case, he or she can exercise some degree of control over the specification so that programming may be simplified and the value of the final product to its users enhanced. For example, it may be determined that certain information which is difficult to compute is not really necessary until a subsequent phase of the project, when it is easier to obtain. Or, it may be determined that such information is not needed at all. Similarly, it may turn out that some procedure or process is really a very inefficient method of obtaining a result, whereas a simpler method produces the same or similar results at a much lower cost.

In any case, a final, precise, definition of the problem is arrived at—usually with input from both the programmer and the user. It should be pointed out that no programming should be attempted or even outlined before the problem is completely specified. Projects that enter the coding stage prematurely usually end up requiring large amounts of time in constant revision of code as the needs of the final product evolve. Worse yet, such code is frequently patched up to get around sticky points based on invalid initial assumptions which stem from an incomplete understanding of the problem. The time that a programmer spends writing and refining the specification of the problem and its solution will be retrieved by eliminating much debugging, reorganizing, and rewriting portions of code that were written too hastily.

The following are the inputs and outputs for the problem above:

Inputs
    Number of students
    For each student
        Social security number
        Name
        Number of courses
        For each course
            Grade
Outputs
    For each student
        Social security number
        Name
        The student's average
        Class average
        Alphabetical list of the students and their corresponding averages
                             and social security numbers

The practice of explicitly specifying the inputs and outputs of a program is extremely valuable. Aside from serving as a summary of problem specification, such a list helps focus on the question of whether each output can be computed from the given set of inputs. It is often the case that one or two inputs have been unintentionally omitted from the problem specification. This omission can be detected at this point before any programming has been done, at a time when the machinery necessary to obtain missing inputs can be put into effect.

Developing an Algorithm

A list of inputs and outputs naturally leads to the next phase of program development: choosing algorithms and data structures. An *algorithm* is a set of instructions by which the outputs are computed from the inputs. A good programmer realizes that no solution is completely specified unless an algorithm for its solution has been described. In developing such an algorithm, the programmer must ask how each of the outputs can be derived from the inputs, that is, which of the outputs can be derived directly from the inputs and which need intermediate quantities or other output quantities for their derivation. For example, the social security number and name of a student are given by the input. Each student's average must be derived from the input grades. The class average must be derived from the students' averages, which are themselves outputs. This implies that the students' averages must be computed before the class average.

During the process of writing and modifying an algorithm, the good programmer uncovers remaining gaps in the problem specification. In general, programming is not a straight-line activity in which one can proceed from one step to another. Rather, at each stage, decisions that were made in previous stages must be reexamined and sometimes modified. Other decisions which were consciously postponed in previous stages must be made in later stages. For example, in the interest of increasing the efficiency of a program, specifications might be modified during the actual coding. Of course, any such change of specification must be agreed to by the user as well as by the programmer.

A first attempt at an algorithm outline for the college program might be the following:

```
read number of students
for each student
    read social security number
    read name
    read grades of the student
    calculate the student's average
    print the student's social security number, name, and average
calculate the class average
sort the class list alphabetically
print in alphabetical order the names, social security numbers,
    and averages of the students
```

Although the algorithm above can be regarded as a logical description of the solution, it cannot be used directly to construct a program. In order to write a BASIC program from such an algorithm it is necessary to be able to translate every statement in the algorithm into equivalent BASIC code. This requires two things: descriptions of how the data are maintained (i.e., the data structures to be used) and the actual computations involved.

We will return shortly to the problem of how to transform the algorithm into BASIC code. For now, let us examine the data structures that are necessary for the solution of the problem.

Choosing Data Structures

The selection of data structures has profound ramifications on the complexity of the algorithm that is required for the solution of a problem and the ease with which this algorithm is implemented. Indeed, the major subject of this book concerns the selection of data structures for problem solving.

In the example above, the choice of data structures is straightforward. Each of the entities required in the program may be retained in a simple variable suitably created for this purpose. In general, variables that are read as a group (e.g., the grades of an individual student) need not be placed in an array unless they must be processed together, as, for example, in a sort routine. Economy of space is achieved by reusing an individual variable, rather than using an array. On the other hand, it is sometimes easier to perform certain tasks on an array than on a set of simple variables. The student averages, names, and social security numbers, for example, should be retained in arrays in order to sort and print the list in alphabetical order. Since we require the average of a set of values at two distinct points, we will use a subroutine for this purpose. This subroutine will accept an array of numbers and the number of items whose average is to be computed and will compute the average of these values. In order to use this subroutine to compute the average of each individual student, it will be necessary to store the set of grades for each student in an array. Although this is not technically necessary and does require some extra space, it will make some of the programming easier. We present the main program.

```
10   'program college
20   'read each student's social security number, name, and grades
30   'and calculate and print the following information
40   '      social security number of each student
50   '      name of each student
60   '      average of each student
70   '      average of the students' averages
80   'also print the averages in alphabetical order
```

```
 90   DEFSTR N
100   DIM ARR(100), NAM(100), NSEC(100), STAVG(100)
110   READ SNUM
120   FOR I = 1 TO SNUM
130       READ NSEC(I), NAM(I)
140       READ CNT
150       FOR J = 1 TO CNT
160           READ ARR(J)
170       NEXT J
180       GOSUB 1000: 'subroutine avg accepts ARR and CNT
                        'and sets the variable AVG
190       STAVG(I) = AVG
200       PRINT NSEC(I), NAM(I), STAVG(I)
210   NEXT I
220   'the names and averages of the individual students
230   'have been printed
240   FOR I = 1 TO SNUM
250       ARR(I) = STAVG(I)
260   NEXT I
270   CNT = SNUM
280   GOSUB 1000 :        'subroutine avg
290   CLASAVG = AVG
300   PRINT "THE CLASS AVERAGE IS "; CLASAVG
310   GOSUB 2000 :        'subroutine sort accepts SNUM, NAM, NSEC, and
                           'STAVG and sorts the list in alphabetical order
320   PRINT "ALPHABETICAL CLASS LIST"
330   FOR I = 1 TO SNUM
340       PRINT NSEC(I), NAM(I), STAVG(I)
350   NEXT I
360   END
800   DATA . . .
            . . .
1000   'subroutine avg goes here
            . . .
2000   'subroutine sort goes here
            . . .
```

The main program should act only in a supervisory fashion. In other words, it should act as a manager which organizes the work that is to be done and assigns various tasks to specific subroutines. Each routine, in turn, organizes the job that it must do and breaks up the work into components to be assigned to still other, lower-level routines. This process continues until the lowest-level routines are written. These routines can perform their job easily enough without calling other routines.

The programmer then proceeds to solve the subproblems. At this time it is necessary to specify those subproblems more precisely. In particular, it is necessary to determine exactly what information the subroutine can access when it is called and what actions it is expected to take. Once the purpose of the subroutine is completely specified, the subroutine may be coded using the same techniques that were used in coding the calling program. This process continues until there are no more algorithms to refine and no more subgoals to accomplish. The routine to calculate the average is straightforward.

```
1000    'subroutine avg
1010    'inputs: ARR, CNT
1020    'outputs: AVG
1030    'locals: K, SUM
1040    'subroutine avg sets AVG to the average of
            'the values in ARR(1) through ARR(CNT)
1050    SUM = 0
1060    FOR K = 1 TO CNT
1070        SUM = SUM + ARR(K)
1080    NEXT K
1090    AVG = SUM / CNT
1100    RETURN
1110    'endsub
```

Let us consider the problem of sorting the list. In the process of sorting the list alphabetically, we must remember that the information associated with a particular student must be kept with that student (i.e., it is not sufficient to rearrange only the names; the social security numbers and averages must be rearranged as well). Once we have precisely defined the task of the subroutine, we proceed to code it:

```
3000    'subroutine sort
3010    'inputs: NAM, NSEC, SNUM, STAVG
3020    'outputs: NAM, NSEC, STAVG
3030    'locals: K, L, NTMP, TEMP
3040    'subroutine sort rearranges the first SNUM entries in the list alphabetically
3050    FOR K = 1 TO SNUM − 1
3060        FOR L = K + 1 TO SNUM
3070            IF NAM(K) <= NAM(L) THEN GOTO 3120
3080                'else do statements 3090-3110
                    'interchange the data for student K with that of student L
3090                TEMP = STAVG(K): STAVG(K) = STAVG(L):
                                                        STAVG(L) = TEMP
3100                NTMP = NAM(K): NAM(K) = NAM(L): NAM(L) = NTMP
3110                NTMP = NSEC(K): NSEC(K) = NSEC(L): NSEC(L) = NTMP
3120        NEXT L
3130    NEXT K
3140    RETURN
3150    'endsub
```

Note that whereas statements 240–270 are used to initialize the inputs to *avg*, there is no initialization of the inputs to *avg* before the call in line 180. This is because the inputs (the array ARR and CNT) were directly initialized from the input stream. Similarly, there are no initializations for the call to *sort*, because it uses the variables of the main program directly. It is also possible to eliminate the extra work of initializing inputs when several routines have the same inputs. However, it is important to ascertain that the inputs have not been changed between the two calls. Often, when a program must be efficient, initialization of an array input to a subroutine takes too much time. This is especially true if it must be done repeatedly (unlike our example, where initialization of ARR from STAVG need be done only once because the class average is computed only once). In such cases, it may be advisable to eliminate the subroutine and to place code to perform its processing directly into the calling program. A more recommended practice, to keep the program structured and maintainable, is to use the array which already contains the data in the calling program as the input to the subroutine; as was done in the case of the *sort* subroutine. This may mean several copies of the same subroutine, each operating on a different input array. The same is true when an array is an output of a subroutine. (Other programming languages use a different mechanism for passing array parameters which does not involve the inefficiency of copying the entire array.)

Note also that NAM, NSEC, and STAVG are both input and output parameters of *sort* since the values of the arrays are being rearranged.

Finally, it is interesting to note that the routine *sort* only sorts the data into alphabetical order. It if were necessary to sort into some other order (e.g., order of increasing average), a separate subroutine would have to be written. It is often the case that separate routines must be written even if they perform the same or similar operations on different types of data.

A question that must be answered for each problem solution is how to divide the chores among a main routine and its subroutines. This question does not have a clear answer, and must be answered by the programmer for each individual program. However, there are two general guidelines that are helpful in selecting those tasks which are to be performed in a calling program and those which are relegated to a subprogram.

The first criterion is that segments of a program that include a large amount of detail which is secondary to the solution of the problem should be placed in a subroutine. When writing and reading a routine, a programmer does not want to be concerned with the details of how certain subtasks are accomplished; he or she merely wants to be able to be sure that they are done. Included in this category is any task whose actual actions may be modified at a later date. A program that is permeated with code that is "to be improved" may prove to be very difficult to improve. On the other hand, if that code is isolated in compact subroutines, each subroutine can be modified and tested independently of the calling routine so that the calling routine need not be changed at all. When the modification is complete, the new subroutine replaces the old one and the total program works correctly. This concept of being able to replace one version of a routine by another is called **modularity** and the individual routines are called **modules**. Programming in a modular style, in which each routine is a self-contained unit that is easily replaceable, enables subsequent modifications to be performed efficiently, correctly, and without worrying about possible side effects of one piece of code on all the others. During the remainder of the text we will be structuring our solutions in this **top-down** modular manner.

A second criterion for placing a specific operation or set of operations in a subroutine is its usefulness to other programs or other portions of the same program. For example, if a particular process (such as sorting) is required at several points in a program, it is helpful to code this process as a subroutine and access the routine through subroutine calls. Thus the code need not be repeated at several points in the program, and hence it need not be debugged several times. Similarly, if one has developed a working sort subroutine, it can be used intact whenever a program that requires sorting is being written. (Of course, all inputs must be initialized properly in the program).

Program Layout

In addition to the difficult issue of how a program should be developed, there are a number of simple, almost mechanical techniques for creating readable, modifiable, and correct programs. The first of these techniques involves the layout of a program.

Consider the following program segment:

```
10   INPUT A,B,C: IF A < B THEN
     GOTO 20 ELSE IF B < C THEN GOTO
     30 ELSE D = C: GOTO 50: 'unconditional branch
20   IF A < C THEN GOTO 40 ELSE D = C:
     GOTO 50: 'unconditional branch
30   D = B: GOTO 50: 'unconditional branch
40   D = A: 'assign A to D
50   PRINT D
```

Before reading further, see if you can determine what this program segment does. The code above reads three numbers A, B, and C, assigns the smallest to D, and prints D. Although it accomplishes its task, this sample is a far cry from the type of program one would like to read and modify. First, the layout of the code is very disorganized. While the BASIC language imposes few restrictions on the format of code, good programmers use formats that are consistent with easy reading and understanding. In particular, rarely should more than one statement appear on a line. In addition, an ELSE clause need never be used after a THEN clause ending in a GOTO. The statements in the ELSE clause will be executed only if the condition is false, regardless of whether an ELSE appears, since if the condition is true, the GOTO will have branched elsewhere.

The following version incorporates these improvements:

```
10   INPUT A, B, C
20   IF A < B THEN GOTO 60: 'branch to 60
30   IF B < C THEN GOTO 90
40   D = C
50   GOTO 120: 'unconditional branch
60   IF A < C THEN GOTO 110
70   D = C
80   GOTO 120: 'unconditional branch
90   D = B
100  GOTO 120: 'unconditional branch
110  D = A: 'assign A to D
120  PRINT D
```

Certainly, the second version is better than the first, although it is far from a "good" program. One of the difficulties in reading the code above is that little is done to help the reader decipher which portions of code do what. There are several steps that can be taken to improve program readability further.

Meaningful Variable Names

It is helpful to use variable names that promote an understanding of the purpose of the variable (subject to the limitations of the version of BASIC being used, as discussed in Section 1). Even if the programmer has no control over the names A, B, and C (they might have been passed on from some previous portion of the program), he or she can still select a more meaningful name than D for the smallest number. Simply by using a variable name such as SMALL, the programmer gives a good indication of what the program does. As another illustration, suppose that the variables of a program to compute interest on a principal could be named PRINC, AMT, YEARS, and RATE rather than A, B, C, and D. Such an assignment of variable names helps reduce the time required to understand a program.

In some cases the programmer may feel that it is more expedient to use "simple" variable names such as X and Y. However, the added time spent in trying to determine, at some later date, just what these variables represent probably costs more than any time initially spent in selecting meaningful names. However, it is usually considered acceptable to use simple variable names such as I, J, or K as indices of a loop.

Documentation

Another way in which the programmer can aid the reader in understanding programs is by providing good documentation. Documentation, in its most general interpretation, refers to any supporting material that the programmer provides (in addition to the code) to help explain the program to the user and to any other programmer who wants to make changes in the future. Included are flowcharts, instructions on the format of the inputs, and explanations of the outputs. More narrowly, documentation has been used to refer to remarks in the actual code.

There are several points to be made concerning remarks. If a program is well written, it is not necessary to insert remarks at each elementary stage. A good program is self-explanatory, so that the reader does not have to plow through a long series of remarks in order to determine what a small portion of code is doing.

Let us analyze the remarks in the second version of our program segment above. One thing that is worse than no remark is a useless remark. Each of the three different remarks in the above program fits remarkably well into this category. The remark

>   *'branch to* 60

says nothing more than the statement

>   GOTO 60

immediately preceding it. The same is true of the remark

>   *'assign A to D*

Such remarks serve only to clutter the layout of the code and perhaps mislead the reader into thinking that something more substantial than actually indicated by the code is really going on. Similarly, the remark

>   *'unconditional branch*

is of use only to the novice programmer who is totally unfamiliar with the terminology of programming. Cluttering up code with such meaningless remarks serves only to confuse the reader.

How, then, should remarks be used to help rather than hinder the reader of a program? First, as mentioned earlier, the code should be written in such a way that many remarks are not necessary. Among the techniques that promote this goal are the use of meaningful identifiers and the use of constructs such as *while* loops and *if* statements in the development of programs.

Yet, even if all the right techniques are used, an explanation should be provided at the beginning of a process or self-contained block of code. These remarks should be concise but complete so that the reader knows the function of the code. In addition, there should usually be a remark at the beginning of a loop explaining the purpose of the loop, and unless it is completely obvious, the remark should also specify the conditions for exiting the loop. Finally, those portions of code whose actions are not clear should be fully documented. These ideas should be used as guidelines and not as rules; the programmer must make the ultimate decision in deciding which statements or groups of statements should be documented.

Another useful documentation technique is to include explanatory output messages. A program that produces a page of numbers is often useless. Make sure that output statements include a message that identifies the final result.

To improve readability, code should be interspersed with blank lines so that individual groups of statements stand out as being related to each other. Incorporating these suggestions, the example above can be rewritten as follows:

```
10    'compute the smallest of three numbers
20    PRINT "ENTER THREE NUMBERS"
30    INPUT A, B, C
40    IF A < B THEN GOTO 90
50    IF B < C THEN GOTO 140
60    SMALL = C
70    GOTO 200
80    '
90    'check whether A or C is smallest
100   IF A < C THEN GOTO 180
110   SMALL = C
120   GOTO 200
130   '
140   'B is smallest
150   SMALL = B
160   GOTO 200
170   '
180   'A is smallest
190   SMALL = A
200   '
210   PRINT "SMALLEST IS "; SMALL
```

Avoiding Needless Branches

Unfortunately, although we have improved the layout of the code and the documentation, there is very little that can be done to make an inherently poor program understandable. The major problem with the code above is its structure and organization. Upon findng a condition to be true or false, control is transferred to a different portion of code. Upon completing that second portion of code, control is again transferred around some third portion of code. As the complexity of a program increases, this problem is compounded until the final product becomes totally unreadable "spaghetti code."

Whenever a GOTO statement is used to transfer control from one portion of a program to another, the resultant code lacks both structure and organization. The complete elimination of the GOTO statement, however, is not feasible. As we have shown in the preceding section, the GOTO statement is often (properly) used to implement various higher-level structures (e.g., *while*, *if-then-else*). Rather than transferring control from one portion of the program to another, the GOTO statement serves to create a unified programming structure. Indeed, when used in this disciplined manner, the GOTO statement contributes to a highly desirable structured programming style. The problem of unstructured or "spaghetti" organization is one that cannot be easily remedied by patching up poorly structured code; it requires careful planning and attention from the start.

The smallest of a set of numbers must be less than or equal to each of the other numbers in the set. However, it is not necessary to compare each number with every other number in order to locate this smallest number. Suppose that as the set of numbers is scanned, the program keeps track of the smallest number encountered thus far in a variable SMALL. Then each time a new number is considered, it need be compared only with SMALL. If the new number is less than SMALL, then it is also less than each of the numbers encountered previously; if the new number is not less than SMALL, then SMALL retains the property of being the smallest. Using this analysis, the solution can be coded in either of the following ways:

```
10   PRINT "ENTER THREE NUMBERS"
20   INPUT A, B, C
30   'SMALL is set to the smallest of A, B and C
40   IF A <= B THEN SMALL = A
               ELSE SMALL = B
50   IF C < SMALL THEN SMALL = C
60   PRINT "SMALLEST IS "; SMALL
```

or

```
10   PRINT "ENTER THREE NUMBERS"
20   INPUT A, B, C
30   'SMALL is set to the smallest of A, B and C
40   SMALL = A
50   IF B < SMALL THEN SMALL = B
60   IF C < SMALL THEN SMALL = C
70   PRINT "SMALLEST IS "; SMALL
```

Contrast either of these versions with any of the three preceding versions. These new versions solve the problem directly by making use of the simple relationship described above. As soon as a condition that requires an action is detected, the appropriate action is performed by a statement that is in close proximity to the condition. No branching is used. Even the casual reader should have little difficulty in following the actions since the program reads sequentially. It is unnecessary to intersperse comments to explain the more intricate parts of the code since there are no intricate parts to explain. The earlier versions, on the other hand, contain an additional comparison and five branches. Of course, not all of these branches are taken on any single run of the program. Yet, for a reader to determine just what is actually going on, it is necessary to understand every possible sequence of statements.

Program Readability

There are several other things the programmer can do in order to make programs more readable. One of these is the use of visual spacing for portions of code. Such spacing includes the use of blank lines to group together different portions of code. This enables the reader to detect logical sections of the program by their physical separation. In addition to using blank lines, separate routines should be given line numbers which differ markedly from the line numbers preceding them. Certainly, major subroutines should be given their own series of line numbers. Perhaps each subroutine should begin on a new ''thousand'' so that the main program might begin at line number 10 while successive major routines should begin at line numbers 1000, 2000, and so on. By separating logical portions of code through the use of blank lines and using separate numbering schemes the programmer can provide simple visual aids to the reader.

Still another visual feature that enhances program readability is the use of indentation. BASIC is a free-form language in that there are almost no restrictions as to the position of parts of a statement on a physical line. For example, a statement may span two or more lines of code, and conversely, two or more statements may be placed on a single line. Some programmers use this freedom to code programs haphazardly, paying little attention to the position and the layout of the statements. This carelessness yields a program that is difficult to read. In Section 1 we have outlined useful indentation patterns for BASIC code which follow elementary pseudocode structures. This indentation pattern is used in the remainder of this book.

"Clever" Code

Finally, the programmer should stay away from ''clever'' code. For example, the following statements compute the bigger and smaller of two numbers, A and B:

```
100   BIG = (A + B + ABS(A − B))/2
110   SMALL = (A + B − ABS(A − B))/2
```

This is a prime example of the type of coding that should never be used (except perhaps to show off a repertoire of clever tricks). Let us see how it works.

$A + B$ is the sum of the bigger number and the smaller. $ABS(A − B)$, the absolute value of the difference between the two numbers, equals the bigger number minus the smaller. If BIG represents the bigger number and SMALL the smaller, then A + B equals BIG + SMALL, and ABS(A − B) equals BIG − SMALL, so A + B + ABS(A − B) equals (BIG + SMALL) + (BIG − SMALL), which equals 2*BIG, and A + B − ABS(A − B) equals (BIG + SMALL) − (BIG − SMALL), which equals 2 * SMALL. Therefore, dividing by 2 yields BIG and SMALL, respectively. The two statements do indeed set BIG and SMALL to the correct values.

A program that is loaded with such "clever" code is doomed to failure, should it ever be modified. Unless the original author remembers precisely how the program works, it is almost impossible to decipher. Unfortunately, many programs in use today are permeated with tricks that only the original author understands. Although such tactics do make the author indispensable to the maintenance of the program (and may for this reason be a guarantee of a lifetime job), they have no place in an environment where well-styled and modifiable programs are run. A simpler version of the code above would be

```
100 IF A > B THEN BIG = A: SMALL = B
        ELSE BIG = B: SMALL = A
```

This second version is clearer than its predecessor and does not require any extra code.

Signaling the End of Data

It is generally helpful for a programmer to have available a set of programming techniques to solve specific problems or parts of problems. This is useful when decomposing programs into tasks for which code has already been designed. Possible techniques include signaling the end of data, searching for an element of an array, and so on.

Suppose that it is necessary to read pairs of values from DATA lines and insert the second of these values at the position in the array specified by the first. Consider the loop

$$\textit{while true do}$$
$$\textit{read } i,\ a(i)$$
$$\textit{endwhile}$$

Since the *while* loop continues indefinitely, we eventually arrive at the situation in which a read is attempted with no data present. Naturally, an error occurs and program execution is terminated. There are two methods used to signal the end of data before the error condition occurs. These are known as the *header method* and the *trailer method*. If the number of data items is known in advance, a header data item consisting of the number of subsequent data items is placed prior to the actual data. Using this number, we may loop through the READ statement the exact number of times necessary. As an example, suppose that we wish to read five names and insert the names into the array. Using the header method, we can write

```
10   DEFSTR A
20   DIM A(100)
30   READ N
40   FOR I = 1 TO N
50       READ K, A(K)
60   NEXT I
70   END
     . . .
500  DATA 5
510  DATA 2, "GAIL"
520  DATA 1, "VIVIENNE"
530  DATA 5, "CHRIS"
540  DATA 3, "MIRIAM"
550  DATA 4, "LINDA"
```

Alternatively, a trailer card containing an "impossible" value may be used to signal the end of data. This method must be used when the number of data items is unknown. Modifying the preceding example, suppose that we wish to read an undetermined number of names and insert them into an array. Using the trailer 0, "XXX" to signal the end of data we may write

```
10   DEFSTR A,P
20   DIM A(100)
30   READ K, PRSN
40       IF K = 0 THEN GOTO 70
50       A(K) = PRSN
60   GOTO 30
70   END
500  DATA 2, "GAIL"
510  DATA 1, "VIVIENNE"
520  DATA 5, "CHRIS"
530  DATA 3, "MIRIAM"
540  DATA 4, "LINDA"
550  DATA 0, "XXX"
```

Conclusion

In this section we have mentioned many points which form a list of dos and don'ts in writing code. We summarize this list.

- Code only one statement per line.
- Use meaningful identifiers.
- Use proper documentation, including proper remarks and explanatory output for the user.

- •Use blank lines and distinct line numbering schemes.
- •Use indentation (for FOR, IF-THEN-ELSE, etc.).
- •Avoid needless transfers.
- •Avoid clever code.
- •Use standard techniques.

The rules above should be used as a guide, but they are not inflexible. The programmer must make the decision as to when rules may be broken and when exceptions should be made. Programming does require initiative and originality. However, a style built on these suggestions contributes to making the final program easy to read and therefore easier to debug and easier to modify when necessary.

EXERCISES

1. Write a program that reads a sequence of numbers and prints the longest ascending subsequence of those numbers.
2. Write a program that reads monetary amounts (under $1.00) and prints the number of each coin necessary to yield that amount using the smallest total number of coins (e.g., $0.42 = 1 quarter, 1 dime, 1 nickel, and 2 pennies). When all the amounts have been processed, print the total number of coins of each type required.
3. Do the same as in Exercise 2, but generate all possible combinations of change rather than only the one with the fewest number of coins.
4. The standard formula for compound interest is

$$a = p * (1 + r/n) \uparrow (n*t)$$

   where p is the original principal, r the annual percentage rate, n the number of periods per year at which compounding is done, t the number of years of the investment or the loan, and a the amount to which the principal has grown.
   (a) Compute the final value of $100 invested at 5% for 25 years compounded annually by an explicit loop and also by the formula above.
   (b) Do the same as in part (a) using successive values of $n = 1, 2, \ldots, 365$ (annual compounding to daily compounding) and observe the results. Can you derive a formula for "continuous" compounding?
5. Another common problem that can be solved by computer is the solution of n equations in n unknowns, using **Gaussian elimination**. For example, a system of three equations in three unknowns might appear as follows:

$$a(1,1)*x + a(1,2)*y + a(1,3)*z = b(1)$$
$$a(2,1)*x + a(2,2)*y + a(2,3)*z = b(2)$$
$$a(3,1)*x + a(3,2)*y + a(3,3)*z = b(3)$$

   The algorithm to solve for x, y, and z proceeds as follows:

(a) Interchange equations (if necessary) so that $a(1,1)$ does not equal 0. (At least one leading coefficient must be nonzero. Why?)

(b) Eliminate the coefficient of x in the second equation by replacing that equation by a new equation formed in the following way. Multiply the first equation by $a(2,1)/a(1,1)$ and subtract the result from the second equation. Do the same for the third equation, but this time multiply by $a(3,1)/a(1,1)$.

(c) Eliminate the coefficient of y from the third equation by performing a similar process using the second and third equations.

(d) When the process has been completed, the form of the equations is (asterisks represent nonzero coefficients)

$$*x + *y + *z = c(1)$$
$$*y + *z = c(2)$$
$$*z = c(3)$$

where each leading coefficient is nonzero and $c(1)$, $c(2)$, and $c(3)$ are the respective constants. The value of z is $c(3)$ divided by the coefficient of z in the last equation, and the values of y and x can be obtained by substituting into the previous equations. Write a program that inputs the two-dimensional array a and the one-dimensional array b and computes the values of x, y, and z.

6. Write a program to trace a path through a maze. The form of the maze is such that each square is either open or closed. If the square is open, it can be entered from either side, above or below (but not diagonally). If the square is closed, it may not be entered. The program reads the dimensions of the maze followed by a series of 0s and 1s representing the status of the squares (0 represents an open square and 1 a closed square). The program finds a path through the maze (if one exists) from the upper left square to the lower right square. Both of these squares must be open. After the path has been found, the program prints the maze with an asterisk representing each closed square and a blank for each open square. Then the program reprints the maze using the digit 1 to represent squares on the actual path taken.

7. A company manufactures three items. The cost of each item is kept in an array declared by DIM COST(2,3). COST(1,I) is the cost of item I to a preferred customer, and COST(2,I) is the cost of item I to a regular customer. The company maintains records on its customers in the following data aggregate:

```
DEFSTR N
'customer records
DIM NAME(20):          'name information
DIM ONORD(20,3):       'order information
DIM BAL(20):           'customers' balances
```

NAME(I) is the name of the Ith customer, ONORD(I,J) is the amount of the Jth item placed on order by customer I, and BAL(I) is the amount owed by the Ith customer. Write a main program and series of routines to do the following:

(a) Read the arrays COST and NAME. Initialize the ONORD array and the BAL array to zeros.

(b) Read a set of DATA lines, each containing a customer name, the type of the customer (preferred or regular), and three integers representing changes to the ONORD array for that customer. If a change is positive (additional items are being ordered), the cost to that customer type (preferred or regular) is to be used in updating the BAL amount for that customer. If the change is negative (an order is being canceled), the smaller cost is to be used. A customer may not cancel more of an item than he has on order. If, after all three changes are made, the new balance is less than the old balance, a 10% surcharge on the difference is to be added. The appropriate fields in the customer record are to be adjusted by a routine called *update*. The appropriate customer record to be updated is to be determined by a routine *find* which accepts a customer name and determines the index of that customer's record within the array NAME.

(c) When a DATA line containing a blank customer name is encountered, print all the customers' names, ONORD amounts, and BAL values, and terminate the program.

3. *PROGRAM RELIABILITY*

Let us summarize the stages of the program development process. We start with a possibly imprecise problem statement. The problem statement is refined to clarify exactly what the inputs to the program are and exactly what outputs are expected of it. An algorithm for solution is chosen; this algorithm might be well known or it might be one that the programmer has to derive personally. The algorithm contains several statements which can be translated directly into a programming language. Others are vague in that they specify only that some task be done without specifying how. Such statements require further clarification and are usually specified by a subalgorithm. This subalgorithm may, in turn, require other subalgorithms. This process continues until the lowest-level algorithms can be readily translated into program statements. In the course of developing each algorithm, the data structures that must be used in its implementation are specified.

Once the algorithms have been written, they can be translated into actual code. If the programmer follows the coding suggestions of the previous sections, the resulting program will be easy to read, understand, and modify. The programmer might congratulate himself or herself on a job well done.

Or are such congratulations a bit premature? It would seem that the programmer should be able to answer some questions about the program. The first question is: Does it work? If a program does not work, it is worthless, regardless of how well it was planned or how nicely the code is documented or how neat the output looks. A "yes" answer to the question of whether a program works requires that the program always works and not just sometimes. The program that fails to work only for certain inputs in exceptional cases will invariably be presented with just those inputs in just those cases and will, of course, fail to work.

Even if a program does work, the question arises: How well does it work? If a payroll program that is to be run on a machine with 2 hours of available time requires 8 hours to run, that program is of no help to the user. Efficiency may seem at times to be an academic question, but when programming on a real machine with real constraints, the question may become crucial.

Questions of whether a program works, and if so, how well, form the subject of *program reliability*. Throughout the remainder of this section we consider some aspects of program reliability. It is not possible to cover all aspects of reliability because there is no general way of determining whether an arbitrary program does what it is supposed to do for all inputs within specific time and space constraints. However, if programmers avoid obvious blunders and make a strong effort to program properly, they improve the chances that their programs are correct and do not require an exorbitant amount of resources.

In this section we consider three major questions in program reliability: "Is the algorithm correct?", "Does the program produce the results intended by the algorithm?" and "Is the program reasonably efficient?"

Program Correctness

A *logic error* reflects a serious flaw in the programmed solution which cannot be attributed to its implementation. As a trivial example, consider the following problem and proposed solution, both in algorithmic and program form. Suppose that it is necessary to read two numbers from data and to compute and print their sum. The following is a proposed algorithmic solution.

> **read** $n1,n2$
> $ans = n1*n2$
> **print** ans

To implement the algorithm above as a program, we can code

```
10   'program solution
20   READ N1, N2
30   ANS = N1*N2
40   PRINT "THE ANSWER IS "; ANS
50   END
60   DATA . . .
```

The solution above is obviously incorrect but it is important to understand where its fault lies. A casual reader of the problem statement and the program *solution* might say that the error is a keying error (an "*" was typed instead of a "+"). However, the reader who has followed the solution from start to finish should note that the program is a correct implementation of the algorithm given above. In fact, the program is correct—but it solves the "wrong problem." The real mistake in this case is in the algorithm—instead of adding two numbers, it multiplies them. Such an error is one of the most difficult errors to find. (In fact, if the programmer tests the program using the inputs 2 and 2, he or she will not even know that there is anything wrong with it.)

How does one ascertain that a program is logically correct? There is no easy answer to this question. In some cases, as in the example above, it is possible to verify by inspection whether a program is correct or not. In fact, most programs that require only that a set of computations be done can be verified for correctness in this way. However, most programs that do anything substantial involve conditional executions and loops. Such control structures are not as easy to follow, especially if the number of iterations through a loop is variable.

There are formal methods that can be used to determine whether a program is correct. However, these are quite tedious and are usually far more complex than the program itself. For this reason, they are rarely used in practice.

Thus it is necessary to rely on techniques that are less than perfect for verifying program correctness. Such techniques when combined with good programming practice and common sense can help eliminate logic errors. The programmer should code all logical portions of the program as separate entities. Each of these entities should be preceded by a remark describing the state of affairs before that portion of the program is executed. This is particularly important in the case of loops. Each portion of the code should be written clearly so that the reader who understands the situation before the code is executed should be able to understand the situation after that portion of code is executed. If any portion of the code is unclear, it should be documented more fully, with an explanation of precisely what actions are to be taken.

If this process is followed consistently from the beginning of the program to its end, the program includes, as remarks, a series of assertions about the values of the program variables. The code of the program should read as proof that each assertion is valid, based on the previous assertion and the code between the two assertions. Thus the reader should be able to follow the transformations of the program variables from start to finish. If the transformations imply that the desired output is not correct, there is something wrong with the logic of the program.

We have actually discovered another argument for simplicity. In theory, one should be able to prove the correctness of every program submitted as correct. In reality, however, this is not always possible. If a program is short and simple, it is easier to analyze. Even if it is not possible to prove that a program is correct, it should be possible to justify intuitively the appropriateness of each portion of the program toward the final solution. These intuitive justifications properly belong as remarks separating major segments of the program. These substitute for more formal proofs and should be paid as much attention as the coding itself. For if one cannot justify the individual portions of the program, the overall solution is very likely incorrect.

Testing and Debugging

Even after the logic of a program has been validated, the question remains whether the program does what it is supposed to. From a logical point of view, an approach may indeed be correct, but the actual implementation of that approach as a program may be incorrect. There are many areas where a program can go wrong. It is the responsibility of the programmer to test a program to the point where he or she is reasonably certain that the code is correct. It may not always be clear just when the testing phase is complete enough to ensure validity, but some general guidelines are helpful.

Testing is the process of detecting errors or "bugs" in a program; *debugging* is the process of correcting the program in such a way that existing errors are removed without introducing new ones. In practice, the removal of errors in a way that does not affect other parts of a program is not at all easy.

An important distinction must be made between the symptom of an error and its cause. For example, suppose that array A has upper bound 10 and an attempt is made to reference A(I), where I is 11. It may be possible to suppress the error and obtain output by rerunning the program with the upper bound of A changed to 11 and A(11) initialized to 0. However, such a modification rarely corrects the error; it merely eliminates its symptom. The actual cause of the error may be a loop that is executing once too often. The proper response is to modify the loop rather than the declaration. It is crucial that the programmer learn to recognize an indication of error for what it is—a symptom and not necessarily a cause. In all cases, debugging should aim at removing the cause and not the symptom. In subsequent examples, we address our attention to the symptoms of errors and their possible causes. We do not consider the underlying logic of the problem because we consider only isolated program segments. However, the programmer should always be on the lookout for errors that stem from the method of problem solution rather than only from the program as written.

How can one determine that there are errors in a program? In general, there are three possibilities: Either there is some form of output indicating an error (e.g., a message indicating division by zero or a system message indicating that the program has exceeded its space allocation), or there are no error messages, but the output is obviously incorrect (e.g., a program that is supposed to compute the sum of squares produces a negative number), or there may be no obvious indication that anything is wrong. In the first two cases there is clearly something wrong; it remains only to determine just what. This determination may not always be easy but it is certainly easier than in the third case, where the programmer has no idea that something is wrong. The most dangerous of all errors is the one that gives no indication of its presence. The fact that such an error can go undetected is a reflection that the testing phase was not sufficiently thorough. Unfortunately, there are many programs that "work" for long periods of time before a particular set of inputs uncovers an error "that was never there before." Although the programmer can rarely be absolutely certain that a program is correct, he or she should do all within his or her power to eliminate all possible errors.

We now consider several types of errors that frequently arise in programming.

Syntax and Execution Errors

Syntax errors are errors that are detected during program translation. They are usually easy to correct, unless they involve some little-used feature of the language. Frequently, a possible source of error is given as part of the system message. Although blindly following the suggestions supplied may eliminate the error message, it will probably not eliminate the error and may even introduce another. Thus, although such error messages are very helpful in pinpointing the existence of an error, the programmer should be the final judge of how to correct it.

Most errors that a programmer faces in debugging programs are execution errors—errors that occur during the actual running of the program. These errors are not always easy to pinpoint and are usually even more difficult to correct. We mention some of the most common causes of execution errors in BASIC.

Reusing Variable Names

A common source of error in BASIC programs is the use of a variable name for more than one purpose. The simplest example of such an error occurs when a programmer mistakenly sets a variable equal to two distinct values. The programmer might mistakenly believe that the original value is no longer necessary or the programmer might have overlooked the fact that the variable was already assigned a value in an earlier part of the program. This error sometimes occurs when the programmer inadvertently uses two variables which share the same first two characters in those versions of BASIC where the first two characters identify a variable uniquely.

There are several steps that can be taken to eliminate such oversights. First, the programmer should describe the purpose of each variable within the program. This description should be inserted as a remark at the beginning of a program or subroutine. Second, the programmer can make use of a cross-reference listing that may be obtained by using special utility programs which are available for most versions of BASIC. This listing contains the statement numbers of all statements that reference each variable within the program. A careful check of this cross-reference should point to those statements in the program that should not be making reference to a particular variable.

There is a related problem that may not yield an error message, although the results are almost certainly incorrect. This problem arises when a local variable within a subroutine has not been identified. For example, consider a program to compute the amount of money that is accumulated if an amount, PRINC, is invested at a rate, RATE, for a period of years, YEARS, where the interest is compounded annually. Suppose that this computation is to be repeated for a variable number of input sets.

A sample program might be the following:

```
10   'program prog
20   READ NUMBER
30   FOR I = 1 TO NUMBER
40       READ PRINC, RATE, YEARS
50       GOSUB 1000: 'subroutine final sets the variable AMT
60       PRINT PRINC; RATE; YEARS; AMT
70   NEXT I
80   END
     . . .
500  DATA . . .
     . . .
1000 'subroutine final
1010 'inputs: PRINC, RATE, YEARS
1020 'outputs: AMT
1030 AMT = PRINC
1040 FOR I = 1 TO YEARS
1050     AMT = AMT * (1 + RATE)
1060 NEXT I
1070 RETURN
1080 'endsub
```

Logically, the program is correct. However, the code as it stands is incorrect. The problem is that the variable name I in the subroutine *final* was already used in the main program. Thus, instead of processing inputs numbered 1, 2, 3, . . . , NUMBER, the program may demand an infinite amount of input. This is because when control returns from the subroutine to the main program, the value of I is the value of YEARS + 1. Of course, the value of YEARS is different for each input, so there is no control over the number of items to be processed. If the value of YEARS is always less than NUMBER − 1, the value of I upon return from *final* is always less than NUMBER and thus the FOR loop is repeated indefinitely. This situation is an infinite loop (which is ended when the program runs out of data). On the other hand, if the value of YEARS exceeds NUMBER − 1 in one input set, the loop is exited upon return from *final* and the program is terminated prematurely.

The problem is that the same variable, I, is used in both the main program and the subroutine. The programmer intended that the loop in the main program execute NUMBER times and the loop in the subroutine execute YEARS times. By mistakenly using the same variable for both of these loops, the error indicated above arose. All variables should be listed in every routine in which the variable is used, and special care must be taken to avoid this type of conflict. If the sub-routine contained the remark

1025   'locals: I

the programmer might realize that I is being used for another purpose.

Counting Errors

Another type of error that often occurs is one that deals with counting. The usual case is that of a loop that is executed once too often (or once too infrequently). This error may or may not yield an error message. But even if it does, the message probably has very little to do with the controls of the loop. As a simple example, consider the problem of finding the average of an arbitrary number of nonzero numbers read into the initial portion of an array, all of whose elements had been previously initialized to zero. One might suggest the following:

```
10   DIM A(100)
       .
       .
       .
100   FOR I = 1 TO 100
110       IF A(I) = 0 THEN GOTO 140
120           SUM = SUM + A(I)
130   NEXT I
140   AVERAGE = SUM / I
```

Unfortunately, the program does not work. The error is that the index I is incremented before A(I) is tested for a zero value. For example, I is set to 5, then A(5) is tested; then I is set to 6, then A(6) is tested; and so on. If there are 20 nonzero numbers, I is set to 21 before the loop is exited. The value of I used to calculate the average in statement 140 is incorrect.

A correct (and easier to understand) solution to the above is the following:

```
10   DIM A(100)
       .
       .
       .
100   FOR I = 1 TO 100
110       IF A(I) = 0 THEN GOTO 140
120           SUM = SUM + A(I)
130   NEXT I
140   'the value of I is the position of the first zero;
          there are I − 1 nonzero numbers
150   CNT = I − 1
160   AVERAGE = SUM / CNT
```

Accuracy of Numerical Results

Even after a program has been written and validated and even after it has been established that the correct process is performed the proper number of times, there are still places where a program can go wrong. One of these is the reuse or misuse of identifiers for too many purposes, as discussed earlier in this section. A second area relates to the accuracy of the results.

Consider, for example, the following program segment, which determines whether a triangle is a right triangle by means of the Pythagorean theorem.

```
10   PRINT "ENTER THREE NUMBERS"
20   INPUT X, Y, Z
30   IF X ↑ 2 + Y ↑ 2 = Z ↑ 2
         THEN PRINT X; Y; Z; " FORM A RIGHT TRIANGLE"
         ELSE PRINT X; Y; Z; " DO NOT FORM A RIGHT TRIANGLE"
```

By executing the program above "by hand" for the values 5, 12, and 13, one would expect that they indeed form a right triangle. Try running the program and you may obtain a different answer. The problem lies in the method used by BASIC to calculate exponentiation. The complex computations often have very slight errors (such as .000001), so that the result of an exponentiation need not be an integer even if both operands are integers. In fact, if one were to print both sides of the equality test in statement 30 by including the statement

```
25   PRINT X ↑ 2 + Y ↑ 2; Z ↑ 2
```

the value 169 would be printed twice. Nonetheless, the test for equality evaluates to false on many microcomputers. This is because numbers are represented internally to greater precision than they are displayed and, therefore, even though 169 is displayed externally, the two sides of the expression are unequal. It is important to remember that the computer produces results according to rigid rules of precision which do not always correspond to programmer intuition. These are often implementation dependent, which makes them even more difficult to detect. Even if the equality test in statement 30 is replaced by

$$X*X + Y*Y = Z*Z$$

the program may not give the expected result. (Although the program may work for the values 5, 12, and 13, it fails to give the correct result when .5, 1.2, and 1.3 are used. This once again illustrates the difficulty in testing a program fully.)

These cases also extend to controls on the number of times a loop is to be executed, as in the index of a FOR loop. As an illustration of this, consider the following code:

```
10   S1 = 0
20   S2 = 0
30   FOR I = −20 TO 20 STEP 2
40        S1 = S1 + 1
50   NEXT I
```

```
60   FOR X  =  − 2 TO 2 STEP .2
70        S2  =  S2 + 1
80   NEXT X
90   PRINT S1, S2
```

One might expect that when the PRINT statement is executed, the values of S1 and S2 are the same, since it appears that each loop is repeated the same number of times (21). Interestingly enough, the values are not the same. The first loop executes correctly so that the value of S1 is 21 (in floating-point form). The value of S2, however, is 20, indicating that the second loop went through 20 iterations.

The reason for this anomaly lies in the method used to represent floating-point numbers. The internal floating-point representation of a number may be a close approximation of its real value. For example, the number 5 may be represented by 4.99999. Sometimes, the difference can be ignored. In cases where a precise count is necessary, as in the example above, the floating-point approximation may yield an incorrect result. Floating-point numbers should not be used where the real intent of the solution is most clearly expressed by the use of integers. Floating-point numbers also cannot be compared for exact equality. Instead, they should be tested for proximity, as in the statement

$$\text{IF ABS}(X − Y) <= \text{DELTA THEN} \ldots$$

DELTA can be made as small as desired, but it should not be 0. Thus, if in the program which tests for a right triangle, statement 30 is replaced by

$$30 \quad \text{IF ABS}((X \uparrow 2 + Y \uparrow 2) − (Z \uparrow 2)) <= 1E − 06 \text{ THEN} \ldots$$

the program gives the correct result.

In general, then, the use of floating-point numbers may be crucial in some cases and disastrous in others. It is the programmer's responsibility to make sure that the attributes of a particular variable are appropriate to the problem at hand.

Testing

For some of the errors mentioned above, the presence of an error is indicated by an error message. In other cases, the program may just run out of time or space because it is in an infinite loop. In many cases, however, unless the programmer tests a program thoroughly, there may be errors in the program that go undetected until just the right combination of inputs is encountered. For this reason, it is extremely important that a program be tested properly before it is put to serious use. Although there exists no uniform method to guarantee that proper testing procedures are used, there are some general guidelines that uncover many of the errors mentioned above. By no means are these suggestions complete; each program requires test cases peculiar to its application.

   Certainly, as a start one should test the program for some simple inputs for which solutions can be computed easily by hand. If the program's solutions do not match those that have been calculated independently, the program is clearly incorrect. However, since the correct answers are known, the temptation exists to adjust the program in the most expedient way so that it produces those correct answers. The most expedient method may not, however, be a valid one. The fact that correct answers are produced for certain inputs does not mean that the program has been corrected. It is necessary to trace the intermediate results of the program from start to finish and to determine which intermediate step is in error. Only when this has been done can a programmer be reasonably sure that the source of error has been located. In fact, even when initial tests indicate that the results for simple cases are correct, the intermediate results should be checked to be sure that correct actions are being taken at each point in the program.

   Another set of test cases consisting of "boundary" values should be used. For example, suppose a tax law specifies that all people with an income of less than $500.00 pay no tax, while those with an income of $500.00 or above pay at a rate of 4%. It is important to test the program for an income which is exactly $500.00 to verify that the proper tax is computed. In some cases, boundary cases can be verified by simply checking that the proper action is taken on equality. In others, it may be necessary to trace the actions of the program on boundary inputs to ascertain that those actions are correct. Besides testing some of these boundary values individually, it is also important to test them together to see how the program behaves on combinations of such inputs.

   After the programmer is satisfied that the program behaves correctly on simple inputs and boundary values, the program should be tested on inputs that are known to be invalid. Very often a program's success depends on its ability to defend itself against invalid inputs as much as on its effects on valid inputs. Even if the user believes that all the input data have been verified before submission to the program, there should be a basic amount of error detection within the program. If there exists a program to validate the input data that fact should be stated, perhaps as a remark, at the outset of the program in question. This will at least absolve the programmer of any responsibility for the validity of the input. Yet, even when the input to a large program has been validated, the inputs to specific subroutines and processes must be validated. For this reason it is a good idea that each routine test that assumptions about its inputs hold. Also, it is important to check that one or more bad items of input do not adversely affect computations on subsequent inputs.

   Finally, the program should be tested for a large random sample of input values. In some cases, it may be possible to test the outputs against results from existing (but perhaps less efficient) programs. In cases where this is not feasible, some of these test cases should be followed through and checked by hand, laborious as this may be. Any time spent in testing the program from the start will probably pay off tenfold by eliminating errors during production runs.

Now that we have described the types of values for which to test the program, how should the testing proceed? If the program has been written in a top-down fashion, the set of routines should be tested individually and as a single program. The routines may be tested in a top-down fashion; that is, the main program is to be tested first, then the subroutines it calls, and finally the entire system as a whole. While testing a routine at a certain level, one assumes that the subroutines it calls already exist. In order to allow the program to run, the programmer has to code dummy routines. For example, consider the following routine:

```
1000    'subroutine rout
1010    'inputs: P1
1020    'outputs: P1, X
1030    'locals: Q1, Q2
        . . .
1040    'group1 of statements giving a value to X
        . . .
1200    Q1 = P1
1210    Q2 = X
1220    GOSUB 2000: 'subroutine sub1 modifies Q1 and Q2
1230    P1 = Q1
1240    X = Q2
        . . .
1250    'group2 of statements modifying P1 and X
        . . .
1400    RETURN
1410    'endsub
```

The purpose of testing the routine above is to determine whether the statements included in *group1* and *group2* are correct. However, in order to allow the subroutine *rout* to execute for testing purposes, a dummy routine for *sub1* must be coded, as in:

```
2000    'subroutine sub1
2010    'inputs: Q1, Q2
2020    'outputs: Q1, Q2
2030    Q1 = 8
2040    Q2 = 9
2050    RETURN
2060    'endsub
```

Before *sub1* is actually coded, the values "computed" by *sub1* in the dummy routine can be altered intentionally to cover all possible cases. In this way the actions of *rout* can be verified for all possibilities. Once *rout* has been tested, routines such as *sub1* can be coded and tested. This type of testing, in which routines at higher levels are tested before those at lower levels, is called ***top-down testing***.

Another type of testing, called ***bottom-up testing***, proceeds in the reverse order. From a logical point of view, the program must be designed in a top-down fashion (one cannnot know what a subroutine is to do before the program using that subroutine has been written). However, once all the routines have been designed, the ones at the lowest levels are written and tested before those at the higher levels. This type of testing is easier, since whenever a program is being tested, all programs on which it depends have already been tested. For this reason, many programmers prefer this technique. The only disadvantage to this method is that the calling programs may not be fully tested. For example, if a subroutine always returns positive numbers, the calling routine is never tested on negative numbers. If the subroutine is subsequently modified so that negative numbers may be returned, a hitherto undiscovered error in the calling routine may occur. However, both of these methods can be used effectively if the testing is done in a comprehensive manner.

Tracing the execution of a program is important in both general testing (so that intermediate results can be checked) and in detecting many types of errors. For example, programs that produce incorrect results for no apparent reason and those that appear to be in an infinite loop can best be debugged by tracing intermediate results. Probably the best way to trace a program is to force the printing of crucial variables at various intervals of execution. Each of these statements should identify the source of the output, as in

$$150 \text{ PRINT ``AT STATEMENT } 150; X = \text{''}; X$$

By following a sequence of such printouts, one can trace the order in which groups of statements are executed and the values of X as they are computed. By narrowing the error down to smaller and smaller segments of the program, the source of an error can be pinpointed precisely.

Tracing can also be done through the use of various debugging features built into an interpreter (e.g., the TRON option). These features can be very helpful. One of their disadvantages, however, is that they sometimes produce voluminous output so that some small but important detail can go undetected. Nevertheless, they can be very effective in tracing errors.

Efficiency

Once it has been established that a program is correct, the program still cannot be considered reliable if it uses an inordinate amount of the machine's resources. For example, if only 2 hours of machine time or 2000 units of memory are available for a particular application and a program requires 25 hours or 25,000 units of memory, the program is not acceptable. Of course, the program may be very efficient but the facilities are simply saturated. However, it may be that rewriting the program would produce a better product.

Good programmers should consider the efficiency of their product when the initial solution is planned. The selection of the overall solution to a program usually has significantly more effect on the efficiency of the resulting program than does the actual form of the source statements. In the remainder of the text, a major part of our attention will be focused on efficient methods to solve problems.

However, there are some ways by which an existing program can be made more efficient. For example, consider the following program segment:

```
10   FOR I = 1 TO 1000
20        READ A(I)
30   NEXT I
40   FOR I = 1 TO 1000
50        IF A(I) > 0 THEN X = X + A(I)
60   NEXT I
```

The code above could be replaced by the following much more efficient version:

```
10   FOR I = 1 TO 1000
20        READ A(I)
30        IF A(I) > 0 THEN X = X + A(I)
40   NEXT I
```

Implicit in every iteration of a loop is at least one branch, one test, and possibly the computation of other functions. In the case above, there is no reason to duplicate this effort needlessly by using the second loop to perform some action that could just as easily have been done in the first loop. There are other "obvious" places where programs can be improved. Programmers should review their code carefully to guarantee that it is as efficient as possible.

But there are also many nontrivial areas in which programs can be improved. For example, consider the following code:

```
10   READ A, B
20   READ X, Y
30   IF X = 0 THEN GOTO 70
40      W = (X + Y) * (A + B) / SQR(10)
50      PRINT X, Y, W
60   GOTO 20
70   END
```

Each iteration through the loop, the value of the square root of 10 is recomputed. However, this value need be computed only once since its value does not change with each repetition of the loop. Similarly, the value of (A + B) does not change within the loop so that it, too, may be computed once outside the loop. A more efficient version of the code above is

```
10   ROOT = SQR(10)
20   READ A, B
30   APLUSB = A + B
40   READ X, Y
50   IF X = 0 THEN GOTO 90
60       W = (X + Y) * APLUSB / ROOT
70       PRINT X, Y, W
80   GOTO 40
90   END
```

If the loop is repeated 1000 times (before being terminated by an OUT OF DATA error), this revision saves 999 additions and 999 executions of the SQR routine. In general, any computation that can be performed outside a loop should not appear within the loop.

      Another example of local inefficiency is the following:

```
10   FOR I = 1 TO 100
20       READ X, Y
30       W = 3 * I * (X + Y)
40       PRINT X, Y, W
50   NEXT I
```

In this example, I is multiplied by 3 each time through the loop. Thus (X + Y) is multiplied by each of the values 3, 6, 9, . . . , 300. I is not used within the loop except at this point. The code above could therefore be performed more efficiently by the following:

```
10   FOR I = 3 TO 300 STEP 3
20       READ X, Y
30       W = I * (X + Y)
40       PRINT X, Y, W
50   NEXT I
```

This eliminates 100 multiplications.

      Another way in which efficiency can be improved is by eliminating needless references to array elements. For example, consider the following code segment:

```
10   FOR I = 1 TO 99 STEP 2
20       READ A(I), A(I + 1)
30       X = (A(I) + A(I + 1)) / 2
40       Y = (A(I) - A(I + 1)) / 2
```

```
50        A(I) = X
60        A(I + 1) = Y
70   NEXT I
```

Each time that an array element is referenced, a computation must be performed (add the base and offset). The code above involves 8×50 such computations. Contrast this with:

```
10   FOR I = 1 TO 99 STEP 2
20        READ X, Y
30        A(I) = (X + Y) / 2
40        A(I + 1) = (X - Y) / 2
50   NEXT I
```

The latter code involves only 2×50 address computations.

Unfortunately, it often happens that the process of making a program more efficient also makes the program less readable. Many of the techniques of good structure outlined in previous sections require more time to execute than do other methods, so that when an entire program is constructed using these techniques, they may add to the overhead of the program. For this reason, some people argue that techniques of good structure should be abandoned if more efficient methods can be found to perform the same task.

This attitude does not promote the development of good programs. There is probably no more efficient method to perform many processes than to code the solution in assembly language and then optimize that code. However, the major purpose of high-level languages such as BASIC is to allow programmers to code solutions to problems without worrying about the details of the lowest-level operations.

Once the decision to use a high-level language has been made, the programmer should exploit the features of that language that make the coding of the solution easier. When coding is done in BASIC, the rules of good structure outlined earlier in this chapter should be followed. These techniques produce programs that are easy to modify and adapt to changing needs.

Related to the question of algorithm efficiency is the method by which the program is translated. As we pointed out at the beginning of the chapter, a program may be translated either by an interpreter or by a compiler. Although an interpreter is more efficient during the development process since it allows easier detection of errors, a program will be most efficient if it is compiled; that is, translated completely into a machine language version which is then executed. Compiled programs often run 5 to 30 times faster than interpreted programs. However, since compiled programs tend to be larger than corresponding interpreted programs, memory limitations may preclude compiling very large programs.

There may be portions of a program that are inefficient. Before a decision is made to rewrite a portion of code, an important question must be answered: What percentage of the total execution time is spent in this section of code? If a particular portion of code represents only 5% of the total execution time of the program and a major rewriting operation can improve it so that it requires only half as much time to run, the net savings to the total program is not 50% but 2.5%.

In selecting an algorithm to solve a problem, efficiency should be the overriding factor after correctness is assured. Once that algorithm has been selected, the program should be coded and tested using the top-down structured approach. That program should be "speeded up" only if the improvement does not make the program less modifiable or if it can be established that the newer version produces a significant saving in the overall running time of the complete program.

EXERCISES

1. Write a program that declares an array of size 100 × 100, initializes each of its elements to zero, and repeatedly inputs groups of three integers. The third integer is to be assigned to the array element at the row and column specified by the first two integers. If either the row or column number is out of bounds, that particular group of three integers is ignored. At the end of the program, print the number of data groups for which only the row number is out of bounds, the number of groups for which only the column number is out of bounds, and the number of data groups for which both are out of bounds. Then print the array.

2. What is the error in the following section of code?

```
10    DIM FACT(10)
20    FOR I = 1 TO 10
30        X = I
40        GOSUB 100
50        FACT(I) = PROD
60        PRINT I, FACT(I)
70    NEXT I
80    'end
100   'subroutine fact
110   'inputs: X
120   'outputs: PROD
130   'locals: I
140   PROD = 1
150   FOR I = X TO 2 STEP -1
160       PROD = PROD * I
170   NEXT I
180   RETURN
190   'endsub
```

3. Show how each of the following pieces of code can be made more efficient.

   (a) 100   FOR I = 1 TO 10
           110   B(I) = A(I) + A(3)
           120   NEXT I

   (b) 100   FOR I = 1 TO 10
           110   X = X + 5 * I
           120   NEXT I

   (c) 100   FOR I = 100 TO 1 STEP − 1
           110   TEMP = A(I)
           120   A(I) = A(I − 1)
           130   A(I − 1) = TEMP
           140   NEXT I

   (d) 100   X = A/2 + B/2

3

The Stack

One of the most useful concepts in computer science is that of the stack. In this chapter we examine this deceptively simple data structure and see why it plays such a prominent role in the areas of programming and programming languages. We define the abstract concept of a stack and show how that concept can be made into a concrete and valuable tool in problem solving. Section 1 introduces the stack as an abstract data structure using pseudocode operations. Section 2 presents an implementation of the stack in BASIC. Sections 3 and 4 present examples of the use of stacks.

1. DEFINITION AND EXAMPLES

A *stack* is an ordered collection of items into which new items may be inserted and from which items may be deleted at one end, called the *top* of the stack. Let us see what this definition means. Given any two items in a stack, one of them can be thought of as "higher" in the stack than the other. Thus we can picture a stack as in Figure 3.1.1. Item F is higher in the stack than all the other items. Item D is higher than items A, B, and C but is lower than items E and F.

You may protest that if Figure 3.1.1 were turned upside down a very similar picture would result, but A rather than F would be the highest element. If a stack were a static, unchanging object, your objection would be quite correct. However, the definition of a stack provides for insertion and deletion of items so that a stack is really a dynamic, constantly changing object. Figure 3.1.1 is only a

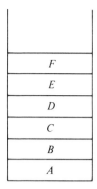

Figure 3.1.1 A stack containing six items.

snapshot of a stack at a particular point in its continuing evolution. To have a true view of a stack, a motion picture is necessary.

The question therefore arises: How does a stack change? From the definition, note that a single end of the stack must be designated as the stack top. A new item may be placed on top of the stack (in which case the top of the stack moves upward to correspond to the new highest element) or the item that is at the top of the stack may be removed (in which case the top of the stack moves downward to correspond to the new highest element). To answer the question "Which way is up?" we must decide which end of the stack is designated as its top—that is, at which end will items be added or deleted. By drawing Figure 3.1.1 so that *F* is physically higher on the page than all the other items in the stack, we mean to imply that *F* is the current top element of the stack. If any new items are to be added to the stack, they will be placed on top of *F*, and if any items are to be deleted, *F* will be the first to be deleted. This is also indicated by the vertical lines that extend past the items of the stack in the direction of the stack top.

Of course, stacks may be drawn in many different ways, as shown in Figure 3.1.2, as long as it is clearly understood which end is the top of the stack. Ordinarily, we will illustrate stacks as in Figure 3.1.1, with the stack top facing the top of the page.

Let us now view a motion picture of a stack to see how it expands and shrinks with the passage of time. Such a picture is given by Figure 3.1.3. In Figure 3.1.3(a) we see the stack as it exists at the time that the snapshot of Figure 3.1.1 was taken. In Figure 3.1.3(b), item *G* is added to the stack. According to the definition, there is only one place on the stack where it can be placed—on the top. The top element on the stack is now *G*. As our motion picture progresses through frames (c), (d), and (e), we see items *H*, *I*, and *J* successively added onto the stack. Notice that the last item inserted (in this case *J*) is at the top of the stack. Beginning with frame (f), however, the stack begins to shrink as first *J*, then *I*, *H*, *G*, and *F*, are successively removed. At each point, the top element is removed since a deletion can be made only from the top. Item *G* could not be removed from the stack before items *J*, *I*, and *H* were gone. This illustrates the

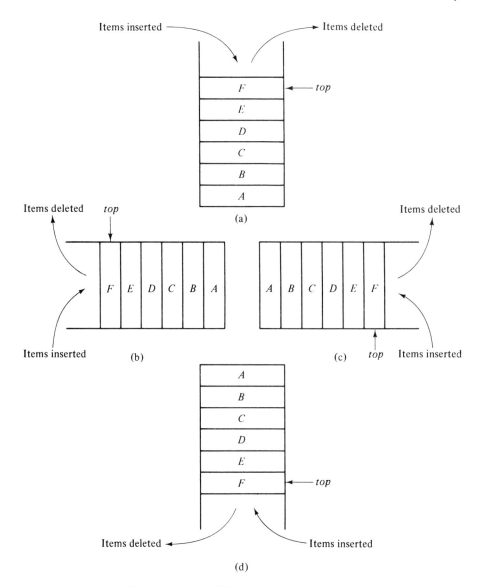

Figure 3.1.2 Four different views of the same stack.

most important attribute of a stack—that the last element inserted into a stack is the first element deleted. Thus J is deleted before I because J was inserted after I. For this reason a stack is sometimes called a last-in, first-out (or **lifo**) list.

Between frames (j) and (k), the stack has stopped shrinking and begins to expand again as item K is added. However, this expansion is short-lived, as the stack then shrinks to only three items in frame (n).

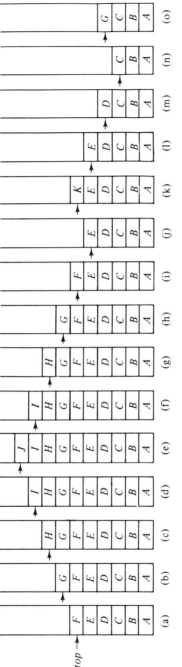

Figure 3.1.3 A motion picture of a stack.

111

Note that there is no way to distinguish between frame (a) and frame (i) by looking at the stack's state at the two instances. In both cases, the stack contains the identical items in the same order and has the same stack top. No record is kept on the stack of the fact that four items had been inserted and deleted in the meantime. Similarly, there is no way to distinguish between frames (d) and (f) or (j) and (l). If a record is needed of the intermediate items having been on the stack, that record must be kept elsewhere; it does not exist within the stack.

In fact, we have actually taken an extended view of what is really observed in a stack. The true picture of a stack is given by a view from the top looking down, rather than from a side looking in. Thus there is no perceptible difference between frames (h) and (o) in Figure 3.1.3. In each case the element at the top is G. Although we know that the stack at (h) and the stack at (o) are not equal, the only way to determine this is to remove all the elements on both stacks and compare them individually. We have been looking at cross sections of stacks to make our understanding clearer, but you should remember that this is an added liberty and there is no real provision for taking such a picture.

Primitive Operations

The two changes that can be made to a stack are given special names. When an item is added to a stack, it is **pushed** onto the stack. Given a stack *s*, and an item *i*, performing the operation *push(s,i)* is defined as adding the item *i* to the top of stack *s*. Similarly, the operation *pop(s)* removes the top element and returns it as a function value. Thus the assignment operation

$$i = pop(s)$$

removes the element at the top of *s* and assigns its value to *i*.

For example, if *s* is the stack of Figure 3.1.3, we performed the operation *push(s,G)* in going from frame (a) to frame (b). We then performed, in turn, the operations:

push(s,H)	[frame (c)]
push(s,I)	[frame (d)]
push(s,J)	[frame (e)]
pop(s)	[frame (f)]
pop(s)	[frame (g)]
pop(s)	[frame (h)]
pop(s)	[frame (i)]
pop(s)	[frame (j)]
push(s,K)	[frame (k)]
pop(s)	[frame (l)]
pop(s)	[frame (m)]
pop(s)	[frame (n)]
push(s,G)	[frame (o)]

Because of the push operation, which adds elements to a stack, a stack is some times called a *pushdown list.*

There is no upper limit on the number of items that may be kept in a stack since no mention was made in the definition as to how many items are allowed in the collection. Pushing another item onto a stack merely produces a larger collection of items. However, if a stack contains a single item and the stack is popped, the resulting stack contains no items and is called the **empty stack.** Although the *push* operation is applicable to any stack, the *pop* operation cannot be applied to the empty stack because such a stack has no elements to delete. Therefore, before applying the *pop* operator to a stack, we must ensure that the stack is not empty. The operation *empty(s)* determines whether or not a stack *s* is empty. If the stack is empty, *empty(s)* returns the value *true:* otherwise, it returns the value *false*.

Another operation that can be performed on a stack is to determine what the top item on a stack is without removing it. This operation is written *stacktop(s)* and returns as its value the top element of stack *s*. The operation *stacktop(s)* is not really a new operation since it can be decomposed into a pop and a push.

$$i = stacktop(s)$$

is equivalent to

$$i = pop(s)$$
$$push(s,i)$$

Like the operation *pop, stacktop* is not defined for an empty stack. The result of an illegal attempt to pop or access an item from an empty stack is called **underflow.** Underflow can be avoided by ensuring that *empty(s)* is *false* before attempting the operation *pop(s)* or *stacktop(s)*.

An Example

Now that we have defined a stack and have indicated the operations which can be performed on it, let us see how we may use the stack in problem solving. Suppose a mathematical expression is given which includes several sets of nested parentheses; for example,

$$7 - ((X * ((X + Y) / (J - 3)) + Y) / (4 - 2.5))$$

and we want to ensure that the parentheses are nested correctly. That is, we want to check that

1. There are an equal number of right and left parentheses.

2. Every right parenthesis is preceded by a matching left parenthesis.

Expressions such as

$$((A + B) \qquad \text{or} \qquad A + B($$

would violate condition 1, while

$$)A + B(- C \qquad \text{or} \qquad (A + B)) - (C + D$$

would violate condition 2.

In order to solve this problem, think of each left parenthesis as opening a scope and each right parenthesis as closing a scope. The ***nesting depth*** at a particular point in an expression is the number of scopes which have been opened but not yet closed at that point. This is the same as the number of left parentheses encountered whose matching right parentheses have not yet been encountered. Let us define the ***parenthesis count*** at a particular point in an expression as the number of left parentheses minus the number of right parentheses which have been encountered in scanning the expression from its left end up to that particular point. If the parenthesis count is nonnegative, it is the same as the nesting depth. The two conditions that must hold if the parentheses in an expression are to form an admissible pattern are:

1. The parenthesis count at the end of the expression is 0. This implies that no scopes have been left open or that exactly as many right parentheses as left parentheses have been found.
2. The parenthesis count at each point in the expression is nonnegative. This implies that no right parenthesis has been encountered for which a matching left parenthesis had not previously been encountered.

In Figure 3.1.4, the count at each point in each of the previous five strings is given directly below that point. Since only the first string meets the two conditions listed above, it is the only one among the five with a correct parenthesis pattern.

Let us now change the problem slightly and assume that three different types of scopes exist. These types are indicated by parentheses (''('' and '')''), brackets (''['' and '']''), and braces (''{'' and '}''). A scope ender must be of the same type as its scope opener. Thus strings such as

$$(A+B], \qquad [(A+B]), \qquad \{A- (B]\}$$

are illegal.

It is necessary to keep track not only of how many scopes have been opened, but also of their types. This information is needed because when a scope ender is encountered, we must know the symbol with which the scope was opened to ensure that it is being closed properly.

A stack may be used to keep track of the types of scopes encountered. Whenever a scope opener is encountered, it is pushed onto the stack. Whenever a scope ender is encountered, the stack is examined. If the stack is empty, the scope ender does not have a matching opener and the string is invalid. If, however, the stack is nonempty, we pop the stack and check whether the popped item corresponds to the scope ender. If a match occurs, we continue. If it does not, the string is invalid. When the end of the string is reached, we make sure that the stack is empty; otherwise, one or more scopes have been opened which have not been closed, making the string invalid. The algorithm for this procedure is outlined below. Figure 3.1.5 shows the state of the stack after reading parts of the string $\{x+(y - [a+b])*c - [(d+e)]\}/(h - (j-(k-[l-n])))$.

```
7 - ( ( X * ( ( X + Y ) / ( J - 3 ) ) + Y ) / ( 4 - 2.5 ) )
0 0 1 2 2 2 3 4 4 4 4 3 3 4 4 4 4 3 2 2 2 1 1 2 2 2   2 1 0
```

```
( ( A + B )
1 2 2 2 2 1
```

```
A + B (
0 0 0   1
```

```
) A + B ( - C
-1 -1 -1 -1 0 0 0
```

```
( A + B ) )   - ( C + D
1 1 1 1 0 -1 -1 0 0 0 0
```

Figure 3.1.4 Parenthesis count at various points of strings.

valid = true
s = the empty stack
while (we have not read the entire string) **and** (*valid = true*) **do**
        read the next symbol (*symb*) of the string
        if *symb* = ''('' **or** *symb* = ''['' **or** *symb* = ''{''
            then *push* (*s,symb*)
        endif
        if *symb* = '')'' **or** *symb* = '']'' **or** *symb* = ''}''
            then if *empty(s)*
                    then *valid = false*
                    else *i = pop(s)*
                        if *i* is not the matching opener for *symb*
                            then *valid = false*
                        endif
                endif
        endif
endwhile
if *empty(s) = false*
    then *valid = false*
endif
if *valid = true*
    then print (''the string is valid'')
    else print (''the string is invalid'')
endif
```
```

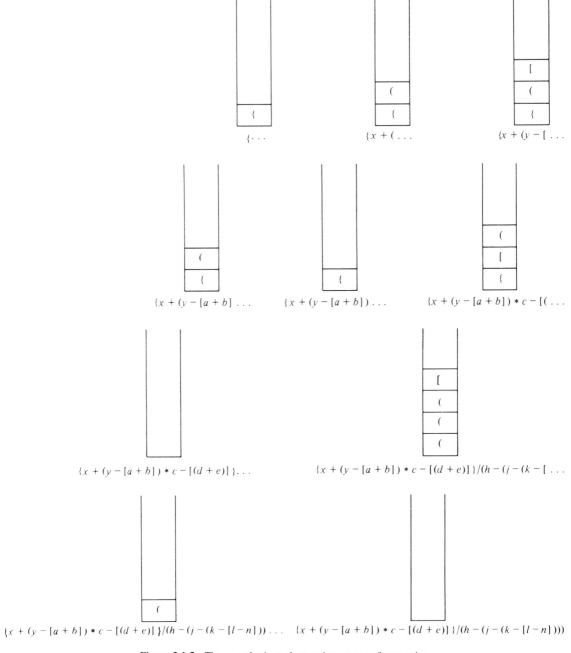

Figure 3.1.5 The parenthesis stack at various stages of processing.

Let us see why the solution to this problem calls for the use of a stack. The last scope to be opened must be the first to be closed. This is precisely simulated by a stack where the last element arriving is the first to leave. Each item on the stack represents a scope that has been opened but which has not yet been closed. Pushing an item onto the stack corresponds to the opening of a scope and popping an item from the stack corresponds to the closing of a scope, leaving one less scope open.

Notice the correspondence between the number of elements on the stack in this example and the parenthesis count in the previous example. When the stack is empty (parenthesis count = 0), and a scope ender is encountered, an attempt is being made to close a scope that has never been opened, so the parentheses pattern is invalid. In the first example, this is indicated by a negative parenthesis count and in the second example by the inability to pop the stack. The reason a simple parenthesis count is inadequate for the second example is that we must keep track of the actual scope openers themselves. This can be done by the use of a stack. Notice also that at any point we examine only the element at the top. The particular configuration of parentheses below the top element is irrelevant while we are examining this top element. It is only after the top element has been popped that we concern ourselves with subsequent elements in a stack.

In general, a stack can be used in any situation that calls for a last-in, first-out discipline or which displays a nesting pattern. We shall see more examples of the use of stacks in the remaining sections of this chapter and, indeed, throughout the text.

EXERCISES

1. Use the operations *push, pop, stacktop,* and *empty* to construct operations that do each of the following:
   (a) Set i to the second element from the top of the stack, leaving the stack without its top two elements.
   (b) Set i to the second element from the top of the stack, leaving the stack unchanged.
   (c) Given an integer n, set i to the nth element from the top of the stack, leaving the stack without its top n elements.
   (d) Given an integer n, set i to the nth element from the top of the stack, leaving the stack unchanged.
   (e) Set i to the bottom element of the stack, leaving the stack empty.
   (f) Set i to the bottom element of the stack, leaving the stack unchanged (*Hint:* Use another, auxiliary stack.)
   (g) Set i to the third element from the bottom of the stack.
2. Simulate the action of the algorithm in this section for each of the following strings by showing the contents of the stack at each point.

(a) $(A + B\})$

(b) $\{[A + B] - [(C - D)]$

(c) $(A + B) - \{C + D\} - [F + G]$

(d) $((H) * \{([J + K])\})$

(e) $(((A))))$

3. Write an algorithm to determine if an input character string is of the form

$$x \, C \, y$$

where x is a string consisting of the letters "A" and "B" and where y is the reverse of x (i.e., if x = "ABABBA", then y must equal "ABBABA"). At each point you may read only the next character of the string.

4. Write an algorithm to determine if an input character string is of the form

$$a \, D \, b \, D \, c \, D \, . \, . \, . \, D \, z$$

where each string $a, b, . . . , z$ is of the form of the string defined in Exercise 3. (Thus a string is in the proper form if it consists of any number of such strings separated by the character "D".) At each point you may read only the next character of the string.

5. Design an algorithm that does not use a stack which reads a sequence of *push* and *pop* operations and determines whether or not underflow occurs on some *pop* operation. Implement the algorithm as a BASIC program.

6. What set of conditions are necessary and sufficient for a sequence of *push* and *pop* operations on a single stack (initially empty) to leave the stack empty and not to cause underflow? What set of conditions are necessary for such a sequence to leave a nonempty stack unchanged?

2. REPRESENTING STACKS IN BASIC

Before programming a problem solution that calls for the use of a stack, we must decide how to represent a stack using the data structures that exist in our programming language. As we shall see, there are several ways to represent a stack in BASIC. We will now consider the simplest of these. In subsequent sections of the book you will be introduced to other possible representations. Each of them, however, is merely an implementation of the concept introduced in Section 1 of this chapter. Each has its advantages and disadvantages in terms of how close it comes to mirroring the abstract concept of a stack and how much effort must be made by the programmer and the computer in using it.

A stack is an ordered collection of items and BASIC already contains a data type that is an ordered collection of items—the array. Whenever a problem solution calls for use of a stack, therefore, it is tempting to begin a program by declaring a variable STACK to be an array. Unfortunately, however, a stack and an array are two entirely different things. The number of elements in an array is fixed and is assigned by the declaration for the array. In general, the user cannot change this number. A stack, on the other hand, is fundamentally a dynamic object whose size is constantly changing as items are popped and pushed.

However, although an array cannot be a stack, it can be the home of a stack. That is, an array can be declared with a range that is large enough for the maximum size of the stack. During the course of program execution, the stack will grow and shrink within the space reserved for it. One end of the array will be the fixed bottom of the stack, while the top of the stack will constantly shift as items are popped and pushed. Thus another variable is needed which, at each point during program execution, will keep track of the current position of the top of the stack.

A stack in BASIC may therefore be declared and initalized using an array SITEM to hold the elements of the stack, and an integer TP to indicate the position of the current stack top within the array. This may be done by the statements:

```
10  MAXSTACK = 100
20  DIM SITEM(MAXSTACK)
30  TP = 0
```

Here we use the variable MAXSTACK to hold the value of the maximum stack size and assume that the stack will at no time contain more than this many numbers in locations SITEM(1) through SITEM(MAXSTACK). In this example, the maximum stack size is set to 100. For consistency among various versions of BASIC, SITEM(0) is not used.

We use a variable MAXSTACK to ensure that modification of the maximum stack size involves changing only a single number, the value of MAXSTACK. If SITEM were directly dimensioned to be of size 100, the constant 100 would have to be changed in every reference to the maximum stack size. The more changes that must be made, the less likely that a program modification will be successful. Programs should be written initally so that they are easily modifiable. Some versions of BASIC may not allow dimensioning an array using a variable bound and in those versions the constant 100 must be used instead of MAXSTACK in the DIM statement. However, even there the variable MAXSTACK should be used in all other references to the maximum stack size to reduce the number of changes to no more than two.

We also assume that the items in the stack are single-precision numbers. There is, of course, no reason to restrict a stack to contain only single-precision numbers; SITEM could just as easily have been given the type integer, double precision, or character string by means of the DEFINT, DEFBL, or DEFSTR statements, respectively. The value of TP, however, must be an integer between 0 and 100 since its value represents the position within the array SITEM of the topmost stack element. (We do not declare TP to be an integer using the DEFINT statement since that would require that all variables in the program beginning with T be declared integers as well.) Thus, if the value of TP is 5, there are five elements on the stack. These are SITEM(1), SITEM(2), SITEM(3), SITEM(4), and SITEM(5). When the stack is popped, the value of TP must be changed to 4 to indicate that there are now only four elements on the stack and that SITEM(4) is the top element. On the other hand, if a new object is pushed onto the stack, the value of TP must be increased by 1 to 6 and the new object inserted into SITEM(6).

The empty stack contains no elements and can therefore be indicated by TP equaling 0. In order to initialize the stack to the empty state, we execute TP = 0. (It is good programming practice to assign initial values explicitly to all variables rather than relying on language or system defaults.)

To determine during the course of execution whether or not a stack is empty, the condition TP = 0 may be tested by means of an IF statement, as follows:

```
100   IF TP = 0
      THEN 'stack is empty
      ELSE 'stack is not empty
```

This test corresponds to the operation *empty(s)*, which was introduced in Section 1. Alternatively, assuming that the variable TRUE has been set to 1 and the variable FALSE to 0, we may write a subroutine that sets a variable to TRUE if the stack is empty and FALSE if it is not empty. Such a subroutine may be written as follows:

```
3000   'subroutine empty
3010   'inputs: TP
3020   'outputs: EMPTY
3030   'locals: none
3040   IF TP = 0 THEN EMPTY = TRUE
                ELSE EMPTY = FALSE
3050   RETURN
3060   'endsub
```

Once this subroutine exists, a test for the empty stack is implemented by the statements

```
100   GOSUB 3000: 'subroutine empty sets the variable EMPTY
110   IF EMPTY = TRUE THEN 'the stack is empty
                       ELSE 'the stack is not empty
```

You may wonder why we bother to define the subroutine *empty* when we could just as easily write IF TP = 0 each time that we want to test for the empty condition. The answer is that we wish to make our programs more comprehensible and to make the use of a stack independent of its implementation. Once we understand the concept of a stack, the phrase "EMPTY = TRUE" is more meaningful than the phrase "TP = 0." If we should later introduce a better implementation of a stack so that "TP = 0" becomes meaningless, we would have to change every reference to the identifier TP throughout our entire program. On the other hand, the phrase "EMPTY = TRUE" would still retain its meaning, since it is an inherent attribute of the stack concept rather than of an implementation of that concept. All that would be required to revise our program to accommodate a new implementation of the stack would be a revision of the declaration of the stack in the main program and the rewriting of the subroutine *empty*. Aggregating the set of implementation-dependent trouble spots into small, easily identifiable units is an important method of making a program more understandable and modifiable. This concept is known as **modularization,** in which individual functions are isolated into low-level **modules** whose properties are easily provable. These low-level modules can then be used by more complex routines which do not have to concern themselves with the details of the low-level modules but only with their function. The complex routines may then themselves be viewed as modules by still-higher-level routines which use them independently of their internal details.

To implement the *pop* operation, the possibility of underflow must be considered since the user may inadvertantly attempt to pop an element from an empty stack. Of course, such an attempt is illegal and should be avoided. However, if such an attempt should be made, the user should be informed of the underflow condition. We therefore introduce a function *pop,* which consists of the following three actions:

1. If the stack is empty, it prints a warning message and halts execution.
2. It removes the top element from the stack.
3. It makes this element available to the calling program.

```
2000   'subroutine pop
2010   'inputs: SITEM, TP
2020   'outputs: POPS, TP
2030   'locals: none
2040   GOSUB 3000:          'subroutine empty sets the variable EMPTY
2050   IF EMPTY = TRUE THEN PRINT "STACK UNDERFLOW": STOP
                           ELSE POPS = SITEM(TP): TP = TP − 1
2060   RETURN
2070   'endsub
```

Note that the output variable of *pop* is named POPS since POP is a reserved word in some versions of BASIC.

Testing for Exceptional Conditions

Let us look at the *pop* function more closely. If the stack is not empty, the top element of the stack is saved as the returned value. This element is then removed from the stack by the statement TP = TP − 1. Let us assume that when *pop* is called, TP equals 87; that is, there are 87 items on the stack. The value of SITEM(87) is returned and the value of TP is changed to 86. Note that SITEM(87) still retains its old value; the array SITEM remains unchanged by the call to *pop*. However, the stack is changed since it now contains only 86 elements rather than 87. Recall that an array and a stack are two different objects. The array only provides a home for the stack. The stack itself contains only those elements between the first item of the array and the TPth element. Thus, reducing the value of TP by 1 effectively removes an element from the stack. This is true despite the fact that SITEM(87) retains its old value.

In order to use the subroutine *pop,* the programmer can write

```
100   GOSUB 2000:       'subroutine pop sets the variable POPS
110   X = POPS
```

X will then contain the value popped from the stack. If the intent of the *pop* operation was not to retrieve the element on the top of the stack but only to remove it from the stack, the variable X need not be used. Of course, the programmer should ensure that the stack is not empty when he or she calls the subroutine *pop.* If unsure of the state of the stack, the programmer may write

```
100   GOSUB 3000:  'subroutine empty sets the variable EMPTY
110   IF EMPTY <> TRUE THEN GOSUB 2000: X = POPS
                    ELSE 'take remedial action
```

If the programmer unwittingly does call *pop* with an empty stack, the subroutine prints the error message STACK UNDERFLOW and execution halts. Although this is an unfortunate state of affairs, it is far better than what would occur had the IF statement in the *pop* routine been omitted entirely. In that case, the value of TP would be 0 and an attempt would be made to access the uninitialized (or nonexistent) element SITEM(0).

A programmer should always provide for the almost certain possibility of error. This is done by including diagnostics that are meaningful in the context of the problem. By doing so, if and when an error does occur, the programmer will be able to pinpoint its source and take corrective action immediately.

However, within the context of a given problem, it may not be necessary to halt execution immediately upon the detection of underflow. Instead, it might be more desirable for the *pop* routine to signal the calling program that an underflow has occurred. The calling routine, upon detecting this signal, can take corrective action. Let us call the subroutine that pops the stack and returns an indication as to whether underflow has occurred, *popandtest.*

```
7000   'subroutine popandtest
7010   'inputs: SITEM, TP
7020   'outputs: POPS, TP, UND
7030   'locals: none
7040   GOSUB 3000: 'subroutine empty sets the variable EMPTY
7050   IF EMPTY = TRUE THEN UND = TRUE
                    ELSE UND = FALSE: POPS = SITEM(TP):
                         TP = TP − 1
7060   RETURN
7070   'endsub
```

In the calling program the programmer would write

110   GOSUB 7000: *'subroutine* popandtest *sets UND and possibly POPS*
120   IF UND = TRUE THEN *'take corrective action*
                        ELSE X = POPS: *'X is the element popped off the stack*

Implementing the push Operation

Let us now examine the *push* operation. It seems that this operation should be quite easy to implement using the array representation of a stack. Assume that a variable X contains the value to be pushed onto the stack. Then a first attempt at a *push* subroutine might be the following:

```
1000  'subroutine push
1010  'inputs: TP, X
1020  'outputs: SITEM, TP
1030  'locals: none
1040  TP = TP + 1
1050  SITEM(TP) = X
1060  RETURN
1070  'endsub
```

This routine makes room for the item X to be pushed onto the stack by incrementing TP by 1, and then it inserts X into the array SITEM.

The subroutine directly implements the *push* operation which was introduced in the preceding section. Yet, as it stands, it is quite incorrect. It allows a subtle error to creep in, caused by using the array representation of the stack. See if you can spot this error before reading further.

Recall that a stack is a dynamic structure that is constantly allowed to grow and shrink and thus change its size. An array, on the other hand, is a fixed object of predetermined size. Thus it is quite conceivable that a stack will outgrow the array that was set aside to contain it. This will occur when the array is full, that is, when the stack contains as many elements as the array—and an attempt is made to push yet another element onto the stack. The result of such an attempt is called an *overflow*.

Assume that the array is full and that the *push* routine above is called. The full array is indicated by the condition TP = 100, so that the 100th (and last) element of the array is the current top of the stack. When *push* is called, TP is increased to 101 and an attempt is made to insert X into the 101th position of the array SITEM. Of course, SITEM contains only 100 elements, so this attempt at insertion will result in an error and produce an appropriate error message. This message is totally meaningless within the context of the original algorithm, since it does not indicate an error in the algorithm, but rather an error in the computer implementation of that algorithm. It would be far more desirable for the programmer to provide for the possibility of overflow and to print out a more meaningful message.

The subroutine *push* may therefore be revised so that it reads as follows:

```
1000    'subroutine push
1010    'inputs: MAXSTACK, TP, X
1020    'outputs: SITEM, TP
1030    'locals: none
1040    IF TP = MAXSTACK THEN PRINT "STACK OVERFLOW": STOP
1050    TP = TP + 1
1060    SITEM(TP) = X
1070    RETURN
1080    'endsub
```

Here a check is made to determine whether the array is full before attempting to push another element onto the stack. The array will be full if TP = MAXSTACK.

You should again note that if and when the overflow condition is detected in *push*, execution halts immediately after printing an error message. This action, as in the case of *pop*, may not be the most desirable. It might, in some cases, make more sense for the calling routine to be able to invoke the push operation in the following manner:

> *pushandtest(overflow, stack, x)*
> *if* overflow = *true*
>   *then* ' Overflow has been detected. x was not
>   ' pushed on stack. Take remedial action.
>   *else* ' x was successfully pushed on the stack.
>   '   Continue processing.

This will allow the program to proceed after returning from *pushandtest* whether or not overflow was detected. The subroutine *pushandtest* is left as an exercise for the reader.

It is useful to compare the subroutine *push* with the earlier subroutine *pop*. Although the overflow and underflow conditions are handled similarly in the two routines, there is a fundamental difference between them. Underflow indicates that the *pop* operation cannot be performed on the stack and may indicate an error in the algorithm or the data. No other implementation or representation of the stack will cure the underflow condition. Rather, the entire problem must be re-thought. (Of course, it is possible that the programmer wishes an underflow to occur as a signal to end one process and begin another. However, in such a case, it would be necessary to use the subroutine *popandtest* rather than the subroutine *pop*.)

Overflow, however, is not a condition that is applicable to a stack as an abstract data structure. As we saw in the preceding section, it is always possible to push an element onto a stack since a stack is just an ordered set and there is no limit to the number of elements such a set can contain. The possibility of an overflow is introduced when a stack is implemented using an array with only a finite number of elements, thereby prohibiting the growth of the stack beyond that number. It may very well be that the algorithm which the programmer used is correct; he or she just did not anticipate that the stack would become so large. Thus, in some cases, a possible way to correct an overflow condition is to change the initialization of the stack so that the array SITEM contains more elements. Note that this can be done simply by increasing the initial value of MAXSTACK. No change is needed to the subroutine *push* since it refers to whatever value MAXSTACK was given in the main program. This illustrates another advantage of using a variable to hold the maximum stack size: modularity and portability. The same subroutine *push* can be used regardless of the particular size of the array SITEM.

However, more often than not, an overflow does indicate an error in the program which cannot be attributed to a simple lack of space. The program may be in an infinite loop, where things are constantly being pushed onto the stack and nothing is ever popped. Thus the stack will outgrow the array bound no matter how high that bound is set. The programmer should always check that this is not the case before indiscriminately raising the array bound. Often, the maximum stack size can easily be determined from the program and its inputs, so that if the stack does overflow, there is probably something wrong with the algorithm the program represents.

Let us now look at our last operation on stacks, *stacktop(s)*, which returns the top element of a stack without removing it from the stack. As we noted in the preceding section, *stacktop* is not really a primitive operation because it can be decomposed into the two operations

$$x = pop(s)$$
$$push(s,x)$$

However, this is a rather awkward way to retrieve the top element of a stack. Why not ignore the decomposition noted above and retrieve the proper value directly? Of course, a check for the empty stack and underflow must then be explicitly stated since the test is no longer handled within *pop*.

We present a BASIC subroutine *stacktop* which sets a variable STKTP to the top element of the stack without removing it from the stack, as follows:

```
4000    'subroutine stacktop
4010    'inputs: SITEM, TP
4020    'outputs: STKTP
4030    'locals: none
4040    GOSUB 3000: 'subroutine empty sets the variable EMPTY
4050    IF EMPTY = TRUE THEN PRINT "STACK UNDERFLOW": STOP
4060    STKTP = SITEM(TP)
4070    RETURN
4080    'endsub
```

You may wonder why we bother writing a separate routine *stacktop* when a reference to SITEM(TP) would serve just as well. There are several reasons for this.

First, the routine *stacktop* incorporates a test for underflow so that no mysterious errors will occur if the stack is empty. Second, it allows the programmer to use a stack without worrying about its internal makeup. Third, if a different implementation of a stack is introduced, the programmer need not comb through all of the places that refer to SITEM(TP) in order to make those references compatible with the new implementation. He or she need only change the *stacktop* routine.

Armed with this set of BASIC routines, we can begin attacking problems that call for the use of stacks and presenting BASIC solutions. We shall do this in the succeeding sections. In the next chapter, we present other implementations of stacks.

EXERCISES

1. Write BASIC programs that use the routines presented in this chapter to implement the operations of Exercise 3.1.1.
2. Given a sequence of *push* and *pop* operations and an integer representing the size of an array in which a stack is to be implemented, design an algorithm to determine whether or not overflow occurs. The algorithm should not use a stack. Implement the algorithm as a BASIC program.
3. Implement the algorithms of Exercises 3.1.3 and 3.1.4 as BASIC programs.
4. Show how to implement a stack of integers in BASIC by using an array S, where S(0) (rather than a separate variable TP) is used to contain the index of the top element of the stack and where S(1) through S(MAXSTACK) contain the elements on the stack. Write a declaration and routines *pop, push, empty, popandtest, stacktop,* and *pushandtest* for this implementation.
5. Using the array implementation of stacks, write a BASIC program to read a character string containing the three sets of scope enclosers (''('' and '')''), (''<'' and ''>''), and (''['' and '']'') and to check whether or not the string contains a correct scoping pattern.
6. Consider a language that does not have arrays but does have stacks as a data type. That is, one can declare

DEFSTACK S

and the *push, pop, popandtest,* and *stacktop* operations are defined as part of the language. Show how a one-dimensional array can be implemented by using these operations on two stacks.
7. Design a method for keeping two stacks within a single linear array *s* in such a way that neither stack overflows until all of the array is used and an entire stack is never shifted to a different location within the array. Write BASIC routines *push1, push2, pop1,* and *pop2* to manipulate the two stacks. (*Hint:* The two stacks grow toward each other.)

8. The Bashemin Parking Garage contains a single lane which can hold up to 10 cars. There is only a single entrance/exit to the garage at one end of the lane. If a customer arrives to pick up a car that is not nearest the exit, all cars blocking its path are moved out, the customer's car is driven out, and the other cars are restored in the order they were in originally.

   Write a program that processes a group of input lines. Each input line contains an ''A'' for arrival or a ''D'' for departure, and a license plate number. Cars are assumed to arrive and depart in the order specified by the input. The program should print a message whenever a car arrives or departs. When a car arrives, the message should specify whether or not there is room for the car in the garage. If there is no room, the car leaves without entering the garage. When a car departs, the message should include the number of times that the car was moved out of the garage to allow other cars to depart.

9. The XYZ Widget Store receives shipments of widgets at various costs. The store's policy is to charge a 20% markup and to sell widgets that were received later before widgets that were received earlier (because widgets received later are at a higher price—this is called a LIFO policy). Write a BASIC program that reads a deck of transactions of two types: sales transactions and receipt transactions. A sales transaction contains an ''S'' and a quantity and represents a sale of that quantity of widgets. A receipt card contains an ''R'', a quantity, and a cost per widget and represents a receipt of a quantity of widgets at that cost per widget. When a receipt transaction is read, print a message. After a sales transaction is read, print a message stating the number sold and the price for each widget. For example, if 200 widgets were sold and there were 50 widgets from a shipment at $1.25, 100 at $1.10, and 50 at $1.00, print (recall the 20% markup)

```
200   WIDGETS SOLD
 50   AT $1.50 EACH    SALES:    $      75.00
100   AT $1.32 EACH    SALES:    $     132.00
 50   AT $1.20 EACH    SALES:    $      60.00
            TOTAL      SALES:    $     267.00
```

If there are an insufficient number of widgets in stock to fill an order, sell as many as are available and then print

REMAINDER OF XXX WIDGETS NOT AVAILABLE.

3. AN EXAMPLE: BASIC SCOPE NESTING

Statement of Problem

To illustrate the usefulness of stacks, let us consider the rules for FOR-NEXT nesting in BASIC. A BASIC FOR statement begins the scope of a loop and a NEXT statement ends that scope. FOR-NEXT loops may be nested as long as each subsequently nested loop is contained entirely within the surrounding loop.

For the programmer's convenience, in order to keep track of the nesting order, each NEXT statement may contain a variable corresponding to the variable in the FOR statement. We may consider the variable as identifying the particular loop referenced by the FOR-NEXT statements. If a NEXT statement does not contain a variable after the keyword NEXT, the NEXT statement closes the most recently opened scope which has not yet been closed. Although the use of an identifying variable in a NEXT statement is optional, if such a variable does appear in a NEXT statement, it must correspond to the innermost (most recently opened) scope that is still open. Thus scopes are closed in the opposite order in which they were opened. (Many popular versions of BASIC allow a single NEXT statement to contain several variables and to terminate multiply nested loops, provided that the variables are specified in the proper order in the NEXT statement. Other BASIC interpreters do not allow a NEXT statement without an identifying variable.)

For an illustration of these rules, let us examine the program segment of Figure 3.3.1. At line 10 of the program, the scope of the loop labeled I is opened and at line 20 the scope of loop J is opened. At line 30, yet another scope (of loop K) is opened, so that three scopes are open at that point. Line 40 indicates that the scope K is to be closed. A new scope (L) is opened in line 50, so that once again three scopes (L, J, I) are open. Scope L is closed in line 60, J in line 70, and I in line 80.

Note that lines 30 and 50 are equally indented since they are both contained within the scope of loop 20 but not contained within each other. While the interpreter ignores all indentation and processes a program solely based on the pattern of FORs and NEXTs that appear, the human reader (including the programmer) will be better able to understand the program that is indented.

We wish to write a BASIC program which associates the NEXT statement

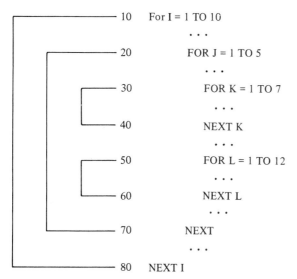

10   For I = 1 TO 10
         . . .
20   FOR J = 1 TO 5
            . . .
30   FOR K = 1 TO 7
               . . .
40   NEXT K
               . . .
50   FOR L = 1 TO 12
               . . .
60   NEXT L
               . . .
70   NEXT
            . . .
80   NEXT I

Figure 3.3.1   A BASIC program segment illustrating FOR-NEXT nesting.

that closes a scope with the FOR statement that begins it. To simplify the input process, we assume that the input consists of DATA statements each of which contains a character string in one of the two forms

FOR variable

or

NEXT variable

where variable is either a valid BASIC identifier or a blank. For example, input corresponding to the FOR-NEXT structure of Figure 3.3.1 is as follows:

<pre>
300   DATA "FOR I"
310   DATA "FOR J"
320   DATA "FOR K"
330   DATA "NEXT K"
340   DATA "FOR L"
350   DATA "NEXT L"
360   DATA "NEXT "
370   DATA "NEXT I"
</pre>

The program should first read and print a character string. If the string represents a FOR statement, the program should print a message of the form

SCOPE variable OPENED

If the string represents a NEXT statement, the program should print a message of the form

SCOPE variable CLOSED

For input corresponding to Figure 3.3.1 the output should be

<pre>
FOR I
SCOPE I OPENED
FOR J
SCOPE J OPENED
FOR K
SCOPE K OPENED
NEXT K
SCOPE K CLOSED
FOR L
SCOPE L OPENED
NEXT L
SCOPE L CLOSED
NEXT
SCOPE J CLOSED
NEXT I
SCOPE I CLOSED
</pre>

We also wish the program to alert us should the variable in the NEXT statement not correspond to the appropriate scope, in which case a suitable error message should be printed.

Algorithm for Solution

We can outline an algorithm as follows:

```
 1.  while there is more input do
 2.      read stmt
 3.      print stmt
 4.      scope = the first word of stmt
 5.      vrble = the second word of stmt
 6.      if scope = ''for''
 7.        then print an appropriate message
 8.              store away vrble
 9.      else if scope = ''next''
10.          then if vrble = ''''
11.              then print a message closing the last scope
12.              else if vrble = the variable on the most recently opened scope
13.                  then print a message closing that scope
14.                  else print an error message and stop
15.                  endif
16.              endif
17.          else print an error message and perform appropriate error recovery
18.          endif
19.      endif
20.  endwhile
```

This outline is quite imprecise and cannot be immediately translated into a program. Rather, it is an attempt to mirror the specification statement (which is even more ambiguous) and to mold it into a framework around which a program can be written. In formulating such an outline, ambiguities in the specification are highlighted. (See if you can spot the ambiguities in specification that are illustrated by the outline example.) Once this outline has been written, each part of it can be isolated separately and refined until it has the precision necessary to be directly translatable into BASIC. During this refinement process you may find that certain parts of the specification have been omitted or must be made more precise. In that case, the outline must be revised and the entire process reiterated. However, revision of the outline is a much simpler task than attempting to patch up a BASIC program that has been written directly from an English description. The relation between a BASIC statement and a specific English phrase in the specification is often very difficult to uncover since English and BASIC are very different from each other. By using an outline as a bridge between the two languages, the path between them becomes more visible. This isolation and refinement process has become a very important tool in writing correct programs and has resulted in large savings of both machine time and programmer time.

Refining the Outline

Let us therefore begin refining the program outline. Line 1 begins a loop that will terminate when the input is exhausted. Let us assume that the end of the input is indicated by the use of a trailer. Thus the main loop of the program may be written as

```
 10   'program scope
 30   DEFSTR S
             . . .
 90   READ STMT
100   IF STMT = "FINISH" THEN GOTO 320
110       PRINT STMT
             . . .
310   GO TO 90
320   END
             . . .
500   DATA . . .
```

Of course, the variable STMT must be declared as a character string (using the statement DEFSTR S). In lines 4 and 5 of the algorithm, we are asked to extract the first and second "words" from the string STMT. Since this is a possibly complicated operation (an arbitrary number of blanks may be interspersed among the words, or we may want to ensure that the words are valid BASIC identifiers), it is best left isolated in a subroutine of its own. We will therefore assume the existence of a subroutine *word* which accepts two inputs: the first is a character string X and the second is an integer N. *word* sets the variable WRD to the Nth word in X, or the null string if there is no Nth word.

We can therefore translate lines 4 and 5 of the outline into the following lines of code:

```
 30   DEFSTR S, V, W, X
             . . .
120   'scope = word(stmt,1)
130   N = 1
140   X = STMT
150   GOSUB 8000:        'subroutine word sets the variable WRD
160   SCOPE = WRD
170   'vrble = word(stmt,2)
180   N = 2
190   X = STMT
200   GOSUB 8000:        'subroutine word sets the variable WRD
210   VRBLE = WRD
```

Eventually, the subroutine *word* must be programmed in BASIC. However, by isolating it as a separate subroutine, we can postpone consideration of the details of character-string extraction and focus instead on the main goals of the program. Later, when the program has been completed, we can fill in the details of the subroutine *word*. This is a further step in the outline/refinement process in which programs are broken up into separately manageable modules.

Let us now turn our attention to lines 6–19 of the outline, which represent the heart of the program. Line 8 instructs us to "store away VRBLE." Note the deliberate vagueness of this instruction. Where are we to store this variable? How are we to retrieve it? By the previous analysis, we have seen that FOR-NEXT loop scoping represents a last-in, first-out discipline; the last scope to be opened must be the first to be closed. Thus a stack is the natural data structure to use for this problem. (Hopefully, you had already realized that fact by now.)

We will, therefore, declare a stack of character strings as follows:

```
30   DEFSTR S, V, W, X
       . . .
60   MAXSTACK = 100
70   DIM SITEM(MAXSTACK)
80   TP = 0
```

We are assuming that no more than 100 scopes will be open simultaneously (many BASIC interpreters impose practical limitations on the number of FOR-NEXT loops that may be nested). Thus "store away VRBLE" is translated as "push VRBLE onto a stack."

Another point must be clarified before continuing with the program. Line 7 refers to an "appropriate message" to be printed upon opening a scope. By the original specification of the problem the program must print

SCOPE *variable* OPENED

We can now translate lines 6–8 of the outline:

```
220   IF SCOPE = "FOR" THEN PRINT "SCOPE "; VRBLE; " OPENED":
                         X = VRBLE: GOSUB 1000: GOTO 310:
                         'push(sitem,vrble)
```

Let us now turn our attention to lines 9–13 of the outline. The message that is printed in lines 11 and 13 must refer to the variable of the last scope opened. This variable can be retrieved by popping the stack. Thus the program continues:

```
230   'else do statements 240-300
240   'if scope = "NEXT" then pop(sitem) else print error message
250   IF SCOPE = "NEXT" THEN GOSUB 2000: VB = POPS
                         ELSE GOTO 290
260   IF VRBLE = "" OR VRBLE = VB
         THEN PRINT "SCOPE "; VB; " CLOSED ": GOTO 310
```

Line 14 refers to the case where the label on a NEXT statement does not correspond to the label identifying the most recently opened scope. This indicates an illegal nesting of FOR-NEXT loops and would cause execution to be terminated. This may be accomplished by the statements

```
270    'else do statement 280
280    PRINT "ERROR. NEXT WITHOUT FOR": STOP
```

Line 17 refers to the case where a statement has been read whose instruction is neither FOR nor NEXT. We must decide what to print to indicate the error and what to do once an error has been found. Perhaps the easiest thing to do is to print

ERROR. INSTRUCTION IS ILLEGAL, STATEMENT IGNORED

and then ignore the statement and continue processing as though it had never been encountered. This can be accomplished by the statements

```
290    'instruction is neither FOR nor NEXT
300    PRINT "ERROR. INSTRUCTION IS ILLEGAL, STATEMENT IGNORED."
```

The Complete Program

Let us now put all the pieces together, add appropriate declarations, and examine the complete program.

```
 10    'program scope
 20    'the statement CLEAR 100 is required on TRS-80 microcomputers
 30    DEFSTR P, S, V, W, X
 40    TRUE = 1
 50    FALSE = 0
 60    MAXSTACK = 100
 70    DIM SITEM(MAXSTACK)
 80    TP = 0
 90    READ STMT
100    IF STMT = "FINISH" THEN GOTO 320
110    PRINT STMT
120    'scope = word(stmt,1)
130    N = 1
140    X = STMT
150    GOSUB 8000:           'subroutine word sets the variable WRD
160    SCOPE = WRD
170    'vrble = word(stmt,2)
180    N = 2
190    X = STMT
200    GOSUB 8000:           'subroutine word
210    VRBLE = WRD
```

```
220   IF SCOPE = "FOR" THEN PRINT "SCOPE "; VRBLE; " OPENED":
                                  X = VRBLE: GOSUB 1000: GOTO 310:
                                  'push(sitem,vrble)
230   'else do statements 240-300
240   'if scope = "NEXT" then pop(sitem) else print error message
250   IF SCOPE = "NEXT" THEN GOSUB 2000: VB = POPS
                                  ELSE GOTO 290
260   IF VRBLE = "" OR VRBLE = VB
         THEN PRINT "SCOPE "; VB; " CLOSED": GOTO 310
270   'else do statement 280
280   PRINT "ERROR. NEXT WITHOUT FOR": STOP
290   'instruction is neither FOR nor NEXT
300   PRINT "ERROR. INSTRUCTION IS ILLEGAL, STATEMENT IGNORED."
310   GOTO 90
320   END
          . . .
500   DATA . . .

          . . .
1000   'subroutine push

          . . .
2000   'subroutine pop

          . . .
3000   'subroutine empty

          . . .
8000   'subroutine word

          . . .
```

We must, of course, include the subroutine *word* and appropriate versions of *pop* and *push* which apply to stacks of character strings. We leave these as exercises for the student. The reader is urged to use the nesting structure of Figure 3.3.1 as input to the program above, and to note the following points:

1. The program produces the correct output for those inputs.
2. At each point of the program, the stack contains the variables of scopes that have been opened but not yet closed.

Note that only minimal error recovery has been incorporated into our program. A cardinal rule of programming is that program design should anticipate erroneous input. Upon reading a FOR statement, a message opening the scope is to be printed and the variable is to be pushed onto the stack for later comparison with the variable identifying the NEXT statement. However, suppose that a FOR statement erroneously contains no variable. Upon encountering the NEXT statement which was to have closed this scope, the program would (according to line 14 of the algorithm) print an error message and stop without noting that the error was in the FOR statement opening that scope. An even more serious problem could occur if the corresponding NEXT statement also did not contain an identifying variable. In such a case the condition in line 12 of the algorithm would be true and the program would continue, giving no indication that an error had occurred. Although we may want to halt program execution upon occurrence of an error, more frequently we would like to take some appropriate action. We must decide what corrective action to take. Upon reading a FOR statement without an identifying variable, a reasonable course would be to print an error message, ignore the FOR statement, and continue processing.

Another error situation that can occur is for scopes to remain open after the input has been exhausted. This occurs when not enough NEXT statements have been placed in the input to match the FOR statements. A simple message at the end of the output, listing all unclosed scopes, should suffice to note this error.

EXERCISES

1. Program the subroutine *word* that sets WRD to the Nth BASIC identifier in a string STR or "" if STR has no Nth identifier.

2. Write versions of *pop, push, empty,* and *popandtest* for stacks of character strings. Note that if two independent stacks, one of integers and one of character strings, appear in the same program, two versions of *pop, push, empty,* and *popandtest* must be included.

3. Assume that FOR statements are of the form

$$\#\# \text{ FOR } var = init \text{ TO } final \text{ STEP } step$$

where $\#\#$ is a line number; *var* is a BASIC identifier; *init, final,* and *step* are either integers or BASIC identifiers; and *step* is assumed positive. Write a program that accepts input consisting of such FOR and NEXT statements and translates them into IF, assignment, and GOTO statements. For example, the following input:

```
10   FOR I = 1 TO N STEP 3
20   FOR J = N TO 500 STEP 1
30   NEXT J
40   NEXT I
50   FOR I = 1 TO 5 STEP K
60   NEXT I
```

would be translated into

```
10   I = 1
20   IF I > N THEN GOTO 90
30   J = N
40   IF J > 500 THEN GOTO 70
```

```
 50   J = J + 1
 60   GOTO 40
 70   I = I + 3
 80   GOTO 20
 90   I = 1
100   IF I > 5 THEN GOTO 130
110   I = I + K
120   GOTO 100
130   'remainder of program
```

(*Hint*: Use stacks of variables, line numbers, and increments.)

4. Assume that a single NEXT statement containing several variables may terminate multiply nested loops provided that the variables are specified in the proper order. Modify the program in this section so that upon encountering a statement of the form

50   NEXT X, Y, Z

the scopes identified by the variables X, Y, and Z are properly closed, and messages of the form

SCOPE X CLOSED
SCOPE Y CLOSED
SCOPE Z CLOSED

are printed. Your program should detect incorrectly nested FOR-NEXT loops.

5. Consider a language in which a NEXT statement containing a variable closes all open scopes nested within the scope identified by that variable. Thus any scopes that have been opened beyond the FOR statement containing the variable but which have not yet been closed, as well as the scope identified by that variable, are to be ended by the same NEXT statement. Modify the program in this section so that a NEXT statement containing a variable closes all such scopes, printing multiple messages indicating which scopes have been closed.

4. AN EXAMPLE: INFIX, POSTFIX, AND PREFIX

Basic Definitions and Examples

In this section we examine a major application of stacks. Although it is one of the most prominent applications, it is by no means the only one. The reason that we consider this application is that it illustrates so well the different types of stacks and the various operations we have defined upon them. The example is also an important topic of computer science in its own right.

Before proceeding with the algorithms and programs of this section it is necessary to provide some groundwork. Consider the sum of *A* and *B*. We think of applying the *operator* "+" to the *operands* *A* and *B* and write the sum as

$A + B$. This particular representation is called *infix*. There are two alternative notations for expressing the sum of A and B using the symbols A, B, and $+$. These are:

$$+ \, A \, B \qquad \textit{prefix}$$
$$A \, B \, + \qquad \textit{postfix}$$

The prefixes "pre," "post," and "in" refer to the relative position of the operator with respect to the two operands. In prefix notation the operator precedes the two operands, in postfix notation the operator follows the two operands, and in infix notation the operator is between the two operands. The prefix and postfix notations are not really as awkward to use as they might first appear. For example, in many versions of BASIC, we can invoke a defined function FNADD to return the sum of the two arguments A and B by writing T = FNADD(A,B). The operator precedes the operands A and B.

Let us now consider some additional examples. The evaluation of the expression $A + B*C$ as written in standard infix notation requires knowledge of which of the two operations, $+$ or $*$, is to be performed first. In the case of $+$ and $*$, we "know" that multiplication is to be done before addition (in the absence of parentheses to the contrary). Thus $A + B*C$ is interpreted as $A + (B*C)$ unless otherwise specified. We say that multiplication takes *precedence* over addition. Suppose that we would like to rewrite $A + B*C$ in postfix. Applying the rules of precedence, we first convert the portion of the expression that is evaluated first, the multiplication. By doing this conversion in stages, we obtain

$A + (B*C)$	parentheses for emphasis
$A + (BC*)$	convert the multiplication
$A(BC*)+$	convert the addition
$ABC*+$	postfix form

The only rules to remember during the conversion process are that the operations with highest precedence are converted first and that after a portion of the expression has been converted to postfix it is to be treated as a single operand. Let us now consider the same example with the precedence of the operators reversed by the deliberate insertion of parentheses.

$(A+B)*C$	infix form
$(AB+)*C$	convert the addition
$(AB+)C*$	convert the multiplication
$AB+C*$	postfix form

In the example above, the addition was converted before the multiplication because of the parentheses. In going from $(A+B)*C$ to $(AB+)*C$, A and B are the operands and $+$ is the operator. In going from $(AB+)*C$ to $(AB+)C*$, $(AB+)$ and C are the operands and $*$ is the operator. The rules for converting from infix to postfix are simple, provided that you know the order of precedence.

We will consider five binary operations: addition, subtraction, multiplication, division, and exponentiation. These operations are denoted by the usual operators $+$, $-$, $*$, $/$, and $\uparrow$. For these binary operators the following is the order of precedence (highest to lowest):

Exponentiation
Multiplication/division
Addition/subtraction

By using parentheses we can override the default precedence.

We give the following additional examples of converting from infix to postfix. Be sure that you understand each of these examples (and can do them on your own) before proceeding to the remainder of this section. We follow the convention that when unparenthesized operators of the same precedence are scanned, the order is assumed to be left to right except in the case of exponentiation, where the order is assumed to be from right to left. Thus $A - B - C$ means $(A - B) - C$, while $A\uparrow B\uparrow C$ means $A\uparrow(B\uparrow C)$.

Infix	Postfix
$A + B$	$AB +$
$A + B - C$	$AB + C -$
$(A + B)*(C - D)$	$AB + CD - *$
$A\uparrow B*C - D + E/F/(G + H)$	$AB\uparrow C*D - EF/GH + / +$
$((A + B)*C - (D - E))\uparrow(F + G)$	$AB + C*DE - FG +$
$A - B/(C*D\uparrow E)$	$ABCDE\uparrow*/ -$

The precedence rules for converting an expression from infix to prefix are identical. The only change from postfix conversion is that the operator is placed before the operands rather than after them. We present the prefix forms of the expressions above. Again, you should attempt to make the transformations on your own.

Infix	Prefix
$A + B$	$+ AB$
$A + B - C$	$- + ABC$
$(A + B)*(C - D)$	$* + AB - CD$
$A\uparrow B*C - D + E/F/(G + H)$	$+ - * ABCD/EF + GH$
$((A + B)*C-(D - E))\uparrow(F + G)$	$\uparrow- * + ABC - DE + FG$
$A - B/(C*D\uparrow E)$	$- A/B*C\uparrow DE$

Note that the prefix form of a complex expression is not the mirror image of the postfix form, as can be seen from the second of the examples above, $A + B - C$. We will henceforth be concerned with the postfix transformations and will leave to the reader as exercises most of the work involving prefix.

One point immediately obvious about the postfix form of an expression is that it requires no parentheses. Let us consider the two expressions $A + (B*C)$ and $(A+B)*C$. Whereas the parentheses in one of the two expressions is superfluous [by convention $A+B*C = A+(B*C)$], the parentheses in the second expression is necessary to avoid confusion with the first. The postfix forms of these expressions are

Infix	Postfix
$A+(B*C)$	$ABC*+$
$(A+B)*C$	$AB+C*$

There are no parentheses in either of the two transformed expressions. A close look tells us that the order of the operators in the postfix expressions determines the actual order of operations in evaluating the expression, making the use of parentheses unnecessary. In going from infix to postfix we are sacrificing the ability to note at a glance the operands associated with a particular operator. We are gaining, however, an unambiguous form of the original expression without the use of cumbersome parentheses. In fact, you may argue that the postfix form of the original expression might look simpler were it not for the fact that it appears difficult to evaluate. For example, how do we know that if $A = 3, B = 4$, and $C = 5$ in the examples above, then 3 4 5 * + equals 23 and 3 4 + 5 * equals 35?

Evaluating a Postfix Expression

The answer to this question lies in the development of an algorithm for evaluating an expression in postfix. Each operator in a postfix string refers to the preceding two operands in the string. (Of course, one of these two operands may itself be the result of applying a previous operator.) Suppose that each time we read an operand, we push it onto a stack. When we reach an operator, its operands will then be the top two elements on the stack. We can then pop these two elements, perform the indicated operation on them, and push the result on the stack so that it will be available for use as an operand of the next operator. The following algorithm evaluates an expression in postfix using this method.

```
initialize a stack s to be empty
'scan the input string reading one element at a time into symb
while there are more characters in the input string do
        symb = next input character
        if symb is an operand
          then push(s,symb)
```

> **else** *secoper* = *pop*(*s*)
> *oper*1 = *pop*(*s*)
> *value* = result of applying *symb* to *oper*1 and *secoper*
> *push*(*s*,*value*)
> **endif**
> **endwhile**
> *result* = *pop*(*s*)

Let us now consider an example. Suppose that we are asked to evaluate the following expression in postfix:

$$6\ 2\ 3\ +\ -\ 3\ 8\ 2\ /\ +\ *\ 2\uparrow 3\ +$$

We show the contents of the operand stack *s* and the variables *symb*, *oper*1, *secoper*, and *value* after each successive iteration of the loop. The top of *s* is to the right.

symb	oper1	secoper	value	s
6				6
2				6,2
3				6,2,3
+	2	3	5	6,5
−	6	5	1	1
3	6	5	1	1,3
8	6	5	1	1,3,8
2	6	5	1	1,3,8,2
/	8	2	4	1,3,4
+	3	4	7	1,7
*	1	7	7	7
2	1	7	7	7,2
↑	7	2	49	49
3	7	2	49	49,3
+	49	3	52	52

Note that *s* is a stack of operands. Each operand is pushed onto the stack when it is encountered. Therefore, the maximum size of the stack is the number of operands that appear in the input expression. However, in dealing with most postfix expressions, the actual size of the stack needed is less than this maximum since an operator removes operands from the stack. In the previous example the stack never contained more than four elements, despite the fact that eight operands appeared in the postfix expression.

Program to Evaluate a Postfix Expression

We are now prepared to plan a program to evaluate an expression in postfix notation. There are a number of questions that we must consider before we can actually write the program. A primary consideration, as in all programs, is to define precisely the form and restrictions, if any, on the input. Usually, the programmer is presented with the form of the input and is required to design a program to accommodate the given data. On the other hand, we are in the fortunate position of being able to choose the form of our input. This enables us to construct a program that is not overburdened with transformation problems that overshadow the actual intent of the routine. Had we been confronted with data in a form that is awkward and cumbersome to work with, we could relegate the transformations to various subroutines and use the output of these subroutines as input to the primary routine. In the "real world," recognition and transformation of input is a major concern.

Let us assume in this case that each input expression is in the form of a string of digits and operator symbols. We will assume that operands are single nonnegative digits (e.g., 0, 1, 2, . . . , 8, 9). For example, an input string might be "345*+". We would like to write a program that inputs expressions in this format and prints for each expression the original input string and the result of the evaluated expression.

Since the symbols are read as characters, we must find a method to convert the operand characters to numbers and the operator characters to operations. For example, we must have a method for converting the character "5" to the number 5 and the character " + " to the addition operation. The conversion of a character to an integer can be handled easily in BASIC. If X$ is the string representation of a number in BASIC, the function VAL(X$) returns the numerical value of that string. [Similarly, STR$(Y) can be used to convert a number Y to its string representation.] To convert an operator symbol into the corresponding action, we use a subroutine *apply* that accepts the character representation of an operator and two operands as inputs. The subroutine sets the variable APPLY to the value of the expression obtained by applying the operator to the two operands. The body of this subroutine will be given below.

The main part of the program is presented below. The routine is merely the BASIC implementation of the evaluation algorithm, taking into account the specific environment and format of the input data and calculated outputs.

```
 10    'program evaluate
 20    'the statement CLEAR 100 is required on TRS-80 microcomputers
 30    DEFSTR A, O, P, S, X
 40    TRUE = 1
 50    FALSE = 0
 60    MAXSTACK = 100
 70    DIM SITEM(MAXSTACK):          'contains stack items 1–100
 80    TP = 0
 90    INPUT "ENTER STRING"; STRING
100    FOR CHAR = 1 TO LEN(STRING)
110        SYMB = MID$(STRING,CHAR,1): 'extract the next character
```

```
120        'if SYMB is a digit, push it on to the stack
130        IF SYMB > = "0" AND SYMB < = "9"
               THEN X = SYMB: GOSUB 1000: GOTO 230
140            'else do stmts 150–220
150        GOSUB 2000:                'subroutine pop sets the variable POP
160        SECOPER = POPS
170        GOSUB 2000:                'subroutine pop
180        OPER1 = POPS
190        GOSUB 6000:                'subroutine apply sets the variable APPLY
200        'we apply the operator to the top two items in the stack and
           'push the resulting value onto the stack in their place
210        X = APPLY
220        GOSUB 1000:                'subroutine push
230    NEXT CHAR
240    GOSUB 2000:                    'subroutine pop
250    RESULT = VAL(POPS)
260    PRINT STRING; " = "; RESULT
270    GOTO 80:                       'repeat for another expression
280    END
1000   'subroutine push
           . . .
2000   'subroutine pop
           . . .
3000   'subroutine empty
           . . .
6000   'subroutine apply
           . . .
```

The subroutine *apply* checks to ensure that SYMB is a valid operator and if it is, determines the results of its operation on the operands OPER1 and SECOPER.

```
6000   'subroutine apply
6010   'inputs: OPER1, SECOPER, SYMB
6020   'outputs: APPLY
6030   'locals: Y
6040   IF NOT (SYMB = "+" OR SYMB = "−" OR SYMB = "*" OR
                               SYMB = "/" OR SYMB = "↑")
           THEN PRINT "INVALID OPERATOR": STOP
6050   IF SYMB = "+" THEN Y = VAL(OPER1) + VAL(SECOPER)
6060   IF SYMB = "−" THEN Y = VAL(OPER1) − VAL(SECOPER)
6070   IF SYMB = "*"  THEN Y = VAL(OPER1) * VAL(SECOPER)
6080   IF SYMB = "/"  THEN Y = VAL(OPER1) / VAL(SECOPER)
6090   IF SYMB = "↑"  THEN Y = VAL(OPER1) ↑ VAL(SECOPER)
6100   APPLY = STR$(Y)
6110   RETURN
6120   'endsub
```

Limitations of the Program

Before we leave the program, we should note some of its deficiencies. Understanding what a program cannot do is as important as knowing what it can do. It should be obvious that attempting to use a program to solve a problem for which it was not intended will lead to chaos. Worse still is the case where an attempt is made to solve a problem with an incorrect program only to have the program produce incorrect results, without the slightest trace of an error message. In these cases the programmer has no indication that the results are wrong, and may therefore make faulty judgments based on those results. For this reason it is important for the programmer to understand the limitations of a program.

A major criticism of this program is that it does nothing in terms of error detection and recovery. If the data on each input line comprise a valid postfix expression, the program works. Suppose, however, that one input line has too many operators or operands or that they are not in a proper sequence. These problems could come about as a result of someone innocently using the program on a postfix expression that contains two-digit numbers, yielding an excessive number of operands. Or, possibly, the user of the program was under the impression that negative numbers could be handled by the program and that they are to be entered with the minus sign, the same sign that is used to represent subtraction. These minus signs are treated as subtraction operators, resulting in an excess number of operators. Depending on the specific type of error, the computer may take one of several actions (e.g., halt execution, print erroneous results, etc.). As another example suppose that at the final statement of the program, the stack is not empty. We get no error messages (because we asked for none) and produce a numerical value for an expression that was probably incorrectly stated in the first place. Suppose that one of the calls to the *pop* routine raises the underflow condition. Since we did not use the *popandtest* routine to pop elements from the stack, the program stops. This seems unreasonable since faulty data in one expression should not prevent the processing of additional expressions. By no means are these the only problems that could arise. As exercises, you may wish to write programs that accommodate less restrictive inputs and some others that will test for and detect some of the errors listed above.

Converting an Expression from Infix to Postfix

We have thus far presented routines to evaluate a postfix expression. Although we have discussed a method for transforming infix to postfix, we have not as yet presented an algorithm for doing so. It is to this task that we now direct our attention. Once such an algorithm has been constructed, we will have the capability of reading an infix expression and evaluating it by first converting it to postfix and then evaluating the postfix expression.

In our previous discussion, we mentioned that subexpressions within innermost parentheses must first be converted to postfix so that they can then be treated as single operands. In this fashion, parentheses can be successively eliminated until the entire expression is converted. The last pair of parentheses to be opened within a group of parentheses encloses the first subexpression within that group to be transformed. This last-in first-out behavior should immediately suggest the use of a stack.

Consider the two infix expressions $A + B*C$ and $(A + B)*C$ and their respective postfix versions, $ABC*+$ and $AB+C*$. In each case the order of the operands is the same as the order of the operands in the original infix expressions. In scanning the first expression, $A+B*C$, the first operand A can be inserted immediately into the postfix expression. Clearly, the $+$ symbol cannot be inserted until after its second operand, which has not yet been scanned, is inserted. Therefore, it must be stored away to be retrieved and inserted in its proper position. When the operand B is scanned, it is inserted immediately after A. Now, however, two operands have been scanned. What prevents the symbol $+$ from being retrieved and inserted? The answer is, of course, the $*$ symbol that follows, which has precedence over $+$. In the case of the second expression the closing parentheses indicates that the $+$ operation should be performed first. Remember that in postfix, unlike infix, the operator that appears earlier in the string is the one that is applied first.

Since precedence plays such an important role in transforming infix to postfix, let us assume the existence of a function $prcd(oper1, secoper)$, where $oper1$ and $secoper$ are characters representing operators. This function returns *true* if $oper1$ has precedence over $secoper$ when $oper1$ appears to the left of $secoper$ in an infix expression without parentheses. $prcd(oper1, secoper)$ returns *false* otherwise. For example, $prcd(``*", ``+")$ and $prcd(``+", ``+")$ are *true,* while $prcd(``+", ``*")$ is *false.* Let us now present an outline of an algorithm to convert an infix string without parentheses into a postfix string. Since we are assuming no parentheses in our input string, the only governor of the order in which operators appear in the postfix string is precedence.

1. initialize the postfix string to ``"
2. initialize the stack *opstk* to empty
3. **while** there are more input symbols **do**
4.   **read** *symb*
5.   **if** *symb* is an operand
6.   **then** add *symb* to postfix string
7.   **else** 'the symbol is an operator
8.   **while** (*empty(stack)* = *false*) **and**
                              (*prcd(stacktop(opstk), symb)* = *true*) **do**
9.   *smbtp* = *pop(opstk)*
                    'smbtp has precedence over *symb* so it can
                    'be added to the postfix string
10.   add *smbtp* to the postfix string
11.   **endwhile**

'at this point, either *opstk* is empty or *symb* has
'precedence over *stacktop(opstk)*. We cannot output
'*symb* into the postfix string until we have read
'the next operator which may have precedence. We
'must, therefore, store *symb*.
12.   *push (opstk,symb)*
13.   *endif*
14. *endwhile*
'at this point, we have reached the end of the
'string. We must output the operators remaining
'on the stack into the postfix string.
15. *while empty(opstk)* = *false do*
16.   *smbtp* = *pop(opstk)*
17.   add *smbtp* to the postfix string
18. *endwhile*

Simulate the algorithm with such infix strings as "$A*B+C*D$" and
"$A+B*C{\uparrow}D{\uparrow}E$" [where *prcd* ("$\uparrow$", "$\uparrow$") = *false*] to convince yourself that it
is correct. Note that at each point of the simulation, an operator on the stack has a
lower precedence than all the operators above it. This is because the initial empty
stack trivially satisfies this condition, and an operator is pushed onto the stack
(line 12) only if the operator currently on top of the stack has a lower precedence
than the incoming one.

You should also note the liberty that we have taken in line 8 in forming the
condition

$$(empty(opstk) = false) \text{ and } (prcd(stacktop(opstk),symb) = true)$$

Make sure that you understand why such a condition cannot be used in an actual
program.

What modification must be made to this algorithm to accommodate parentheses? The answer is surprisingly little. When an opening parenthesis is read, it
must be pushed onto the stack. This can be done by establishing the convention
that *prcd(op,"(")* = *false*, for any operator symbol *op* other than a right parenthesis. We also define *prcd("(",op)* = *false* to ensure that an operator symbol
appearing after a left parenthesis will be pushed onto the stack.

When a closing parenthesis is read, all operators up to the first opening parenthesis must be popped from the stack onto the postfix string. This can be done
by setting *prcd(op,")")* = *true* for all operators *op* other than a left parenthesis.
When these operators have been popped off the stack and the opening parenthesis
is uncovered, special action must be taken. The opening parenthesis must be
popped off the stack, and it and the closing parenthesis must be discarded rather

than placed in the postfix string or on the stack. Let us set $prcd($ "(", ") ") to *false*. This will ensure that upon reaching an opening parenthesis, the loop beginning at line 8 will be skipped so that the opening parenthesis will not be inserted into the postfix string. Execution will therefore proceed to line 12. However, since the closing parenthesis should not be pushed onto the stack, line 12 is replaced by the statement

> 12. **if** *(empty(opstk)* = *true)* **or** *(symb* <> ")")*
>   **then** *push(opstk,symb)*
>   **else** *smbtp* = *pop(opstk)*

With these conventions for the *prcd* function and the revision to line 12, the algorithm can be used to convert any infix string to postfix. We summarize the precedence rules for parentheses:

$prcd($ "(",op$)$ = *false*	for any operator *op*
$prcd(op,$ "("$)$ = *false*	for any operator *op* other than ")"
$prcd(op,$ ")"$)$ = *true*	for any operator *op* other than "("
$prcd($ ")",op$)$ = undefined	for any operator *op* (an attempt to compare the two indicates an error)

We illustrate this algorithm with some examples

Example 1: $A + B*C$

The contents of *symb,* the postfix string, and *opstk* are shown after scanning each symbol. *opstk* is shown with its top to the right.

Line	*symb*	Postfix string	*opstk*
1	A	A	
2	+	A	+
3	B	AB	+
4	*	AB	+ *
5	C	ABC	+ *
6		ABC*	+
7		ABC* +	

Lines 1, 3, and 5 correspond to the scanning of an operand, so the symbol (*symb*) is immediately placed on the postfix string. In line 2 an operator was scanned and the stack was found to be empty, so the operator is placed on the stack. In line 4 the precedence of the new symbol (*) is greater than the precedence of the symbol on the top of the stack (+), so the new symbol is pushed onto the stack. In steps 6 and 7 the input string is empty, so the stack is popped and its contents placed on the postfix string.

Example 2: $(A + B)*C$

symb	Postfix string	opstk
(		(
A	A	(
+	A	(+
B	AB	(+
)	AB +	
*	AB +	*
C	AB + C	*
	AB + C*	

In this example, when the right parenthesis is encountered the stack is popped until a left parenthesis is encountered, at which point both parentheses are discarded. By using parentheses to force an order of precedence different from the default, the order of appearance of the operators in the postfix string is different from that in Example 1.

Example 3: $((A - (B + C))*D)\uparrow(E + F)$

symb	Postfix string	opstk
(		(
(		((
A	A	((
−	A	((−
(	A	((− (
B	AB	((− (
+	AB	((− (+
C	ABC	((− (+
)	ABC +	((−
)	ABC + −	(
*	ABC + −	(*
D	ABC + − D	(*
)	ABC + − D*	
↑	ABC + − D*	↑
(	ABC + − D*	↑(
E	ABC + − D*E	↑(
+	ABC + − D*E	↑(+
F	ABC + − D*EF	↑(+
)	ABC + − D*EF +	↑
	ABC + − D*EF + ↑	

Why does the conversion algorithm seem so involved, whereas the evaluation algorithm seems so simple? The answer is that the former converts from one order of precedence (governed by the *prcd* function and the appearance of parentheses) to the natural order (i.e., the operation to be executed first appears first). Because of the many combinations of elements at the top of the stack (if not empty) and possible incoming symbol, a large number of statements are necessary to cover each possibility. In the latter algorithm, on the other hand, the operators appear in precisely the order in which they are to be executed. For this reason the operands can be stacked until an operator is found, at which point the operation is performed immediately.

The motivation behind the conversion algorithm is the desire to output the operators in the order in which they are to be executed. In solving this problem by hand we could follow vague instructions that require us to convert from the inside out. This works very well for human beings doing a problem with pencil and paper (if they do not become confused or make a mistake). However, when writing a program or an algorithm, we must be more precise in our instructions. We cannot be sure that we have reached the innermost parentheses or the operator with the highest precedence until we have actually scanned many additional symbols. At that time, we must backtrack to some previous point.

Rather than backtrack continuously, we make use of the stack to "remember" the operators encountered previously. If an incoming operator is of greater precedence than the one on top of the stack, this new operator is pushed onto the stack. This means that when all the elements in the stack are finally popped, this new operator will precede the former top in the postfix string (which is correct since it has higher precedence). If, on the other hand, the precedence of the new operator is less than that of the top of the stack, the operator at the top of the stack should be executed first. Therefore, the stack is popped, the popped operator placed on the output string, and the incoming symbol is compared with the new top; and so on. By including parentheses in our input string, we may override the order of operations. Thus when a left parenthesis is scanned, it is pushed on the stack. When its associated right parenthesis is found, all the operators between the two parentheses are placed on the output string, because they are to be executed before any operators appearing following the parentheses.

Program to Convert
an Expression from Infix
to Postfix

There are two things that we must do before we actually write the program. The first is to define precisely the format of the input and output. The second is to construct, or at least define, those routines on which the main routine depends. We assume that the input consists of strings of characters, one string per input line. The end of the string is signaled by the occurrence of a blank. For the sake of simplicity, we assume that all operands are single-character letters or digits. The output is a character string, so the output of the conversion process will be suitable for the evaluation process, provided that all the single-character operands in the initial infix string are digits.

In transforming the conversion algorithm into a program, we make use of several routines. Among these are *empty, pop, push,* and *popandtest,* all suitably modified so that the elements on the stack are characters.

Note that we cannot use the variable PRCD for the output of the *prcd* subroutine since all variables beginning with the letter P have already been defined to be character strings. This was necessary because both the *pop* and *popandtest* subroutines produce character-string output in the variable POPS. For this reason we use the variable ZPRCD as the output of the *prcd* subroutine. *prcd* accepts two single-character operator symbols as arguments and sets ZPRCD to TRUE if the first has precedence over the second when it appears to the left of the second in an infix string, and FALSE otherwise. The subroutine should, of course, incorporate the parentheses conventions previously introduced. Similarly, we cannot use the variable STKTP for the output of the *stacktop* subroutine, since in many versions of BASIC only the first two characters will be used by the computer to distinguish between variables. Thus STKTP and STRING will be treated as one and the same variable. For this reason we use the variable XSTKTP as the output of the *stacktop* subroutine.

Once these auxiliary subroutines have been written, we can write the program. We assume that the program inputs a line containing an expression in infix, performs the conversion procedures, and prints the original string and the postfix string. The body of the program follows:

```
10    'program postfix
20    'the statement CLEAR 100 is required on TRS-80 microcomputers
30    DEFSTR O, P, S, X
40    TRUE = 1
50    FALSE = 0
60    MAXSTACK = 100
70    DIM SITEM(MAXSTACK): 'contains opstk items 1–100
80    TP = 0
90    PSTFX = ""
100   'stack is initially empty
110   INPUT "ENTER STRING"; STRING
120   'begin scanning symbols one at a time
130   'line 3 of the conversion algorithm
140   FOR CHAR = 1 TO LEN(STRING)
150       'line 4
160       SYMB = MID$(STRING,CHAR,1): 'extract the next input symbol
170       'check if SYMB is an operand
180       'lines 5 and 6
190       IF SYMB >= "0" AND SYMB <= "9"
              THEN PSTFX = PSTFX + SYMB: GOTO 310
```

```
200   'else do stmts 210–300
210   'lines 8 through 11
220   GOSUB 3000:      'subroutine empty
230   IF EMPTY = TRUE THEN GOTO 290
240   GOSUB 4000:      'subroutine stacktop sets XSTKTP
250   OPER1 = XSTKTP
260   SECOPER = SYMB
270   GOSUB 8000:      'subroutine prcd sets ZPRCD
280   IF ZPRCD = TRUE
         THEN GOSUB 2000: SMBTP = POPS:
             PSTFX = PSTFX + SMBTP: GOTO 210
290   'line 12 (as revised)
300   IF (EMPTY = TRUE) OR (SYMB <> '')'')
         THEN X = SYMB: GOSUB 1000
         ELSE GOSUB 2000
310   NEXT CHAR
320   'lines 15 through 18
330   GOSUB 3000: 'subroutine empty
340   IF EMPTY = TRUE THEN GOTO 380
350   GOSUB 2000: 'subroutine pop
360   PSTFX = PSTFX + POPS
370   GOTO 330
380   PRINT "INFIX STRING = "; STRING
390   PRINT "POSTFIX STRING = "; PSTFX
400   PRINT
410   GOTO 80: 'get the next input string
420   END
1000  'subroutine push

         . . .

2000  'subroutine pop

         . . .

3000  'subroutine empty

         . . .

4000  'subroutine stacktop

         . . .

8000  'subroutine prcd
8010  'inputs: OPER1, SECOPER
8020  'outputs: ZPRCD
8030  'locals: none
8040  ZPRCD = TRUE
8050  IF (OPER1 = ''('' OR SECOPER = ''('')
         THEN ZPRCD = FALSE
8060  IF SECOPER = ''↑'' THEN ZPRCD = FALSE
```

8070   IF (OPER1 = ''+'' OR OPER1 = ''−'') AND (SECOPER = ''*'' OR

SECOPER = ''/'')

THEN ZPRCD = FALSE
8080   RETURN
8090   *'endsub*

The program has one major flaw—it does not check that the input string is a valid infix expression. In fact, it would be instructive for you to examine the operation of this program when it is presented with a valid postfix string as input. As an exercise you are asked to write a program that checks whether or not an input string is a valid infix expression.

We can now write a program to read an infix string and find its numerical value. If the original input strings consist of single-digit operands with no letter operands, then combining programs may be accomplished by linking the output of procedure *postfix* for each input string with the input of procedure *evaluate*. A single set of stack manipulation routines may be defined and used by both the conversion and evaluation routines.

Most of our attention in this section has been devoted to transformations involving postfix expressions. The algorithm to convert an infix expression into postfix scans characters from left to right, stacking and unstacking as necessary. If it were necessary to convert from infix to prefix, the infix string could be scanned from right to left and the appropriate symbols entered in the prefix string from right to left. Since most algebraic expressions are read from left to right, postfix is a more natural choice.

The programs above are merely indicative of the types of routines one could write to manipulate and evaluate postfix expressions. They are by no means comprehensive or unique. There are many variations of the routines discussed above that are equally acceptable. Some of the older high-level-language compilers actually used routines such as *evaluate* and *postfix* to handle algebraic expressions. Since that time, more sophisticated schemes have been developed to handle these problems.

EXERCISES

1. Transform each of the following expressions to prefix and postfix.
   (a) $A + B - C$
   (b) $(A + B)*(C - D)\uparrow E*F$
   (c) $(A + B)*(C\uparrow(D - E) + F) - G$
   (d) $A + (((B - C)*(D - E) + F)/G)\uparrow(H - J)$

2. Transform each of the following prefix expressions to infix.
   (a) $+ - ABC$
   (b) $+A - BC$

(c) $+ + A -\uparrow* \; BCD/+ \; EF*GHI$
(d) $+ - \uparrow ABC*D**EFG$

3. Transform each of the following postfix expressions to infix.
   (a) $AB + C -$
   (b) $ABC + -$
   (c) $AB - C + DEF - +\uparrow$
   (d) $ABCDE - +\uparrow*EF* -$

4. Apply the evaluation algorithm in the text to evaluate the following postfix expressions. Assume that $A = 1, B = 2, C = 3$.
   (a) $AB + C - BA + C\uparrow-$
   (b) $ABC + *CBA - + *$

5. Modify the infix to postfix conversion program to accept as input a character string of operators and operands representing a postfix expression and to create the fully parenthesized infix form of the original postfix. For example, $AB +$ would be transformed into $(A + B)$, and $AB + C -$ would be transformed into $((A + B) - C)$.

6. Write a single program to evaluate a string given in infix. You are to use two stacks, one for operands and the other for operators. You should not first convert the infix string to postfix and then evaluate the postfix string, but rather evaluate as you go along.

7. Write a program *prefix* to accept an input string in infix and create the prefix form of that string, assuming that the string is read from right to left and that the prefix string is created from right to left.

8. Write a BASIC program to convert
   (a) A prefix string to postfix.
   (b) A postfix string to prefix.
   (c) A prefix string to infix.
   (d) A postfix string to infix.

9. Write a BASIC program that accepts an infix string and forms an equivalent infix string with all superfluous parentheses removed. Can this be done without using a stack?

10. Assume a machine that has a single register and six instructions.

LD	A	which places the operand A into the register
ST	A	which places the contents of the register into the variable A
AD	A	which adds the contents of the variable A to the register
SB	A	which subtracts the contents of the variable A from the register
ML	A	which multiplies the contents of the register by the variable A
DV	A	which divides the contents of the register by the variable A

    Write a program that accepts a postfix expression containing single-letter operands and the operators $+$, $-$, $*$, and $/$, and which prints a sequence of instructions to evaluate the expression and leave the result in the register. Use variables of the form

Tn as temporary variables. For example, the postfix expression $ABC* + DE - /$ should yield the printout

LD	B
ML	C
ST	T1
LD	A
AD	T1
ST	T2
LD	D
SB	E
ST	T3
LD	T2
DV	T3
ST	T4

4

Queues and Lists

This chapter introduces the queue, an important data structure which is often used to simulate real-world situations. The concepts of the stack and queue are then extended to a new structure, the list. Various forms of lists and their associated operations are examined and several applications are presented.

1. THE QUEUE AND ITS SEQUENTIAL REPRESENTATION

A *queue* is an ordered collection of items from which items may be deleted at one end (called the *front* of the queue) and into which items may be inserted at the other end (called the *rear* of the queue).

Figure 4.1.1(a) illustrates a queue containing three elements, A, B, and C. A is at the front of the queue and C is at the rear. In Figure 4.1.1(b), an element has been deleted from the queue. Since elements may be deleted only from the front of the queue, A is removed and B is now at the front. In Figure 4.1.1(c), when items D and E are inserted, they must be inserted at the rear of the queue.

Since D has been inserted into the queue before E, it will be removed earlier. The first element inserted into a queue is the first element to be removed. For this reason a queue is sometimes called a *fifo* (first-in, first-out) list, as opposed to a stack, which is a *lifo* (last-in, first-out) list. Examples of queues abound in the real world. A line at a bank or at a bus stop, and a batch of jobs waiting to be processed by a computer, are familiar examples of queues.

There are three primitive operations that can be applied to a queue. The operation *insert(q,x)* inserts item x at the rear of the queue q. The operation

154

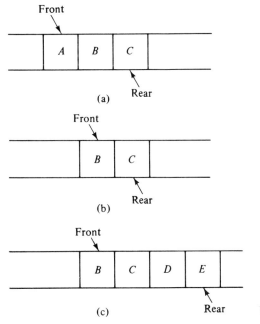

Figure 4.1.1 A queue.

$x = remove(q)$ deletes the element at the front of the queue q and sets x to its contents. The third operation, *empty(q)*, returns *true* or *false*, depending on whether or not the queue is empty. The queue in Figure 4.1.1 can be obtained by the following sequence of operations. We assume that the queue is initially empty.

> *insert(q,A)*
> *insert(q,B)*
> *insert(q,C)*   [Figure 4.1.1(a)]
> $x = remove(q)$ [Figure 4.1.1(b); x is set to A]
> *insert(q,D)*
> *insert(q,E)*   [Figure 4.1.1(c)]

The *insert* operation can always be performed since there is no limit to the number of elements a queue may contain. The *remove* operation, however, can be applied only if the queue is nonempty—there is no way to remove an element from a queue that contains no elements. The result of an illegal attempt to remove an element from an empty queue is called **underflow**. The *empty* operation is, of course, always applicable.

How shall a queue be represented in BASIC? An idea that comes immediately to mind is to use an array to hold the elements of the queue, and to use two variables, FRNT and REAR, to hold the positions within the array of the first and last elements of the queue. Initially, REAR is set to 0 and FRNT is set to 1, and the queue is empty whenever REAR < FRNT. The number of elements in the queue at any time is equal to the value of REAR − FRNT + 1. Thus an empty queue of numbers might be initialized by

        10   MAXQUEUE = 100
        20   DIM QITEMS(MAXQUEUE)
        30   FRNT = 1
        40   REAR = 0

Of course, using an array to hold a queue introduces the possibility of **overflow** if the queue contains more elements than were allocated for the array. Ignoring the possibility of underflow and overflow for the moment, the operation *insert(q,x)* could be implemented by the statements

        3000   REAR = REAR + 1
        3010   QITEMS(REAR) = X

and the operation *x = remove(q)* could be implemented by

        2000   X = QITEMS(FRNT)
        2010   FRNT = FRNT + 1

Let us examine what might happen under this representation. Figure 4.1.2 illustrates an array of five elements (again ignoring a possible element at index 0) used to represent a queue (i.e., MAXQUEUE = 5). Initially [Figure 4.1.2(a)],

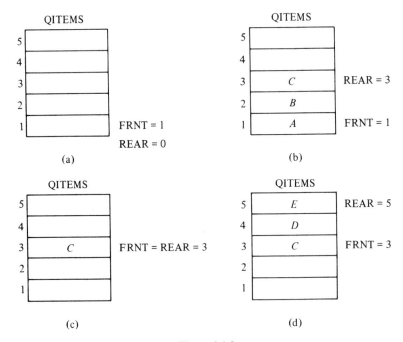

Figure 4.1.2

the queue is empty. In Figure 4.1.2(b) items A, B, and C have been inserted. In Figure 4.1.2(c) two items have been deleted and in Figure 4.1.2(d) two new items, D and E, have been inserted. The value of FRNT is 3 and the value of REAR is 5, so there are only $5 - 3 + 1 = 3$ elements in the queue. Since the array contains five elements, there should be room for the queue to expand without the worry of overflow. However, to insert F into the queue, REAR must be increased by 1 to 6 and QITEMS(6) must be set to the value F. But QITEMS is an array of only five elements, so the insertion cannot be made. It is possible to reach the absurd situation where the queue is empty, yet no new element can be inserted (see if you can come up with a sequence of insertions and deletions to reach that situation). Clearly, the array representation as outlined above is unacceptable.

One solution is to modify the *remove* operation so that when an item is deleted, the entire queue is shifted to the beginning of the array. The operation $x = remove(q)$ would then be implemented (again, ignoring the possibility of underflow) by

```
2000   X = QITEMS(1)
2010   FOR I = 1 TO REAR - 1
2020       QITEMS(I) = QITEMS(I + 1)
2030   NEXT I
2040   REAR = REAR - 1
```

The variable FRNT need no longer be specified as part of a queue, since the first element of the array is always at the front of the queue. The empty queue is represented by the queue in which REAR equals zero. Figure 4.1.3 shows the queue of Figure 4.1.2 under this new representation.

This method, however, is too inefficient to be satisfactory. Each deletion involves moving every remaining element of the queue. If a queue contains 500 or 1000 elements, this is clearly too high a price to pay. Further, the operation of removing an element from a queue logically involves manipulation of only one element—the one currently at the front of the queue. The implementation of that operation should reflect this and should not involve a host of extraneous operations. For a somewhat more efficient alternative, see Exercise 3.

Another solution is to treat the array that holds the queue as a circle rather than as a straight line. That is, we imagine the first element of the array as immediately following its last element. This implies that even if the last element is occupied, a new value can be inserted behind it in the first element of the array as long as that first element is empty.

Let us look at an example. Assume that a queue contains three items in positions 3, 4, and 5 of a five-element array. This is the situation of Figure 4.1.2(d), reproduced as Figure 4.1.4(a). Although the array is not full, the last element of the array is occupied. If an attempt is now made to insert item F into the queue, it can be placed in position 1 of the array, as shown in Figure 4.1.4(b). The first item of the queue is in QITEMS(3), which is followed in the

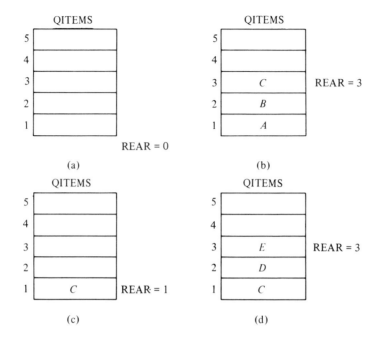

Figure 4.1.3

queue by QITEMS(4), QITEMS(5), and QITEMS(1). Figure 4.1.4(c), (d), and (e) show the status of the queue as the first two items, C and D, are deleted, then G is inserted, and finally E is deleted.

Unfortunately, it is difficult under this representation to determine when the queue is empty. The condition REAR < FRNT is no longer valid as a test for the empty queue since Figure 4.1.4(b), (c) and (d) all illustrate situations in which the condition is true, yet the queue is not empty.

One way of solving this problem is to establish the convention that the value of FRNT is the index of the array element immediately preceding the first element of the queue rather than the index of the first element itself. Thus, since REAR contains the index of the last element of the queue, the condition FRNT = REAR implies that the queue is empty.

A queue of numbers may therefore be declared and initialized by

```
10   MAXQUEUE = 100
20   DIM QITEMS(MAXQUEUE)
30   FRNT = MAXQUEUE
40   REAR = MAXQUEUE
```

Note that FRNT and REAR are initialized to the last index of the array, rather than 0 or 1, because the last element of the array immediately precedes the first one within the queue under this representation. Since REAR = FRNT, the queue is initially empty.

The *empty* subroutine may be coded as

```
1000   'subroutine empty
1010   'inputs: FRNT, REAR
1020   'outputs: EMPTY
1030   'locals: none
1040   IF FRNT = REAR THEN EMPTY = TRUE ELSE EMPTY = FALSE
1050   RETURN
1060   'endsub
```

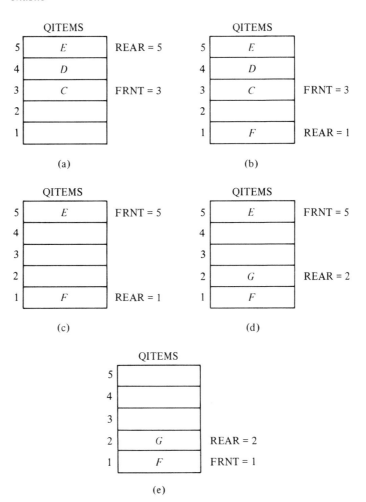

Figure 4.1.4

The operation *remove(q)* may be coded as

```
2000  'subroutine remove
2010  'inputs: FRNT, MAXQUEUE, QITEMS
2020  'outputs: RMOVE
2030  'locals: EMPTY
2040  GOSUB 1000: 'subroutine empty sets the variable EMPTY
2050  IF EMPTY = TRUE THEN PRINT "QUEUE UNDERFLOW": STOP
2060  IF FRNT = MAXQUEUE THEN FRNT = 1 ELSE FRNT = FRNT + 1
2070  RMOVE = QITEMS(FRNT)
2080  RETURN
2090  'endsub
```

Note that FRNT must be updated before an element is extracted.

Of course, often an underflow condition is meaningful and serves as a signal for a new phase of processing. We may wish to use a subroutine *rmovandtest* at statement number 9000, which would be invoked by

```
100 GOSUB 9000:              'subroutine removeandtest sets the
                             'variables RMOVE and UND
110 IF UND = TRUE THEN       'take corrective action
              ELSE           'RMOVE is the element removed
                             'from the queue
```

removeandtest sets UND to FALSE and RMOVE to the element removed from the queue if the queue is nonempty and sets UND to TRUE if underflow occurs. The coding of the routine is left to the reader.

The insert *Operation*

In order to code the *insert* operation, the question of overflow must be considered. Overflow occurs when the entire array is occupied by items of the queue and an attempt is made to insert yet another element into the queue. For example, consider the queue of Figure 4.1.5(a). There are three elements in the queue: C, D, and E in QITEMS(3), QITEMS(4), and QITEMS(5), respectively. Since the last item of the queue occupies QITEMS(5), REAR equals 5. Since the first element of the queue is in QITEMS(3), FRNT equals 2. In Figure 4.1.5(b) and (c), items F and G are inserted into the queue and the value of REAR is changed accordingly. At that point, the array is full and an attempt to perform any more insertions will cause an overflow. But this is indicated by the fact that FRNT = REAR, which is precisely the indication for underflow. It seems that there is no way to distinguish between the empty queue and the full queue under this implementation. Such a situation is clearly unsatisfactory.

One solution is to sacrifice one element of the array and to allow a queue to

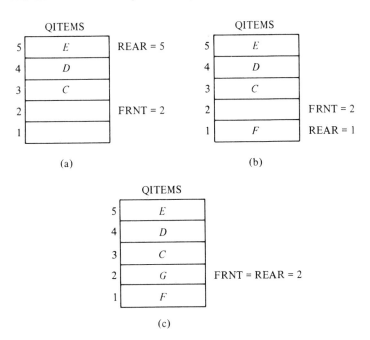

Figure 4.1.5

grow only as large as one less than the size of the array. Thus, if an array of 100 elements is declared as a queue, the queue may have up to 99 members. An attempt to insert a 100th element into the queue will result in an overflow. The *insert* routine may then be written as follows:

```
3000    'subroutine insert
3010    'inputs: FRNT, MAXQUEUE, QITEMS, REAR, X
3020    'outputs: QITEMS, REAR
3030    'locals: none
3040    'make room for new element
3050    IF REAR = MAXQUEUE THEN REAR = 1 ELSE REAR = REAR + 1
3060    'check for overflow
3070    IF REAR = FRNT THEN PRINT "QUEUE OVERFLOW": STOP
3080    QITEMS(REAR) = X
3090    RETURN
3100    'endsub
```

The test for overflow in *insert* occurs after REAR has been adjusted, whereas the test for underflow in *remove* occurs immediately upon entering the routine, before FRNT is updated.

An Alternative BASIC Representation

An alternative technique for representing a queue in BASIC is to declare arrays QUEUE and QITEMS and initialize variables FRNT, REAR, and the array QUEUE as follows:

```
10  MAXQUEUE = 100
20  DIM QITEMS(MAXQUEUE)
30  DIM QUEUE(2)
40      FRNT = 1
50      REAR = 2
60  QUEUE(FRNT) = MAXQUEUE
70  QUEUE(REAR) = MAXQUEUE
```

Under this representation, QUEUE(FRNT) and QUEUE(REAR), rather than FRNT and REAR, point to the front and rear of the queue. The advantage of this representation is that it allows both queue pointers to be contained in a single entity (QUEUE). However, the *insert* and *remove* routines become somewhat more cumbersome.

EXERCISES

1. Write the subroutine *removeandtest*, which sets UND to FALSE and X to the item removed from a nonempty queue, and sets UND to TRUE if the queue is empty.

2. What set of conditions is necessary and sufficient for a sequence of *insert* and *remove* operations on a single empty queue to leave the queue empty without causing underflow? What set of conditions is necessary and sufficient for such a sequence to leave a nonempty queue unchanged?

3. If an array is not considered circular, the text suggests that each *remove* operation must shift down every remaining element of a queue. An alternative method is to postpone shifting until REAR equals the last index of the array. When that situation occurs and an attempt is made to insert an element into the queue, the entire queue is shifted down so that the first element of the queue is in the first position of the array. What are the advantages of this method over performing a shift at each *remove* operation? What are the disadvantages? Rewrite the routines *remove, insert*, and *empty* using this method.

4. Show how a sequence of insertions and removals from a queue represented by a linear array can cause an overflow to occur upon an attempt to insert an element into an empty queue.

5. We can avoid sacrificing one element of a queue if a variable EMPTY is added to the queue representation. Show how this can be done and rewrite the queue manipulation routines under that representation.

6. How would you implement a queue of stacks? a stack of queues? a queue of queues? Write routines to implement the appropriate operations for each of these data structures.

7. Show how to implement a queue of integers in BASIC (assuming that arrays start at index 0) by using an array QITEMS where QITEMS(0) is used to indicate the front of the queue, QITEMS(MAXQUEUE + 1) is used to indicate its rear, and QITEMS(1) through QITEMS(MAXQUEUE) are used to contain the queue elements. Show how to initialize such an array to represent the empty queue, and write routines *remove, insert*, and *empty* for such an implementation.

8. Show how to implement a queue in BASIC in which each item consists of three integers.

9. A *deque* is an ordered set of items from which items may be deleted at either end and into which items may be inserted at either end. Call the two ends of a deque *left* and *right*. How can a deque be represented as a BASIC array? Write four BASIC routines,

remvleft, remvright, insrtleft, insrtright

to remove and insert elements at the left and right ends of a deque. Make sure that the routines work properly for the empty deque and that they detect overflow and underflow.

10. Define an *input-restricted deque* as a deque (see Exercise 9) for which only the operations *remvleft, remvright*, and *insrtleft* are valid, and an *output-restricted deque* as a deque for which only the operations *remvleft, insrtleft*, and *insrtright* are valid. Show how each of these can be used to represent both a stack and a queue.

11. The Scratchemup Parking Garage contains a single lane which can hold up to 10 cars. Cars arrive at the south end of the garage and leave from the north end. If a customer arrives to pick up a car that is not the northernmost, all cars to the north of the customer's car are moved out, his or her car is driven out, and the other cars are restored in the order they were in originally. Whenever a car leaves, all cars to the south are moved forward so that at all times all the empty spaces are in the southern part of the garage.

    Write a program that reads a group of DATA lines. Each line contains an "A" for arrival or a "D" for departure, and a license plate number. Cars are assumed to arrive and depart in the order specified by the input. The program should print a message each time a car arrives or departs. When a car arrives, the message should specify whether or not there is room for the car in the garage. If there is no room for a car, the car waits until there is room or until a departure card is read for the car. When room becomes available, another message should be printed. When a car departs, the message should include the number of times the car was moved within the garage (including the departure itself but not the arrival; this number is 0 if the car departs from the waiting line).

12. The ABC Widget Store receives shipments of widgets at various costs. The store's policy is to charge a 20% markup and to sell widgets that were received earlier be-

fore widgets that were received later (a FIFO policy). Thus widgets from the first shipment are sold at 20% above their cost; when there are no more first-shipment widgets left, widgets from the second shipment are sold at 20% above their cost; and so on. Write a program that reads transactions of two types: sales transactions and receipt transactions. A sales transaction contains an "S" and a quantity, and represents a sale of that quantity of widgets. A receipt transaction contains an "R", a quantity, and a cost per widget, and represents a receipt of a quantity of widgets at a given cost per widget. After a receipt transaction is read, print the transaction. After a sales transaction, print the transaction and then print a message stating the price at which the widgets were sold. For example, if 200 widgets were sold and there were 50 widgets from a shipment at $1.00, 100 widgets from a shipment at $1.10, and 50 widgets from a shipment at $1.25, print (recall the 20% markup)

200	WIDGETS	SOLD			
50	AT	$ 1.20	PRICE	$	60.00
100	AT	$ 1.32	PRICE	$	132.00
50	AT	$ 1.50	PRICE	$	75.00
			TOTAL PRICE	$	267.00

If there is an insufficient number of widgets in stock to fill an order, sell as many as are available and then print

REMAINDER OF XXX WIDGETS ARE NOT AVAILABLE.

2. LINKED LISTS

What are the drawbacks of using sequential storage to represent stacks and queues? One major drawback is that a fixed amount of storage remains allocated to the stack or queue even when the structure is actually using a smaller amount or possibly no storage at all. Further, no more than that fixed amount of storage may be allocated, thus introducing the possibility of overflow.

Assume that a program uses two stacks implemented in two separate arrays, S1ITEMS and S2ITEMS. Further, assume that each of these arrays has 100 elements. Then despite the fact that 200 elements are available for the two stacks, neither can grow beyond 100 items. Even if the first stack contains only 25 items, the second cannot contain more than 100. One solution to this problem is to allocate a single array SITEMS of 200 elements. The first stack will occupy SITEMS(1), SITEMS(2), . . . , SITEMS(T1), while the second stack will be allocated from the other end of the array, occupying SITEMS(200), SITEMS(199), . . . , SITEMS(T2) (where T1 < T2). Thus, when one of the stacks is not occupying storage, the other stack may make use of that storage. Of course, two distinct sets of *pop, push,* and *empty* routines are necessary for the two stacks since one grows by increasing T1 while the other grows by decreasing T2.

Unfortunately, while such a scheme allows two stacks to share a common

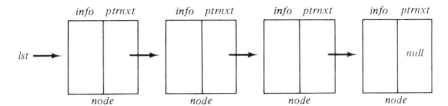

Figure 4.2.1 A linear linked list.

area, no such simple solution exists for three or more stacks or even for two queues. Instead, one must keep track of the tops and bottoms (or fronts and rears) of all the structures sharing a single large array. Each time that the growth of one structure is about to impinge on the storage currently being used by another, all the structures must be shifted within the single array to allow for the growth.

In a sequential representation, the items of a stack or queue are implicitly ordered by the sequential order of storage. Thus, if QITEMS(X) represents an element of a queue, the next element will be QITEMS(X + 1) [or QITEMS(1) if X = MAXQUEUE]. Suppose that the items of a stack or a queue were explicitly ordered; that is, each item contains within itself the address of the next item. Such an explicit ordering gives rise to a data structure pictured in Figure 4.2.1, which is known as a *linear linked list.* Each item in the list is called a *node* and contains two fields, an *information* field and a *next address* field. The information field holds the actual element on the list. The next address field contains the address of the next node in the list. Such an address, which is used to access a particular node, is known as a *pointer.* The entire linked list is accessed from an external pointer *lst* which points to (contains the address of) the first node in the list. (By an "external" pointer, we mean one that is not included within a node. Rather, its value can be accessed directly by referencing a variable.) The next address field of the last node in the list contains a special value, known as *null,* which is not a valid address. This *null pointer* is used to signal the end of a list.

The list with no nodes on it is called the *empty list* or the *null list.* The value of the external pointer *lst* to such a list is the null pointer. Thus a list can be initialized to the empty list by the operation *lst = null.*

We now introduce some notation for use in algorithms (but not in BASIC programs). If *p* is a pointer to a node, *node(p)* refers to the node pointed to by *p, info(p)* refers to the information portion of that node, and *ptrnxt(p)* refers to the next address portion and is therefore a pointer. Thus, if *ptrnxt(p)* is not *null, info(ptrnxt(p))* refers to the information portion of the node that follows *node(p)* in the list.

Inserting and Removing Nodes from a List

A list is a dynamic data structure. The number of nodes on a list may vary dramatically as elements are inserted and removed. The dynamic nature of a list may be contrasted with the static nature of an array whose size remains constant. For example, suppose that we are given a list of integers, as illustrated in Figure 4.2.2(a) and we desire to insert the integer 6 at the front of that list. That is, we wish to change the list so that it appears as in Figure 4.2.2(f).

The first step is to obtain a node in which to house the additional integer. If a list is to grow and shrink, there must be some mechanism for obtaining empty nodes to be inserted onto the list. Note that, unlike an array, a list does not come with a presupplied set of storage locations into which elements can be placed.

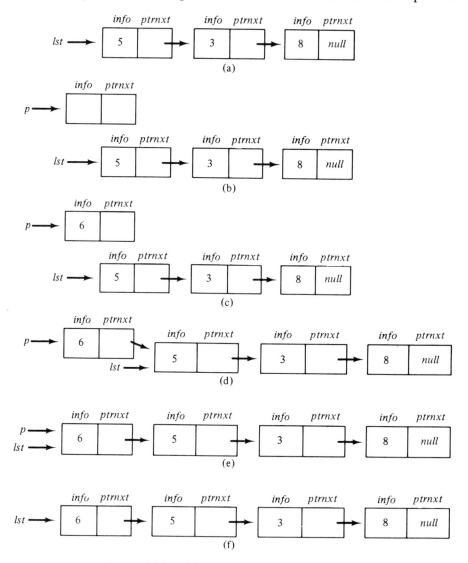

Figure 4.2.2   Adding an element to the front of a list.

Let us assume the existence of a mechanism for obtaining empty nodes. The operation

$$p = getnode$$

obtains an empty node and sets the contents of a variable named p to the address of that node. This means that p is a pointer to this newly allocated node. Figure 4.2.2(b) illustrates the list and the new node after performing the *getnode* operation. The details of how this operation can be implemented will be explained shortly.

The next step is to insert the integer 6 into the *info* portion of the newly allocated node. This is done by the operation

$$info(p) = 6$$

The result of this operation is illustrated in Figure 4.2.2(c).

After setting the *info* portion of *node(p)*, it is necessary to set the *ptrnxt* portion of that node. Since *node(p)* is to be inserted at the front of the list, the node that follows should be the current first node on the list. Since the variable *lst* contains the address of that first node, *node(p)* can be added to the list by performing the operation

$$ptrnxt(p) = lst$$

This operation places the value of *lst* (which is the address of the first node on the list) into the *ptrnxt* field of *node(p)*. Figure 4.2.2(d) illustrates the result of this operation.

At this point, p points to the list with the additional item included. However, since *lst* is the external pointer to the desired list, its value must be modified to the address of the new first node of the list. This can be done by performing the operation

$$lst = p$$

which changes the value of *lst* to the value of p. Figure 4.2.2(e) illustrates the result of this operation. Note that Figure 4.2.2(e) and (f) are identical except that the value of p is not shown in Figure 4.2.2(f). This is because p is used as an auxiliary variable during the process of modifying the list but its value is irrelevant to the status of the list before and after the process. Once the operations above have been performed, the value of p may be changed without affecting the list.

Putting all the steps together, we have an algorithm for inserting the integer 6 onto the front of the list *lst:*

$$p = getnode$$
$$info(p) = 6$$
$$ptrnxt(p) = lst$$
$$lst = p$$

The algorithm can obviously be generalized so that it inserts any object x onto the front of a list *lst* by replacing the operation *info*(p) = 6 with *info*(p) = x. Convince yourself that the algorithm works correctly even if the list is initially empty (*lst* = *null*).

Figure 4.2.3 illustrates the process of removing the first node of a nonempty list and storing the value of its *info* field into a variable x. The initial configuration is shown in Figure 4.2.3(a) and the final configuration is shown in Figure 4.2.3(f). The process itself is almost the exact opposite of the process to add a

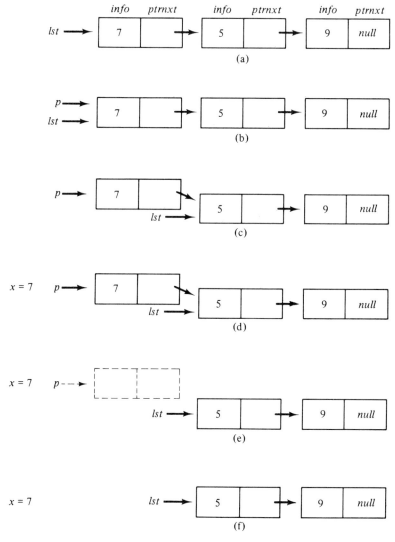

Figure 4.2.3 Removing a node from the front of a list.

node to the front of a list. To obtain Figure 4.2.3(d) from Figure 4.2.3(a), the following operations (whose actions should be clear) are performed:

$$p = lst \qquad \text{[Figure 4.2.3(b)]}$$
$$lst = ptrnxt(p) \qquad \text{[Figure 4.2.3(c)]}$$
$$x = info(p) \qquad \text{[Figure 4.2.3(d)]}$$

At this point, the algorithm has accomplished what it was supposed to do: The first node has been removed from lst and x has been set to the desired value. However, the algorithm is not yet complete. In Figure 4.2.3(d), p still points to the node that was formerly first on the list. However, that node is currently useless because it is no longer on the list and its information has been stored in x. [The node is not considered to be on the list despite the fact that $ptrnxt(p)$ points to a node on the list, since there is no way to reach $node(p)$ from the external pointer lst.] The variable p was used as an auxiliary variable during the process of removing the first node from the list. The starting and ending configurations of the list make no reference to p. It is therefore reasonable to expect that p will be used for some other purpose in a short while after this operation has been performed. But once the value of p is changed, there is no way to access the node at all, since neither an external pointer nor a $ptrnxt$ field contains its address. Therefore, the node is currently useless and cannot be reused; yet it is taking up valuable storage.

It would also be desirable to have some mechanism for making $node(p)$ available for reuse even if the value of the pointer p is changed. The operation that does this is

$$freenode(p) \qquad \text{[Figure 4.2.3(e)]}$$

Once this operation has been performed, it becomes illegal to reference $node(p)$ since the node is no longer allocated. Since the value of p is a pointer to a node that has been freed, any reference to that value is also illegal.

However, the node might be reallocated and a pointer to it reassigned to p by the operation $p = getnode$. Note that we say that the node "might be" reallocated, since the $getnode$ operation returns a pointer to some newly allocated node. There is no guarantee that this new node is the same as the one that has just been freed.

Another way of thinking of $getnode$ and $freenode$ is that $getnode$ creates a new node, while $freenode$ destroys a node. Under this view, nodes are not used and reused but are rather created and destroyed. We shall say more about the two operations $getnode$ and $freenode$ and about the concepts they represent in a moment, but first we make the following interesting observation.

Linked Implementation of Stacks

The operation of adding an element to the front of a linked list is quite similar to that of pushing an element onto a stack. In both cases, a new item is added as the only immediately accessible item in a collection. A stack can be accessed only through its top element and a list can be accessed only from the pointer to its first element. Similarly, the operation of removing the first element from a linked list is analogous to popping a stack. In both cases, the only immediately accessible item of a collection is removed from that collection, and the next item becomes immediately accessible.

Thus we have discovered another way of implementing a stack. A stack may be represented by a linear linked list. The first node of the list is the top of the stack. If an external pointer *stack* points to such a linked list, the operation *push(stack,x)* may be implemented by

$$p = getnode$$
$$info(p) = x$$
$$ptrnxt(p) = stack$$
$$stack = p$$

The operation *empty(stack)* is merely a test as to whether *stack* equals *null*. The operation $x = pop(stack)$ is the operation of removing the first node from a non-empty list and signaling underflow if the list is empty:

if *empty(stack)* = *true*
    then print ''underflow''
        stop
endif
$p = stack$
$stack = ptrnxt(p)$
$x = info(p)$
freenode(p)

Figure 4.2.4(a) illustrates a stack implemented as a linked list, and Figure 4.2.4(b) illustrates the same stack after another element has been pushed onto it.

The getnode *and* freenode *Operations*

We now return to a discussion of the *getnode* and *freenode* operations. In an abstract, idealized world it is possible to postulate an infinite number of unused nodes available for use by abstract algorithms. The *getnode* operation finds one such node and makes it available to the algorithm. Alternatively, the *getnode* operation may be regarded as a machine that manufactures nodes and never breaks down. Thus each time that *getnode* is invoked, it presents its caller with a brand new node, different from all the nodes previously in use.

In such an ideal world, the *freenode* operation would be unnecessary to make a node available for reuse. Why use an old secondhand node when a simple call to *getnode* can produce a new, never-before-used node? The only harm that an unused node can do is to reduce the number of nodes which can possibly be

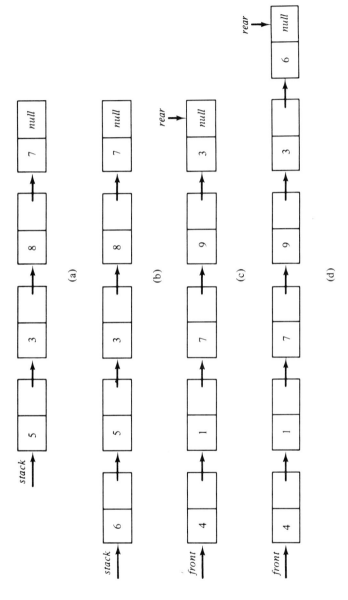

Figure 4.2.4 A stack and a queue as linked lists.

used, but if an infinite supply of nodes is available, such a reduction is meaningless. Therefore, there is never a reason to reuse a node.

Unfortunately, we live in a real world. Computers do not have an infinite amount of storage and cannot manufacture more storage for immediate utilization (at least, not yet). Therefore, there are a finite number of nodes available and it is impossible to use more than that number at any given instant. If it is desired to use more than that number over a given period of time, some nodes must be reused. The function of *freenode* is to make a node that is no longer being used in its current context available for reuse in a different context.

We might think of a finite pool of empty nodes existing initially. This pool cannot be accessed by the programmer except through the *getnode* and *freenode* operations. *getnode* removes a node from the pool, while *freenode* returns a node to the pool. Since any unused node is as good as any other, it makes no difference which node is retrieved by *getnode* or where within the pool a node is placed by *freenode*.

The most natural form for this pool to take is that of a linked list acting as a stack. The list is linked together by the *ptrnxt* field in each node. The *getnode* operation removes the first node from this list and makes it available for use. The *freenode* operation adds a node to the front of the list, making it available for reallocation by the next *getnode*. The list of available nodes is called the **available list**.

What happens when the available list is empty? This means that all nodes are currently in use and it is impossible to allocate any additional nodes. If a program calls on *getnode* when the available list is empty, the amount of storage assigned for that program's data structures is too small. Therefore, overflow occurs. This is similar to the situation of a stack implemented in an array overflowing the array bounds.

As long as data structures are abstract, theoretical concepts in a world of infinite space, there is no possibility of overflow. It is only when they are implemented as real objects in a finite area that the possibility of overflow arises.

Let us assume that the external pointer *avail* points to the list of available nodes. Then the operation

$$p = getnode$$

is implemented as follows:

$$
\begin{aligned}
&\textbf{\textit{if}}\ avail\ =\ null \\
&\quad \textbf{\textit{then print}}\ \text{``overflow''} \\
&\qquad\quad \textbf{\textit{stop}} \\
&\textbf{\textit{endif}} \\
&p\ =\ avail \\
&avail\ =\ ptrnxt(avail)
\end{aligned}
$$

Since the possibility of overflow is accounted for in the *getnode* operation, it need not be mentioned in the list implementation of *push*. If a stack is about to overflow all available nodes, the statement $p = getnode$ within the *push* operation will result in an overflow.

The implementation of *freenode*(p) is straightforward:

$$ptrnxt(p) = avail$$
$$avail = p$$

The advantage of the list implementation of stacks is that all the stacks being used by a program can share the same available list. When any stack needs a node, it can obtain it from the single available list. When any stack no longer needs a node, it returns the node to that same available list. As long as the total amount of space needed by all the stacks at any one time is less than the amount of space initially available to them all, each stack is able to grow and shrink to any size. No space has been preallocated to any single stack and no stack is using space which it does not need. Furthermore, other data structures such as queues may also share the same set of nodes.

Linked Implementation of Queues

Let us now examine how to represent a queue as a linked list. Recall that items are deleted from the front of a queue and inserted at the rear. Let the list pointer that points to the first element of a list represent the front of the queue. Another pointer to the last element of the list represents the rear of the queue, as shown in Figure 4.2.4(c). Figure 4.2.4(d) illustrates the same queue after a new item has been inserted.

If we let a queue *queue* consist of a list and two pointers, *frnt* and *rear,* the operations *empty*(*queue*) and $x = remove(queue)$ are completely analogous to *empty*(*stack*) and $x = pop(stack)$ with the pointer *frnt* replacing *stack*. However, special attention must be paid to the case in which the last element is removed from a queue. In this case, *rear* must also be set to *null* since in an empty queue both *frnt* and *rear* are *null*. The operation $x = remove(queue)$ may therefore be implemented as follows:

> **if** *empty*(*queue*) = *true*
>   **then print** ''queue underflow''
>   **stop**
> **endif**
> $p = frnt$
> $x = info(p)$
> $frnt = ptrnxt(p)$
> **if** $frnt = null$
>   **then** $rear = null$
> **endif**
> *freenode*(p)

The operation *insert(queue,x)* can be implemented by

$$p = getnode$$
$$info(p) = x$$
$$ptrnxt(p) = null$$
if *rear = null*
   then *frnt = p*
   else *ptrnxt(rear) = p*
endif
$$rear = p$$

What are the disadvantages of representing a stack or queue by a linked list? Clearly, a node in a linked list occupies more storage than a corresponding element in an array since two pieces of information are necessary in a list node for each item (*info* and *ptrnxt*), whereas only one piece of information is needed in the array implementation. However, the space used for a list node is usually not twice the space used by an array element since the elements in such a list usually consist of records with many subfields. For example, if each element on a stack were a record occupying 10 words, the addition of an eleventh word to contain a pointer increases the space requirement by only 10%. Further, in many machine languages it is possible to compress information and a pointer into a single word so that there is no space degradation.

Another disadvantage is the additional time that must be spent in managing the available list. Each addition and deletion of an element from a stack or a queue involves a corresponding deletion or addition to the available list.

The advantage of using linked lists is that all the stacks and queues of a program have access to the same available list of nodes. Nodes that are unused by one stack may be used by another, as long as the total number of nodes in use at any one time is not greater than the total number of nodes available.

The Linked List as a Data Structure

Linked lists are important not only as a means of implementing stacks and queues, but as data structures in their own right. An item is accessed in a linked list by traversing the list from its beginning. An array implementation allows access to the nth item in a group using a single operation, while a list implementation requires n operations. It is necessary to pass through each of the first $n - 1$ elements before reaching the nth element because there is no relation between the memory location occupied by an element of a list and its position within that list.

The advantage of a list over an array occurs when it is necessary to insert or delete an element in the middle of a group of other elements. For example, suppose that we wish to insert an element x between the third and fourth elements in an array of size 10 which currently contains seven items. Items 7 through 4 must first be moved one slot and the new element inserted in the newly available position 4. This process is illustrated by Figure 4.2.5(a). In this case, insertion of one item involves moving four items in addition to the insertion itself. If the array contained 500 or 1000 elements, a correspondingly larger number of elements would have to be moved. Similarly, to delete an element from an array, all the elements past the element deleted must be moved one position.

On the other hand, if the items are stored as a list, then, if p is a pointer to a given element of the list, inserting a new element after $node(p)$ involves allocating a node, inserting the information, and adjusting two pointers. The amount of work required is independent of the size of the list. This is illustrated in Figure 4.2.5(b).

Let $insafter(p,x)$ denote the operation of inserting an item x into a list following a node pointed to by p. This operation may be implemented as follows:

$$q \; = \; getnode$$
$$info(q) \; = \; x$$
$$ptrnxt(q) \; = \; ptrnxt(p)$$
$$ptrnxt(p) \; = \; q$$

An item can be inserted only after a given node, not before the node. This is because there is no way to proceed from a given node to its predecessor in a linear list without traversing the list from its beginning. To insert an item before $node(p)$, the $ptrnxt$ field of its predecessor must be changed to point to a newly allocated node. But, given p, there is no way to find that predecessor. However, it is possible to achieve the effect of inserting an element before a given node in a

(a)   **Figure 4.2.5**

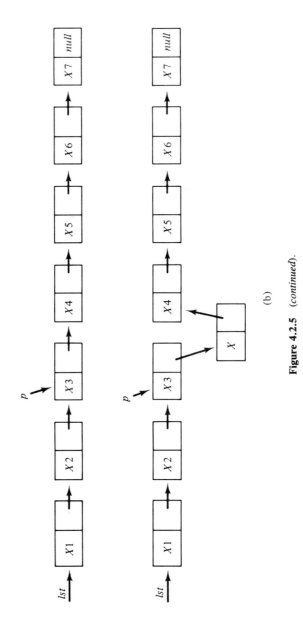

Figure 4.2.5 *(continued).*

linked list by inserting the element after the node and then switching the contents of the given node and its newly created successor. We leave the details for the reader.

Similarly, to delete a node from a linear list it is not sufficient to be given a pointer to that node. This is because the *ptrnxt* field of the node's predecessor must be changed to point to the node's successor and there is no direct way of reaching the predecessor of a given node. The best that can be done is to delete a node following a given node. (However, it is possible to save the contents of the following node, delete the following node, and then replace the contents of the given node with the information saved. This achieves the effect of deleting a given node.) Let *delafter(p,x)* denote the operation of deleting the node following *node(p)* and assigning its contents to the variable *x*. This operation may be implemented as follows:

$$q = ptrnxt(p)$$
$$x = info(q)$$
$$ptrnxt(p) = ptrnxt(q)$$
$$freenode(q)$$

The freed node is placed back onto the available list so that it may be reused in the future.

Examples of List Operations

We illustrate these two operations as well as the *push* and *pop* operations for lists with some simple examples. The first example is to delete all occurrences of the number 4 from a list *lst*. The list is traversed in a search for nodes that contain 4 in their *info* fields. Each such node must be deleted from the list. But to delete a node from a list, its predecessor must be known. For this reason, two pointers, *p* and *q*, are used. *p* is used to traverse the list and *q* always points to the predecessor of *p*. The algorithm makes use of the *pop* operation to remove nodes from the beginning of the list, and the *delafter* operation to remove nodes from the middle of the list.

```
q = null
p = lst
while p <> null do
        if info(p) = 4
            then if q = null
                    then 'remove first node of lst
                        x = pop(lst)
                        freenode(p)
                        p = lst
                    else 'advance p and delete the node following node(q)
                        p = ptrnxt(p)
                        delafter(q,x)
                endif
```

        else 'continue traversing the list
          'advance p and q
          $q = p$
          $p = ptrnxt(p)$
    endif
  endwhile

The practice of using two pointers, one following the other, is a common one in working with lists. This technique is used in the next example as well. Assume that a list *lst* is ordered so that smaller items precede larger ones. It is desired to insert an item x into this list in its proper position. The algorithm to do this makes use of the *push* operation to add a node to the front of the list and the *insafter* operation to add a node in the middle of the list:

  $q = null$
  $p = lst$
  while $(p <> null)$ **and** $(x > info(p))$ **do**
    $q = p$
    $p = ptrnxt(p)$
  endwhile
  'at this point, a node containing x must be inserted
  if $q = null$
    then 'insert x at the head of the list
      $push(lst,x)$
    else $insafter(q,x)$
  endif

This is a very common operation and will be denoted by *place(lst,x)*.

Lists in BASIC

How can linear lists be represented in BASIC? Since a list is simply a collection of nodes, an array of nodes immediately suggests itself. However, the nodes cannot be ordered by the array ordering; each node must contain within itself a pointer to its successor. However, BASIC has no facilities for referring to a single node with two fields (let alone an array of such nodes). Therefore, we declare two arrays, INFO and PTRNXT, as follows:

    10 DIM INFO(500)
    20 DIM PTRNXT(500)

In this scheme, a pointer to a node is an integer between 1 and 500. The null pointer is represented by the integer 0. We use the notation "*node*(P)," where P is a BASIC variable representing a pointer, to represent the collection of {IN-FO(P), PTRNXT(P)}. This INFO(P) represents the information contained in *node*(P) and PTRNXT(P) represents the pointer to the node following *node*(P) (or 0). Since BASIC cannot manipulate entire nodes, we cannot use the notation "NODE(P)" in programs. It is merely useful to refer to *node*(P) in algorithms or discussions. It should be noted that although INFO and PTRNXT are independent BASIC variables, it is the programmer's responsibility to preserve their logical relationship in any programs that use linked lists.

Let the variable LST represent a pointer to a list. Suppose that LST has the value 7. Then INFO(7) is the first data item on the list. The second node of the list is given by PTRNXT(7). Suppose that PTRNXT(7) equals 385. Then INFO(385) is the second data item on the list and PTRNXT(385) points to the third node. The nodes of a list may be scattered throughout the array in any arbitrary order. Each node carries within itself the address of its successor. The PTRNXT field of the last node in the list contains 0, which is the null pointer. There is no relation between the contents of a node and the pointer to it. The pointer P to a node merely specifies which node is being referenced; it is INFO(P) that represents the information contained within that node.

Figure 4.2.6 illustrates a portion of the arrays INFO and PTRNXT that con-

	INFO	PTRNXT
1	26	0
2	11	10
3	5	16
L4 = 4	1	25
L2 = 5	17	1
6	13	2
7		
8	19	19
9	14	13
10	4	22
11		
L3 = 12	31	8
13	6	3
14		
15		
16	37	24
L1 = 17	3	21
18		
19	32	0
20		
21	7	9
22	15	0
23		
24	12	0
25	18	6
26		
27		

Figure 4.2.6   Arrays of nodes containing four linked lists.

tain four linked lists. The list L1 starts at *node*(17) and contains the integers 3, 7, 14, 6, 5, 37, 12. The nodes that contain these integers in their INFO fields are scattered throughout the array. The corresponding PTRNXT field of each node contains the index within the arrays of the node containing the next element of the list. The last node on the list is *node*(24), which contains the integer 12 in its INFO field and the null pointer (0) in its PTRNXT field to indicate that it is last on the list. Similarly, L2 begins at *node*(5) and contains the integers 17 and 26; L3 begins at *node*(12) and contains the integers 31, 19, and 32; and L4 begins at *node*(4) and contains the integers 1, 18, 13, 11, 4, and 15. The variables L1, L2, L3, and L4 are integers representing external pointers to the four lists. Thus the fact that the variable L2 has the value 5 represents the fact that the list to which it points begins at *node*(5).

Initially, all nodes are unused since no lists have yet been formed. Therefore, they must all be placed on the available list. If the variable AVAIL is used to point to the available list, we may initially organize that list as follows:

```
50   AVAIL = 1
60   FOR I = 1 TO 499
70        PTRNXT(I) = I + 1
80   NEXT I
90   PTRNXT(500) = 0
```

The 500 nodes are initially linked in their natural order, so that PTRNXT(I) points to *node*(I + 1). Thus *node*(1) is the first node on the available list, *node*(2) is the second, and so on; *node*(500) is the last node on the list since PTRNXT(500) equals 0. There is no reason other than convenience for initially ordering the nodes in this fashion. We could just as well have set PTRNXT(1) to 500, PTRNXT(500) to 2, PTRNXT(2) to 499, and so on, until PTRNXT(250) is set to 251 and PTRNXT(251) to 0. The important point is that the ordering is explicit within the nodes themselves and is not implied by some other underlying structure.

When a node is needed for use in a particular list, it is obtained from the available list. Similarly, when a node is no longer necessary, it is returned to the available list. These two operations are implemented by the BASIC routines *getnode* and *freenode*. *getnode* is a function that removes a node from the available list and returns a pointer to it.

```
1000   'subroutine getnode
1010   'inputs: AVAIL, PTRNXT
1020   'outputs: AVAIL, GTNODE
1030   'locals: none
1040   IF AVAIL = 0 THEN PRINT "OVERFLOW": STOP
1050   GTNODE = AVAIL
1060   AVAIL = PTRNXT(AVAIL)
1070   RETURN
1080   'endsub
```

If AVAIL equals 0 when this routine is called, there are no nodes available. This means that the list structures of a particular program have overflowed the available space.

The subroutine *freenode* accepts a pointer *FRNODE* to a node and returns that node to the available list:

```
2000   'subroutine freenode
2010   'inputs: AVAIL, FRNODE
2020   'outputs: AVAIL, PTRNXT
2030   'locals: none
2040   PTRNXT(FRNODE) = AVAIL
2050   AVAIL = FRNODE
2060   RETURN
2070   'endsub
```

For the remaining subroutines in this chapter, we assume that the variables INFO, PTRNXT, and AVAIL have been initialized properly in the program and can therefore be used by any routine. We therefore do not indicate the use of these three variables as explicit inputs or outputs of our list manipulation routines.

The primitive operations for lists are straightforward BASIC versions of the corresponding algorithms. The routine *insafter* accepts a pointer PNTR to a node and an item X as parameters. It first ensures that PNTR is not null and then inserts X into a node following the node pointed to by PNTR.

```
3000   'subroutine insafter
3010   'inputs: PNTR, X
3020   'outputs: none
3030   'locals: GTNODE, Q
3040   IF PNTR = 0 THEN PRINT "VOID INSERTION": RETURN
3050   GOSUB 1000: 'subroutine getnode sets the variable GTNODE
3060   Q = GTNODE
3070   INFO(Q) = X
3080   PTRNXT(Q) = PTRNXT(PNTR)
3090   PTRNXT(PNTR) = Q
3100   RETURN
3110   'endsub
```

The routine *delafter* accepts a pointer PNTR to a node and deletes the following node [i.e., the node pointed to by PTRNXT(PNTR)] and stores its contents in X.

```
4000   'subroutine delafter
4010   'inputs: PNTR
4020   'outputs: X
4030   'locals: FRNODE, Q
```

```
4040    IF PNTR = 0 THEN PRINT "VOID DELETION": RETURN
4050    IF PTRNXT(PNTR) = 0 THEN PRINT "VOID DELETION": RETURN
4060    Q = PTRNXT(PNTR)
4070    X = INFO(Q)
4080    PTRNXT(PNTR) = PTRNXT(Q)
4090    FRNODE = Q
4100    GOSUB 2000: 'subroutine freenode accepts the variable FRNODE
4110    RETURN
4120    'endsub
```

Before calling *insafter* we must be sure that PNTR is not null. Before calling *delafter* we must be sure that neither PNTR nor PTRNXT(PNTR) is null.

Queues as Lists in BASIC

We now present BASIC routines for manipulating a queue represented as a linear list, leaving routines for manipulating a stack as exercises for the reader. A queue may be represented as follows:

```
10    DIM QUEUE(2)
20    FRNT = 1
30    REAR = 2
```

QUEUE(FRNT) and QUEUE(REAR) are pointers to the first and last nodes of a queue represented as a list. (This representation is similar to the alternative method for representing a queue mentioned at the end of the preceding section.) In an empty queue, both QUEUE(FRNT) and QUEUE(REAR) equal 0, the null pointer. The *empty* subroutine need check only one of these pointers since in a nonempty queue, neither QUEUE(FRNT) nor QUEUE(REAR) will be 0. (Because the values of FRNT and REAR remain constant throughout the queue manipulation routines, we do not list them explicitly among the inputs.)

```
5000    'subroutine empty
5010    'inputs: QUEUE
5020    'outputs: EMPTY
5030    'locals: none
5040    IF QUEUE(FRNT) = 0 THEN EMPTY = TRUE ELSE EMPTY = FALSE
5050    RETURN
5060    'endsub
```

The routine to insert an element into a queue may be written as follows:

```
6000    'subroutine insert
6010    'inputs: QUEUE, X
6020    'outputs: QUEUE
6030    'locals: GTNODE, P
```

```
6040   GOSUB 1000: 'subroutine getnode sets the variable GTNODE
6050   P = GTNODE
6060   INFO(P) = X
6070   PTRNXT(P) = 0
6080   IF QUEUE(REAR) = 0 THEN QUEUE(FRNT) = P
                              ELSE PTRNXT(QUEUE(REAR)) = P
6090   QUEUE(REAR) = P
6100   RETURN
6110   'endsub
```

The function *remove*, which deletes the first element from a queue and returns its value, may be written as follows. (Note that we cannot use the variable FRNODE for the input of the *freenode* subroutine since FRNODE and FRNT will be treated as the same variable in some versions of BASIC. For this reason we use the variable ZFRNODE as the input variable to the *freenode* subroutine.)

```
7000   'subroutine remove
7010   'inputs: QUEUE
7020   'outputs: QUEUE, RMOVE
7030   'locals: P, ZFRNODE
7040   GOSUB 5000: 'subroutine empty sets the variable EMPTY
7050   IF EMPTY = TRUE THEN PRINT "QUEUE UNDERFLOW": STOP
7060   P = QUEUE(FRNT)
7070   RMOVE = INFO(P)
7080   QUEUE(FRNT) = PTRNXT(P)
7090   IF QUEUE(FRNT) = 0 THEN QUEUE(REAR) = 0
7100   ZFRNODE = P
7110   GOSUB 2000: 'subroutine freenode accepts the variable ZFRNODE
7120   RETURN
7130   'endsub
```

Example of a List Operation in BASIC

Let us look at a somewhat more complex list operation implemented in BASIC. We have defined the operation *place(lst,x)*, where *lst* points to an ordered linear list and *x* is an element to be inserted into its proper position within the list. Ordinarily, the algorithm for performing that operation could be translated directly into BASIC. However, that algorithm contains the line

$$\textbf{while } (p <> null) \textbf{ and } (x > info(p)) \textbf{ do}$$

If P is equal to 0 (which is the null pointer under this BASIC implementation of lists), then INFO(P) is undefined (under those versions of BASIC in which arrays do not start with an index of 0) or has not been initialized explicitly (under those versions of BASIC that do) and a reference to INFO(0) should be avoided. Thus we want to avoid the evaluation of the second condition in the **while** statement in the case that P equals 0. We assume that we have already implemented the stack operation *push* at statement 9000, which accepts a list pointer STACK and an element X. The code to implement the *place* operation is as follows:

```
8000   'subroutine place
8010   'inputs: LST, X
8020   'outputs: LST
8030   'locals: P, Q
8040   P = LST
8050   Q = 0
8060   'search section
8070   IF P = 0 THEN GOTO 8130
8080   IF X < = INFO(P) THEN GOTO 8130
8090       'else advance the pointers P and Q
8100       Q = P
8110       P = PTRNXT(P)
8120   GOTO 8070
8130   'insertion section
8140   'if Q = 0 then subroutine push inserts X at the head of the list
       '          else subroutine insafter inserts X following node(Q)
8150   IF Q = 0 THEN STACK = LST: GOSUB 9000: LST = STACK
             ELSE PNTR = Q: GOSUB 3000
8160   RETURN
8170   'endsub
```

Noninteger Lists

Of course, a node on a list need not contain an integer. For example, to represent a stack of character strings by a linked list, nodes containing character strings in their INFO fields are needed. Such nodes could be declared by

```
10   DEFSTR I
20   DIM INFO(500)
30   DIM PTRNXT(500)
```

A particular application may call for nodes containing more than one item of information. For example, each student node in a list of students may contain the following information: the student's name, college identification number, address, grade-point index, major, and so on. Nodes for such an application may be declared as follows:

```
10   DEFSTR A, I, M, S
20   DIM STUDENT(500)
```

```
30   DIM ID(500)
40   DIM ADDRESS(500)
50   DIM GPINDX(500)
60   DIM MAJR(500)
70   DIM PTRNXT(500)
```

The arrays STUDENT, ID, ADDRESS, GPINDX, and MAJR make up the "info" portions of the list nodes. These arrays, together with the array PTRNXT, represent the complete set of nodes. A separate set of BASIC routines must be written to manipulate lists containing each type of node.

Header Nodes

Sometimes it is desirable to keep an extra node at the front of a list. Such a node does not represent an item in the list and is called a *header node* or a *list header*. The INFO portion of such a header node might be unused, as illustrated in Figure 4.2.7(a). More often, the INFO portion of such a node could be used to keep global information about the entire list. For example, Figure 4.2.7(b) illustrates a list in which the INFO portion of the header node contains the number of nodes (not including the header) in the list. In such a data structure more work is needed to add or delete an item from the list since the count in the header node must be adjusted properly. However, the number of items in the list may be obtained directly from the header node so that the entire list need not be traversed.

Another example of the use of header nodes is the following. Suppose that a factory assembles machinery out of smaller units. A particular machine (inventory number $A746$) might be composed of a number of different parts (numbers $B841$, $K321$, $A087$, $J492$, $G593$). This assembly could be represented by a list such as the one illustrated in Figure 4.2.7(c), where each item on the list represents a component and where the header node represents the entire assembly.

The empty list would no longer be represented by the null pointer, but rather by a list with a single header node, as in Figure 4.2.7(d).

Of course, routines such as *empty, push, pop, insert,* and *remove* must be rewritten to account for the presence of a header node. Most of the routines become a bit more complex, but some, like *insert,* become simpler since an external list pointer is never null. We leave the rewriting of the routines as an exercise for the reader. The routines *insafter* and *delafter* need not be changed at all. In fact, *insafter* and *delafter* can be used instead of *push* and *pop* since the first item in such a list appears in the node that follows the header node, rather than in the first node on the list.

If the *info* portion of a node can contain a pointer (as is true in our BASIC implementation of a list of integers where a pointer is represented by an integer), additional possibilities for the use of a header node present themselves. For example, the *info* portion of a list header might contain a pointer to the last node

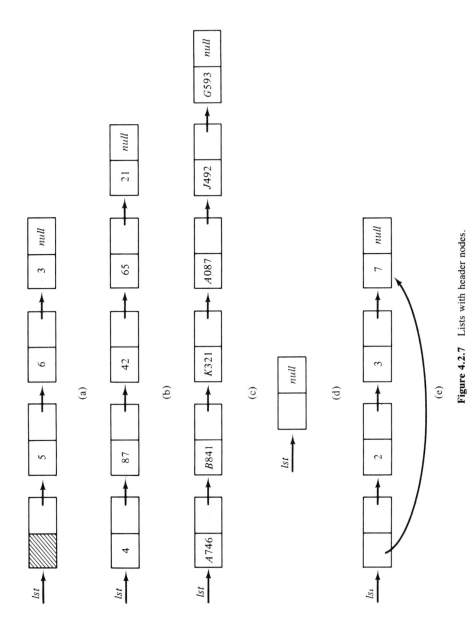

Figure 4.2.7 Lists with header nodes.

in the list, as in Figure 4.2.7(e). Such an implementation would simplify the representation of a queue. Until now, two external pointers, *queue(frnt)* and *queue(rear)*, were necessary for a list to represent a queue. However, now only a single external pointer *q* to the header node of the list is necessary. *ptrnxt(q)* would point to the front of the queue and *info(q)* to its rear.

Another possibility for the use of the INFO portion of a list header is as a pointer to a "current" node in the list during a traversal process. This would eliminate the need for an external pointer during traversal.

EXERCISES

1. Write a set of routines for implementing several stacks and queues within a single array.
2. What are the advantages and disadvantages of representing a group of items as an array versus a linear linked list?
3. Present four methods of implementing a queue of queues using the list and array implementations of a queue. Write each of the following routines for each implementation:

    remvq   which removes a queue from the queue
                    of queues *qq* and assigns it to *q*

    insrtq   which inserts queue *q* on *qq*

    remvonq   which removes an element from the
                    first queue of *qq* and assigns it to *x*

    insrtonq   which inserts an element *x* on the first
                    queue on *qq*

    Define analogous implementations and operations for a stack of stacks, a stack of queues, and a queue of stacks.
4. Write an algorithm and a BASIC routine to perform each of the following operations.
    (a) Append an element to the end of a list.
    (b) Concatenate two lists.
    (c) Free all the nodes in a list.
    (d) Reverse a list, so that the last element becomes the first, and so on.
    (e) Delete the last element from a list.
    (f) Delete the *n*th element from a list.
    (g) Combine two ordered lists into a single ordered list.
    (h) Form a list containing the union of the elements of two lists.
    (i) Form a list containing the intersection of the elements of two lists.
    (j) Insert an element after the *n*th element of a list.

(k) Delete every second element from a list.

(l) Place the elements of a list in increasing order.

(m) Return the sum of the integers in a list.

(n) Return the number of elements in a list.

(o) Move *node*(p) forward n positions in a list.

(p) Make a copy of a list.

5. Write an algorithm and a BASIC routine to perform each of the operations of Exercise 4 on a group of elements in contiguous positions of an array.

6. Write a BASIC routine to interchange the mth and nth elements of a list.

7. Write a routine *inssub* to insert the elements of list *l2* beginning at the *i2*th element and continuing for *len* elements into the list *l1* beginning at position *i1*. No elements of the list *l1* are to be removed or replaced. If $i1 > length(l1) + 1$ [where $length(l1)$ denotes the number of nodes in the list *l1*], or if $i2 + len - 1 > length(l2)$, or if $i1 < 1$, or if $i2 < 1$, print an error message. The list *l2* should remain unchanged.

8. Write a BASIC routine *search* which accepts a pointer L to a list of integers and an integer X and returns a pointer to a node containing X if it exists, and the null pointer otherwise. Write another routine *srchinsrt* which adds X to L if it is not found and always returns a pointer to a node containing X.

9. Write a BASIC program to read a group of DATA lines, each containing one word. Print each word that appears in the input and the number of times that it appears.

10. **(a)** Consider a factory that assembles machinery from smaller units. An ***elementary part*** is one that is not assembled from smaller parts. Write a program that reads a set of DATA lines containing four-character part numbers. The first such number on the line identifies a nonelementary part and the remaining numbers identify the parts from which the nonelementary part is assembled. These constituent parts may be elementary, or may in turn be assembled from other parts (in which case their numbers appear as the first number on some DATA line). The program creates a list with a header node for each nonelementary part. The header node contains the name of the nonelementary part and a pointer to a list of nodes describing the constituent parts, as discussed in the text at the end of this section. Pointers to the header nodes of each of the lists are placed in successive elements of an array PARTS. The program then prints all nonelementary parts.

(b) Write a program that accepts an array PARTS and a set of lists as constructed in part (a) and prints for each nonelementary part a list of all the elementary parts that are contained within its assembly. (For example, if part A contains parts B, C, and D, where B contains elementary parts E and F, C is elementary, and D contains G, which contains elementary parts H and I, and D also contains elementary part J, then A contains the elementary parts C, E, F, H, I, and J.)

(c) Show how part (b) is simplified if each node includes an additional pointer field. Explain the use of such an additional field in this application and rewrite the programs of parts (a) and (b) so that such a field is included.

3. AN EXAMPLE: SIMULATION USING LINKED LISTS

One of the most useful applications of queues and linked lists is in *simulation.* A simulation program is one that attempts to model a real-world situation in order to learn something about it. Each object and action in the real situation has its counterpart in the program. If the simulation is accurate, that is, if the program successfully mirrors the real world, the result of the program should mirror the result of the actual actions being simulated. Thus it is possible to understand what occurs in the real-world situation without actually observing its occurrence.

Let us look at an example. Suppose that there is a bank with four tellers. A customer enters the bank at a specific time $t1$, desiring to conduct a transaction with any teller. The transaction may be expected to take a certain period of time $t2$ before it is completed. If a teller is free, the teller can process the customer's transaction immediately and the customer leaves the bank as soon as the transaction has been completed, at time $t1 + t2$. The total time spent in the bank by the customer is exactly equal to the duration of the transaction, $t2$.

However, it is possible that none of the tellers are free; they are all servicing customers who arrived previously. In that case, there is a line waiting at each teller's window. The line for a particular teller may consist of a single person— the one currently transacting business with the teller, or it may be a very long line. The customer proceeds to the back of the shortest line and waits until all previous customers in the line have completed their transactions and have left the bank. At that time, he may transact his business. The customer leaves the bank at $t2$ time units after reaching the front of a teller's line. In this case the time spent in the bank is $t2$ plus the time spent waiting on line.

Given such a system, we would like to compute the average time spent by a customer in the bank. One way of doing so is to stand in the bank doorway, ask departing customers the time of their arrival and record the time of their departure, subtract the first from the second, and take the average over all customers. However, this would not be very practical. It would be difficult to ensure that no customer is overlooked leaving the bank. Furthermore, it is doubtful that most customers would remember the exact time of their arrival.

Instead, we write a program to simulate the customer actions. Each part of the real-world situation has its analog in the program. Each DATA line of the program represents a customer. The real-world action of a customer arriving is modeled by a DATA line being read. As each customer arrives, two facts are known: the time of the customer's arrival and the duration of the customer's transaction (since, presumably, when a customer arrives, he or she knows what he or she wishes to do at the bank). Thus each DATA line contains two numbers: the time (in minutes since the bank opened) of the customer's arrival and the amount of time (again, in minutes) necessary for the transaction. These DATA lines are ordered by increasing arrival time. The input is ended by a trailer on which the arrival time and the transaction duration are both zero. We assume at least one DATA line.

The four lines in the bank are represented by four queues. Each node of the queues represents a customer waiting in a line, with the node at the front of a queue representing the customer currently being served by a teller.

Suppose that at a given instant of time the four lines each contain a specific number of customers. What can happen to alter the status of the lines? Either a new customer enters the bank, in which case one of the lines will have an additional customer, or the first customer in one of the four lines completes a transaction, in which case that line will have one less customer. Thus there are a total of five actions (a customer entering, plus four cases of a customer leaving) which can change the status of the lines. Each of these five actions is called an *event.*

The simulation proceeds by finding the next event to occur and effecting the change in the queues which mirrors the change in the lines at the bank due to that event. In order to keep track of events, the program uses an *event list.* This list contains at most five nodes, each representing the next occurrence of one of the five types of event. Thus the event list contains one node representing the next customer arriving and up to four nodes representing each of the four customers at the head of a line completing a transaction and leaving the bank. Of course, it is possible that one or more of the lines in the bank are empty, or that the doors of the bank have been closed for the day so that no more customers are arriving. In such cases, the event list contains fewer than five nodes.

An event node representing a customer's arrival is called an *arrival node,* and a node representing a departure is called a *departure node.* At each point in the simulation, it is necessary to know the next event to occur. For this reason, the event list is ordered by increasing time of event occurrence so that the first event node on the list represents the next event to occur.

The first event to occur is the arrival of the first customer. The event list is therefore initialized by reading the first DATA line and placing an arrival node representing the first customer's arrival on the event list. Initially, of course, all four queues are empty. The simulation then proceeds as follows: The first node is removed from the event list and the changes which that event causes are made to the queues. As we shall soon see, these changes may also cause additional events to be placed on the event list. The process of removing the first node from the event list and effecting the changes that it causes is repeated until the event list is empty.

When an arrival node is removed from the event list, a node representing the arriving customer is placed on the shortest of the queues representing the four lines. If that customer is the only one on a queue, a node representing her departure is also placed on the event list, since she is at the front of her queue. At the same time, the next DATA line is read and an arrival node representing the next customer to arrive is placed on the event list. Thus there will always be an arrival node on the event list (as long as the input is not exhausted, at which point no more customers arrive) since as soon as one arrival node is removed from the event list, another is added to it.

When a departure node is removed from the event list, the node representing the departing customer is removed from the front of one of the four queues. At that point, the amount of time that the departing customer has spent in the bank is computed and added to a total. At the end of the simulation, this total will be divided by the number of customers to yield the average time spent by a customer. After a customer node has been deleted from the front of its queue, the next customer on the queue (if any) becomes the one being serviced by that teller and a departure node for that next customer is added to the event list.

This process continues until the event list is empty, at which point the average time is computed and printed. Note that the event list itself does not mirror any part of the real-world situation. It is used as part of the program to control the entire process. A simulation such as this one, which proceeds by changing the simulated situation in response to the occurrence of one of several events, is called an *event-driven simulation.*

We now examine the data structures required by this program. The nodes on the queues represent customers and therefore must contain fields representing the arrival time and the transaction duration, in addition to a PTRNXT field to link the nodes in a list. The nodes on the event list represent events and therefore must contain the time that the event occurs, the type of the event, and any other information associated with that event, as well as a PTRNXT field. Thus it would seem that two separate node pools are needed for the two different types of node. This would entail two *getnode* and *freenode* routines and two sets of list manipulation routines. To avoid this cumbersome set of duplicate routines, let us try to use a single type of node for both events and customers.

We can declare such a pool of nodes as follows:

```
20   DIM INFO(500,3)
30   TIME = 1
40   ELAPSEDTIME = 2
50   TYPE = 3
60   DIM PTRNXT(500)
```

For a customer node I, INFO(I,TIME) is the customer's arrival time and INFO(I,ELAPSEDTIME) is the transaction's duration. INFO(I,TYPE) is unused in a customer node. The PTRNXT field is used as a pointer to link the nodes of a queue together. For an event node I, INFO(I,TIME) is used to hold the time of the event's occurrence; INFO(I, ELAPSEDTIME) is used for the transaction duration of the arriving customer in an arrival node and is unused in a departure node. INFO(I,TYPE) is an integer between 0 and 4, depending on whether the event is an arrival [INFO(I,TYPE) = 0] or a departure from line one, two, three, or four [INFO(I,TYPE) = 1, 2, 3 or 4]. PTRNXT holds a pointer linking the nodes of the event list together. (Note that we compress the arrival time, duration, and type into a single array INFO because they are all represented by integers, although the integer array PTRNXT is a separate array. The reason for doing this is that we wish to make an explicit distinction between the information and pointer portions of a node. If the various pieces of information needed in a node were of different types, we would have to separate INFO into several distinct arrays as we did for the student nodes at the end of the preceding section.)

The four queues are defined by arrays Q and NUM introduced by the statements

```
80   DIM Q(4,2)
90   FRNT = 1
100  REAR = 2
110  DIM NUM(4)
```

Q(I,FRNT) and Q(I,REAR) contain pointers to the front and rear of the Ith queue, while NUM(I) contains the number of customers on the Ith queue.

An additional variable, EVLST, points to the front of the event list, another variable, TTLTIME, is used to keep track of the total time spent by all customers, and a third variable, COUNT, keeps count of the number of customers who have passed through the bank. An auxiliary array, AUXINFO, is used to store temporarily the information portion of a node.

The program first declares all the global variables mentioned above, initializes all lists and queues, and repeatedly removes the next node from the event list to drive the simulation until the event list is empty. It calls on the subroutine *placeaux* to insert a node whose information is given by AUXINFO into its proper place in the event list. The event list is ordered by increasing value of the TIME field. The program also calls on subroutine *popaux* to remove the first node from the event list and place its information into AUXINFO. These routines are equivalent to the routines *place* and *pop* introduced earlier except that they reference the array AUXINFO rather than the variables X and POPS.

The main program also calls on subroutines *arrive* and *depart,* which effect the changes in the event list and the queues caused by an arrival and a departure. Specifically, subroutine *arrive* reflects the arrival of a customer at time ATIME with a transaction of duration DUR, and subroutine *depart* reflects the departure of the first customer from the QINDXth queue at time DTIME. The coding of these routines will be given shortly.

```
10   'program bank
20   DIM INFO(500,3):      'information portion of list node
30   TIME = 1
40   ELAPSEDTIME = 2
50   TYPE = 3
60   DIM PTRNXT(500):      next address portion of list node
70   DIM AUXINFO(3):       'temporary storage; input to insafter, insert,
                           'placeaux, push; output of popaux, remove
```

```
 80   DIM Q(4,2):            'pointers to teller queues
 90   FRNT = 1
100   REAR = 2
110   DIM NUM(4)             'number of nodes on teller queues
120   DIM QUEUE(2):          'used as an input and output of routines
                             'insert and remove
130   'initialize variables and lists
140   TRUE = 1
150   FALSE = 0
160   EVLST = 0:             'pointer to event list
170   COUNT = 0:             'number of customers
180   TTLTIME = 0:           'total time spent by all customers
190   'initialize available list
200   AVAIL = 1
210   FOR I = 1 TO 499
220       PTRNXT(I) = I + 1
230   NEXT I
240   PTRNXT(500) = 0
250   'initialize queues
260   FOR I = 1 TO 4
270       Q(I,FRNT) = 0
280       Q(I,REAR) = 0
290       NUM(I) = 0
300   NEXT I
310   'initialize the event list with the first arrival
320   READ AUXINFO(TIME), AUXINFO(ELAPSEDTIME)
330   AUXINFO(TYPE) = 0
340   LST = EVLST
350   GOSUB 8000:            'subroutine placeaux may reset LST
360   EVLST = LST
370   'begin the event-driven simulation
380   IF EVLST = 0 THEN GOTO 540
390       STACK = EVLST
400       GOSUB 4000:        'subroutine popaux resets the variables STACK
                             'and AUXINFO
410       EVLST = STACK
420       'check if the next event is an arrival or a departure
430       IF AUXINFO(TYPE) > 0 THEN GOTO 490
440       'arrival
450       ATIME = AUXINFO(TIME)
460       DUR = AUXINFO(ELAPSEDTIME)
470       GOSUB 9000:        'subroutine arrive accepts ATIME and DUR and
                             'resets EVLST, NUM, and Q
480       GOTO 380
```

```
490     'departure
500     QINDX = AUXINFO(TYPE)
510     DTIME = AUXINFO(TIME)
520     GOSUB 10000:      'subroutine depart accepts QINDX and DTIME
                          'and resets EVLST, NUM, Q, COUNT, and TTLTIME
530     GOTO 380
540     PRINT "AVERAGE TIME IS"; TTLTIME / COUNT
550     END
600     DATA . . . , . . .
610     DATA . . . , . . .
            . . .
700     DATA 0, 0
1000    'subroutine getnode
            . . .
2000    'subroutine freenode
            . . .
3000    'subroutine insafter
            . . .
4000    'subroutine popaux
            . . .
5000    'subroutine empty (stack)
            . . .
6000    'subroutine insert
            . . .
7000    'subroutine remove
            . . .
8000    'subroutine placeaux
            . . .
9000    'subroutine arrive
            . . .
10000   'subroutine depart
            . . .
11000   'subroutine push
            . . .
12000   'subroutine empty (queue)
            . . .
```

The subroutine *arrive* modifies the queues and the event list to reflect a new arrival at time ATIME with a transaction of duration DUR. It inserts a new customer node at the rear of the shortest queue by calling the subroutine *insert*, which must be suitably modified to handle the type of node in this example. *arrive* must then increase the NUM field of that queue by 1. If the customer is the only one on his queue, a node representing his departure is added to the event list by calling the subroutine *placeaux*. Then the next data item (if any) is read and an arrival node is placed on the event list to replace the arrival that has just been processed. If there is no more input (as signaled by two zeros), subroutine *arrive* returns without adding a new arrival node and the main program processes any remaining (departure) nodes on the event list.

```
9000   'subroutine arrive
9010   'inputs: ATIME, DUR, EVLST, NUM, Q
9020   'outputs: EVLST, NUM, Q
9030   'locals: I, J, SMALL
9040   'Find the shortest queue
9050   J = 1
9060   SMALL = NUM(1)
9070   FOR I = 2 TO 4
9080       IF NUM(I) < SMALL THEN SMALL = NUM(I): J = I
9090   NEXT I
9100   'Queue J is the shortest. Insert a new node representing
9110   'the new arrival
9120   AUXINFO(TIME) = ATIME
9130   AUXINFO(ELAPSEDTIME) = DUR
9140   AUXINFO(TYPE) = J
9150   QUEUE(FRNT) = Q(J, FRNT)
9160   QUEUE(REAR) = Q(J, REAR)
9170   GOSUB 6000: 'subroutine insert modifies the array QUEUE
9180   Q(J, FRNT) = QUEUE(FRNT)
9190   Q(J, REAR) = QUEUE(REAR)
9200   NUM(J) = NUM(J) + 1
9210   'Check if this is the only node on the queue. If it is, the
9220   'customer's departure must be placed on the event list.
9230   IF NUM(J) <> 1 THEN GOTO 9290
9240   'else do stmnts 9250-9280
9250   AUXINFO(TIME) = ATIME + DUR
9260   LST = EVLST
9270   GOSUB 8000: 'subroutine placeaux may reset the variable LST
9280   EVLST = LST
9290   'Read the new arrival line. Place the arrival on the event list.
9300   READ AUXINFO(TIME), AUXINFO(ELAPSEDTIME)
9310   IF AUXINFO(TIME) = 0 AND AUXINFO(ELAPSEDTIME) = 0
           THEN RETURN: 'trailer card
9320   AUXINFO(TYPE) = 0
9330   LST = EVLST
9340   GOSUB 8000: 'subroutine placeaux
9350   EVLST = LST
9360   RETURN
9370   'endsub
```

The routine *depart* modifies the QINDXth queue and the event list to reflect the departure of the first customer on the queue at time DTIME. The customer is removed from the queue by calling subroutine *remove,* which must be suitably modified to handle the type of node in this example. *depart* must then decrement the queue's NUM field by 1. The departure node of the next customer on the queue (if any) replaces the departure node that has just been removed from the event list.

```
10000    'subroutine depart
10010    'inputs: COUNT, DTIME, EVLST, NUM, Q, QINDX, TTLTIME
10020    'outputs: COUNT, EVLST, NUM, Q, TTLTIME
10030    'locals: P
10040    'remove the customer node from the queue and gather statistics
10050    QUEUE(FRNT) = Q(QINDX, FRNT)
10060    QUEUE(REAR) = Q(QINDX, REAR)
10070    GOSUB 7000: 'subroutine remove modifies the array QUEUE
10080    Q(QINDX, FRNT) = QUEUE(FRNT)
10090    Q(QINDX, REAR) = QUEUE(REAR)
10100    NUM(QINDX) = NUM(QINDX) − 1
10110    TTLTIME = TTLTIME + (DTIME − AUXINFO(TIME))
10120    COUNT = COUNT + 1
10130    'if there are any more customers on the queue, place the
10140    'departure of the next customer onto the event list after
10150    'computing its departure time
10160    IF NUM(QINDX) = 0 THEN RETURN
10170    P = Q(QINDX, FRNT)
10180    AUXINFO(TIME) = DTIME + INFO(P, ELAPSEDTIME)
10190    AUXINFO(TYPE) = QINDX
10200    LST = EVLST
10210    GOSUB 8000: 'subroutine placeaux may reset the variable LST
10220    EVLST = LST
10230    RETURN
10240    'endsub
```

Simulation programs are rich in their use of list structures. The reader is urged to explore the use of BASIC for simulation and the use of special-purpose simulation languages.

EXERCISES

1. In the bank simulation program of the text, a departure node on the event list represents the same customer as the first node on a customer queue. Is it possible to use a single node for a customer currently being served? Rewrite the program of the text so that only a single node is used. Is there any advantage to using two nodes?

2. The program in the text uses the same type of node for both customer and event nodes. Rewrite the program using two different types of nodes for these two purposes. Does this save space?

3. Revise the bank simulation program of the text to determine the average length of the four lines.

4. The *standard deviation* of a group of n numbers is given by

$$\frac{1}{n} \sum_{i=1}^{n} (x_i - m)^2$$

where x_i are the individual numbers and m their mean. Modify the bank simulation program to compute the standard deviation of the time spent by a customer in the bank. Write another program which simulates a single line for all four tellers with the customer at the head of the single line going to the next available teller. Compare the means and standard deviations of the two methods.

5. Modify the bank simulation program so that whenever the length of one line exceeds the length of another by more than two, the last customer on the longer line moves to the rear of the shorter.

6. Write a BASIC program to simulate a simple multiuser computer system as follows. Each user has a unique ID and wishes to perform a number of transactions on the computer. However, only one transaction may be processed by the computer at any given moment. Each input line represents a single user and contains the user's ID followed by a starting time followed by a series of integers representing the duration of each of the user's transactions. The input is sorted by increasing starting time, and all times and durations are in seconds. Assume that a user does not request time for a transaction until the preceding transaction is complete and that the computer accepts transactions on a first-come, first-served basis. The program should simulate the system and print a message containing the user ID and the time whenever a transaction begins and ends. At the end of the simulation it should print the average waiting time for a transaction. (The waiting time is the amount of time between the time that the transaction was requested and the time it was started.)

7. Many simulations do not simulate events given by input data, but rather generate events according to some probability distribution. The following exercises explain how. Most computer systems have a random-number generating function RND(X). (The name and parameters of the function vary from computer to computer. RND is used as an example only.) X is initialized to a value between 0 and 1 called a *seed*. The statement X = RND(X) resets the value of the variable X to a uniform random real number between 0 and 1. By this we mean that if the statement is executed a sufficient number of times and any two equal-length intervals between 0 and 1 are chosen, approximately as many of the successive values of X fall into one interval as into the other. Thus the probability of a value of X falling in an interval of length

$l <= 1$ equals l. Find out the name of the random-number generating function on your computer and verify that the above is true.

Given a random number generator RND, consider the following statements:

$$100 \ X = RND(X)$$
$$110 \ Y = (B-A)*X + A$$

(a) Show that, given any two equal-sized intervals within the interval from A to B, if the statements are repeated sufficiently often, an approximately equal number of successive values of Y fall into each of the two intervals. The variable Y is said to be a **uniformly distributed random variable.** What is the average of the values of Y in terms of A and B?

(b) Rewrite the bank simulation of the text assuming that the transaction duration is uniformly distributed between 1 and 15. Each input line represents an arriving customer and contains only the time of arrival. Upon reading an input line, generate a transaction duration for that customer by computing the next value according to the method outlined above.

8. The successive values of Y that are generated by the following statements are called **normally distributed** with mean M and standard deviation S. (Actually, they are approximately normally distributed, but the approximation is close enough.)

```
 10   DEFDBL M, S, Y, X
 20   DEFINT I
 30   DIM X(15)
 40   'statements initializing the values of S, M and
 50   'the array X go here
 60   SUM = 0
 70   FOR I = 1 TO 15
 80       X(I) = RND(X(I))
 90       SUM = SUM + X(I)
100   NEXT I
110   Y = S * (SUM-7.5) / SQR(1.25) + M
120   'statements that use the value of Y go here
130   IF condition THEN GOTO 60
140   END
```

(a) Verify that the average of the values of Y (the mean of the distribution) equals M and that the standard deviation (see Exercise 4) equals S.

(b) A certain factory produces items according to the following process: an item must be assembled and polished. Assembly time is uniformly distributed between 100 and 300 seconds and polishing time is normally distributed with a mean of 20 seconds and a standard deviation of 7 seconds (but values below 5 are discarded). After an item is assembled, a polishing machine must be used and a worker cannot begin assembling the next item until the item he has just assembled has been polished. There are 10 workers but only one polishing machine. If the machine is not available, workers who have finished assembling their items must wait for the machine to be free. Compute the average waiting time per item by means of a simulation. Do the same under the assumption of two and three polishing machines.

9. (a) The XYZ Widget Store has expanded! Instead of selling only superior-quality widgets, it now also sells thingamijigs and dohickies. The store still charges a 20% markup on widgets, but in order to attract customers to its new products, it charges only a 15% markup on thingamijigs and dohickies. Whenever the store's inventory of a particular product falls below a certain number (called the ***reorder point***), the store reorders a certain amount (called the ***reorder amount***) of the product. Once a given item is reordered, it takes a certain number of days (called the ***reorder period***) for the item to arrive at the store. However, if customers have placed orders in excess of the reorder amount, the quantity that is reordered equals the reorder amount plus the amount demanded by the customers. If additional customers ask for the item after the item has already been reordered but the reorder amount would not cover the additional demand, another order is placed for the item. The amount of the additional order is equal to the reorder amount plus the total amount demanded minus the amount already ordered.

Write a program to read the reorder point, reorder amount, reorder period, and an initial factory price for each of the three items. Initially, assume that on day 1 the reorder amount of each item has been ordered. Then read a group of two types of transactions: a customer transaction containing a "C", the customer's name, and three numbers representing the amounts of each item that the customer wishes to buy, and a price transaction containing a "P" and three prices representing new factory prices for each of the items that the store sells. Each transaction also contains a day number. The transactions are sorted by increasing day number. If the store has quantities of a particular item at varying prices, it uses a LIFO policy and first sells those items which it received last (and presumably are higher priced).

The output of the program is a series of messages ordered by increasing day number. The initial message is that on day 1 a specific amount of each item has been ordered at a specific cost. (The cost for an order is the price that is in effect on the day of the order, not that in effect on the day of delivery.) Messages are printed whenever an order is placed, whenever a shipment is received, whenever a customer requests a sale, and whenever items are sent to a customer. Whenever more than one customer is waiting for items in a shipment, the rule used is first come, first served. If only part of a sale can be filled, it is filled and the remainder is filled upon receipt of a shipment. When all the items in a given sale have been sent out, the total price for the sale is computed and a message is printed.

(b) What changes would have to be introduced to the program under each of the following altered conditions?

(1) The store uses a FIFO policy instead of a LIFO policy (e.g., shipments received earlier are sold first).

(2) The store always sells items from shipments at higher costs before items at lower cost, regardless of time of receipt.

(3) If more than one customer is waiting for a given shipment, the shipment is sold to the customer with the greatest total sale.

4. OTHER LIST STRUCTURES

Although a linked linear list is a rather useful data structure, it has several short-comings. In this section we present other methods of organizing a list and show how they can be used to overcome these shortcomings.

Circular Lists

One of the shortcomings of linear lists is that given a pointer p to a node in such a list, we cannot reach any of the nodes that precede $node(p)$. If a list is traversed, the original pointer to the beginning of the list must be preserved in order to be able to reference the list again.

Suppose that a small change is made to the structure of a linear list so that the *ptrnxt* field in the last node contains a pointer back to the first node rather than the null pointer. Such a list is called a *circular list* and is illustrated in Figure 4.4.1. From any point in such a list it is possible to reach any other point in the list. If we begin at a given node and traverse the entire list, we ultimately end up at the starting point. Note that a circular list does not have a natural "first" or "last" node. We must, therefore, establish a first and last node by convention. One useful convention is to let the external pointer to the circular list point to the last node, and to allow the following node to be the first node, as illustrated in Figure 4.4.2. We also establish the convention that a null pointer represents an empty circular list.

The Stack as a Circular List

A circular list can be used to represent a stack or a queue. Let *stack* be a pointer to the last node of a circular list and let us adopt the convention that the first node is the top of the stack. The following is a BASIC subroutine to push a number X onto the stack, assuming a set of *nodes* and an auxiliary routine *getnode* at statement 1000 as presented in previous sections. The *push* subroutine calls on the *empty* subroutine at statement 4000, which tests whether STACK equals zero.

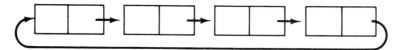

Figure 4.4.1   A circular list.

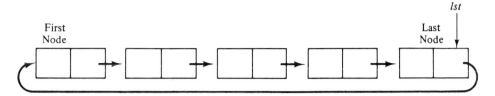

Figure 4.4.2   The first and last nodes of a circular list.

```
5000    'subroutine push
5010    'inputs: STACK, X
5020    'outputs: STACK
5030    'locals: EMPTY, GTNODE, P
5040    GOSUB 1000: 'subroutine getnode sets the variable GTNODE
5050    P = GTNODE
5060    INFO(P) = X
5070    GOSUB 4000: 'subroutine empty sets the variable EMPTY
5080    IF EMPTY = TRUE THEN STACK = P
                        ELSE PTRNXT(P) = PTRNXT(STACK)
5090    PTRNXT(STACK) = P
5100    RETURN
5110    'endsub
```

Note that the *push* subroutine is slightly more complex for circular lists than it is for linear lists.

The BASIC *pop* subroutine for a stack of numbers implemented as a circular list is as follows. It calls the subroutine *freenode* at statement 2000 introduced earlier.

```
6000    'subroutine pop
6010    'inputs: STACK
6020    'outputs: POPS, STACK
6030    'locals: EMPTY, P
6040    GOSUB 4000: 'subroutine empty sets the variable EMPTY
6050    IF EMPTY = TRUE THEN PRINT "STACK OVERFLOW": STOP
6060    P = PTRNXT(STACK)
6070    POPS = INFO(P)
6080    'if P = STACK then there is only one node in the stack
6090    IF P = STACK THEN STACK = 0 ELSE PTRNXT(STACK) = PTRNXT(P)
6100    FRNODE = P
6110    GOSUB 2000: 'subroutine freenode
6120    RETURN
6130    'endsub
```

The Queue as a Circular List

It is easier to represent a queue as a circular list than as a linear list. As a linear list, a queue is specified by two pointers, one to the front of the list and the other to its rear. However, by using a circular list, a queue may be specified by a single pointer QUEUE to that list. The node pointed to by QUEUE is the rear of the queue and the following node is its front. The routine *remove* (accepting a variable QUEUE) is identical to *pop* (accepting STACK) except that all references to STACK are replaced by QUEUE and all references to POPS are replaced by RMOVE. *empty* must also be modified to accept QUEUE, rather than STACK, as an input. The BASIC routine *insert* may be coded as follows:

```
7000   'subroutine insert
7010   'inputs: QUEUE, X
7020   'outputs: QUEUE
7030   'locals: GTNODE, P
7040   GOSUB 1000: 'subroutine getnode sets the variable GTNODE
7050   P = GTNODE
7060   INFO(P) = X
7070   GOSUB 4000: 'subroutine empty sets the variable EMPTY
7080   IF EMPTY = TRUE THEN QUEUE = P
                         ELSE PTRNXT(P) = PTRNXT(QUEUE)
7090   PTRNXT(QUEUE) = P
7100   QUEUE = P
7110   RETURN
7120   'endsub
```

Note that this is equivalent to the code

```
90    STACK = PTRNXT(QUEUE)
100   X = 'element to be inserted
110   GOSUB 9000: 'subroutine push
120   QUEUE = PTRNXT(QUEUE)
```

That is, to insert an element into the rear of a circular queue, the element is inserted into the front of the queue and the queue pointer is then advanced one element, so that the new element becomes the rear.

Primitive Operations on Circular Lists

The routines *insafter,* which inserts a node containing X after *node*(PNTR), and *delafter,* which deletes the node following *node*(PNTR) and stores its contents in X, are similar to the routines for linear lists as presented in Section 2. Let us now consider the *delafter* subroutine in more detail. Looking at the corresponding routine for linear lists in Section 2, we note an additional consideration in the case of a circular list. Suppose that PNTR points to the only node in the list. In a linear list, PTRNXT(PNTR) is null in that case, making the deletion invalid. In the case of a circular list, however, PTRNXT(PNTR) points to *node*(PNTR) so that *node*(PNTR) follows itself. The question is whether it is desirable to delete *node*(PNTR) from the list in this case. It is unlikely that we would want to do so, since the operation *delafter* is usually invoked when pointers to each of two nodes are available, one immediately following another, and it is desired to delete the second. *delafter* for circular lists is therefore implemented as follows:

```
8000    'subroutine delafter
8010    'inputs: PNTR
8020    'outputs: X
8030    'locals: FRNODE, Q
8040    'if PNTR = 0 then the list is empty
8050    IF PNTR = 0 THEN PRINT "VOID DELETION": RETURN
8060    'if PNTR = PTRNXT(PNTR) then the list contains only a single node
8070    IF PNTR = PTRNXT(PNTR) THEN PRINT "VOID DELETION": RETURN
8080    Q = PTRNXT(PNTR)
8090    X = INFO(Q)
8100    PTRNXT(PNTR) = PTRNXT(Q)
8110    FRNODE = Q
8120    GOSUB 2000: 'subroutine freenode
8130    RETURN
8140    'endsub
```

Note, however, that *insafter* cannot be used to insert a node following the last node in a circular list and *delafter* cannot be used to delete the last node of a circular list. In both cases, the external pointer to the list must be modified to point to the new last node. The routines can be modified to accept LST as an additional parameter and to change its value when necessary. An alternative is to write separate routines *insend* and *dellast* for these cases. (*insend* is identical to the *insert* operation for a queue implemented as a circular list.) The calling routine would be responsible for determining which routine to call. Another alternative is to give the calling routine the responsibility of adjusting the external pointer LST if necessary. We leave the exploration of these possibilities to the reader.

It is also easier to free all the nodes of a circular list than to free all the nodes of a linear list. In the case of a linear list, the entire list must be traversed, as one node at a time is returned to the available list or until the last node is reached and the entire list is appended to the available list. For a circular list, we can write a routine *freelist*, which effectively frees an entire list without traversing the list:

```
9000   'subroutine freelist
9010   'inputs: LST
9020   'outputs: LST
9030   'locals: P
9040   P = PTRNXT(LST)
9050   PTRNXT(LST) = AVAIL
9060   AVAIL = P
9070   LST = 0
9080   RETURN
9090   'endsub
```

Similarly, we may write a routine *concat*, which concatenates two lists—that is, it appends the circular list pointed to by L2 to the end of the circular list pointed to by L1:

```
10000   'subroutine concat
10010   'inputs: L1, L2
10020   'outputs: L1
10030   IF L2 = 0 THEN RETURN
10040   IF L1 = 0 THEN L1 = L2: RETURN
10050   P = PTRNXT(L1)
10060   PTRNXT(L1) = PTRNXT(L2)
10070   PTRNXT(L2) = P
10080   L1 = L2
10090   RETURN
10100   'endsub
```

The Josephus Problem

Let us consider a problem that can be solved in a straightforward manner by using a circular list. The problem is known as the Josephus problem and postulates a group of soldiers surrounded by an overwhelming enemy force. There is no hope for victory without reinforcements, but there is only a single horse available for escape. The soldiers agree to a pact to determine which of them is to escape and summon help. They form a circle and a number n is picked from a hat. One of their names is also picked from a hat. Beginning with the soldier whose name is picked, they begin to count clockwise around the circle. When the count reaches n, that soldier is removed from the circle, and the count begins again with the next soldier. The process continues so that each time the count reaches n, a soldier is removed from the circle. Once a soldier is removed from the circle, of course, he is no longer counted. The last soldier remaining is to take the horse and escape. The problem is, given a number n, the ordering of the soldiers in the circle, and the soldier from whom the count begins, to determine the order in which soldiers are eliminated from the circle, and which soldier escapes.

The input to the program is the number n and a list of names which is the clockwise ordering of the soldiers in the circle, beginning with the soldier from whom the count is to start. The last input line contains the string ''END,'' indicating the end of the input. The program should print the names of the soldiers in the order in which they are eliminated and the name of the soldier who escapes.

For example, suppose that *n* equals 3 and there are five soldiers, named *A*, *B*, *C*, *D* and *E*. We count three soldiers starting at *A*, so that *C* is eliminated first. We then begin at *D* and count *D*, *E*, and back to *A*, so *A* is eliminated next. Then we count *B*, *D*, and *E* (*C* has already been eliminated) and finally *B*, *D*, and *B*, so *D* is the soldier who escapes.

Clearly, a circular list in which each node represents one soldier is a natural data structure to use in solving this problem. It is possible to reach any node from any other by counting around the circle. To represent the removal of a soldier from the circle, that soldier's node is deleted from the circular list. Finally, when only one node remains on the list, the result is determined.

An outline of the program might be the following:

> ***read*** *n*
> ***read*** *soldier*
> ***while*** *soldier* is not ''end'' ***do***
>   insert *soldier* on the circular list
>   ***read*** *soldier*
> ***endwhile***
> ***while*** there is more than one node on the list ***do***
>   count through *n*-1 nodes on the list
>   ***print*** the name of the soldier in the *n*th node
>   delete the *n*th node
> ***endwhile***
> ***print*** the name of the soldier in the only node on the list

We assume at least one name in the input. The program uses the routines *insert, delafter,* and *freenode*.

```
10    'program josephus
20    DEFSTR I, S, X
30    DIM INFO(500)
40    DIM PTRNXT(500)
50    TRUE = 1
60    FALSE = 0
70    LST = 0
80    AVAIL = 1
90    FOR K = 1 TO 499
100        PTRNXT(K) = K + 1
110   NEXT K
120   PTRNXT(500) = 0
130   READ N
140   PRINT "THE ORDER IN WHICH THE SOLDIERS ARE ELIMINATED IS:"
```

```
150   'read the names, placing each at the rear of the list
160   READ SOLDIER
170   IF SOLDIER = "END" THEN GOTO 230
180      QUEUE = LST
190      X = SOLDIER
200      GOSUB 7000:    'subroutine insert accepts QUEUE and X
                        'and resets QUEUE
210      LST = QUEUE
220   GOTO 160
230   'repeat as long as more than one node remains on the list
240   IF LST = PTRNXT(LST) THEN GOTO 350
250      'else do statements 260-330
260      FOR J = 1 TO N - 1
270         LST = PTRNXT(LST)
280            'at this point LST points to the Jth node counted
290      NEXT J
300      'PTRNXT(LST) points to the Nth node; delete that node
310      PNTR = LST
320      GOSUB 8000: 'subroutine delafter sets the variable X
330      PRINT X
340   GOTO 240
350   'print the only name remaining on the list and free its node
360   PRINT "THE SOLDIER WHO ESCAPES IS "; INFO(LST)
370   FRNODE = LST
380   GOSUB 2000: 'subroutine freenode
390   END
500   DATA . . .
         . . .
990   DATA "END"
1000  'subroutine getnode
         . . .
2000  'subroutine freenode
         . . .
4000  'subroutine empty
         . . .
7000  'subroutine insert
         . . .
8000  'subroutine delafter
         . . .
```

Header Nodes

Suppose that we wish to traverse a circular list. This can be done by repeatedly executing the statement P = PTRNXT(P), where P is initially a pointer to the

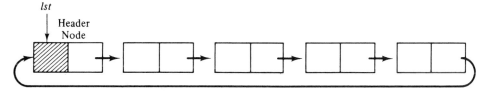

Figure 4.4.3 A circular list with a header node.

beginning of the list. However, since the list is circular, we will not know when the entire list has been traversed unless another pointer LST points to the first node and a test is made for the condition P = LST.

An alternative method is to place a header node as the first node of a circular list. This list header may be recognized by a special value in its INFO field, which cannot be the valid contents of a list node in the context of the problem, or it may contain a flag marking it as a header. The list can then be traversed using a single pointer, with the traversal halting when the header node is reached. The external pointer to the list is to its header node, as illustrated in Figure 4.4.3. This means that a node cannot be added easily onto the rear of such a circular list, as could be done when the external pointer was to the last node of the list. Of course, it may be possible to keep a pointer to the last node of a circular list within the header node or to keep an additional external pointer to the last node.

If a stationary external pointer to a circular list is present in addition to the pointer used for traversal, the header node need not contain a special flag but can be used in much the same way as a header node of a linear list to contain global information about the list. The end of a traversal would be signaled by the equality of the traversing pointer and the external stationary pointer.

Addition of Long Positive Integers Using Circular Lists

We now present an example of an application that uses circular lists with header nodes. The hardware of most computers allows integers of only a specific maximum length. Suppose that we wish to represent positive integers of arbitrary length and to write a function that returns the sum of two such integers. To add two integers, their digits are traversed from right to left and corresponding digits and a possible carry from the previous digits' sum are added. This suggests representing long integers by storing their digits from right to left in a list so that the first node on the list contains the least significant digit (rightmost) and the last node contains the most significant (leftmost). However, in order to save space, we will keep five digits in each node. We may declare the set of nodes by

```
20   DIM INFO(500)
30   DIM PTRNXT(500)
```

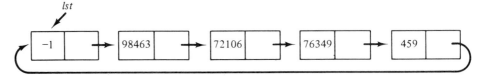

Figure 4.4.4   A large integer as a circular list.

Since we wish to traverse the lists during the addition but wish eventually to restore the list pointers to their original values, we use circular lists with headers. The header node is distinguished by an INFO value of -1. For example, the integer 459763497210698463 is represented by the list illustrated in Figure 4.4.4.

Now let us write a subroutine *addnum*, which accepts pointers to two such lists representing integers, creates a list representing the sum of the integers, and returns a pointer to the sum list. Both lists are traversed in parallel and five digits are added at a time. If the sum of two five digit numbers is SUM, the carry of the sum, CARRY, is given by INT(SUM / 100000). The low-order five digits of SUM are then given by SUM–100000*CARRY. When the end of one list is reached, the carry is propagated to the remaining digits of the other list. The subroutine follows and uses the routines *getnode* at statement 1000 and *insafter* at statement 11000.

```
20000   'subroutine addnum
20010   'inputs: PLST, QLST
20020   'outputs: ADDNUM
20030   'locals: CARRY, GTNODE, HUNTHOU, PPTR, QPTR, S, SUM
20040   HUNTHOU = 100000
20050   'PLST and QLST are pointers to the header nodes of two
        'lists representing long integers
20060   'set PPNTR and QPNTR to the nodes following the headers
20070   PPNTR = PTRNXT(PLST)
20080   QPNTR = PTRNXT(QLST)
20090   'set up header node for the sum
20100   GOSUB 1000: 'subroutine getnode sets the variable GTNODE
20110   S = GTNODE
20120   INFO(S) = -1
20130   PTRNXT(S) = S
20140   'initially there is no carry
20150   CARRY = 0
20160   'traverse section
20170   IF INFO(PPNTR) = -1 OR INFO(QPNTR) = -1 THEN GOTO 20310
20180       'add the info of two nodes and previous carry
20190       SUM = INFO(PPNTR) + INFO(QPNTR) + CARRY
```

```
20200    'determine whether there is a carry
20210    CARRY = INT(SUM / HUNTHOU)
20220    'determine the low-order five digits of SUM
20230    X = SUM - HUNTHOU * CARRY
20240    'insert into the list. advance the traversals.
20250    PNTR = S
20260    GOSUB 11000: 'subroutine insafter accepts PNTR and X
20270    S = PTRNXT(S)
20280    PPNTR = PTRNXT(PPNTR)
20290    QPNTR = PTRNXT(QPNTR)
20300  GOTO 20170
20310  'at this point there may be nodes left in one of PLST or QLST
20320  'traverse the remainder of PLST
20330  IF INFO(PPNTR) = -1 THEN GOTO 20420
20340    SUM = INFO(PPNTR) + CARRY
20350    CARRY = INT(SUM / HUNTHOU)
20360    X = SUM - HUNTHOU * CARRY
20370    PNTR = S
20380    GOSUB 11000: 'subroutine insafter
20390    S = PTRNXT(S)
20400    PPNTR = PTRNXT(PPNTR)
20410  GOTO 20320
20420  'traverse the remainder of QLST
20430  IF INFO(QPNTR) = -1 THEN GOTO 20520
20440    SUM = INFO(QPNTR) + CARRY
20450    CARRY = INT(SUM / HUNTHOU)
20460    X = SUM - HUNTHOU * CARRY
20470    PNTR = S
20480    GOSUB 11000: 'subroutine insafter
20490    S = PTRNXT(S)
20500    QPNTR = PTRNXT(QPNTR)
20510  GOTO 20430
20520  'check if there is an extra carry from the first five digits
20530  IF CARRY = 0 THEN GOTO 20590
20540  'else do stmnts 20550-20580
20550  PNTR = S
20560  X = CARRY
20570  GOSUB 11000: 'subroutine insafter
20580  S = PTRNXT(S)
20590  'S points to the last node in the sum
20600  ADDNUM = PTRNXT(S)
20610  RETURN
20620  'endsub
```

Doubly Linked Lists

Although a circularly linked list has advantages over a linear list, it still has several drawbacks. One cannot traverse such a list backward nor can a node be deleted from a circularly linked list given only a pointer to that node. In cases where these facilities are required, the appropriate data structure is a ***doubly linked list.*** Each node in such a list contains two pointers, one to its predecessor and another to its successor. In fact, in the context of doubly linked lists, the terms *predecessor* and *successor* are meaningless, since the list is entirely symmetric. Doubly linked lists may be either linear or circular and may or may not contain a header node, as illustrated in Figure 4.4.5.

We may consider the nodes on a doubly linked list as consisting of three fields: an *info* field, which contains the information stored in the node, and *left* and *right* fields, which contain pointers to the nodes on either side. We may declare variables to represent such nodes by

$$
\begin{array}{ll}
30 & \text{DIM INFO(500)} \\
40 & \text{DIM LEFT(500)} \\
50 & \text{DIM RIGHT(500)}
\end{array}
$$

LEFT(I) and RIGHT(I) point to the nodes to the left and right of *node*(I), respectively.

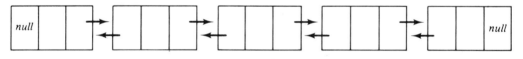

(a) A linear doubly linked list.

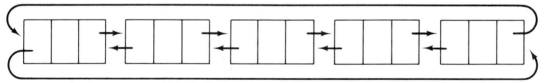

(b) A circular doubly linked list without a header.

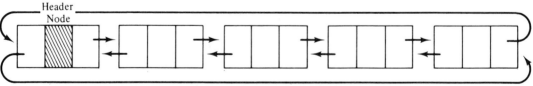

(c) A circular doubly linked list with a header.

Figure 4.4.5   Doubly linked lists.

Alternatively, we may declare a set of such nodes by

```
30   DIM INFO(500)
40   DIM PTRNXT(500,2)
50   LEFT = 1
60   RIGHT = 2
```

Under this representation, PTRNXT(I,LEFT) and PTRNXT(I,RIGHT) point to the nodes to the left and right of *node*(I), respectively. It is the latter representation that we use in the remainder of the text.

Note that the available list for such a set of nodes need not be doubly linked, since it is not traversed bidirectionally. The available list may be linked together by using either PTRNXT(I,LEFT) or PTRNXT(I,RIGHT). Of course, appropriate *getnode* and *freenode* routines must be written.

We now present routines to operate on doubly linked circular lists. A convenient property of such a list is that if *p* is a pointer to any node in a doubly linked circular list, then

$$left(right(p)) = p = right(left(p))$$

One operation that can be performed on doubly linked lists but not on ordinary linked lists is to delete a given node, given only a pointer to that node. The following BASIC routine deletes the node pointed to by PNTR from a doubly linked list and stores its contents in X.

```
15000   'subroutine delete (doubly linked list)
15010   'inputs: PNTR
15020   'outputs: X
15030   'locals: FRNODE, Q, R
15040   IF PNTR = 0 THEN PRINT "VOID DELETION": RETURN
15050   X = INFO(PNTR)
15060   Q = PTRNXT(PNTR,LEFT)
15070   R = PTRNXT(PNTR,RIGHT)
15080   PTRNXT(Q,RIGHT) = R
15090   PTRNXT(R,LEFT) = Q
15100   FRNODE = PNTR
15110   GOSUB 2000: 'subroutine freenode
15120   RETURN
15130   'endsub
```

The routine *insertright* inserts a node with information field X to the right of *node*(PNTR) in a doubly linked list.

```
16000   'subroutine insertright
16010   'inputs: PNTR, X
16020   'outputs: none
16030   'locals: GTNODE, Q, R
16040   IF PNTR = 0 THEN PRINT "VOID INSERTION": RETURN
16050   GOSUB 1000: 'subroutine getnode sets the variable GTNODE
16060   Q = GTNODE
16070   INFO(Q) = X
16080   R = PTRNXT(PNTR,RIGHT)
16090   PTRNXT(R,LEFT) = Q
16100   PTRNXT(Q,RIGHT) = R
16110   PTRNXT(Q,LEFT) = PNTR
16120   PTRNXT(PNTR,RIGHT) = Q
16130   RETURN
16140   'endsub
```

A routine *insertleft* to insert a node with information field X to the left of *node*(PNTR) in a doubly linked list is similar and is left as an exercise for the reader.

In programming for microcomputers, space efficiency is often a crucial consideration. A program may not be able to afford the overhead of two pointers for each element of a list. There are several techniques for compressing the left and right pointers of a node into a single field. For example, a single pointer field PTR in each node can contain the sum of pointers to its left and right neighbors. Given two external pointers, P and Q, to two adjacent nodes such that P = LEFT(Q), RIGHT(Q) can be computed as PTR(Q) − P and LEFT(P) can be computed as PTR(P) − Q. Given P and Q, it is possible to delete either node and reset its pointer to the preceding or succeeding node. It is also possible to insert a node to the left of *node*(P) or to the right of *node*(Q) or to insert a node between *node*(P) and *node*(Q) and reset either P or Q to the newly inserted node. In using such a scheme, it is crucial always to maintain two external pointers to two adjacent nodes in the list.

Addition of Long Integers Using Doubly Linked Lists

As an illustration of the use of doubly linked lists, let us consider extending the implementation of long integers to include negative as well as positive integers. The header node of a circular list representing a long integer will contain an indication of whether the integer is positive or negative. When we wanted to add two positive integers, we traversed the integers from the least significant digit to the most significant. However, to add a positive and a negative integer, the smaller absolute value must be subtracted from the larger absolute value and the result must be given the sign of the integer with the larger absolute value. Thus some method is needed for testing which of two integers represented as circular lists has the larger absolute value.

The first criterion that may be used to identify the integer with the larger absolute value is the length of the integers (assuming that they do not contain leading zeros). Thus, we can count the number of nodes in each list, and the list that has more nodes represents the integer with the larger absolute value. However, this count involves an extra traversal of the list. Instead of counting the number of nodes, the count could be kept as part of the header node and referred to as needed.

However, if both lists have the same number of nodes, it is necessary to traverse the lists from the most significant digit to the least significant to determine which number is larger. Note that this traversal is in the opposite direction of the traversal that must be used in actually adding two integers. For this reason, doubly linked lists are used to represent such integers.

Consider the format of the header node. In addition to a right and left pointer, the header must contain the length of the list and an indication of whether the number is positive or negative. These two items of information can be combined into a single integer whose absolute value is the length of the list and whose sign is the sign of the number being represented. However, in doing so, the ability to identify the header node by examining the sign of its INFO field is destroyed. When a positive integer was represented as a singly linked circular list, an INFO field of -1 indicated a header node. Under the new representation, however, a header node may contain an INFO field such as 5, which is a valid INFO value for any other node in the list.

There are several ways to remedy this problem. One way is to add another field to each node to indicate whether or not it is a header node. Such a flag could contain the value 1 if the node is a header and 0 if it is not. This means, of course, that each node would require more space. Alternatively, the count could be eliminated from the header node and the INFO value -1 would indicate a positive number and -2 a negative number. A header node could then be identified by its negative INFO field. However, this would increase the time needed to compare two numbers since it would be necessary to count the number of nodes in each list. Such space/time trade-offs are very common in computing, and a decision must be made as to which efficiency should be sacrificed and which retained. In our case, we choose yet a third option, which is to retain an external pointer to the list header. A pointer P can be identified as pointing to a header if it equals the original external pointer; otherwise, *node*(P) is not a header.

Figure 4.4.6 indicates a sample node and the representation of four integers as doubly linked lists. Note that the least significant digits are to the right of the header and that the counts in the header nodes do not include the header node itself.

Using the representation above, we present a routine *compare*, which compares the absolute values of two integers represented as doubly linked lists. This routine accepts as inputs two variables which are pointers to the list headers. The output variable COMPARE is set to 1 if the first integer has the greater absolute

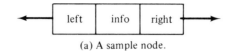

(a) A sample node.

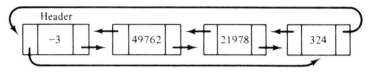

(b) The integer −3242197849762.

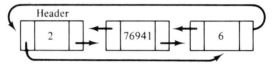

(c) The integer 676941.

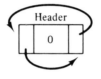

(d) The integer 0.

Figure 4.4.6   Integers as doubly linked lists.

value, − 1 if the second integer has the greater absolute value, and 0 if the absolute values of the two integers are equal.

```
30000   'subroutine compare
30010   'inputs: PPNTR, QPNTR
30020   'outputs: COMPARE
30030   'locals: R, S
30040   'compare the counts
30050   IF ABS(INFO(PPNTR)) > ABS(INFO(QPNTR))
            THEN COMPARE = 1: RETURN
30060   IF ABS(INFO(PPNTR)) < ABS(INFO(QPNTR))
            THEN COMPARE = −1: RETURN
30070   'the counts are equal
30080   R = PTRNXT(PPNTR, LEFT)
30090   S = PTRNXT(QPNTR, LEFT)
```

```
30100   'traverse the list from the most significant digit
30110   IF R = PPNTR THEN GOTO 30170
30120      IF INFO(R) > INFO(S) THEN COMPARE = 1: RETURN
30130      IF INFO(R) < INFO(S) THEN COMPARE = −1: RETURN
30140      R = PTRNXT(R, LEFT)
30150      S = PTRNXT(S, LEFT)
30160   GOTO 30110
30170   'the absolute values are equal
30180   COMPARE = 0
30190   RETURN
30200   'endsub
```

We are now ready to write a subroutine *oppsignadd* that accepts two pointers to lists representing long integers of opposite sign where the absolute value of the first is not less than that of the second. *oppsignadd* outputs a pointer to a list representing the sum of the integers. We must, of course, be careful to eliminate leading zeros from the sum. To do this, we use the variable ZEROPTR to traverse the list, deleting those nodes containing leading zeros.

In this routine PPNTR points to the integer with the larger absolute value and QPNTR points to the integer with the smaller absolute value. The values of these variables do not change. Auxiliary variables P1 and Q1 are used to traverse the lists. The sum is formed in a list pointed to by the variable RPNTR.

```
35000   'subroutine oppsignadd
35010   'inputs: PPNTR, QPNTR
35020   'outputs: OPPSIGNADD
35030   'locals: BRROW, CNTR, GTNODE, HUNTHOU, P1, PNTR, Q1, RPNTR, X,
            ZEROPTR
35040   HUNTHOU = 100000
35050   CNTR = 0: 'counter for number of nodes in result
35060   BRROW = 0: '1 if a borrow was required, 0 if not; initially no 'borrow
35070   'generate a header node for the sum
35080   GOSUB 1000: 'subroutine getnode sets the variable GTNODE
35090   RPNTR = GTNODE
35100   PTRNXT(RPNTR, LEFT) = RPNTR
35110   PTRNXT(RPNTR, RIGHT) = RPNTR

35120   'traverse the two lists
35130   P1 = PTRNXT(PPNTR, RIGHT)
35140   Q1 = PTRNXT(QPNTR, RIGHT)
35150   IF Q1 = QPNTR THEN GOTO 35250
35160      X = INFO(P1) − BRROW − INFO(Q1)
35170      IF X >= 0 THEN BRROW = 0
                   ELSE X = X + HUNTHOU: BRROW = 1
```

```
35180    'generate a node and insert it to the left of the header in the sum
35190    PNTR = RPNTR
35200    GOSUB 16500: 'subroutine insertleft accepts PNTR and X
35210    CNTR = CNTR + 1
35220    P1 = PTRNXT(P1, RIGHT)
35230    Q1 = PTRNXT(Q1, RIGHT)
35240  GOTO 35150


35250  'traverse remainder of PPNTR list
35260  IF P1 = PPNTR THEN GOTO 35340
35270    X = INFO(P1) − BRROW
35280    IF X >= 0 THEN BRROW = 0
                      ELSE X = X + HUNTHOU: BRROW = 1
35290    PNTR = RPNTR
35300    GOSUB 16500: 'subroutine insertleft
35310    CNTR = CNTR + 1
35320    P1 = PTRNXT(P1, RIGHT)
35330  GOTO 35260


35340  'delete leading zeros
35350  ZEROPTR = PTRNXT(RPNTR, LEFT)
35360  IF INFO(ZEROPTR) <> 0 OR ZEROPTR = RPNTR THEN GOTO 35420
35370    PNTR = ZEROPTR
35380    ZEROPTR = PTRNXT(ZEROPTR, LEFT)
35390    GOSUB 15000: 'subroutine delete accepts PNTR
35400    CNTR = CNTR − 1
35410  GOTO 35360


35420  'insert count and sign into header
35430  IF INFO(PPNTR) > 0 THEN INFO(RPNTR) = CNTR
                      ELSE INFO(RPNTR) = − CNTR
35440  OPPSIGNADD = RPNTR
35450  RETURN
35460  'endsub
```

We can also write a subroutine *samesignadd* at line 25000, which adds two integers with like signs. This is very similar to the subroutine *addnum* of the previous implementation except that it deals with a doubly linked list and must keep track of the number of nodes in the sum.

Using these routines, we can write a new version of *addnum*, which adds two integers represented by doubly linked lists.

```
20000   'subroutine addnum
20010   'inputs: PLST, QLST
20020   'outputs: ADDNUM
20030   'locals: COMPARE, OPPSIGNADD, PPTR, QPTR, TEMP
20040   PPNTR = PLST
20050   QPNTR = QLST
20060   'check if integers are of like sign;
        'if they are call the samesignadd routine
20070   IF INFO(PPNTR) * INFO(QPNTR) > 0
            THEN GOSUB 25000: ADDNUM = SAMESIGNADD: RETURN
20080   'check which integer has the greater absolute value
20090   GOSUB 30000: 'subroutine compare sets the variable COMPARE
20100   'if necessary, reverse pointers so that PPNTR points
        'to the larger integer
20110   IF COMPARE < 0
            THEN TEMP = PPNTR: PPNTR = QPNTR: QPNTR = TEMP
20120   GOSUB 35000: 'subroutine oppsignadd
20130   ADDNUM = OPPSIGNADD
20140   RETURN
20150   'endsub
```

Multilists

Sometimes, it is desirable to have a particular item of data on more than one list without repeating the item in several nodes. For example, consider a public health survey on the effects of cigarette smoking and alcohol. Researchers have collected the medical histories of a large number of people, each of whom has been categorized as a nonsmoker, a light smoker, or a heavy smoker, and as a nondrinker, a light drinker, or a heavy drinker. The researchers wish to be able to maintain this information so that they can obtain various statistics or follow-up mailing labels for specific subgroups (e.g., what is the incidence rate of a particular disease for heavy smokers who are also heavy drinkers?). One solution is to maintain each person's medical record in a node that is kept on two lists: one indicating the level of smoking, and the other indicating the level of alcohol consumption.

In order to keep a node on more than one list, the node must contain a pointer for each list in which it resides. A data structure containing such nodes is called a *multilist*. In the example above, a node would contain a person's name and medical history in the information portion, one pointer to the next node with the same level of smoking and another pointer to the next node with the same level of alcohol consumption. It is also a good idea to keep fields in a node indicating which lists contain the node so that when traversing one list it is possible to determine the other lists that contain each particular node. Such a node for the example above is illustrated in Figure 4.4.7. Figure 4.4.8 illustrates a portion of a multilist for that example, showing eight nodes representing people responding as follows:

Name	Alcohol level	Smoking level
A	No	No
B	Heavy	No
C	Light	Heavy
D	No	No
E	Heavy	Heavy
F	Light	Light
G	No	Heavy
H	Heavy	Light

In this figure, each list is ordered alphabetically. The pointers in the figure are labeled for the reader's convenience to indicate the list of which they are a part (e.g., LA represents "light alcohol," NS represents "no smoking," etc.). For example, the list for light smoking contains nodes *F* and *H,* while the one for heavy alcohol consumption contains nodes *B, E,* and *H.* Thus, if we wanted to determine all light smokers who were also heavy drinkers, we could traverse either the list of light smokers and check every light smoker as to whether he was a heavy drinker, or traverse the list of heavy drinkers and check for light smoking. In either case, the result would be node *H.*

The lists in a multilist may be linear or circular, singly or doubly linked. Of course, if they are doubly linked, twice as many pointers are required. Also, they may or may not contain a header node. For example, suppose that each list had a header containing the number of nodes in the list. Then, if we wished to find all heavy drinkers who are light smokers, we could check the headers of the two lists

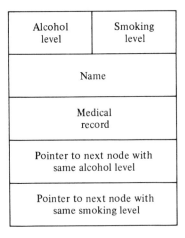

Figure 4.4.7   A node in a multilist.

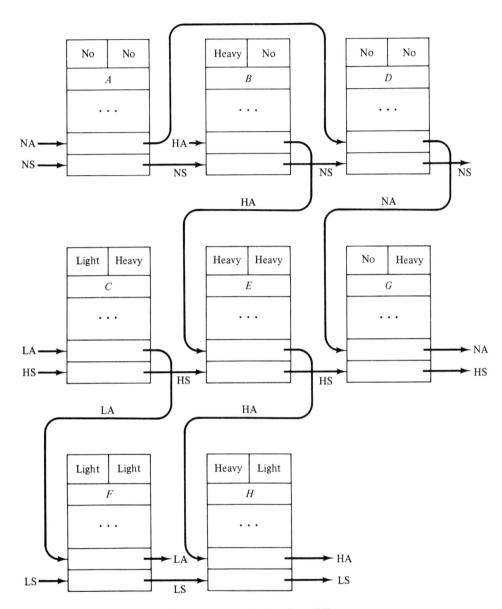

Figure 4.4.8 A portion of a multilist.

to determine which list is smaller. By traversing the smaller list, we can avoid a great deal of extra work.

EXERCISES

1. Write an algorithm and a BASIC routine to perform each of the operations of Exercise 4.2.4 for circular lists. Which are more efficient on circular lists than on linear lists? Which are less efficient?

2. Rewrite the subroutine *place* of Section 2 to insert a new item in an ordered circular list.

3. Write a program to solve the Josephus problem by using an array rather than a circular list. Why is a circular list more efficient?

4. Consider the following variation of the Josephus problem. A group of people stand in a circle and each chooses a positive integer. One of their names and a positive integer *n* are chosen. Starting with the person whose name is chosen, they count around the circle clockwise and eliminate the *n*th person. The positive integer which that person chose is then used to continue the count. Each time a person is eliminated, the number that person chose is used to determine the next person eliminated. For example, suppose that the five people are *A, B, C, D,* and *E* and they choose integers *3, 4, 6, 2,* and *7*, respectively, and person *A* and the integer 2 are initially chosen. Then if they start from *A*, the order in which people are eliminated from the circle is *B, A, E, C*, leaving *D* as the last one in the circle.

   Write a program that reads a group of DATA lines. Each DATA line except the first and last contains a name and a positive integer chosen by that person. The order of the names in the data is the clockwise ordering of the people in the circle and the count is to start with the first name in the input. The first input line contains the number of people in the circle. The last input line contains a single positive integer representing the initial count. The program prints the order in which the people are eliminated from the circle.

5. Write a BASIC routine that prints an arbitrarily long integer represented by a list. Note that if a node contains fewer than five digits, its contents must be padded with leading zeros prior to printing unless it represents the most significant digits of the number.

6. Write a BASIC subroutine *multnum* to multiply two long positive integers represented by singly linked circular lists.

7. Write an algorithm and a BASIC routine to perform each of the operations of Exercise 4.2.4 for doubly linked circular lists. Which are more efficient on doubly linked than on singly linked lists? Which are less efficient?

8. Assume that a single pointer field in each node of a doubly linked list contains the sum of pointers to the node's predecessor and successor, as described in the text. Given pointers P and Q to two adjacent nodes in such a list, write BASIC routines to

insert a node to the right of *node*(Q), to the left of *node*(P), and between *node*(P) and *node*(Q) modifying P to point to the newly inserted node. Write an additional routine to delete *node*(Q), resetting Q to its successor.

9. Assume that FIRST and LAST are external pointers to the first and last nodes of a doubly linked list represented as in Exercise 8. Write BASIC routines to implement the operations of Exercise 4.2.4 for such a list.

10. Write the routine *samesignadd* to add two long integers of the same sign represented by doubly linked lists.

11. Rewrite the routine *oppsignadd* for the doubly-linked-list representation of Exercise 8.

12. Write a BASIC subroutine *multnum* to multiply two long integers represented by doubly linked circular lists.

13. How can you represent a polynomial in three variables (*x*, *y*, and *z*) as a circular list? Each node should represent a term of the polynomial and should contain the powers of *x*, *y*, and *z* as well as the coefficient of that term. The nodes should be ordered in decreasing powers of *x*, then in decreasing powers of *y*, then in decreasing powers of *z*. Write BASIC subroutines to do the following:
    (a) Add two such polynomials.
    (b) Multiply two such polynomials.
    (c) Take the partial derivative of such a polynomial with respect to any of its variables.
    (d) Evaluate such a polynomial for given values of *x*, *y* and *z*.
    (e) Divide one such polynomial by another, creating a quotient and a remainder polynomial.
    (f) Integrate such a polynomial with respect to any of its variables.
    (g) Print the representation of such a polynomial.
    (h) Given four such polynomials, $f(x,y,z)$, $g(x,y,z)$, $h(x,y,z)$, and $i(x,y,z)$, compute the polynomial $f(g(x,y,z), h(x,y,z), i(x,y,z))$.

14. Write a BASIC program that reads two groups of DATA lines. Each line of the first group consists of a name, a smoking level, and an alcohol consumption level. This first group is terminated by a line that contains the name END. After reading the first group, the program should form a multilist as outlined in the text. The program then reads the second group, each line of which contains a smoking level and an alcohol consumption level. For each DATA line of the second group, the program should print the number of people with both the smoking and alcohol consumption levels given on that line.

5

Recursion

This chapter introduces recursion, a problem-solving tool which is one of the most powerful and at the same time one of the least understood by beginning students of programming. We define recursion, present several examples, and show how it can be an effective tool in problem solving. In some languages that are more powerful than BASIC, recursion is implemented as part of the language; this is not true in BASIC. We therefore examine how recursive algorithms can be implemented in BASIC using stacks. Finally, we discuss the advantages and disadvantages of using recursion in problem solving.

1. RECURSIVE DEFINITION AND PROCESSES

Many objects in mathematics are defined by presenting a process to produce that object. For example, π is defined as the ratio of the circumference of a circle to its diameter. This is equivalent to the following set of instructions: Obtain the circumference of a circle and its diameter, divide the former by the latter, and call the result π. Clearly, the process specified must terminate with a definite result.

The Factorial Function

Another example of a definition specified by a process is that of the factorial function, a function that plays an important role in mathematics and statistics. Given a positive integer n, *n factorial* is defined as the product of all integers between n and 1. For example, 5 factorial is equal to 5*4*3*2*1 = 120 and 3 factorial equals 3*2*1 = 6. 0 factorial is defined as 1. In mathematics, the exclamation mark (!) is often used to denote the factorial function. We may therefore write the definition of this function as follows:

$$n! = 1 \qquad \text{if } n = 0$$
$$n! = n*(n-1)*(n-2)*\ldots*1 \qquad \text{if } n > 0$$

Note that the three dots are really a shorthand notation for the product of all the numbers between $n-3$ and 2 (assuming that $n > 5$). To avoid this shorthand in the definition of $n!$, we would have to list a formula for $n!$ for each value of n separately, as follows:

$$0! = 1$$
$$1! = 1$$
$$2! = 2*1$$
$$3! = 3*2*1$$
$$4! = 4*3*2*1$$
$$\ldots\ldots\ldots$$

Of course, we cannot hope to list a formula for the factorial of each integer. In order to avoid any shorthand and to avoid an infinite set of definitions, yet to define the function precisely, we may present an algorithm that accepts an integer n and computes the value of $n!$ in a variable *fact:*

```
x = n
prod = 1
while x > 0 do
    prod = x * prod
    x = x - 1
endwhile
fact = prod
return
```

Such an algorithm is called *iterative* because it calls for the explicit repetition of some process as long as a certain condition is met. An algorithm may be thought of as a program for an "ideal" machine without any of the practical limitations of a real computer and may therefore be used to define a mathematical function. Although the algorithm above may be readily translated into a BASIC subroutine, this subroutine cannot serve as the definition of the factorial function because of such limitations as precision and the finite size of a real machine.

Let us look more closely at the definition of $n!$, which lists a separate formula for each value of n. We may note, for example, that 4! equals 4*3*2*1, which equals 4*3!. In fact, for any $n > 0$, we see that $n!$ equals $n*(n-1)!$. Multiplying n by the product of all integers from $n-1$ to 1 yields the product of all integers from n to 1. We may therefore define

$$0! = 1$$
$$1! = 1*0!$$
$$2! = 2*1!$$
$$3! = 3*2!$$
$$4! = 4*3!$$
$$. . .$$

or, using the mathematical notation used earlier,

$$n! = 1 \qquad \text{if } n = 0$$
$$n! = n*(n-1)! \qquad \text{if } n > 0$$

This definition may appear quite strange since it defines the factorial function in terms of itself. This seems to be a circular definition and totally unacceptable until we realize that the mathematical notation is simply a concise way of writing the infinite number of equations necessary to define $n!$ for each n. 0! is defined directly as 1. Once 0! has been defined, defining 1! as 1*0! is not circular at all. Similarly, once 1! has been defined, defining 2! as 2*1! is equally straightforward. It may be argued that the latter notation is more precise than the definition of $n!$ as $n*(n-1)*$ . . . $*1$ for $n > 0$ because it does not resort to three dots to be filled in by the hopefully logical intuition of the reader. Such a definition, which defines an object in terms of a simpler case of itself, is called a ***recursive definition***.

Let us see how the recursive definition of the factorial function may be used to evaluate 5!. The definition states that 5! equals 5*4!. Thus, before we can evaluate 5!, we must first evaluate 4!. Using the definition once more, we find that 4! = 4*3!. Therefore, we must evaluate 3!. Repeating this process, we have

```
1.   5! = 5*4!
2.        4! = 4*3!
3.             3! = 3*2!
4.                  2! = 2*1!
5.                       1! = 1*0!
6.                            0! = 1
```

Each case is reduced to a simpler case until we reach the case of 0!, which is, of course, 1. At line 6 we have a value which is defined directly rather than as the factorial of another number. We may therefore backtrack from line 6 to line 1, returning the value computed in one line to evaluate the result of the previous line. This produces

```
6'.  0! = 1
5'.  1! = 1*0! = 1*1 = 1
4'.  2! = 2*1! = 2*1 = 2
3'.  3! = 3*2! = 3*2 = 6
2'.  4! = 4*3! = 4*6 = 24
1'.  5! = 5*4! = 5*24 = 120
```

Let us attempt to incorporate this process into an algorithm. Again, we want the algorithm to accept a nonnegative integer n as input and to return in a variable *fact* the nonnegative integer which is n factorial.

```
1.   if n = 0
2.     then fact = 1
3.          return
4.     else
5.          x = n - 1
6.          find the value of x!. call it y.
7.          fact = n * y
8.          return
9.   endif
```

This algorithm exhibits the process used to compute $n!$ by the recursive definition. The key to the algorithm is, of course, line 6, where we are told to "find the value of $x!$". We can view this step as suspending temporarily the execution of the algorithm with input n on the machine we are now using and then initiating execution of the same algorithm on a different machine with input x. (That is, n on the second machine is set to x before beginning to execute the algorithm.) In the process of computing x factorial, the second machine may call upon yet a third machine, and so on.

Eventually, the second machine will complete its task. When it has done so, it has computed the result of x factorial and it then sends that result back to the first machine. The first machine sets y to the resulting value and resumes execution. To see that this process will eventually halt, note that at the start of line 6, x equals $n-1$. Each time that the algorithm is executed on a different machine, its input is one less than the preceding time, so that (since the original input n was a nonnegative integer) 0 will eventually be input. At that point, the algorithm will simply calculate the value 1 in the variable *fact*. This value is returned to a previous machine in line 6, which asked for the evaluation of $0!$. The multiplication of $y \ (= 1)$ by $n \ (= 1)$ is then performed on that previous machine and the result is returned. This sequence of multiplications and returns continues until the original $n!$ has been evaluated.

Of course, the assumption of an arbitrary number of machines for the calculation of a seemingly simple problem is both impractical and unrealistic. In the next section we examine how to convert this process into a BASIC program that can be run on a single machine.

We note that it is much simpler and more straightforward to use the iterative method for evaluation of the factorial function. We present the recursive method as a simple example to introduce recursion, not as a more effective method of solving this particular problem. Indeed, all the problems in the first part of this section can be solved more effectively by iteration. However, later in this section and in subsequent chapters, we will come across examples which are solved more easily by recursive methods.

Multiplication of Natural Numbers

Another example of a recursive definition is the definition of multiplication of natural numbers. The product $a*b$, where a and b are positive integers, may be defined as a added to itself b times. This is an iterative definition. An equivalent recursive definition is

$$a*b = a \qquad\qquad \text{if } b = 1$$
$$a*b = a*(b-1)+a \qquad \text{if } b > 1$$

To evaluate 6*3 by this definition, we must first evaluate 6*2 and then add 6. To evaluate 6*2, we must first evaluate 6*1 and add 6. But 6*1 equals 6, by the first part of the definition. Thus

$$6*3 = 6*2+6 = 6*1+6+6 = 6+6+6 = 18$$

The reader is urged to convert the definition above to a recursive algorithm as a simple exercise.

Note the pattern that exists in recursive definitions. A simple case of the term to be defined is defined explicitly (in the case of the factorial, 0! was defined as 1; in the case of multiplication, $a*1$ was defined as a). The other cases are defined by applying some operation to the result of evaluating a simpler case. Thus, $n!$ is defined in terms of $(n-1)!$ and $a*b$ in terms of $a*(b-1)$. Successive simplifications of any particular case must eventually lead to the explicitly defined trivial case. In the case of the factorial function, successively subtracting 1 from n will eventually yield 0. In the case of multiplication, successively subtracting 1 from b will eventually yield 1. If this were not the case, the definition would be invalid. For example, if we defined

$$n! = (n+1)!/(n+1)$$

or

$$a*b = a*(b+1) - a$$

we would be unable to determine the values of 5! or 6*3. (You are invited to attempt to determine these values using the definitions above.) This is true despite the fact that the two equations are mathematically valid. Continually adding 1 to n or b does not eventually produce an explicitly defined case. Even if 100! were defined explicitly, how could the value of 101! be determined?

The Fibonacci Sequence

Let us examine a less familiar example. The **Fibonacci sequence** is the sequence of integers

$$0, 1, 1, 2, 3, 5, 8, 13, 21, 34, \ldots$$

Each element in this sequence after the first two is the sum of the two preceding elements (e.g., $0 + 1 = 1, 1 + 1 = 2, 1 + 2 = 3, 2 + 3 = 5, \ldots$). If we let $fib(0) = 0, fib(1) = 1$, and so on, we may define the Fibonacci sequence by the following recursive definition:

$$fib(n) = n \qquad\qquad\qquad \text{if } n = 0 \text{ or } 1$$
$$fib(n) = fib(n-2) + fib(n-1) \qquad \text{if } n >= 2$$

To compute $fib(6)$, for example, we may apply the definition recursively to obtain

$$
\begin{aligned}
fib(6) &= fib(4) + fib(5) = fib(2) + fib(3) + fib(5)\\
&= fib(0) + fib(1) + fib(3) + fib(5) = 0 + 1 + fib(3) + fib(5)\\
&= 1 + fib(1) + fib(2) + fib(5)\\
&= 1 + 1 + fib(0) + fib(1) + fib(5) = 2 + 0 + 1 + fib(5)\\
&= 3 + fib(3) + fib(4)\\
&= 3 + fib(1) + fib(2) + fib(4) = 3 + 1 + fib(0) + fib(1) + fib(4)\\
&= 4 + 0 + 1 + fib(2) + fib(3)\\
&= 5 + fib(0) + fib(1) + fib(3) = 5 + 0 + 1 + fib(1) + fib(2)\\
&= 6 + 1 + fib(0) + fib(1) = 7 + 0 + 1 = 8
\end{aligned}
$$

Notice that the recursive definition of the Fibonacci numbers differs from the recursive definitions of the factorial function and multiplication. The recursive definition of fib refers to itself twice. For example, $fib(6) = fib(4) + fib(5)$, so that in computing $fib(6)$, fib must be applied recursively twice. However, part of the computation of $fib(5)$ involves determining $fib(4)$ so that a great deal of computational redundancy occurs in applying the definition. In the example above, $fib(3)$ was computed three separate times. It would have been much more efficient to "remember" the value of $fib(3)$ the first time it was evaluated and reuse it each time that it was needed. An iterative method of computing $fib(n)$ such as the following is much more efficient (the result is placed in the variable fib):

```
if n <= 1
    then fib = n
    else
        lofib = 0
        hifib = 1
        for i = 2 to n
            x = lofib
            lofib = hifib
            hifib = x + lofib
        next i
        fib = hifib
endif
return
```

Essentially, this algorithm enumerates all the Fibonacci numbers successively in the variable *hifib*.

Compare the number of additions (not including increments of the index variable *i*) which are performed in computing *fib*(6) by this algorithm and by using the recursive definition. In the case of the factorial function, the same number of multiplications must be performed in computing *n*! by the recursive and iterative methods. The same is true of the number of additions in the two methods of computing multiplication. However, in the case of the Fibonacci numbers, the recursive method is far more expensive than its iterative counterpart.

The Binary Search

You may have received the erroneous impression that recursion is a very handy tool for defining mathematical functions but has no influence in more practical computing activities. The next example will illustrate an application of recursion to one of the most common activities in computing—that of searching.

Consider an array of elements in which objects have been placed in some order. For example, a dictionary or telephone book may be thought of as an array whose entries are in alphabetical order. A company payroll file may be in the order of employees' social security numbers. Suppose that such an array exists and we wish to find a particular element in it. For example, we wish to look up a name in a telephone book, a word in a dictionary, or a particular employee in a personnel file. The process used to find such an entry is called a **search**. Since searching is such a common activity in computing, it is desirable to find an efficient method for performing it. Perhaps the crudest search method is the **sequential** or **linear** search, in which each item of the array is examined in turn, and compared to the item being searched for until a match occurs. If the list is unordered and haphazardly constructed, the linear search may be the only way to find anything in it (unless, of course, the list is first rearranged). However, such a method would never be used in looking up a name in a telephone book. Rather, the book is opened to a random page and the names on that page are examined. Since the names are ordered alphabetically, such an examination would determine whether the search should continue in the first or second part of the book.

Let us apply this idea to searching an array. If the array contains only one element, the problem is trivial. Otherwise, compare the item being searched for with the item at the middle of the array. If they are equal, the search has been completed successfully. If the middle element is greater than the item being searched for, the search process is repeated in the first half of the array (since if the item appears anywhere it must appear in the first half); otherwise, the process is repeated in the second half. Note that each time a comparison is made, the number of elements remaining to be searched is divided in half. For large arrays, this method is superior to the sequential search, in which each comparison reduces the number of elements remaining to be searched by only one. Because of the division of the array to be searched into two equal parts, this search method is called the ***binary search***.

Notice that we have quite naturally defined a binary search recursively. If the item being searched for is not equal to the middle element of the array, the instructions are to search a subarray using the same method. Thus the search method is defined in terms of itself with a smaller array as input. We are sure that the process will terminate because the input arrays become smaller and smaller, and the search of a one element array can be found nonrecursively since the middle element of such an array is its only element.

We now present a recursive algorithm to search a sorted array a for an element x between $a(low)$ and $a(high)$. The algorithm places in a variable *binsrch* an index of a such that $a(binsrch) = x$, if such an index exists between *low* and *high*. If x is not found in that portion of the array, *binsrch* is set to 0. (We assume that *low* is greater than zero.)

```
1.   if low > high
2.      then binsrch = 0
3.            return
4.   endif
5.   mid = int((low + high)/2)
6.   if x = a(mid)
7.      then binsrch = mid
8.      else if x < a(mid)
9.              then search for x in a(low) to a(mid − 1)
10.             else search for x in a(mid + 1) to a(high)
11.          endif
12.  endif
13.  return
```

Since the possibility of an unsuccessful search is included (i.e., the element may not exist in the array), the trivial case has been altered somewhat. A search on a one-element array (when $low = high$) is not defined directly as the appropriate index. Instead, that element [the element $a(mid)$, where $mid = low = high$] is compared to the item being searched for. If the two items are not equal, the search continues in the "first" or "second" half—each of which contains no elements. This trivial case of no elements is indicated by the condition $low > high$ and its result is defined directly as 0.

Let us apply this algorithm to an example. Suppose that the array a contains the elements 1, 3, 4, 5, 17, 18, 31, 33 in that order and we wish to search for 17 (i.e., $n = 17$) between item 1 and item 8 (i.e., $low = 1$, $high = 8$). Applying the algorithm, we have:

Line   1:   Is $low > high$? It is not, so continue with line 5.
Line   5: $mid = int((1 + 8)/2) = 4$.

Line 6:   Is $x = a(4)$? 17 is not equal to 5, so execute the **else** clause.

Line 8:   Is $x < a(4)$? 17 is not less than 5, so perform the **else** clause at line 10.

Line 10:   Repeat the algorithm with $low = mid + 1 = 5$ and $high = high = 8$ (i.e., search the upper half of the array).

Line 1:   Is $5 > 8$? No, so continue with line 5.

Line 5: $mid = int((5 + 8)/2) = 6$.

Line 6:   Is $x = a(6)$? 17 does not equal 18, so execute the **else** clause.

Line 8:   Is $x < a(6)$? Yes, since $17 < 18$, so execute the **then** clause.

Line 9:   Repeat the algorithm with $low = low = 5$ and $high = mid - 1 = 5$. We have isolated x between the fifth and the fifth elements of a.

Line 1:   Is $5 > 5$? No, so continue with line 5.

Line 5: $mid = int((5 + 5)/2) = 5$.

Line 6:   Since $a(5) = 17$, *binsrch* is set to 5. 17 is indeed the fifth element of the array.

Note the pattern of calls to and returns from the algorithm. A diagram tracing this pattern appears in Figure 5.1.1. The solid arrows indicate the flow of control through the algorithm and the recursive calls. The dotted lines indicate returns.

Let us examine how the algorithm works in searching for an item that does

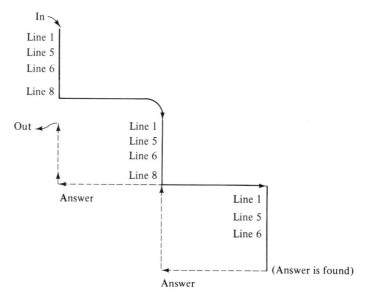

Figure 5.1.1   A diagrammatic representation of the binary search algorithm.

not appear in the array. Assume the array a as in the previous example and assume that we are searching for $x = 2$.

Line 1:   Is *low* > *high*? 1 is not greater than 8, so continue with line 5.

Line 5:   *mid* = *int*((1 + 8)/2) = 4.

Line 6:   Is $x = a(4)$? 2 does not equal 5, so execute the ***else*** clause.

Line 8:   Is $x < a(4)$? Yes, 2 < 5, so perform the ***then*** clause.

Line 9:   Repeat the algorithm with *low* = *low* = 1 and
            high = *mid* − 1 = 3. If 2 appears in the array, it must appear
            between $a(1)$ and $a(3)$ inclusive.

Line 1:   Is 1 > 3? No, continue with line 5.

Line 5:   *mid* = *int*((1 + 3)/2) = 2.

Line 6:   Is 2 = $a(2)$? No, execute the ***else*** clause.

Line 8:   Is 2 < $a(2)$? Yes, since 2 < 3. Perform the ***then*** clause.

Line 9:   Repeat the algorithm with *low* = *low* = 1 and
            high = *mid* − 1 = 1. If x exists in a, it must be the first
            element.

Line 1:   Is 1 > 1? No, continue with line 5.

Line 5:   *mid* = *int*((1 + 1)/2) = 1.

Line 6:   Is 2 = $a(1)$? No, execute the ***else*** clause.

Line 8:   Is 2 < $a(1)$? 2 is not less than 1, so perform the ***else*** clause.

Line 10:   Repeat the algorithm with *low* = *mid* + 1 = 2 and
            high = *high* = 1.

Line 1:   Is *low* > *high*? 2 is greater than 1, so *binsrch* is 0. The item 2
            does not exist in the array.

This example illustrates the value of recursion in problem solving. While a recursive solution may be more expensive than an iterative solution, it is often easier to discover the recursive solution by identifying a trivial case and formulating the solution of a complex case in terms of one or more simpler cases. Once the recursive solution has been formulated, a recursive algorithm can be developed quite naturally. As we shall see in the next section, a program can be developed for such a recursive algorithm using a few simple techniques. Although this program may be quite complex, it can often be simplified to produce a more efficient iterative solution. In the next section we examine how to implement a recursive algorithm as a BASIC program and how to simplify that program subsequently. For now, however, let us give one more example of developing a solution to a problem by use of recursion.

The Towers of Hanoi Problem

Let us look at another problem that can be solved logically and elegantly by use of recursion. This is the "Towers of Hanoi" problem, whose initial setup is shown in Figure 5.1.2. Three pegs, *A*, *B*, and *C*, exist. Four disks with different diameters are placed on peg *A* so that a larger disk is always below a smaller disk. The object is to move the four disks to peg *C* using peg *B* as auxiliary in a series of steps. Only the top disk on any peg may be moved to any other peg in each step, and a larger disk may never rest on a smaller one. See if you can produce a solution. Indeed, it is not even apparent that a solution exists.

Let us see if we can develop a solution. Instead of focusing our attention on a solution for four disks, let us consider the general case of *n* disks. Suppose that we had a solution for *n* − 1 disks and we could state a solution for *n* disks in terms of the solution for *n* − 1 disks. Then the problem would be solved. This is true because in the trivial case of one disk (continually subtracting 1 from *n* will eventually produce 1), the solution is simple: Merely move the single disk from peg *A* to peg *C*. Therefore, we will have developed a recursive solution if we can state a solution for *n* disks in terms of *n* − 1. See if you can find such a relationship. In particular, for the case of four disks, suppose that we knew how to move the top three disks from peg *A* to another peg without violating the rules. How could we then complete the job of moving all four? Recall that there are three pegs available.

Suppose that we could move three disks from peg *A* to peg *C*. Then we could just as easily move them to *B*, using *C* as auxiliary. This would result in the situation depicted in Figure 5.1.3(a). We could then move the largest disk from *A* to *C* [Figure 5.1.3(b)] and finally apply the solution for three disks a second time to move the three disks from *B* to *C*, using the now empty peg *A* as an auxiliary [Figure 5.1.3(c)]. Thus we may state a recursive solution to the Towers of Hanoi problem as follows:

To move *n* disks from *A* to *C*, using *B* as auxiliary:

1. If *n* = 1, then move the single disk from *A* to *C* and stop.
2. Move the top *n* − 1 disks from *A* to *B*, using *C* as auxiliary.
3. Move the remaining disk from *A* to *C*.
4. Move the *n* − 1 disks from *B* to *C*, using *A* as auxiliary.

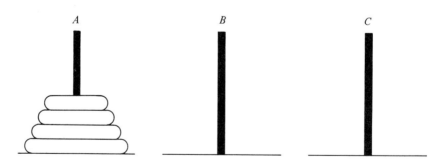

Figure 5.1.2   The initial setup of the Towers of Hanoi.

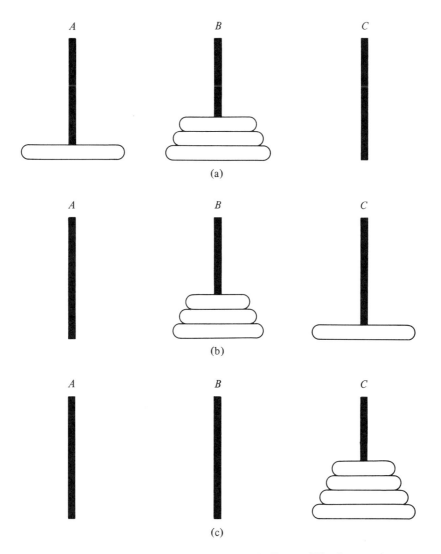

Figure 5.1.3   Recursive solution to the Towers of Hanoi.

We are sure that this method will produce a correct solution for any value of n. If $n = 1$, step 1 will result in the correct solution. If $n = 2$, we know that we already have a solution for $n - 1 = 1$, so that steps 2 and 4 will perform correct-ly. Similarly, when $n = 3$, we have already produced a solution for $n - 1 = 2$, so that steps 2 and 4 can be performed. In this fashion, we can show that the solution works for $n = 1, 2, 3, 4, 5, \ldots$ up to any value for which we desire a solution. Notice that we developed the solution by identifying a trivial case

($n = 1$) and a solution for a general complex case (n) in terms of a simpler case ($n-1$).

How can this solution be converted into an algorithm? We are no longer dealing with a mathematical function such as factorial, but rather with concrete actions such as "move a disk." How are we to represent such actions algorithmically? The problem is not completely specified. What are its inputs? What are its outputs to be? Whenever you are told to write an algorithm, you must receive specific instructions as to exactly what the algorithm is expected to do. A problem statement such as "Solve the Towers of Hanoi problem" is quite insufficient. What is usually meant when such a problem is specified is that not only the algorithm but also the inputs and outputs must be designed so that they correspond reasonably to the problem description. The design of inputs and outputs is an important phase of a solution and should be given as much attention as the rest of a program. There are two reasons for this. The first is that the user (who must ultimately evaluate and pass judgment on your work) will not see the elegant method you incorporated in your algorithm but will struggle mightily to decipher the output or to adapt input data to your particular input conventions. The failure to agree early on input and output details has been the cause of much grief to programmers and users alike. The second reason is that a slight change in the input or output format may make the algorithm much simpler to design.

Let us, then, proceed to design the inputs and outputs for this algorithm. At first glance it appears that the only input needed is the value of n, the number of disks. A reasonable form for the output would be a list of statements such as

move disk nnn from peg yyy to peg zzz

where *nnn* is the number of the disk to be moved and *yyy* and *zzz* are the names of the pegs involved. The action to be taken for a solution would be to perform each of the output statements in the order in which it appears in the output.

The programmer then decides to write an algorithm *towers* (he or she is purposely vague about the inputs at this point) to print the output noted above. The algorithm would be invoked by

towers (inputs)

Let us assume that the user will be satisfied to name the disks $1, 2, 3, \ldots, n$ and the pegs A, B, and C. What should the input variables to *towers* be? Clearly, they should include n, the number of disks to be moved. This not only includes information about how many disks there are but also what their names are. The programmer then notices that in the recursive algorithm, it is necessary to move $n-1$ disks using a recursive call to *towers*. Thus, on the recursive call, the first input variable to *towers* will be $n-1$. But this implies that the top $n-1$ disks are numbered $1, 2, 3, \ldots, n-1$ and that the smallest disk is numbered 1. This is a good example of programming convenience determining problem representation.

There is no a priori reason for labeling the smallest disk 1; logically, the largest disk could have been labeled 1 and the smallest disk *n*. However, since it leads to a simpler and more direct approach, we will choose to label the disks so that the smallest disk has the smallest number.

What are the other input variables to *towers?* At first glance, it might appear that no additional input variables are necessary since the pegs are named *A, B,* and *C* by default. However, a closer look at the recursive solution leads us to the realization that on the recursive calls disks will be moved not from *A* to *C* using *B* as auxiliary but rather from *A* to *B* using *C* (step 2) or from *B* to *C* using *A* (step 4). We therefore include three additional input variables in *towers.* The first, *source,* represents the peg from which we are removing disks; the second, *dest,* represents the peg to which we will take the disks; and the third, *aux,* represents the auxiliary peg. This situation is one which is quite typical of recursive routines; additional input variables are necessary to handle the recursive call situation. We already saw one example of this in the binary search algorithm, where the input variables *low* and *high* were necessary despite the fact that the initial call will always have *low* equal to 1 and *high* equal to the size of the array being searched. Thus our particular Towers of Hanoi problem would be solved by calling

$$towers(4, \text{``}A\text{''}, \text{``}C\text{''}, \text{``}B\text{''})$$

The complete algorithm to solve the Towers of Hanoi problem, closely following the original recursive solution, may be written as follows:

> **subroutine** *towers* (*n, source, dest, aux*)
> '*initially in our example,* source *is A,* dest *is C, and* aux *is B*
> '*if only one disk, make the move and return*
> **if** *n* = 1
>   **then print** "move disk 1 from peg" ; *source;* "to peg" ; *dest*
>   **return**
> **endif**
> '*move top* $n - 1$ *disks from A to B, using C as auxiliary*
> *towers* ($n - 1,$ *source, aux, dest*)
> '*move remaining disk from A to C*
> **print** " move disk " ; *n;* " from peg " ; *source;* " to peg " ; *dest*
> '*move* $n - 1$ *disks from B to C, using A as auxiliary*
> *towers* ($n - 1,$ *aux, dest, source*)
> **return**

Trace the actions of the algorithm above when it inputs the value 4 for *n,* "*A*" for *source,* "*C*" for *dest,* and "*B*" for *aux.* Be careful to keep track of the changing values of the input variables *source, aux,* and *dest.* Verify that it produces the following output:

> move disk 1 from peg *A* to peg *B*
> move disk 2 from peg *A* to peg *C*
> move disk 1 from peg *B* to peg *C*
> move disk 3 from peg *A* to peg *B*
> move disk 1 from peg *C* to peg *A*
> move disk 2 from peg *C* to peg *B*
> move disk 1 from peg *A* to peg *B*
> move disk 4 from peg *A* to peg *C*
> move disk 1 from peg *B* to peg *C*
> move disk 2 from peg *B* to peg *A*
> move disk 1 from peg *C* to peg *A*
> move disk 3 from peg *B* to peg *C*
> move disk 1 from peg *A* to peg *B*
> move disk 2 from peg *A* to peg *C*
> move disk 1 from peg *B* to peg *C*

Verify that the solution above actually works and does not violate any of the rules.

Properties of Recursive Definitions or Algorithms

Let us summarize what is involved in a recursive definition or algorithm. One important requirement for a recursive algorithm to be correct is that it not generate an infinite sequence of calls on itself. Clearly, any algorithm that does generate such a sequence will never terminate. For at least one input or group of inputs, a recursive process *p* must be defined in terms that do not involve *p*. There must be a "way out" of the sequence of recursive calls. In the examples of this section, the nonrecursive portions of the definitions were

Factorial:	$0! = 1$
Multiplication:	$a*1 = a$
Fibonacci sequence:	$fib(0) = 0 \quad fib(1) = 1$
Binary search:	**if** $low > high$ **then** $binsrch = 0$
	if $x = a(mid)$ **then** $binsrch = mid$
Towers of Hanoi:	**if** $n = 1$ **then print** "move disk 1 from peg" ; *source;*
	"to peg" ; *dest*

Without such a nonrecursive exit, no recursive function can ever be computed.

The second ingredient of a recursive definition or algorithm is to be able to represent a complex case in terms of a simpler one. In the examples of this section these representations were

Factorial:	$n! = n*(n-1)!$ for $n > 0$
Multiplication:	$a*b = a*(b-1)+a$ for $b > 1$
Fibonacci sequence:	$fib(n) = fib(n-1) + fib(n-2)$ for $n >= 2$
Binary search:	search for *x* in $a(low)$ to $a(mid-1)$ for $x < a\ (mid)$
	search for *x* in $a(mid+1)$ to $a(high)$ for $x > a\ (mid)$

Towers of Hanoi: $towers(n-1, source, aux, dest)$ and
$towers(n-1, aux, dest, source)$ for $n > 1$

Any instance of a recursive definition or invocation of a recursive algorithm must contain a general representation of a complex case in terms of a simpler one and must eventually reduce to some manipulation of one or more simple, nonrecursive cases.

EXERCISES

1. Write iterative and recursive algorithms to evaluate $a * b$ by using addition, where a and b are nonnegative integers.
2. Let a be an array of integers. Present recursive algorithms to compute:
   (a) The maximum element of the array
   (b) The minimum element of the array
   (c) The sum of the elements of the array
   (d) The product of the elements of the array
   (e) The average of the elements of the array
3. Evaluate each of the following, using both the iterative and recursive definitions.
   (a) 6!   (b) 9!
   (c) 100 * 3   (d) 6 * 4
   (e) $fib(10)$ (f) $fib(11)$
4. Assume that an array of 10 integers contains the elements

   1, 3, 7, 15, 21, 22, 36, 78, 95, 106

   Use the recursive binary search to find each of the following items in the array (if they exist).
   (a) 1   (b) 20   (c) 36   (d) 200
5. Write an iterative version of the binary search algorithm. (*Hint:* Modify the values of *low* and *high* directly.)
6. Ackerman's function is defined recursively on the nonnegative integers as follows:

   $a(m,n) = n+1$ if $m = 0$
   $a(m,n) = a(m-1, 1)$ if $m <> 0, n = 0$
   $a(m,n) = a(m-1, a(m,n-1))$ if $m <> 0, n <> 0$

   (a) Using the definition above, show that $a(2,2) = 7$.
   (b) Prove that $a(m,n)$ is defined for all nonnegative integers m and n.
   (c) Can you find an iterative method of computing $a(m,n)$?
7. Count the number of additions necessary to compute $fib(n)$ for $0 <= n <= 10$ by the iterative and recursive methods. Does any pattern emerge?

8. If an array contains n elements, what are the maximum number of recursive calls made by the binary search algorithm?

9. Develop recursive algorithms to do the following.

    (a) Find the sum of all the integers in a linked linear list.

    (b) Reverse a linked linear list so that the first element is last, the second is next to last, and so on.

2. BASIC IMPLEMENTATION OF RECURSIVE ALGORITHMS

In this section we examine the mechanisms used to implement recursion. Some computer languages (such as Algol, Pascal, and PI/I) allow recursive programs, so that a subroutine may, indeed, call itself. Other languages (such as BASIC, FORTRAN, and COBOL) do not have recursion built in as a language mechanism. Therefore, to implement a recursive solution in such a language, it is necessary to simulate mechanisms for implementing recursion using nonrecursive techniques. A problem such as the Towers of Hanoi whose solution can be derived and stated quite simply using recursive techniques can be programmed in these languages by simulating the recursive solution using more elementary operations. If we know that the recursive solution is correct (and it is often fairly easy to prove such a solution correct) and we have established techniques for converting a recursive solution to a nonrecursive one, we can create a correct solution in a nonrecursive language. It is not an uncommon occurrence for a programmer to be able to state a solution to a problem in the form of a recursive algorithm. The ability to generate a nonrecursive solution from this algorithm is indispensable when using a language that does not support recursion.

Let us examine the recursive algorithm for the factorial function more closely to determine why it cannot be implemented in BASIC directly. We repeat the algorithm for that process:

1.   **if** $n = 0$
2.   **then** $fact = 1$
3.   **return**
4.   **else**
5. $x = n - 1$
6.   find the value of $x!$. call it y.
7. $fact = n * y$
8.   **return**
9.   **endif**

In presenting this algorithm in Section 1, we described its operation as temporarily suspending itself on its current machine when it reached line 6 (the recursive call), and beginning execution on a new machine, with the input variable n on the second machine initialized to the value of x on the first machine. The reason for this conceptualization was that, in BASIC, there is only a single variable named n. Therefore, if n were reset to x on the first machine, its old value would be lost forever. But once the value of $x!$ has been computed, the old value of n is required again (in line 7) so that it can be multiplied by the value of $x!$ to yield the value of $n!$. Therefore, several values of n must be maintained simultaneously, one for each concurrent recursive call. The easiest way to conceptualize this is to think of each recursive execution as executing on its own machine. In that case, it is perfectly reasonable to have several variables named n, one on each machine.

However, we note that at any single instant, we must have access to only a single copy of n—that copy which exists within the current call. That is, only one of our "machines" is active at any time. The others are waiting for the active machine to complete its calculation of factorial and return its result. Furthermore, once a cursive call has terminated, the values of its variables are no longer required.

This description suggests the use of a stack to keep the successive generations of variables. Each item on the stack represents a new machine executing a recursive call and consists of the variables of the algorithm executing on the new machine. Each time that a recursive routine is entered, a new allocation of its variables is pushed on top of the stack. Any reference to a variable in that routine is through the current top of the stack. When the routine returns, the stack is popped, the top allocation is freed, and the previous allocation becomes the current stack top to be used for referencing variables. This represents a machine, having computed its factorial value and returned that value to the previous machine and halting execution as the previous machine resumes execution.

Figure 5.2.1 contains a series of snapshots of the stacks for the variables n, x, and y as execution of the *fact* algorithm proceeds. Initially, the stacks are empty, as illustrated by Figure 5.2.1(a). After the first call on *fact* by the calling procedure, the situation is as shown in Figure 5.2.1(b), with $n = 4$. Copies of the variables x and y exist but are not initialized. Since n does not equal 0, x is set to 3 and *fact*(3) is called [Figure 5.2.1(c)]. The new value of n again does not equal 0, so x is set to 2 and *fact*(2) is called [Figure 5.2.1(d)]. This continues until n equals 0 [Figure 5.2.1(f)]. At that point, the value 1 is returned from the call to *fact*(0). Execution resumes from the point at which *fact*(0) was called, which is the assignment of the returned value to the copy of y declared in *fact*(1). This is illustrated by the status of the stack shown in Figure 5.2.1(g), where the variables allocated for *fact*(0) have been freed and y is set to 1.

The statement *fact* $= n*y$ is then executed, multiplying the top values of n and y to obtain 1, and returning this value to *fact*(2) [Figure 5.2.1(h)]. This process is repeated twice more, until finally the value of y in *fact*(4) equals 6 [Figure 5.2.1(j)]. The statement *fact* $= n*y$ is executed one more time. The product 24 is returned to the calling routine.

Note that each time a recursive routine returns, it returns to the point immediately following the point from which it was called. Thus the recursive call to *fact*(3) returns to the assignment of the result to y within *fact*(4), but the recursive

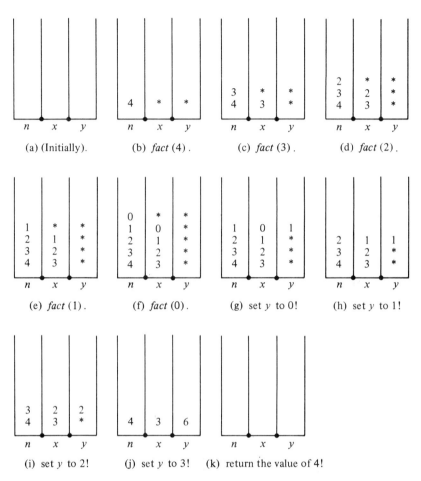

Figure 5.2.1   The stack at various times during execution. (An asterisk indicates an uninitialized value.)

call to *fact*(4) returns to the statement in the calling routine or the main program from which it was invoked.

Note that as we have presented the implementation of recursion, all three variables (*n*, *x*, and *y*) used by the recursive algorithm are stacked. However, it is only necessary to stack *n*. To see why this is so, recall the reason for using a stack in the first place. It is necessary to push the old value of *n* on a stack because that old value will be required after we return from the recursive invocation in which the value of *n* is reset. This illustrates that both of the following two conditions must be true in order to require that a variable be stacked:

1. The variable must have been assigned a value before a recursive invocation takes place. (*n* has been assigned such a value by virtue of its being an input variable to the algorithm.)

2. The value assigned before the recursive invocation must be used within the algorithm after the recursive invocation. (The value of n that has been input is used in line 7.)

To determine whether or not x and y must be stacked, we must examine whether or not both these conditions are true for these two variables. In the case of x, condition 1 is most certainly true. x is assigned a value in line 5, before the recursive invocation of line 6. However, condition 2 is not true for x. Nowhere in lines 7–9 is any use made of the previous value of x. Therefore, the value of x can be modified by the recursive invocation without stacking the old value, since that old value is never used again.

In the case of y, we have a different situation. y was never assigned a value before the recursive invocation. It is not an input variable, nor is it given a value in lines 1–5. Therefore, y does not meet condition 1 and does not have to be stacked. (In fact, even if y were given a value in lines 1–5, it would still not have to be stacked, since it does not meet condition 2 either. Although the value of y is used in line 7, that value is the one that was assigned in line 6 after the recursive invocation. To meet condition 2, the value that must be used after the recursive invocation must be one which was assigned to the variable before that invocation.)

To verify the fact that x and y need not be stacked, review the actions of the algorithm with $n = 4$ as depicted in Figure 5.2.1, but ignoring the stacks for x and y. Assume single variables x and y whose values are modified regardless of recursive invocations. Of course, n is still stacked. Notice that executing the algorithm under this model yields the same results as when x and y were stacked.

Factorial in BASIC

We have just described the action of the recursive factorial algorithm using a stack to represent the successive allocations of the variables. By using a stack, we should therefore be able to mimic these actions in BASIC. However, one problem remains. Many versions of BASIC do not allow a subroutine to call itself. That is, the group of statements executed following the execution of a GOSUB statement and before the execution of a RETURN statement may not contain a GOSUB to another statement within that group. Other versions of BASIC do not impose (or do not enforce) this restriction, but have other restrictions (which we discuss shortly) which severely limit the usefulness of such a GOSUB. Thus it may not be possible or practical to implement a recursive call by executing a GOSUB to the recursive routine since the GOSUB is contained within the group of statements making up the subroutine. In the interest of clarity of presentation, however, we will ignore all such restrictions for the moment and present a method to implement the recursive factorial algorithm in BASIC by actually using recursive GOSUBs.

We make one further modification from the illustration of Figure 5.2.1.

Rather than using the top of the stack as the current value of the variable N, we use a separate variable CN, which is pushed onto and popped from the stack that contains all the previous values of this variable. The stack itself is kept in an array PARAM and is declared by

```
10   MXSTACK = 50
20   DIM PARAM(MXSTACK)
```

The subroutine *push* (at statement 1000) accepts CN and pushes its value onto the stack; the subroutine *pop* (at statement 2000) pops the stack and sets the variable POPS to the popped value. The simulated factorial routine, called *simfact*, begins by initializing the stack to empty, CN to the input value N, and pushes a dummy data area onto the stack to reflect the initial call from the main program. (This is necessary so that the final return to the main program does not find the stack empty.) A recursive call is implemented by pushing CN onto the stack, resetting CN to the new input value and executing a GOSUB. A return is implemented by popping the stack onto CN and executing a RETURN. The output of the routine is kept in the variable SIMFACT.

```
10000   'subroutine simfact
10010   'inputs: N
10020   'outputs: SIMFACT
10030   'locals: CN, POPS, TP, X, Y
10040   'initialization
10050   TP = 0: 'the stack is initially empty
10060   CN = N
10070   'push a dummy data area onto the stack
10080   GOSUB 1000: 'subroutine push accepts CN

10090   'this is the beginning of the simulated routine
10100   IF CN = 0 THEN SIMFACT = 1: GOTO 10190:
                                     'lines 1 - 2 of the algorithm
10110   X = CN - 1
10120   'call fact recursively (line 6)
10130   GOSUB 1000: 'subroutine push
10140   CN = X
10150   GOSUB 10090: 'the actual call

10160   'return to this point after the recursive call
10170   Y = SIMFACT: 'second half of line 6
10180   SIMFACT = CN*Y: 'line 7

10190   'the following is a simulation of the return in lines 3 and 8
10200   GOSUB 2000: 'subroutine pop sets the variable POPS
10210   CN = POPS
10220   RETURN: 'to line 10160 or the main program
10230   'endsub
```

You are invited to trace through the actions of this routine for N = 4 to see how it mirrors the actions of the recursive algorithm.

The Call / Return Mechanism

Now that we have seen how to manage multiple allocations of variables in recursive algorithms, we turn to the question of the recursive call/return mechanism and how it can be simulated. We must do this because many versions of BASIC prohibit recursive calls such as the one in line 10150 of the preceding program. This call is recursive because between 10090 (which is the target of the GOSUB) and line 10220 (which is the RETURN), the program may execute line 10150 again (which is a GOSUB to the same group of statements.) Other versions of BASIC permit such a call, but limit the nesting depth of subroutine calls. This nesting depth equals the number of GOSUB statements that have been executed whose corresponding RETURN statements have not yet been executed. The nesting depth of most programs stays safely below this maximum, since the nesting depth is always less than the number of subroutines contained in the program. (Indeed, it is rare for the nesting depth to equal this number since one routine directly calls many others, so that one subroutine will have returned before another is called.) But a program containing a recursive routine can easily exceed the nesting depth if it is called with a large input because the routine repeatedly calls itself. Thus there are situations where the use of direct recursion in BASIC is not possible.

If a GOSUB is prohibited as a means of implementing recursion, we must find some other mechanism. To discover a method of doing this, let us examine how an ordinary GOSUB and RETURN are implemented. When a subroutine is called, it must eventually return control to the statement following the GOSUB. This means that a record must be maintained of this location, called the **return address.** If several subroutines have been called but have not yet returned, a return address must be maintained for each one. Thus if the main program executes GOSUB *xxx,* the subroutine at *xxx* executes GOSUB *yyy,* and the subroutine at *yyy* executes GOSUB *zzz,* then three return addresses are maintained: the location *lz* of the statement following GOSUB *zzz* to which the subroutine at *zzz* must return, the location *ly* of the statement following GOSUB *yyy* to which the subroutine at *yyy* must return, and the location *lx* of the statement following GOSUB *xxx* to which the subroutine at *xxx* must return.

These return addresses can be maintained in a stack. A GOSUB pushes the address of its following statement on the return address stack and branches (executes a GOTO) to its target. When GOSUB *xxx* is executed, *lx* is pushed onto the stack and we branch to *xxx.* When GOSUB *yyy* is executed, *ly* is pushed on top of *lx* and we branch to *yyy.* Finally, when GOSUB *zzz* is executed, *lz* is pushed on top of *ly* and *lz* and we branch to *zzz.* Figure 5.2.2(a) illustrates this situation and the corresponding return address stack.

When a subroutine executes a RETURN, the return address stack is popped

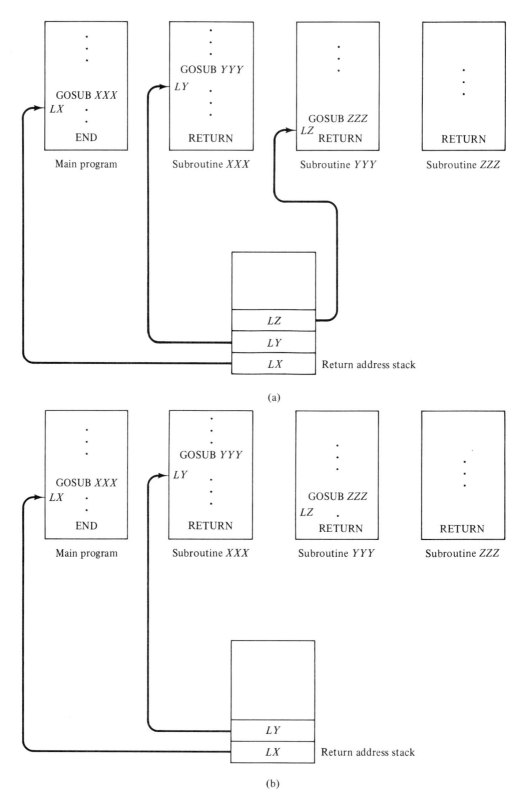

(a)

(b)

244

Figure 5.2.2

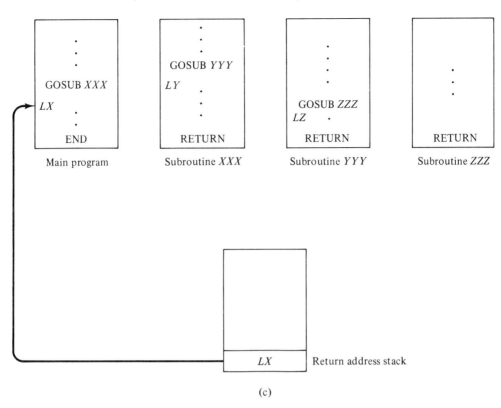

Figure 5.2.2   *(continued).*

and a branch is executed to the return address popped off the stack. Thus when the subroutine at *zzz* executes RETURN, *lz* is popped off the stack and the program branches to *lz*, which follows GOSUB *zzz* in the subroutine at *yyy*. This is illustrated in Figure 5.2.2(b). When this routine returns in turn, *ly* is popped and the program branches to *ly*, following GOSUB *yyy* in the subroutine at *xxx* [Figure 5.2.2(c)]. Then this routine returns by popping *lx* from the stack and branching to *lx* following GOSUB *xxx*. Note that the return address for a routine is not determined by that routine but by the routine that calls it. The same routine may be called from several different locations in several different routines and the return address is determined by the location from which it is called.

The same mechanism can be used by a recursive call and return. We can consider the data area that must be pushed onto a stack in simulating a recursive call and popped from the stack in simulating a recursive return as containing a return address as well as the values of program variables that must be preserved.

How can we manipulate return addresses in BASIC? We cannot access the actual addresses themselves or push statement numbers onto a stack. Instead, we use a variable called a ***return indicator*** whose integer value indicates the location to which the routine must return. For example, the factorial function can return to one of two locations: the assignment of X! to Y or to the statement in the program that initially invoked *fact*.

Suppose that a variable CRETADDR, used as a return indicator, can assume the value 1 or 2. The value 1 indicates that the current invocation of the recursive routine is the initial invocation and that, upon completion, the routine is to return to the main program. Upon initial entry to the factorial routine, CRETADDR is therefore set to 1. The value 2 indicates that the current invocation is a recursive invocation that is to return to the previous invocation. When the routine calls itself recursively, the value of CRETADDR is saved on a stack. Thus when the called invocation returns, that previous value of CRETADDR can be restored, thereby enabling the calling routine to return to the proper location. After the current value of CRETADDR has been stacked, CRETADDR is reset to 2, indicating that the new invocation is a recursive one. Indeed, we can view the return indicator as an implicit input variable of the recursive algorithm, to be used in effecting its return. Thus we require, in addition to the stack of variables, a stack of return indicators. This stack can be declared by

30   DIM RETADDR (MXSTACK)

Note that a single TP value can be used for both the PARAM and RETADDR stacks since both stacks are pushed and popped at the same time: in simulating a recursive call and a recursive return. Alternatively, and closer to reality, the two stacks can be viewed as a single stack of data areas, each containing two elements or fields: a saved parameter value and a saved return indicator value. There is also a current data area, consisting of the variables CN and CRETADDR. Thus we can use a single specially designed *push* routine which accepts the current data area (CN and CRETADDR) and pushes it onto the stack, and a single specially designed *pop* routine which pops a data area from the stack into the current data area.

Thus the simulation of the recursive factorial call consists of the statements

```
10135   'save the old parameter values on the stack
10140   GOSUB 1000: 'subroutine push
10145   'initialize the new input values
10150   CN = X
10160   CRETADDR = 2: 'the simulated call is to return to the
                       'previous invocation
10165   'simulate the actual recursive call
10170   GOTO . . .: 'the start of the simulated routine
```

The simulation of the return from the recursive factorial routine consists of setting the variable SIMFACT to the result of the factorial computation and then executing

```
10220  I = CRETADDR:          'save the current return indicator
10230  GOSUB 2000:            'subroutine pop resets CN and CRETADDR
10240  IF I = 1 THEN RETURN:  'to the main routine
10250  IF I = 2 THEN GOTO . . .:  'the point following the recursive call
```

We now present the complete simulation of the recursive factorial routine:

```
10000  'subroutine simfact
10010  'inputs: N
10020  'outputs: SIMFACT
10030  'locals: CN, CRETADDR, TP, X, Y
10040  'initialization
10050  TP = 0: 'the stack is initially empty
10060  CN = N
10070  CRETADDR = 1
10080  'push a dummy data area onto the stack
10090  GOSUB 1000: 'subroutine push accepts CN and CRETADDR

10100  'this is the beginning of the simulated routine
10110  IF CN = 0 THEN SIMFACT = 1: GOTO 10210: 'return
10120      X = CN − 1
10130      'call fact recursively
10140      GOSUB 1000: 'subroutine push
10150      CN = X
10160      CRETADDR = 2
10170  GOTO 10100

10180  'return to this point after the recursive call
10190  Y = SIMFACT
10200  SIMFACT = CN * Y

10210  'the following is the simulation of the return
10220  I = CRETADDR
10230  GOSUB 2000: 'subroutine pop resets CN and CRETADDR
10240  IF I = 1 THEN RETURN: 'to the main program
10250  IF I = 2 THEN GOTO 10180: 'the point following the recursive call
10260  'endsub
```

We adopt the convention that the code to simulate a return (statements 10210–10250) is always placed at the end of the routine. Any return that must be executed within the body of the routine (such as in statement 10110) is simulated by transferring control to this block of code.

Although this routine is fairly complex, it has been derived by a direct application of a mechanical process which can be applied to any recursive algorithm. Later in this section we will see how to simplify the complex routine and make it more straightforward.

For completeness, we also present the routines *push* and *pop* as required by *simfact*:

```
1000   'subroutine push
1010   'inputs: CN, CRETADDR, MXSTACK, TP
1020   'outputs: PARAM, RETADDR, TP
1030   'locals: none
1040   IF TP = MXSTACK THEN PRINT "STACK OVERFLOW": STOP
1050   TP = TP + 1
1060   PARAM(TP) = CN
1070   RETADDR(TP) = CRETADDR
1080   RETURN
1090   'endsub

2000   'subroutine pop
2010   'inputs: PARAM, RETADDR, TP
2020   'outputs: CN, CRETADDR, TP
2030   'locals: EMPTY
2040   GOSUB 3000: 'subroutine empty sets the variable EMPTY
2050   IF EMPTY = TRUE THEN PRINT "STACK UNDERFLOW": STOP
2060   CN = PARAM(TP)
2070   CRETADDR = RETADDR(TP)
2080   TP = TP - 1
2090   RETURN
2100   'endsub
```

The Towers of Hanoi in BASIC

Let us now look at a more complex example of recursion, the Towers of Hanoi problem presented in Section 1, and simulate its recursion to produce a nonrecursive BASIC program. We present again the recursive algorithm of Section 1.

```
'subroutine towers (n, source, dest, aux)
'initially, in our example, source is A, dest is C, and aux is B
'if only one disk, make the move and return
if n = 1
   then print " move disk 1 from peg " ; source; " to peg " ; dest
        return
endif
'move top n − 1 disks from source to aux, using dest as auxiliary
towers (n − 1, source, aux, dest)
'move remaining disk from source to dest
print " move disk " ; n; " from peg " ; source; " to peg " ; dest
'move n − 1 disks from aux to dest, using source as auxiliary
towers (n − 1, aux, dest, source)
return
```

Make sure that you understand the problem and the recursive solution before proceeding. If you do not, reread the last portion of Section 1.

There are four input variables in this subroutine, each of which is subject to change in a recursive call. Therefore, the data area must contain elements representing all four. There are three possible points to which the subroutine returns on various calls: the calling program and the statements following the two recursive calls. Therefore, the return indicator can assume three possible values. The return indicator is encoded as an integer (either 1, 2, or 3) within each data area.

The following is a sample main program with a nonrecursive simulation of *towers*. We can use the variables CSOURCE, CAUX, and CDEST as the current values of the algorithm variables *source, aux,* and *dest*. This means that program variables beginning with the letter C are strings, so that the current values of N and the return address are named NC and ZRETADDR (instead of CN and CRETADDR as in the factorial example). Similarly, the stacks for the disk variables are named PSOURCE, PDEST, and PAUX, reserving P as an initial letter for string variables, so that the stacks for N and the return address are named NPARAM and RETADDR.

```
 100   'main program
 110   DEFSTR A, C, D, P, S
 120   DIM NPARAM (50):      'stack for values of N
 130   DIM PSOURCE (50):     'stack for values of SOURCE
 140   DIM PDEST (50):       'stack for values of DEST
 150   DIM PAUX(50):         'stack for values of AUX
 160   DIM RETADDR(50):      'stack for return indicators
 170   INPUT N
 180   SOURCE = "A"
 190   DEST = "C"
 200   AUX = "B"
 210   GOSUB 10000:          'subroutine simtowers
 220   END
 230   '
 240   '
 250   '
1000   'subroutine push goes here
           . . .
2000   'subroutine pop goes here
           . . .
10000  'subroutine simtowers
10010  'inputs: AUX, DEST, N, SOURCE
10020  'outputs: none
10030  'locals: CAUX, CDEST, CSOURCE, CTEMP, NC, TP, ZRETADDR
10040  'initialization
10050  TP = 0
```

```
10060  'set the input variables and the return address of the current
10070  'data area to their proper values
10080  NC = N:                        'the current value of N
10090  CSOURCE = SOURCE:              'the current value of SOURCE
10100  CDEST = DEST:                  'the current value of DEST
10110  CAUX = AUX:                    'the current value of AUX
10120  ZRETADDR = 1:                  'the current return indicator
10130  'push dummy data area onto stack
10140  GOSUB 1000: 'subroutine push pushes NC, CSOURCE, CDEST, CAUX,
                   'and ZRETADDR onto the stack


10150  'this is the beginning of the simulated routine
10160  IF NC = 1 THEN PRINT " MOVE DISK 1 FROM PEG " ; CSOURCE;
                         " TO PEG " ; CDEST: GOTO 10360
10170     'this is the first recursive call
10180     GOSUB 1000:                 'subroutine push
10190     NC = NC - 1
10200     CTEMP = CAUX:               'interchange CAUX and CDEST
10210     CAUX = CDEST
10220     CDEST = CTEMP
10230     ZRETADDR = 2
10240  GOTO 10150
10250     'we return to this point from the first recursive call
10260     PRINT "MOVE DISK "; NC; " FROM PEG "; CSOURCE; " TO PEG ";
             CDEST
10270     'this is the second recursive call
10280     GOSUB 1000: 'subroutine push
10290     NC = NC - 1
10300     CTEMP = CSOURCE: 'interchange CAUX and CSOURCE
10310     CSOURCE = CAUX
10320     CAUX = CTEMP
10330     ZRETADDR = 3
10340  GOTO 10150


10350  'return to this point from the second recursive call
10360  'simulation of a return
10370  I = ZRETADDR
10380  GOSUB 2000: 'subroutine pop resets the variables NC, CSOURCE,
                   'CDEST, CAUX, TP, and ZRETADDR
10390  IF I = 1 THEN RETURN
10400  IF I = 2 THEN GOTO 10250
10410  IF I = 3 THEN GOTO 10350
10420  'endsub
```

Improving the Simulating Routines

There are a number of techniques which we can frequently use to simplify simulations of recursion. In our discussion of the simulation of the factorial routine, we have already come across one of these techniques: not all variables of a recursive algorithm need be stacked. We now examine some additional techniques which can eliminate some of the complexity of recursive invocation and reduce or even eliminate the need for the return indicator stack.

Let us reexamine the second simulation of the recursive factorial algorithm. There is only one textual recursive call of the factorial routine (in algorithm line 6 and program statements 10130–10170), so there is only one return address within *simfact* (at statement 10180). The other return address is to the main routine which originally called *simfact*. But suppose that a dummy data area had not been stacked upon initialization of the simulation. Then a data area is placed on the stack only in simulating a recursive call. When the stack is popped in returning from a recursive call, that area is removed from the stack. However, when an attempt is made to pop the stack in simulating a return to the main procedure, an underflow will occur. We can test for this underflow by using *popandtest* rather than *pop*, and when it does occur we can return directly to the outside calling routine rather than through a return indicator. This means that one of the return addresses can be eliminated. Since this leaves only a single possible return address, it need not be placed on the stack.

Thus the current data area has been reduced to contain the single variable CN and the stack to the single array PARAM. The program is now quite compact and comprehensible.

```
10000   'subroutine simfact
10010   'inputs: N
10020   'outputs: SIMFACT
10030   'locals: CN, TP, UND, X, Y
10040   'initialization
10050   TP = 0
10060   CN = N
10070   'this is the beginning of the simulated routine
10080   IF CN = 0 THEN SIMFACT = 1: GOTO 10170:   'return
10090      X = CN − 1
10100      'call fact recursively
10110      GOSUB 1000: 'subroutine push accepts CN
10120      CN = X
10130   GOTO 10070

10140   'return to this point after the recursive call
10150      Y = SIMFACT
10160      SIMFACT = CN*Y
```

```
10170      'statements 10180–10200 simulate the return
10180         GOSUB 4000: 'subroutine popandtest resets CN and UND
10190   IF UND = FALSE THEN GOTO 10140: 'the point after the recursive
                                                              'call
10200   IF UND = TRUE THEN RETURN: 'to the main program
10210   'endsub
```

Note that we have indented statements 10090–10120 and 10150–10180 to illustrate that the program actually consists of two loops, although we did not originally design it that way. We will explain the significance of this shortly.

Eliminating GOTO

Although the program above is certainly simpler than the preceding one, it is still far from an "ideal" program. If you were to look at the program without having seen its derivation, it is doubtful that you could identify it as computing the factorial function. The statements:

$$10130 \quad \text{GOTO } 10070$$

and

$$10190 \quad \text{IF UND = FALSE THEN GOTO } 10140$$

are particularly irritating since they interrupt the flow of thought at a time that one might otherwise come to an understanding of what is happening. Let us see if we can transform this program into a still more readable version.

The two variables X and CN are assigned values from each other and are never in use simultaneously, so they may be combined and referred to as one variable X. A similar statement may be made about the variables SIMFACT and Y, which can be combined and referred to as the single variable Y, which is assigned to the output variable SIMFACT only upon return to the main program. Performing these transformations leads to the following version of *simfact*:

```
10000   'subroutine simfact
10010   'inputs: N
10020   'outputs: SIMFACT
10030   'locals: TP, UND, X, Y
10040   'initialization
10050   TP = 0
10060   X = N
10070   'this is the beginning of the simulated routine
10080   IF X = 0 THEN Y = 1: GOTO 10150: 'return
10090      'call fact recursively
10100         GOSUB 1000: 'subroutine push accepts X
10110      X = X − 1
10120   GOTO 10070
```

```
10130    'return to this point after the recursive call
10140        Y = X * Y
10150        'the following is a simulation of the return
10160        GOSUB 4000: 'subroutine popandtest resets X and UND
10170        IF UND = TRUE THEN SIMFACT = Y: RETURN
10180    GOTO 10130: 'return to the point following the recursive call
10190    'endsub
```

We are now beginning to approach a readable program. The program consists of two loops:

1. The subtraction loop, which consists of statements 10070–10120.
   This loop is exited when X = 0, at which point Y is set to 1 and execution
   proceeds to the statement labeled 10150.
2. The multiplication loop, which begins at 10130 and ends with GOTO 10130
   at statement 10180. This loop is exited when the stack has been emptied and
   underflow occurs, at which point a return is executed.

Let us examine these two loops more closely. X starts off at the value of the
input parameter N and is reduced by 1 each time the subtraction loop is repeated.
Each time X is set to a new value, the old value of X is saved on the stack. This
continues until X is 0. Thus after the first loop has been executed, the stack contains, from top to bottom, the integers 1 to N.

The multiplication loop merely removes each of these values from the stack
and sets Y to the product of the popped value and the old value of Y. Since we
know what the stack contains at the start of the multiplication loop, why bother
popping the stack? We can use those values directly. We can eliminate the stack
and the first loop entirely and replace the multiplication loop with a loop that
multiplies Y by each of the integers from 1 to N in turn. The resulting program is

```
10000    'subroutine simfact
10010    'inputs: N
10020    'outputs: SIMFACT
10030    'locals: X,Y
10040    Y = 1
10050    FOR X = 1 TO N
10060        Y = Y * X
10070    NEXT X
10080    SIMFACT = Y
10090    RETURN
10100    'endsub
```

But this program is a direct BASIC implementation of the iterative version of the
factorial function as presented in Section 1. The only change is that X varies from
1 to N rather than from N to 1.

Thus a series of simplifications, beginning with the brute-force simulation of a recursive algorithm, has brought us to a direct and efficient program for solving a problem. Although this direct program is apparent for the factorial algorithm, there are many other problems for which a direct program is not so apparent but for which a recursive solution is available. The techniques we have presented form powerful tools for implementing solutions to these problems. We illustrate the simplification techniques once again for a more complex problem, Towers of Hanoi.

Simplifying Towers of Hanoi

Let us reexamine the routine *simtower* presented earlier to solve the Towers of Hanoi problem.

First, notice that three return indicator values were used: one for each of the two recursive calls and one for the return to the main program. However, the return to the main program can be signaled by an underflow in the stack, exactly as in the second version of *simfact*. This leaves two return indicator values. If we could eliminate one more such value, it would no longer be necessary to stack a return indicator, since there would be only one point remaining to which control may be passed if the stack is popped successfully. We focus our attention on the second recursive call of the algorithm and the following statements:

$$towers(n-1, aux, dest, source)$$
$$\textit{return}$$

The actions that occur in simulating this call are:

1. Push the current data area, $A1$, onto the stack.
2. Set the parameters in the new current data area, $A2$, to their respective values: $n-1$, *aux*, *dest*, and *source*.
3. Set the return indicator in the current data area, $A2$, to indicate the address of the statement immediately following the call.
4. Branch to the beginning of the simulated routine.

After the simulated routine has completed, it is ready to return. The following actions occur:

5. Save the return indicator, i, from the current data area $A2$.
6. Pop the stack and set the current data area to the popped data area, $A1$.
7. Branch to the statement indicated by the value of i.

But the statement indicated by the value of i is the **return** statement since **return** immediately follows the second recursive call to *towers*. Thus the next step is to pop the stack again and return once more. We never again make use of the information in the current data area $A1$, since it is immediately destroyed by popping the stack as soon as it has been restored. Since there is no reason to use this data area again, there is no reason to save it on the stack in simulating the call. Data need be saved on the stack only if they are to be reused. Therefore, in this case, the call may be simulated simply by

1. Changing the parameters in the current data area to their respective values
2. Branching to the beginning of the simulated routine.

When the simulated routine returns it can return directly to the routine that called the current version. There is no reason to execute a return to the current version, only to return immediately to the preceding version. Since there is only one possible return indicator value left, it is unnecessary to keep it in the data area, to be pushed and popped with the rest of the data. Whenever the stack is popped successfully, there is only one address to which a branch can be executed: the statement following the first call. If an underflow is encountered, the routine returns to the calling routine.

Our revised main program and nonrecursive simulation of *towers* follows:

```
100    'main program
110    DEPSTR A, C, D, P, S
120    DIM NPARAM (50)
130    DIM PSOURCE(50)
140    DIM PDEST(50)
150    DIM PAUX(50)
160    TRUE = 1
170    FALSE = 0
180    INPUT N
190    SOURCE = ''A''
200    DEST = ''C''
210    AUX = ''B''
220    GOSUB 10000:          'subroutine simtowers
230    END
240    '
250    '
260    '

              . . .
10000  'subroutine simtowers
10010  'inputs: AUX, DEST, N, SOURCE
10020  'outputs: none
10030  'locals: CAUX, CDEST, CSOURCE, CTEMP, NC, TP, UND
10040  'initialization
10050  TP = 0
10060  NC = N
10070  CSOURCE = SOURCE
10080  CDEST = DEST
10090  CAUX = AUX
```

```
10100   'the simulated routine begins here
10110   IF NC = 1 THEN PRINT "MOVE DISK 1 FROM PEG "; CSOURCE;
                                        " TO PEG "; CDEST: GOTO 10270
10120      'simulation of first recursive call
10130      GOSUB 1000:          'subroutine push
10140      NC = NC − 1
10150      CTEMP = CDEST
10160      CDEST = CAUX
10170      CAUX = CTEMP
10180   GOTO 10100

10190      'this is the point of return from the first recursive call
10200      PRINT "MOVE DISK "; NC; " FROM PEG "; CSOURCE; " TO PEG ";
                                                                 CDEST

10210      'simulation of second recursive call
10220      NC = NC − 1
10230      CTEMP = CSOURCE
10240      CSOURCE = CAUX
10250      CAUX = CTEMP
10260   GOTO 10100

10270   'simulation of a return
10280   GOSUB 4000: 'subroutine popandtest sets the variables NC,
                    'CSOURCE, CDEST, CAUX, and UND
10290   IF UND = TRUE THEN RETURN: 'return to main program
10300   'otherwise go to the point after the recursive call
10310   GOTO 10190
10320   'endsub
```

Trace through the actions of this program and see how it reflects the actions of the original recursive version.

Additional Comments

There is one additional point that should be made regarding the implementation of recursive functions. In our naive implementation of the factorial function, we used a single variable *simfact* to contain the result of the factorial evaluation at each point in the recursive process. The reason this could be done is because it was never necessary to maintain more than one factorial value, so a single variable was sufficient. Contrast this with an algorithm for the computation of the

Fibonacci function with input n which might contain the line

$$fib = fib(n-2) + fib(n-1)$$

That is, given a value n for which we wish to compute the Fibonacci function, first compute the Fibonacci function with the input value $n-2$, then compute the Fibonacci function with the input value $n-1$, and then add the two values together and use the sum as the result of the Fibonacci function with input value n. If we used only a single variable *simfib* to hold the result of the Fibonacci function, that variable would be set by the invocation of $fib(n-2)$ but would be reset by the invocation of $fib(n-1)$, thus destroying the value of $fib(n-2)$.

It is therefore necessary to implement the recursions as though the algorithm had been written

$$x = fib(n-2)$$
$$y = fib(n-1)$$
$$fib = x+y$$

In implementing this version, a single variable *simfib* can be used for the result of the Fibonacci function since its value for $fib(n-2)$ is saved in the variable x before it is reset by $fib(n-1)$. Of course, the variable x would have to be stacked since a recursive call intervenes between its definition and use. (Note that the variable y does not meet this criteria and thus need not be stacked.)

Another point to make about recursive algorithms and their implementation is that errors in such processes are quite common and very difficult to trace. The reason for this is that a recursive process works by successively invoking itself on simpler inputs until it reaches an input for which the results are directly defined. If, however, an invalid input is presented to the process, it may continually attempt to "simplify" that invalid input without ever reaching the directly defined input value. For example, if a negative number is input to the factorial function, the routine might continually subtract 1 and call itself on increasingly negative numbers, never reaching the number 0 for which the factorial function is directly defined. However, the cause of the error might be very difficult to determine since its symptom is the computer running around a loop indefinitely until some value becomes too negative. It is therefore particularly important for a recursive routine to guard against invalid inputs. In our example, one should implement the factorial algorithm as though the statement

> **if** $n < 0$
>   **then print** "negative input to factorial function"
>   *stop*
> **endif**

were placed at its beginning.

EXERCISES

1. Suppose that another provision were added to the Towers of Hanoi problem: that one disk may not rest on another disk which is more than one size larger (e.g., disk 1 may only rest on disk 2 or on the ground, disk 2 may only rest on disk 3 or on the ground, etc.). Why does the solution in the text fail to work? What is faulty about the logic that led to it under the new rules?

2. Prove that the number of moves performed by *simtowers* in moving n disks equals $2^n - 1$. Can you find a method of solving the Towers of Hanoi problem in fewer moves? Either find such a method for some n or prove that none exists.

3. Write a nonrecursive simulation of the recursive binary search procedure, and transform it into an iterative procedure.

4. Write a nonrecursive simulation of *fib*. Can you transform it into an iterative method?

5. Determine what the following recursive algorithm computes. Write an iterative subroutine to accomplish the same purpose.

$$
\begin{aligned}
&\textbf{function } func(n) \\
&\textbf{if } n = 0 \\
&\quad \textbf{then } func = 0 \\
&\quad \textbf{else } func = n + func(n-1) \\
&\textbf{endif} \\
&\textbf{return}
\end{aligned}
$$

6. The expression $mod(m,n)$ yields the remainder of m upon division by n. Define the *greatest common divisor* (*gcd*) of two integers x and y by

$$
\begin{array}{ll}
gcd(x,y) = y & \text{if } y <= x \text{ and } mod(x,y) = 0 \\
gcd(x,y) = gcd(y,x) & \text{if } x < y \\
gcd(x,y) = gcd(y, mod(x,y)) & \text{otherwise}
\end{array}
$$

Write a BASIC subroutine that simulates a recursive algorithm to compute $gcd(x,y)$. Find an iterative method for computing this function.

7. Let $comm(n,k)$ represent the number of different committees of k people that can be formed, given n people to choose from. For example, $comm(4,3) = 4$ since given four people A, B, C, and D there are four possible three-person committees: ABC, ABD, ACD, and BCD. Prove the identity

$$
comm(n,k) = comm(n-1, k) + comm(n-1, k-1)
$$

Write and test a BASIC subroutine that simulates the recursive algorithm to compute $comm(n,k)$ for $n,k >= 1$.

8. Define a ***generalized Fibonacci sequence of $f0$ and $f1$*** as the sequence $gfib(f0, f1,0)$, $gfib(f0,f1,1)$, $gfib(f0,f1,2)$, . . ., where

$$gfib(f0,f1,0) = f0$$
$$gfib(f0,f1,1) = f1$$
$$gfib(f0,f1,n) = gfib(f0,f1,n-1) + gfib(f0,f1,n-2) \quad \text{if } n > 1$$

Write a BASIC subroutine that simulates the recursive algorithm to compute $gfib(f0,f1,n)$. Find an iterative method for computing this subroutine.

9. An ***order n matrix*** is an $n \times n$ array of numbers. For example,

$$(3)$$

is a 1×1 matrix,

$$\begin{pmatrix} 1 & 3 \\ -2 & 8 \end{pmatrix}$$

is a 2×2 matrix, and

$$\begin{pmatrix} 1 & 3 & 4 & 6 \\ 2 & -5 & 0 & 8 \\ 3 & 7 & 6 & 4 \\ 2 & 0 & 9 & -1 \end{pmatrix}$$

is a 4×4 matrix. Define the ***minor*** of an element x in a matrix as the submatrix formed by deleting the row and column containing x. In the foregoing example of a 4×4 matrix, the minor of the element 7 is the 3×3 matrix

$$\begin{pmatrix} 1 & 4 & 6 \\ 2 & 0 & 8 \\ 2 & 9 & -1 \end{pmatrix}$$

Clearly, the order of a minor of any element is 1 less than the order of the original matrix. Denote the minor of an element $a(i,j)$ by $minor(a(i,j))$.

Define the ***determinant*** of a matrix a [written $det(a)$] recursively as follows:

(1) If a is a 1×1 matrix (x), then $det(a) = x$.
(2) If a is of order greater than 1, compute the determinant of a as follows:
  (a) Choose any row or column. For each element $a(i,j)$ in this row or column, form the product

$$(-1)^{i+j} * a(i,j) * det(minor(a(i,j)))$$

where i and j are the row and column positions of the element chosen, $a(i,j)$ is the element chosen, and $det(minor(a(i,j)))$ is the determinant of the minor of $a(i,j)$.

(b) $det(a)$ = sum of all these products.

[More concisely, if n is the order of a, then

$$det(a) = \sum_{i=1}^{n} (-1)^{i+j} * a(i,j) * det(minor(a(i,j))), \qquad \text{for any } j$$

or

$$det(a) = \sum_{j=1}^{n} (-1)^{i+j} * a(i,j) * det(minor(a(i,j))), \qquad \text{for any } i.$$

Write a BASIC program that will read the matrix A, print A in matrix form, and print $det(A)$, where det is a subroutine that computes the determinant of a matrix.

3. WRITING RECURSIVE PROGRAMS

In the preceding section we saw how to transform a recursive definition or algo-rithm into a BASIC program. It is a much more difficult task to develop a recur-sive solution to a problem specification whose algorithm is not supplied. It is not only the program but also the original definitions and algorithms that must be developed. In general, when faced with the task of writing a program to solve a problem, there is no reason to look for a recursive solution. Most problems can be solved in a straightforward manner using nonrecursive methods. However, some problems can be solved logically and most elegantly by recursion. In this section we try to identify some problems that can be solved recursively, develop a technique for finding recursive solutions, and present some examples.

Let us examine once again the factorial function. Factorial is probably a prime example of a problem that should not be solved recursively since the itera-tive solution is so direct and simple. However, let us examine the elements that make the recursive solution work. First, we can recognize a large number of dis-tinct cases to solve. That is, we want to write a program to compute 0!, 1!, 2!, and so on. We can also identify a "trivial" case for which a nonrecursive solu-tion can be obtained directly. This is the case of 0!, which is defined as 1. The next step is to find a method of solving a "complex" case in terms of a "sim-pler" case. This will allow reduction of a complex problem to a simpler problem. The transformation of the complex case to the simpler case should eventually re-sult in the trivial case. This would mean that the complex case is ultimately de-fined in terms of the trivial case.

Let us examine what this means when applied to the factorial function. 4! is a more "complex" case than 3!. The transformation that is applied to the number

4 to obtain the number 3 is simply the subtraction of 1. Repeatedly subtracting 1 from 4 eventually results in 0, which is a "trivial" case. Thus if we are able to define 4! in terms of 3!, and in general $n!$ in terms of $(n-1)!$, we will be able to compute 4! by first working our way down to 0! and then working our way back up to 4! using the definition of $n!$ in terms of $(n-1)!$. In the case of the factorial function we have such a definition, since

$$n! = n*(n-1)!$$

Thus $4! = 4*3! = 4*3*2! = 4*3*2*1! = 4*3*2*1*0! = 4*3*2*1*1 = 24.$

These are the essential ingredients of a recursive algorithm—being able to define a "complex" case in terms of a "simpler" case and having a directly solvable (nonrecursive) "trivial" case. Once this has been done, one can develop a solution to the complex case using the assumption that the simpler case has already been solved. The recursive algorithm for the factorial function assumes that $(n-1)!$ is defined and uses that quantity in computing $n!$.

Let us see how these ideas apply to other examples of Section 1. In defining $a*b$ recursively, the case of $b = 1$ is trivial since in that case, $a*b$ is defined as a. In general, $a*b$ may be defined in terms of $a*(b-1)$ by the definition $a*b = a*(b-1) + a$. Again the complex case is transformed into a simpler case by subtracting 1, eventually leading to the trivial case of $b = 1$. Here the recursion is based on the second parameter b alone.

In the case of the Fibonacci function, two trivial cases were defined: $fib(0) = 0$ and $fib(1) = 1$. A complex case, $fib(n)$, is then reduced to two simpler cases, $fib(n-2)$ and $fib(n-1)$. It is because of the definition of $fib(n)$ as $fib(n-2) + fib(n-1)$ that two trivial cases directly defined are necessary. $fib(1)$ cannot be defined as $fib(0) + fib(-1)$, because the Fibonacci function is not defined for negative numbers.

The binary search function is an interesting example of recursion. The recursion is based on the number of elements in the array that must be searched. Each time the routine is called recursively, the number of elements to be searched is halved (approximately). The trivial case is the one in which there are either no elements to be searched or the element being searched for is at the middle of the array. If $low > high$, then the first of these two conditions holds and 0 is returned. If $x = a(mid)$, the second condition holds and mid is returned as the answer. In the more complex case of $high - low + 1$ elements to be searched, the search is reduced to taking place in one of two subregions:

1. The first half of the array from low to $mid - 1$
2. The second half of the array from $mid + 1$ to $high$

Thus a complex case (a large area to be searched) is reduced to a simpler case (an area to be searched of approximately half the size of the original area). This eventually reduces to a comparison with a single element $[a(mid)]$ or a search within an array of no elements.

Translation from Prefix to Postfix Using Recursion

Let us examine another problem for which the recursive solution is the most direct and elegant one. This is the problem of converting a prefix expression to postfix. Prefix and postfix notation were discussed in Chapter 3. Briefly, prefix and postfix notations are methods of writing mathematical expressions without parentheses. In prefix notation each operator immediately precedes its operands. In postfix notation each operator immediately follows its operands. To refresh your memory, here are a few conventional (infix) mathematical expressions with their prefix and postfix equivalents:

Infix	Prefix	Postfix
$A+B$	$+AB$	$AB+$
$A+B*C$	$+A*BC$	$ABC*+$
$A*(B+C)$	$*A+BC$	$ABC+*$
$A*B+C$	$+*ABC$	$AB*C+$
$A+B*C+D-E*F$	$-++A*BCD*EF$	$ABC*+D+EF*-$
$(A+B)*(C+D-E)*F$	$**+AB-+CDEF$	$AB+CD+E-*F*$

The most convenient way to define postfix and prefix is by using recursion. Assuming only single-letter variables as operands, a prefix expression is a single letter or an operator followed by two prefix expressions. A postfix expression may be defined similarly as a single letter or as an operator preceded by two postfix expressions. The definitions above assume that all operations are binary (i.e., each requires two operands). Examples of such operations are addition, subtraction, multiplication, division, and exponentiation. It is easy to extend the definitions of prefix and postfix given above to include unary operations such as negation or factorial, but in the interest of simplicity we will not do so here. Verify that each of the prefix and postfix expressions above is valid by showing that they satisfy the definitions, and make sure that you can identify the two operands of each operator.

We will put these recursive definitions to use in a moment, but first let us return to our problem. Given a prefix expression, how can we convert it into a postfix expression? We can immediately identify a trivial case: If a prefix expression consists of only a single variable, that expression is its own postfix equivalent. That is, an expression such as A is valid as both a prefix and a postfix expression.

Now consider a longer prefix string. If we knew how to convert any shorter prefix string to postfix, could we convert this longer prefix string? The answer is yes, with one proviso. Every prefix string longer than a single variable contains an operator, a first operand, and a second operand (remember that we are assuming binary operators only). Assume that we are able to identify the first and second operands, which are necessarily shorter than the original string. We can then convert the long prefix string to postfix by first converting the first operand to postfix, then converting the second operand to postfix and appending it to the end of the first converted operand, and finally appending the initial operator to the end of the resultant string. Thus we have developed a recursive algorithm for converting a prefix string to postfix with the provision that we must specify a method for identifying the operands in a prefix expression. We can summarize this algorithm as follows:

1. If the prefix string is a single variable, it is its own postfix equivalent.
2. Let *op* be the first operator of the prefix string.
3. Find the first operand *opnd1* of the string. Convert it to postfix and call it *post1*.
4. Find the second operand *opnd2* of the string. Convert it to postfix and call it *post2*.
5. The desired string is formed by appending *post1*, *post2*, and *op*.

Before transforming the conversion algorithm into a BASIC program, let us examine its inputs and outputs. We wish to write a function *convert* which accepts a character string. This string represents a prefix expression in which all variables are single letters and the allowable operators are " + ", " − ", "*", "/", and "↑". The function returns a string which is the postfix equivalent of the prefix input.

Assume the existence of another function *find,* which accepts a string and a position and returns an integer which is the length of the longest prefix expression contained within the input string which starts at that position. For example, *find*("*a + cd*",1) returns 1, since "*a*" is the longest prefix string starting at position 1 of the string "*a + cd*". *find*(" + *abcd + gh*",1) returns 5 since " + *abc*" is the longest prefix string starting at the beginning of " + *abcd + gh*"; *find*("*a + cd*",2) returns 3 since " + *cd*" is the longest prefix string starting at position 2 of "*a + cd*". If no prefix string exists within the input string starting at the specified position, *find* returns 0. [For example, *find*("* + ab*",1) and *find*(" + *a − c*d*",6) both return 0.] This function is used to identify the first and second operands of a prefix operator. Assuming the existence of the function *find,* an algorithm for a conversion routine that accepts a prefix string *prefix* and sets the variable *convert* to its postfix equivalent may be written as follows.

```
    function convert(prefix)
    if len(prefix) = 1
       then 'check for variable
               if prefix is a single letter
                  then convert = prefix
                  else print "invalid prefix string"
                       convert = " "
               endif
               return
    endif
```

```
'the prefix string is longer than a single character;
'extract the operator and the two operand lengths
op = mid$(prefix,1,1)
m = find(prefix,2)
n = find(prefix,m + 2)
if (op is not an operator) or (m = 0) or (n = 0) or (m + n + 1 <> len(prefix))
   then print "invalid prefix string"
         convert = " "
         return
endif
opnd1 = mid$(prefix,2,m)
opnd2 = mid$(prefix,m + 2,n)
post1 = convert(opnd1)
post2 = convert(opnd2)
convert = post1 + post2 + op
return
```

Note that we are using the convention for presenting a function in pseudo-code that was introduced at the end of Section 2.1. Under that convention, the name of the function (in this case *convert*) is used as its returned value. In a recursive function, the function definition includes a recursive call.

Note also that several checks have been incorporated into the algorithm to ensure that the input is a valid prefix string. One of the most difficult classes of errors to detect are those resulting from invalid inputs and the programmer's neglect to check for validity.

We now turn our attention to the function *find*, which accepts a character string and a starting position and returns the length of the longest prefix string which is contained in that input string starting at that position. The word "longest" in this definition is superfluous since there is at most one substring starting at a given position of a given string which is a valid prefix expression. We first show that there is at most one valid prefix expression starting at the beginning of a string. To see this, note that it is trivially true in a string of length 1. Assume that it is true for a short string. Then a long string which contains a prefix expression as an initial substring must begin with either a variable, in which case that variable is the desired substring, or with an operator. Deleting the initial operator, the remaining string is shorter than the original string and can therefore have at most a single initial prefix expression. This expression is the first operand of the initial operator. Similarly, the remaining substring (after deleting the first operand) can have only a single initial substring which is a prefix expression. This expression must be the second operand. Therefore, we have uniquely identified the operator and operands of the prefix expression starting at the beginning of an arbitrary string, if such an expression exists. Since there is at most one valid prefix string starting at the beginning of any string, there is at most one such string starting at any position of an arbitrary string. This is obvious when we consider the substring of the given string starting at the given position.

Notice that this proof has given us a recursive method for finding a prefix expression in a string. We now incorporate this method into the function *find*, which finds the length of the substring of a string *prefix* beginning at position *y* which forms a valid prefix expression:

```
function find(prefix,x)
if x > len(prefix)
  then find = 0
       return
endif
first = mid$(prefix,x,1)
if first is a letter
  then 'the first character is the desired postfix substring
       find = 1
       return
endif
'find the two operands
mm = find(prefix,x + 1)
nn = find(prefix,x + mm + 1)
if (mm = 0) or (nn = 0) or ((mm + nn + 1) > len(prefix))
  then find = 0
  else find = mm + nn + 1
endif
return
```

Make sure that you understand how these algorithms work by tracing their actions on both valid and invalid prefix expressions. More important, make sure that you understand how they were developed and how logical analysis led to a natural recursive solution.

Conversion Programs in BASIC

Let us now present BASIC routines that implement the algorithms above, using the techniques of the preceding section.

In the function *convert,* the algorithm variables that must be stacked on the recursive calls are *op, opnd2,* and *post1,* since all of them are assigned a value before a recursive call which is used afterward. The current values of these algorithm variables will be maintained in the program variables COP, C2OPND, and CPST1, and the stacks of their values in previous invocations will be maintained in the arrays SOP, S2OPND, and SPST1. The value of the algorithm variable *opnd1* will be maintained in the variable C1OPND, although it does not have to be stacked. The value of the algorithm variable *post2* will be maintained in the variable PTFX2. (We use these names because we assume that only the first two characters of a variable name are significant, a reserved word such as POS may not be embedded in a variable name, and that an array and variable cannot have the same name, although many versions of BASIC do not have these restrictions. We also assume the statement DEFSTR C,P,S at the beginning of the program so that we begin all string-variable names with one of these three letters). The top of the stack will be maintained in the variable TP, and routines *push*1 and *popandtest*1 at statements 1000 and 4000, respectively, will be used to push and pop from the stack. The output variable of *convert* will be named PCNVERT (so as not to conflict with COP and because ON is a reserved word and may not be embedded in a variable name in many versions of BASIC).

Note that *convert* contains two recursive calls, neither of which can be eliminated. Thus although a version of *popandtest,* rather than *pop,* is used to maintain the recursion stack, it is still necessary to keep a return indicator. The current value of this indicator is kept in the variable ZRETADDR, and the stack of the previous values in the array RETADDR. Thus *push*1 pushes COP, C2OPND, CPST1, and ZRETADDR onto the stack, and *popandtest*1 resets the values of all these variables from the stack if the stack is nonempty. *popandtest*1 also sets the variable UND to TRUE if an underflow occurs (i.e., the stack is empty and cannot be popped) and FALSE otherwise. We use the return indicator values 2 and 3 to indicate returns from the first and second recursive calls to *convert.*

We also use two routines, *ltr* and *optr,* at statements 5000 and 6000 to determine if a character is a letter (operand) or an operator symbol. The character is input in the variable PP. The variable LTR is set to TRUE if PP is a letter and FALSE otherwise. The variable OPTR is set to TRUE if PP is an operator symbol and FALSE otherwise. We also use an auxiliary variable PAUX to hold the value of the input prefix string so as not to modify the variable PREFIX, which is the input to the simulating routine. The variable PAUX, rather than PREFIX, is used as the first input to the *find* routine.

Thus, assuming the conventions and routines noted above, the BASIC routine *convert* may be written as follows:

```
20000   'subroutine convert
20010   'inputs: PREFIX
20020   'outputs: PCNVERT
20030   'locals: COP, CPST1, C1OPND, FIND, LTR, M, N, OPTR,
            PAUX, PP, PTFX2, TP, UND, X, ZRETADDR
20040   TP = 0
20050   PAUX = PREFIX
20060   IF LEN(PAUX) > 1 THEN GOTO 20120
20070   'check for a variable
20080   PP = PAUX
20090   GOSUB 5000: 'subroutine ltr accepts PP and sets the variable LTR
```

```
20100   IF LTR = TRUE
            THEN PCNVERT = PAUX
            ELSE PRINT "INVALID PREFIX STRING": PCNVERT = " "
20110   GOTO 20410: 'return from recursive routine


20120   'the prefix string consists of an operator and two operands
20130   'extract the operator and the two operand lengths
20140   COP = MID$(PAUX,1,1)
20150   X = 2
20160   GOSUB 30000: 'subroutine find accepts PAUX and X and sets FIND
20170   M = FIND
20180   X = M+2
20190   GOSUB 30000: 'subroutine find
20200   N = FIND
20210   PP = COP
20220   GOSUB 6000: 'subroutine optr accepts PP and sets the variable OPTR
20230   IF OPTR = FALSE OR M = 0 OR N = 0 OR M+N+1 <>LEN(PAUX)
            THEN PRINT "INVALID PREFIX STRING":
                PSTFX = " ": GOTO 20410
20240   C1OPND = MID$(PAUX,2,M)
20250   C2OPND = MID$(PAUX,M+2,N)
20260   ZRETADDR = 2: 'return to point after first recursive call
20270   GOSUB 1000: 'subroutine push1 places COP, C2OPND, CPST1,
                'and ZRETADDR on the stack
20280   'set the input to the first recursive call
20290   PAUX = C1OPND
20300   GOTO 20060: 'first recursive call


20310   'this is the point of return from the first recursive call
20320   CPST1 = PCNVERT
20330   'set up the second recursive call
20340   ZRETADDR = 3: 'return to point after second recursive call
20350   GOSUB 1000: 'subroutine push1
20360   PAUX = C2OPND
20370   GOTO 20060: 'second recursive call


20380   'this is the point of return from the second recursive call
20390   PTFX2 = PCNVERT
20400   PCNVERT = CPST1 + PTFX2 + COP


20410   'this is the return from the recursive routine
20420   GOSUB 4000: 'subroutine popandtest1 resets COP, C2OPND,
                'CPST1, ZRETADDR, and UND
```

```
20430   IF UND = TRUE THEN RETURN: 'to main program
20440   IF ZRETADDR = 2 THEN GOTO 20310
20450   IF ZRETADDR = 3 THEN GOTO 20380
20460   'endsub
```

(You may note that it is not really necessary to stack all the variables COP, C2OPND, and CPST1 on both recursive calls. Indeed, CPST1 has not been given a meaningful value before the first recursive call and the value of C2OPND is not used after the second recursive call. Thus CPST1 need not be stacked on the first call and C2OPND need not be stacked on the second. Thus it would be possible to maintain three separate stacks: the first would consist of the arrays SOP and RETADDR, the second of the array S2OPND, and the third of the array SPST1. Two different *push* routines would be needed. The first, used in the first call, would push COP on the SOP stack, ZRETADDR on the RETADDR stack, and C2OPND on the S2OPND stack. The second, used in the second call, would push COP on the SOP stack, ZRETADDR on the RETADDR stack, and CPST1 on the SPST1 stack. Only one *popandtest* routine is required: It would first pop the SOP and ZRETADDR stack to determine whether we are returning from the first or second call, and based on that would pop either S2OPND or SPST1. Although this might save some space, it does not seem worthwhile in terms of either machine time or programmer time. You may also note that the variable PTFX2 may be eliminated and statements 20390 and 20400 combined into the single statement PCNVERT = CPST1 + PCNVERT + COP.)

In the subroutine *find*, the algorithm variables that must be stacked on recursive calls are x and mm (again, x need only be stacked on the first call and mm need only be stacked on the second, but we will stack them both on both calls). We use program variables ZX and ZMM for their current values and arrays XX and MM for their stacks. Note that we use separate stacks for *find* and *convert*. The stack top for *find* is kept in the variable TTP, and routines *push2* and *popandtest2* at statements 1200 and 4200 are used to push and pop from that stack.

As in the case with *convert, find* contains two recursive calls, neither of which can be eliminated, and therefore requires maintaining a return indicator. The current value of this indicator is in the variable Z2RETADDR and it is stacked in the array R2RETADDR. Thus *push2* pushes ZX, ZMM, and Z2RETADDR on the stack, and *popandtest2* resets these variables from the stack. Again, we use return indicator values of 2 and 3. *find* also makes use of the subroutine *ltr* described earlier.

```
30000   'subroutine find
30010   'inputs: PAUX, X
30020   'outputs: FIND
30030   'locals: LTR, NN, PFIRST, PP, TTP, UND, ZRETADDR, ZX
30040   TTP = 0
30050   ZX = X
```

30060   IF ZX > LEN(*PAUX*) THEN FIND = 0: GOTO 30280: *'return*
30070   PFIRST = MID$(*PAUX*,ZX,1)
30080   PP = PFIRST
30090   GOSUB 5000: *'subroutine* ltr *accepts PP and sets the variable LTR*
30100   IF LTR = TRUE THEN FIND = 1: GOTO 30280: *'return*
30110   *'find the two operands*
30120   *'prepare for first recursive call*
30130   Z2RETADDR = 2
30140   GOSUB 1200: *'subroutine* push2 *places ZX, ZMM, and Z2RETADDR*
                              'on the stack
30150   *'set input and issue first recursive call*
30160   ZX = ZX+1
30170   GOTO 30060: *'first recursive call*

30180   *'return to this point after first recursive call*
30190   ZMM = FIND
30200   *'prepare for second recursive call*
30210   Z2RETADDR = 3
30220   GOSUB 1200: *'subroutine* push2
30230   ZX = ZX + ZMM + 1
30240   GOTO 30060: *'second recursive call*

30250   *'return to this point after second recursive call*
30260   NN = FIND
30270   IF NN = 0 OR ZMM = 0 OR ZMM+NN+1 > LEN(PAUX)
              THEN FIND = 0
              ELSE FIND = ZMM + NN + 1

30280   *'return from the recursive routine*
30290   GOSUB 4200: *'subroutine* popandtest2 *restores ZX, ZMM,*
                              'Z2RETADDR, and UND
30300   IF UND = TRUE THEN RETURN: *'to calling routine*
30310   IF Z2RETADDR = 2 THEN GOTO 30180
30320   IF Z2RETADDR = 3 THEN GOTO 30250
30330   *'endsub*

Recursive List Processing

One important application of recursion is in managing complex data structures. For example, a list of integers may be defined recursively as the null list or a single node containing an integer and a pointer to another list of integers. Thus a list containing a single integer qualifies as a list of integers because its only node contains an integer and a pointer to the null list; a list of two integers has its first node containing an integer and a pointer to a single-integer list; and a list of *n* integers consists of a first node containing an integer and a pointer to a list of $n - 1$ integers.

We can use this recursive definition to design an algorithm, *reverse*, to reverse a list *lst* so that its last element becomes the first, and so on. The technique used rests on the observation that the reversal of a null list or a one element list is the list itself. If the list has more than one element, the reversal can be performed by reversing the list formed by all the nodes except the first and then appending the first node to the end of the list.

```
 1.  function reverse(lst)
 2.  if lst = null
 3.      then reverse = lst
 4.              return
 5.  endif
 6.  p = ptrnxt(lst)
 7.  if p = null
 8.      then reverse = lst
 9.              return
10.  endif
11.  q = reverse(p)
12.  ptrnxt(lst) = null
13.  ptrnxt(p) = lst
14.  reverse = q
15.  return
```

To understand this algorithm, observe that lines 2–10 ensure that the reversal of the null list or a one-element list is the list itself. The reversal of a two-element list is illustrated in Figure 5.3.1. Since *lst* is not *null*, *p* is set to point to the second node on the list by line 6. This is the situation depicted by Figure 5.3.1(a). Since *p* is not *null*, the algorithm resumes at line 11 by calling itself recursively. (Note that during the recursive call the values of *lst* and *p* are stacked, *lst* is reset to *p*, *p* to *null*, and *reverse* to *p*. When the recursive invocation returns, *q* is set to *reverse*, and *lst* and *p* are restored to their former values.) Since the recursive call is on a one-element list, it returns a pointer to that list which is stored in the variable *q* by line 11. *lst* and *p* are unchanged. This is depicted in Figure 5.3.1(b).

Lines 12 and 13 place the first node of the list at its rear, as depicted in Figure 5.3.1(c). Finally, lines 14 and 15 return the reversed list. Note that upon return, *lst* points to the same node as it did before the call, but that node is now at the rear rather than the front of the list. To reset *lst* to the first node of the reversed list, we could execute *lst = reverse(lst)*.

Figure 5.3.1(d)–(f) show the reversal of a four-element list. Note that after return from the recursive call (line 11), *p* points to the last node on the reversed sublist, which was formerly the second node on the input list. It would be instructive for you to trace the recursive invocations in more detail, including the recursion stack for *lst* and *p*.

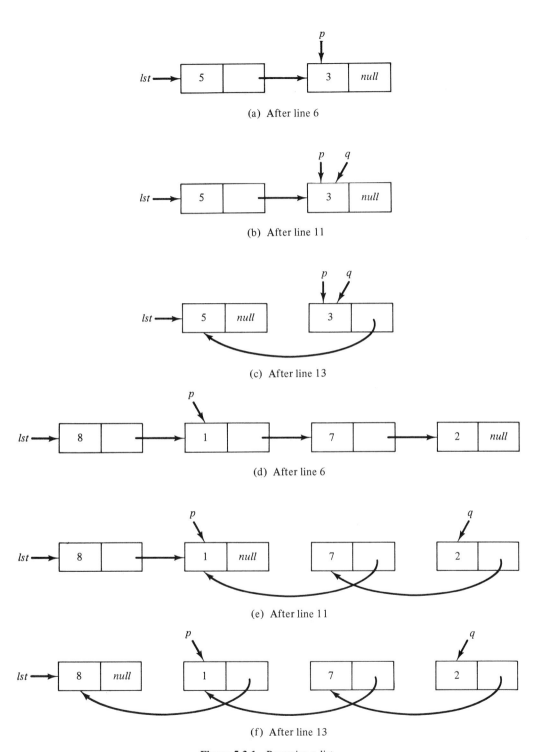

(a) After line 6

(b) After line 11

(c) After line 13

(d) After line 6

(e) After line 11

(f) After line 13

Figure 5.3.1 Reversing a list.

We should note that a nonrecursive algorithm to reverse a list, although not as intuitive, is fairly straightforward:

```
function reverse(lst)
if lst = null
    then reverse = lst
          return
endif
p = ptrnxt(lst)
if p = null
    then reverse = lst
          return
endif
ptrnxt(lst) = null
q = lst                 'q is one step behind p
r = ptrnxt(p)           'r is one step ahead of p
while r <> null do
      ptrnxt(p) = q
      q = p
      p = r
      r = ptrnxt(p)
endwhile
ptrnxt(p) = q
reverse = p
return
```

You are invited to confirm that this algorithm reverses the lists of Figures 5.3.1(a) and (d). You are also invited to write BASIC programs to implement the recursive and nonrecursive algorithm and to derive one from the other.

Although most recursive algorithms for simple lists can be implemented nonrecursively without use of a stack, in the next chapter we will be introduced to more complex data structures where use of recursion is essential.

Recursive Chains

A recursive algorithm need not call itself directly. Rather, it may call itself indirectly, as in the following example:

```
'algorithm a              'algorithm b
_____                    _____
_____                    _____
_____                    _____
'call to algorithm b      'call to algorithm a
_____                    _____
_____                    _____
_____                    _____
'end of algorithm a       'end of algorithm b
```

In this example, algorithm *a* calls algorithm *b*, which may in turn call *a*, which may again call *b*. Thus both *a* and *b* are recursive since they indirectly call themselves. However, the fact that they are recursive is not evident from examining the body of either of the routines individually. Algorithm *a* seems to be calling a separate algorithm *b* and it is impossible to determine by examining *a* alone that it will indirectly call itself.

More than two algorithms may participate in a ***recursive chain***. Thus an algorithm *a* may call *b*, which calls *c*, . . ., which calls *z*, which calls *a*. Each algorithm in the chain may potentially call itself and is therefore recursive. The programmer must ensure that the system does not generate an infinite sequence of recursive calls. Of course, in converting a chain of recursive algorithms into a BASIC program, the programmer must also ensure that the variables and return indicators are stacked properly, so that the simulated execution of each RETURN statement will restore these elements to their proper values.

Recursive Definition of Algebraic Expressions

Let us consider an example of such a recursive chain of algorithms and convert these algorithms into BASIC programs. Consider the following recursive group of definitions:

1. An ***expression*** is a *term* followed by a *plus sign* followed by a *term*, or a *term* alone.
2. A ***term*** is a *factor* followed by an *asterisk* followed by a *factor*, or a *factor* alone.
3. A ***factor*** is either a *letter* or an *expression* enclosed in *parentheses*.

Before looking at some examples, note that none of the three items above is defined directly in terms of itself. However, each is defined in terms of itself indirectly. An expression is defined in terms of a term, a term in terms of a factor, and a factor in terms of an expression. Similarly, a factor is defined in terms of an expression, which is defined in terms of a term, which is defined in terms of a factor. Thus the entire set of definitions forms a recursive chain.

Let us now give some examples. The simplest form of a factor is a letter. Thus *A*, *B*, *C*, *Q*, *Z*, and *M* are all factors. They are also terms, since a term may be a factor alone. They are also expressions, since an expression may be a term alone. Since *A* is an expression, (*A*) is a factor and therefore a term as well as an expression. *A* + *B* is an example of an expression that is neither a term nor a factor. (*A* + *B*), however, is all three. *A**B is a term and therefore an expression, but it is not a factor. *A**B + *C* is an expression that is neither a term nor a factor. *A**(*B* + *C*) is a term and an expression but not a factor.

Each of the examples above is a valid expression. This can be shown by applying the definition of an expression to each of them. Consider, however, the string $A + *B$. It is neither an expression, a term, nor a factor. It would be instructive for you to attempt to apply the definitions of expression, term, and factor to see that none of them describe the string $A + *B$. Similarly, $(A + B*)C$ and $A + B + C$ are not valid expressions according to the definitions above.

Let us write an algorithm that reads a character string, prints the string, and then prints *valid* if it is a valid expression and *invalid* if it is not. We will use three separate functions to recognize expressions, terms, and factors, respectively. First, however, we present an algorithm for an auxiliary routine *getsymb* which has two inputs: *str* and *pos*. *str* contains the input character string and *pos* is the position in *str* of the next character we wish to process. Upon entry to *getsymb*, *pos* is compared to the length of the string. If $pos <= len(str)$, then *getsymb* returns the character at position *pos* of *str* and *pos* is incremented by 1. If $pos > len(str)$, then *getsymb* returns a blank.

```
function getsymb(str,pos)
if pos > len(str)
    then getsymb = " "
    else getsymb = mid$(str,pos,1)
        pos = pos + 1
endif
return
```

The function that recognizes an expression is called *expr*. It, too, inputs *str* and *pos*. *expr* returns *true* if a valid expression begins at position *pos* of *str* and *false* otherwise. It also resets *pos* to the position following the longest expression it can find. The functions *factor* and *term* are much like *expr* except that they are responsible for recognizing factors and terms, respectively. They also reposition *pos* to the position following the longest factor or term within the string *str* that they can find. We can write the algorithm for the main routine as follows:

```
read str
print str
pos = 1
ok = expr(str,pos)
if ok = true and pos >len(str)
    then print "valid"
    else print "invalid"
        'The condition can fail for one (or both) of two reasons.
        'If ok is false, there is no valid expression beginning at pos.
        'If pos <=len(str), there may be a valid expression starting
        'at the beginning of str but it does not occupy the entire string.
endif
```

The algorithms for the functions *expr, term,* and *factor* adhere closely to the definitions given earlier. Each of the routines attempts to satisfy one of the criteria for the entity being recognized. If one of these criteria is satisfied, *true* is returned. If none of these criteria are satisfied, *false* is returned.

```
function expr(str,pos)
'look for a term
ok = term(str,pos)
if ok = false
   then expr = false
        return
endif
'look at the next symbol
c = getsymb(str,pos)
if c <> "+"
   then ' We have found the longest expression (a single term).
        ' Reposition pos so that it refers to the position
        ' immediately following the expression.
        pos = pos - 1
        expr = true
        return
endif
'At this point we have found a term and a plus sign.
'We must look for another term.
ok = term(str,pos)
if ok = true
   then expr = true
   else expr = false
endif
return
```

The routine *term* that recognizes terms is very similar and we present it without comment.

```
function term(str,pos)
ok = factor(str, pos)
if ok = false
   then term =false
        return
endif
c = getsymb(str,pos)
if c <> "*"
   then pos = pos - 1
        term = true
        return
   endif
```

$$ok \ = \ factor(str,pos)$$
if $ok \ = \ true$
   then $term \ = \ true$
   else $term \ = \ false$
endif
return

The routine *factor* recognizes factors and should now be fairly straightforward. It uses a subroutine *ltr* which returns *true* if its character parameter is a letter and *false* otherwise.

function $factor(str,pos)$
$c \ = \ getsymb(str,pos)$
if $c <> \ "("$
   then 'check for a letter
        $factor \ = \ ltr(c)$
        return
endif
'the factor is a parenthesized expression
$ok \ = \ expr(str,pos)$
if $ok \ = \ false$
   then $factor \ = \ false$
        return
endif
$c \ = \ getsymb(str,pos)$
if $c <> \ ")"$
   then $factor \ = \ false$
   else $factor \ = \ true$
endif
return

We note that in each of the three algorithms, *expr, term,* and *factor,* the input variable *str* is never modified, so it need not be stacked. The input/output variable *pos* is modified, but since its modified value is used subsequently by each of the calling routines (by virtue of its being an output variable), its old value need not be saved, so it, too, need not be stacked. The variables *c* and *ok* also need not have their values stacked because values assigned to these variables before a recursive call are never used afterward (note that in this instance, the recursive call is not to the routine of the same name but to one of the other routines which might then call the caller). Similarly, the return variables *expr, term,* and *factor* are never given a value before the recursive call, so they need not be stacked either. Thus we have the unusual situation in which no variables need be stacked in a recursive routine. It is therefore tempting to implement these routines using actual recursive *gosubs*, as presented in the first part of Section 2, so that we need not stack return indicators either. We now present such a BASIC program. We emphasize, however, that the program will not work under all BASICs, or might work for simple expressions in which the recursion is not too complex but not for more complicated expressions.

The following is a complete program that processes an expression according to the rules above. In implementing the algorithms, we use the variable *PS* instead of *pos,* *FCTR* instead of *factor,* *XPR* instead of *expr,* and *GTSYMB* instead of *getsymb.*

```
 10   'program findexp
 20   DEFSTR A, C, S
 30   TRUE = 1
 40   FALSE = 0
 50   PS = 1
 60   INPUT STR
 70   PRINT STR
 80   GOSUB 3000:    'subroutine expr sets the variable XPR
 90   OK = XPR
100   IF OK = TRUE AND PS > LEN(STR) THEN PRINT "VALID"
                                     ELSE PRINT "INVALID"
110   'The condition can fail for one (or both) of two reasons.
120   'If OK is FALSE, there is no valid expression beginning
130   'at PS. If PS <= LEN(STR), there may be a valid
140   'expression starting at PS, but it does not occupy the
150   'entire string.
160   END
170   '
180   '
190   '
2000  'subroutine getsymb
2010  'inputs: PS, STR
2020  'outputs: GTSYMB, PS
2030  'locals: none
2040  IF PS > LEN(STR)
          THEN GTSYMB = " "
          ELSE GTSYM = MID$(STR, PS, 1): PS = PS + 1
2050  RETURN
2060  'endsub
2070  '
2080  '
2090  '
3000  'subroutine expr
3010  'inputs: PS, STR
3020  'outputs: PS, XPR
3030  'locals: C, GTSYMB, OK, TERM
```

```
3040   GOSUB 4000:    'subroutine term sets the variable TERM
3050   OK = TERM
3060   IF OK = TRUE THEN GOTO 3100
3070   'else do stmts 3080–3090
3080     XPR = FALSE
3090     RETURN
3100   GOSUB 2000:    'subroutine getsymb sets the variable GTSYMB
3110   C = GTSYMB
3120   IF C = ''+'' THEN GOTO 3170
3130   'else do stmts 3140–3160
3140     PS = PS − 1
3150     XPR = TRUE
3160     RETURN
3170   GOSUB 4000:    'subroutine term
3180   OK = TERM
3190   IF OK = TRUE THEN XPR = TRUE
                       ELSE XPR = FALSE
3200   RETURN
3210   'endsub
3220   '
3230   '
3240   '
4000   'subroutine term
4010   'inputs: PS, STR
4020   'outputs: PS, TERM
4030   'locals: C, FCTR, GTSYMB, OK
4040   GOSUB 5000:    'subroutine factor sets the variable FCTR
4050   OK = FCTR
4060   IF OK = TRUE THEN GOTO 4100
4070   'else do stmts 4080–4090
4080     TERM = FALSE
4090     RETURN
4100   GOSUB 2000:    'subroutine getsymb sets the variable GTSYMB
4110   C = GTSYMB
4120   IF C = ''*'' THEN GOTO 4170
4130   'else do stmts 4140–4160
4140     PS = PS − 1
4150     TERM = TRUE
4160     RETURN
4170   GOSUB 5000:    'subroutine factor
4180   OK = FCTR
```

```
4190  IF OK = TRUE THEN TERM = TRUE
                    ELSE TERM = FALSE
4200  RETURN
4210  'endsub
4220  '
4230  '
4240  '
5000  'subroutine factor
5010  'inputs: PS, STR
5020  'outputs: FCTR, PS
5030  'locals: C, GTSYMB, LTR, OK
5040  GOSUB 2000:    'subroutine getsymb sets the variable GTSYMB
5050  C = GTSYMB
5060  IF C = "(" THEN GOTO 5110
5070  'else do stmts 5080–5100
5080      GOSUB 6000: 'subroutine ltr accepts the variable C and sets
                         'the variable LTR
5090      FCTR = LTR
5100      RETURN
5110  GOSUB 3000:    'subroutine expr sets the variable XPR
5120  OK = XPR
5130  IF OK = TRUE THEN GOTO 5170
5140  'else do stmts 5150–5160
5150      FCTR = FALSE
5160      RETURN
5170  GOSUB 2000:    'subroutine gtsymb
5180  C = GTSYMB
5190  IF C = ")" THEN FCTR = TRUE
                    ELSE FCTR = FALSE
5200  RETURN
5210  'endsub
5220  '
5230  '
5240  '
6000  'subroutine ltr
6010  'inputs: C
6020  'outputs: LTR
6030  'locals: ALPH, I
6040  ALPH = "ABCDEFGHIJKLMNOPQRSTUVWXYZ"
6050  FOR I = 1 to 26
6060      IF MID$(ALPH, I, 1) = C THEN LTR = TRUE: RETURN
6070  NEXT I
6080  LTR = FALSE
6090  RETURN
6100  'endsub
```

All three routines are recursive since each may call itself indirectly. For example, if you trace through the actions of the program *findexp* for the input string "(A*B*C*D) + (F*(F)+G)", you will find that each of the routines *expr*, *term*, and *factor* calls on itself.

We leave to the reader the implementation of this program without using recursive GOSUBs, but using a return indicator stack instead.

EXERCISES

1. Define a postfix and prefix expression to include the possibility of unary operators. Write a program to convert a prefix expression possibly containing the unary negation operator (represented by the symbol "@") to postfix.

2. Rewrite the subroutine *find* in the text so that it is nonrecursive and computes the length of a prefix string by counting the number of operators and single-letter operands.

3. Write a recursive algorithm and its BASIC simulation which accepts a prefix expression consisting of binary operators and single-digit integer operands and returns the value of the expression.

4. Modify the recursive and nonrecursive algorithm *reverse* of the text to reverse a singly linked circular list.

5. Write a BASIC subroutine to implement the recursive algorithm *reverse* presented in the text. Then simplify the routine so that it does not use a stack.

6. Develop a recursive algorithm to find the sum of all the numbers in an integer list.

7. Rewrite the program *findexp* so that it does not use recursive GOSUBs.

8. Write a BASIC subroutine that simulates a recursive algorithm to compute the number of sequences of n binary digits which do not contain two 1's in a row. (*Hint*: Compute how many such sequences exist which start with 0, and how many exist which start with 1.)

9. Write a BASIC program that simulates a recursive algorithm to sort an array A as follows:
   (a) Let K be the index of the middle element of the array.
   (b) Sort the elements up to and including A(K).
   (c) Sort the elements past A(K).
   (d) Merge the two subarrays into a single sorted array.
   This method is called a ***merge sort.***

10. Develop a recursive method (and program it) to compute the number of different ways in which an integer k can be written as a sum, each of whose operands is less than n.

11. Develop a recursive method (and program it) to print in alphabetical order all possible permutations of the letters stored in a character array of size n.

12. Write a BASIC subroutine that simulates a recursive algorithm to find the kth smallest element of an array a of numbers by choosing any element $a(i)$ of a and partitioning a into those elements smaller than, equal to, and greater than $a(i)$.

13. The Eight Queens problem is to place eight queens on a chessboard so that no queen is attacking any other queen. The following is a recursive algorithm to solve the problem. *board* is an 8 by 8 array which represents a chessboard. *board(i,j)* equals *true* if there is a queen at position *(i,j)*, and *false* otherwise. *good(board)* is a function that returns *true* if no two queens on the chessboard are attacking each other and *false* otherwise. At the end of the program, the status of *board* represents a solution to the problem.

```
program queens
for i = 1 to 8
    for j = 1 to 8
        board(i,j) = false
    next j
next i
b = try(1)
end

function try(n)
if n > 8
  then try = true
       return
  else for i = 1 to 8
           board(n,i) = true
           if good(board) = true and try(n+1) = true
             then try = true
                  return
             else board(n,i) = false
           endif
       next i
       try = false
       return
endif
```

The recursive subroutine *try* returns *true* if it is possible, given the *board* at the time that it is called, to add queens in rows *n* through 8 to achieve a solution. *try* returns *false* if there is no solution which has queens at the positions in *board* that already contain *true*. If *true* is returned, the subroutine also adds queens in rows *n* through 8 to produce a solution. Implement these algorithms and verify that the program produces a solution.

[The idea behind the solution is as follows: *board* represents the global situation during an attempt to find a solution. The next step toward finding a solution is chosen arbitrarily (place a queen in the next untried position in row *n*) and recursively test whether it is possible to produce a solution which includes that step. If it is, return. If it is not, backtrack from the attempted next step [*board(n,i)* = *false*] and try another possibility. This method is called **backtracking**.]

14. A 10 × 10 array *maze* of 0's and 1's represents a maze in which a traveler must find a path from *maze*(1,1) to *maze*(10,10). The traveler may move from a square into any adjacent square in the same row or column, but may not skip over any squares or move diagonally. In addition, the traveler may not move into any square that contains a 1. *maze*(1,1) and *maze*(10,10) contain 0's. Write a routine that accepts such a *maze* and either prints a message that no path through the maze exists, or prints a list of positions representing a path from (1,1) to (10,10).

15. Convert the following recursive program scheme into an iterative version which does not use a stack. *f(n)* is a function that returns a logical value based on the value of *n*, and *g(n)* is a function that returns a value of the same type as *n* without modifying *n*.

> **subroutine** *rec*(n)
> **if not** *f(n)*
>   **then**
>   'any group of statements
>   'which do not change the value of *n*
>   *rec*(g(n))
>   **endif**
>   **return**

Generalize your result to the case in which *rec* is a function.

16. Let *f(n)* be a logical-valued function and *g(n)* and *h(n)* be functions that return a value of the same type as *n* without modifying *n*. Let *(stmts)* represent any group of statements that do not modify the value of *n*. Show that the recursive algorithm *rec* is equivalent to the iterative algorithm *iter*:

> **subroutine** *rec*(n)
> **if not** *f(n)*
>   **then** (*stmts*)
>   *rec*(g(n))
>   *rec*(h(n))
>   **endif**
>   **return**

> **subroutine** *iter*(n)
> *push*(s,n)
> **while not** *empty*(s) **do**
>   *n* = *pop*(s)
>   **if not** *f(n)*
>   **then** (*stmts*)
>   *push*(s,h(n))
>   *push*(s,g(n))
>   **endif**
>   **endwhile**
>   **return**

Show that the *if* statement in *iter* can be replaced by the loop

$$
\begin{aligned}
&\textbf{\textit{while}}\ f(n)\ =\ \textit{false}\ \textbf{\textit{do}}\\
&\quad (\textit{stmts})\\
&\quad \textit{push}(s, h(n))\\
&\quad n\ =\ g(n)\\
&\textbf{\textit{endwhile}}
\end{aligned}
$$

6

Trees

In this chapter we focus our attention on a data structure that has been found to be extremely useful in many applications—the tree. We define different forms of this data structure and show how they can be represented in BASIC and how they can be applied to solving a wide variety of problems.

1. BINARY TREES

A *binary tree* is a finite set of elements which is either empty or contains a single element called the *root* of the tree and whose remaining elements are partitioned into two disjoint subsets each of which is itself a binary tree. These two subsets are called the *left* and *right subtrees* of the original tree. Each element of a binary tree is called a *node* of the tree.

A conventional method of picturing a binary tree is shown in Figure 6.1.1. This tree consists of nine nodes with *A* as its root. Its left subtree is rooted at *B* and its right subtree is rooted at *C*. This is indicated by the two branches emanating from *A*: to *B* on the left and to *C* on the right. The absence of a branch indicates an empty subtree. For example, the left subtree of the binary tree rooted at *C* and the right subtree of the binary tree rooted at *E* are both empty. The binary trees rooted at *D*, *G*, *H*, and *I* have empty right and left subtrees.

Figure 6.1.2 illustrates some structures which are not binary trees. Be sure that you understand why each of them is not a binary tree as defined above.

If *A* is the root of a binary tree and *B* is the root of its left or right subtree, *A* is said to be the *father* of *B* and *B* is said to be the *left* or *right son* of *A*. A node

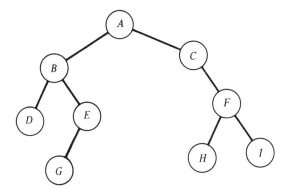

Figure 6.1.1   A binary tree.

that has no sons (such as *D*, *G*, *H*, or *I* of Figure 6.1.1) is called a *leaf*. Node *n*1 is an *ancestor* of node *n*2 (and *n*2 is a *descendant* of *n*1) if *n*1 is either the father of *n*2 or the father of some ancestor of *n*2. For example, in the tree of Figure 6.1.1, *A* is an ancestor of *G* and *H* is a descendant of *C*, but *E* is neither an ancestor nor a descendant of *C*. A node *n*2 is a *left descendant* of node *n*1 if *n*2 is either the left son of *n*1 or a descendant of the left son of *n*1. A *right descendant* may be defined in a similar manner. Two nodes are *brothers* if they are sons of the same father.

If every nonleaf node in a binary tree has nonempty right and left subtrees, the tree is termed a *strictly binary tree*. Thus the tree of Figure 6.1.3 is strictly binary, while that of Figure 6.1.1 is not (because nodes *C* and *E* have one son each). A strictly binary tree with *n* leafs always contains $2n - 1$ nodes. The proof of this fact is left as an exercise for the reader.

The *level* of a node in a binary tree may be defined as follows. The root of the tree has level 0 and the level of any other node in the tree is 1 more than the level of its father. For example, in the binary tree of Figure 6.1.1, node *E* is at level 2 and node *H* is at level 3. The *depth* of a binary tree is the maximum level of any leaf in the tree. This equals the length of the longest path from the root to any leaf. Thus the depth of the tree of Figure 6.1.1 is 3. A *complete binary tree of level n* is one in which each node at level *n* is a leaf and in which each node at level less than *n* has nonempty left and right subtrees. Figure 6.1.4 illustrates a complete binary tree of level 3.

We also define an *almost complete binary tree* as a binary tree for which there is a nonnegative integer *k* such that

1. Each leaf in the tree is either at level *k* or at level $k + 1$.
2. If a node in the tree has a right descendant at level $k + 1$, then all of its left descendants which are leafs are also at level $k + 1$.

The strictly binary tree of Figure 6.1.5(a) is not almost complete since it contains leafs at levels 1, 2, and 3, thereby violating condition 1. The strictly binary tree of Figure 6.1.5(b) satisfies condition 1 since every leaf is either at level 2 or at

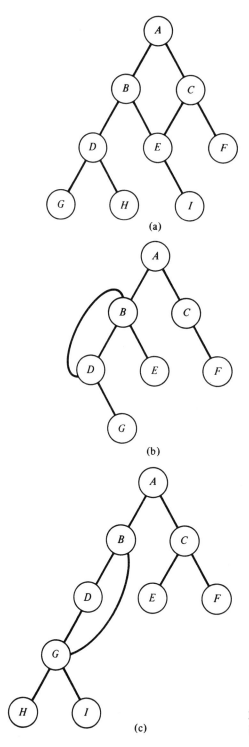

(a)

(b)

(c)

Figure 6.1.2 Structures which are not binary trees.

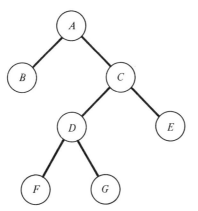

Figure 6.1.3 A strictly binary tree.

level 3. However, condition 2 is violated since *A* has a right descendant at level 3 (*J*) but also has a left descendant which is a leaf at level 2 (*E*). The strictly binary tree of Figure 6.1.5(c) satisfies both conditions 1 and 2 and is therefore an almost complete binary tree. The binary tree of Figure 6.1.5(d) is also an almost complete binary tree but is not strictly binary since node *E* has a left son but not a right son. (We should note that many texts refer to such a tree as a "complete binary tree" rather than as an "almost complete binary tree." Still other texts use the term "complete" or "fully binary" to refer to the concept which we call "strictly binary." We use the terms "strictly binary," "complete," and "almost complete" as we have defined them here.)

The nodes of an almost complete binary tree can be numbered so that the root is assigned the number 1, a left son is assigned twice the number assigned its father, and a right son is assigned one more than twice the number assigned its father. Figure 6.1.5(e) illustrates the numbering of the nodes of the tree of Figure 6.1.5(c). Under this numbering scheme each node in an almost complete binary tree is assigned a unique number which defines the node's position within the

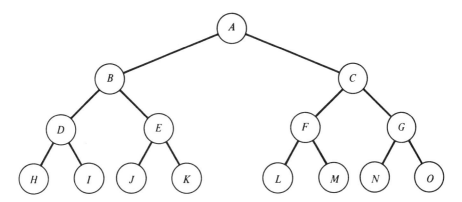

Figure 6.1.4 A complete binary tree of level 3.

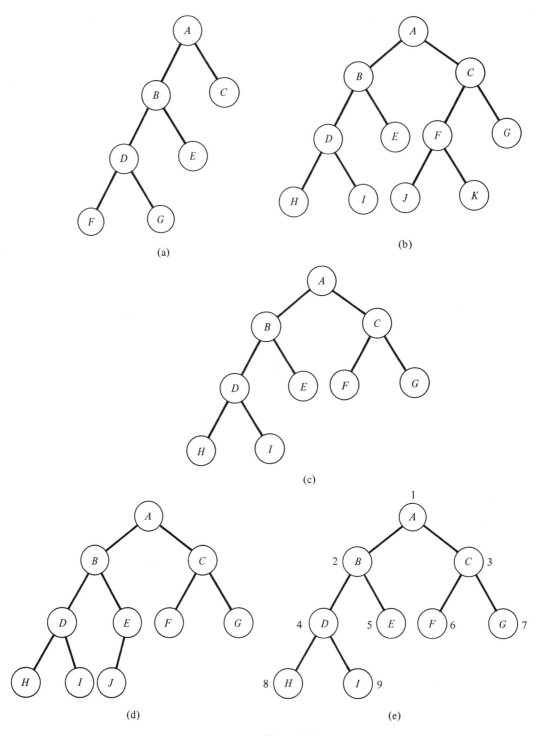

(a)

(b)

(c)

(d)

(e)

Figure 6.1.5

tree. An almost complete strictly binary tree with n leafs has $2n-1$ nodes, as does any other strictly binary tree with n leafs. An almost complete binary tree with n leafs which is not strictly binary has $2n$ nodes. There are two distinct almost complete binary trees with n leafs, one of which is strictly binary and one of which is not. For example, the trees of Figure 6.1.5(c) and (d) are both almost complete and have five leafs; however, the tree of Figure 6.1.5(c) is strictly binary, whereas that of Figure 6.1.5(d) is not. There is only a single almost complete binary tree with n nodes. This tree is strictly binary if and only if n is odd. Thus the tree of Figure 6.1.5(c) is the only almost complete binary tree with nine nodes and is strictly binary because 9 is odd, while the tree of Figure 6.1.5(d) is the only almost complete binary tree with 10 nodes and is not strictly binary because 10 is even.

Operations on Binary Trees

There are a number of primitive operations that can be applied to a binary tree. If p is a pointer to a node nd of a binary tree, the function $info(p)$ returns the contents of nd. The functions $left(p)$, $right(p)$, $father(p)$, and $brother(p)$ return pointers to the left son of nd, the right son of nd, the father of nd, and the brother of nd, respectively. These functions return the null pointer if nd has no left son, right son, father, or brother. Finally, the logical functions $isleft(p)$ and $isright(p)$ return the value *true* if nd is a left or right son, respectively, of some other node in the tree, and *false* otherwise.

Note that the functions $isleft(p)$, $isright(p)$, and $brother(p)$ can be implemented using the functions $left(p)$, $right(p)$, and $father(p)$. *isleft* may be implemented as follows:

```
function isleft(p)
q = father(p)
if q = null
    then isleft = false        'p points to the root
    else if left(q) = p
            then isleft = true
            else isleft = false
        endif
endif
return
```

isright may be implemented in a similar manner, or by calling *isleft*. *brother(p)* may be implemented using *isleft* or *isright* as follows:

```
            function brother(p)
            if father(p) = null
              then brother = null   'p points to the root
              else if isleft(p)
                      then brother = right (father(p))
                      else brother = left(father(p))
                   endif
            endif
            return
```

In constructing a binary tree, the operations *maketree, setleft,* and *setright* are useful. The function *maketree(x)* creates a new binary tree consisting of a single node with information field *x* and returns a pointer to that node. *setleft(p,x)* accepts a pointer *p* to a binary tree node *nd* with no left son and an item *x*. It creates a new left son of *nd* with information field *x*. *setright(p,x)* is analogous to *setleft* except that it creates a right son of *nd*.

Applications of Binary Trees

A binary tree is a useful data structure when two-way decisions must be made at each point in a process. For example, suppose that we want to find all duplicates in a list of numbers. One way of doing this is to compare each number with all those that precede it. However, this involves a large number of comparisons. The number of comparisons can be reduced by using a binary tree. The first number is read and placed in a node which is established as the root of a binary tree with empty left and right subtrees. Each successive number in the list is then compared to the number in the root. If it matches, we have a duplicate. If it is smaller, the process is repeated with the left subtree, and if it is larger, the process is repeated with the right subtree. This continues until either a duplicate is found or an empty subtree is reached. When an empty subtree is reached, the number is placed into a new node at that position in the tree. An algorithm for doing this follows.

```
        'read the first number and insert it into a single-node binary tree
        read number
        tree = maketree(number)
        while there are numbers left in the input do
            read number
            q = tree
            p = tree
            while (q <> null) and (number <> info(p)) do
                p = q
                if number < info(p)
                  then q = left(p)
                  else q = right(p)
                endif
            endwhile
```

> **if** number = info(p)
> > **then print** number, "is a duplicate"
> > **else if** number < info(p)
> > > **then** setleft(p, number)
> > > **else** setright (p, number)
> > > *endif*
> > *endif*
> *endwhile*

Figure 6.1.6 illustrates the tree that would be constructed from the input

$$14 \quad 15 \quad 4 \quad 9 \quad 7 \quad 18 \quad 3 \quad 5 \quad 16 \quad 4 \quad 20 \quad 17 \quad 9 \quad 14 \quad 5$$

The output would indicate that 4, 9, 14, and 5 are duplicates.

Another common operation is to ***traverse*** a binary tree, that is, to pass through the tree, enumerating each of its nodes once. We may simply wish to print the contents of each node as we enumerate it, or we may wish to process it in some other fashion. In either case, we speak of ***visiting*** the nodes of a binary tree.

The order in which the nodes of a linear list are visited in a traversal is clearly from first to last. However, there is no such "natural" linear order for the nodes of a tree. Thus different orderings are used for traversal in different cases. We shall define three of these traversal methods. In each of these methods, nothing need be done to traverse an empty binary tree. The methods will all be defined recursively so that traversing a binary tree involves visiting the root and traversing its left and right subtrees. The only difference among the methods is the order in which these three operations are performed.

To traverse a nonempty binary tree in ***preorder*** (also known as ***depth-first order***), we perform the following three operations:

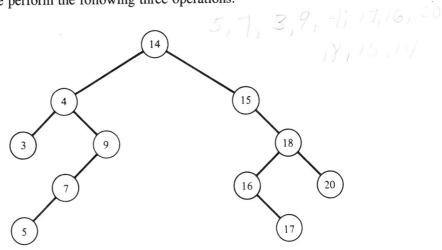

Figure 6.1.6 A binary tree constructed for finding duplicates.

1. Visit the root.
2. Traverse the left subtree in preorder.
3. Traverse the right subtree in preorder.

To traverse a nonempty binary tree in *inorder* or *symmetric order*:

1. Traverse the left subtree in inorder.
2. Visit the root.
3. Traverse the right subtree in inorder.

To traverse a nonempty binary tree in *postorder:*

1. Traverse the left subtree in postorder.
2. Traverse the right subtree in postorder.
3. Visit the root.

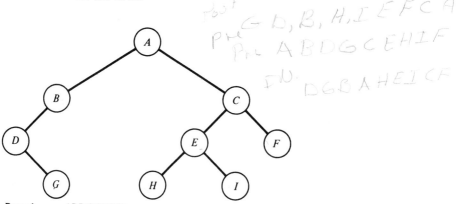

Preorder: *ABDGCEHIF*
Inorder: *DGBAHEICF*
Postorder: *GDBHIEFCA*

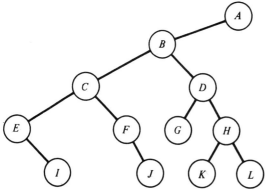

Preorder: *ABCEIFJDGHKL*
Inorder: *EICFJBGDKHLA*
Postorder: *IEJFCGKLHDBA*

Figure 6.1.7 Binary trees and their traversals.

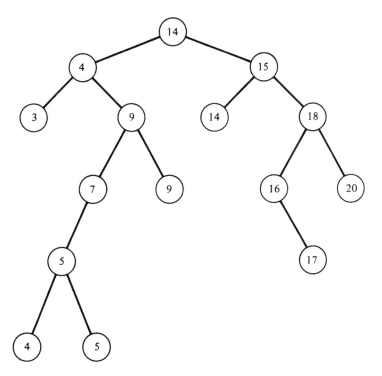

Figure 6.1.8   A binary tree constructed for sorting.

Figure 6.1.7 illustrates two binary trees and their traversals in preorder, inorder, and postorder.

Many algorithms and processes that use binary trees proceed in two phases. The first phase builds a binary tree and the second phase traverses the tree. As an example of such an algorithm, consider the following sorting method. Given a list of numbers in an input file, we wish to print them in ascending order. As we read the numbers, they can be inserted into a binary tree such as the one of Figure 6.1.6. However, unlike the previous algorithm which was used to find duplicates, duplicate values are also placed in the tree. When a number is compared to the contents of a node in the tree, a left branch is taken if the number is smaller than the contents of the node and a right branch if it is greater or equal to the contents of the node. Thus if the input list is

$$14 \quad 15 \quad 4 \quad 9 \quad 7 \quad 18 \quad 3 \quad 5 \quad 16 \quad 4 \quad 20 \quad 17 \quad 9 \quad 14 \quad 5$$

the binary tree of Figure 6.1.8 is produced. Such a binary tree has the property that the contents of each node in the left subtree of a node n are less than the contents of n, and the contents of each node in the right subtree of n are greater than or equal to the contents of n. Thus, if the tree is traversed in inorder (left, root, right), the numbers are printed in ascending order. (You are asked to prove this as an exercise.) The use of binary trees in sorting and searching will be discussed further in Chapters 8 and 9.

Let us denote the operation of traversing a binary tree in inorder and printing the contents of each of its nodes by *intrav(tree)*. Then the sorting algorithm may be written as follows:

```
read number
tree = maketree(number)
while there are numbers left in the input do
        read number
        q = tree
        while q <> null do
                p = q
                if number < info(p)
                    then q = left(p)
                    else q = right(p)
                endif
        endwhile
        if number < info(p)
            then setleft(p, number)
            else setright(p,number)
        endif
endwhile
'traverse the tree
intrav(tree)
```

As another application of binary trees, consider the following method of representing an expression containing operands and binary operators by a strictly binary tree. The root of such a binary tree contains an operator which is to be applied to the results of evaluating the expressions represented by the left and right subtrees. A node representing an operator has two nonempty subtrees, while a node representing an operand has two empty subtrees. Figure 6.1.9 illustrates some expressions and their tree representations. Note that parentheses are not required in the tree since the tree structure defines the order of operations.

Let us see what happens when these binary trees are traversed. Traversing such a tree in preorder means that the operator (the root) will precede its two operands (the subtrees). Thus a preorder traversal should yield the prefix form of the expression. (For definitions of the prefix and postfix forms of an arithmetic expression, see Sections 3.3 and 5.3.) This is indeed the case. Traversing the binary trees of Figure 6.1.9 yields the prefix forms

$+A*BC$	[Figure 6.1.9(a)]
$*+ABC$	[Figure 6.1.9(b)]
$+A*-BC{\uparrow}D*EF$	[Figure 6.1.9(c)]
${\uparrow}+A*BC*+ABC$	[Figure 6.1.9(d)]

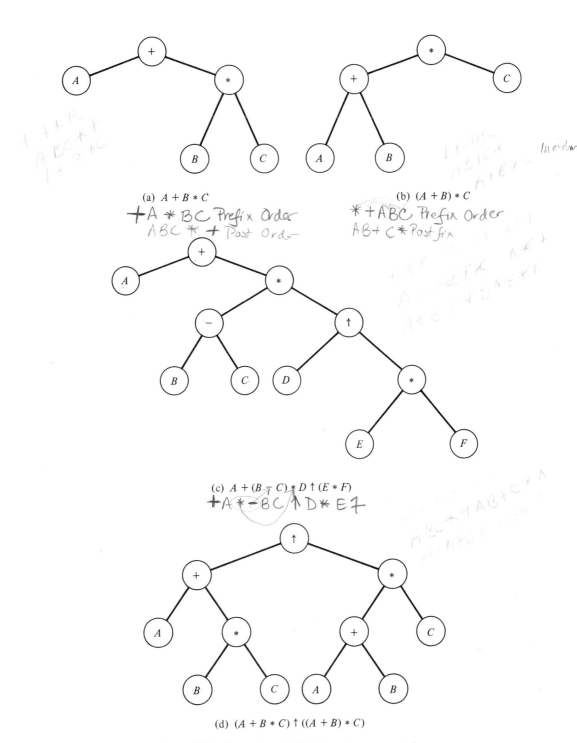

(a) $A + B * C$

[handwritten] $+ A * BC$ Prefix Order
$ABC * +$ Post Order

(b) $(A + B) * C$

[handwritten] $* + ABC$ Prefix Order
$AB + C *$ Postfix

[handwritten top left] $ABC * +$

[handwritten right] Inorder

(c) $A + (B - C) * D \uparrow (E * F)$

[handwritten] $+ A * - BC \uparrow D * EF$

(d) $(A + B * C) \uparrow ((A + B) * C)$

Figure 6.1.9 Expressions and their binary tree representation.

Similarly, traversing such a binary tree in postorder places the operator after its two operands so that a postorder traversal produces the postfix form of the expression. Thus postorder traversals of the binary trees of Figure 6.1.9 yield the postfix forms

$$ABC*+ \qquad \text{[Figure 6.1.9(a)]}$$
$$AB+C* \qquad \text{[Figure 6.1.9(b)]}$$
$$ABC-DEF*{\uparrow}*+ \qquad \text{[Figure 6.1.9(c)]}$$
$$ABC*+AB+C*{\uparrow} \qquad \text{[Figure 6.1.9(d)]}$$

What happens when such binary trees are traversed in inorder? Since the root (operator) is visited after the nodes of the left subtree (the first operand) and before the nodes of the right subtree (the second operand), we might expect an inorder traversal to yield the infix form of the expression. Indeed, if the binary tree of Figure 6.1.9(a) is traversed, the infix expression $A+B*C$ is obtained. However, since the binary tree does not contain parentheses, an expression whose infix form requires parentheses to override explicitly the conventional precedence rules cannot be retrieved by a simple inorder traversal. The inorder traversals of the trees of Figure 6.1.9 yield the expressions

$$A+B*C \qquad \text{[Figure 6.1.9(a)]}$$
$$A+B*C \qquad \text{[Figure 6.1.9(b)]}$$
$$A+B-C*D{\uparrow}E*F \qquad \text{[Figure 6.1.9(c)]}$$
$$A+B*C{\uparrow}A+B*C \qquad \text{[Figure 6.1.9(d)]}$$

which are correct except for parentheses.

EXERCISES

1. Prove that the root of a binary tree is an ancestor of every node in the tree except itself.

2. Prove that a node of a binary tree has at most one father.

3. How many ancestors does a node at level n in a binary tree have? Prove your answer.

4. What are the maximum number of nodes at level n in a binary tree?

5. Write an algorithm to determine if a binary tree is
   (a) strictly binary.
   (b) complete.
   (c) almost complete.

6. Prove that a strictly binary tree with n leafs contains $2n-1$ nodes.

7. Given a strictly binary tree with n leafs, let $level(i)$ for i between 1 and n equal the level of the ith leaf. Prove that the sum of $1/2^{level(i)}$ for all i between 1 and n equals 1.

8. Prove that the nodes of an almost complete binary tree with n nodes can be numbered from 1 to n in such a way that the number assigned to the left son of the node numbered i is $2i$ and the number assigned to the right son of the node numbered i is $2i + 1$.

9. Two binary trees are *similar* if they are both empty or if they are both nonempty, their left subtrees are similar, and their right subtrees are similar. Write an algorithm that determines if two binary trees are similar.

10. Two binary trees are *mirror similar* if they are both empty or if they are both non-empty and the left subtree of each is mirror similar to the right subtree of the other. Write an algorithm that determines if two binary trees are mirror similar.

11. Write algorithms to determine whether or not one binary tree is similar or mirror similar (see Exercises 9 and 10) to some subtree of another.

12. Develop an algorithm to find duplicates in a list of numbers without using a binary tree. If there are n distinct numbers in the list, how many times must two numbers be compared for equality in your algorithm? What if all n numbers are equal?

13. Write an algorithm that accepts a pointer to a binary tree representing an expression and returns the infix version of the expression which contains only those parentheses that are necessary.

2. BINARY TREE REPRESENTATIONS

In this section we examine various methods of implementing binary trees in BASIC and present routines that build and traverse binary trees. We also present some applications of binary trees.

Node Representation of Binary Trees

As in the case of list nodes, tree nodes may be implemented as array elements. Typically, each node would contain INFO, LEFT, RIGHT, and FTHER fields. (We use FTHER rather than FATHER to avoid conflict with the variable FALSE under those versions of BASIC in which only the first two characters of a variable name are significant.) The LEFT, RIGHT, and FTHER fields of a node point to the node's left son, right son, and father, respectively. We may declare

```
10   MXNODE = 500
20   DIM INFO(MXNODE)
30   DIM LEFT(MXNODE)
40   DIM RIGHT(MXNODE)
50   DIM FTHER(MXNODE)
```

Under this representation, the operations *info*(p), *left*(p), *right*(p), and *father*(p) would be implemented by direct references to INFO(P), LEFT(P), RIGHT(P), and FTHER(P).

Alternatively, nodes may be represented by

```
10   MXNODE = 500
20   DIM INFO(MXNODE)
30   DIM PTR(MXNODE,3)
40       LEFT = 1
50       RIGHT = 2
60       FTHER = 3
```

Under this representation, the operations *info(p)*, *left(p)*, *right(p)*, and *father(p)* would be implemented by references to INFO(P), PTR(P,LEFT), PTR(P,RIGHT), and PTR(P,FTHER). We use this implementation in the remainder of this section.

The operations *isleft(p)*, *isright(p)*, and *brother(p)* can be implemented in terms of the operations *left(p)*, *right(p)*, and *father(p)*, as described in the preceding section. To implement *isleft* and *isright* more efficiently, we can include an additional field ISLEFT containing the value TRUE (or 1) if that node is a left son of some other node and the value FALSE (or 0) if it is a right son of some other node or the root of the tree. Of course, the root is uniquely identified by a null (zero) value in its FTHER field. Alternatively, these operations may be implemented by setting the sign of the FTHER field negative if the node is a left son or positive if it is a right son and using the BASIC SGN function. The pointer to a node's father is then given by the absolute value of the FTHER field. To implement *brother(p)* more efficiently, we can include an additional BROTHER field in each node.

We create an available list from which we can obtain binary tree nodes by

```
70   AVAIL = 1
80   FOR I = 1 TO MXNODE − 1
90       PTR(I,LEFT) = I + 1
100  NEXT I
110  PTR(MXNODE,LEFT) = 0
```

The routines *getnode* and *freenode* are straightforward and are left as exercises. Note that the available list is not a binary tree but a linear list whose nodes are linked together by the LEFT field. We call this representation the ***node implementation*** of a binary tree.

Under the node implementation, the *maketree* operation, which allocates a node and sets it as the root of a binary tree with empty left and right subtrees, can be implemented as follows. (In *maketree* and in the following subroutines, we do not indicate explicitly that the variables MXNODE, INFO, PTR, AVAIL, LEFT, RIGHT, and FTHER may be inputs and outputs, since that is implied by the binary tree context.)

```
13000   'subroutine maketree
13010   'inputs: X
13020   'outputs: MAKETREE
13030   'locals: GTNODE, PX
13040   GOSUB 1000: 'subroutine getnode sets the variable GTNODE
13050   PX = GTNODE
13060   INFO(PX) = X
13070   PTR(PX,LEFT) = 0
13080   PTR(PX,RIGHT) = 0
13090   PTR(PX,FTHER) = 0
13100   MAKETREE = PX
13110   RETURN
13120   'endsub
```

The subroutine *setleft* sets a node with contents X as the left son of *node*(P).

```
14000   'subroutine setleft
14010   'inputs: P, X
14020   'outputs: none
14030   'locals: MAKETREE, QX
14040   IF P = 0 THEN PRINT "VOID INSERTION": STOP
14050   IF PTR(P, LEFT) <> 0 THEN PRINT "INVALID INSERTION": STOP
14060   GOSUB 13000: 'subroutine maketree sets the variable MAKETREE
14070   QX = MAKETREE
14080   PTR(P,LEFT) = QX
14090   PTR(QX, FTHER) = P
14100   RETURN
14110   'endsub
```

The routine *setright,* which creates a right son of *node*(P) with contents X, is similar and is left as an exercise for the reader.

It is not always necessary to use FTHER, LEFT, and RIGHT fields. If a tree is always traversed in downward fashion (from the root to the leafs), the *father* operation is never used; in that case, a FTHER field is unnecessary. Similarly, if a tree is always traversed in upward fashion (from the leafs to the root), the *left* and *right* operations are never used and LEFT and RIGHT fields are not needed. It would still be possible to perform the *isleft* and *isright* operations by using a signed pointer in the FTHER field, as discussed earlier; a right son contains a positive FTHER value and a left son contains a negative FTHER value. Of course, the routines *maketree, setleft,* and *setright* must be suitably modified for these representations. We generally assume that all three fields (FTHER, LEFT, and RIGHT) are present, but you may wish to conserve space by eliminating those that are unnecessary in a particular situation.

The following program uses a binary tree to find duplicate numbers. It closely follows the algorithm of Section 1.

```
 10  'program dup
 20  DEFINT A, F, I, L, M, P, Q, R, T
 30  'establish the set of tree nodes
 40  MXNODE = 500: 'maximum number of nodes
 50  DIM INFO(MXNODE), PTR(MXNODE,3)
 60       LEFT = 1
 70       RIGHT = 2
 80       FTHER = 3
 90  'initialize the available list
100  AVAIL = 1
110  FOR I = 1 TO MXNODE − 1
120       PTR(I,LEFT) = I + 1
130  NEXT I
140  PTR(MXNODE,LEFT) = 0
150  'initialize the tree from the first input value
160  READ X
170  GOSUB 13000: 'subroutine maketree sets the variable MAKETREE
180  TREE = MAKETREE
190  'begin looking for duplicates
200  READ NUMBER
210  IF NUMBER = −99 THEN STOP
220     PPNTR = TREE
230     QPNTR = TREE
240     'travel down the tree
250     IF QPNTR = 0 OR NUMBER = INFO(PPNTR) THEN GOTO 290
260        PPNTR = QPNTR
270        IF NUMBER < INFO(PPNTR) THEN QPNTR = PTR(PPNTR,LEFT)
                                     ELSE QPNTR = PTR(PPNTR,RIGHT)
280     GOTO 250
290     'if the number is in the tree, it is a duplicate
300     IF NUMBER = INFO(PPNTR)
           THEN PRINT NUMBER; "IS A DUPLICATE": GOTO 200
310     'otherwise, insert the number into the tree
320     X = NUMBER
330     P = PPNTR
340     'call either setleft (at 14000) or setright (at 15000); both accept P and X
350     IF NUMBER < INFO(PPNTR) THEN GOSUB 14000
                                  ELSE GOSUB 15000
360  GOTO 200
```

370   END
   . . .
500   DATA . . .

Almost Complete Array Representation of Binary Trees

Recall from Section 1 that the nodes of an almost complete binary tree can be numbered in such a way that the number assigned a left son is twice the number assigned its father and the number assigned a right son is one more than twice the number assigned its father. To represent an almost complete binary tree, we do not need father, left, or right links. Instead, the node assigned the number p is the implicit father of the nodes assigned the numbers $2p$ and $2p+1$. A tree with n leafs is represented by an array *info* of size $2n-1$ if the tree is strictly binary and of size $2n$ if it is not. A pointer to a node is therefore an integer between 1 and $2n$. The root of the tree is at position 1, so that *tree* equals 1. The left son of the node at position p is at position $2p$ and its right son is at position $2p+1$. Thus *left*(p) may be translated into $2p$ and *right*(p) into $2p+1$. Similarly, given a left son at position p, its right brother may be found at $p+1$. *father*(p) may be computed by truncating the value of $p/2$ to an integer. p points to a left son if and only if it is a multiple of 2. Thus the test for whether p points to a left son (the *isleft* subroutine) is to check whether or not $2*int(p/2)$ equals p. Figure 6.2.1 illustrates arrays that represent the almost complete binary trees of Figure 6.1.5(c) and (d).

We can extend this array representation of almost complete binary trees to an array representation of binary trees generally. We do this by identifying an almost complete binary tree which contains the binary tree that is to be represented. Figure 6.2.2(a) illustrates two (non-almost-complete) binary trees and Figure 6.2.2(b) illustrates the smallest almost complete binary trees that contain them. Finally, Figure 6.2.2(c) illustrates the array representations of these almost complete binary trees, and by extension, of the original binary trees.

Under this representation, an array element is allocated whether or not it serves to contain a node of a tree. We must, therefore, flag unused array elements as null tree nodes. This may be accomplished by one of two methods. One method is to place a special value in the positions of the array that represent null tree nodes. This special value should be invalid as the information content of a legitimate tree mode. For example, in a tree containing positive numbers, a null node may be indicated by a negative number. Alternatively, we may declare a parallel array, *flag,* containing the value 1 in positions corresponding to actual tree nodes and 0 in positions corresponding to null tree nodes.

We now present the program that uses a binary tree to find duplicate numbers in an input list using the latter representation of binary trees, together with the routines *maketree* and *setleft*.

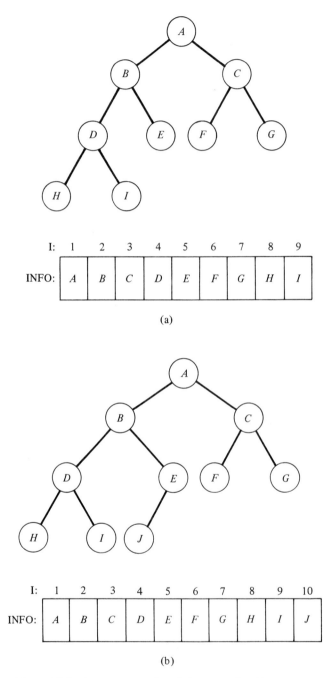

(a)

(b)

Figure 6.2.1 Array representation of almost complete binary trees.

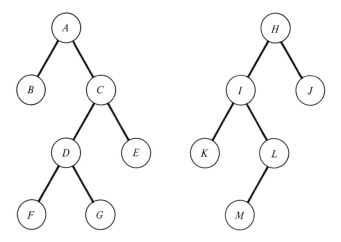

(a) Two binary trees

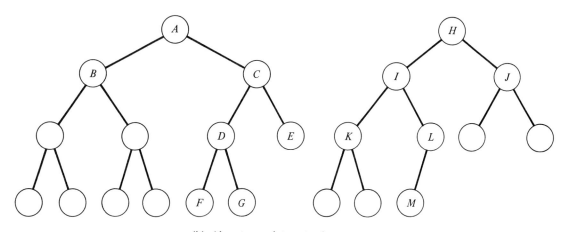

(b) Almost complete extensions

1	2	3	4	5	6	7	8	9	10	11	12	13
A	B	C			D	E					F	G

1	2	3	4	5	6	7	8	9	10
H	I	J	K	L					M

(c) Array representations

Figure 6.2.2

```
 10  'program dup2
 20  MXNODE = 500
 30  DIM INFO(MXNODE), FLAG(MXNODE)
 40  READ X
 50  GOSUB 13000: 'subroutine maketree initializes the tree root
 60  READ NUMBER
 70  IF NUMBER = -99 THEN STOP
 80     PPNTR = 1
 90     QPNTR = 1
100     IF QPNTR > MXNODE THEN GOTO 150
110     IF FLAG(QPNTR) = 0 OR NUMBER = INFO(PPNTR)
            THEN GOTO 150
120        PPNTR = QPNTR
130        IF NUMBER < INFO(PPNTR) THEN QPNTR = 2 * PPNTR
                               ELSE QPNTR = 2 * PPNTR + 1
140     GOTO 100
150     'if the number is in the tree, it is a duplicate
160     IF NUMBER = INFO(PPNTR)
            THEN PRINT NUMBER; "IS A DUPLICATE": GOTO 60
170     'otherwise, insert the number into the tree
180     X = NUMBER
190     P = PPNTR
200     'call either setleft or setright
210     IF NUMBER < INFO(PPNTR) THEN GOSUB 14000
                               ELSE GOSUB 15000
220  GOTO 60
230  END
       . . .
500  DATA
       . . .
13000  'subroutine maketree
13010  'inputs: X
13020  'outputs: none (the tree is always rooted at node 1)
13030  'locals: II
13040  FOR II = 2 to MXNODE
13050       FLAG(II) = 0
13060  NEXT II
13070  INFO(1) = X
13080  FLAG(1) = 1
13090  RETURN
13100  'endsub
```

```
14000   'subroutine setleft
14010   'inputs: P,X
14020   'outputs: none
14030   'locals: PX
14040   PX = 2*P
14050   IF PX < 1 OR PX > MXNODE
            THEN PRINT "ARRAY OVERFLOW": STOP
14060   IF FLAG(PX) <> 0 THEN PRINT "INVALID INSERTION": STOP
14070   INFO(PX) = X
14080   FLAG(PX) = 1
14090   RETURN
14100   'endsub

15000   'subroutine setright
        . . .
```

Note that under this implementation, the routine *maketree* is used to initialize the arrays INFO and FLAG to represent a tree with a single node. The variable MAKETREE is unnecessary since under this representation the single binary tree represented by INFO and FLAG is always rooted at node 1. That is the reason PPNTR is initialized to 1 in statement 80. Note also that under this representation it is always necessary to check that the array bound (MXNODE) has not been exceeded whenever we move down the tree (see statements 100 and 14050).

Choosing a Binary Tree Representation

Which representation of binary trees is preferable? There is no general answer to this question. The almost complete array representation is somewhat simpler, although it is necessary to ensure that all pointers are within the array bounds. The almost complete array representation clearly saves storage space for trees that are known to be almost complete, since it eliminates the need for the arrays LEFT, RIGHT, and FTHER, and does not even require a FLAG array. It is also space efficient for trees which are only a few nodes short of being almost complete, or when nodes are successively eliminated from a tree that is initially almost complete, although a FLAG array might then be required.

However, the almost complete array representation can be used only in a context in which only a single tree is required, or where the number of trees needed is fixed in advance. Even when this number is known, separate arrays are required for each tree; unused space in one array cannot be utilized for a tree housed in another array. Further, separate routines (e.g., *maketree, setleft,* etc.) would be required for each tree unless large arrays or variables indicating the appropriate array are transmitted as inputs and outputs. By contrast, the node representation requires LEFT, RIGHT, and FTHER arrays (although we have seen that one or two of these may be eliminated in specific situations) but allows much more flexible use of the collection of nodes. In the node representation, a node may be placed at any location in any tree, whereas in the almost complete array representation a node can be utilized only if it is needed at a specific location in a specific tree. Thus the node representation is preferable in the general, dynamic situation of many trees of unpredictable shape.

The program that finds duplicates is a good illustration of the trade-offs involved. The program *dup*, which utilized the node representation of binary trees, required LEFT and RIGHT arrays in addition to INFO. (The array FTHER was not really necessary in that program.) *dup2*, which utilized the almost complete binary representation, required only an additional array FLAG (and this, too, could have been eliminated if only positive numbers or integers were allowed in the input so that a null tree node could be represented by a specific negative or noninteger INFO value). The almost complete array representation could be used for this example because only a single tree was required. However, *dup2* might not work for as many input cases as *dup*. For example, suppose that the input was in ascending order. Then the tree that is formed has all null left subtrees (you are invited to verify that this is the case by simulating the programs for such input). In this case the only elements of INFO that are occupied in *dup2* are 1, 3, 7, 15, and so on (each position is 1 more than twice the previous one). If the value of MXNODE is kept at 500, a maximum of only 16 distinct ascending numbers can be accommodated in the input (the last one will be at position 255). This can be contrasted with *dup*, which permits any 500 distinct numbers in any order before it runs out of space.

Traversing Binary Trees

The methods for traversing binary trees are best described by recursive algorithms that mirror the traversal definitions. The three algorithms *pretrav, intrav,* and *postrav* print the contents of a binary tree in preorder, inorder, and postorder, respectively. The input variable to each algorithm is a pointer to the root node of a binary tree.

> **subroutine** *pretrav(tree)*
> **if** *tree = null*
>   **then return**
> **endif**
> **print** *info(tree)*
> *pretrav(left(tree))*
> *pretrav(right(tree))*
> **return**
>
> **subroutine** *intrav(tree)*
> **if** *tree = null*
>   **then return**
> **endif**
>
> *intrav(left(tree))*
> **print** *info(tree)*
> *intrav(right(tree))*
> **return**

> **subroutine** *postrav*(*tree*)
> **if** *tree* = *null*
>   **then return**
> **endif**
> *postrav*(*left*(*tree*))
> *postrav*(*right*(*tree*))
> **print** *info*(*tree*)
> **return**

The reader is invited to simulate the actions of these algorithms on the trees of Figures 6.1.7 and 6.1.8.

Of course, BASIC routines to perform these traversals must explicitly perform the necessary stacking and unstacking. For example, a BASIC routine to traverse in inorder a binary tree using the node representation may be written as follows. (We use STMAX as the maximum stack size so as not to conflict with MXNODES and MAKETREE.)

```
16000   'subroutine intrav
16010   'inputs: TREE
16020   'outputs: none
16030   'locals: EMPTY, P, POPS, SITEM, STMAX, TP, X
16040   'declare the recursion stack
16050   STMAX = 500
16060   DIM SITEM(STMAX)
16070   TP = 0
16080   P = TREE:   'begin at the tree root
16090   'travel down left branches as far as possible saving pointers to nodes passed
16100   IF P = 0 THEN GOTO 16150
16110      X = P
16120      GOSUB 1000: 'subroutine push pushes X onto the stack
16130      P = PTR(P,LEFT)
16140   GOTO 16100
16150   'check if finished
16160   GOSUB 3000: 'subroutine empty sets the variable EMPTY
16170   IF EMPTY = TRUE THEN RETURN
16180   'at this point the left subtree is empty, visit the root
16190   GOSUB 2000: 'subroutine pop sets the variable POPS
16200   P = POPS
16210   PRINT INFO(P)
16220   'traverse the right subtree
16230   P = PTR(P,RIGHT)
16240   GOTO 16090
16250   'endsub
```

The nonrecursive routines to traverse a binary tree in postorder and preorder as well as the nonrecursive traversal of binary trees using the almost complete array representation are left as exercises for the reader.

Threaded Binary Trees

Since traversing a binary tree is such a common operation, it would be helpful to find a more efficient method to perform the operation. Let us examine the routine *intrav* to discover the reason a stack is needed. The stack is popped when P equals *null* (0 under the node implementation). This happens in one of two cases: one case is when the loop consisting of statements 16090–16140 is exited after having been executed one or more times. This implies that the program has traveled down left branches until it reached a null pointer, stacking each node as it was passed. Thus the top element of the stack is the value of P before it became 0. If an auxiliary pointer Q is kept one step behind P, the value of Q can be used directly and need not be popped.

The other case in which P is 0 is when the loop consisting of statements 16090–16140 is skipped entirely. This occurs after reaching a node with an empty right subtree, executing statement 16230 [P = PTR(P,RIGHT)], which may set P to 0, and returning to statement 16090 and then to 16150. At this point, we would have lost our way were it not for the stack whose top points to the node whose left subtree was just traversed. Suppose, however, that instead of a null pointer, a node with an empty right subtree contained a pointer to the node which would be on top of the stack at that point in the algorithm. Then there would no longer be a need for the stack, since the node points directly to its inrder successor. Such a pointer is called a *thread* and must be differentiable from a tree pointer, which is used to link a node to its left or right subtree. Figure 6.2.3 shows the binary trees of Figure 6.1.7 with threads replacing null pointers in nodes with empty right subtrees. The threads are drawn with dotted lines to differentiate them from tree pointers. Note that the rightmost node in each tree still has a null right pointer since it has no inorder successor. Such trees are called *right in-threaded* binary trees.

How can threads be represented in the BASIC implementation of binary trees? In the node implementation, a thread can be represented by a negative value of PTR(P,RIGHT). The absolute value of a negative PTR(P,RIGHT) is the index of the node which is the inorder successor of *node*(P). The sign of PTR(P, RIGHT) indicates whether its absolute value represents a thread (minus) or a pointer to a nonempty subtree (plus).

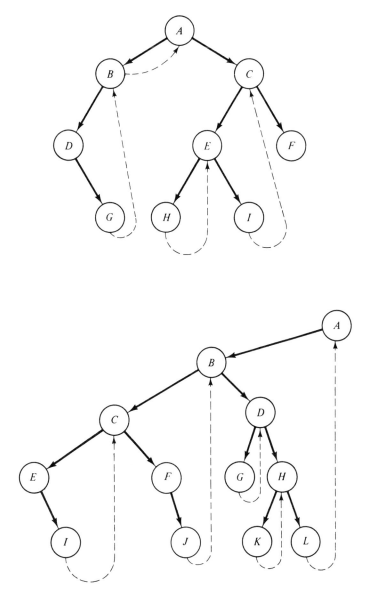

Figure 6.2.3 Right in-threaded binary trees.

Under this implementation, the following routine traverses a right in-thread-ed binary tree in inorder:

```
16000   'subroutine intrav2
16010   'inputs: TREE
16020   'outputs: none
16030   'locals: P, Q
16040   P = TREE
16050   'travel down left links keeping Q behind P
16060   Q = 0
16070   IF P = 0 THEN GOTO 16110
16080      Q = P
16090      P = PTR(P,LEFT)
16100   GOTO 16070
16110   IF Q = 0 THEN RETURN: 'check if finished
16120   PRINT INFO(Q)
16130   P = PTR(Q,RIGHT)
16140   IF P >= 0 THEN GOTO 16050: 'if node(Q) has a right subtree, traverse it
16150      'follow the thread to Q's inorder successor
16160      Q = -P
16170      PRINT INFO(Q)
16180      P = PTR(Q,RIGHT)
16190   GOTO 16140
16200   'endsub
```

Under the almost complete array implementation of binary trees, the FLAG array can be used to contain threads. As before, FLAG(I) equals 0 if I does not represent a node. If I represents a node with a right son, FLAG(I) equals 1 and its right son is at $2*I+1$. However, if I represents a node with no right son, FLAG(I) contains the negative of the index of its inorder successor. (Note that we must use negative numbers to allow us to distinguish a node with a right son from a node whose inorder successor is the root of the tree.) If I is the rightmost node of the tree, so that it has no inorder successor, FLAG(I) can contain the value $-(MXNODE+1)$. We leave the implementation of traversal algorithms for this representation as an exercise for the reader.

In a right in-threaded binary tree, the inorder successor of any node can be found efficiently. Such a tree can also be constructed in a straightforward manner. Under the node representation, the function *maketree* remains unchanged from the unthreaded version and the routines *setleft* and *setright* are as follows:

```
14000   'subroutine setleft
14010   'inputs: P, X
14020   'outputs: none
14030   'locals: GTNODE, QX
```

```
14040   IF P = 0 THEN PRINT "VOID INSERTION": STOP
14050   IF PTR(P,LEFT) <> 0 THEN PRINT "INVALID INSERTION": STOP
14060   GOSUB 10000: 'subroutine getnode sets the variable GTNODE
                              'to point to a newly allocated node
14070   QX = GTNODE
14080   INFO(QX) = X
14090   PTR(P,LEFT) = QX
14100   PTR(QX,RIGHT) = − P: 'the inorder successor of node(QX) is node(P)
14110   PTR(QX,LEFT) = 0
14120   PTR(QX,FTHER) = P
14130   RETURN
14140   'endsub

15000   'subroutine setright
15010   'inputs: P, X
15020   'outputs: none
15030   'locals: GTNODE, QX, RX
15040   IF P = 0 THEN PRINT "VOID INSERTION": STOP
15050   IF PTR(P,RIGHT) > 0 THEN PRINT "INVALID INSERTION": STOP
15060   GOSUB 10000: 'subroutine getnode sets the variable GTNODE
                              'to point to a newly allocated node
15070   QX = GTNODE
15080   INFO(QX) = X
15090   RX = PTR(P,RIGHT): 'save the inorder successor of node(P)
15100   PTR(P,RIGHT) = QX
15110   PTR(QX,LEFT) = 0
15120   PTR(QX,RIGHT) = RX: 'the inorder successor of node(QX) is the
                              'previous successor of node(P)
15130   PTR(QX,FTHER) = P
15140   RETURN
15150   'endsub
```

We leave to the reader to provide appropriate *maketree, setleft,* and *setright* routines for right in-threaded binary trees under the almost complete array implementation.

A *left in-threaded* binary tree may be defined similarly as one in which each null left pointer is altered to contain a thread to that node's inorder predecessor, and an *in-threaded* binary tree may be defined as a binary tree which is both left in-threaded and right in-threaded. However, left in-threading does not yield the advantages of right in-threading. We may also define right and left *prethreaded* binary trees, in which null right and left pointers of nodes are replaced by their preorder successors and predecessors, respectively. A right prethreaded binary tree may be traversed efficiently in preorder without the use of a stack. A right in-threaded binary tree may also be traversed in preorder without the use of a stack. The traversal algorithms are left as exercises for the reader.

Heterogeneous Binary Trees

Often, the information contained in different nodes of a binary tree do not all have the same attributes. For example, in representing a binary expression with numerical operands, we may wish to use a binary tree whose leafs contain numbers but whose nonleaf nodes contain characters representing operators. Figure 6.2.4(a) illustrates such a binary tree. To represent such a tree in BASIC, we may place a pointer in the INFO field of each node. This pointer is an index into an array of the type appropriate for that node. For example, if the node is to represent an integer, the pointer in its INFO field is to an element of an integer array. Each tree node must also contain within itself an indication of the type of object to which its INFO field points. Figure 6.2.4(b) shows such a representation of the binary tree in Figure 6.2.4(a). The figure shows two arrays: OPER to hold the possible operators, and NUM to hold operands. Each tree node contains two fields (in addition to left, right, and father pointers). The first is a character that represents the type of the node. If this character is "N", the node represents an operand and the second field in the node is the position of the operand in the array NUM. If this character is "O", the node represents an operator and the second field is the position of the operator in the array OPER. In this example we may preinitialize an array of characters containing the five arithmetic operations and use an additional array to contain the operands.

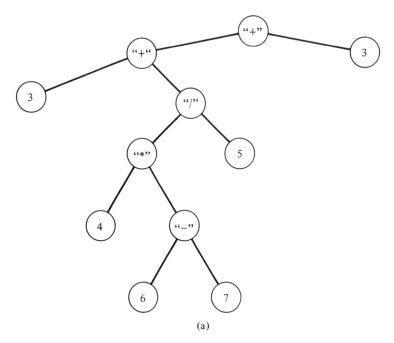

(a)

Figure 6.2.4 Binary tree representing $3 + 4 * (6 - 7)/5 + 3$.

```
 10    DEFSTR O
 20    DIM INFO(500):    'points into the array NUM or OPER
 30    DIM OTYPE(500): ' "N" = operand "O" = operator
 40    DIM PTR(500,3)
 50        LEFT = 1
 60        RIGHT = 2
 70        FTHER = 3
 80    DIM OPER(5): 'holds operators
 90    OPER(1) = " + "
100    OPER(2) = " − "
110    OPER(3) = " * "
120    OPER(4) = " / "
130    OPER(5) = " ↑ "
140    DIM NUM(500): 'holds operands
```

Note that only one copy of each operator exists in OPER (since all the operators to be used are known in advance), but that several copies of an operand (e.g., 3)

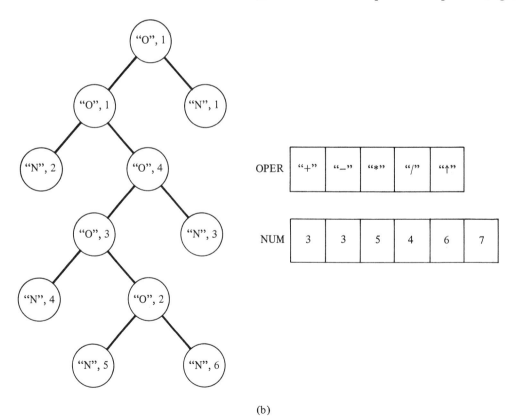

(b)

Figure 6.2.4   *(continued)*

may exist in NUM (since the number of possible operands is too large to keep permanently only one copy of each in an array. Further, it may be too much work to search the entire array to determine the location of an operand that is already present within the array.)

Alternatively, we may represent the operators by a string OPER initialized to "$+-*/\uparrow$" and use the MID\$ function to extract the appropriate operator. Another option would be to use the INFO portion of the node to contain, depending on the contents of OTYPE, either the numerical operand itself or a pointer to the proper operator in OPER (provided that all the operands and the intermediate results are integer). Thus the space needed for NUM would be saved. Yet another option is to store both the operators and operands in character-string form in the INFO portion of the node, and use the VAL function to convert an operand to numeric form. This would make both OPER and NUM unnecessary.

Let us write a BASIC subroutine *evbtree* which accepts a pointer to a tree representing a binary expression and calculates the value of the expression represented by the tree. It uses the auxiliary subroutine *apply*. The first input variable of *apply* is a character representing an operator and the last two are numbers which are two operands. The subroutine *apply* returns a number that is the result of applying the operator to the two operands.

evbtree may best be defined recursively as an algorithm for a function that accepts a pointer to such a tree, evaluates the left and right subtrees, and then applies the operator of the root to the two results. We use the first representation described above. However, we note that a separate field OTYPE is unnecessary since a node contains an operand if and only if it is a leaf. Thus the test whether *node(p)* contains an operand is equivalent to whether *ptr(p,left)* equals *null*.

```
function evbtree(tree)
if ptr(tree,left) = null
    then 'the expression is a single operand
            evbtree = num(info(tree))
            return
    else 'evaluate the left subtree
            frsoper = evbtree(ptr(tree,left))
            'evaluate the right subtree
            secoper = evbtree(ptr(tree,right))
            'extract the operator
            osymb = oper(info(tree))
            'apply the operator and return the result
            evbtree = apply(osymb,frsoper,secoper)
            return
endif
```

Using the techniques of Chapter 5, we may now implement this algorithm as a BASIC program.

```
21000   'subroutine evbtree
21010   'inputs: TREE
21020   'outputs: EVBTREE
21030   'locals: APPLY, CFRSOPER, CPARAM, CRETADDR, FRSOPER, I,
                  OSYMB, PARAM, Q1, Q2, RETADDR, SECOPER
21040   'define the recursion stack; each stack element consists of
        'a tree pointer parameter, a return address indicator,
        'and a value for the first operand
21050   DIM PARAM(50), RETADDR(50), FRSOPER(50)
21060   TP = 0: 'initialize the stack to empty
21070   'push an initial record onto the stack
21080   CPARAM = TREE: 'CPARAM is the current tree pointer parameter
21090   CRETADDR = 1: 'CRETADDR is the current return address
                              'indicator.
21100                         '1 represents a return to the main program
                              '2 represents a return after the first recursive call
                              '3 represents a return after the second recursive call
21110   CFRSOPER = 0:     'CFRSOPER is the current first operand
                              'initialized to the dummy value 0
21120   GOSUB 1000:          'subroutine push saves CPARAM, CRETADDR,
                              'and CFRSOPER on the stack
21130   'beginning of simulated recursive routine
21140   'statements 21160–21210 traverse the left side of the
        'tree until a leaf (operand) is found
21150   'when a leaf is found, return its operand value in the
        'variable EVBTREE
21160   IF PTR(CPARAM,LEFT) = 0
            THEN EVBTREE = NUM(INFO(CPARAM)): GOTO 21380
21170       'simulation of the recursive call evbtree(ptr(tree,left))
21180       GOSUB 1000: 'subroutine push
21190       CRETADDR = 2
21200       CPARAM = PTR(CPARAM,LEFT)
21210   GOTO 21130

21220   'return to this point after evaluating evbtree(ptr(tree,left))
21230   CFRSOPER = EVBTREE
21240   'the first operand has been found; compute the
        'second operand by calling evbtree(ptr(tree,right))
21250   GOSUB 1000: 'subroutine push
21260   CRETADDR = 3
21270   CPARAM = PTR(CPARAM,RIGHT)
21280   GOTO 21130
```

```
21290   'return to this point after evaluating evbtree(ptr(tree,right))
21300   SECOPER = EVBTREE
21310   'apply the operator to the two operands
21320   OSYMB = OPER(INFO(CPARAM)): 'operator
21330   Q1 = CFRSOPER:                'first operand
21340   Q2 = SECOPER:                 'second operand
21350   GOSUB 6000: 'subroutine apply accepts OSYMB, Q1, and
                        'Q2 and sets the variable APPLY
21360   EVBTREE = APPLY
21370   'simulate a return from the evaluation of evbtree(tree) when tree
        'points to an operator node
21380   'simulation of a return from evbtree
21390   I = CRETADDR: 'save the current return address
21400   GOSUB 2000:     'subroutine pop pops the stack and restores the
                          'variables CPARAM, CRETADDR, and CFRSOPER
21410   IF I = 1 THEN RETURN
21420   IF I = 2 THEN GOTO 21220
21430   IF I = 3 THEN GOTO 21290
21440   'endsub
```

Note that not all of the variables used in the algorithm (e.g., *secoper*) are stored in the stack; variables are stacked only if their values may be changed by a subsequent recursive call.

EXERCISES

1. Write a BASIC subroutine that accepts a pointer to a node and returns TRUE if that node is the root of a valid binary tree and FALSE otherwise.

2. Write a BASIC subroutine that accepts a pointer to a node of a binary tree and returns the level of the node in the tree.

3. Write a BASIC subroutine (for both representations presented in this section) that accepts a pointer to a binary tree and creates a new binary tree which is the mirror image of the first (i.e., all left subtrees are now right subtrees, and vice versa; see Exercises 6.1.10 and 6.1.11).

4. Write BASIC subroutines that convert a binary tree represented solely by a FTHER array (in which a left son's FTHER field contains the negative of the pointer to its father and a right son's FTHER contains a pointer to its father) to its representation using LEFT and RIGHT arrays, and vice versa.

5. Write a BASIC program to perform the following experiments. Generate 100 distinct random numbers. As each number is generated, insert it into an initially empty binary tree so that all numbers in a left subtree of a node are smaller than the number in the node, which is in turn smaller than the numbers in the right subtree of the node.

When all 100 numbers have been inserted, print the level of the leaf with largest level and the level of the leaf with smallest level. Repeat this process 50 times. Print a table with a count of how many of the 50 runs resulted in a difference between the maximum and minimum leaf level of 1, 2, 3, and so on.

6. Write a BASIC subroutine that accepts two pointers to non-root nodes in a binary tree and returns a pointer to the youngest common ancestor of the two nodes.

7. Write BASIC subroutines to traverse a binary tree in preorder and postorder using the node representation.

8. Write BASIC subroutines to traverse a binary tree in inorder, preorder, and postorder using the almost complete array representation.

9. Write a BASIC subroutine to create a binary tree given
   (**a**) The preorder and inorder traversals of that tree.
   (**b**) The preorder and postorder traversals of that tree.
   Each subroutine should accept two character strings as inputs. The tree created should contain a single character in each node.

10. How do you account for the similarity between the nonrecursive subroutine for inorder traversal presented in this section and the nonrecursive routine to solve the Towers of Hanoi problem of Section 5.2?

11. An index of a textbook consists of major terms, ordered alphabetically, each of which is accompanied by a set of page numbers and a set of subterms. The subterms are printed on successive lines following the major term and are arranged alphabetically within the major term. Each subterm is accompanied by a set of page numbers.

   Design a data structure to represent such an index and write a BASIC program to print an index from data as follows. Each input line begins with an M (major term) or an S (subterm). An M line contains an M followed by a major term followed by an integer n (possibly zero) followed by n page numbers where the major term appears. An S line is similar except that it contains a subterm rather than a major term. The input lines appear in no particular order except that each subterm is considered to be a subterm of the major term that last precedes it. There may be many input lines for a single major term or subterm (all page numbers appearing on any line for a particular term should be printed with that term).

   The index should be printed with one term on a line followed by all the pages on which the term appears, in ascending order. Major terms should be printed in alphabetical order. Subterms should appear in alphabetical order immediately following their major term. Subterms should be indented beneath their major term.

   The set of major terms should be organized as a binary tree. Each node in the tree contains (in addition to left and right pointers and the major term itself) pointers to two other binary trees. One of these represents the set of page numbers in which the major term occurs and the other represents the set of subterms of the major term. Each node on a subterm binary tree contains (in addition to left and right pointers and the subterm) a pointer to a binary tree representing the set of page numbers in which the subterm occurs.

12. Define a ternary tree and extend to it the concepts of the preceding two sections.

3. AN EXAMPLE: THE HUFFMAN ALGORITHM

Consider the following problem. Suppose that we have an alphabet of n symbols and a long message consisting of symbols from this alphabet. We wish to encode the message as a long bit string (we define a bit to be either 0 or 1) as follows. Assign a bit string code to each symbol of the alphabet. Then concatenate (string together) the individual codes of the symbols making up the message to produce an encoding for the message. For example, suppose that the alphabet consists of the four symbols A, B, C, D and that codes are assigned to these symbols as follows:

Symbol	Code
A	010
B	100
C	000
D	111

The message *ABACCDA* would then be encoded as 010100010000000111010. However, such an encoding would be inefficient since 3 bits are used for each symbol, so that 21 bits are needed to encode the entire message. Suppose that a 2-bit code is assigned to each symbol, as follows:

Symbol	Code
A	00
B	01
C	10
D	11

Then the code for the message would be 00010010101100, which requires only 14 bits. We wish to find a code that minimizes the length of the encoded message.

Let us reexamine the example above. Each of the letters B and D appears only once in the message, while the letter A appears three times. Thus if a code is chosen in which the letter A is assigned a shorter bit string than the letters B and D, the length of the encoded message would be small. This is because the short code (representing the letter A) would appear more frequently than the long code. Indeed, codes can be assigned as follows:

Symbol	Frequency	Code
A	3	0
B	1	110
C	2	10
D	1	111

Using this code, the message *ABACCDA* is encoded as 0110010101110, which requires only 13 bits. In very long messages that contain symbols which appear very infrequently, the savings are substantial. Ordinarily, codes are not constructed on the basis of the frequency of the occurrence of characters within a single message alone, but on the basis of their frequency within a whole set of messages. The same code set is used for each message. For example, if messages consist of English words, the known relative frequency of occurrence of the letters of the alphabet in the English language would be used.

Note that if variable-length codes are used, the code for one symbol may not be a prefix of the code for another. This must be true if the decoding is to proceed from left to right. If the code for a symbol x, $c(x)$, were a prefix of the code of a symbol y, $c(y)$, then when $c(x)$ is encountered it is unclear whether it represents the symbol x or whether it is the first part of $c(y)$.

In our example the bit string for a message is scanned from left to right. If a 0 is encountered as the first bit, the symbol is an *A;* otherwise, it is a *B, C,* or *D* and the next bit is examined. If the second bit is a 0, the symbol is a *C;* otherwise, it must be a *B* or a *D* and the third bit must be examined. If the third bit is a 0, the symbol is a *B;* if it is a 1, the symbol is a *D.* As soon as the first symbol has been identified, the process is repeated starting at the next bit to find the second symbol.

This suggests a method for developing an optimal encoding scheme given the frequency of occurrence of each symbol in a message. Find the two symbols that appear least frequently. In our example, these are *B* and *D*. The last bit of their codes will differentiate between them: 0 for *B* and 1 for *D*. Combine these two symbols into the single symbol *BD*, whose code represents the knowledge that a symbol is either a *B* or a *D*. The frequency of occurrence of this new symbol is the sum of the frequencies of its two constituent symbols. Thus the frequency of *BD* is 2. There are now three symbols: *A* (frequency 3), *C* (frequency 2), and *BD* (frequency 2). Again choose the two symbols with smallest frequency: *C* and *BD*. The last bit of their codes will differentiate between them: 0 for *C* and 1 for *BD*. The two symbols are then combined into the single symbol *CBD* with frequency 4. There are now only two symbols remaining: *A* and *CBD*. These are combined into the single symbol *ACBD*. The last bits of the codes for *A* and *CBD* will differentiate between them: 0 for *A* and 1 for *CBD*.

The symbol *ACBD* now contains the entire alphabet; it is assigned the null bit string of length zero as its code. This means that at the start of the decoding, before any bits have been examined, it is certain that any symbol is contained in *ACBD*. The two symbols that comprise *ACBD* (*A* and *CBD*) are assigned the codes 0 and 1, respectively. If a 0 is encountered, the encoded symbol is an *A*; if a 1 is encountered, it is a *C, B,* or *D*. Similarly, the two symbols that constitute *CBD* (*C* and *BD*) are assigned the codes 10 and 11, respectively. The first bit indicates that the symbol is one of the constituents of *CBD* and the second bit indicates whether it is a *C* or a *BD*. The symbols that comprise *BD* (*B* and *D*) are then assigned the codes 110 and 111. By this process, symbols that appear fre-

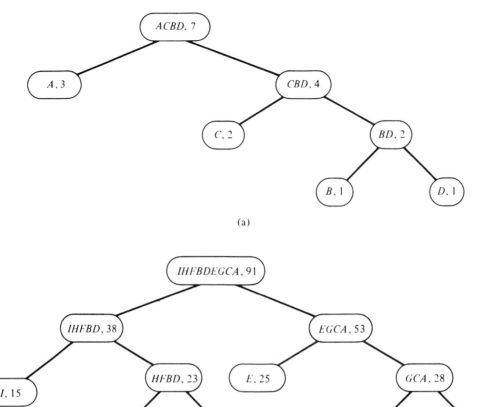

(a)

(b)

Symbol	Frequency	Code	Symbol	Frequency	Code	Symbol	Frequency	Code
A	15	111	D	12	011	G	6	1100
B	6	0101	E	25	10	H	1	01000
C	7	1101	F	4	01001	I	15	00

(c)

Figure 6.3.1 Huffman trees.

quently in the message are assigned shorter codes than symbols that appear infrequently.

The action of combining two symbols into one suggests the use of a strictly binary tree. Each leaf node represents a symbol of the original alphabet. Each nonleaf node represents an aggregate of the symbols in its descendant leaf nodes. Figure 6.3.1(a) shows the binary tree constructed using the preceding example. Each node in the illustration contains a symbol and its frequency. Figure 6.3.1(b) shows the binary tree constructed by this method for the alphabet and frequency table of Figure 6.3.1(c). Such trees are called *Huffman trees*, after the discoverer of this encoding method.

Once a Huffman tree is constructed, the code of any symbol in the alphabet can be determined by starting at the leaf which represents that symbol and climbing up to the root. The code is initialized to the null string. Each time a left branch is climbed, 0 is appended to the left of the code; each time a right branch is climbed, 1 is appended to the left of the code.

The *info* portion of a tree node contains the frequency of the occurrence of the symbol represented by that node. The inputs to the algorithm are n, the number of symbols in the original alphabet, and *frqncy,* an array of size at least n such that *frqncy(i)* is the relative frequency of the ith symbol. The algorithm is to assign values to an array *code* of size at least n so that *code(i)* contains the code assigned to the ith symbol. The algorithm also constructs an array *pstn* of size at least n such that *pstn(i)* points to the node representing the ith symbol. This array is necessary to identify the point in the tree from which to start in constructing the code for a particular symbol in the alphabet. The *isleft* operation introduced earlier can be used once the tree has been constructed as we climb the tree in order to determine whether 0 or 1 should be placed at the front of the code.

Using these routines, we may outline Huffman's algorithm as follows. (The set *rootnodes* contains pointers to the roots of partial binary trees which are not yet left or right subtrees.)

```
rootnodes = the empty set
'construct a node for each symbol
for i = 1 to n
    p = maketree(frqncy(i))
    pstn(i) = p
    add p to rootnodes
next i
'construct the tree
while rootnodes contains more than one item do
        p1 = the element in rootnodes with smallest info value
        remove p1 from rootnodes
        p2 = the element in rootnodes with smallest info value
        remove p2 from rootnodes
```

```
        'combine p1 and p2 as branches of a single tree
        p = maketree(info(p1) + info(p2))
        set p1 and p2 as the sons of node(p)
        add p to rootnodes
endwhile
'the tree is now constructed; use it to find codes
root = the single element in rootnodes
for i = 1 to n
    code(i) = ""
    p = pstn(i)
    'travel up the tree
    while p <> root do
        if isleft(p)
            then code(i) = "0" + code(i)
            else code(i) = "1" + code(i)
        endif
        p = father(p)
    endwhile
next i
```

Note that the Huffman tree is strictly binary. Thus if there are n symbols in the alphabet, the Huffman tree (which has n leafs) can be represented by an array of nodes of size $2n - 1$. Since the amount of storage needed for the tree is known, it may be allocated in advance. We also note that the Huffman tree is traversed from the leafs to the root. This means that LEFT and RIGHT fields are not needed; a FTHER field alone is sufficient to represent the tree structure. The sign of the FTHER field can be used to determine if a node is a left or right son, while its absolute value is the pointer to the node's father. A left son holds a negative FTHER value; a right son holds a positive FTHER value. The nodes of the tree are therefore declared by

$$80 \quad \text{DIM INFO}(2*N - 1), \text{FTHER}(2*N - 1)$$

Let us write a program to encode the characters of a message using Huffman's algorithm. The input ot the program consists of a number N, which is the number of symbols in the alphabet followed by a set of N pairs, each of which consists of a symbol and its relative frequency. The program first constructs a string ALPHA, which consists of all the symbols in the alphabet, and an array CODE such that CODE(I) is the code assigned to the Ith symbol in ALPHA. The program then prints each character, its relative frequency, and its code. Note that it is unnecessary to construct the array PSTN since $node(I)$ represents the Ith symbol of the alphabet under this representation.

```
10   'program findcode
20   'the statement CLEAR 100 is required on TRS-80 microcomputers
30   DEFSTR A, C, S
40   DEFINT F, I, J, N, P, Q, T
```

```
 50   TRUE = 1
 60   FALSE = 0
 70   READ N
 80   DIM CODE(N), FRQNCY(N)
 90   DIM INFO(2*N − 1), FTHER(2*N − 1)
100   FOR I = 1 TO 2*N − 1: 'initialize arrays
110       INFO(I) = 0
120       FTHER(I) = 0
130   NEXT I
140   FOR I = 1 TO N: 'initialize alphabet and frequencies
150       READ SYMB, FRQNCY(I)
160       ALPHA = ALPHA + SYMB
170   NEXT I
180   'build the Huffman tree
190   FOR I = 1 TO N
200       INFO(I) = FRQNCY(I)
210   NEXT I
220   FOR I = N + 1 TO 2*N − 1
230       'I is the next available node; search all previous nodes for
          'the two root nodes P1 and P2 with smallest frequencies
240       J1 = 9999
250       J2 = 9999
260       P1 = 0
270       P2 = 0
280       FOR Q = 1 TO I − 1
290       IF FTHER(Q) = 0
              THEN IF INFO(Q) < J1
                      THEN P2 = P1: J2 = J1: P1 = Q: J1 = INFO(Q)
                      ELSE IF INFO(Q)<J2 THEN P2 = Q: J2 = INFO(Q)

300       NEXT Q
310       P = I: 'allocate node(P)
320       INFO(P) = J1 + J2
330       'set P1 to the left subtree of P and P2 to the right subtree
340       FTHER(P1) = −P
350       FTHER(P2) = P
360   NEXT I
370   'extract the codes from the tree
380   FOR I = 1 TO N
390       CODE(I) = '' ''
400       P = I
410       IF FTHER(P) = 0 THEN GOTO 450
420       IF FTHER(P) < 0 THEN CODE(I) = ''0'' + CODE(I)
                          ELSE CODE(I) = ''1'' + CODE(I)
```

```
430        P = ABS(FTHER(P))
440        GOTO 410
450   NEXT I
460   FOR I = 1 TO N
470        PRINT MID$(ALPHA,I,1), INFO(I), CODE(I)
480   NEXT I
490   END
      . . .
800   DATA . . .
```

The reader is referred to Section 9.4, which suggests further improvements to this program. We leave to the reader the coding of the subroutine *encode*. This subroutine accepts the string ALPHA and the array CODE constructed in the program above and a message MSGE and returns the bit-string encoding of the message.

Given the encoding of a message and the Huffman tree used in constructing the code, the original message can be recovered as follows. Begin at the root of the tree. Each time a 0 is encountered, move down a left branch, and each time a 1 is encountered, move down a right branch. Repeat this process until a leaf is encountered. The next character of the original message is the symbol that corresponds to that leaf. See if you can decode 1110100010111011 using the Huffman tree of Figure 6.3.1(b).

In order to decode, it is necessary to travel from the root of the tree down to its leafs. This means that the fields LEFT and RIGHT are needed to hold the left and right sons of a particular node. It is straightforward to construct the arrays LEFT and RIGHT from the array FTHER. Alternatively, the arrays LEFT and RIGHT can be constructed directly from the frequency information for the symbols of the alphabet using an approach similar to that used in constructing the array FTHER. (Of course, if the trees are to be identical, the symbol/frequency pairs must be presented in the same order under the two methods.) We leave these algorithms, as well as the decoding algorithm, as exercises for the reader.

EXERCISES

1. Write a BASIC subroutine *encode*. The subroutine accepts the string ALPHA and the array CODE produced by the program *findcode* in the text and a message MSGE. The subroutine outputs the Huffman encoding of that message.

2. Write a BASIC subroutine *decode* that accepts the string ALPHA produced by the program *findcode* in the text, arrays LEFT and RIGHT used to represent a Huffman tree, and a string MSGE. The subroutine should output the Huffman decoding of MSGE.

3. Is it possible to have two different Huffman trees for a set of symbols with given frequencies? Either give an example where two such trees exist or prove that there is only a single such tree.

4. Define a **Fibonacci binary tree of order n** as follows: If $n = 0$ or $n = 1$, the tree consists of a single node. If $n > 1$, the tree consists of a root, with the Fibonacci binary tree of order $n-1$ as the left subtree and the Fibonacci binary tree of order $n-2$ as the right subtree.
   (a) Write a BASIC subroutine that returns a pointer to the Fibonacci binary tree of order n.
   (b) Is such a tree strictly binary?
   (c) What is the number of leafs in the Fibonacci binary tree of order n?
   (d) What is the depth of the Fibonacci binary tree of order n?

5. Given a binary tree t, its **extension** is defined as the binary tree $e(t)$ formed from t by adding a new node at each null left and right pointer in t. The new nodes are called **external** nodes and the original nodes are called **internal** nodes. $e(t)$ is called an **extended binary tree**.
   (a) Prove that an extended binary tree is strictly binary.
   (b) If t has n nodes, how many nodes does $e(t)$ have?
   (c) Prove that all leafs in an extended binary tree are external nodes.
   (d) Write a BASIC subroutine that extends a binary tree t.
   (e) Prove that any strictly binary tree with more than one node is an extension of one and only one binary tree.
   (f) Write a BASIC subroutine that accepts a pointer to a strictly binary tree $t1$ containing more than one node and deletes nodes from $t1$ creating a binary tree $t2$ such that $t1 = e(t2)$.
   (g) Show that the complete binary tree of order n is the nth extension of the binary tree consisting of a single node.

6. Given a strictly binary tree t in which the n leafs are labeled as nodes 1 through n, let $level(i)$ be the level of node i and let $frq(i)$ be an integer assigned to node i. Define the **weighted path length** of t as the sum of $frq(i)*level(i)$ over all leafs of t.
   (a) Write a BASIC subroutine to compute the weighted path length given fields frq and $fther$.
   (b) Show that the Huffman tree is the strictly binary tree with minimum weighted path length if $frq(i)$ is interpreted as $frqncy(i)$.

4. REPRESENTING LISTS AS BINARY TREES

There are several operations that can be performed on a list of elements. Included among these operations are adding a new element to the front or rear of the list, deleting the existing first or last elements of the list, retrieving the kth element or the last element of the list, inserting an element following or preceding a given element, deleting a given element, and deleting the predecessor or successor of a given element. Building a list with given elements is an additional operation which is frequently required.

Depending on the representation chosen for a list, some of these operations may or may not be possible with varying degrees of efficiency. For example, a list may be represented by successive elements in an array or as nodes in a linked structure. Inserting an element following a given element is relatively efficient in a linked list (involving modifications to a few pointers aside from the actual insertion) but relatively inefficient in an array (involving moving all subsequent elements in the array one position). However, finding the kth element of a list is far more efficient in an array (involving only the computation of an offset) than in a linked structure (which requires passing through the first $k-1$ elements). Similarly, it is not possible to delete a specific element in a singly linked linear list given only a pointer to that element and it is only possible to do so inefficiently in a singly linked circular list (by traversing the entire list to reach the previous element, and then performing the deletion). The same operation, however, is quite efficient in a doubly linked (linear or circular) list.

In this section we introduce a tree representation of a linear list in which the operations of finding the kth element of a list and deleting a specific element are relatively efficient. It is also possible to build a list with given elements using this representation. We also consider briefly the operation of inserting a single new element.

A list may be represented by a binary tree as illustrated in Figure 6.4.1. Figure 6.4.1(a) shows a list in the usual linked format, while Figure 6.4.1(b) and (c) show two binary tree representations of the list. Elements of the original list are represented by leafs of the tree (shown as squares in the figure), while nonleaf nodes of the tree (shown as circles in the figure) are present as part of the internal tree structure. Associated with each leaf node are the contents of the corresponding list element. Associated with each nonleaf node is a count representing the number of leafs in the node's left subtree. (Although this count can be computed from the tree structure, it is maintained as a data element to avoid recomputing its value each time it is needed.) The elements of the list in their original sequence are assigned to the leafs of the tree in the inorder sequence of the leafs. Note from Figure 6.4.1 that several binary trees can represent the same list.

Finding the kth Element of a List

To justify using so many extra tree nodes to represent a list, we present an algorithm to find the kth element of a list represented by a tree. Let *tree* point to the root of the tree, and let *lcount*(p) represent the count associated with the nonleaf node pointed to by p [*lcount*(p) is the number of leafs in the tree rooted at *node* (*left*(p))]. The following algorithm sets the variable *find* to point to the leaf containing the kth element of the list. The algorithm maintains a variable r containing the number of list elements remaining to be counted. r is initialized to k at

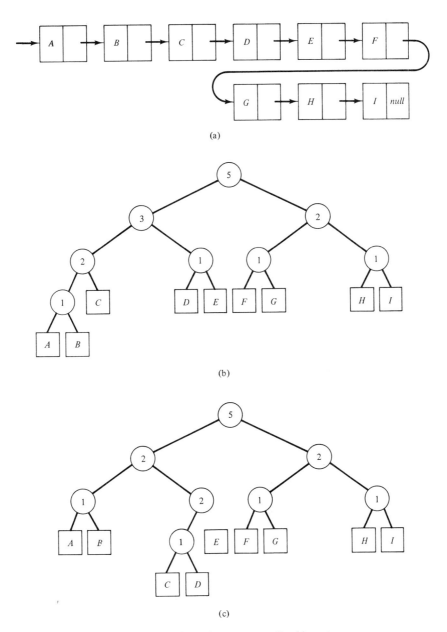

(a)

(b)

(c)

Figure 6.4.1 A list and two corresponding binary trees.

the beginning of the algorithm. At each nonleaf node p the algorithm determines from the values of r and $lcount(p)$ whether the desired leaf is located in the left or right subtree. If the leaf is in the left subtree, the algorithm proceeds to that subtree without modifying the value of r. If the desired leaf is in the right subtree, the algorithm proceeds to that subtree after reducing the value of r by the value of $lcount(p)$.

$$r = k$$
$$p = tree$$
while p is not a leaf node **do**
      if $r <= lcount(p)$
        then $p = left(p)$
        else $r = r - lcount(p)$
             $p = right(p)$
      endif
endwhile
$find = p$

Figure 6.4.2(a) illustrates finding the fifth element of a list in the tree of Figure 6.4.1(b), while Figure 6.4.2(b) illustrates finding the eighth element in the tree of Figure 6.4.1(c). The dashed line represents the path taken by the algorithm down the tree to the appropriate leaf. We indicate the value of r (the remaining number of elements to be counted) next to each node that is encountered by the algorithm.

We note that the number of tree nodes examined in finding the kth list element is less than or equal to one more than the depth of the tree (the longest path in the tree from the root to a leaf). Thus four nodes are examined in Figure 6.4.2(a) in finding the fifth element of the list and also in Figure 6.4.2(b) in finding the eighth element. If a list is represented as a linked structure, four nodes are traversed [i.e., the operation $p = next(p)$ would be performed four times] in finding the fifth element of a list and seven nodes are traversed in finding the eighth element. Although this is not a very impressive saving, consider a list with 1000 elements. A binary tree of depth 10 is sufficient to represent such a list. Thus, finding the kth element (regardless of whether k was 3, 253, 708, or 999) using a binary tree would require examining no more than 11 nodes. Since the number of leafs of a binary tree increases as 2 raised to the power of its depth, such a tree represents a relatively efficient data structure for finding the kth element of a list.

Deleting an Element

How can an element be deleted from a list represented by a tree? The deletion itself is relatively easy. It involves only resetting to null a left or right pointer in the father of the deleted node dn. However, to enable subsequent accesses, the

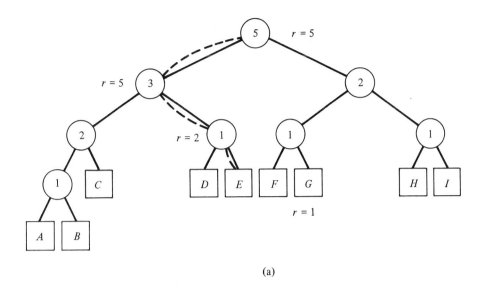

(a)

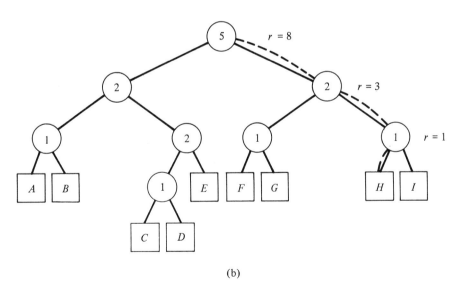

(b)

Figure 6.4.2 Finding the *m*th element in a tree-represented list.

counts in all ancestors of *dn* may have to be modified. The modification consists of reducing *lcount* by 1 in each node *nd* of which *dn* was a left descendant, since the number of leafs in the left subtree of *nd* is 1 fewer. At the same time, if the brother of *dn* is a leaf, it can be moved up the tree to take the place of its father. We can then move that node up even farther if it has no brother in its new position. This may reduce the depth of the resulting tree, making subsequent accesses slightly more efficient.

We may therefore present an algorithm to delete a leaf pointed to by *p* from a tree (and thus an element from a list) as follows. (The line numbers at the left are for future reference.)

```
 1.   if p = tree
 2.     then tree = null
 3.           freenode(p)
 4.           return
 5.   endif
 6.   f = father(p)
 7.   'remove node(p) and set b to point to its brother
 8.   if p = left(f)
 9.     then left(f) = null
10.           b = right(f)
11.           lcount(f) = lcount(f)-1
12.     else right(f) = null
13.           b = left(f)
14.   endif
15.   if node(b) is a leaf
16.     then 'move the contents of node(b) up to its father and free node(b)
17.           info(f) = info(b)
18.           left(f) = null
19.           right(f) = null
20.           lcount(f) = 0
21.           freenode(b)
22.   endif
23.   freenode(p)
24.   'climb up the tree
25.   q = f
26.   while q <> tree do
27.         f = father(q)
28.         if q = left(f)
29.         then 'the deleted leaf was a left descendant of node(f)
30.               lcount(f) = lcount(f)-1
31.               b = right(f)   'node(b) is the brother of node(q)
32.         else b = left(f)      'node(b) is the brother of node(q)
33.         endif
```

```
34.          if b = null and node(q) is a leaf
35.             then 'move up the contents of node(q)
                      'to its father and free node(q)
36.                info(f) = info(q)
37.                left(f) = null
38.                right(f) = null
39.                lcount(f) = 0
40.                freenode(q)
41.          endif
42.          q = f
43.    endwhile
44.    return
```

Figure 6.4.3 illustrates the results of this algorithm for such a tree in which the nodes C, D, and B are deleted in that order. Make sure that you follow the actions of the algorithm on these examples. Note that the algorithm maintains a zero count in leaf nodes for consistency, although the count is not required for such nodes. Note also that the algorithm never moves up a nonleaf node even if this could be done. [For example, the father of A and B in Figure 6.4.3(b) has not been moved up.] We can easily modify the algorithm to do this (the modification is left to the reader), but have not done so, for reasons that will become apparent shortly.

This algorithm involves inspection of up to two nodes (the ancestor of the node being deleted and that ancestor's brother) at each level. Thus the operation of deleting the kth element of a list represented by a tree (which involves finding the element and then deleting it) requires a number of node accesses approximately equal to three times the tree depth. Whereas deletion from a linked list requires accesses to only three nodes (the node preceding and following the deleted node as well as the deleted node), deleting the kth element requires a total of $k + 2$ accesses ($k - 1$ of which are to locate the node preceding the kth). For large lists, therefore, the tree representation is more efficient.

Similarly, we can compare the efficiency of tree-represented lists favorably with array-represented lists. If an n-element list is kept sequentially in the first n elements of an array, finding the kth element involves only a single array access, but deleting it requires shifting the $n - k$ elements that had followed the deleted element. If gaps are allowed in the array so that deletion can be implemented efficiently (by setting a flag in the array position of the deleted element without shifting any subsequent elements), finding the kth element requires at least k array accesses. The reason for this is that it is no longer possible to know the array position of the kth element in the list since gaps may exist among the elements in the array. [We should note, however, that if the order of the elements in the list is irrelevant, the kth element in an array can be deleted efficiently by overwriting it with the element in position n (the last element) and adjusting the count to $n - 1$.

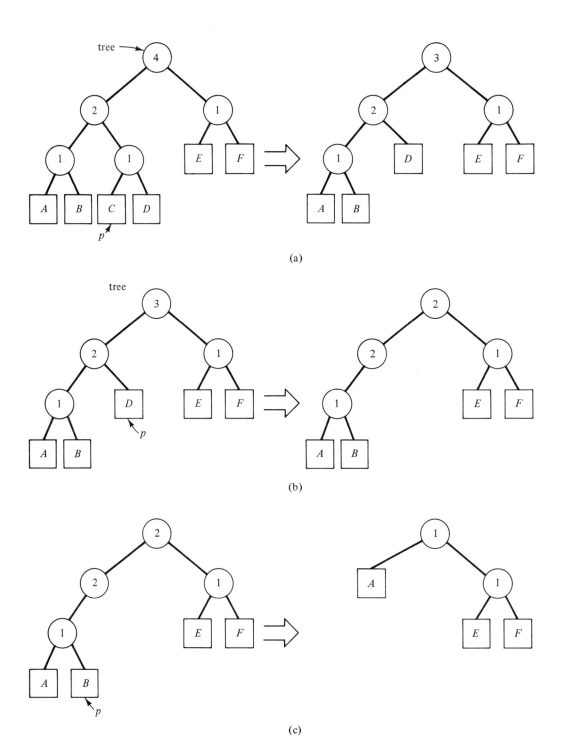

Figure 6.4.3 The deletion algorithm.

However, it is unlikely that we would want to delete the kth element from a list in which the order is irrelevant since then there would be no significance in the kth element over any of the others.]

Inserting a new kth element into a tree-represented list (between the $(k-1)$st and the previous kth) is also a relatively efficient operation. The insertion consists of locating the kth element, replacing it with a new nonleaf node which has a leaf containing the new element as its left son and a leaf containing the old kth element as its right son, and adjusting appropriate counts among its ancestors. We leave the details to the reader. (We should note, however, that repeatedly adding a new kth element by this method would cause the tree to become highly unbalanced, so that the branch containing the kth element becomes disproportionately long compared to the other branches. This means that the efficiency of finding the kth element is not as great as it would be in a balanced tree in which all branches are approximately the same length. The reader is encouraged to find a "balancing" strategy which would alleviate this problem. Despite this problem, if insertions into the tree are made randomly so that it is equally likely for an element to be inserted at any given position, the resulting tree remains fairly balanced and finding the kth element remains efficient.)

Implementing Tree-Represented Lists in BASIC

The BASIC implementations of the search and deletion algorithms are straightforward using the node representation of binary trees. However, such a representation requires INFO, LCOUNT, FTHER, LEFT, and RIGHT fields for each tree node, while a list node requires only INFO and NXT fields. Coupled with the fact that the tree representation requires approximately twice as many nodes as a linked list, this space requirement may make the tree representation impractical.

However, under the almost complete array representation, the space requirements are not nearly so great. If we assume that no insertions are required and that the initial list size is known, we can set aside an array to hold an almost complete strictly binary tree representation of the list. As we shall soon show, it is always possible to construct such a binary tree representation of a list. Once the tree has been constructed, the only fields that are required are INFO, LCOUNT, and a field FLAG which indicates whether or not an array element represents an existing or a deleted tree node. Also, as we have noted before, LCOUNT is required only for the nonleaf nodes of the tree. It is also possible to eliminate the need for the FLAG field at some expense to efficiency (see Exercises 6 and 7). Thus we assume the declarations (given N elements in the list)

```
10   DEFSTR E
     . . .
30   DIM EINFO(2*N-1):   'the list contains string elements
40   DIM LCOUNT(N-1):    'for nonleaf nodes only
50   DIM FLAG(2*N-1):    'whether or not node(I) is in the tree
```

A nonleaf node can be recognized by an EINFO value equal to the null string (""). *father(p)*, *left(p)*, and *right(p)* can be implemented in the usual way as INT(P/2), 2*P, and 2*P + 1, respectively.

A BASIC routine to find the Kth element follows:

```
1000    'subroutine findelement
1010    'inputs: EINFO, K, LCOUNT
1020    'outputs: FIND
1030    'locals: P, R
1040    R = K
1050    P = 1
1060    IF EINFO(P) <>" " THEN GOTO 1090
1070        IF R <= LCOUNT(P) THEN P = 2*P
                        ELSE R = R-LCOUNT(P): P = 2*P+1
1080    GOTO 1060
1090    FIND = P
1100    RETURN
1110    'endsub
```

The BASIC routine to delete the leaf pointed to by P using an almost complete tree representation is somewhat simpler than the algorithm given above. We can ignore all assignments of *null* (lines 2, 9, 18, 19, 37, and 38) since pointers are not used. We can also ignore all assignments of zero to an *lcount* field (lines 20 and 39) since such an assignment is part of the conversion of a nonleaf node to a leaf. However, in our BASIC representation, leaf nodes do not contain an LCOUNT field, as noted earlier. A node can be recognized as a leaf (lines 15 and 34) by a nonnull EINFO value, and the pointer B as null (line 34) by a zero value for FLAG(B). Freeing a node (lines 3, 21, and 40) is accomplished by setting its FLAG field to zero.

```
2000    'subroutine delete
2010    'inputs: EINFO, FLAG, LCOUNT, P
2020    'outputs: EINFO, FLAG, LCOUNT
2030    'locals: B, F, Q
2040    IF P = 1 THEN FLAG(P) = 0: RETURN: 'algorithm lines 1-5
2050    F = INT(P/2):                       'algorithm line 6
2060    IF F = P/2 THEN B = 2*F+1: LCOUNT(F) = LCOUNT(F)-1
                    ELSE B = 2*F:           'algorithm lines 7-14
2070    IF EINFO(B) <> " " THEN EINFO(F) = EINFO(B): FLAG(B) = 0:
                                            'algorithm lines 15-22
2080    FLAG(P) = 0:                        'algorithm line 23
2090    Q = F:                              'algorithm line 25
```

```
2100   IF Q = 1 THEN RETURN
2110      F = INT(Q/2):                        'algorithm line 27
2120      IF F = Q/2 THEN LCOUNT(F) = LCOUNT(F)−1: B = 2*F+1
                  ELSE B = 2*F:                'algorithm lines 27−33
2130      IF FLAG(B) = 0 AND EINFO(Q) <> " "
                  THEN EINFO(F) = EINFO(Q): FLAG(Q) = 0:
                                               'algorithm lines 34−41
2140      Q = F:                               'algorithm line 42
2150   GOTO 2100
2160   'endsub
```

Our use of the almost complete array representation explains the reason for not moving a nonleaf node without a brother farther up in a tree during deletion. Such a moving-up process would involve copying the contents of all nodes in the subtree within the array, whereas it involves modifying only a single pointer if the node representation is used.

Constructing a Tree-Represented List

We now return to the claim that given a list of n elements, it is possible to construct an almost complete strictly binary tree representing the list. We have already seen in Section 1 that it is possible to construct an almost complete strictly binary tree with n leafs and $2n-1$ nodes. The leafs of such a tree occupy nodes numbered n through $2n-1$. If d is the smallest integer such that 2^d is greater or equal to n, then d is equal to the depth of the tree and 2^d is the number assigned to the first node on the bottom level of the tree. The first elements of the list are assigned to nodes numbered 2^d through $2n-1$ and the remainder (if any) to nodes numbered n through 2^d-1. We can therefore assign elements of the list to the EINFO fields of tree leafs in this sequence, and assign the null string to the EINFO fields of nonleaf nodes numbered 1 through $n-1$. It is also a simple matter to initialize the FLAG field to 1 in all nodes numbered from 1 to $2n-1$.

Initializing the values of the LCOUNT array is more difficult. Two methods can be used: one involving more time and a second involving more space. In the first method, all LCOUNT fields are initialized to zero. Then the tree is climbed from each leaf to the tree root in turn. Each time a node is reached from its left son, one is added to its LCOUNT field. After this process is performed for each leaf, the LCOUNT values have been properly assigned. The following routine uses this method to construct a tree from a list of input data:

```
3000   'subroutine buildtree
3010   'inputs: N
3020   'outputs: EINFO, FLAG, LCOUNT
3030   'locals: D, F, I, P, POWER, SIZE
```

```
3040   'compute the tree depth D and the value of 2↑D
3050   D = 0
3060   POWER = 1: 'POWER is 2↑D
3070   IF POWER > = N THEN GOTO 3110
3080      D = D+1
3090      POWER = POWER*2
3100   GOTO 3070
3110   'assign the elements of the list and the flags
       'and initialize LCOUNT to zero in all nonleafs
3120   SIZE = 2*N−1
3130   FOR I = POWER TO SIZE
3140      READ EINFO(I)
3150      FLAG(I) = 1
3160   NEXT I
3170   FOR I = N TO POWER−1
3180      READ EINFO(I)
3190      FLAG(I) = 1
3200   NEXT I
3210   FOR I = 1 TO N−1
3220      FLAG(I) = 1
3230      LCOUNT(I) = 0
3240      EINFO(I) = " "
3250   NEXT I
3260   'set the LCOUNT fields
3270   FOR I = N TO SIZE: 'begin from each leaf to the root
3280      P = I
3290      IF P = 1 THEN GOTO 3340
3300         F = INT(P/2)
3310         IF F = P/2 THEN LCOUNT(F) = LCOUNT(F) + 1
3320         P = F
3330      GOTO 3290
3340   NEXT I
3350   RETURN
3360   'endsub
```

The second method uses an additional array RCOUNT to hold the number of leafs in the right subtree of each nonleaf node. This field as well as the LCOUNT field is set to 1 in each nonleaf which is the father of two leafs. Additionally, if N is odd, so that there is a node [numbered INT(N/2)] which is the father of a leaf and a nonleaf node, LCOUNT in that node is set to 2 and RCOUNT to 1. The algorithm then goes through the remaining array elements in reverse order, setting LCOUNT in each node to the sum of LCOUNT and RCOUNT in the node's left son and RCOUNT to the sum of LCOUNT and

RCOUNT in the node's right son. A BASIC routine to implement this technique follows:

```
3000  'subroutine buildtree
3010  'inputs: N
3020  'outputs: EINFO, FLAG, LCOUNT
3030  'locals: D, I, NN, POWER, SIZE
3040  'compute the tree depth D and the value of 2↑D
3050  D = 0
3060  POWER = 1: 'POWER is 2↑D
3070  IF POWER >= N THEN GOTO 3110
3080      D = D+1
3090      POWER = POWER*2
3100  GOTO 3070
3110  'assign the elements of the list and the flag
3120  SIZE = 2*N-1
3130  FOR I = POWER TO SIZE
3140      READ EINFO(I)
3150      FLAG(I) = 1
3160  NEXT I
3170  FOR I = N TO POWER-1
3180      READ EINFO(I)
3190      FLAG(I) = 1
3200  NEXT I
3210  'set the LCOUNT and RCOUNT fields in the leafs' fathers
3220  'assume a declaration DIM RCOUNT(N-1)
3230  NN = INT(N/2)
3240  FOR I = NN TO N-1
3250      LCOUNT(I) = 1
3260      RCOUNT(I) = 1
3270      FLAG(I) = 1
3280      EINFO(I) = " "
3290  NEXT I
3300  IF NN <> N/2 THEN LCOUNT(NN) = 2
3310  I = NN-1
3320  IF I = 0 THEN RETURN
3330      LCOUNT(I) = LCOUNT(2*I)+RCOUNT(2*I)
3340      RCOUNT(I) = LCOUNT(2*I+1)+RCOUNT(2*I+1)
3350      FLAG(I) = 1
3360      EINFO(I) = " "
3370      I = I-1
3380  GOTO 3320
3390  'endsub
```

Note that RCOUNT is not listed as an output of *buildtree* since it is not needed once the tree is built; it is only used internally to set the value of LCOUNT properly. In fact, if a FLAG field is used, it can be used to hold the RCOUNT value as the values of LCOUNT are being set and then reset to 1 after all LCOUNT values have been computed. This would eliminate the need for a separate RCOUNT array. However, as we noted earlier and in the exercises, the FLAG field is not really required, so this technique does involve additional space requirements.

We also note that we did not actually require the value of D, so statements 3050 and 3080 can be omitted in both of the routines above. They were included to make the routines more comprehensible.

The Josephus Problem Revisited

The Josephus problem of Section 4.4 is a perfect example of the utility of the binary tree representation of a list. In that problem it was necessary to repeatedly find the Mth next element of a list and then delete that element. These are operations that can be performed efficiently in a tree-represented list.

If C equals the number of elements currently in a list, the position of the Mth node following the node in position K that has just been deleted is given by one more than the remainder obtained on dividing $K-2+M$ by C. For example, if a list has five elements and the third element is deleted, and we wish to find the fourth element following the deleted element, then $C = 4$, $K = 3$, and $M = 4$. The remainder obtained on dividing $K-2+M$ (which equals 5) by C (which equals 4 after the deletion) is 1, so that the element is in position 2. (After deleting element 3, we count elements 4, 5, 1, and 2.) We can therefore write a BASIC routine *follower* to find the Mth node following a node in position K which has just been deleted and reset K to its position. The routine calls the routine *findelement* presented earlier.

```
4000   'subroutine follower
4010   'inputs: C, EINFO, K, LCOUNT, M
4020   'outputs: FIND, K
4030   'locals: D1, D2, J
4040   J = K-2+M
4050   D1 = J/C
4060   D2 = INT(D1)
4070   K = J-D2*C+1
4080   GOSUB 1000: 'subroutine findelement sets the variable FIND
4090   RETURN
4100   'endsub
```

A program to read the number of people in the circle, the number of the count, and the names of the people, and to determine the order in which the people are eliminated from the circle follows:

```
  10  'program josephus
  20  DEFSTR E
  30  READ N, M: 'number of people and the count
  40  DIM EINFO(2*N−1), LCOUNT(N − 1), FLAG(2*N−1)
  50  GOSUB 3000: 'subroutine buildtree initializes EINFO, LCOUNT, FLAG
  60  K = N+1:    'initially we have "deleted" the (N+1)st person
  70  C = N:      'initially there are N people in the list
  80  'repeat until only one person left
  90  IF C = 1 THEN GOTO 160
 100     GOSUB 4000: 'subroutine follower sets FIND and resets K
 110     P = FIND
 120     PRINT EINFO(P)
 130     GOSUB 2000: 'subroutine delete accepts P
 140     C = C−1
 150  GOTO 90
 160  PRINT EINFO(1)
 170  END
1000  'routines buildtree, follower, findelement, and delete go here
         . . .
9000  DATA . . .
```

EXERCISES

1. Prove that under the numbering scheme of Section 1, the leftmost node at level n in an almost complete strictly binary tree is assigned the number 2^n.

2. Prove that the depth of an almost complete strictly binary tree is the smallest integer d such that 2^d is greater than or equal to the number of leafs.

3. In an almost complete binary tree that is not strictly binary, which of the statements in Exercises 1 and 2 remain true?

4. Prove that the extension (see Exercise 6.3.5) of an almost complete binary tree is almost complete.

5. For what values of n and m is the solution to the Josephus problem given in this section faster in execution than the solution given in Section 4.4? Why is this so?

6. Explain how we can eliminate the need for a FLAG field if we elect not to move up a newly created leaf with no brother.

7. Explain how we can eliminate the need for a FLAG field if we set LCOUNT to -1 in a nonleaf node which is converted to a leaf node, and reset EINFO to `` `` in a deleted node.

8. Show how to represent a linked list as an almost complete binary tree in which each list element is represented by one tree node and no additional tree nodes are required. Write a BASIC routine to return a pointer to the Kth element of such a list.

5. TREES AND THEIR APPLICATIONS

In this section we consider general trees and their representations. We also investigate some of their applications.

A *tree* is a finite nonempty set of elements in which one element is called the *root* and the remaining elements are partitioned into a number of disjoint subsets, each of which is itself a tree. Each element in a tree is called a *node* of the tree.

Figure 6.5.1 illustrates some trees. Each node is the root of a tree with zero or more subtrees. A node with no subtrees is a *leaf*. We use the terms *father*, *son*, *ancestor*, *descendant*, *level*, and *depth* in the same sense that we used them for binary trees. Two nodes that have the same father are *brothers*. We also define the *degree* of a node in a tree as the number of its sons. Thus in Figure 6.5.1(a), node C has degree 0 (and is therefore a leaf), node D has degree 1, node B has degree 2, and node A has degree 3. There is no upper limit on the degree of a node.

Let us compare the trees of Figure 6.5.1(a) and (c). They are equivalent as trees. Each has A as its root and three subtrees. One of those subtrees has root C with no subtrees, another has root D with a single subtree rooted at G, and the third has root B with two subtrees rooted at E and F. The only difference between the two illustrations is the order in which the subtrees are arranged. The definition of a tree makes no distinction among subtrees of a general tree as opposed to the case of a binary tree, where a distinction is made between the left and right subtrees. An *ordered tree* is defined as a tree in which the subtrees of each node form an ordered set. Thus, in an ordered tree, we may speak of the first, second, or last son of a particular node. The first son of a node in an ordered tree is often called the *oldest* son of that node and the last son is called the *youngest*. Although the trees of Figure 6.5.1(a) and (c) are equivalent as unordered trees, they are different as ordered trees. In the remainder of this chapter we use the word ``tree'' to refer to ``ordered tree.'' A *forest* is an ordered set of ordered trees.

The question arises as to whether a binary tree is a tree. Every binary tree except for the empty binary tree is indeed a tree. However, not every tree is binary since a tree node may have more than two sons, whereas a binary tree node may not. Even a tree whose nodes have at most two sons is not necessarily a binary tree. This is because an only son in a general tree is not designated as

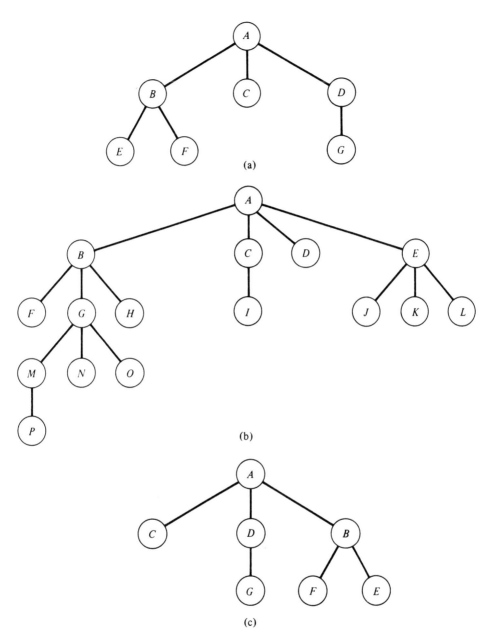

(a)

(b)

(c)

Figure 6.5.1 Examples of trees.

being a "left" or a "right" son, whereas in a binary tree, every son must be either a "left" son or a "right" son. In fact, although a nonempty binary tree is a tree, the designations of left and right have no meaning within the context of a tree (except perhaps to order the two subtrees of those nodes with two sons). A nonempty binary tree is a tree each of whose nodes has a maximum of two subtrees which have the added designation of "left" or "right."

BASIC Representations of Trees

An ordered tree can be represented in BASIC by means of an array of tree nodes. However, what should the structure of each individual node be? In the representation of a binary tree, each node contains an information field and three pointers to its two sons and its father. But how many pointers should a tree node contain? The number of sons of a node is variable and may be as large or as small as desired. If we arbitrarily declare

```
10   DIM INFO(500)
20   DIM FTHER(500)
30   DIM SN(500,20)
```

then we are limiting the number of sons a node may have to a maximum of 20. (We do not use the name SON for the array of sons since it contains the keyword ON and is therefore illegal in some versions of BASIC.) Although it is true that, in most cases, this will be sufficient, it is inadequate when it is necessary to create dynamically a node with 21 or 100 sons. Far worse than this remote possibility is the fact that 20 units of storage are reserved in each node in the tree even though a node may actually have only one or two (or even zero) sons. This is a tremendous waste of space.

One alternative is to link all the sons of a node together in a linear list. Thus the set of available nodes might be declared as follows:

```
10   DIM INFO(500)
20   DIM FTHER(500)
30   DIM SN(500)
40   DIM NXT(500)
```

SN(P) points to the oldest son of *node*(P) and NXT(P) points to the next younger brother of *node*(P). Of course, the FTHER field may be omitted if all traversals are from a node to its sons. Even if it is necessary to go from the sons to the father, the FTHER field can be omitted by placing a pointer to the father in the NXT field of the youngest son instead of leaving it null. A negative value can indicate that the NXT field in this node is a pointer to the node's father rather than to its brother, and the absolute value of the NXT field yields the actual pointer. This is similar to the representation of threads in binary trees. Figure 6.5.2 illustrates the representations of the trees of Figure 6.5.1 assuming that no access from a son to a father is required.

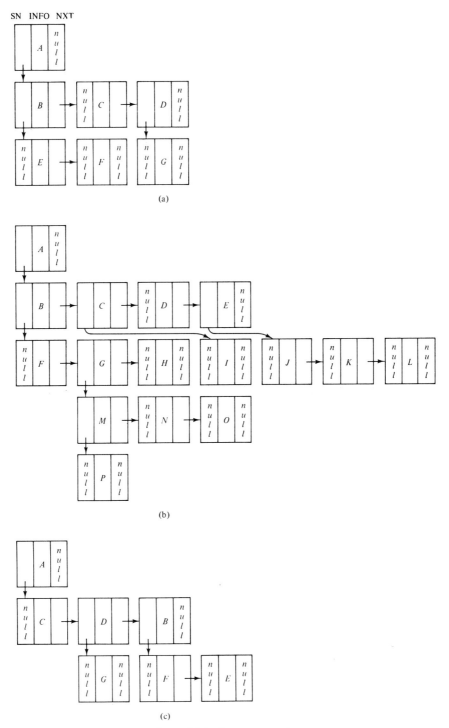

Figure 6.5.2 Tree representations.

Note that under this implementation, each tree node contains two pointers, SN and NXT. If we think of SN as corresponding to the left pointer of a binary tree node and NXT as corresponding to its right pointer, this method actually represents a general ordered tree by a binary tree. We may view this binary tree as the original tree tilted 45 degrees counterclockwise with all father-to-son links removed except for those between a node and its oldest son, and with links added between each node and its next younger brother. Figure 6.5.3 illustrates the binary trees corresponding to the trees of Figure 6.5.1

In fact, a binary tree may be used to represent an entire forest, since the NXT pointer in the root of a tree can be used to point to the next tree of the forest. Figure 6.5.4 illustrates a forest and its corresponding binary tree.

Tree Traversals

The traversal methods for binary trees induce corresponding traversal methods for forests. The preorder, inorder, or postorder traversals of a forest may be defined as the preorder, inorder, or postorder traversals of its corresponding binary tree. If a forest is represented as a set of nodes with *sn* and *nxt* pointers as given above, a recursive algorithm to print the contents of its nodes in inorder may be written as follows:

> **subroutine** *intrav(p)*
> **if** *p* = *null*
>   **then return**
> **endif**
> *intrav(sn(p))*
> **print** *info(p)*
> *intrav(nxt(p))*
> **return**

Algorithms for preorder and postorder traversals are similar.

These traversals of a forest may also be defined directly as follows:

Preorder
  1. Visit the root of the first tree in the forest.
  2. Traverse in preorder the forest formed by the subtrees of the first tree, if any.
  3. Traverse in preorder the forest formed by the remaining trees in the forest, if any.

Inorder
  1. Traverse in inorder the forest formed by the subtrees of the first tree in the forest, if any.
  2. Visit the root of the first tree.
  3. Traverse in inorder the forest formed by the remaining trees in the forest, if any.

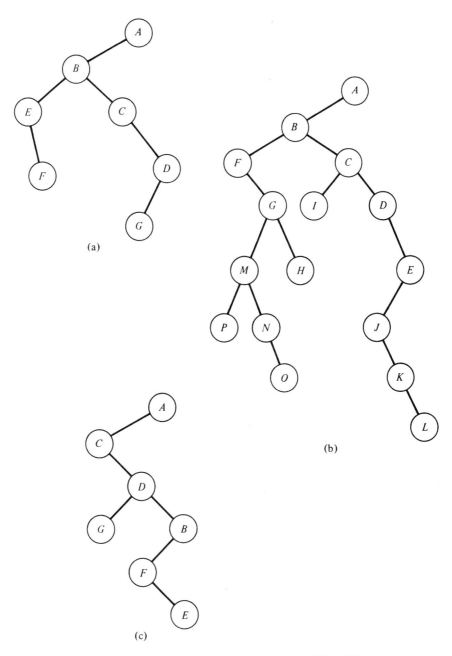

(a)

(b)

(c)

Figure 6.5.3 Binary trees corresponding to trees of Figure 6.5.1.

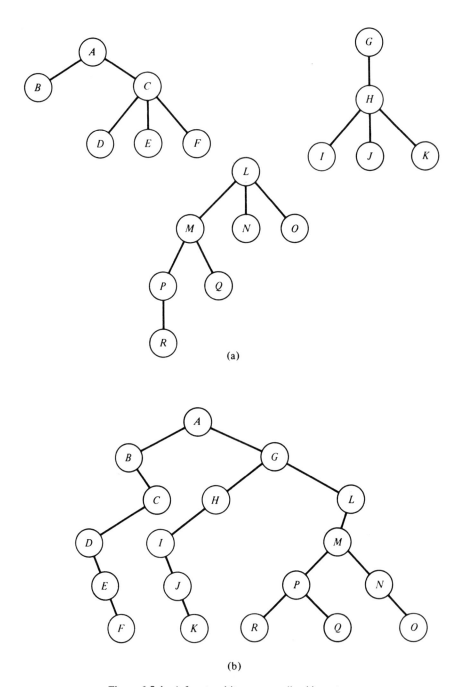

(a)

(b)

Figure 6.5.4 A forest and its corresponding binary tree.

Postorder
   1. Traverse in postorder the forest formed by the subtrees of the first tree in the forest, if any.
   2. Traverse in postorder the forest formed by the remaining trees in the forest, if any.
   3. Visit the root of the first tree in the forest.

The nodes of the forest in Figure 6.5.4(a) may be listed in preorder as *ABC DEFGHIJKLMPRQNO*, in inorder as *BDEFCAIJKHGRPQMNOL*, and in postorder as *FEDCBKJIHRQPONMLGA*. Let us call a traversal of a binary tree a *binary traversal*, and a traversal of an ordered general tree a *general traversal*.

General Expressions as Trees

An ordered tree may be used to represent a general expression in much the same way that a binary tree may be used to represent a binary expression. Since a node may have any number of sons, nonleaf nodes need not represent only binary operators but can represent operators with any number of operands. Figure 6.5.5 illustrates two expressions and their tree representations. The symbol "%" is used to represent unary negation to avoid confusing it with binary subtraction, which is represented by a minus sign. A function reference such as $f(G,H,I,J)$ is viewed as the operator f applied to the operands $G,H,I,$ and J.

A traversal of the trees of Figure 6.5.5 in preorder results in the strings $* \% + A B - + C \log + D ! E f G H I J$ and $q + A B \sin C * X + Y Z$, respectively. These are the prefix versions of those two expressions. Thus we see that a preorder general traversal of an expression tree produces its prefix expression. Inorder general traversal yields the respective strings $A B + \% C D E ! + \log + G H I J f - *$ and $A B + C \sin X Y Z + * q$, which are the postfix versions of the two expressions.

The fact that an inorder general traversal yields a postfix expression might be surprising at first glance. However, the reason for it becomes clear upon examination of the transformation that takes place when a general ordered tree is represented by a binary tree. Consider an ordered tree in which each node has zero or two sons. Such a tree is shown in Figure 6.5.6(a) and its binary tree equivalent in Figure 6.5.6(b). A binary traversal of the binary tree of Figure 6.5.6(b) is the same as a general traversal of the ordered tree of Figure 6.5.6(a). However, a tree such as the one in Figure 6.5.6(a) may be considered as a binary tree in its own right, rather than as an ordered tree. Thus it is possible to perform a binary traversal (rather than a general traversal) directly on the tree of Figure 6.5.6(a). Beneath that figure are the binary traversals of that tree, while beneath Figure 6.5.6(b) are the binary traversals of the tree in that figure which are the same as the general traversals of the tree of Figure 6.5.6(a).

Note that the preorder binary traversals of the two trees are the same. Thus if a preorder binary traversal of a tree representing a binary expression yields the

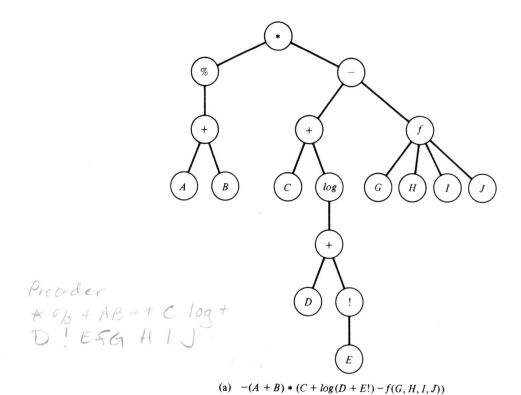

Preorder
* % + AB − + C log +
D ! ESG HIJ

(a) $-(A + B) * (C + log (D + E!)) - f(G, H, I, J))$

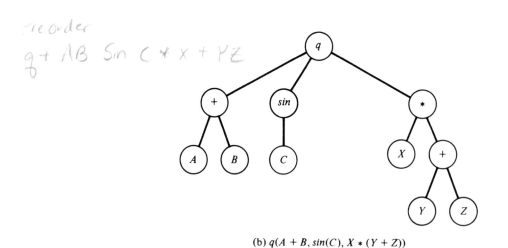

reorder
q + AB Sin C * X + YZ

(b) $q(A + B, sin(C), X * (Y + Z))$

Figure 6.5.5 Tree representation of an arithmetic expression.

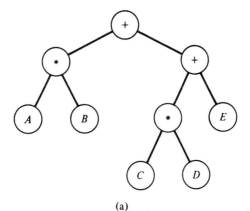

(a)

Preorder: $+ * AB + * CDE$
Inorder: $A * B + C * D + E$
Postorder: $AB * CD * E + +$

$* - a - bc / - de \cdot + fgh$

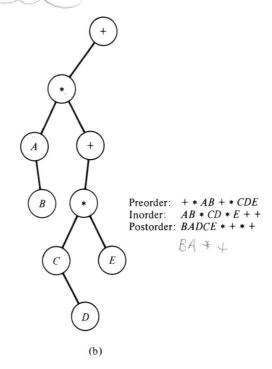

Preorder: $+ * AB + * CDE$
Inorder: $AB * CD * E + +$
Postorder: $BADCE * + * +$

$BA * +$

(b)

Figure 6.5.6

prefix of the expression, the preorder general traversal of a tree representing a general expression that happens to have only binary operators yields the prefix form of the expression as well. However, the postorder binary traversals of the trees are not the same. Instead, the inorder binary traversal of the second (which is the same as the inorder general traversal of the first) is the same as the postorder binary traversal of the first. Thus the inorder general traversal of an ordered tree representing a binary expression is equivalent to the postorder binary traversal of the binary tree representing that expression, which yields postfix.

Suppose that it is desired to evaluate an expression whose operands are all numerical constants. Such an expression can be represented in BASIC by a tree whose nodes are defined by

```
10   DIM INFO(500)
20   DIM SN(500)
30   DIM NXT(500)
```

The SN and NXT pointers are used to link together the nodes of a tree as previously illustrated. Since a node may contain information that may be either a number (operand) or a character string (operator), the information portion of the node points to either an element in an array OPER of operators or an element in an array NUM of operands. These arrays are declared by

```
10   DEFSTR O
20   DIM OPER(20)
30   DIM NUM(500)
```

in which we assume a maximum of 20 different operators and 500 operands. As in the case of binary expression trees, operand and operator nodes may be distinguished from each other since operands are leafs and therefore have null SN fields, while operators are nonleafs.

We wish to write a BASIC subroutine *evtree* which accepts a pointer to such a tree and returns the value of the expression represented by that tree. The routine *evbtree* presented in Section 2 performs a similar operation on binary expression trees. *evbtree* utilizes a subroutine *apply* which accepts an operator symbol and two numerical operands and returns the numerical result of applying the operator to the operands. However, in the case of a general expression we cannot use such a function since the number of operands (and hence the number of arguments) varies with the operator. We therefore introduce a new variation of the subroutine *apply* which accepts a pointer to an expression tree that contains a single operator and its numerical operands and returns the result of applying the operator to its operands. For example, the result of calling the routine *apply* with input variable P pointing to the tree in Figure 6.5.7 is 24. If the root of the tree that is passed to *evtree* represents an operator, each of its subtrees must be replaced by tree nodes representing the numerical results of their evaluation so that the subroutine *apply* may be called. As the expression is evaluated, the tree nodes

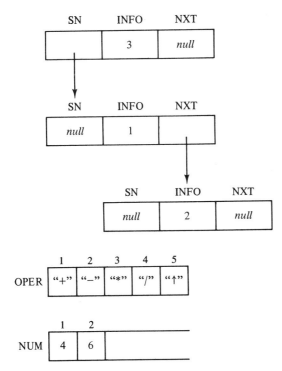

Figure 6.5.7 An expression tree.

representing operands must be freed and operator nodes must be converted to operand nodes. Note that this means that *evtree*, unlike *evbtree*, destroys the expression tree in the course of evaluating it.

We now present a routine *replace*, which accepts a pointer to an expression tree and replaces the tree with a single tree node containing the numerical result of the expression's evaluation. *replace* is most naturally developed as a recursive algorithm, which can then be transformed into a BASIC routine using the methods of Chapter 5. The algorithm calls upon the operation *apply* discussed above and the operation *newop*. *newop* accepts an operand, inserts the operand into the array *num*, and returns a pointer to that position of *num*. Thus *newop* creates a new operand.

```
subroutine replace(pp)
q = sn(pp)
if q = null
   then return
endif
```

'traverse the list of sons, replacing each operator by its result
while q <> null **do**
    if sn(q) <> null
      then replace(q)
    endif
    q = nxt(q)
endwhile
'all the sons are now operands
'find the result of applying the operator in the tree root to its
'operands and replace the operator by the result
info(pp) = newop(apply(pp))
'free all the sons of the tree root
rl = sn(pp)
sn(pp) = null
while r1 <> null **do**
    r2 = r1
    r1 = nxt(r1)
    freenode(r2)
endwhile
return

The following are BASIC versions of *replace* and *newop*.

```
23000   'subroutine replace
23010   'inputs: PP
23020   'outputs: none
23030   'locals: APPLY, CPARAM, CQ, CRETADDR, FRNODE, I, NWOP,
               PARAM, PX, QQ, R1, R2, RETADDR, TP
23040   'define the recursion stack; each stack position contains a tree
        'pointer parameter, a value for the variable q in the
        'recursive algorithm, and a return address
23050   DIM PARAM(50), RETADDR(50), QQ(50)
23060   TP = 0:        'initialize the stack to empty
23070   'push an initial record onto the stack
23080   CPARAM = 0:    'CPARAM is the current tree pointer
23090   CRETADDR = 0:  'CRETADDR is the current return address
                       '1 represents a return to the calling program
                       '2 represents a return after the recursive call
23100   CQ = 0:        'CQ is a pointer to a son of CPARAM corresponding
                       'to the variable q in the algorithm
23110   GOSUB 1000:    'subroutine push
23120   'initialize variables to their values from the external call
23130   CPARAM = PP
23140   CRETADDR = 1
```

```
23150   'begin the body of replace
23160   CQ = SN(CPARAM)
23170   IF CQ = 0 THEN GOTO 23440: 'return
23180   'simulation of the first while loop
23190   IF CQ = 0 THEN GOTO 23290
23200     IF SN(CQ) = 0 THEN GOTO 23270
23210     'simulation of the recursive call replace(q)
23220     GOSUB 1000: 'subroutine push
23230     CPARAM = CQ
23240     CRETADDR = 2
23250     GOTO 23150
23260     'return here after a recursive call
23270     CQ = NXT(CQ)
23280   GOTO 23190

23290   'all the sons of node(CPARAM) are now operands
23300   PX = CPARAM
23310   GOSUB 6000:        'subroutine apply accepts PX and
                           'sets the variable APPLY
23320   X = APPLY
23330   GOSUB 24000:       'subroutine newop accepts X and
                           'sets the variable NWOP
23340   INFO(CPARAM) = NWOP

23350   'free the sons of the tree node
23360   R1 = SN(CPARAM)
23370   SN(CPARAM) = 0
23380   IF R1 = 0 THEN GOTO 23440: 'return
23390     R2 = R1
23400     R1 = NXT(R1)
23410     FRNODE = R2
23420     GOSUB 12000: 'subroutine freenode accepts the variable FRNODE
23430   GOTO 23380

23440   'simulation of return from replace
23450   I = CRETADDR
23460   GOSUB 2000:        'subroutine pop pops the stack and resets the
                           'variables CPARAM, CRETADDR, and CQ
23470   IF I = 1 THEN RETURN
23480   IF I = 2 THEN GOTO 23260: 'return after recursive call within
                                  'replace
23490   'endsub
```

. . .

```
24000   'subroutine newop
24010   'inputs: LAST, NUM, X
24020   'outputs: LAST, NUM, NWOP
24030   'locals: none
24040   'the variable LAST (which is initialized when the tree is built)
        'holds the last position in the array NUM which is occupied;
        'increase LAST and insert the operand X
24050   LAST = LAST + 1
24060   IF LAST > 500 THEN PRINT "TOO MANY OPERANDS": STOP
24070   NUM(LAST) = X
24080   NWOP = LAST
24090   RETURN
24100   'endsub
```

[Note that the contents of the array NUM are always added to but never compacted. If we are in a context which builds a single tree and evaluates it and then builds another tree while reusing NUM, this is feasible. However, if many trees are being built and evaluated simultaneously so that an arbitrary number of trees exist at any point, NUM will quickly overflow. A solution would be to let LAST point to the first unused element in NUM and each unused element would contain a pointer to the next unused element. The routine *freenode* would be responsible for adding newly freed elements of NUM to this available list and *newop* would execute LAST = NUM(LAST) rather than executing LAST = LAST + 1 before the insertion. The main program would initialize LAST to 1 and NUM(I) to I + 1 for all I.]

The routine *evtree* may now be written as follows:

```
22000   'subroutine evtree
22010   'inputs: TREE
22020   'outputs: EVTREE
22030   'locals: FRNODE, PP, QQ
22040   PP = TREE
22050   GOSUB 23000: 'subroutine replace
22060   QQ = INFO(TREE)
22070   EVTREE = NUM(QQ)
22080   FRNODE = TREE
22090   GOSUB 12000: 'subroutine freenode
22100   RETURN
22110   'endsub
```

Other Tree Operations

In constructing a tree there are several operations which are frequently used. One of these is *setsons*, which accepts a node of a tree that has no sons and a linear list of nodes linked together through the NXT field. *setsons* establishes the nodes in the list as the sons of the node in the tree. The BASIC routine to implement this operation is straightforward. (We assume that no father pointers are needed so that the FTHER field is eliminated and the NXT pointer in the youngest node is null. The routines would be slightly more complex and less efficient if this were not the case.)

```
22000   'subroutine setsons
22010   'inputs: Q, LST
22020   'outputs: none
22030   'locals: none
22040   IF Q = 0 THEN PRINT "VOID INSERTION": STOP
22050   IF SN(Q) <> 0 THEN PRINT "INVALID INSERTION": STOP
22060   SN(Q) = LST
22070   RETURN
22080   'endsub
```

Another common operation is *addson*, where Q points to a node in a tree and it is desired to add a node containing X as the youngest son of *node*(Q). The BASIC routine to implement *addson* is as follows. The routine calls the auxiliary routine *getnode*, which removes a node from the available list and returns a pointer to it.

```
23000   'subroutine addson
23010   'inputs: Q, X
23020   'outputs: none
23030   'locals: GTNODE, P, R
23040   IF Q = 0 THEN PRINT "INVALID INSERTION": STOP
23050   R = 0
23060   P = SN(Q)
23070   IF P = 0 THEN GOTO 23110
23080     R = P
23090     P = NXT(P)
23100   GOTO 23070
23110   GOSUB 1000: 'subroutine getnode sets the variable GTNODE
23120   P = GTNODE
23130   INFO(P) = X
23140   NXT(P) = 0
23150   IF R = 0 THEN SN(Q) = P
                  ELSE NXT(R) = P
23160   RETURN
23170   'endsub
```

Note that in order to add a new son to a node, the list of existing sons must be traversed. Since adding a son is a common operation, a representation is often used which makes this operation more efficient. Under this alternative representation, the list of sons is ordered from youngest to oldest rather than vice versa. Thus SN(Q) points to the youngest son of *node*(Q), and NXT(Q) points to its

next older brother. Under this representation the routine *addson* may be written
as follows:

```
23000  'subroutine addson
23010  'inputs: Q, X
23020  'outputs: none
23030  'locals: GTNODE, P
23040  IF Q = 0 THE PRINT "INVALID INSERTION": STOP
23050  GOSUB 1000: 'subroutine getnode sets the variable GTNODE
23060  P = GTNODE
23070  INFO(P) = X
23080  NXT(P) = SN(Q)
23090  SN(Q) = P
23100  RETURN
23110  'endsub
```

EXERCISES

1. How many distinct trees can be constructed with n nodes?

2. How many distinct trees can be constructed with n nodes and maximum level m?

3. Prove that if m pointer fields are set aside in each node of a general tree to point to a
   maximum of m sons, and if the number of nodes in the tree is n, then the number of
   null son pointer fields is $n(m-1)+1$.

4. If a forest is represented by a binary tree as in the text, show that the number of null
   right links is 1 greater than the number of nonleafs of the forest.

5. Define the **breadth-first order** of the nodes of a general tree as the root followed by all
   nodes on level 1, followed by all nodes on level 2, and so on. Within each level, the
   nodes should be ordered so that children of the same father appear in the same order as
   they appear in the tree, and if $n1$ and $n2$ have different fathers, $n1$ appears before $n2$ if
   the father of $n1$ appears before the father of $n2$. Extend the definition to a forest. Write
   a BASIC program to traverse a forest represented as a binary tree in breadth-first order.

6. Consider the following method of transforming a general tree gt into a strictly binary
   tree bt. Each node of gt is represented by a leaf of bt. If gt consists of a single node,
   then bt consists of a single node. Otherwise, bt consists of a new root node and a left
   subtree lt and a right subtree rt. lt is the strictly binary tree formed recursively from the
   oldest subtree of gt, and rt is the strictly binary tree formed recursively from gt without
   its oldest subtree. Write a BASIC routine to convert a general tree into such a strictly
   binary tree.

7. Write a BASIC routine *compute* which accepts a pointer to a tree representing an expression with constant operands and sets the variable COMPUTE to the result of evaluating the expression without destroying the tree.

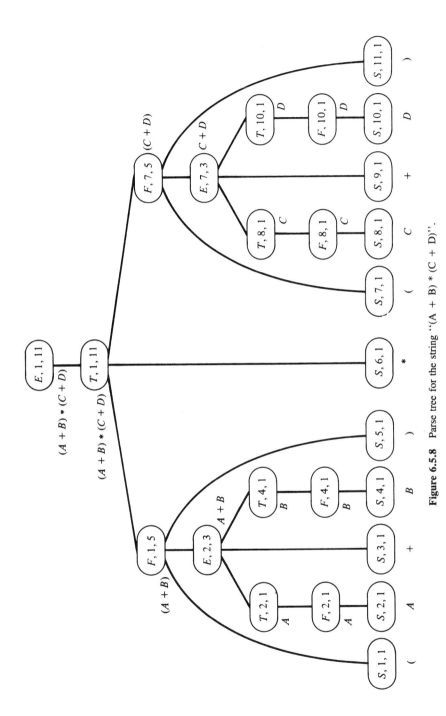

Figure 6.5.8 Parse tree for the string "(A + B) * (C + D)".

8. Write a BASIC program to convert an infix expression into an expression tree. Assume that all nonbinary operators precede their operands. Let the input expression be represented as follows: an operand is represented by the character "N" followed by a number, an operator by the character "T" followed by a character representing the operator, and a function by the character "F" followed by the name of the function.

9. Consider the definition of an expression, term, and factor given at the end of Section 5.3. Given a string of letters, plus signs, asterisks, and parentheses which form a valid expression, a **parse tree** can be formed for the string. Such a tree is illustrated in Figure 6.5.8 for the string "$(A+B)*(C+D)$". Each node in such a tree represents a substring and contains a letter (E for expression, T for term, F for factor, or S for symbol) and two integers. The first is the position within the input string where the substring represented by that node begins, and the second is the length of the substring. (The substring represented by each node is shown below that node in the figure.) The leafs are all S nodes and represent single symbols of the original input. The root of the tree must be an E node. The sons of any non-S node n represent the substrings that make up the grammatical object represented by n. Write a BASIC routine that accepts such a string and constructs a parse tree for it.

6. AN EXAMPLE: GAME TREES

One application of trees is to game playing by computer. We illustrate this application by writing a BASIC program to determine the "best" move in tic-tac-toe from a given board position. Assume that there is a function *evaluate* which accepts a board position and an indication of a player (X or O) and returns a numerical value which represents how "good" the position seems to be for that player (the larger the value returned by *evaluate,* the better the position). Of course, a winning postion yields the largest possible value and a losing position yields the smallest. An example of such an evaluation function for tic-tac-toe is the number of rows, columns, and diagonals remaining open for one player minus the number remaining open for his opponent (except that the value 9 would be returned for a position that wins, and −9 for a position that loses). This function does not "look ahead" to consider any possible board positions that might result from the current position—it merely evaluates a static board position.

Given a board position, the best next move could be determined by considering all possible moves and resulting positions. That move which results in the board position with the highest evaluation should be selected. However, such an analysis does not necessarily yield the best move, as can be seen from Figure 6.6.1. This figure illustrates a position and the five possible moves which X can make from that position. Applying the evaluation function described above to the five resulting positions yields the values shown. Four moves yield the same maximum evaluation, although three of them are distinctly inferior to the fourth. (The fourth position yields a certain victory for X, while the other three can be drawn by O.) In fact, the move that yields the smallest evaluation is as good as or better

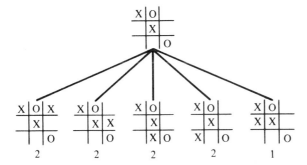

Figure 6.6.1

than the moves that yield a higher evaluation. Such a static evaluation function is not good enough to predict the outcome of the game. Although a better evaluation function could easily be produced for the game of tic-tac-toe (even if it were by the brute-force method of listing all positions and the appropriate response), most games are too complex for static evaluators to determine the best response.

Suppose that it were possible to look ahead several moves. Then the choice of a move could be improved considerably. Define the *look ahead level* as the number of future moves to be considered. Starting at any position, it is possible to construct a tree of the possible board positions that may result from each move. Such a tree is called a *game tree*. The game tree for the opening tic-tac-toe position with a look-ahead level of 2 is illustrated in Figure 6.6.2 (Actually, other positions do exist, but because of symmetry considerations, these are effectively the same as the positions shown.) Note that the maximum level (called the *depth*) of the nodes in such a tree is equal to the look-ahead level.

Let us designate the player who must move at the root's game position as *plus* and his opponent as *minus*. We attempt to find the best move for plus from the root's game position. The remaining nodes of the tree may be designated as *plus nodes* or *minus nodes*, depending upon which player must move from that node's position. Each node of Figure 6.6.2 is marked as a plus or minus node.

Suppose that the game positions of all the sons of a plus node have been evaluated for player plus. Then, clearly, plus should choose the move that yields the maximum evaluation. Thus the value of a plus node to player plus is the maximum of the values of its sons. On the other hand, once plus has made his move, minus will select the move that yields the minimum evaluation for player plus. Thus the value of a minus node to player plus is the minimum of the values of its sons.

Therefore, to decide the best move for player plus from the root, the positions in the leafs must be evaluated for player plus using a static evaluation function. These values are then moved up the game tree by assigning to each plus node the maximum of its sons' values and to each minus node the minimum of its sons' values on the assumption that minus will select the move that is worst for plus. The value assigned to each node of Figure 6.6.2 by this process is indicated in that figure immediately below the node. The move that plus should select, giv-

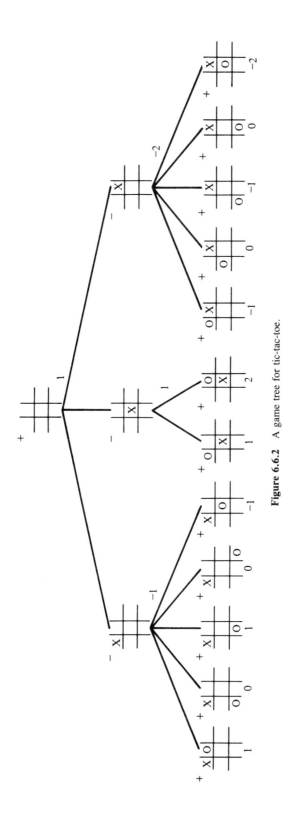

Figure 6.6.2 A game tree for tic-tac-toe.

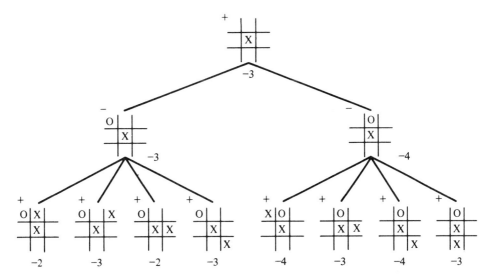

Figure 6.6.3 Computing O's reply.

en the board position in the root node, is the one that maximizes its value. Thus the opening move for X should be the middle square, as illustrated in Figure 6.6.2. Figure 6.6.3 illustrates the determination of O's best reply. Note that the designation of "plus" and "minus" depends on whose move is being calculated. Thus, in Figure 6.6.2, X is designated as plus, while in Figure 6.6.3, O is designated as plus. In applying the static evaluation function to a board position, the value of the position to whichever player is designated as plus is computed. This method is called the ***minimax*** method because, as the tree is climbed, the maximum and minimum functions are applied alternately.

The best move for a player from a given position may be determined by first constructing the game tree and applying a static evaluation function to the leafs. These values are then moved up the tree by applying the minimum and maximum at minus and plus nodes, respectively. Each node of the game tree must include a representation of the board and an indication of whether the node is a plus node or a minus node. An array of nodes may be defined by

```
10   DEFSTR B
20   DIM BOARD(500,3,3)
30   DIM TURN(500)
40   DIM SN(500)
50   DIM NXT(500)
```

BOARD(P,ROW,COL) has the value "X", "O", or " ", depending on whether the square in row ROW and column COL of the board position in *node*(P) is occupied by either of the players or is unoccupied. TURN(P) has the value 1 or

−1, depending on whether *node*(P) is a plus or minus node, respectively. The remaining two fields of a node are used to position the node within the tree. SN(P) points to the oldest son of *node*(P), while NXT(P) points to its next younger brother. We assume that an available list of nodes has been established and that appropriate *getnode* and *freenode* routines have been written.

The BASIC routine *nextmove* accepts three inputs, BRD, DEPTH, and XO, and computes the best next move. BRD is a 3 by 3 array representing the current board position. DEPTH is the desired look-ahead level. XO is an indication of whose move is being computed ("X" or "O"). *nextmove* outputs the array B, which represents the best board position that can be achieved by a particular player from position BRD. *nextmove* uses two auxiliary routines, *buildtree* and *bestbranch*. The routine *buildtree* builds the game tree whose root contains the board position BRD and returns a pointer to that root. The routine *bestbranch* accepts a pointer ND to a node and computes the value of two output variables: HIGH, which is a pointer to the son of *node*(ND) representing the best move, and VLUE, which is the evaluation of that move using the minimax technique. We will present these two routines shortly. In all the routines of this section we do not list explicitly the arrays BOARD, TURN, SN, or NXT as inputs or outputs, although most of the routines use them as such.

```
2000    'subroutine nextmove
2010    'inputs: BRD, DEPTH, XO
2020    'outputs: B
2030    'locals: COL, ND, ROW
2040    GOSUB 3000: 'subroutine buildtree sets the variable TREE
2050    ND = TREE
2060    GOSUB 6000: 'subroutine bestbranch sets the variable HIGH
2070    FOR ROW = 1 TO 3
2080        FOR COL = 1 TO 3
2090            B(ROW,COL) = BOARD(HIGH,ROW,COL)
2100        NEXT COL
2110    NEXT ROW
2120    RETURN
2130    'endsub
```

The function *buildtree* returns a pointer to the root of a game tree. It accepts two variables: BRD, representing a board position, and DEPTH, representing the depth of a tree to be constructed. *buildtree* sets the variable TREE to point to a newly constructed tree of proper depth with BRD as the board position in its root. *buildtree* uses the auxiliary routine *getnode*, which removes a node from the available list and returns a pointer to it. It also uses a routine *expand*, which accepts P, a pointer to a node in a game tree, and DEPTH, the depth of the game tree that is to be constructed. *expand* produces the subtree rooted at P to the proper depth.

```
3000   'subroutine buildtree
3010   'inputs: BRD, DEPTH
3020   'outputs: TREE
3030   'locals: COL, P, ROW
3040   GOSUB 1000: 'subroutine getnode sets the variable GTNODE
3050   TREE = GTNODE: 'initialize the root of the tree
3060   FOR ROW = 1 to 3
3070       FOR COL = 1 to 3
3080           BOARD(TREE,ROW,COL) = BRD(ROW,COL)
3090       NEXT COL
3100   NEXT ROW
3110   TURN(TREE) = 1: 'the root is a plus node by definition
3120   SN(TREE) = 0
3130   NXT(TREE) = 0
3140   P = TREE
3150   GOSUB 4000: 'subroutine expand creates the rest of the game tree
3160   RETURN
3170   'endsub
```

expand may be implemented by calling upon an auxiliary recursive algorithm *expand2* which accepts an additional input variable, *level,* whose value is the level of *node*(P) in the tree. *expand2* generates all board positions that may be obtained from the board position of *node*(P) and establishes them as the sons of P in the game tree. *expand2* then calls itself recursively using each of these sons as an input in turn until the desired depth is reached. *expand2* uses an auxiliary routine *generate* which accepts P and returns a pointer to a list of nodes containing the board positions that can be obtained from the board contained in *node*(P). This list is linked together by the NXT field. We leave the coding of *generate* as an exercise for the reader. We now present a recursive algorithm for *expand,* followed by a BASIC routine to implement that algorithm.

$$\textbf{subroutine } expand(p,depth)$$
$$level = 0 \text{ 'the level of } node(p)$$
$$expand2(p,level,depth)$$
$$\textbf{return}$$

$$\textbf{subroutine } expand2(p,level,depth)$$
$$\textbf{if } level = depth$$
    then 'p is already at the maximum level
        return
endif
$$q = generate(p)$$
$$sn(p) = q$$

```
'traverse the list of nodes
while q <> 0 do
    turn(q) = −turn(p)
    sn(q) = 0
    expand2 (q,level + 1,depth)
    q = nxt (q)
endwhile
return
```

There are several points to consider about this implementation before presenting its BASIC version. First, since the BASIC program is not itself recursive, there is no need for a separate routine *expand2*. The values of the variable *level* of the algorithm (maintained in a stack of the same name in the program, together with its current value, CLEVEL) is initialized and pushed and popped within the routine *expand* itself.

It is also necessary to note that the game tree program includes two recursive simulations; one is in the routine *expand,* as discussed, and the other is in the routine *bestbranch,* to be presented shortly. Each of these routines require its own, separate recursion stacks. Therefore, two separate sets of stack manipulation routines are also required. For this reason, we assume the existence of routines *push*1 and *pop*1 (at statements 10000 and 20000, respectively) to be called by *expand*, and *push*2 and *pop*2 (at 11000 and 21000) to be called by *bestbranch*. In addition, since neither routine calls the other, they can share a single array, RETADDR, to hold the two return address stacks. If this were not the case, two separate arrays would be required. (Actually, the remaining recursion stacks can be shared as well, but this would create some confusion regarding their names and the names of the variables that hold their current values.) Therefore, we assume that the array RETADDR is dimensioned in the main program, to be shared by both routines.

We may now present the BASIC implementation of *expand*:

```
4000   'subroutine expand
4010   'inputs: DEPTH, MAXSTACK, P
4020   'outputs: none
4030   'locals: CLEVEL, CP, CQ, CRETADDR, I, P1, Q, TP
4040   'define a recursion stack; each stack position I contains a tree
       'pointer P1(I), the level of that tree node LEVEL(I) and the
       'value Q(I) of the variable CQ; the return address stack RETADDR
       'is DIMensioned in the main program.
4050   DIM P1(MAXSTACK), LEVEL(MAXSTACK), Q(MAXSTACK)
4060   TP = 0
4070   CRETADDR = 1
4080   CP = P
4090   CLEVEL = 0
4100   CQ = 0
```

```
4110   GOSUB 10000: 'subroutine push1
4120   'if CLEVEL = DEPTH then CP is already at the maximum level
4130   IF CLEVEL = DEPTH THEN GOTO 4300
4140   GOSUB 5000: 'subroutine generate accepts CP and sets the variable
                   'GNERATE
4150   CQ = GNERATE
4160   SN(CP) = CQ
4170   IF CQ = 0 THEN GOTO 4300
4180      'if CQ <> 0 then traverse the list of nodes
4190      TURN(CQ) = −TURN(CP)
4200      SN(CQ) = 0
4210      'simulation of the recursive call expand2(q,level + 1, depth)
4220      GOSUB 10000: 'subroutine push1
4230      CP = CQ
4240      CLEVEL = CLEVEL + 1
4250      CRETADDR = 2
4260      GOTO 4120
4270      'return point for the recursive call
4280      CQ = NXT(CQ)
4290   GOTO 4170
4300   'simulation of return from EXPAND
4310   I = CRETADDR
4320   GOSUB 20000: 'subroutine pop1
4330   IF I = 1 THEN RETURN
4340   IF I = 2 THEN GOTO 4270
4350   'endsub
```

Once the game tree has been created, *bestbranch* evaluates the nodes of the tree. When a pointer to a leaf is passed to *bestbranch,* it calls a routine *evaluate,* which statically evaluates the board position of that leaf for the player whose move we are determining. The coding of *evaluate* is left as an exercise. When a pointer to a nonleaf is passed to *bestbranch,* the routine calls itself recursively on each of its sons and then assigns the maximum of its sons' values to the nonleaf if it is a plus node, and the minimum if it is a minus node. *bestbranch* also keeps track of which son yielded this minimum or maximum value.

If TURN(P) is −1, then *node*(P) is a minus node and it is to be assigned the minimum of the values assigned to its sons. If, however, TURN(P) is +1, *node*(P) is a plus node and its value should be the maximum of the values assigned to the sons of *node*(P). If $min(x,y)$ is the minimum of x and y, and $max(x,y)$ is their maximum, then $min(x,y) = -max(-x,-y)$ (you are invited to prove this as a trivial exercise). Thus the correct maximum or minimum can be found as follows. In the case of a plus node, compute the maximum; in the case of a minus node, compute the maximum of the negatives of the values and then reverse the sign of the result. These ideas are incorporated into *bestbranch.* When the value of a son of *node* (ND) is computed, it is multiplied by TURN(ND) (either 1 or −1, depending on whether ND is a plus or a minus node). If that result is greater than the largest result obtained from the other sons of ND, that son is established as the next move after ND. To obtain the value of that move to the player being evaluated, we again multiply by TURN(ND), effectively computing either the minimum or maximum as appropriate.

The input variables to *bestbranch* are ND, a pointer to the tree node whose best next move we are determining, and XO, which represents the player for whom we are evaluating the best next move. The output variables HIGH and VLUE are, respectively, a pointer to that son of *node*(ND) which maximizes or minimizes its value and the value of that son which then becomes the value of *node*(ND).

A recursive algorithm for *bestbranch* is given below, followed by the BASIC implementation.

```
subroutine bestbranch(nd,xo)
if sn(nd) = 0
   then vlue = evaluate(nd,xo)
        high = nd
        return
endif
'determine the value of the oldest son
p = sn(nd)
bestbranch(p,xo)  'sets vlue to the value of node(p)
'The variable tvlue is used to hold the highest value of all sons
'examined so far, and temp is used to point to the son that produces
'that value; initialize these so that the oldest son represents the best
'move of all sons examined so far.
tvlue = turn(nd) * vlue
temp = p
'traverse the remaining sons and reset tvlue and temp.
p = nxt(p)
while p <> 0 do
        bestbranch(p,xo)  'sets vlue to the value of node(p)
        v2 = turn(nd) * vlue
        if v2 > tvlue
           then tvlue = v2
                temp = p
        endif
        p = nxt(p)
endwhile
vlue = turn(nd) * tvlue
high = temp
return
```

The BASIC implementation of *bestbranch* now follows. We assume the declaration DEFSTR X and that the BASIC routine *evaluate* accepts CND and XO and sets EVLUATE.

```
6000    'subroutine bestbranch
6010    'inputs: MAXSTACK, ND, XO
6020    'outputs: HIGH, VLUE
6030    'locals: CND, CP, CRETADDR, I, NSTACK, PSTACK, TEMP, TSTACK,
                TVLUE, V2, VSTACK
6040    'define the recursion stack; each stack position I, contains a tree
        'pointer NSTACK (I) and values for the variables CP, TVLUE, and
        'TEMP (these values are PSTACK(I), VSTACK(I) and RSTACK(I),
        'respectively); the return address stack RETADDR is DIMensioned in
        'the main program
6050    DIM NSTACK(MAXSTACK), PSTACK(MAXSTACK)
6060    DIM TSTACK(MAXSTACK), VSTACK(MAXSTACK)
6070    'push an initial record on the stack
6080    CRETADDR = 1
6090    CND = ND
6100    CP = 0
6110    TEMP = 0
6120    TVLUE = 0
6130    GOSUB 11000: 'subroutine push2
6140    'if SN(CND) = 0 then the node is a leaf; call evaluate at 7000
6150    IF SN(CND) = 0 THEN GOSUB 7000: VLUE =EVLUATE: HIGH = CND:
                                                              GOTO 6410
6160        'the node is not a leaf; traverse its sons
6170        CP = SN(CND)
6180        'simulation of the first recursive call bestbranch(p,xo)
6190        GOSUB 11000: 'subroutine push2
6200        CND = CP
6210        CRETADDR = 2
6220    GOTO 6140
6230    'return point after the first recursive call
6240    'if CND is a minus node, multiply by −1
6250    TVLUE = TURN(CND)*VLUE
6260    TEMP = CP
6270    CP = NXT(CP)
6280    IF CP = 0 THEN GOTO 6390
6290        'simulation of the second recursive call bestbranch(p,xo)
6300        GOSUB 11000: 'subroutine push2
6310        CND = CP
6320        CRETADDR = 3
6330        GOTO 6140
```

```
6340    'return point after the second recursive call
6350    V2 = TURN(CND)*VLUE
6360    IF V2 >  TVLUE THEN TVLUE = V2: TEMP = CP
6370    CP = NXT(CP)
6380  GOTO 6280
6390  VLUE = TURN(CND)*TVLUE
6400  HIGH = TEMP
6410  'simulation of a return from bestbranch
6420  I = CRETADDR
6430  GOSUB 21000: 'subroutine pop2
6440  IF I = 1 THEN RETURN
6450  IF I = 2 THEN GOTO 6230
6460  IF I = 3 THEN GOTO 6340
6470  'endsub
```

EXERCISES

1. Write the BASIC routines *generate* and *evaluate* as described in the text.

2. Rewrite the programs of this and the preceding section under the implementation in which each tree node includes a field FTHER, which contains a pointer to its father. Under which implementation are the programs more efficient?

3. Modify the routine *bestbranch* in the text so that the nodes of the tree are freed when they are no longer needed.

4. Combine the processes of building the game tree and evaluating its nodes into a single process so that the entire game tree need not exist at any one time and nodes are freed when no longer necessary.

5. Modify the program of Exercise 3 so that if the evaluation of a minus node is greater than the minimum of the values of its father's older brothers, the program does not bother expanding that minus node's younger brothers, and if the evaluation of a plus node is less than the maximum of the values of its father's older brothers, the program does not bother expanding that plus node's younger brothers. This method is called the **alpha-beta minimax** method. Explain why it is correct.

6. The game of **kalah** is played as follows. Two players each have seven holes, six of which are called **pits** and the seventh a **kalah**. These are arranged according to the following diagram.

Player 1

K P P P P P
   P P P P P K

Player 2

Initially, there are six stones in each pit and no stones in either kalah, so the opening position looks like this:

0 6 6 6 6 6 6

6 6 6 6 6 6 0

The players alternate turns, each turn consisting of one or more moves. To make a move, a player chooses one of his nonempty pits. The stones are removed from that pit and are distributed counterclockwise into the pits and into that player's kalah (the opponent's kalah is skipped), one stone per pit, until there are no stones remaining. For example, if player 1 moves first, a possible opening move might result in the following board position:

1 7 7 7 7 7 0

6 6 6 6 6 6 0

If a player's last stone lands in his own kalah, the player gets another move. If the last stone lands in one of his own pits which is empty, that stone and the stones in the opponent's pit directly opposite are removed and placed in the player's kalah. The game ends when either player has no stones remaining in his pits. At that point, all of the stones in his opponent's pits are placed in the opponent's kalah and the game ends. The player with the most stones in his kalah is the winner. Write a program that accepts a kalah board position and an indication of whose turn it is and produces that player's best move.

7. How would you modify the ideas of the tic-tac-toe program to compute the best move in a game that contains an element of chance, such as backgammon?

8. Why have computers been programmed to play perfect tic-tac-toe but not perfect chess or checkers?

9. The game of *nim* is played as follows. Some number of sticks are placed in a pile. Two players alternate in removing either one or two sticks from the pile. The player to remove the last stick is the loser. Write a BASIC routine to determine the best move in nim.

7

Graphs and Their Applications

In this chapter we consider a new data structure—the graph. We define some terms associated with graphs and show how to implement graphs in BASIC. We also present several applications of graphs.

1. GRAPHS

A *graph* consists of a set of *nodes* (or *vertices*) and a set of *arcs*. Each arc in a graph is specified by a pair of nodes. Figure 7.1.1(a) illustrates a graph. The set of nodes is {*A,B,C,D,E,F,G,H*} and the set of arcs is {(*A,B*), (*A,D*), (*A,C*), (*C,D*), (*C,F*), (*E,G*), (*A,A*)}. If the pairs of nodes that make up the arcs are ordered pairs, the graph is said to be a *directed graph* (or *digraph*). Figure 7.1.1(b), (c), and (d) illustrate three digraphs. The arrows between nodes represent arcs. The head of each arrow represents the second node in the ordered pair of nodes making up an arc, while the tail of each arrow represents the first node in the pair. The set of arcs for the graph of Figure 7.1.1(b) is {<*A,B*>, <*A,C*>,<*A,D*>,<*C,D*>,<*F,C*>,<*E,G*>,<*A,A*>}. We use parentheses to indicate an unordered pair and angled brackets to indicate an ordered pair. In the remainder of this chapter we restrict our attention to digraphs.

Note that a graph need not be a tree [Figure 7.1.1(a), (b), and (d)] but that a tree must be a graph, where we may consider the pointer from a father to a son as an arc of the graph [Figure 7.1.1(c)]. Note also that a node need not have any arcs associated with it [node *H* in Figure 7.1.1(a) and (b)].

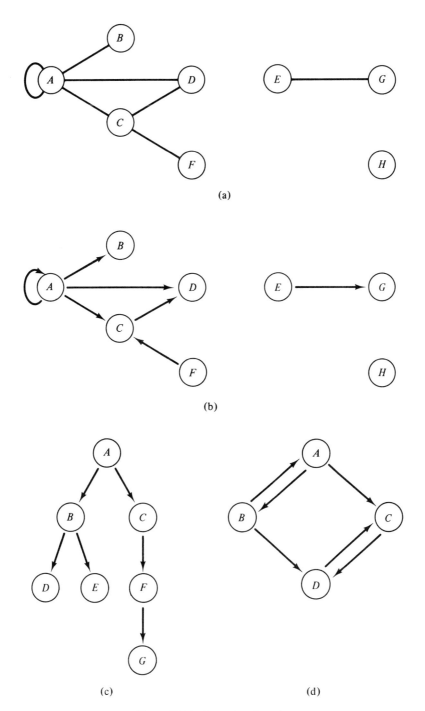

Figure 7.1.1 Examples of graphs.

A node n is *incident* to an arc x if n is one of the two nodes in the ordered pair of nodes that comprise x. (We also say that x is incident to n.) The *degree* of a node is the number of arcs incident to it. The *indegree* of a node n is the number of arcs that have n as the head and the *outdegree* of n is the number of arcs that have n as the tail. For example, node A in Figure 7.1.1(d) has indegree 1, outdegree 2, and degree 3. A node n is *adjacent* to a node m if there is an arc from m to n.

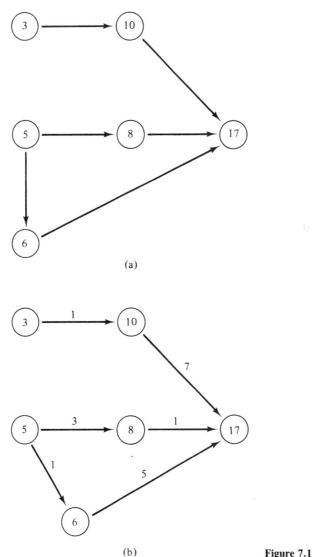

Figure 7.1.2 Relations and graphs.

A *relation R* on a set *A* is a set of ordered pairs of elements of *A*. If $<x,y>$ is a member of a relation *R*, then *x* is said to be *related* to *y* in *R*. For example, if *A* is the set {3,5,6,8,10,17}, the set {$<3,10>,<5,6>,<5,8>,$ $<6,17>,<8,17>,<10,17>$} is a relation on *A*. This particular relation may be described by saying that *x* is related to *y* if *x* and *y* are in *A*, *x* is less than *y*, and the remainder obtained by dividing *y* by *x* is odd. $<8,17>$ is a member of this relation since 8 is smaller than 17 and the remainder on dividing 17 by 8 is 1, which is odd. A relation may be represented by a graph in which the nodes represent the underlying set and the arcs represent the ordered pairs of the relation. Figure 7.1.2(a) illustrates the graph representing the relation described above.

A value may be associated with each arc of a graph as in Figure 7.1.2(b). In that figure, the value associated with each arc is the remainder obtained by dividing the integer at the head of the arc by the integer at the tail. Such a graph, in which a value is associated with each arc, is called a *weighted graph* or a *network*. The value associated with an arc is called its *weight*.

We identify several primitive operations which are useful in dealing with graphs. The operation *join (a,b)* adds an arc from node *a* to node *b* if one does not already exist. *joinwt (a,b,x)* adds an arc from node *a* to node *b* with weight *x* in a weighted graph. *remv(a,b)* and *remvwt(a,b,x)* remove an arc from *a* to *b* if one exists (*remvwt* also sets *x* to its weight). Although we may also want to add or delete nodes from a graph, we postpone a discussion of these possibilities until a later section. The function *adjacent(a,b)* returns *true* if node *b* is adjacent to node *a*, and *false* otherwise.

A *path of length k* from node *a* to node *b* is defined as a sequence of $k+1$ nodes $n_1, n_2, \ldots, n_{k+1}$ such that $n_1 = a$, $n_{k+1} = b$, and $adjacent(n_i, n_i+1)$ is *true* for all *i* between 1 and *k*. If for some integer *r*, a path of length *k* exists between *a* and *b*, then there is a *path* from *a* to *b*. A path from a node to itself is called a *cycle*. If a graph contains a cycle, it is *cyclic*; otherwise, it is *acyclic*.

Consider the graph of Figure 7.1.3. There is a path of length 1 from *A* to *C*, two paths of length 2 from *B* to *G*, and a path of length 3 from *A* to *F*. There is no path from *B* to *C*. There are cycles from *B* to *B*, from *F* to *F*, and from *H* to *H*. Be sure that you can find all paths of length less than 9 and all cycles in the figure.

BASIC Representation of Graphs

Let us now turn to the question of how to represent a graph in BASIC. Suppose that the number of nodes in the graph is constant; that is, arcs may be added or deleted but nodes may not. A graph with five nodes could then be declared as follows:

```
10   N = 5
20   DIM INFO(N)
30   DIM ADJ(N,N)
```

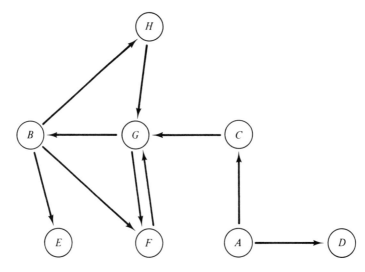

Figure 7.1.3

Each node of the graph is represented by an integer between 1 and N and the array element INFO(I) represents the information associated with node I. The value of ADJ(I,J) is either TRUE or FALSE (i.e., 1 or 0), depending on whether or not node J is adjacent to node I. The two-dimensional array ADJ is called an *adjacency matrix*. The *order* of such an adjacency matrix is defined as the number of nodes in the underlying graph (which equals N). In the case of a weighted graph, each arc can also be assigned information in a two-dimensional array declared by

40   DIM WEIGHT(N,N)

Frequently, the nodes of an unweighted graph are numbered from 1 to N and no information is associated with them. We are then interested only in the existence of arcs between nodes; we are not concerned with any other information about either the nodes or the arcs. In such cases, the graph could be declared simply by

20   DIM ADJ(N,N)

In effect, the graph is totally described by its adjacency matrix. We present the code for the primitive operations described above in the case where a graph is described by its adjacency matrix.

```
1000   'subroutine join
1010   'inputs: ADJ, N1, N2
1020   'outputs: ADJ
1030   'locals: none
1040   'add an arc from node N1 to N2
1050   ADJ(N1, N2) = TRUE
1060   RETURN
1070   'endsub
```

```
2000   'subroutine remv
2010   'inputs: ADJ, N1, N2
2020   'outputs: ADJ
2030   'locals: none
2040   'delete an arc from node N1 to node N2 if one exists
2050   ADJ(N1, N2) = FALSE
2060   RETURN
2070   'endsub


3000   'subroutine adjacent
3010   'inputs: ADJ, N1, N2
3020   'outputs: AJACENT
3030   'locals: none
3040   'tests whether there is an arc from node N1 to node N2
3050   IF ADJ(N1,N2) = TRUE THEN AJACENT = TRUE
                            ELSE AJACENT = FALSE
3060   RETURN
3070   'endsub
```

A weighted graph with a fixed number of nodes may be declared by

```
20   DIM ADJ(N,N)
30   DIM WEIGHT(N,N)
```

The routine *joinwt*, which adds an arc from N1 to N2 with weight WT, may be coded as follows:

```
4000   'subroutine joinwt
4010   'inputs: ADJ, WEIGHT, N1, N2, WT
4020   'outputs: ADJ, WEIGHT
4030   'locals: none
4040   ADJ(N1, N2) = TRUE
4050   WEIGHT(N1, N2) = WT
4060   RETURN
4070   'endsub
```

The routine *remvwt* is left to the reader as an exercise.

Path Matrices

There are two binary operations which are useful in dealing with values that are either *true* or *false*. These operations, **and** and **or**, are called **logical operations**. If x and y are variables with the values *true* or *false,* then x **and** y is *true* if and only if both x and y are *true*; otherwise, it is *false*. x **or** y is *true* if and only if either or both of x and y are *true*. Thus x **or** y is *false* if and only if both x and y

are *false*. The **and** operation is called **conjunction** and the **or** operation is called **disjunction**.

Let us assume that a graph of *n* nodes is completely described by its adjacency matrix, *adj* (i.e., no data are associated with the nodes and the graph is not weighted). Consider the logical expression *adj(i,k)* **and** *adj(k,j)*. Its value is *true* if and only if the values of both *adj(i,k)* and *adj(k,j)* are *true*, which implies that there is an arc from node *i* to node *k* and an arc from node *k* to node *j*. Thus *adj(i,k)* **and** *adj(k,j)* equals *true* if and only if there is a path of length two from *i* to *j* passing through *k*.

Now consider the expression

$(adj(i,1)$ **and** $adj(1,j))$ **or** $(adj(i,2)$ **and** $adj(2,j))$ **or** . . .
$$\text{or } (adj(i,n) \text{ } \textbf{and} \text{ } adj(n,j))$$

The value of this expression is *true* if and only if there is a path of length 2 from node *i* to node *j* either through node 1 or through node 2, . . . , or through node *n*. This is the same as saying that the expression evaluates to *true* if and only if there is some path of length 2 from node *i* to node *j*. Consider a two-dimensional array *adj₂* such that $adj_2(i,j)$ is the value of the expression above. *adj₂* is called the **path matrix of length 2** for the graph. The value of $adj_2(i,j)$ indicates whether or not there is a path of length 2 between *i* and *j*. If you are familiar with matrix multiplication, you may realize that *adj₂* is the product of *adj* with itself, with numerical multiplication replaced by conjunction and addition replaced by disjunction. *adj₂* is said to be the **Boolean product** of *adj* with itself.

Figure 7.1.4 illustrates this process. Figure 7.1.4(a) depicts a graph and its adjacency matrix in which *true* is represented by 1 and *false* is represented by 0. Figure 7.1.4(b) is the Boolean product of that matrix with itself and is thus the path matrix of length 2 for the graph. Convince yourself that a 1 appears in row *i*, column *j* of the matrix of Figure 7.1.4(b) if and only if there is a path of length 2 from node *i* to node *j* in the graph.

Similarly, define *adj₃*, the path matrix of length 3, as the Boolean product of *adj₂* with *adj*. $adj_3(i,j)$ equals *true* if and only if there is a path of length 3 from *i* to *j*. In general, to compute the path matrix of length *l*, form the Boolean product of the path matrix of length *l*−1 with the adjacency matrix. Figure 7.1.5 illustrates the matrices *adj₃* and *adj₄* of the graph in Figure 7.1.4(a).

We may write a routine *prod*, which computes the Boolean product C of an array A with an array B, as follows. A is assumed to be of size A1 by A2, B is assumed to be of size B1 by B2, and C is assumed to be of size A1 by B2.

```
6000   'subroutine prod
6010   'inputs: A, A1, A2, B, B1, B2
6020   'outputs: C
6030   'locals: CIJ, II, JJ, KK
```

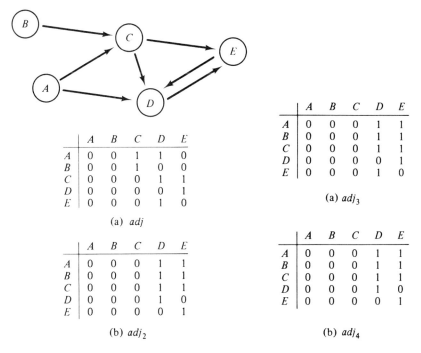

	A	B	C	D	E
A	0	0	1	1	0
B	0	0	1	0	0
C	0	0	0	1	1
D	0	0	0	0	1
E	0	0	0	1	0

(a) *adj*

	A	B	C	D	E
A	0	0	0	1	1
B	0	0	0	1	1
C	0	0	0	1	1
D	0	0	0	1	0
E	0	0	0	0	1

(b) *adj*₂

Figure 7.1.4

	A	B	C	D	E
A	0	0	0	1	1
B	0	0	0	1	1
C	0	0	0	1	1
D	0	0	0	0	1
E	0	0	0	1	0

(a) adj_3

	A	B	C	D	E
A	0	0	0	1	1
B	0	0	0	1	1
C	0	0	0	1	1
D	0	0	0	1	0
E	0	0	0	0	1

(b) adj_4

Figure 7.1.5

```
6040   IF A2 <> B1 THEN PRINT ''PRODUCT CANNOT BE FORMED'' : STOP
6050   FOR II = 1 TO A1
6060       FOR JJ = 1 TO B2
6070           CIJ = FALSE
6080           FOR KK = 1 TO A2
6090               IF A(II,KK) = TRUE AND B(KK,JJ) = TRUE
                          THEN CIJ = TRUE
6100           NEXT KK
6110           C(II,JJ) = CIJ
6120       NEXT JJ
6130   NEXT II
6140   RETURN
6150   'endsub
```

We may also write a routine that accepts an adjacency matrix, ADJ, its order N, and a positive integer K and computes the matrix ADJ_K in the array variable APROD, as follows:

```
7000   'subroutine adjprod
7010   'inputs: ADJ, K, N
7020   'outputs: APROD
```

```
7030    'locals: A, A1, A2, B, B1, B2, C, I, J, NUM
7040    'initialize B and C to ADJ
7050    FOR I = 1 TO N
7060        FOR J = 1 TO N
7070            B(I,J) = ADJ(I,J)
7080            C(I,J) = ADJ(I,J)
7090        NEXT J
7100    NEXT I
7110    'initialize the other inputs to the subroutine prod
7120    A1 = N
7130    A2 = N
7140    B1 = N
7150    B2 = N
7160    'call prod K-1 times
7170    NUM = 1
7180    IF NUM = K THEN GOTO 7280
7190        'set A to C
7200        FOR I = 1 TO N
7210            FOR J = 1 to N
7220                A(I,J) = C(I,J)
7230            NEXT J
7240        NEXT I
7250        GOSUB 6000: 'subroutine prod sets C equal to the Boolean
                        'product of A and B
7260        NUM = NUM + 1
7270    GOTO 7180
7280    'set APROD to C
7290    FOR I = 1 TO N
7300        FOR J = 1 TO N
7310            APROD(I,J) = C(I,J)
7320        NEXT J
7330    NEXT I
7340    RETURN
7350    'endsub
```

Transitive Closure

Assume that we want to know whether a path of length 3 or less exists between two nodes of a graph. If such a path exists between nodes i and j, it must be of length 1, 2, or 3. If there is a path of length 3 or less between nodes i and j, the value of

$$adj(i, j) \; \textbf{or} \; adj_2(i, j) \; \textbf{or} \; adj_3(i, j)$$

must be *true*. Figure 7.1.6 shows the matrix formed by *or*ing the matrices *adj*, *adj*$_2$, and *adj*$_3$. This matrix contains the value *true* (represented by the value 1 in the figure) in row *i*, column *j* if and only if there is a path of length 3 or less from node *i* to node *j*.

Suppose we wish to construct a matrix *path* such that *path*(*i*, *j*) equals *true* if and only if there is some path from node *i* to node *j* (of any length). Clearly,

$$path(i, j) \; = \; adj(i, j) \; \textbf{or} \; adj_2(i, j) \; \textbf{or} \ldots$$

However, the equation above cannot be used in computing *path* since the process that it describes is an infinite one. However, if the graph has *n* nodes, it must be true that

$$path(i, j) \; = \; adj(i, j) \; \textbf{or} \; adj_2(i, j) \; \textbf{or} \ldots \textbf{or} \; adj_n (i, j).$$

This is because if there is a path of length $m > n$ from *i* to *j* (such as *i*, i_2, i_3, . . . , i_m, *j*), there must be another path from *i* to *j* of length less than or equal to *n*. To see why this is so, note that since there are only *n* nodes in the graph, at least one node *k* must appear in the path twice. The path from *i* to *j* can be shortened by removing the cycle from *k* to *k*. This process is repeated until no two nodes in the path (except possibly *i* and *j*) are equal and therefore the path is of length *n* or less. Figure 7.1.7 illustrates the matrix *path* for the graph of Figure 7.1.4(a). The matrix *path* is often called the ***transitive closure*** of the matrix *adj*.

We may write a BASIC routine that accepts an adjacency matrix ADJ and computes its transitive closure PATH. This routine uses the auxiliary routine *prod*.

```
5000   'subroutine transclose
5010   'inputs: ADJ, N
5020   'outputs: PATH
5030   'locals: A, A1, A2, B, B1, B2, C, I, J, R
5040   'we assume a prior declaration
5050   'DIM A(N,N), B(N,N), C(N,N), PATH(N,N)
```

	A	B	C	D	E
A	0	0	1	1	1
B	0	0	1	1	1
C	0	0	0	1	1
D	0	0	0	1	1
E	0	0	0	1	1

	A	B	C	D	E
A	0	0	1	1	1
B	0	0	1	1	1
C	0	0	0	1	1
D	0	0	0	1	1
E	0	0	0	1	1

Figure 7.1.6

Figure 7.1.7   *path* = *adj* or *adj*$_2$ or *adj*$_3$ or *adj*$_4$ or *adj*$_5$.

```
5060   FOR I = 1 TO N
5070       FOR J = 1 TO N
5080           C(I,J) = ADJ(I,J)
5090           PATH(I,J) = ADJ(I,J)
5100           B(I,J) = ADJ(I,J)
5110       NEXT J
5120   NEXT I
5130   A1 = N: 'the variables A1, A2, B1, B2 are used by the routine prod
5140   A2 = N
5150   B1 = N
5160   B2 = N
5170   FOR R = 1 TO N - 1
5180       'R represents the number of times ADJ has been multiplied by
             'itself to obtain C
5190       'at this point PATH represents all paths of length R or less
5200       'reset C to the Boolean product of C and ADJ by setting A to C,
             'and calling the subroutine prod to reset C to the product of
             'A and B
5210       FOR I = 1 TO N
5220           FOR J = 1 TO N
5230               A(I,J) = C(I,J)
5240           NEXT J
5250       NEXT I
5260       GOSUB 6000 : 'subroutine prod sets C equal to the Boolean
                            'product of A and B
5270       'set PATH to PATH OR C
5280       FOR I = 1 TO N
5290           FOR J = 1 TO N
5300               IF C(I,J) = TRUE THEN PATH(I,J) = TRUE
5310           NEXT J
5320       NEXT I
5330   NEXT R
5340   RETURN
5350   'endsub
```

We can make some improvement in the efficiency of this program in many practical cases by checking whether PATH remains unchanged after a repetition of the FOR loop consisting of statements 5170–5330. However, in the interests of clarity and simplicity, we do not include this check.

Warshall's Algorithm

The method described above is quite inefficient. Let us see if we can find a more efficient method of computing *path*. Let us define the matrix $path_k$ such that

$path_k(i, j)$ equals true if and only if there is a path from node i to node j which does not pass through any nodes numbered higher than k (except, possibly, for i and j themselves). How can the value of $path_{k+1}(i,j)$ be obtained from $path_k$? Clearly, for any i or j such that $path_k(i,j) = true$, $path_{k+1}(i, j)$ must equal *true* (why?). The only situation in which $path_{k+1}(i, j)$ can equal *true* while $path_k(i,j)$ equals *false* is if there is a path from i to j passing through node $k+1$ but there is no path from i to j passing through only nodes 1 through k. But this means that there must be a path from i to $k+1$ passing through only nodes 1 through k and a similar path from $k+1$ to j. Thus $path_{k+1}(i, j) = true$ if and only if one of the following two conditions holds:

1. $path_k(i, j) = true$
2. $path_k(i,k+1) = true$ and $path_k(k+1,j) = true$

This means that $path_{k+1}(i, j)$ equals $path_k(i, j)$ **or** $(path_k(i,k+1)$ **and** $path_k(k+1,j))$. An algorithm to obtain the matrix $path_k$ from the matrix $path_{k-1}$ based on this observation follows:

```
for i = 1 to n
    for j = 1 to n
        pathₖ(i, j) = pathₖ₋₁(i, j) or (pathₖ₋₁(i,k) and pathₖ₋₁(k, j))
    next j
next i
```

This may be logically simplified and made more efficient as follows:

```
pathₖ = pathₖ₋₁
for i = 1 to n
    if pathₖ₋₁(i,k)
        then for j = 1 to n
                pathₖ(i, j) = pathₖ₋₁(i, j) or pathₖ₋₁(k, j)
             next j
    endif
next i
```

Clearly, $path_0(i,j) = adj(i,j)$ since the only way to go from node i to node j without passing through any other nodes is to go directly from i to j. Further, $path_n(i, j) = path(i, j)$ since any path from node i to node j passes through nodes numbered from 1 to n. The following BASIC routine may therefore be used to compute the transitive closure.

```
4000    'subroutine transclose
4010    'inputs: ADJ, N
4020    'outputs: PATH
4030    'locals: I, J, K
```

```
4040  'PATH is initialized to ADJ
4050  FOR I = 1 TO N
4060      FOR J = 1 TO N
4070          PATH(I,J) = ADJ(I,J)
4080      NEXT J
4090  NEXT I
4100  FOR K = 1 TO N
4110      'compute successive values of PATH
4120      FOR I = 1 TO N
4130          IF PATH(I,K) = FALSE THEN GOTO 4170
4140          FOR J = 1 TO N
4150              IF PATH(K,J) = TRUE THEN PATH(I,J) = TRUE
4160          NEXT J
4170      NEXT I
4180  NEXT K
4190  RETURN
4200  'endsub
```

This method of finding the transitive closure is often called **Warshall's algorithm**, after its discoverer.

EXERCISES

1. For the graph of Figure 7.1.1:
   (a) Find its adjacency matrix.
   (b) Find its path matrix using powers of the adjacency matrix.
   (c) Find its path matrix using Warshall's algorithm.
2. Draw a digraph to correspond to each of the following relations on the integers from 1 to 12:
   (a) x is related to y if $x-y$ is evenly divisible by 3.
   (b) x is related to y if $x + 10*y < x*y$.
   (c) x is related to y if the remainder on division of x by y is 2.
   Compute the adjacency and path matrices for each of these relations.
3. A node $n1$ is **reachable** from a node $n2$ in a graph if $n1$ equals $n2$ or there is a path from $n2$ to $n1$. Write a BASIC subroutine *reach* which accepts an adjacency matrix *adj* and two integers i and j, and determines if node j in the digraph is reachable from node i.
4. Write BASIC routines which, given an adjacency matrix and two nodes of a graph, compute
   (a) The number of paths of a given length existing between the two nodes.
   (b) The total number of paths existing between the two nodes.
   (c) The length of the shortest path between the two nodes.

5. A relation on a set S (and its corresponding digraph) is *reflexive* if every element of S is related to itself.
   (a) What must be true of a digraph if it represents a reflexive relation?
   (b) Give an example of a reflexive relation and draw its corresponding digraph.
   (c) What must be true of the adjacency matrix of a reflexive digraph?
   (d) Write a BASIC routine that accepts an adjacency matrix and determines if the digraph represents a reflexive relation.

6. A relation on a set of S (and its corresponding digraph) is *irreflexive* if no element of S is related to itself.
   (a) What must be true of a digraph if it represents an irreflexive relation?
   (b) Give an example of an irreflexive relation and draw its corresponding digraph.
   (c) Does there exist a relation that is neither reflexive nor irreflexive? (See Exercise 5.)
   (d) What must be true of the adjacency matrix of an irreflexive digraph?
   (e) Write a BASIC routine that accepts an adjacency matrix and determines if the digraph it represents is irreflexive.

7. A relation on a set S (and its corresponding digraph) is *symmetric* if for any two elements x and y in S such that x is related to y, y is also related to x.
   (a) What must be true of a digraph if it represents a symmetric relation?
   (b) Give an example of a symmetric relation and draw its digraph.
   (c) What must be true of the adjacency matrix of a symmetric digraph?
   (d) Write a BASIC routine that accepts an adjacency matrix and determines if the digraph it represents is symmetric.

8. A relation on a set S (and its corresponding digraph) is *antisymmetric* if for any two distinct elements x and y in S such that x is related to y, y is not related to x.
   (a) What must be true of a digraph if it represents an antisymmetric relation?
   (b) Give an example of an antisymmetric relation and its digraph.
   (c) Does there exist a relation that is both symmetric and antisymmetric? (See Exercise 7.)
   (d) What must be true of the adjacency matrix of an antisymmetric digraph?
   (e) Write a BASIC routine that accepts an adjacency matrix and determines if the digraph it represents is antisymmetric.

9. A relation on a set S (and its corresponding digraph) is *transitive* if for any three elements x, y, and z in S such that if x is related to y and y is related to z, it is also true that x is related to z.
   (a) What must be true of a digraph if it represents a transitive relation?
   (b) Give an example of a transitive relation and draw its digraph.
   (c) What must be true of the Boolean product of the adjacency matrix of a transitive digraph with itself?
   (d) Write a BASIC routine that accepts an adjacency matrix and determines if the digraph it represents is transitive.
   (e) Prove that the transitive closure of any digraph is transitive.
   (f) Prove that the smallest transitive digraph which includes all nodes and arcs of a given digraph is the transitive closure of that digraph.

10. Given a digraph, prove that it is possible to renumber its nodes so that the resultant adjacency matrix is lower triangular (see Exercise 1.2.13) if and only if the digraph is acyclic. Write a BASIC program *lowtri* which accepts an adjacency matrix ADJ of an acyclic graph and creates a lower triangular adjacency matrix LTADJ which represents the same graph. The program should also set the values of a one-dimensional array PERM of size N so that PERM(I) is set to the new number assigned to the node that was numbered I in the matrix ADJ.

2. A FLOW PROBLEM

In this section we consider a real-world problem and illustrate a solution that uses a weighted graph. There are a number of formulations of this problem whose solutions carry over to a wide range of applications. We present one such formulation here and refer the reader to the literature for alternative versions.

Assume a water pipe system as in Figure 7.2.1(a). Each arc represents a pipe and the number above each arc represents the capacity of that pipe in gallons per minute. The nodes represent points at which pipes are joined and water is transferred from one pipe to another. Two nodes, S and T, are designated as a *source* of water and a *user* of water (or a *sink*), respectively. This means that water originating at S must be carried through the pipe system to T. Water may flow through a pipe in only one direction (pressure-sensitive valves may be used to prevent water from flowing backward) and there are no pipes entering S or leaving T. A weighted directed graph, as in Figure 7.2.1(a), is an ideal data structure to model the situation.

We would like to maximize the amount of water flowing from the source to the sink. Although the source may be able to produce water at a prodigious rate and the sink may be able to consume water at a comparable rate, the pipe system may not have the capacity to carry it all from the source to the sink. Thus the limiting factor of the entire system is the pipe capacity. Many other real-world problems are similar in nature. The system could be an electrical network, a railway system, a communications network, or any other distribution system in which one wants to maximize the amount of an item being delivered from one point to another.

Define a *capacity function*, $c(a,b)$, where a and b are nodes, as follows: if *adjacent* (a,b) is true (i.e., if there is a pipe from a to b), then $c(a,b)$ is the capacity of the pipe from a to b. If there is no pipe from a to b, then $c(a,b) = 0$. At any point in the operation of the system, a given amount of water (possibly 0) flows through each pipe. Define a *flow function*, $f(a,b)$, where a and b are nodes, as 0 if b is not adjacent to a, and as the amount of water flowing through the pipe from a to b otherwise. Clearly, $f(a,b) \geq 0$ for all nodes a and b. Furthermore, $f(a,b) \leq c(a,b)$ for all nodes a and b, since a pipe may not carry more water than its capacity. Let v be the amount of water that flows through the system from S to T. Then the amount of water leaving S through all pipes equals the

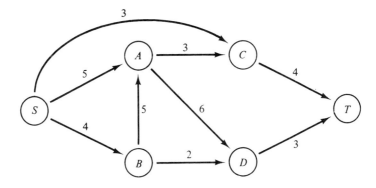

(a) A flow problem.

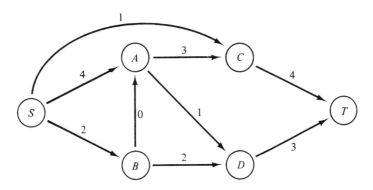

(b) A flow function.

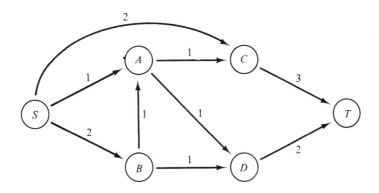

(c) A flow function.

Figure 7.2.1

amount of water entering T through all pipes and both these amounts equal v. This can be stated by the equality

$$\sum_{x \,\epsilon\, \text{nodes}} f(S,x) = v = \sum_{x \,\epsilon\, \text{nodes}} f(x,T)$$

No node other than S can produce water, and no node other than T can absorb water. Thus the amount of water leaving any node other than S or T is equal to the amount of water entering that node. This can be stated by

$$\sum_{y \,\epsilon\, \text{nodes}} f(x,y) = \sum_{y \,\epsilon\, \text{nodes}} f(y,x) \qquad \text{for all nodes } x \neq S, T.$$

Define the *inflow* of a node x as the total flow entering x and the *outflow* as the total flow leaving x. The conditions above may be rewritten as

$$\text{outflow}(S) = \text{inflow}(T) = v$$
$$\text{inflow}(x) = \text{outflow}(x) \qquad \text{for all } x \neq S,T$$

Several flow functions may exist for a given graph and capacity function. Figure 7.2.1(b) and (c) illustrate two possible flow functions for the graph of Figure 7.2.1(a). Make sure that you understand why both of them are valid flow functions and why both satisfy the equations and inequalities above.

We wish to find a flow function that maximizes the value of v, the amount of water going from S to T. Such a flow function is called *optimal*. Clearly, the flow function of Figure 7.2.1(b) is better than the one of Figure 7.2.1(c), since v equals 7 in the former but only 5 in the latter. See if you can find a flow function that is better than the one of Figure 7.2.1(b).

One valid flow function can be achieved by setting $f(a,b)$ to 0 for all nodes a and b. Of course, this flow function is least optimal since no water flows from S to T. It may be possible to improve a given flow function so that the flow from S to T is increased. However, the improved version must satisfy all the conditions for a valid flow function. In particular, if the flow entering any node (except for S or T) is increased or decreased, the flow leaving that node must be increased or decreased correspondingly. The strategy for producing an optimal flow function is to begin with the zero flow function and to improve upon it successively until an optimal flow function is produced.

Improving a Flow Function

Given a flow function f, there are two ways to improve upon it. One way consists of finding a path $S = x_1, x_2, \ldots, x_n = T$ from S to T such that the flow along each arc in the path is strictly less than its capacity [i.e., $f(x_{k-1}, x_k) < c(x_{k-1}, x_k)$ for all k between 2 and n]. The flow can be increased on each arc in such a path by the minimum value of $c(x_{k-1}, x_k) - f(x_{k-1}, x_k)$ for all k between 2 and n [so that when the flow has been increased along the entire path there is at least one arc $\langle x_{k-1}, x_k \rangle$ in the path for which $f(x_{k-1}, x_k) = c(x_{k-1}, x_k)$ and through which the flow may not be increased].

This may be illustrated by the graph of Figure 7.2.2(a), which gives the capacity and the current flow, respectively, for each arc. There are two paths from S to T with positive flow [(S,A,C,T) and (S,B,D,T)]. However, each of these paths contains one arc ($\langle A,C \rangle$ and $\langle B,D \rangle$) in which the flow equals the capacity. Thus the flow along these paths may not be improved. However, the path (S,A,D,T) is such that the capacity of each arc in the path is greater than its current flow. The maximum amount by which the flow can be increased along this path is 1 since the flow along arc $\langle D,T \rangle$ cannot exceed 3. The resulting flow function is shown in Figure 7.2.2(b). The total flow from S to T has been increased from 5 to 6. To see that the result is still a valid flow function, note that for each node (except T) whose inflow is increased, the outflow is increased by the same amount.

Are there any other paths whose flow can be improved? In this example, you should satisfy yourself that there are not. However, given the graph of Figure 7.2.2(a) we could have chosen to improve the path (S,B,A,D,T). The resulting flow function is illustrated in Figure 7.2.2(c). This function also provides for a net flow of 6 from S to T and is therefore neither better nor worse than the flow function of Figure 7.2.2(b).

Even if there is no path whose flow may be improved, there may be another method of improving the net flow from the source to the sink. This is illustrated by Figure 7.2.3. In Figure 7.2.3(a) there is no path from S to T whose flow may be improved. But if the flow from X to Y is reduced, the flow from X to T can be increased. To compensate for the decrease in the inflow to Y, the flow from S to Y could be increased. The result of the entire process is an increase in the net flow from S to T. The flow from X to Y can be redirected to T as shown in Figure 7.2.3(b) and the net flow from S to T can thereby be increased from 4 to 7.

We may generalize this second method as follows. Suppose that there is a path from S to some node y, a path from some node x to T, and a path from x to y with positive flow. Then the flow along the path from x to y may be reduced and the flows from x to T and from S to y may be increased by the same amount. This amount is the minimum of the flow from x to y and the differences between capacities and flows in the paths from S to y and x to T.

These two methods may be combined by proceeding through the graph from S to T as follows. The amount of water emanating from S to T can be increased by any amount (since we have assumed no limit on the amount that can be produced by the source) only if the pipes from S to T can carry the increase. Suppose that the pipe capacity from S to x allows the amount of water entering x to be increased by an amount a. Then if a node y is adjacent to x (i.e., there is an arc $\langle x,y \rangle$), the amount of water emanating from x to T can be increased by the minimum of a and the unused capacity of arc $\langle x,y \rangle$. This is an application of the first method. Similarly, if node x is adjacent to some node y (i.e., there is an arc $\langle y,x \rangle$), the amount of water emanating from y toward T can be increased by

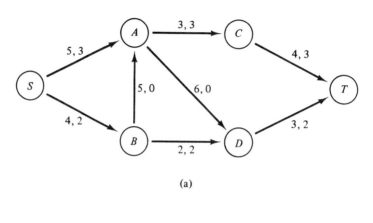

(a)

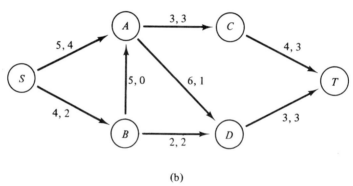

(b)

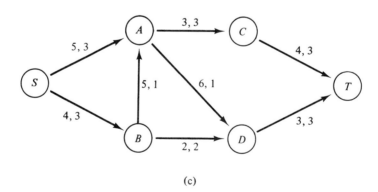

(c)

Figure 7.2.2 Increasing the flow in a graph.

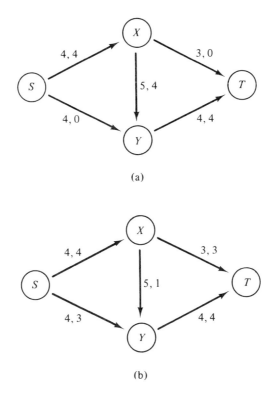

(a)

(b)

Figure 7.2.3   Increasing the flow in a graph.

the minimum of a and the existing flow from y to x. This can be done by reducing the flow from y to x as in the second method. The resultant decrease in inflow to x can be remedied since the capacity from S to x allows an increase in inflow to x of up to a. Proceeding in this fashion from S to T, the amount by which the flow to T may be increased can be determined.

Define a *semipath* from S to T as a sequence of nodes $S = x, x_2, \ldots, x_n = T$ such that, for all $1 < i \leq n$, either $<x_{i-1}, x_i>$ or $<x_i, x_{i-1}>$ is an arc. Using the technique above, we may describe an algorithm to discover a semipath from S to T such that the flow to each node in the semipath may be increased. This is done by building on already recognized partial semipaths from S. If the last node in a recognized partial semipath from S is x, the algorithm considers extending it to any node y such that either $<x,y>$ or $<y,x>$ is an arc. The partial semipath is extended to y only if the extension can be made in such a way that the inflow to y can be increased. Once a partial semipath has been extended to a node y, that node is removed from consideration as an extension of some other partial semipath. (This is because at this point we are trying to discover a single semipath from S to T.) The algorithm, of course, keeps track of the amount by which the inflow to y may be increased and whether its increase is due to consideration of the arc $<x,y>$ or $<y,x>$.

This process continues until some partial semipath from S has been completed by extending it to T. The algorithm then proceeds backward along that semipath, adjusting all flows until S is reached. (This will be illustrated shortly with an example.) The entire process is then repeated in an attempt to discover yet another such semipath from S to T. When no partial semipath may be successfully extended, the flow cannot be increased and the existing flow is optimal. (You are asked to prove this as an exercise.)

An Example

Let us illustrate this process with an example. Consider the arcs and capacities of the weighted graph of Figure 7.2.4. We begin by assuming a flow of 0 and attempt to discover an optimal flow. Figure 7.2.4(a) illustrates the initial situation. The two numbers along each arc represent the capacity and current flow, respectively. We may extend a semipath from S to (S,X) and (S,Z), respectively. The flow from S to X may be increased by 4 and the flow from S to Z may be increased by 6. The semipath (S,X) may be extended to (S,X,W) and (S,X,Y) with corresponding increases of flow to W and Y of 3 and 4, respectively. The semipath (S,X,Y) may be extended to (S,X,Y,T) with an increase of flow to T of 4. [Note that at this point we could have chosen to extend (S,X,W) to (S,X,W,T). Similarly, we could have extended (S,Z) to (S,Z,Y) rather than (S,X) to (S,X,W) and (S,X,Y). These decisions are arbitrary.]

Since we have reached T by the semipath (S,X,Y,T) with a net increase of 4, we increase the flow along each forward arc of the semipath by this amount. The results are depicted in Figure 7.2.4(b).

We now repeat the process above with the flow of Figure 7.2.4(b). (S) may be extended to (S,Z) only, since the flow in arc $<S,X>$ is already at capacity. The net increase to Z through this semipath is 6. (S,Z) may be extended to (S,Z,Y), yielding a net increase of 4 to Y. (S,Z,Y) cannot be extended to (S,Z,Y,T), since the flow in arc $<Y,T>$ is at capacity. However, it can be extended to (S,Z,Y,X) with a net increase to node X of 4. (Note that since this semipath includes a backward arc $<Y,X>$, it implies a possible reduction in the flow from X to Y of up to 4.) The semipath (S,Z,Y,X) may be extended to (S,Z,Y,X,W) with a net increase of 3 (the unused capacity of $<X,W>$) to W. This semipath may then be extended to (S,Z,Y,X,W,T) with a net increase of 3 in the flow to T. Since we have reached T with an increase of 3, we proceed backward along this semipath. Since $<W,T>$ and $<X,W>$ are forward arcs, their flow may each be increased by 3. Since $<Y,X>$ is a backward arc, the flow along $<X,Y>$ is reduced by 3. Since $<Z,Y>$ and $<S,Z>$ are forward arcs, their flow may be increased by 3. This results in the flow shown in Figure 7.2.4(c).

We then attempt to repeat the process. (S) may be extended to (S,Z) with an increase of 3 to Z, (S,Z) may be extended to (S,Z,Y) with an increase of 1 to Y, and (S,Z,Y) may be extended to (S,Z,Y,X) with an increase of 1 to X. However,

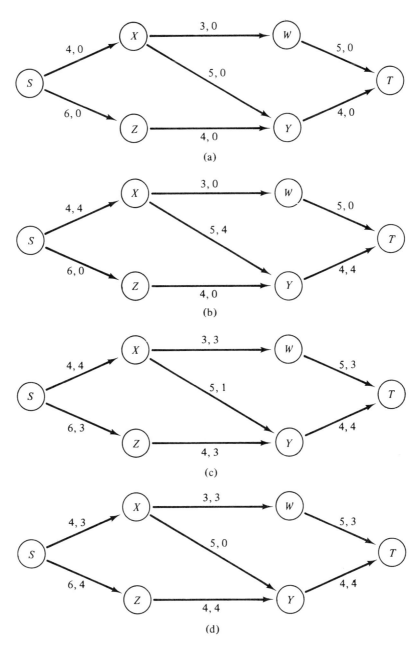

Figure 7.2.4   Producing an optimum flow.

since arcs $<S,X>$, $<Y,T>$, and $<X,W>$ are at capacity, no semipath may be extended further and an optimum flow has been found. Note that this optimum flow need not be unique. Figure 7.2.4(d) illustrates another optimum flow for the same graph, which was obtained from Figure 7.2.4(a) by considering the semipaths (S,X,W,T) and (S,Z,Y,T).

The Algorithm and Program

Given a weighted graph (an adjacency matrix and a capacity matrix) with a source S and a sink T, the algorithm to produce an optimum flow function for that graph may be outlined as follows:

1. initialize the flow function to 0 at each arc
2. attempt to find a semipath from S to T which increases the flow to T by $a > 0$
3. *if* a semipath cannot be found *then return*
4. increase the flow to each node (except S) in the semipath by a
5. *goto* step 2

   Of course, the heart of the algorithm lies in step 2. Once a node has been placed on a partial semipath, it can no longer be used to extend a different semipath. Thus the algorithm uses an array *opath* such that *opath(node)* is *true* or *false* depending on whether or not *node* is on some semipath. It also needs an indication of which nodes are at the ends of partial semipaths so that such partial semipaths can be extended by adding adjacent nodes. *epath(node)* indicates whether or not *node* is at the end of a partial semipath. For each node on a semipath, the algorithm must keep track of what node precedes it on that semipath and the direction of the arc. *precede(node)* points to the node that precedes *node* on its semipath and *forward(node)* has the value *true* if and only if the arc is from *precede(node)* to *node*. *improve(node)* indicates the amount by which the flow to *node* may be increased along its semipath. The algorithm that attempts to find a semipath from S to T along which the flow may be increased may be written as follows. [We assume that $c(x,y)$ is the capacity of the arc from x to y and that $f(x,y)$ is the current flow from x to y.]

set *epath(node)* and *opath(node)* to *false* for all nodes
epath(S) = *true*
opath(S) = *true*
'compute maximum flow from S which the arcs can carry
improve(S) = sum of $c(S,node)$ over all nodes *node*
while (*opath(T)* = *false*) **and** (there exists a node *nd* such that *epath(nd)* = *true*) **do**
    epath(nd) = *false*

while there exists a node *i* such that (*adjacent*(*nd*,*i*) = *true*
                      and *opath*(*i*) = *false* **and** *f*(*nd*,*i*) < *c*(*nd*,*i*)) **do**
  'the flow from *nd* to *i* may be increased; place *i* on the semipath
  opath(*i*) = *true*
  epath(*i*) = *true*
  precede(*i*) = *nd*
  forward(*i*) = *true*
  temp = *c*(*nd*,*i*) − *f*(*nd*,*i*)
  if *improve*(*nd*) < *temp*
    then *improve*(*i*) = *improve*(*nd*)
    else *improve*(*i*) = *temp*
  endif
endwhile
while there exists a node *i* such that (*adjacent*(*i*,*nd*) = *true*
                      and *opath*(*i*) = *false* **and** *f*(*i*,*nd*)>0) **do**
  'the flow from *i* to *nd* may be decreased; place *i* on the semipath
  opath(*i*) = *true*
  epath(*i*) = *true*
  precede(*i*) = *nd*
  forward(*i*) = *false*
  if *improve*(*nd*) < *f*(*i*,*nd*)
    then *improve*(*i*) = *improve*(*nd*)
    else *improve*(*i*) = *f*(*i*,*nd*)
  endif
endwhile
endwhile
if *opath*(*T*) = *true*
  then we have found a semipath from *S* to *T*
  else the flow is already optimal
endif

Once a semipath from *S* to *T* has been found, the flow may be increased along that semipath (line 4 above) by the following algorithm:

$$a = improve(T)$$
$$nd = T$$
while *nd* <> *S* **do**
  pd = *precede*(*nd*)
  if *forward*(*nd*) = *true*
    then *f*(*pd*,*nd*) = *f*(*pd*,*nd*) + *a*
    else *f*(*nd*,*pd*) = *f*(*nd*,*pd*) − *a*
  endif
  nd = *pd*
endwhile

This method of solving the flow problem is known as the ***Ford–Fulkerson algorithm***, after its discoverers.

Let us now convert these algorithms into a BASIC routine *maxflow* where the array CAP is an input variable representing a capacity function defined on a weighted graph and declared by

20   DIM CAP (N,N): *'N is the number of nodes in the graph*

S and T are inputs representing the source and sink, the two-dimensional array FLOW is an ouput variable representing the maximum flow function, and TTLFLOW is an output variable representing the amount of flow from S to T under the flow function represented by FLOW.

The previous algorithms may be converted easily into BASIC programs. Two arrays EPATH and OPATH whose elements hold the values TRUE or FALSE are required as well as two integer arrays PRECEDE and IMPROVE. The array *forward* of the algorithm may be combined with the array *precede* to produce the BASIC array PRECEDE, in which PRECEDE(ND) is positive or negative depending on whether *forward(nd)* is *true* or *false* in the algorithm. The absolute value of PRECEDE(ND) is the node that precedes ND on a semipath. Similarly, the question of whether J is adjacent to I can be answered by checking whether or not CAP(I,J) = 0.

We present the routine here as a straightforward implementation of the algorithms.

```
1000   'subroutine maxflow
1010   'inputs: CAP, N, S, T
1020   'outputs: FLOW, TTLFLOW
1030   'locals: A, EPATH, I, IMPROVE, J, K, ND, OPATH, PD, PRECEDE
1040   'initialize
1050   FOR I = 1 TO N
1060       FOR J = 1 TO N
1070           FLOW(I,J) = 0
1080       NEXT J
1090   NEXT I
1100   TTLFLOW = 0
1110   'attempt to find a semipath from S to T
1120   IMPROVE(S) = 0
1130   FOR K = 1 TO N
1140       EPATH(K) = FALSE
1150       OPATH(K) = FALSE
1160       IMPROVE(S) = IMPROVE(S) + CAP(S,K)
1170   NEXT K
1180   EPATH(S) = TRUE
```

```
1190   OPATH(S) = TRUE
1200   IF OPATH(T) = TRUE THEN GOTO 1400: 'a semipath has been found
1210       FOR ND = 1 TO N
1220           IF EPATH(ND) = TRUE THEN GOTO 1250
1230       NEXT ND
1240   GOTO 1400
1250       EPATH(ND) = FALSE
1260       FOR I = 1 TO N: 'combine the two loops of the algorithm into one
1270           IF OPATH(I) = TRUE OR FLOW(ND,I) = CAP(ND,I)
                   THEN GOTO 1330
1280           OPATH(I) = TRUE
1290           EPATH(I) = TRUE
1300           PRECEDE(I) = ND
1310           TEMP = CAP(ND,I) − FLOW(ND,I)
1320           IF IMPROVE(ND) < TEMP THEN IMPROVE(I) = IMPROVE(ND)
                                          ELSE IMPROVE(I) = TEMP
1330           IF OPATH(I) = TRUE OR FLOW(I,ND) = 0 THEN GOTO 1380
1340           OPATH(I) = TRUE
1350           EPATH(I) = TRUE
1360           PRECEDE(I) = −ND
1370           IF IMPROVE(ND) < FLOW(I,ND)
                   THEN IMPROVE(I) = IMPROVE(ND)
                   ELSE IMPROVE(I) = FLOW(I,ND)
1380       NEXT I
1390   GOTO 1200
1400   'if no semipath has been found, the flow is optimal
1410   IF OPATH(T) = FALSE THEN RETURN
1420   A = IMPROVE(T)
1430   TTLFLOW = TTLFLOW + A
1440   ND = T
1450   IF ND = S THEN GOTO 1110: 'attempt to find another semipath from S to T
1460       PD = PRECEDE(ND)
1470       IF PD > 0 THEN FLOW(PD,ND) = FLOW(PD,ND) + A
                   ELSE PD = −PD : FLOW(ND,PD) = FLOW(ND,PD) − A
1480       ND = PD
1490   GOTO 1450
1500   'endsub
```

For large graphs with many nodes, the arrays IMPROVE and EPATH may be prohibitively expensive in terms of space. Furthermore, a search through all nodes to find one such that EPATH(ND) = TRUE may be very inefficient in terms of time. An alternative solution might be to note that the value of IMPROVE is required only for those nodes ND such that

EPATH(ND) = TRUE. Those graph nodes that are at the end of semipaths may be kept in a list whose nodes are declared by

```
10   DIM GRAPHNODE(100)
20   DIM IMPROVE(100)
30   DIM NXT(100)
```

When a node that is at the end of a semipath is required, remove the first element from the list. We can similarly dispense with the array PRECEDE by maintaining a separate list of nodes for each semipath. However, this suggestion is of dubious value in saving space since almost all nodes will be on some semipath. You are invited to write the routine *maxflow* as an exercise, using these suggestions to save time and space.

EXERCISES

1. Find the maximum flows for the graphs in Figure 7.2.1 using the Ford–Fulkerson method (the capacities are shown next to the arcs).
2. Given a graph and a capacity function as in this section, define a **cut** as any set of nodes x containing S but not T. Define the **capacity of the cut x** as the sum of the capacities of all the arcs leaving the set x minus the sum of the capacities of all the arcs entering x.
   (a) Show that for any flow function f, the value of the total flow v is less than or equal to the capacity of any cut.
   (b) Show that equality in part (a) is achieved when the flow is maximum and the cut has minimum capacity.
3. Prove that the Ford–Fulkerson algorithm produces an optimum flow function, using the statements of Exercise 2.
4. Rewrite the routine *maxflow* using a linked list to contain nodes at the end of semi-paths, as suggested in the text.
5. Assume that in addition to a capacity for every arc, there is also a cost function, *cost*. *cost* is the cost of each unit of flow from node a to node b. Modify the program of the text to produce the flow function that maximizes the total flow from source to sink at the lowest cost (i.e., if there are two flow functions, both of which produce the same maximum flow, choose the one with the least cost).
6. Assuming a cost function as in Exercise 5, write a program to produce the maximum cheapest flow, that is, a flow function such that the total flow divided by the cost of the flow is greatest.
7. A **probabilistic** directed graph is one in which a probability function associates a probability with each arc. The sum of the probabilities of all arcs emanating from any node is 1. Consider an acyclic probabilistic digraph representing a tunnel system. A man is placed at one node in the tunnel. At each node, he chooses to take a particular arc to

another node with probability given by the probability function. Write a program to compute, for each node of the graph, the probability that the man passes through that node. What if the graph were cyclic?

8. Write a BASIC program that reads the following information about an electrical network:
   (a) N, the number of wires in the network,
   (b) the amount of current entering through the first wire and leaving through the Nth,
   (c) the resistance of each of the wires 2 through N-1,
   (d) a set of ordered pairs <I,J> indicating that wire I is connected to wire J and that electricity flows through wire I to wire J.

   The program should compute the amount of current flowing through each of wires 2 through N-1 by applying Kirchhoff's law and Ohm's law. Kirchhoff's law states that the amount of current flowing into a junction equals the amount leaving a junction. Ohm's law states that if two paths exist between two junctions the sum of the currents times the resistances over all wires in the first path is equal to the sum of the currents times the resistances over all the wires in the second path.

3. THE LINKED REPRESENTATION OF GRAPHS

The adjacency matrix representation of a graph is frequently inadequate because it requires advance knowledge of the number of nodes. If a graph must be constructed in the course of solving a problem, or if it must be updated dynamically as the program proceeds, a new matrix must be created for each addition or deletion of a node. This is extremely dificult in BASIC and prohibitively inefficient, especially in a real-world situation, where a graph may have 100 or more nodes. Further, even if a graph has very few arcs, so that the adjacency matrix (and the weight matrix for a weighted graph) consists mostly of zeros, space must be reserved for every possible arc between two nodes whether or not such an arc exists. If the graph contains n nodes, a total of n^2 locations must be used.

As you might expect, the remedy is to use a linked structure, allocating and freeing nodes from an available pool. This is similar to the methods used to represent dynamic binary and general trees. In the linked representation of trees, each allocated node corresponds to a tree node. This is possible because each tree node is the son of only one other tree node and is therefore contained in only a single list of sons. However, in a graph an arc may exist between any two graph nodes. It is possible to keep an adjacency list for every node in a graph (such a list contains all nodes adjacent to a given node) and a node might find itself on many different adjacency lists (one for each node to which it is adjacent). But this requires that each allocated node contain a variable number of pointers, depending on the number of nodes to which it is adjacent. This solution is clearly impractical, as we saw in attempting to represent general trees with nodes containing pointers to each of its sons.

An alternative is to construct a multilinked structure in the following way.

The nodes of the graph (hereafter referred to as **graph nodes**) are represented by a linked list of **header nodes**. Each such header node contains three fields: *info, nxtnode,* and *arcptr*. If *p* points to a header node representing a graph node *a*, then *info(p)* contains any information associated with graph node *a*. *nxtnode(p)* is a pointer to the header node representing the next graph node in the header node list, if any. Each header node is at the head of a list of nodes of a second type called **list nodes** or **arc nodes**. This list is called the **adjacency list**. Each node on an adjacency list represents an arc of the graph. *arcptr(p)* points to the adjacency list of nodes representing the arcs emanating from the graph node *a*.

Each node on an adjacency list contains two fields: *ndptr* and *nexarc*. If *q* points to a list node representing an arc $<a,b>$, *ndptr(q)* is a pointer to the header node representing the graph node *b*. *nexarc(q)* points to a list node representing the next arc emanating from graph node *a*, if any. Each list node is contained in a single adjacency list representing all arcs emanating from a given graph node. The term **allocated nodes** is used to refer to both header and list nodes of a multilinked structure representing a graph.

Figure 7.3.1 illustrates this representation. If each graph node carries some information but (since the graph is not weighted) the arcs do not, two types of allocated nodes are needed: one for header nodes (graph nodes) and the other for adjacency list nodes (arcs). These are illustrated in Figure 7.3.1(a). Each header node contains an *info* field and two pointers. The first of these is to the adjacency list of arcs emanating from the graph node, and the second is to the next header node in the list of graph nodes. Each arc node contains two pointers, one to the next arc node in the adjacency list and the other to the header node representing the graph node that terminates the arc. Figure 7.3.1(b) depicts a graph and 7.3.1(c) its linked representation.

Note that header nodes and list nodes have different formats and must be represented by different sets of BASIC variables, which in turn necessitates keeping two distinct available lists. Even in the case of a weighted graph in which each list node contains an *info* field to hold the weight of an arc, if the information in the header nodes is not numeric, two different node formats may be necessary. However, for simplicity we modify the representation slightly and make the assumption that both header and list nodes have the same format, each containing two pointers and a single integer information field. These nodes are declared by

```
10   MAXNODES = 100
20   DIM INFO(MAXNODES)
30   DIM PNT(MAXNODES)
40   DIM NXT(MAXNODES)
```

If P points to a header node, *node*(P) represents a graph node A. INFO(P) represents the information associated with the graph node A, NXT(P) points to the next graph node in the list of graph nodes, and PNT(P) points to the first list node representing an arc emanating from A. If P points to a list node, *node*(P) represents an arc $<A,B>$, INFO(P) represents the weight of the arc, NXT(P)

A sample header node representing a graph node.　　　A sample list node representing an arc.

(a)

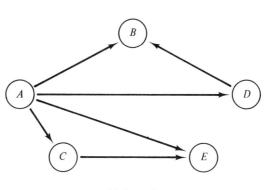

(b) A graph.

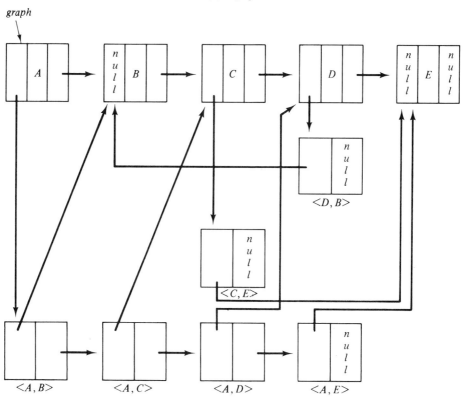

(c) Linked representation of a graph.

Figure 7.3.1　Linked representation of a graph.

points to the next arc emanating from *A* in the adjacency list of *A*, and PNT(P) points to the header node representing the graph node *B*. We use this implementation in the remainder of this section and assume the existence of routines *getnode* and *freenode*.

We now present the implementation of the primitive graph operations using the linked representation. The subroutine *joinwt* accepts two pointers P and Q to two header nodes and creates an arc between them with weight WT. If an arc already exists between the nodes, the weight of that arc is set to WT.

```
1000   'subroutine joinwt
1010   'inputs: P,Q, WT
1020   'outputs: none
1030   'locals: GTNODE, R, R2
1040   'search the list of arcs emanating
       'from node(P) for an arc to node(Q)
1050   R2 = 0
1060   R = PNT(P)
1070   IF R = 0 THEN GOTO 1120
1080      IF PNT(R) = Q THEN INFO(R) = WT : RETURN
1090      R2 = R
1100      R = NXT(R)
1110   GOTO 1070
1120   'an arc from node(P) to node(Q) does not exist
       'such an arc must be created
1130   GOSUB 6000: 'subroutine getnode sets the variable GTNODE
1140   R = GTNODE
1150   PNT(R) = Q
1160   NXT(R) = 0
1170   INFO(R) = WT
1180   IF R2 = 0 THEN PNT(P) = R
                    ELSE NXT(R2) = R
1190   RETURN
1200   'ensub
```

We leave the implementation of the operation *join* for an unweighted graph as an exercise for the reader. The subroutine *remv* accepts two pointers P and Q to two header nodes and removes the arc between them, if one exists.

```
2000   'subroutine remv
2010   'inputs: P, Q
2020   'outputs: none
2030   'locals: FRNODE, R, R2
2040   R2 = 0
2050   R = PNT(P)
```

```
2060   IF R = 0 THEN RETURN: 'no arc exists from node(P) to node(Q)
2070   IF PNT(R) <> Q THEN R2 = R: R = NXT(R): GOTO 2060
2080   'PNT(R) equals Q so that
       'R points to an arc from node(P) to node(Q)
2090   IF R2 = 0 THEN PNT(P) = NXT(R)
                 ELSE NXT(R2) = NXT(R)
2100   FRNODE = R
2110   GOSUB 7000: 'subroutine freenode accepts the variable FRNODE
2120   RETURN
2130   'endsub
```

We leave the implementation of the operation *remvwt*, which sets X to the weight of the arc from the graph node represented by *node*(P) to the graph node represented by *node*(Q) in a weighted graph and then removes the arc from the graph, as an exercise for the reader.

The subroutine *adjacent* accepts two pointers P and Q to two header nodes and determines whether *node*(Q) is adjacent to *node*(P).

```
3000   'subroutine adjacent
3010   'inputs: P, Q
3020   'outputs: AJACENT
3030   'locals: R
3040   R = PNT(P)
3050   IF R = 0 THEN GOTO 3090
3060      IF PNT(R) = Q THEN AJACENT = TRUE : RETURN
3070      R = NXT(R)
3080   GOTO 3050
3090   AJACENT = FALSE
3100   RETURN
3110   'endsub
```

Another useful subroutine is *findnode*, which returns a pointer to a header node with information field X if such a header node exists, and returns the null pointer (0) otherwise.

```
4000   'subroutine findnode
4010   'inputs: GRAPH, X
4020   'outputs: FINDNODE
4030   'locals: PP
4040   PP = GRAPH
4050   IF PP = 0 THEN FINDNODE = PP: RETURN
4060      IF INFO(PP) = X THEN FINDNODE = PP: RETURN
4070      PP = NXT(PP)
4080   GOTO 4050
4090   'endsub
```

The subroutine *addnode* adds a node with information field X to a graph and returns a pointer to that node.

```
5000   'subroutine addnode
5010   'inputs: GRAPH, X
5020   'outputs: ADDNODE, GRAPH
5030   'locals: GTNODE, PP
5040   GOSUB 6000: 'subroutine getnode sets the variable GTNODE
5050   PP = GTNODE
5060   INFO(PP) = X
5070   PNT(PP) = 0
5080   NXT(PP) = GRAPH
5090   GRAPH = PP
5100   ADDNODE = PP
5110   RETURN
5120   'endsub
```

The reader should be aware of another important difference between the adjacency matrix representation and the linked representation of graphs. Implicit in the matrix representation is the ability to traverse a row or column of the matrix. Traversing a row is equivalent to identifying all arcs emanating from a given node. This can be done efficiently in the linked representation by traversing the list of arc nodes starting at a given header node. Traversing a column of an adjacency matrix, however, is equivalent to identifying all arcs that terminate at a given node; there is no corresponding method for accomplishing this under the linked representation. Of course, the linked representation could be modified to include two lists emanating from each header node: one for the arcs emanating from the graph node and the other for the arcs terminating at the graph node. However, this would require allocating two nodes for each arc, thus increasing the complexity of adding or deleting an arc. Alternatively, each arc node could be placed on two lists. In this case, an arc node would contain four pointers: one to the next arc emanating from the same node, one to the next arc terminating at the same node, one to the header node at which it terminates, and one to the header node from which it emanates. A header node would contain three pointers: one to the next header node, one to the list of arcs emanating from it, and one to the list of arcs terminating at it. The programmer must, of course, choose from among these representations by examining the needs of the specific problem and considering both time and storage efficiency. We invite the reader to write a routine *remvnode*, which accepts two pointers, GRAPH and P, and removes a header node pointed to by P from a graph pointed to by GRAPH using the various graph representations that we have outlined above. Of course, when a node is removed from a graph, all arcs emanating and terminating at that node must also be removed. In the linked representation that we have presented there is no easy way of removing a node from a graph since the arcs terminating at the node cannot be obtained directly.

An Application to Scheduling

Let us now consider an application using the linked representation of graphs. Suppose that a chef in a diner receives an order for a fried egg. The job of frying an egg can be decomposed into a number of distinct subtasks:

Get egg	Crack egg	Get grease
Grease pan	Heat grease	Pour egg into pan
Wait until egg is done		Remove egg

Some of these tasks must precede others (e.g., ''get egg'' must precede ''crack egg''). Others may be done simultaneously (e.g., ''get egg'' and ''heat grease''). The chef wishes to provide the quickest service possible and is assumed to have an unlimited number of assistants. The problem is to assign tasks to the assistants so as to complete the job in the least possible time.

Although this example may seem frivolous, it is typical of many real-world scheduling problems. A large computer system may schedule jobs to minimize turnaround time; a compiler may schedule machine language operations to minimize execution time; a plant manager may organize an assembly line to minimize production time; and so on. All of these problems are closely related and can be solved by the use of graphs.

Let us represent the foregoing problem as a graph. Each node of the graph represents a subtask and each arc $<x,y>$ represents the requirement that subtask y cannot be performed until subtask x has been completed. This graph G is shown in Figure 7.3.2.

Consider the transitive closure of G. The transitive closure is the graph T such that $<x,y>$ is an arc of T if and only if there is a path from x to y in G. This transitive closure is shown in Figure 7.3.3.

In the graph T, an arc exists from node x to node y if and only if subtask x must be performed before subtask y. Note that neither G nor T can contain a cycle since if a cycle existed from a node x to itself, subtask x could not be performed until after subtask x had been completed. This is clearly an impossible situation in the context of the problem.

Since G does not contain a cycle, there must be at least one node in G which

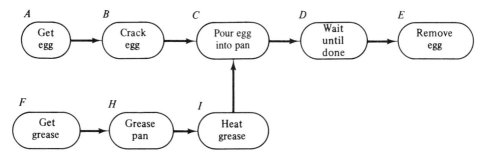

Figure 7.3.2   The graph G.

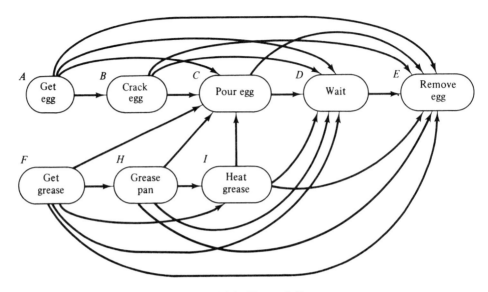

Figure 7.3.3 The graph *T*.

has no predecessors. To see this, suppose that every node in the graph did have a predecessor. In particular, let us choose a node z which has a predecessor y. y cannot equal z or the graph would have a cycle from z to itself. Since every node has a predecessor, y must also have a predecessor x which is not equal to either y or z. Continuing in this fashion, a sequence of distinct nodes

$$z,y,x,w,v,u,\ \cdots$$

is obtained. If any two nodes in this sequence were equal, a cycle would exist from that node to itself. However, the graph contains only a finite number of nodes, so that eventually, two of the nodes must be equal. This is a contradiction. Thus there must be at least one node without a predecessor.

In the graphs of Figures 7.3.2 and 7.3.3, the nodes A and F do not have predecessors. Since they have no predecessors, the subtasks which they represent may be performed immediately and simultaneously without waiting for any other subtasks to be completed. Every other subtask must wait until at least one of these is completed. Once these two subtasks have been performed, their nodes and any incident arcs can be removed from the graph. Note that the resulting graph does not contain any cycles since nodes and arcs have been removed from a graph which originally contained no cycles. Therefore, the resulting graph must also contain at least one node with no predecessors. In the example, B and H are two such nodes. Thus the subtasks B and H may be performed simultaneously in the second time period.

Continuing in this fashion, we find that the minimum time in which the egg can be fried is six time periods (assuming that every subtask takes exactly one time period) and that a maximum of two assistants need be employed, as follows:

The process above can be outlined as follows:

Time period	Assistant 1	Assistant 2
1	Get egg	Get grease
2	Crack egg	Grease pan
3	Heat grease	
4	Pour egg into pan	
5	Wait until done	
6	Remove egg	

Step 1. Read the precedences and construct the graph.
Step 2. Use the graph to determine subtasks that can be done simultaneously.

Let us refine each of these two steps. Two crucial decisions must be made in refining step 1. The first is to decide the format of the input; the second is to decide on the representation of the graph. Clearly, the input must contain indications of which subtasks must precede others. The most convenient way to represent these requirements is by ordered pairs of subtasks; each input line contains the names of two subtasks where the first subtask on a line must precede the second. Of course, the data must be valid in the sense that no subtask may precede itself (no cycles are permitted in the graph). Only those precedences that are implied by the data and the transitive closure of the resulting graph are assumed to hold. A subtask may be represented by a character string such as ''GET EGG'' or by a number. We choose to represent subtasks by character strings so that the input data reflect the real-world situation as closely as possible. If the number of subtasks at the start of execution is known, an adjacency matrix in which each element is initialized to the value *false* could be used to represent the graph. As each precedence is read, the value *true* could be inserted in the matrix at an appropriate position. However, let us assume that this information is unavailable at the start of execution and that it is necessary to provide for an arbitrary number of nodes. For this reason the linked representation of a graph is used.

What information should be kept with each node of the graph? Clearly, the name of the subtask that the node represents is needed for output purposes. This name will be kept as a character string. The remaining information depends on how the graph is used. This will become apparent only after step 2 is refined. Here is a good example of how the various parts of a program outline interact with each other to produce a single unit.

Step 2 can be refined into the following algorithm:

> ***while*** the graph is not empty ***do***
>   determine which nodes have no predecessors
>   output this group of nodes with an indication that they
>   can be performed simultaneously in the next time period
>   remove these nodes and their incident arcs from the graph
> ***endwhile***

How can it be determined which nodes have no predecessors? One method is to maintain a *count* field in each node containing the number of nodes that precede it. Note that we are not interested in which nodes precede a given node—only in how many. If the *count* of a node is 0, that node is known to have no predecessors and may be placed on an output list. Each time a node x is output, its adjacency list of arcs must be traversed and the *count* field decremented in every node adjacent to x. During each simulated time period, the list of nodes remaining in the graph is traversed, in a search for those whose *count* field is 0 and which may now be output. Thus the refinement of step 2 may be rewritten as follows:

```
period = 1
while graph <> null do
    'initialize the output list to empty
    output = null
    'traverse the graph searching for nodes which may be placed on the output list
    p = graph
    while p <= null do
        if count(p) = 0
            then remove node(p) from the list of graph nodes and place it on the output list
        endif
        set p to the next graph node
    endwhile
    if output = null
        then error–every node in the graph has a predecessor and therefore the graph
                                                       contains a cycle
            stop
    endif
    print period
    'traverse the output list
    p = output
    while p <>null do
        print info(p)
        traverse the list of arcs emanating from node(p), reducing the count of each
                        terminating node by 1 and freeing each arc node as it is encountered
        q = next node in output list
        freenode(p)
        p = q
    endwhile
    period = period + 1
endwhile
```

Note in the example that it is possible to delete nodes from the linked representation efficiently only because the only nodes deleted are those with no predecessors. Thus deleted nodes have no arcs terminating in them.

The BASIC Program

At this point in the refinement of step 2, we can indicate the structure of the nodes that we shall need. The header nodes which represent graph nodes contain the following fields:

SUBTASK   the name of the subtask represented by this node
COUNT   the number of predecessors of this graph node
ARCPTR   a pointer to the list of arcs emanating from this node
NXTNODE   a pointer to the next node in the graph or in the output list

Each list node representing an arc contains two pointer fields:

NDPTR   a pointer to its terminating node
NEXARC   a pointer to the next arc in the adjacency list

Thus two types of nodes are required: one to represent graph nodes and one to represent arcs. Using the array representation of lists, these may be declared by

```
 30  DEFSTR S
 40  NMAX = 100: 'maximum number of nodes
 50  DIM SUBTASK(NMAX)
 60  DIM COUNT(NMAX)
 70  DIM ARCPTR(NMAX)
 80  DIM NXTNODE(NMAX)
 90  AMAX = 200: 'maximum number of arcs
100  DIM NDPTR(AMAX)
110  DIM NEXARC(AMAX)
```

Of course, there are two available lists (pointed to by NAVAIL and AAVAIL and two sets of routines (*getnode, freenode* and *getarc, freearc*) to allocate and free allocated nodes. We also assume the existence of a function *find*, which searches a list of graph nodes pointed to by GRAPH for one such node whose SUBTASK field equals STASK. If no such graph node exists, *find* allocates a new graph node ND and sets SUBTASK(ND) to STASK, COUNT(ND) to 0, and ARCPTR(ND) to 0. *find* then adds ND to the list of graph nodes. In either case, *find* returns a pointer to the graph node containing STASK. The routine *join* described above (but modified to account for the formats of our nodes) is also used.

We may now write a BASIC scheduling program:

```
10   'program schedule
20   'the statement CLEAR 100 is required on TRS-80 microcomputers
30   DEFSTR S
40   NMAX = 100
50   DIM SUBTASK(NMAX)
60   DIM COUNT(NMAX)
70   DIM ARCPTR(NMAX)
80   DIM NXTNODE(NMAX)
90   AMAX = 200
100  DIM NDPTR(AMAX)
110  DIM NEXARC(AMAX)
120  'initialize the available lists
130  NAVAIL = 1
140  AAVAIL = 1
150  FOR I = 1 TO NMAX - 1
160      NXTNODE(I) = I + 1
170  NEXT I
180  NXTNODE(NMAX) = 0
190  FOR I = 1 TO AMAX - 1
200      NEXARC(I) = I + 1
210  NEXT I
220  NEXARC(AMAX) - 0
230  GRAPH = 0
240  'construct the graph
250  'read a precedence and place the arc representing it into the graph
260  READ S1TASK, S2TASK
270  IF S1TASK = "FINISH" THEN GOTO 380
280      STASK = S1TASK
290      GOSUB 1000: 'subroutine find sets the variable FIND to point to
                          'the graph node whose SUBTASK field equals STASK
300      P = FIND
310      STASK = S2TASK
320      GOSUB 1000: 'subroutine find
330      Q = FIND
340      GOSUB 1500: 'subroutine join accepts P and Q
350      'increment the count of the terminal node
360      COUNT(Q) = COUNT(Q) + 1
370  GOTO 250
380  'the graph has been constructed
390  PERIOD = 1
400  IF GRAPH = 0 THEN GOTO 780
410    OTPT = 0: 'OTPT is a pointer to the output list
420    P = GRAPH
430    Q = 0
440    'Q remains one node behind P during traversal
```

```
450     IF P = 0 THEN GOTO 550
460        R = NXTNODE(P)
470        IF COUNT(P) <> 0 THEN Q = P: GOTO 530
480        'remove graphnode(P) from the graph
490        IF Q = 0 THEN GRAPH = R
                     ELSE NXTNODE(Q) = R
500        'place graphnode(P) on the output list
510        NXTNODE(P) = OTPT
520        OTPT = P
530        P = R
540     GOTO 450
550     IF OTPT = 0
           THEN PRINT "ERROR IN INPUT- GRAPH CONTAINS A CYCLE":
                STOP
560     PRINT "PERIOD", PERIOD
570     'traverse the output list
580     P = OTPT
590     IF P = 0 THEN GOTO 760
600        PRINT SUBTASK(P)
610        'traverse arcs emanating from graphnode(P)
620        Q = ARCPTR(P)
630        IF Q = 0 THEN GOTO 710
640           T = NDPTR(Q)
650           COUNT(T) = COUNT(T) − 1
660           R = NEXARC(Q)
670           FRARC = Q
680           GOSUB 2000: 'subroutine freearc accepts the variable FRARC
690           Q = R
700        GOTO 630
710        R = NXTNODE(P)
720        FRNODE = P
730        GOSUB 2500: 'subroutine freenode accepts the variable FRNODE
740        P = R
750     GOTO 590
760     PERIOD = PERIOD + 1
770  GOTO 400
780  END
        . . .
900  DATA . . .
        . . .
1000  'subroutine find
        . . .
1500  'subroutine join
        . . .
2000  'subroutine freearc
        . . .
2500  'subroutine freenode
        . . .
```

Improving the Program

Although the program above is correct, it is highly inefficient. See if you can spot the reason for this before reading further. Consider the fact that in a typical real-world situation, there may be hundreds of subtasks, yet no more than three or four of them can be performed in a single time period. Thus the entire program may require 100 or more time periods to complete. This means that the loop consisting of statements 400–770 is repeated many times. Each time it is repeated, the entire list of 50 graph nodes (on the average) must be traversed in order to locate the few whose COUNT field is 0. (This average of 50 assumes that the graph initially has 100 nodes. Justify this estimate as an exercise.) This is very inefficient.

As each time period is simulated, those nodes whose subtasks can be performed in the next time period can be identified. This can be done when the COUNT in a node is reduced by 1 and becomes 0. At that point, why not remove the node from the list of graph nodes and place it on a new list of those nodes that can be output in the next time period? Then, in the next time period, this new list can be traversed to produce the output, so that the entire graph need not be searched for nodes with a COUNT field of 0. The reader is encouraged at this point to discover the reason for not using this seemingly simple system.

Consider the method that would be used to remove a node from the list of graph nodes. Since this list is a linear linked list, we cannot remove a node from it unless we have a pointer to its predecessor on the list. However, when we identify a node with zero count from the arc which it terminates, we have a pointer only to that node itself and not to its predecessor on the list of graph nodes. In order to reach the predecessor we have to traverse the list from its beginning, which is the source of the original inefficiency.

There are several possible solutions to this problem. One possible solution is deferred to Example 9.4.2, at which point we will have introduced the concepts necessary for its implementation. Another solution, which the thoughtful reader should have discovered, is to link the graph nodes in a doubly linked list rather than in a singly linked linear list so that a node's predecessor is accessible directly from the node itself, instead of through a traversal of the entire list from its beginning.

Although the graph nodes are linked in a doubly linked list, the output list may remain a singly linked linear list, since it actually behaves like a stack, for which a linear list is sufficient. After performing step 1, which creates the graph, the doubly linked list of graph nodes is traversed once in order to initialize the output list to contain those graph nodes which initially have no predecessors. As each time period is subsequently simulated, the output list created in the previous time period is traversed, the subtask represented by each node in the list is output, the counts in the graph nodes adjacent to each node in the output list are reduced, and if the count in an adjacent node becomes zero, that adjacent node is placed in the output list for the next period. This means that two output lists are needed: one for the current period, which was created in the previous period and is now being traversed, and one that is being created in the current period and will be traversed in the next.

The refinement of step 2 under this implementation may be outlined as follows:

```
'traverse the list of graph nodes and place all nodes
'with zero count on the initial output list
p = graph
output = null
while p <> null do
    q = nextnode(p)
    if count(p) = 0
        then remove node(p) from the graph list
             place node(p) on the output list
    endif
    p = q
endwhile
'simulate the time periods
period = 1
while output <> null do
    print period
    'initialize the output list for the next period
    nextout = null
    'traverse the output list
    p = output
    while p <> null do
        print info(p)
        'traverse the list of arcs emanating from node(p)
        r = arcptr(p)
        while r <> null do
            'reduce the count in the terminating node
            t = nodeptr(r)
            count(t) = count(t) − 1
            if count(t) = 0
                then remove node(t) from the graph
                     'add node(t) to the nextout list
                     nextnode(t) = nextout
                     nextout = t
            endif
```

$$rr \ = \ nextarc(r)$$
$$freearc(r)$$
$$r \ = \ rr$$
endwhile
$$q \ = \ nextnode(p)$$
$$freenode(p)$$
$$p \ = \ q$$
endwhile
$$output \ = \ nextout$$
$$period \ = \ period \ + \ 1$$
endwhile
if $graph <> null$
   then error—there is a cycle in the graph
        stop
endif

In order to accommodate the pointers of the doubly linked list, the graph nodes must include an extra field PREVNODE, containing a pointer to the previous graph node in the list. The graph nodes can therefore be declared:

```
40   NMAX = 100
50   DIM SUBTASK(NMAX)
60   DIM COUNT(NMAX)
70   DIM ARCPTR(NMAX)
80   DIM PREVNODE(NMAX)
90   DIM NXTNODE(NMAX)
```

The available list of graph nodes and the two output lists need not be doubly linked, so that the contents of PREVNODE are irrelevant for nodes on these lists. The routine *find* must be suitably modified to accommodate doubly linked lists. The routine *join* is used as well. We may write a BASIC program for the scheduling problem using our improved algorithm as follows:

```
10   'program schedule (improved)
20   'the statement CLEAR 100 is required on TRS-80 microcomputers
30   DEFSTR S
40   NMAX = 100: 'maximum number of nodes
50   DIM SUBTASK(NMAX)
60   DIM COUNT(NMAX)
70   DIM ARCPTR(NMAX)
80   DIM PREVNODE(NMAX)
90   DIM NXTNODE(NMAX)
100  AMAX = 200: 'maximum number of arcs
110  DIM NDPTR(AMAX)
120  DIM NEXARC(AMAX)
```

```
130   'initialize the available lists
140   NAVAIL = 1
150   FOR I = 1 TO NMAX − 1
160       NXTNODE(I) = I + 1
170   NEXT I
180   NXTNODE(NMAX) = 0
190   AAVAIL = 1
200   FOR I = 1 TO AMAX − 1
210       NEXARC(I) = I + 1
220   NEXT I
230   NEXARC(AMAX) = 0
240   'construct the graph
250   GRAPH = 0
260   READ S1TASK, S2TASK
270   IF S1TASK = "FINISH" THEN GOTO 380
280       'the subroutine find will adjust all necessary forward and
          'backward pointers and the count field in adding a graph node
          'with SUBTASK field STASK to the doubly linked list of graph nodes
290       STASK = S1TASK
300       GOSUB 1000: 'subroutine find sets the variable FIND
310       P = FIND
320       STASK = S2TASK
330       GOSUB 1000: 'subroutine find
340       Q = FIND
350       GOSUB 1500: 'subroutine join accepts P and Q
360       COUNT(Q) = COUNT(Q) + 1
370   GOTO 260
380   'traverse the list of graph nodes and place all graph nodes
      'with zero count on the output list
390   OTPT = 0
400   P = GRAPH
410   IF P = 0 THEN GOTO 540
420     Q = NXTNODE(P)
430     IF COUNT(P) <> 0 THEN GOTO 510
440     'remove graphnode(P) from the graph list
450     R = PREVNODE(P)
460     IF Q <> 0 THEN PREVNODE(Q) = R
470     IF R = 0 THEN GRAPH = Q
                  ELSE NXTNODE(R) = Q
480     'place node(P) on the output list
490     NXTNODE(P) = OTPT
500     OTPT = P
510     'go on to the next graph node
520     P = Q
530   GOTO 410
```

```
540   'simulate the time periods
550   PERIOD = 1
560   IF OTPT = 0 THEN GOTO 950
570      PRINT "PERIOD", PERIOD
580      'initialize the output list for the next period,
         'and traverse the current output list
590      NEXOT = 0
600      P = OTPT
610      IF P = 0 THEN GOTO 910
620         PRINT SUBTASK(P)
630         'traverse arcs emanating from node(P)
640         R = ARCPTR(P)
650         IF R = 0 THEN GOTO 850
660            'reduce count in the terminating node
670            T = NDPTR(R)
680            COUNT(T) = COUNT(T) - 1
690            IF COUNT(T) <> 0 THEN GOTO 790
700            'once the subtask represented by node (P) has been
               'performed the subtask represented by node(T) may be performed
710            'remove graphnode(T) from the graph list
720            V = NXTNODE(T)
730            W = PREVNODE(T)
740            IF V <> 0 THEN PREVNODE(V) = W
750            IF W <> 0 THEN NXTNODE(W) = V
                        ELSE GRAPH = V
760            'place node(T) on the new output list
770            NXTNODE(T) = NEXOT
780            NEXOT = T
790            'free arcnode(R) and continue traversing the list of
               'arc nodes emanating from graphnode(P)
800            RR = NEXARC(R)
810            FRARC = R
820            GOSUB 2000: 'subroutine freearc accepts the variable FRARC
830            R = RR
840         GOTO 650
850         'continue traversing the output list
860         Q = NXTNODE(P)
870         FRNODE = P
880         GOSUB 2500: 'subroutine freenode accepts the variable FRNODE
890         P = Q
900      GOTO 610
```

910   *'reset the output list for the next period*
920   OTPT = NEXOT
930   PERIOD = PERIOD + 1
940 GOTO 560
950 IF GRAPH <> 0 THEN PRINT "ERROR − GRAPH CONTAINS A CYCLE"
960 END
970 DATA . . .

. . .

1000   *'subroutine* find

. . .

1500   *'subroutine* join

. . .

2000 *'subroutine* freearc

. . .

2500 *'subroutine* freenode

. . .

EXERCISES

1. Implement a graph using linked lists so that each header node heads two lists: one containing the arcs emanating from the graph node and the other containing the arcs terminating at the graph node.
2. Implement a graph so that the lists of header nodes and arc nodes are circular.
3. Implement a graph using a list of adjacency lists. Under this representation, a graph of n nodes consists of n header nodes, each containing an integer from 1 to n and a pointer. The pointer is to a list of list nodes each of which contains the node number of a node adjacent to the node represented by the header node.
4. There may be more than one way to organize a set of subtasks in a minimum number of time periods. For example, the subtasks in Figure 7.3.2 may be completed in six time periods in one of three different methods:

Period	Method 1	Method 2	Method 3
1	*A,F*	*F*	*A,F*
2	*B,H*	*A,H*	*H*
3	*I*	*B,I*	*B,I*
4	*C*	*C*	*C*
5	*D*	*D*	*D*
6	*E*	*F.*	*E*

Write a program that will generate all possible methods of organizing the subtasks in the minimum number of time periods.

5. Consider the graph of Figure 7.3.4. The program *schedule* outputs the following organization of tasks:

Time	Subtasks
1	A,B,C
2	D,E
3	F
4	G

This requires three assistants (for time period 1). Can you find a method of organizing the subtasks so that only two assistants are required at any time period, yet the entire job can be accomplished in the same four time periods? Write a program that organizes subtasks so that a minimum number of assistants are needed to complete the entire job in the minimum number of time periods.

6. If there is only one worker available, it will take k time periods to complete an entire job, where k is the number of subtasks. Write a program to list a valid order in which the worker can perform the tasks. Note that this program is simpler than *schedule*, since an output list is not needed; as soon as the COUNT field reaches 0 the task may be output. The process of converting a set of precedences into a single linear list in which no later element precedes an earlier one is called a ***topological sort.***

7. A ***PERT network*** is a weighted acyclic directed graph in which each arc represents an activity and its weight represents the time needed to perform that activity. If arcs $<A,B>$ and $<B,C>$ exist in the network, the activity represented by arc $<A,B>$ must be completed before the activity represented by $<B,C>$ can be started. Each node x of the network represents a time at which all activities represented by arcs terminating at x can be completed.

(**a**) Write a BASIC routine that accepts a representation of such a network and assigns to each node x the earliest time that all activities terminating in that node can be completed. Call this quantity $et(x)$. [*Hint*: Assign time 0 to all nodes with no pre-

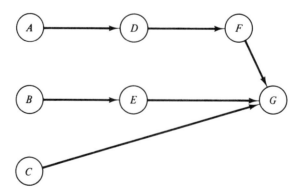

Figure 7.3.4

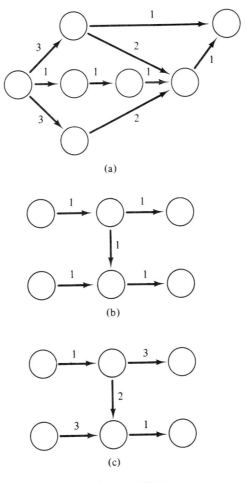

Figure 7.3.5   Some PERT networks.

decessors. If all predecessors of a node x have been assigned times, then $et(x)$ is the maximum over all predecessors of the sum of the time assigned to a predecessor and the weight of the arc from that predecessor to x.]

(b) Given the assignment of times in part (a), write a BASIC routine that assigns to each node x the latest time that all activities terminating in x can be completed without delaying the completion of all the activities. Call this quantity $lt(x)$. [*Hint:* Assign time $et(x)$ to all nodes x with no successors. If all successors of a node x have been assigned times, $lt(x)$ is the minimum over all successors of the difference between the time assigned to a successor and the weight of the arc from x to the successor.]

(c) Prove that there is at least one path in the graph from a node with no predecessors to a node with no successors such that $et(x) = lt(x)$ for every node x on the path. Such a path is called a ***critical path***.

(**d**) Explain the significance of a critical path by showing that reducing the time of the activities along every critical path reduces the earliest time by which the entire job can be completed.

(**e**) Write a BASIC routine to find all critical paths in a PERT network.

(**f**) Find the critical paths in the networks of Figure 7.3.5.

8. Write a BASIC program that accepts a representation of a PERT network as given above and computes the earliest time in which the entire job can be finished if as many activities as possible may be performed in parallel. The program should also print the starting and ending time of each activity in the network. Write another BASIC program to schedule the activities so that the entire job can be completed at the earliest possible time subject to the constraint that at most m activities can be performed in parallel.

8

Sorting

Sorting and searching are among the most common ingredients of programming systems. In the first section of this chapter we discuss some of the overall considerations involved in sorting. In the remainder of the chapter we discuss some of the more common sorting techniques and the advantages or disadvantages of one technique over another. In Chapter 9 we discuss searching and some applications.

1. GENERAL BACKGROUND

The concept of an ordered set of elements is one which has considerable impact on our daily lives. Consider, for example, the process of finding a telephone number in a telephone directory. This process, called a *search*, is simplified considerably by the fact that the names in the directory are listed in alphabetical order. Consider the trouble you might have in attempting to locate a telephone number if the names were listed in the order in which the customers placed their phone orders with the telephone company. In such a case, the names might as well have been entered in random order. Since the entries are sorted in alphabetical rather than in chronological order, the process of searching is simplified. Or, consider the case of someone searching for a book in a library. Because the books are shelved in a specific order (Library of Congress, Dewey Decimal System, etc.), each book is assigned a specific position relative to the others and can be retrieved in a reasonable amount of time (if it is there). Or, consider a set of numbers sorted sequentially in a computer's memory. As we shall see in Chapter

9, it is usually easier to find a particular element of that set if the numbers are maintained in sorted order. In general, a set of items is kept sorted in order either to produce a report (to simplify manual retrieval of information, as in a telephone book or a library shelf) or to make machine access to data more efficient.

We now present some basic terminology. A *file of size n* is a sequence of *n* items $r(1)$, $r(2)$, . . . , $r(n)$. Each item in the file is called a *record.* (The use of the term "file" in this context differs from its standard BASIC usage.) A *key,* $k(i)$, is associated with each record $r(i)$. The key is usually (but not always) a field of the entire record. The file is said to be *sorted on the key* if $i < j$ implies that $k(i)$ precedes $k(j)$ in some ordering on the keys. In the example of the telephone book, the file consists of all the entries in the book. Each entry is a record. The key upon which the file is sorted is the name field of the record. Each record also contains fields for an address and a telephone number.

A sort can be classified as being *internal* if the records that it is sorting are in main memory, or *external* if some of the records that it is sorting are in auxiliary storage. We restrict our attention to internal sorts.

It is possible for two records in a file to have the same key. A sorting technique is called *stable* if for all records i and j such that $k(i) = k(j)$, if $r(i)$ precedes $r(j)$ in the original file then $r(i)$ precedes $r(j)$ in the sorted file.

A sort takes place either on the records themselves or on an auxiliary table of pointers. For example, consider Figure 8.1.1(a), in which a file of five records is shown. If the file is sorted in increasing order on the numeric key shown, the resulting file is as shown in Figure 8.1.1(b). In this case the actual records themselves have been sorted

Suppose, however, that the amount of data stored in each of the records in the file of Figure 8.1.1(a) is so large that the overhead involved in moving the actual data is prohibitive. In this case an auxiliary table of pointers may be used, so that these pointers are moved instead of the actual data, as shown in Figure 8.1.2. (This is called *sorting by address.*) The table in the center is the file and

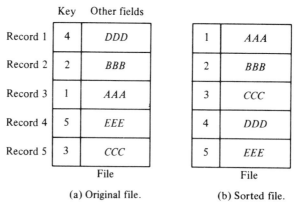

Key   Other fields

Record 1	4	*DDD*		1	*AAA*
Record 2	2	*BBB*		2	*BBB*
Record 3	1	*AAA*		3	*CCC*
Record 4	5	*EEE*		4	*DDD*
Record 5	3	*CCC*		5	*EEE*

File   File

(a) Original file.   (b) Sorted file.

Figure 8.1.1   Sorting actual records.

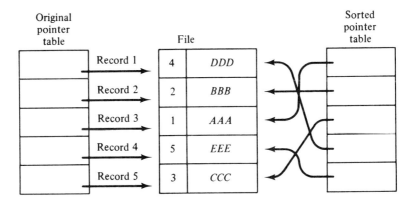

Figure 8.1.2   Sorting by using an auxiliary table of pointers.

the table at the left is the initial table of pointers. The entry in position j in the table of pointers points to record j. During the sorting process, the entries in the pointer table are adjusted so that the final table is as shown at the right. Originally, the first pointer was to the first entry in the file; upon completion the first pointer is to the fourth entry in the table. Note that none of the original file entries are moved. In most of the programs in this chapter we illustrate techniques of sorting actual records. The extension of these techniques to sorting by address is straightforward and will be left as an exercise for the reader. (Actually, for the sake of simplicity, in the examples presented in this chapter we sort only the keys; we leave to the reader to modify the programs to sort full records.)

Because of the relationship between sorting and searching, the first question to ask in any application is whether a file should be sorted. Sometimes, there is less work involved in searching a set of elements for a particular one than first to sort the entire set and then to extract the desired element. On the other hand, if frequent use of the file is required for the purpose of retrieving specific elements, it might be more efficient to sort the file. This is because the overhead of successive searches may far exceed the overhead involved in sorting the file once and subsequently retrieving elements from the sorted file. Thus it cannot be said that it is more efficient either to sort or not to sort. The programmer must make a decision based on individual circumstances. Once a decision to sort has been made, other decisions must be made, including what is to be sorted and what methods are to be used. There is no one sorting method that is universally superior to all others. The programmer must carefully examine the problem and the desired results before deciding these very important questions.

Efficiency Considerations

As we shall see in this chapter, there are a great number of methods that can be used to sort a file. The programmer must be aware of several interrelated and often conflicting efficiency considerations to make an intelligent choice as to which sorting method is most appropriate to a particular problem. Three of the most important of these considerations include: the length of time which must be spent by the programmer in coding a particular sorting program, the amount of machine time necessary for running the program, and the amount of space necessary for the program.

If a file is small, sophisticated sorting techniques designed to minimize space and time requirements are usually worse or only marginally better in achieving efficiencies than are simpler, generally less efficient methods. Similarly, if a particular sorting program is to be run only once and there is sufficient machine time and space in which to run it, it would be ludicrous for a programmer to spend days investigating the best methods of obtaining the last ounce of efficiency. In such cases, the amount of time that must be spent by the programmer is properly the overriding consideration in determining which sorting method to use. However, a strong word of caution must be inserted. Programming time is never a valid excuse for using an incorrect program. A sort that is run only once may be able to afford the luxury of an inefficient technique, but it cannot afford an incorrect one. The presumably sorted data may be used in an application in which the assumption of ordered data is crucial.

However, a programmer must be able to recognize the fact that a particular sort is inefficient and must be able to justify its use in a particular situation. Too often, programmers take the easy way out and code an inefficient sort which is then incorporated into a larger system in which the sort is a key component. The designers and planners of the system are then surprised at the inadequacy of their creation. To maximize his or her efficiency, a programmer must be knowledgeable of a wide range of sorting techniques and be cognizant of the advantages and disadvantages of each, so that when the need for a sort arises, he or she can supply the one that is most appropriate for the particular situation.

This brings us to the other two efficiency considerations: time and space. As in most computer applications, the programmer must often optimize one of these at the expense of the other. In considering the time necessary to sort a file of size n, we do not concern ourselves with actual time units, as these will vary from one machine to another, from one program to another, and from one set of data to another. Rather, we are interested in the corresponding change in the amount of time required to sort a file induced by a change in the file size n. Let us see if we can make this concept more precise. We say that y is **proportional** to x if the relation between y and x is such that multiplying x by a constant multiplies y by that same constant. Thus, if y is proportional to x, doubling x will double y and multiplying x by 10 will multiply y by 10. Similarly, if y is proportional to x, doubling x will multiply y by 4 and multiplying x by 10 will multiply y by 100.

Often we do not measure the time efficiency of a sort by the number of time units required but by the number of critical operations performed. Examples of such critical operations are key comparisons (i.e., the comparisons of the keys of two records in the file to determine which is greater), movement of records or pointers to records, or interchanges of two records. The critical operations chosen are those that take the most time. For example, a key comparison may be a complex operation, especially if the keys themselves are long or the ordering among keys is nontrivial. Thus a key comparison requires much more time than say, a simple increment of an index variable in a *for-next* loop. Also, the number of simple operations required is usually proportional to the number of key comparisons. For this reason, the number of key comparisons is a useful measure of a sort's time efficiency.

There are two ways to determine the time requirements of a sort, neither of which yields results that are applicable to all cases. One method is to go through a sometimes intricate and involved mathematical analysis of various cases (e.g., best case, worst case, average case). The result of this analysis is often a formula giving the average time (or number of operations) required for a particular sort as a function of the file size n. (Actually, the time requirements of a sort depend on factors other than the file size; however, we concern ourselves here only with the dependence on the file size.) Suppose that such a mathematical analysis on a particular sorting program results in the conclusion that the program takes $.01n^2 + 10n$ time units to execute. The first and fourth columns of Figure 8.1.3 show the time needed by the sort of various values of n. You will notice that for small values of n, the quantity $10n$ (third column of Figure 8.1.3) overwhelms the quantity $.01n^2$ (second column). This is because the difference between n^2 and n is small for small values of n and is more than compensated for by the difference between 10 and .01. Thus, for small values of n, an increase in n by a factor of 2 (e.g., from 50 to 100) increases the time needed for sorting by approximately that same factor of 2 (from 525 to 1100). Similarly, an increase in n by a factor of 5 (e.g., from 10 to 50), increases the sorting time by approximately 5 (from 101 to 525). However, as n becomes larger, the difference between n^2 and n increases so quickly that it eventually more than compensates for the difference between 10 and .01. Thus when n equals 1000, the two terms contribute equally to the amount of time needed by the program. As n becomes even larger, the term $.01n^2$ overwhelms the term $10n$ and the contribution of the term $10n$ becomes almost insignificant. Thus, for large values of n, an increase in n by a factor of 2 (e.g., from 50,000 to 100,000) results in an increase in sorting time of approxi-

n	$a = 0.01n^2$	$b = 10n$	$a + b$	$\dfrac{(a + b)}{n^2}$
10	1	100	101	1.01
50	25	500	525	0.21
100	100	1,000	1,100	0.11
500	2,500	5,000	7,500	0.03
1,000	10,000	10,000	20,000	0.02
5,000	250,000	50,000	300,000	0.01
10,000	1,000,000	100,000	1,100,000	0.01
50,000	25,000,000	500,000	25,500,000	0.01
100,000	100,000,000	1,000,000	101,000,000	0.01
500,000	2,500,000,000	5,000,000	2,505,000,000	0.01

Figure 8.1.3

mately 4 (from 25.5 million to 101 million), and an increase in *n* by a factor of 5 (e.g., from 10,000 to 50,000) increases the sorting time by approximately a factor of 25 (from 1.1 million to 25.5 million). Indeed, as *n* becomes larger and larger, the sorting time becomes more closely proportional to n^2, as is clearly illustrated by the last column of Figure 8.1.3. Because of this, we say that the time for such a sort is on the ***order of*** n^2, written $O(n^2)$. Thus for large *n* the time required by the sort is almost proportional to n^2. Of course, for small values of *n*, the sort may exhibit drastically different behavior (as in Figure 8.1.3), a situation that must be taken into account in analyzing its efficiency.

Using this concept of the order of a sort, we can compare various sorting techniques and classify them as being "good" or "bad" in general terms. One might hope to discover the "optimal" sort, which is $O(n)$; unfortunately, however, it can be shown that no such generally useful sort exists. Most of the classical sorts we shall consider have time requirements which range from $O(n \log n)$ to $O(n^2)$. [The ***logarithm*** of a number *n* to the ***base*** *m* is the number of times *m* must be multiplied by itself to obtain *n* and is written $log_m n$. Thus $log_{10} 1000$ is 3 since $10*10*10 = 10^3$ equals 1000 and $log_2 1000$ is slightly less than 10 since 2^{10} equals 1024. You are asked to show as an exercise that the base of the logarithm is irrelevant in determining the order of an $O(n \log n)$ sort.] In the former, multiplying the file size by 100 will multiply the sorting time by less than 200; in the latter, multiplying the file size by 100 multiplies the sorting time by a factor of 10,000. Figure 8.1.4 shows the comparison of *n* log *n* with n^2 for a range of values of *n*. It can be seen from the figure that for large *n*, as *n* increases, n^2 increases at a much more rapid rate than *n* log *n*. However, a sort should not be selected simply because it is $O(n \log n)$. The relation of the file size *n* and the other terms comprising the actual sorting time must be known. In particular, terms that play an insignificant role for large values of *n* may play a very dominant role for small values of *n*. All of these considerations must be considered before an intelligent sort selection can be made.

A second method of determining time requirements of a sorting technique is to run the program and measure its efficiency (either by measuring absolute time units or the number of operations performed). In order to use such results in mea-

n	$n \log_{10} n$	n^2
1×10^1	1.0×10^1	1.0×10^2
5×10^1	8.5×10^1	2.5×10^3
1×10^2	2.0×10^2	1.0×10^4
5×10^2	1.3×10^3	2.5×10^5
1×10^3	3.0×10^3	1.0×10^6
5×10^3	1.8×10^4	2.5×10^7
1×10^4	4.0×10^4	1.0×10^8
5×10^4	2.3×10^5	2.5×10^9
1×10^5	5.0×10^5	1.0×10^{10}
5×10^5	2.8×10^6	2.5×10^{11}
1×10^6	6.0×10^6	1.0×10^{12}
5×10^6	3.3×10^7	2.5×10^{13}
1×10^7	7.0×10^7	1.0×10^{14}

Figure 8.1.4 A comparison of *n* log *n* and n^2 for various values of *n*.

suring the efficiency of a sort, the test must be run on "many" sample files. Even when such statistics have been gathered, the application of that sort to a specific file may not yield results that follow the general pattern. Peculiar attributes of the file in question may make the sorting speed deviate significantly. In the sorts of the subsequent sections we shall give an intuitive explanation as to why a particular sort is classified as $O(n^2)$ or $O(n \log n)$; we leave mathematical analysis and sophisticated testing of empirical data as exercises for the ambitious reader.

In most cases, the time needed by a sort depends on the original sequence of the data. For some sorts, input data that are almost in sorted order can be completely sorted in time $O(n)$, while input data that is in reverse order need time which is $O(n^2)$. For other sorts the time required is $O(n \log n)$ regardless of the original order of the data. Thus, if we have some knowledge about the original sequence of the data, we can make a more intelligent decision as to which sorting method to select. On the other hand, if we have no such knowledge, we may wish to select a sort based on the worst possible case or based on the "average" case. In any event, the only general comment that can be made about sorting techniques is that there is no "best" general sorting technique. The choice of a sort must, of necessity, depend on the specific circumstances.

Once a particular sorting technique has been selected, the programmer should do his or her best to make the program as efficient as possible. In many programming applications it is often necessary to sacrifice efficiency for the sake of clarity. With sorting, the situation is usually the opposite. Once a sorting program has been written and tested, the programmer's chief goal is to improve its speed, even if it becomes less readable. The reason for this is that a sort may account for the major part of a program's efficiency, so that any improvement in sorting time significantly affects overall efficiency. Another reason is that a sort is often used quite frequently, so that a small improvement in its execution speed saves a great deal of computer time. It is usually a good idea to remove subroutine calls, especially from inner loops, and to replace them with the code of the subroutine in line, since the call-return mechanism of a language can be prohibitively expensive in terms of time. In many of the programs we do not do this, so as not to obfuscate the intent of the program with huge blocks of code. Also, the call-return mechanism in BASIC is more efficient than in many other languages. This is because in BASIC the call-return is handled by a transfer with a return address; parameter transmission is accomplished by explicit assignment statements. Under our conventions for passing parameters in BASIC, we might wish to avoid even the explicit assignment of parameters, especially array parameters. Thus it may be more efficient to duplicate subroutine code to operate directly on the different arguments rather than to repeatedly assign arguments to subroutine input variables and output variables to arguments. In other languages, a subroutine call may involve the assignment of storage to local variables, an activity that sometimes requires a call to the operating system.

Space constraints are usually less important than time considerations. One of the reasons for this is that, for most sorting programs, the amount of space needed is closer to $O(n)$ than to $O(n^2)$. A second reason is that if more space is required, it can almost always be found in auxiliary storage. Of course, the usual relationship between time and space holds for sorting algorithms; that is, those programs that require less time usually require more space, and vice versa.

In the remaining sections we investigate some of the more popular sorting techniques and indicate some of their advantages and disadvantages.

EXERCISES

1. Choose any sorting technique with which you are familiar.
   (a) Write a program for the sort.
   (b) Is the sort stable?
   (c) Determine the time requirements of the sort as a function of the file size, both mathematically and empirically.
   (d) What is the order of the sort?
   (e) At what file size does the most dominant term begin to overshadow the others?
2. Show that if a sort is $O(n \log_2 n)$, it is also $O(n \log_{10} n)$, and vice versa.
3. Suppose that a time requirement is given by the formula $a*n^2 + b*n*\log_2 n$, where a and b are constants. Answer the following questions by both proving your results mathematically and writing a program to validate the results empirically.
   (a) For what values of n (expressed in terms of a and b) does the first term dominate the second?
   (b) For what value of n (expressed in terms of a and b) are the two terms equal?
   (c) For what values of n (expressed in terms of a and b) does the second term dominate the first?
4. Show that any process which sorts a file can be extended to find all duplicates in the file.
5. A *sort decision tree* is a binary tree that represents a sorting method based on comparisons. Figure 8.1.5 illustrates such a decision tree for a file of three elements. Each nonleaf of such a tree represents a comparison between two elements. Each leaf represents a completely sorted file. A left branch from a nonleaf indicates that the first key was smaller than the second; a right branch indicates that it was larger. (We assume that all the elements in the file have distinct keys.) For example, the tree of Figure 8.1.5 represents a sort on three elements, $x(1)$, $x(2)$, $x(3)$, which proceeds as follows. Compare $x(1)$ to $x(2)$. If $x(1) < x(2)$, compare $x(2)$ with $x(3)$, and if $x(2) < x(3)$, the sorted order of the file is $x(1)$, $x(2)$, $x(3)$; otherwise, if $x(1) < x(3)$, the sorted order is $x(1)$, $x(3)$, $x(2)$, and if $x(1) > x(3)$, the sorted order is $x(3)$, $x(1)$, $x(2)$. If $x(1) > x(2)$, proceed in a similar fashion down the right subtree.
   (a) Show that a sort decision tree which never makes a redundant comparison [i.e., never compares $x(i)$ and $x(j)$ if the relationship between $x(i)$ and $x(j)$ is known] has $n!$ leafs.

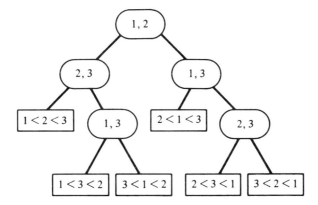

Figure 8.1.5   A decision tree for a file of 3 elements.

(b) Show that the depth of such a decision tree is at least $\log_2(n!)$.

(c) Show that $n^n \geqslant n! \geqslant (n/2)^{n/2}$, so that the depth of such a tree is $O(n \log n)$.

(d) Explain why this proves that any sorting method which uses comparisons on a file of size n must make at least $O(n \log n)$ comparisons.

6. Given a sort decision tree for a file as in Exercise 5, show that if the file contains some equal elements, the result of applying the tree to the file (where either a left or right branch is taken whenever two elements are equal) is a sorted file.

7. Extend the concept of the binary decision tree of Exercises 5 and 6 to a ternary tree which includes the possibility of equality. It is desired to determine which elements of the file are equal, in addition to the order of the distinct elements of the file. How many comparisons are necessary?

8. Show that if k is the smallest integer greater than or equal to $n + \log_2 n - 2$, then k comparisons are necessary and sufficient to find the largest and second largest elements of a set of n distinct elements.

9. How many comparisons are necessary to find the largest and smallest of a set of n distinct elements?

2. EXCHANGE SORTS

Bubble Sort

The first sort we present is probably the most widely known among beginning students of programming—the ***bubble sort.*** One of the characteristics of this sort is that it is easy to understand and program. Yet of all the sorts we shall consider, it is probably the least efficient.

In each of the subsequent examples, x is an array of integers of which the first n are to be sorted so that $x(i) \leqslant x(j)$ for $1 \leqslant i < j \leqslant n$. It is straightforward to extend this simple format to one that is used in sorting n records, each with a subfield key k. In BASIC this could be done by maintaining the other fields of the record in separate arrays. Whenever an operation is performed on $k(i)$, the corresponding operation would be performed on each of the other fields. Comparisons, of course, would be applied only to the key field.

The basic idea underlying the bubble sort is to pass through the file sequentially several times. Each pass consists of comparing each element in the file with its successor [$x(i)$ with $x(i+1)$] and interchanging the two elements if they are not in proper order. Consider the following file:

25   57   48   37   12   92   86   33

The following comparisons are made on the first pass:

$x(1)$	with	$x(2)$	(25 with 57)	no interchange
$x(2)$	with	$x(3)$	(57 with 48)	interchange
$x(3)$	with	$x(4)$	(57 with 37)	interchange
$x(4)$	with	$x(5)$	(57 with 12)	interchange
$x(5)$	with	$x(6)$	(57 with 92)	no interchange
$x(6)$	with	$x(7)$	(92 with 86)	interchange
$x(7)$	with	$x(8)$	(92 with 33)	interchange

Thus, after the first pass, the file is in the order

25   48   37   12   57   86   33   92

Notice that after this first pass, the largest element (in this case 92) is in its proper position within the array. In general, $x(n-i+1)$ will be in its proper position after iteration i. The method is called the bubble sort because each number slowly "bubbles" up to its proper position. After the second pass the file is

25   37   12   48   57   33   86   92

Notice that 86 has now found its way to the second highest position. Since each iteration places a new element into its proper position, a file of n elements requires no more than $n-1$ iterations.

The complete set of iterations is the following:

iteration 0 (original file)	25	57	48	37	12	92	86	33
iteration 1	25	48	37	12	57	86	33	92
iteration 2	25	37	12	48	57	33	86	92
iteration 3	25	12	37	48	33	57	86	92
iteration 4	12	25	37	33	48	57	86	92
iteration 5	12	25	33	37	48	57	86	92
iteration 6	12	25	33	37	48	57	86	92
iteration 7	12	25	33	37	48	57	86	92

On the basis of the discussion above we could proceed to code the bubble sort. However, there are some obvious improvements to the method. First, since

all the elements in positions greater than or equal to $n - i + 1$ are already in proper
position after iteration i, they need not be considered in succeeding iterations.
Thus on the first pass $n - 1$ comparisons are made, on the second pass $n - 2$ comparisons, and on the $(n - 1)$th pass only one comparison is made [between $x(1)$
and $x(2)$]. Therefore, the process speeds up as it proceeds through successive
passes.

   We have shown that $n - 1$ passes are sufficient to sort a file of size n.
However, in the sample file of eight elements above, the file was sorted after five
iterations, making the last two iterations unnecessary. In order to eliminate unnecessary passes we must be able to detect the fact that the file is already sorted.
But this is a simple task since in a sorted file, no interchanges are made on any
pass. By keeping a record of whether or not any interchanges are made in a given
pass it can be determined whether further passes are necessary. Under this method, if the file can be sorted in fewer than $n - 1$ passes, the final pass makes no
interchanges.

   Using these improvements, we present the routine *bubble*, which accepts
two variables X and N. X is an array of numbers and N is an integer representing
the number of elements to be sorted. (N may be less than the upper bound of X.)

```
5000   'subroutine bubble
5010   'inputs: N, X
5020   'outputs: X
5030   'locals: J, P, PASS, SWITCH
5040   'initialization
5050   SWITCH = TRUE
5060   FOR PASS = 1 TO N - 1:                    'outer loop controls
                                                 'the number of passes
5070        IF SWITCH = FALSE THEN RETURN
5080        'else do stmts 5090-5130
5090        SWITCH = FALSE:                      'initially no interchanges
                                                 'have been made on this pass
5100        FOR J = 1 to N - PASS:               'inner loop controls
                                                 'each individual pass
5110             IF X(J) > X(J +1)
                 THEN SWITCH = TRUE:
                      HOLD = X(J): X(J) = X(J + 1): X(J +1) = HOLD
5120                                             'elements were out of order
                                                 'an interchange is necessary
5130        NEXT J
5140   NEXT PASS
5150   RETURN
5160   'endsub
```

   What can be said about the efficiency of the bubble sort? In the case of a
sort that does not include the two improvements outlined above, the analysis is

simple. There are $n-1$ passes and $n-1$ comparisons on each pass. Thus the total number of comparisons is $(n - 1)*(n - 1) = n^2 - 2n + 1$, which is $O(n^2)$. Of course, the number of interchanges depends on the original order of the file. However, the number of interchanges cannot be greater than the number of comparisons. It is likely that it is the number of interchanges rather than the number of comparisons which takes up the most time in the algorithm's execution.

Let us see how the improvements that we introduced affect the speed of the bubble sort. The number of comparisons on iteration i is $n - i$. Thus, if there are k iterations, the total number of comparisons is $(n - 1) + (n - 2) + (n - 3) + \cdots + (n - k)$, which equals $(2kn - k^2 - k)/2$. It can be shown that the average number of iterations, k, is $O(n)$, so that the entire formula is still $O(n^2)$, although the constant multiplier is smaller than before. However, there is additional overhead involved in testing and initializing the variable SWITCH (once per pass) and setting it to TRUE (once for every interchange).

The only redeeming features of the bubble sort are that it requires little additional space (one additional record to hold the temporary value for interchanging and several simple integer variables) and that it is $O(n)$ in the case that the file is completely sorted (or almost completely sorted). This follows from the observation that only one pass of $n-1$ comparisons (and no interchanges) is necessary to establish that a sorted file is sorted.

There are some other ways to improve the bubble sort. One of these is to observe that the number of passes necessary to sort the file is the largest distance by which a number must move "down" in the array. In our example, for instance, 33, which starts at position 8 in the array, ultimately finds its way to position 3 after five iterations. The bubble sort can be speeded up by having successive passes go in opposite directions so that the small elements move quickly to the front of the file in the same way that the large ones move to the rear. This reduces the required number of passes. This version is left as an exercise.

Quicksort

The next sort we consider is the **partition exchange sort** (or **quicksort**). Let x be an array and n the number of elements in the array to be sorted. Choose an element a from a specific position within the array [e.g., a can be chosen as the first element so that $a = x(1)$]. Suppose the elements of x are rearranged so that a is placed into position j and the following conditions hold:

1. Each of the elements in positions 1 through $j-1$ is less than or equal to a.
2. Each of the elements in positions $j+1$ through n is greater than or equal to a.

Notice that if these two conditions hold for a particular a and j, then a is the jth smallest element of x, so that a remains in position j when the array is completely sorted. (You are asked to prove this fact as an exercise.) If the process above is repeated with the subarrays $x(1)$ through $x(j-1)$ and $x(j+1)$ through $x(n)$ and any subarrays created by the process in successive iterations, the final result is a sorted file.

Let us illustrate the quicksort with an example. If an initial array is given as

$$25 \quad 57 \quad 48 \quad 37 \quad 12 \quad 92 \quad 86 \quad 33$$

and the first element (25) is placed in its proper position, the resulting array is

$$12 \quad 25 \quad 57 \quad 48 \quad 37 \quad 92 \quad 86 \quad 33$$

At this point, 25 is in its proper position in the array ($x(2)$), each element below that position (12) is less than or equal to 25, and each element above that position (57, 48, 37, 92, 86, and 33) is greater than or equal to 25. Since 25 is in its final position, the original problem has been decomposed into the problem of sorting the two subarrays

$$(12) \quad \text{and} \quad (57 \quad 48 \quad 37 \quad 92 \quad 86 \quad 33)$$

Nothing need be done to sort the first of these subarrays; a file of one element is already sorted. To sort the second subarray, the process is repeated and the subarray is further subdivided. The entire array may now be viewed as

$$12 \quad 25 \quad (57 \quad 48 \quad 37 \quad 92 \quad 86 \quad 33)$$

where parentheses enclose the subarrays that are yet to be sorted. Repeating the process on the subarray $x(3)$ through $x(8)$ yields

$$12 \quad 25 \quad (48 \quad 37 \quad 33) \quad 57 \quad (92 \quad 86)$$

and further repetitions yield

12	25	(37	33)	48	57	(92	86)
12	25	(33)	37	48	57	(92	86)
12	25	33	37	48	57	(92	86)
12	25	33	37	48	57	(86)	92
12	25	33	37	48	57	86	92

Note that the final array is sorted.

By this time you should have noticed that the quicksort may be defined most conveniently as a recursive procedure. We may outline an algorithm *quick(lb,ub)* to sort all elements in an array x between positions lb and ub (lb is the lower bound, ub the upper bound) as follows:

if lb > ub
    then return   'array is sorted
endif

rearrange (lb,ub,j)   'rearrange the elements of the subarray such that one of the
                                    'elements (possibly $x(lb)$) is now at $x(j)$ (j is an output
                                    'parameter) and:
                                    '1. $x(i) \leq x(j)$ for $lb \leq i < j$
                                    '2. $x(i) > (j)$ for $j < i \leq ub$
                                    '$x(j)$ is now at its final position

quick(lb,j − 1)   'recursively sort the subarray between positions *lb* and
                                    $j − 1$

quick(j + 1,ub)   'recursively sort the subarray
                                    'between positions $j + 1$ and *ub*

There are now two problems. We must produce a mechanism to implement *rearrange* and produce a method to implement the entire process nonrecursively.

    The object of *rearrange* is to allow a specific element to find its proper position with respect to the others in the subarray. Note that the manner in which this rearrangement is performed is irrelevant to the sorting method. All that is required by the sort is that the elements be partitioned properly. In the example above, the elements in each of the two subfiles remain in the same relative order as they appear in the original file. However, such a rearrangement method is relatively inefficient to implement.

    One way to effect a rearrangement efficiently is the following. Let $a = x (lb)$ be the element whose final position is sought. (No appreciable efficiency is gained by selecting the first element of the subarray as the one that is inserted into its proper position; it merely makes some of the programs easier to code.) Two pointers, *up* and *down,* are initialized to the upper and lower bounds of the subarray, respectively. At any point during execution, each element in a position above *up* is greater than or equal to a and each element in a position below *down* is less than or equal to a. The two pointers *up* and *down* are moved toward each other in the following fashion. Execution begins by increasing the pointer *down* one position at a time until $x(down) > a$. At that point the pointer *up* is decreased one position at a time until $x(up) \leq a$. If *up* is still greater than *down*, we proceed to interchange $x(down)$ with $x(up)$. The process is repeated until $up \leq down$, at which point $x(up)$ is interchanged with $x(lb)$ (which equals a), whose final position was sought, and the value of j is set to the position *up*.

    We illustrate this process on the sample file, showing the positions of *up* and *down* as they are adjusted. The direction of the scan is indicated by an arrow at the pointer being moved. An asterisk indicates that an interchange is made.

$a = x(lb) = 25$

down◆							*up*	
25	57	48	37	12	92	86	33	
	down						*up*	
25	57	48	37	12	92	86	33	
	down						◆*up*	
25	57	48	37	12	92	86	33	
	down					◆*up*		
25	57	48	37	12	92	86	33	
	down				◆*up*			
25	57	48	37	12	92	86	33	
	down			*up*				
25	57	48	37	12	92	86	33	
	down			*up*				
25	12	48	37	57	92	86	33	*
	down◆			*up*				
25	12	48	37	57	92	86	33	
		down		*up*				
25	12	48	37	57	92	86	33	
		down		◆*up*				
25	12	48	37	57	92	86	33	
		down	◆*up*					
25	12	48	37	57	92	86	33	
		◆*up,down*						
25	12	48	37	57	92	86	33	
	up	*down*						
25	12	48	37	57	92	86	33	
	up	*down*						
12	25	48	37	57	92	86	33	*

At this point 25 is in its proper position (position 2), every element to its left is less than or equal to 25, and every element to its right is greater than or equal to 25. We could now proceed to sort the two subarrays (12) and (48 37 57 92 86 33) by applying the same method.

An algorithm to implement the subroutine *rearrange* is as follows (*x, lb,* and *ub* are input variables, and *j* and *x* are output variables):

```
a = x (lb)                    'a is the element whose final
                              'position is sought
up = ub
down = lb
while down < up do
     while x(down) <= a do
          down = down + 1     'move down up the array
     endwhile
```

> *while* x(*up*) > a *do*
>   *up* = *up* − 1   'move *up* down the array
> *endwhile*
> *if* *down* < *up*
>   *then* interchange x(*down*) and x(*up*)
> *endif*
> *endwhile*
> x(*lb*) = x(*up*)   'x(*up*) is interchanged
> x(*up*) = a   'with x(*lb*) = a
> j = *up*

Note that if k equals $ub-lb+1$, so that we are rearranging a subarray of size k, the subroutine uses k key comparisons [of x(*down*) with a and x(*up*) with a] to perform the partition.

A program segment for *rearrange* follows:

```
6000   'subroutine rearrange
6010   'inputs: LB, UB, X
6020   'outputs: J, X
6030   'locals: A, DOWN, TEMP, UP
6040   A = X(LB)
6050   UP = UB
6060   DOWN = LB
6070   'move up the array
6080   IF X(DOWN) > A THEN GOTO 6110
6090      DOWN = DOWN + 1
6100   IF DOWN < UP THEN GOTO 6080
6110   'move down the array
6120   IF X (UP) < = A THEN GOTO 6150
6130      UP = UP − 1
6140   GOTO 6120
6150   IF DOWN < UP THEN TEMP = X(DOWN): X(DOWN) = X(UP):
                              X(UP) = TEMP: GOTO 6070
6160   X(LB) = X(UP)
6170   X(UP) = A
6180   J = UP
6190   RETURN
6200   'endsub
```

Note that the routine is a slightly modified version of the algorithm to ensure correctness when DOWN equals N, the (possibly) last element of the array. The routine can be made slightly more efficient by eliminating some of the redundant tests. You are asked to do this as an exercise.

While the recursive quicksort algorithm is relatively clear in terms of what it accomplishes and how, recursion is not available in BASIC. In addition, it is desirable to avoid the overhead of subroutine calls in programs such as sorts in which execution efficiency is a significant consideration. The recursive calls to QUICK can easily be eliminated by using a stack as in Chapter 5. Once *rearrange* has been executed, the current parameters to QUICK are no longer needed, except in computing the arguments to the two subsequent recursive calls. Thus instead of stacking the current parameters upon each recursive call, we can compute and stack the new parameters for each of the two recursive calls. Under this approach, the stack at any point contains the lower and upper bounds of all subarrays that must yet be sorted. Furthermore, since the second recursive call immediately precedes the return to the calling program (as in the Towers of Hanoi problem), it may be eliminated entirely and replaced with a branch. Finally, since the order in which the two recursive calls are made is irrelevant in this problem, we elect in each case to stack the larger subarray and process the smaller subarray immediately. As we will explain shortly, this technique keeps the size of the stack to a minimum.

We may now code a program to implement the quicksort. As in the case of *bubble,* the input variables are the array X and the number of elements of X we wish to sort, N. The subroutine *pushbounds* pushes LB and UB onto the stack, *popbounds* pops them from the stack, and *empty* determines if the stack is empty.

```
5000    'subroutine quicksort
5010    'inputs: N, X
5020    'outputs: X
5030    'locals: J, LB, SITEM, TEMP, TP, UB
5040    TP = 0: 'initialize the stack
5050    LB = 1
5060    UB = N
5070    GOSUB 1000: 'subroutine pushbounds pushes LB and UB onto the stack
5080    'repeat as long as there are any unsorted subarrays on the stack
5090    GOSUB 3000: 'subroutine empty sets the variable EMPTY
5100        IF EMPTY = TRUE THEN RETURN
5110        GOSUB 2000: 'subroutine popbounds pops LB and UB off the stack
5120    IF UB <= LB THEN GOTO 5090
5130        'process the next subarray by rearranging and splitting it into two
5140        GOSUB 6000: 'subroutine rearrange sets the variable J
5150        'stack the larger subarray
5160        IF J–LB > UB–J THEN TEMP = UB: UB = J – 1: GOSUB 1000:
                                    LB = J + 1: UB = TEMP: GOTO 5120
5170                                'stack lower subarray and
                                    'process upper subarray
```

```
5180    'else do stmts 5190–5240, stack upper subarray
5190    TEMP = LB
5200    LB = J + 1
5210    GOSUB 1000: 'subroutine pushbounds
5220    'process lower subarray
5230    UB = J − 1
5240    LB = TEMP
5250  GOTO 5120
5260  'endsub
        . . .
6000  'subroutine rearrange
```

The routines *rearrange, empty, popbounds,* and *pushbounds* could be inserted in line for maximum efficiency. Trace the action of *quicksort* on the sample file.

How efficient is the quicksort? Assume that the file size n is a power of 2, say $n = 2^m$, so that $m = \log_2 n$. Assume also that the proper position for $x(lb)$ always turns out to be the exact middle of the subarray. In that case there will be approximately n comparisons (actually $n − 1$) on the first pass, after which the file is split into two subfiles each of size $n/2$ approximately. For each of these two files there are approximately $n/2$ comparisons, and a total of four files each of size $n/4$ are formed. Each of these files requires $n/4$ comparisons, yielding a total of $n/8$ subfiles. After halving the subfiles m times, there are n files of size 1. Thus the total number of comparisons for the entire sort is approximately.

$$n + 2*(n/2) + 4*(n/4) + 8*(n/8) + \ldots + n*(n/n)$$

or

$$n + n + n + n + \ldots + n \quad (m \text{ terms})$$

comparisons. There are m terms because the file is subdivided m times. Thus the total number of comparisons is $O(n*m)$ or $O(n \log n)$ [recall that $m = \log_2 n$]. Thus if the properties above describe the file, the quicksort is $O(n \log n)$, which is relatively efficient.

The analysis above assumes that the original array and all the resulting subarrays are unsorted, so that $x(lb)$ always finds its proper position at the middle of the subarray. Suppose that the conditions above do not hold and the original array is sorted (or almost sorted). If, for example, $x(lb)$ is in its correct position, the original file is split into subfiles of sizes 0 and $n − 1$. If this process continues, a total of $n − 1$ subfiles are sorted, the first of size n, the second of size $n − 1$, the third of size $n − 2$, and so on. Assuming k comparisons to rearrange a file of size k, the total number of comparisons to sort the entire file is

$$n + (n − 1) + (n − 2) + \ldots + 2$$

which is $O(n^2)$. Similarly, if the original file is sorted in descending order, the final position of $x(lb)$ is ub and the file is again split into two subfiles which are heavily unbalanced (sizes $n - 1$ and 0). Thus the quicksort has the seemingly absurd property that it works best for files that are "completely unsorted" and worst for files that are completely sorted. The situation is precisely the opposite for the bubble sort, which works best for sorted files and worst for unsorted files. The analysis for the case where the file size is not an integral power of 2 is similar but slightly more complex; the results, however, remain the same. It can be shown that on the average (over all files of size n), the quicksort makes $O(n \log n)$ comparisons. Even the worst-case efficiency can be improved by using the techniques of Exercise 11.

The space requirements for the quicksort depend on the number of nested recursive calls or on the size of the stack. Clearly, the stack can never grow larger than the number of elements in the original file. How much smaller than n the stack grows depends on the number of subfiles generated and on their sizes. The size of the stack is somewhat contained by always stacking the larger of the two subarrays and applying the routine to the smaller of the two. This guarantees that all smaller subarrays are subdivided before larger subarrays, giving the net effect of having fewer elements on the stack at any given time. The reason for this is that a smaller subarray will be divided fewer times than a larger subarray. Of course, the larger subarray will ultimately be processed and subdivided, but this will occur after the smaller subarrays have already been sorted and therefore removed from the stack.

EXERCISES

1. Prove that the number of passes necessary in the bubble sort of the text before the file is in sorted order (not including the last pass, which detects the fact that the file is sorted) equals the largest distance by which an element must move from a larger index to a smaller index.

2. Rewrite the program *bubble* so that successive passes go in opposite directions. (This is known as the **cocktail shaker sort**.)

3. Prove that in the sort of Exercise 2, if two elements are not interchanged during two consecutive passes in opposite directions, they are in their final position.

4. A sort by **counting** is performed as follows. Declare an array *count* and set $count(i)$ to the number of elements which are less than or equal to $x(i)$. Then place $x(i)$ in position $count(i)$ of an output array. (However, beware of the possibility of equal elements.) Write a routine to sort an array x of size n using this method.

5. Assume that a file contains integers between a and b, with many numbers repeated several times. A **distribution sort** proceeds as follows. Declare an array *number* of size $b - a + 1$ and set $number(i-a+1)$ to the number of times that integer i appears in the file. Then reset the values in the file appropriately. Write a routine to sort an array x of size n containing integers between a and b by this method.

6. The *odd-even transposition sort* proceeds as follows. Pass through the file several times. On the first pass, compare $x(i)$ with $x(i + 1)$ for all odd i. On the second pass, compare $x(i)$ with $x(i + 1)$ for all even i. Each time that $x(i) > x(i + 1)$, interchange the two. Continue alternating in this fashion until the file is sorted.
   (a) What is the condition for the termination of the sort?
   (b) Write a BASIC routine to implement the sort.
   (c) On the average, what is the efficiency of this sort?

7. Rewrite the program for the quicksort by starting with the recursive algorithm and applying the methods of Chapter 5 to produce a nonrecursive version.

8. Under what circumstances can statement 6100 in the *rearrange* routine be changed from

$$6100 \quad \text{IF DOWN} < \text{UB THEN GOTO } 6080$$

to

$$6100 \quad \text{GOTO } 6080$$

Which version is more efficient, and why?

9. Can statements 6080–6100 of the subroutine *rearrange* be changed from

```
6080   IF X(DOWN) > A THEN GOTO 6110
6090      DOWN = DOWN + 1
6100   IF DOWN < UB THEN GOTO 6080
```

to

```
6080   DOWN = DOWN + 1
6090   IF DOWN < UB
          THEN IF X(DOWN) <= A THEN GOTO 6080
```

What are the advantages and/or disadvantages of this change?

10. Modify the quicksort program of the text so that if a subarray is small, the bubble sort is used. Determine, by actual computer runs, how small the subarray should be so that this mixed strategy will be more efficient than an ordinary quicksort.

11. Modify *rearrange* so that the middle value of $x(lb)$, $x(ub)$, and $x(int((ub+lb)/2))$ is used to partition the array. In what cases is the quicksort using this method more efficient than the version of the text? In what cases is it less efficient?

12. Evaluate the efficiency of each of the following sorting methods with respect to time and space considerations.
   (a) The bubble sort using $n - 1$ passes, in which every pass goes through all the elements of the file.
   (b) The bubble sort in which each pass makes one fewer comparison than the preceding pass.
   (c) The bubble sort of the text, as modified in Exercise 2.
   (d) The counting sort of Exercise 4.
   (e) The distribution sort of Exercise 5.

(**f**) The odd-even transposition sort of Exercise 6.
(**g**) The quicksort as modified in Exercise 10.
(**h**) The quicksort as modified in Exercise 11.

13. (**a**) Rewrite the routines for the bubble sort and the quicksort as presented in the text and the sorts of Exercise 12 so that a record is kept of the actual number of comparisons and the actual number of interchanges made.

   (**b**) Write a random-number generator (or use an existing one if your computer has one) that generates integers between 0 and 9999.

   (**c**) Using the generator of part (b), generate several files of size 10, size 100, and size 1000. Apply the sorting routines of part (a) to measure the time requirements for each of the sorts on each of the files.

   (**d**) Measure the results of part (c) against the theoretical values presented in this section. Do they agree? If not, explain. In particular, rearrange the files so that they are completely sorted and in reverse order and see how the sorts behave with these inputs.

3. SELECTION AND TREE SORTING

Straight Selection Sort

A *selection sort* is one in which successive elements are selected from the file and placed in their proper position. The following program is an example of a *straight selection sort*. The largest number is first placed in the Nth position, the next largest is placed in position $N-1$, and so on.

```
5000   'subroutine select
5010   'inputs: N, X
5020   'outputs: X
5030   'locals: I, IDX, J, LARGE
5040   FOR I = N TO 2 STEP - 1
5050        'place the largest number of X(1) through X(I)
             'into LARGE and its index into IDX
5060        LARGE = X(1)
5070        IDX = 1
5080        FOR J = 2 TO I
5090            IF X(J) > LARGE THEN LARGE = X(J): IDX = J
5100        NEXT J
5110        X(IDX) = X(I)
5120        X(I) = LARGE: 'place LARGE into position I
5130   NEXT I
5140   RETURN
5150   'endsub
```

This sort is also known as the ***push-down*** sort.

Analysis of the straight selection sort is straightforward. The first pass makes $n - 1$ comparisons, the second pass makes $n - 2$, and so on. Therefore, there is a total of

$$(n - 1) + (n - 2) + (n - 3) + \ldots + 1 = n*(n - 1)/2$$

comparisons, which is $O(n^2)$. The number of interchanges is always $n - 1$ (unless a test is added to prevent the interchanging of an element with itself). There is little additional storage required (except to hold a few temporary variables). The sort may therefore be categorized as $O(n^2)$, although it is faster than the bubble sort. There is no improvement if the input file is completely sorted or unsorted since the testing proceeds to completion without regard to the makeup of the file. Despite the fact that it is simple to code, it is unlikely that the straight selection sort would be used on any files but those for which n is small.

Binary Tree Sorts

In the remainder of this section we illustrate several selection sorts that utilize binary trees. Before we do that, however, let us analyze the binary tree sort of Section 6.1. The reader is advised to review that sort before proceeding.

The method involves scanning each element of the input file and placing it into its proper position in a binary tree. To find the proper position of an element, y, a left or right branch is taken at each node depending on whether y is less than the element in the node or greater than or equal to it. Once each input element is in its proper position in the tree, the sorted file can be retrieved by an inorder traversal of the tree. We present the algorithm for this sort, modifying it to accommodate the input as a preexisting array. Translating the algorithm to a BASIC routine is straightforward.

```
'establish the first element as root
tree = maketree(x(1))
'repeat for each successive element
for i = 2 to n
    y = x(i)
    q = tree
    p = q
    'travel down the tree until a leaf is reached
    while p <> null do
        q = p
        if y < info(p)
            then p == left(p)
            else p = right(p)
        endif
    endwhile
```

> **if** $y < info(q)$
>   **then** $setleft(q,y)$
>   **else** $setright(q,y)$
>   **endif**
> **next** i
> 'the tree is built, traverse it in inorder
> $intrav(tree)$

In order to convert the algorithm above into a subroutine to sort an array, it is necessary to revise *intrav* so that visiting a node involves placing the contents of the node into the next position of the original array.

The relative efficiency of this method depends on the original order of the data. If the original array is completely sorted (or sorted in reverse order), the resulting tree appears as a sequence of only right (or left) links, as in Figure 8.3.1. In this case the insertion of the first node requires no comparisons, the second node requires two comparisons, the third node three comparisons, and so on. Thus the total number of comparisons is

$$2 + 3 + \ldots + n = n*(n + 1)/2 - 1$$

which is $O(n^2)$.

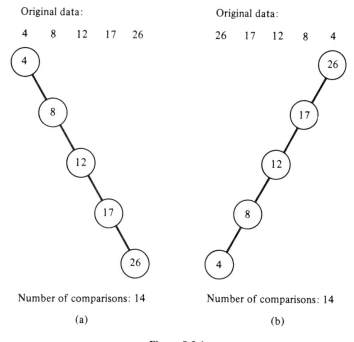

Original data:

4   8   12   17   26

Number of comparisons: 14

(a)

Original data:

26   17   12   8   4

Number of comparisons: 14

(b)

Figure 8.3.1

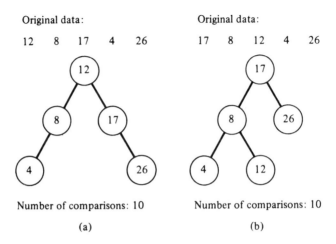

Figure 8.3.2

On the other hand, if the data in the original array are organized so that approximately half the numbers following any given number a in the array are less than a and half are greater than a, trees such as those in Figure 8.3.2 result. In such a case, the depth of the resulting binary tree is the smallest integer d greater than or equal to $\log_2(n+1) - 1$. The number of nodes at any level l (except possibly for the last) is 2^l and the number of comparisons necessary to place a node at level l (except when $l = 0$) is $l + 1$. Thus the total number of comparisons is between

$$d + \sum_{l=1}^{d-1} 2^l(l+1) \qquad \text{and} \qquad \sum_{l=1}^{d} 2^l(l+1)$$

It can be shown (mathematically inclined readers might be interested in proving this fact as an exercise) that the resulting sums are $O(n \log n)$.

Of course, once the tree has been created, time is expended in traversing it. (Note that if the tree is threaded as it is created, the traversal time is sharply reduced.)

This sort requires that one tree node be reserved for each array element. Depending on the method used to implement the tree, space may be required for tree pointers and threads, if any.

Tournament Sort

The next tree sort we consider is frequently called the **tournament sort** because its actions mirror those of a tournament where participants compete against each other to determine the best player. (This sort is also called the ***tree selection sort***.) Consider a tournament that determines the best player from the set {Ed, Gail, Keith, George, Jack, Pat, Barbara, Frank}. The outcome of the tournament can be represented by a binary tree, as in Figure 8.3.3. Each leaf of the tree represents a player in the tournament. Each nonleaf node represents the results of a game between the players represented by its two sons. In Figure 8.3.3(a) it is clear that Gail is the tournament champion.

But suppose that it is also desired to determine the second-best player. Pat is not necessarily the second-best player despite the fact that he played Gail in the championship game. To determine the second-best player, it would be necessary for Keith (who lost to Gail in the quarter finals) to play George (who lost to Gail in the semifinals) and the winner of that match to play Pat.

Let us indicate that a player has been declared a winner by placing an asterisk in the leaf node corresponding to that player. Clearly, if a node is marked with an asterisk, its player does not participate in any future runoffs. If both sons of a node contain an asterisk, those sons both represent players who have completed the tournament, and therefore the father node is also marked with an asterisk and no longer participates in further runoffs. If only one son of a node is marked with an asterisk, the player represented by the other son is moved up to the father node. For example, when the leaf containing Gail in Figure 8.3.3(a) is marked with an asterisk, the name Keith is moved up to replace Gail in the father of that leaf. The tournament is then replayed from that point, with George playing Keith (George wins) and George playing Pat (Pat wins), thus yielding the tree of Figure 8.3.3(b). Pat is indeed the second-best player. This process may be continued [Figure 8.3.3(c) illustrates that George is third best] until all the nodes of the tree are marked with asterisks.

The same technique is used in the tournament sort. Each of the original elements is assigned to a leaf node of a binary tree. The tree is constructed in bottom-up fashion from the leaf nodes to the root as follows. Choose two leaf nodes and establish them as the sons of a newly created father node. The content of the father node is set to the larger of the two numbers represented by its sons. This process is repeated until either one or zero leafs remain. If one remains, move the node itself up to the previous level. Now repeat this process with the newly created father nodes (plus the possible node that had no partner in the previous repetition) until the largest number is placed in the root node of a binary tree whose leafs contain all the numbers of the original file. The contents of this root node may then be output as the largest element. The leaf node containing the value at the root is then replaced with a number smaller than any in the original file (this corresponds to marking it with an asterisk). The contents of all its ancestors are then recomputed from the leafs to the root. This process is repeated until all the original elements have been output.

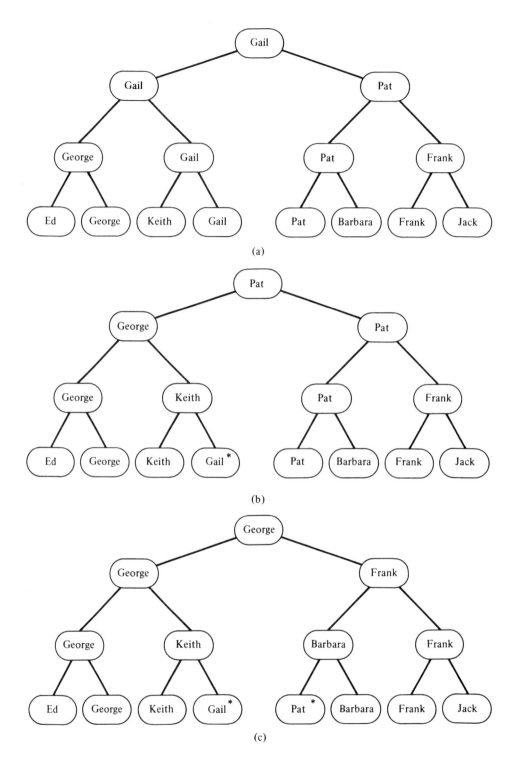

(a)

(b)

(c)

Figure 8.3.3 A tournament.

Figure 8.3.4(a) shows the initial tree using the file presented in the last section:

25   57   48   37   12   92   86   33

After 92 is output, the tree is transformed as in Figure 8.3.4(b), where 92 has been replaced by -1 and 86 is moved up to the root position. Note that it is necessary to recompute the contents of those nodes which were ancestors of the original leaf node that contained 92. Figure 8.3.4(c) shows the tree after 57 has moved up to the root. Note that -1 is used as the smallest value in this example, since the numbers being sorted are all positive. The reader is asked to complete the process until all the elements of the original file have been output.

Before writing a program to implement the tournament sort, we must decide how to implement the tree in BASIC. The linked array representation of Section 6.2 could be used. However, the efficiency of the program can be improved by using the representation in which an almost complete binary tree is represented as an array. In this representation, if index i references a node, then $left(i)$ is referenced by index $2*i$, $right(i)$ is referenced by $2*i + 1$, and $father(i)$ is referenced by $int(i/2)$. To simplify the coding, we use a complete binary tree. In such a tree, only those nodes at the maximum level are leafs. Such a tree with eight leafs is illustrated in Figure 8.3.4. In general, the number of leafs in a complete binary tree is a power of 2. If the original file is of size n which is not a power of 2, the number of leafs is the smallest power of 2 greater than n and the extra leafs are initialized to -1.

A second question is what should the contents of the tree nodes be? Suppose that we allow the tree nodes to contain the actual items to be sorted, as in Figure 8.3.4. Then when the root is output, the leaf node corresponding to that root element must be replaced by a very small number and the contents of all its ancestors must be readjusted. But in order to locate the leaf node corresponding to the root, given only the root, it is necessary to travel from the root down to the leaf making a comparison at each level. Furthermore, this process must be repeated for each new root node. It would certainly be more efficient if it were possible to proceed directly from the root to the leaf that corresponds to its contents. We therefore construct the complete binary tree in the following way. Each leaf contains an element of the original array x. Each nonleaf node contains the index of the leaf node corresponding to the array element which the nonleaf node represents. If the content of a leaf node i, $tree(i)$, is moved up to a nonleaf node j, $tree(j)$ is set to i (the index in the tree of the leaf node corresponding to the element) rather than $tree(i)$ (the actual element itself). The content of a nonleaf node (which is the index of the appropriate leaf node) is subsequently moved up the tree directly. Thus if i is a leaf node, $tree(i)$ contains the actual element that node i represents; if i is a nonleaf node, $tree(i)$ references the index of a leaf node and hence $tree(tree(i))$ references the actual element that node i represents.

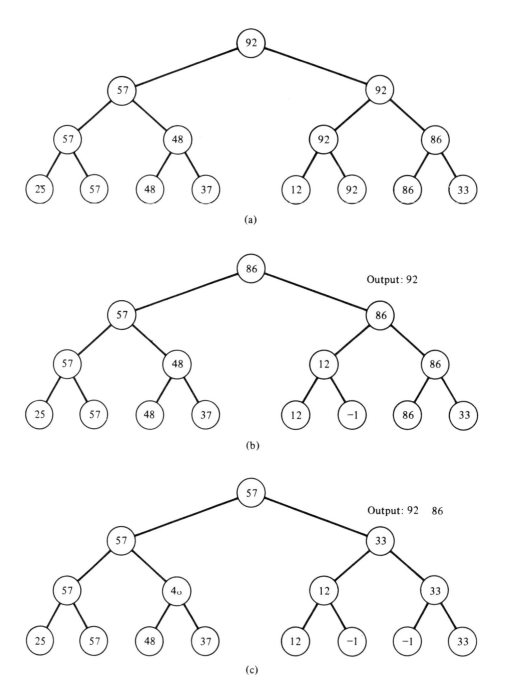

Figure 8.3.4

For example, the array *tree* representing the tree of Figure 8.3.4(a) is initialized as follows. (Nodes 8 through 15 are leafs, nodes 1 through 7 are nonleafs.)

i	*tree(i)*
1	13
2	9
3	13
4	9
5	10
6	13
7	14
8	25
9	57
10	48
11	37
12	12
13	92
14	86
15	33

We may now code the sort routine (assuming that $n > 1$) as follows:

```
5000   'subroutine tournament
5010   'inputs: N, X
5020   'outputs: X
5030   'locals: I, K, SIZE, SMALL, TREE
5040   SIZE = 1
5050   SMALL = − 9999
5060   IF SIZE < N THEN SIZE = SIZE * 2: GOTO 5060
5070   'SIZE is the number of leafs necessary in the complete binary tree
5080   'the number of nodes is 2* SIZE −1
5090   'assume that the array TREE has been dimensioned to size at least
       '2*SIZE − 1
5100   GOSUB 6000:                          'subroutine initialize
5110   'initialize creates the initial tree as described in the text
5120   'now that the tree is constructed, repeatedly place the element
       'represented by the root in the next lower position in the array X
       'and readjust the tree
```

```
5130   FOR K = N TO 2 STEP − 1
5140       I = TREE(1):                      'I is the index of the leaf node
                                             'corresponding to the root
5150       X(K) = TREE(I):                   'place element referenced by root
                                             'in position K
5160       TREE(I) = SMALL
5170       GOSUB 7000:                       'subroutine readjust
                                             'readjusts the tree based on the
                                             'new contents of TREE(I)
5180   NEXT K
5190   X(1) = TREE(TREE(1))
5200   RETURN
5210   'endsub
```

We now present the routines *initialize* and *readjust*. Note that the level directly above the leafs must be treated differently than the other levels.

```
6000   'subroutine initialize
6010   'inputs: N, SIZE, SMALL, X
6020   'outputs: TREE
6030   'locals: J, K
6040   'initialize leafs of tree corresponding to array elements
6050   FOR J = 1 TO N
6060       TREE (SIZE + J − 1) = X(J)
6070   NEXT J
6080   'initialize remaining leafs
6090   FOR J = SIZE + N TO 2*SIZE − 1
6100       TREE(J) = SMALL
6110   NEXT J
6120   'compute upper levels of the tree
6130   'the level directly above the leafs is treated separately
6140   FOR J = SIZE TO 2*SIZE − 1 STEP 2
6150       IF TREE(J) >= TREE(J + 1) THEN TREE(INT(J/2)) = J
                                          ELSE TREE(INT(J/2)) = J + 1
6160   NEXT J
6170   'compute the remaining levels
6180   K = INT (SIZE/2)
6190   IF K <= 1 THEN RETURN
6200      FOR J = K TO 2*K − 1 STEP 2
6210          IF TREE(TREE(J)) >= TREE(TREE(J + 1))
                  THEN TREE(INT(J/2)) = TREE(J)
                  ELSE TREE(INT(J/2)) = TREE(J + 1)
6220      NEXT J
6230      K = INT(K/2)
6240   GOTO 6190
6250   'endsub
```

```
7000    'subroutine readjust
7010    'inputs: I
7020    'outputs: TREE
7030    'locals: J
7040    'now that TREE(I) has a new value (SMALL) we adjust all its ancestors
7050    'adjust the father node
7060    IF INT(I/2) = I/2 THEN TREE (INT(I/2)) = I + 1
                            ELSE TREE(INT(I/2)) = I - 1
7070    'advance to the root
7080    I = INT(I/2)
7090    IF I <= 1 THEN RETURN
7100       'set J to the brother of I
7110       IF INT(I/2) = I/2 THEN J = I + 1
                             ELSE J = I - 1
7120       IF TREE(TREE(I)) > TREE(TREE(J)) THEN TREE(INT(I/2)) = TREE(I)
                                            ELSE TREE(INT(I/2) = TREE(J)
7130       I = INT(I/2)
7140    GOTO 7090
7150    'endsub
```

Measuring the time and space requirements of this sort is straightforward. Observe that after the initial tree has been created and the root has been output, d comparisons are required to readjust the tree and move a new element to the root position, where d is the depth of the tree. Since d is approximately $\log_2(n + 1)$ and $n - 1$ adjustments must be made to the tree, the number of comparisons is approximately $(n - 1)\log_2 (n + 1)$, which is $O(n \log n)$. Of course, comparisons are made in creating the initial tree, but the number of such comparisons is $O(n)$ and is therefore dominated by the $O(n \log n)$ term.

The space requirements, in addition to temporary values, are the $2*size - 1$ memory units reserved for the array *tree*, where *size* is the smallest integral power of 2 which is greater than or equal to n. Since we insisted on a complete binary tree in this program, there may be much wasted space if, for example, the value of n is 33 or 129. Of course, if a linked implementation of trees is used, additional space is required for the links.

Heapsort

Although the program above appears to be relatively efficient in all cases, it does have a serious shortcoming which is easy to remove. The upper levels of the tree contain pointers, while the actual data are kept only at the lowest level. As a by-product of this, many nodes carry duplicate information on several levels of the tree. Because of this, there is considerable work involved in bringing an element from the leaf to the root. Much of this work is unnecessary in the later stages of the sort when most of the leafs (and indirectly, many of the upper levels) contain the value SMALL, causing unnecessary comparisons to be made.

This drawback may be remedied by the **heapsort.** In this sort, only one node is reserved for each of the elements in the original file.This serves to eliminate the large amount of space allocated in the tournament sort and the redundant comparisons of the later stages of that sort. In fact, the original array x is used as a workspace for the sort, so that extra space is required only for temporary variables.

Define a **heap of size n** as an almost complete binary tree of n nodes such that the content of each node is less than or equal to the content of its father. If the array implementation of an almost complete binary tree is used, as was done in the implementation of the tournament sort, this condition reduces to the inequality for all j between 1 and n:

$$info(j) \leq info(k) \qquad \text{for } k = int(j/2)$$

It is clear from this definition of a heap that the root of the tree (or the first element of the array) is the largest element in the heap. Assuming that the routine *createheap(i)* creates a heap of size i consisting of the first i elements of the array x, a sorting method could be implemented as follows:

> **for** i = n **to** 2 **step** $- 1$
>   *createheap(i)*
>   interchange $x(1)$ and $x(i)$
> **next** i

As we shall see, however, it is not necessary to create the entire heap anew on each iteration; we can readjust the heap that was created on the preceding iteration so that it remains a heap even after the interchange. Thus the heapsort consists of the following algorithm.

> *createheap(n)*
> **for** i = n **to** 2 **step** -1
>   interchange $x(1)$ and $x(i)$
>   create a heap of order $i - 1$ by readjusting the position of $x(1)$
> **next** i

We must consider two problems: how to create the original heap and how to adjust the intermediate heaps. To create the original heap, start with a heap of size 1 consisting of $x(1)$ alone and try to create a heap of size 2 consisting of $x(1)$ and $x(2)$. This can be accomplished quite easily by interchanging $x(2)$ and $x(1)$ if $x(1)$ is less than or equal to $x(2)$. In general, in order to create a heap of size i by inserting node i into an existing heap of size $i - 1$, compare node i with its father. If node i is greater, interchange the two and change i to point to the father. Repeat this process until the content of the father of node i is greater than or equal to the content of node i or until i is the root of the heap. Thus an algorithm to create a heap of order k may be written as follows:

```
for node = 2 to k                          'insert x(node) into heap
   i = node
   j = int(i/2)                            'j is father of i
   while (i > 1) and (x(j) <= x(i)) do
        interchange x(i) and x(j)
            i = j                          'advance up the tree
            j = int(i/2)                   'j is father of i
   endwhile
next node
```

To solve the second problem of finding the proper place for $x(1)$ in a tree which satisfies the requirements of a heap (except for the root), initialize i to 1 and repeatedly interchange the content of node i with the content of the larger of its two sons as long as its content is not larger than those of both its sons, resetting i to point to the larger son. The algorithm to readjust the heap of order k may be written as follows:

```
i = 1
'compute the larger of i's two sons and place in j
j = 2
if (k >= 3) and (x(3) > x(2))
   then j = 3
endif
while (j <= k) and (x(j) > x(i)) do
        interchange x(i) and x(j)
        i = j
        'set j to the larger of i's sons
        j = 2 * i
        if (j + 1 <= k) and (x(j + 1) > x(j))
            then j = j + 1
        endif
endwhile
```

At this point, we should note that this algorithm cannot be implemented directly as written. If the condition $j <= k$ in the **while** loop is false, subsequent evaluation of $x(j) > x(i)$ may result in $x(j)$ being out of bounds. Thus the implementation of the compound conditional of the **while** loop will have to proceed in two steps. Similarly, the last **if** statement will have to be implemented as

```
if j+1<= k
   then if x(j + 1) >x(j)
           then j = j + 1
        endif
endif
```

because we must again ensure that the references to $x(j + 1)$ and $x(j)$ are within array bounds. Failure to consider such possibilities is a frequent source of program failure.

Figure 8.3.5 illustrates the creation of a heap of size 8 from the original file:

25   57   48   37   12   92   86   33

The dotted lines in that figure indicate that two elements have been interchanged.

Figure 8.3.6 illustrates the adjustment of the heap as $x(1)$ is moved to its proper position in the original array until all the elements of the heap are pro-

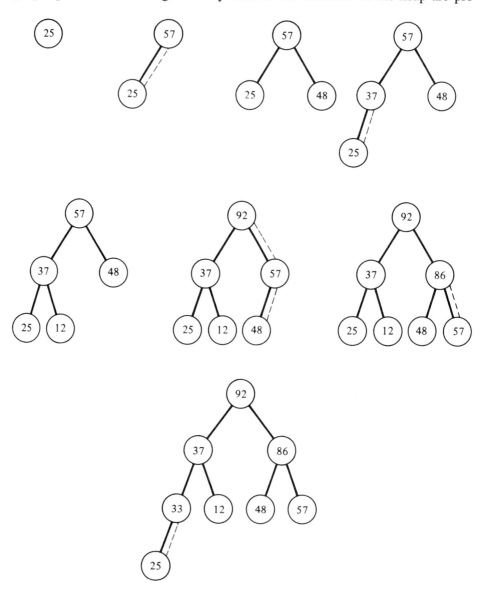

Figure 8.3.5   Creating a heap of size 8.

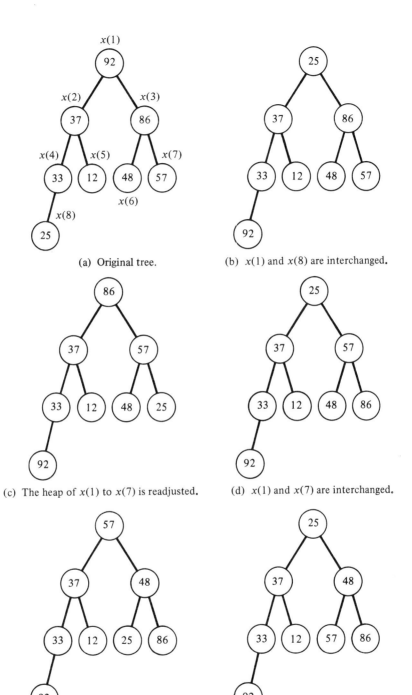

(a) Original tree.

(b) $x(1)$ and $x(8)$ are interchanged.

(c) The heap of $x(1)$ to $x(7)$ is readjusted.

(d) $x(1)$ and $x(7)$ are interchanged.

(e) The heap of $x(1)$ to $x(6)$ is readjusted.

(f) $x(1)$ and $x(6)$ are interchanged.

Figure 8.3.6 Adjusting a heap.

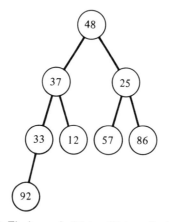

(g) The heap of $x(1)$ to $x(5)$ is readjusted.

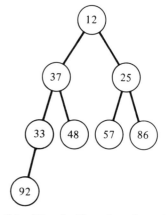

(h) $x(1)$ and $x(5)$ are interchanged.

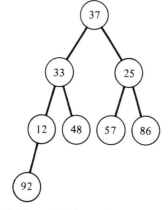

(i) The heap of $x(1)$ to $x(4)$ is readjusted.

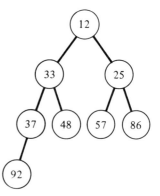

(j) $x(1)$ and $x(4)$ are interchanged.

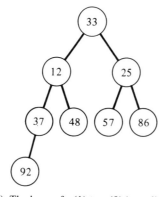

(k) The heap of $x(1)$ to $x(3)$ is readjusted.

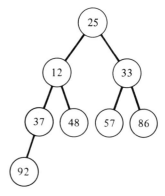

(l) $x(1)$ and $x(3)$ are interchanged.

Figure 8.3.6 (*continued*).

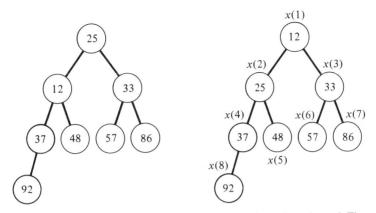

(m) The heap of $x(1)$ to $x(2)$ is readjusted.   (n) $x(1)$ and $x(2)$ are interchanged. The array is sorted.

Figure 8.3.6   *(continued).*

cessed. Note that after an element has been "removed" from the heap it retains its position in the array; it is merely ignored in subsequent processing. Note also that the transformations in Figure 8.3.6 illustrate a tournament in which, after an element is inserted into a father node, the sons below it advance up the tree to take their proper position. This eliminates the redundant nodes and the redundant tests of the tournament sort.

In the program below we implement the heapsort. The statements of the program mirror the description above except that not all the interchanges called for are made immediately. The value whose correct position is being sought is kept in a temporary variable y. Advances up or down the tree are made by adjusting pointers.

We present the program to implement the heapsort. N is assumed to be greater than or equal to 3.

```
5000   'subroutine heap
5010   'inputs: N, X
5020   'outputs: X
5030   'locals: I, J, K, Y
5040   'create initial heap
5050   FOR K = 2 TO N
5060       'insert X(K) into existing heap of size K − 1
5070       I = K
5080       Y = X(K)
5090       J = INT(I/2):      'J is father of I
```

```
5100        IF J <= 0 THEN GOTO 5160
5110        IF Y <= X(J) THEN GOTO 5160
5120           X(I) = X(J)
5130           I = J
5140           J = INT(I/2)
5150        GOTO 5100
5160        X(I) = Y
5170     NEXT K
5180     'we remove X(1) and place it in its proper position in the
         'array; we then adjust the heap
5190     FOR K = N TO 2 STEP - 1
5200        Y = X(K)
5210        X(K) = X(1)
5220        'readjust the heap of order K - 1; move Y down the heap to
            'its proper position
5230        I = 1
5240        J = 2
5250        IF (K - 1 >= 3) AND (X(3) > X(2)) THEN J = 3
5260        'J is the larger son of I in the heap of size K - 1
5270        IF J > K - 1 THEN GOTO 5340
5280        IF X(J) <= Y THEN GOTO 5340
5290           X(I) = X(J)
5300           I = J
5310           J = 2 * I
5320           IF J + 1 <= K - 1 THEN IF X(J + 1) > X(J) THEN J = J + 1
5330        GOTO 5260
5340        X(I) = Y
5350     NEXT K
5360     RETURN
5370     'endsub
```

To analyze the heapsort, note that a complete binary tree with n nodes (where n is 1 less than a power of 2) has $\log_2(n + 1)$ levels. Thus if each element in the array were a leaf, requiring it to be filtered through the entire tree both while creating and adjusting the heap, the sort would still be $O(n \log n)$. However, clearly not every element must pass through the entire tree. Thus while the sort is $O(n \log n)$, the multipliers are not as large as those for the tournament sort. The worst case for the heapsort is $O(n \log n)$; but it is not very efficient for small n. (Why?) The space requirement for the heapsort (aside from array indices) is only one additional record (Y) to hold the temporary for switching, provided that the array implementation of an almost complete binary tree is used.

EXERCISES

1. Explain why the straight selection sort is more efficient than the bubble sort.

2. Consider the following **quadratic selection sort.** Divide the n elements of the file into $\sqrt{n}$ groups of $\sqrt{n}$ elements each. Find the largest element of each group and insert it into an auxiliary array. Find the largest of the elements in this auxiliary array. This is the largest element of the file. Then replace this element in the array by the next largest element of the group from which it came. Again find the largest element of the auxiliary array. This is the second largest element of the file. Repeat the process until the file has been sorted. Write a BASIC routine to implement a quadratic selection sort as efficiently as possible.

3. Rewrite the tournament sort of this section, using linked allocation to store the binary tree.

4. Modify the routines of the tournament sort so that nonleafs as well as leafs contain the actual elements of the original file. When the content of the root is output, move down the tree to find the leaf whose ancestors must be modified.

5. Modify the routine *readjust* of the tournament sort so that when the content of a leaf is set to *small,* the content of its brother (rather than the index of its brother) is moved up the tree. (Note that under this modification, a nonleaf may contain the index of a nonleaf. For example, the array *tree* for the tree of Figure 8.3.4(c) would be as follows:

i	1	2	3	4	5	6	7	8	9	10	11	12	13	14	15
$tree(i)$	9	9	7	9	10	12	33	25	57	48	37	12	-1	-1	33

tree(6) and *tree*(7) both contain actual values and *tree*(3) contains the index of a nonleaf.) Why is this method more efficient?

6. Modify the tournament sort in the following ways. When the initial tree is created and the content of a leaf node is moved up, the content of the leaf is immediately changed to *small.* When the content of a nonleaf is moved up, the winner between its two sons is moved up to take its place. Each time the root of the tree is output, move up its largest son, then move up the largest son of that son, and so on, until the value *small* is moved up.

7. Use the technique of the tournament sort to merge n input files, each of which is sorted in ascending order, into a single output file, as follows. The tree is maintained so that the key represented by each node is the smaller of the keys of its two sons. Each leaf is designated as an input area for a single file. An auxiliary routine *inp(i)* reads the next input value from the ith input file into the appropriate leaf. When all the elements of file i have been input, *inp(i)* returns a value larger than any value in all input fields. An auxiliary routine *writeroot* outputs the element in the tree root into the output file. Each node of the tree contains an element and the input file number from which the element came. An element is contained in only a single node of the tree at any time. When an element is moved from a node *nd* to its father, another element is moved from below to *nd*. When an element is moved up from a leaf, the routine *inp* is called with the appropriate parameter to read a new input value into the leaf.

8. Define an **almost complete ternary tree** as a tree in which every node has at most three sons and such that the nodes can be numbered from 1 to n so that the sons of $node(i)$

are $node(3*i - 1)$, $node(3*i)$, and $node(3*i + 1)$. Define a **ternary heap** as an almost complete ternary tree in which the content of each node is greater than or equal to the contents of all its descendants. Write a sorting routine similar to the heapsort using a ternary heap.

9. Write a routine $combine(x)$ that accepts an array x in which the subtrees rooted at $x(2)$ and $x(3)$ are heaps and which modifies the array x so that it represents a single heap.

4. INSERTION SORTS

Simple Insertion

An *insertion sort* is one that sorts a set of records by inserting records into an existing sorted file. An example of a simple insertion sort is the following subroutine:

```
5000   'subroutine insert
5010   'inputs: N, X
5020   'outputs: X
5030   'locals: I, K
5040   'initially X(1) may be thought of as a sorted file of one element.
       'after each repetition of the following loop, the elements X(1)
       'through X(K) are in order
5050   FOR K = 2 TO N
5060       'insert X(K) into the sorted file
5070       Y = X(K)
5080       'move down one position all numbers greater than Y
5090       FOR I = K - 1 TO 1 STEP - 1
5100           IF Y >= X(I) THEN GOTO 5130
5110               X(I + 1) = X(I)
5120       NEXT I
5130       'insert Y at proper position
5140       X(I + 1) = Y
5150   NEXT K
5160   RETURN
5170   'endsub
```

If the initial file is sorted, only one comparison is made on each pass, so that the sort is $O(n)$. If the file is initially sorted in the reverse order, the sort is $O(n^2)$ since the total number of comparisons is

$$(n - 1) + (n - 2) + \ldots + 3 + 2 + 1 = (n - 1)*n/2$$

which is $O(n^2)$. However, the simple insertion sort is still usually better than the bubble sort. The closer the file is to sorted order, the more efficient the simple insertion sort becomes. The average number of comparisons in the simple insertion sort (by considering all possible permutations of the input array) is also

$O(n^2)$. The space requirements for the sort consist of only one temporary variable y.

The speed of the sort can be improved somewhat by using a binary search (see Section 5.1, 5.2, and 9.1) to find the proper position for $x(k)$ in the sorted file $x(1), \ldots, x(k-1)$. This reduces the total number of comparisons from $O(n^2)$ to $O(n \log n)$. However, even if the correct position i for $x(k)$ is found in $O(\log n)$ steps, each of the elements $x(i+1), \ldots, x(k-1)$ must be moved one position. The latter operation performed n times requires $O(n^2)$ replacements. Unfortunately, therefore, the binary search technique does not significantly improve the overall time requirements of the sort.

Another improvement to the simple insertion sort can be made by using *list insertion*. In this method there is an array *link* of pointers, one for each of the original array elements. Initially, $link(i) = i + 1$ for $1 \leq i < n$ and $link(n) = 0$. Thus the array may be thought of as a linear list pointed to by an external pointer *first* initialized to 1. To insert the kth element, the linked list is traversed until the proper position for $x(k)$ is found, or until the end of the list is reached. At that point $x(k)$ can be inserted into the list by merely adjusting the list pointers without shifting any elements in the array. This reduces the time required for insertion but not the time required for searching for the proper position. The space requirements are also increased because of the extra *link* array. The number of comparisons is still $O(n^2)$, although the number of replacements in the *link* array is $O(n)$. You are asked to code both the binary insertion sort and the list insertion sort as exercises.

Shell Sort

More significant improvement can be achieved by using the *shell sort* (or *diminishing increment sort*), named after its discoverer. This method sorts separate subfiles of the original file. These subfiles contain every kth element of the original file. The value of k is called an *increment*. For example, if k is 5, the subfile consisting of $x(1), x(6), x(11), \ldots$ is first sorted. Five subfiles, each containing one-fifth of the elements of the original file, are sorted in this manner. These are (reading across)

subfile 1	▶	$x(1)$	$x(6)$	$x(11)$	. . .
subfile 2	▶	$x(2)$	$x(7)$	$x(12)$	. . .
subfile 3	▶	$x(3)$	$x(8)$	$x(13)$	. . .
subfile 4	▶	$x(4)$	$x(9)$	$x(14)$	. . .
subfile 5	▶	$x(5)$	$x(10)$	$x(15)$	. . .

In general, the ith element of the jth subfile is $x((i-1)*5+j)$. If a different increment k is chosen, the k subfiles are divided so that the ith element of the jth subfile is $x((i-1)*k+j)$.

After the first k subfiles are sorted (usually by simple insertion), a new smaller value of k is chosen and the file is again partitioned into a new set of

subfiles. Each of these larger subfiles is sorted and the process is repeated yet
again with an even smaller value of k. Eventually, the value of k is set to 1 so that
the subfile consisting of the entire file is sorted. A decreasing sequence of increments is fixed at the start of the entire process. The last value in this sequence
must be 1.

For example, if the original file is

$$25 \quad 57 \quad 48 \quad 37 \quad 12 \quad 92 \quad 86 \quad 33$$

and the sequence (5,3,1) is chosen, then the following subfiles are sorted on each
iteration.

first iteration (increment = 5)

$$(x(1), x(6))$$
$$(x(2), x(7))$$
$$(x(3), x(8))$$
$$(x(4))$$
$$(x(5))$$

second iteration (increment = 3)

$$(x(1), x(4), x(7))$$
$$(x(2), x(5), x(8))$$
$$(x(3), x(6))$$

third iteration (increment = 1)

$$(x(1), x(2), x(3), x(4), x(5), x(6), x(7), x(8))$$

Figure 8.4.1 illustrates the Shell sort on this sample file. The lines under-
neath each array join individual elements of the separate subfiles. Each of the
subfiles is sorted using the simple insertion sort.

We present below a routine to implement the Shell sort. In addition to the
standard parameters X and N, it requires an array INCRMNTS, containing the
diminishing increments of the sort, and NUMINC, the number of elements in the
array INCRMNTS.

```
5000    'subroutine shell
5010    'inputs: INCRMNTS, N, NUMINC, X
5020    'outputs: X
5030    'locals: I, J, K, SPAN
5040    FOR I = 1 TO NUMINC
5050        SPAN = INCRMNTS(I):      'SPAN is the size of the increment
5060        FOR J = SPAN + 1 TO N
5070            'insert element X(J) into its proper position within
                'its subfile
5080            Y = X(J)
```

```
5090                FOR K = J − SPAN TO 1 STEP − SPAN
5100                    IF Y > = X(K) THEN GOTO 5130
5110                        X(K + SPAN) = X(K)
5120                    NEXT K
5130                    X(K + SPAN) = Y
5140            NEXT J
5150    NEXT I
5160    RETURN
5170    'endsub
```

Be sure that you can trace the actions of this program on the sample file of Figure 8.4.1. Notice that on the last iteration where SPAN equals 1 the sort reduces to a simple insertion.

The idea behind the Shell sort is a simple one. We have already noted that the simple insertion sort is highly efficient on a file that is in almost sorted order. It is also important to realize that when the file size n is small, an $O(n^2)$ sort is often more efficient than an $O(n \log n)$ sort. The reason for this is that $O(n^2)$ sorts are generally quite simple to program and involve very few actions other than comparisons and replacements on each pass. Because of this low overhead, the constant of proportionality is rather small. An $O(n \log n)$ sort is generally quite complex and employs a large number of extra operations on each pass in order to reduce the work of subsequent passes. Thus its constant of proportionality is larg-

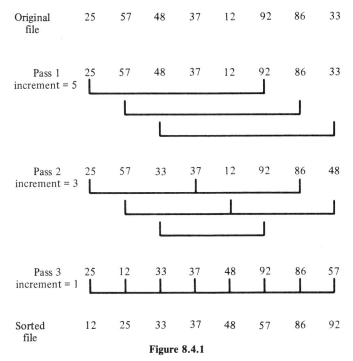

Figure 8.4.1

er. When n is large, n^2 overwhelms $n \log n$, so that the constants of proportional-ity do not play a major role in determining the faster sort. However, when n is small, n^2 is not much larger than $n \log n$, so that a large difference in those con-stants often causes an $O(n^2)$ sort to be faster.

Since the first increment used by the Shell sort is large, the individual sub-files are quite small, so that the simple insertion sorts on those subfiles are fairly fast. Each sort of a subfile causes the entire file to be more nearly sorted. Thus, although successive passes of the Shell sort use smaller increments and therefore deal with larger subfiles, those subfiles are almost sorted due to the actions of previous passes. Thus the insertion sorts on those subfiles are also quite efficient. In this connection, it is significant to note that if a file is partially sorted using an increment k and is subsequently partially sorted using an increment j, the file re-mains partially sorted on the increment k. That is, subsequent partial sorts do not disturb earlier ones.

The efficiency analysis of the Shell sort is mathematically involved and be-yond the scope of this book. The actual time requirements for a specific sort depends on the number of elements in the array *incrmnts* and on their actual val-ues. It has been shown that the order of the Shell sort can be approximated by $O(n(\log n)^2)$ if an appropriate sequence of increments is used. One requirement that is intuitively clear is that the elements of *incrmnts* should be relatively prime (i.e., have no common divisors other than 1). This guarantees that successive iterations intermingle subfiles so that the entire file is indeed almost sorted when the increment equals 1 on the last iteration.

Address Calculation Sort

As a final example of sorting by insertion, consider the following technique, called sorting by ***address calculation*** (sometimes called sorting by ***hashing***). In this method a function f is applied to each key. The result of this function deter-mines into which of several subfiles the record is to be placed. The function should have the property that if $x < y$, then $f(x) < f(y)$. Such a function is called ***order-preserving.*** Thus all of the records in one subfile will have keys which are less than or equal to the keys of the records in another subfile. An item is placed into a subfile in correct sequence by using any sorting method; simple insertion is often used. After all of the items of the original file have been placed into sub-files, the subfiles may be concatenated to produce the sorted result.

For example, consider again the sample file:

$$25 \quad 57 \quad 48 \quad 37 \quad 12 \quad 92 \quad 86 \quad 33$$

Let us create 10 subfiles, one for each of the 10 possible first digits. Initially, each of these subfiles is empty. An array of pointers $f(9)$ having a lower bound of 0 and an upper bound 9 is declared, where $f(i)$ points to the first element in the file whose first digit is i. [Most versions of BASIC assign array indices starting at

$f(0) = null$

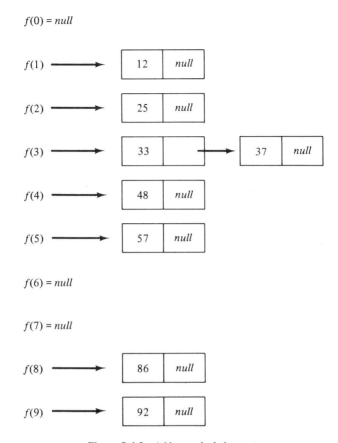

Figure 8.4.2 Address calculation sort.

0. In those versions of BASIC where this is not so, it is necessary to declare the array $f(10)$ and adjust all index references by adding 1 or by using $f(10)$ in place of $f(0)$.] After scanning the first element (25), it is placed into the file headed by $f(2)$. Each of the subfiles is maintained as a sorted linked list of the original array elements. After processing each of the elements in the original file, the subfiles appear as in Figure 8.4.2.

    We present a routine to implement the address calculation sort. The routine assumes an array of two-digit numbers and uses the first digit of each number to assign that number to a subfile. The routine uses the subroutine *place* to insert Z into its proper position in the ordered list LST.

```
5000   'subroutine addr
5010   'inputs: N, X
5020   'outputs: X
5030   'locals: AVAIL, F, I, INFO, J, LST, P, PTRNXT, Z
```

```
5040    DIM INFO(N), PTRNXT(N)
5050    DIM F(9):                   'F(I) points to the first
                                     'element in the file whose first digit is I.
5060    'initialize available list
5070    AVAIL = 1
5080    FOR I = 1 TO N − 1
5090        PTRNXT(I) = I + 1
5100    NEXT I
5110    PTRNXT(N) = 0
5120    'initialize pointers
5130    FOR I = 0 TO 9
5140        F(I) = 0
5150    NEXT I
5160    FOR I = 1 TO N
5170        'we successively insert each element into its respective
            'subfile using list insertion
5180        Z = X(I)
5190        FIRST = INT (Z/10): 'find the first digit of a two-digit number
5200        'search the linked list
5210        LST = F(FIRST)
5220        GOSUB 8000:             'subroutine place inserts Z into its proper
                                     'position in the linked list pointed to by LST.
5230                                'place inputs: AVAIL, INFO, LST, PTRNXT, Z
5240                                'place outputs: AVAIL, PTRNXT
                                     'and possibly LST
5250        F(FIRST) = LST:         'this statement is necessary in the case
                                     'where place modifies LST
5260    NEXT I
5270    'copy numbers back into the array X
5280    I = 0
5290    FOR J = 0 TO 9
5300        P = F(J)
5310        IF P = 0 THEN GOTO 5360
5320            I = I + 1
5330            X(I) = INFO(P)
5340            P = PTRNXT(P)
5350        GOTO 5310
5360    NEXT J
5370    RETURN
5380    'endsub
        . . .
8000    'subroutine place
        . . .
```

The space requirements of the address calculation sort are approximately $2n$ (used by the arrays INFO and PTRNXT) plus some header nodes and temporary variables. Note that if the original data are given in the form of a linked list rather than as a sequential array, it is not necessary to maintain both the array X and the linked structure consisting of INFO and PTRNXT.

To evaluate the time requirements for the sort, note the following. If the n original elements are approximately uniformly distributed over the m subfiles and the value of n/m is approximately 1, the time of the sort is nearly $O(n)$, since the function assigns each element to its proper file and little extra work is required to place the element within the subfile itself. On the other hand, if n/m is much larger than 1, or if the original file is not uniformly distributed over the m subfiles, a significant amount of work is required to insert an element into its proper subfile, and the time is therefore closer to $O(n^2)$.

EXERCISES

1. The *two-way insertion sort* is a modification of the simple insertion sort as follows. A separate output array of size n is set aside. This output array acts as a circular structure, as in Section 4.1. $x(1)$ is placed into the middle element of the array. Once a contiguous group of elements are in the array, room for a new element is made by shifting all smaller elements one step to the left or all larger elements one step to the right. The choice of which shift to perform depends on which would cause the smallest amount of shifting. Write a BASIC subroutine to implement this technique.

2. The *merge insertion sort* proceeds as follows:

   Step 1: For all odd i between 1 and $n-1$, compare $x(i)$ with $x(i+1)$. Place the larger in the next position of an array *large* and the smaller in the next position of an array *small*. If n is odd, place $x(n)$ in the last position of the array *small*. [*large* is of size $int(n/2)$; *small* is of size $int(n/2)$ or $int(n/2)+1$, depending on whether n is even or odd.]

   Step 2: Sort the array *large* using merge insertion recursively. Whenever an element *large(j)* is moved to *large(k)*, *small(j)* is also moved to *small(k)*. [At the end of this step, $large(i) \le large(i+1)$ for all i less than $int(n/2)$ and $small(i) \le large(i)$ for all i less than or equal to $int(n/2)$.]

   Step 3: Copy *small(1)* and all the elements of *large* into $x(1)$ through $x(int(n/2)+1)$.

   Step 4: Define the integer *num(i)* as $(2^{i+1}+(-1)^i)/3$. Beginning with $i = 1$ and proceeding by 1 while $num(i) \le int(n/2)+1$, insert the elements *small(num(i+1))* down to *small(num(i)+1)* into x in turn using binary insertion. [For example, if $n = 20$, the successive values of *num* are:

$num(1) = 1$, $num(2) = 3$, and $num(3) = 5$, $num(4) = 11$, which equals $int(n/2) + 1$. Thus the elements of *small* are inserted in the following order: $small(3)$, $small(2)$; then $small(5)$, $small(4)$; then $small(10)$, $small(9)$, $small(8)$, $small(7)$, $small(6)$. In this example, there is no $small(11)$.]

Write a BASIC subroutine to implement this technique.

3. Modify the quicksort of Section 2 so that it uses a simple insertion sort when a subfile is below some size s. Determine by experiments what value of s should be used for maximum efficiency.

4. Prove that if a file is partially sorted using an increment j in the Shell sort, it remains partially sorted on that increment even after it is partially sorted on another increment, k.

5. Explain why it is desirable to choose all the increments of the Shell sort so that they are relatively prime.

6. Find the number (in terms of file size n) of comparisons and interchanges performed by each of the sorting methods listed below for the following files.

   (1) A sorted file
   (2) A file that is sorted in reverse order (i.e., from largest to smallest)
   (3) A file in which the elements $x(1)$, $x(3)$, $x(5)$, . . . are the smallest elements and are in sorted order and in which the elements $x(2)$, $x(4)$, $x(6)$, . . . are the largest elements and are in reverse sorted order [i.e., $x(1)$ is the smallest, $x(2)$ is the largest, $x(3)$ is next to the smallest, $x(4)$ is the next to the largest, etc.].
   (4) A file in which $x(1)$ through $x(int(n/2))$ are the smallest elements and are sorted and in which $x(int(n/2) + 1)$ through $x(n)$ are the largest elements and are in reverse sorted order
   (5) A file in which $x(1)$, $x(3)$, $x(5)$, . . . are the smallest elements in sorted order and in which $x(2)$, $x(4)$, $x(6)$, . . . are the largest elements in sorted order

   (a) The simple insertion sort.
   (b) The insertion sort using a binary search.
   (c) The list insertion sort.
   (d) The two-way insertion sort of Exercise 1.
   (e) The merge insertion sort of Exercise 2.
   (f) The Shell sort using increments 2 and 1.
   (g) The Shell sort using increments 3, 2, and 1.
   (h) The Shell sort using increments 8, 4, 2, and 1.
   (i) The Shell sort using increments 7, 5, 3, and 1.
   (j) The address calculation sort presented in the text.

7. Under what circumstances would you recommend the use of each of the following sorts over the others?
   (a) Shell sort of this section
   (b) Heapsort of Section 3
   (c) Quicksort of Section 2

8. Determine which of the following sorts is most efficient?
    (a) The simple insertion sort of this section
    (b) The straight selection sort of Section 3
    (c) The bubble sort of Section 2

5. MERGE AND RADIX SORTS

Merge Sorts

Merging is the process of combining two or more sorted files into a third sorted file. An example of a routine that accepts two sorted arrays A and B of AN and BN elements, respectively, and merges them into a third array C containing CN elements is the following:

```
5000   'subroutine mergearr
5010   'inputs: A, AN, B, BN, CN
5020   'outputs: C
5030   'locals: APNT, BPNT, CPNT
5040   IF AN + BN > CN
           THEN PRINT "ARRAY BOUNDS INCOMPATIBLE":
               STOP
5050   'APNT, BPNT, and CPNT are indicators of how far we are in arrays
       'A, B, and C, respectively
5060   APNT = 1
5070   BPNT = 1
5080   CPNT = 1
5090   IF APNT > AN OR BPNT > BN THEN GOTO 5130
5100   IF A (APNT) < B(BPNT)
           THEN C(CPNT) = A(APNT): APNT = APNT + 1
           ELSE C(CPNT) = B(BPNT): BPNT = BPNT + 1
5110      CPNT = CPNT + 1
5120   GOTO 5090
5130   'copy any remaining elements from A to C
5140   IF APNT > AN THEN GOTO 5190
5150      C(CPNT) = A(APNT)
5160      CPNT = CPNT + 1
5170      APNT = APNT + 1
5180   GOTO 5130
5190   'copy any remaining elements from B to C
5200   IF BPNT > BN THEN GOTO 5250
5210      C(CPNT) = B(BPNT)
5220      CPNT = CPNT + 1
5230      BPNT = BPNT + 1
5240   GOTO 5190
5250   RETURN
5260   'endsub
```

We can use this technique to sort a file in the following way. Divide the file into *n* subfiles of size 1 and merge adjacent (disjoint) pairs of files. We then have approximately *n*/2 files of size 2. Repeat this process until there is only one file remaining of size *n*. Figure 8.5.1 illustrates how this process operates on a sample file. Each individual file is contained in brackets.

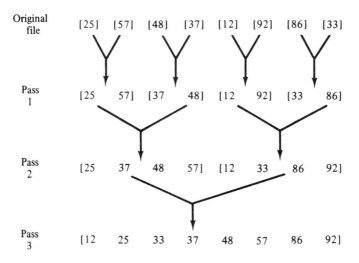

Figure 8.5.1   Successive passes of the merge sort.

We present a routine to implement the description above of a *straight merge sort.* An auxiliary array XAUX of size N is required to hold the results of merging two subarrays of X. The variable SIZE contains the size of the subarrays being merged. Since at any time the two files being merged are both subarrays of X, lower and upper bounds are required to indicate the subfiles of X being merged. ALO and AHI represent the lower and upper bounds of the first file and BLO and BHI represent the lower and upper bounds of the second file, respectively. APNT and BPNT are used to reference elements of the source files being merged and CPNT indexes the destination file XAUX. The routine follows:

```
5000   'subroutine msort
5010   'inputs: N, X
5020   'outputs: X
5030   'locals: AHI, ALO, APNT, BHI, BLO, BPNT, CPNT, SIZE, XAUX
5040   'assume the existence of a declaration   DIM XAUX(N)
5050   SIZE = 1:                    'merge files of size 1
5060   IF SIZE > = N THEN GOTO 5480
5070      ALO = 1:                  'initialize lower bound of first file
5080      CPNT = 1:                 'CPNT is index for auxiliary array
```

```
5090      IF ALO + SIZE > N THEN GOTO 5350:         'check if there is only one
                                                     'subfile left
5100           'compute remaining indices
5110           BLO = ALO + SIZE
5120           AHI = BLO − 1
5130           IF BLO + SIZE − 1 < N THEN BHI = AHI + SIZE
                                      ELSE BHI = N
5140           'proceed through the two subfiles
5150           APNT = ALO
5160           BPNT = BLO
5170           IF APNT > AHI OR BPNT > BHI THEN GOTO 5220
5180               'enter smaller into array XAUX
5190               IF X(APNT) < = X(BPNT)
                       THEN XAUX(CPNT) = X(APNT):   APNT = APNT + 1
                       ELSE XAUX(CPNT) = X(BPNT):   BPNT = BPNT + 1
5200               CPNT = CPNT + 1
5210           GOTO 5170
5220           'at this point one of the subfiles has been exhausted
               'insert any remaining portions of the other file
5230           IF APNT > AHI THEN GOTO 5280
5240               XAUX(CPNT) = X(APNT)
5250               APNT = APNT + 1
5260               CPNT = CPNT + 1
5270           GOTO 5230
5280           IF BPNT > BHI THEN GOTO 5330
5290               XAUX(CPNT) = X(BPNT)
5300               BPNT = BPNT + 1
5310               CPNT = CPNT + 1
5320           GOTO 5280
5330           ALO = BHI + 1:       'advance ALO to start of next pair of files
5340       GOTO 5090
5350       'copy any remaining single file
5360       APNT = ALO
5370       IF CPNT > N THEN GOTO 5420
5380           XAUX(CPNT) = X(APNT)
5390           CPNT = CPNT + 1
5400           APNT = APNT + 1
5410       GOTO 5370
5420       'adjust X and SIZE
5430       FOR APNT = 1 TO N
5440           X(APNT) = XAUX(APNT)
5450       NEXT APNT
5460       SIZE = SIZE * 2
5470   GOTO 5060
5480   RETURN
5490   'endsub
```

There is one deficiency in the procedure described above which is easily remedied if the program is to be practical for sorting large arrays. Instead of merging each set of files into the auxiliary array XAUX and then recopying the array XAUX into X, alternate merges can be performed from X to XAUX and from XAUX to X. We leave this modification as an exercise for the reader.

The time required for the sort is $O(n \log n)$, since there are obviously no more than $\log_2 n$ passes. The sort, however, does require an auxiliary array XAUX into which the merged files can be stored.

There are two modifications of the procedure above which can result in more efficient sorting. The first of these is the *natural merge*. In the straight merge, the files are all the same size (except perhaps for the last file). We can, however, exploit any order that may already exist among the elements and let the subfiles be defined as the longest subarrays of increasing elements. You are asked to code such a routine as an exercise.

The second modification uses linked allocation instead of sequential allocation. By adding a single pointer field to each record, the need for the second array XAUX can be eliminated. This can be done by explicitly linking together each input and output subfile. The modification can be applied to both the straight merge and the natural merge. You are asked to implement these in the exercises.

Radix Sort

The next sorting method that we consider is called the *radix sort*. This sort is based on the values of the actual digits in the positional representations of the numbers being sorted. For example, the number 235 in decimal notation is written with a 2 in the hundreds position, a 3 in the tens position, and a 5 in the units position. The larger of two such integers of equal length can be determined as follows. Start at the most significant digit and advance through the least significant digits as long as the corresponding digits in the two numbers match. The number with the larger digit in the first position in which the digits of the two numbers do not match is the larger of the two numbers. Of course, if all the digits of both numbers match, the numbers are equal.

We can write a sorting routine based on the method described above. Using the decimal base, for example, the numbers can be sorted into 10 groups based on their most significant digit. (For simplicity, we assume that all the numbers have the same number of digits by padding with leading zeros, if necessary.) Thus every element in the "0" group is less than every element in the "1" group all of whose elements are less than every element in the "2" group, and so on. We can then sort within the individual groups based on the next significant digit. We repeat this process until each subgroup has been subdivided so that the least significant digits are sorted. At this point the original file has been sorted. (Note that the division of a subfile into groups with the same digit in a given position is similar to the *rearrange* operation in the quicksort, in which a subfile is divided into two groups based on comparison with a particular element.) This method is sometimes called the **radix-exchange sort:** its coding is left as an exercise for the reader.

Let us now consider an alternative to the method described above. It is apparent from the discussion above that considerable bookkeeping is involved in constantly subdividing files and distributing their contents into subfiles based on particular digits. It would certainly be easier if we could process the entire file as a whole rather than deal with many individual files.

Suppose that we perform the following actions on the file for each digit, beginning with the least significant digit and ending with the most significant digit. Take each number in the order in which it appears in the file and place it into one of 10 queues, depending on the value of the digit currently being processed. Then restore each queue to the original file starting with the queue of numbers with a 0 digit and ending with the queue of numbers with a 9 digit. When these actions have been performed for each digit, starting with the least significant and ending with the most significant, the file is sorted. This sorting method is called the **radix sort.**

Notice that this scheme sorts on the less significant digits first. Thus when all the numbers are sorted on a more significant digit, numbers which have the same digit in that position but different digits in a less significant position are already sorted on the less significant position. This allows processing of the entire file without subdividing the files and keeping track of where each subfile begins and ends. Figure 8.5.2 illustrates this sort on the sample file

$$25 \quad 57 \quad 48 \quad 37 \quad 12 \quad 92 \quad 86 \quad 33$$

Be sure that you can follow the actions depicted in the two passes of Figure 8.5.2.

We can therefore outline an algorithm to sort in the above fashion as follows:

>   *for* k = least significant digit *to* most significant digit
>   *for* i = 1 *to* n
> $y = x(i)$
> $j = k$th digit of y
>   place y at rear of *queue*(j)
>   *next* i
>   *for* qu = 0 *to* 9
>   place elements of *queue*(qu) in next sequential position of x
>   *next* qu
>   *next* k

Original file

     25   57   48   37   12   92   86   33

Queues based on least significant digit.

	Front	Rear
queue (0)		
queue (1)		
queue (2)	12	92
queue (3)	33	
queue (4)		
queue (5)	25	
queue (6)	86	
queue (7)	57	37
queue (8)	48	
queue (9)		

After first pass:

     12   92   33   25   86   57   37   48

Queues based on most significant digit.

	Front	Rear
queue (0)		
queue (1)	12	
queue (2)	25	
queue (3)	33	37
queue (4)	48	
queue (5)	57	
queue (6)		
queue (7)		
queue (8)	86	
queue (9)	92	

Sorted file: 12   25   33   37   48   57   86   92

Figure 8.5.2   Illustration of the radix sort.

We now present a program that implements the foregoing sort on *m*-digit numbers. In order to save a considerable amount of work in processing the queues (especially in the step where we return the queue elements to the original file), we write the program using linked allocation. If the initial input to the subroutine is an array, that input is first converted into a linear linked list; if the original input is already in linked format, this step is not necessary and, in fact, space is saved. This is the same situation as in the subroutine *addr* (address calculation sort) of Section 8.4. As in previous programs, we do not make any internal calls to subroutines but rather perform their actions in place. We again make use of the zeroth element of BASIC arrays.

```
5000   'subroutine radix
5010   'inputs: M, N, X
5020   'outputs: X
5030   'locals: FIRST, FRNT, I, INFO, JTEMP, K, P, PTRNXT, Q, REAR, Y
```

```
5040    'assume global declarations DIM INFO(N), PTRNXT(N),
        'FRNT(9), REAR (9)
5050    'FRNT(I) and REAR(I) define the front and rear of the Ith queue,
        'for all values of I between 0 and 9
5060    'initialize linked list
5070    FOR I = 1 TO N - 1
5080        INFO(I) = X(I)
5090        PTRNXT(I) = I + 1
5100    NEXT I
5110    INFO(N) = X(N)
5120    PTRNXT(N) = 0
5130    FIRST = 1:                  'FIRST points to the head of the linked list
5140    'assume that we have M-digit numbers
5150    FOR K = 1 TO M
5160        'initialize queues
5170        FOR I = 0 TO 9
5180            REAR(I) = 0
5190            FRNT(I) = 0
5200        NEXT I
5210        'process each element on the list
5220        IF FIRST = 0 THEN GOTO 5330
5230          P = FIRST
5240          FIRST = PTRNXT(FIRST)
5250          Y = INFO(P)
5260          'extract Kth digit and assign it to J
5270          JTEMP = INT(Y / 10 ↑ (K - 1))
5280          J = JTEMP - 10*INT(JTEMP/10)
5290          Q = REAR(J)
5300          IF Q = 0 THEN FRNT(J) = P
                        ELSE PTRNXT(Q) = P
5310          REAR(J) = P
5320        GOTO 5220
5330        'At this point each record is in its proper queue based on
            'digit K. We now form a single list of all the queue elements
5340        'find the first element
5350        FOR J = 0 TO 9
5360            IF FRNT(J) <> 0 THEN GOTO 5380
5370        NEXT J
5380        FIRST = FRNT(J)
5390        'link up the remaining queues
5400        IF J > = 9 THEN GOTO 5480:     'check if finished
5410          'find next element
5420          FOR I = J + 1 TO 9
5430              IF FRNT(I) <> 0 THEN GOTO 5450
5440          NEXT I
```

```
5450          IF I <= 9 THEN P = I:  PTRNXT(REAR(J)) = FRNT(I)
5460          J = I
5470       GOTO 5400
5480       PTRNXT(REAR(P)) = 0
5490    NEXT K
5500    'copy back to original array
5510    FOR I = 1 TO N
5520       X(I) = INFO(FIRST)
5530       FIRST = PTRNXT(FIRST)
5540    NEXT I
5550    RETURN
5560    'endsub
```

The time requirements for the radix sorting method clearly depend on the number of digits (m) and the number of elements in the file (n). Since the outer loop FOR K = 1 to M . . . is traversed m times (once for each digit) and the inner loop n times (once for each element in the file), the sort is approximately $O(m*n)$. Thus the sort is reasonably efficient if the number of digits in the keys is not too large. It should be noted, however, that many machines have the hardware facilities to order digits of a number (particularly if they are in binary) much more rapidly than they can execute a compare of two full keys. Therefore, it is not reasonable to compare the $O(m*n)$ estimate with some of the other results we arrived at in this chapter. Note also that if the keys are dense (i.e., if almost every number that can possibly be a key is actually a key), then m approximates log n, so that $O(m*n)$ approximates $O(n$ log $n)$. The sort does require space to store pointers to the fronts and rears of the queues in addition to an extra field in each record to be used as a pointer in the linked lists. If the number of digits is large, it is sometimes more efficient to sort the file by first applying the radix sort to the most significant digits and then using straight insertion on the rearranged file. In cases where most of the records in the file have differing most significant digits, this process eliminates wasteful passes on the least significant digits.

EXERCISES

1. Write an algorithm for a routine $merge(x,lb1,ub1,ub2)$ which assumes that $x(lb1)$ through $x(ub1)$ and $x(ub1+1)$ through $x(ub2)$ are sorted and which merges the two into $x(lb1)$ through $x(ub2)$.

2. Consider the following recursive version of the merge sort, which uses the routine $merge$ of the previous exercise. It inputs the array x, the constant 1, and the variable n. Rewrite the routine by eliminating recursion and simplifying. How does the resulting routine differ from the one in the text?

subroutine msort2(x,lb,ub)
if lb <> ub
   then mid = int((ub + lb)/2)
      msort2(x,lb,mid)
      msort2(x,mid + 1,ub)
      merge(x,lb,mid,ub)
endif
return

3. Let $a(l1,l2)$ be the average number of comparisons necessary to merge two sorted arrays of length $l1$ and $l2$, respectively, where the elements of the arrays are chosen at random from among $l1 + l2$ elements.
   (a) What are the values of $a(l1,0)$ and $a(0,l2)$?
   (b) Show that for $l1 > 0$ and $l2 > 0$, $a(l1,l2)$ is equal to $(l1/(l1+l2))*(1+a(l1-1,l2))+(l2/(l1+l2))*(1+a(l1,l2-1))$. (*Hint:* Express the average number of comparisons in terms of the average number of comparisons after the first comparison.)
   (c) Show that $a(l1,l2)$ equals $(l1*l2*(l1+l2+2))/((l1+1)*(l2+1))$.
   (d) Verify the formula in part (c) for two arrays, one of size 2 and one of size 1.

4. Consider the following method of merging two arrays a and b into c. Perform a binary search for $b(1)$ in the array a. If $b(1)$ is between $a(i)$ and $a(i+1)$, output $a(1)$ through $a(i)$ to the array c, then output $b(1)$ to the array c. Next, perform a binary search for $b(2)$ in the subarray $a(i + 1)$ to $a(la)$ (where la is the number of elements in the array a) and repeat the output process. Repeat this procedure for every element of the array b.
   (a) Write a BASIC routine to implement this method.
   (b) In which cases is this method more efficient than the method of the text? In which cases is it less efficient?

5. Consider the following method (called *binary merging*) of merging two sorted arrays a and b into c. Let la and lb be the number of elements of a and b, respectively, and assume that $la \geq lb$. Divide a into $lb + 1$ approximately equal subarrays. Compare $b(1)$ with the smallest element of the second subarray of a. If $b(1)$ is smaller, then find $a(i)$ such that $a(i) \leq b(1) \leq a(i+1)$ by a binary search in the first subarray. Output all elements of the first subarray up to and including $a(i)$ into c, and then output $b(1)$ into c. Repeat this process with $b(2)$, $b(3)$, . . ., $b(j)$, where $b(j)$ is found to be larger than the smallest element of the second subarray. Output all remaining elements of the first subarray and the first element of the second subarray into c. Then compare $b(j)$ to the smallest element of the third subarray of a, and so on.
   (a) Write a program to implement the binary merge.
   (b) Show that if $la = lb$, the binary merge acts like the merge described in the text.
   (c) Show that if $lb = 1$, the binary merge acts like the merge of Exercise 4.

6. Determine the number of comparisons (as a function of n and m) which are performed in merging two ordered files a and b of sizes n and m, respectively, by each of the following merge methods, on each of the following sets of ordered files:

(1) Merge Methods:
  (a) The merge method presented in the text
  (b) The merge of Exercise 4
  (c) The binary merge of Exercise 5
(2) Sets of Files:
  (a) $m = n$ and $a(i) < b(i) < a(i+1)$ for all i
  (b) $m = n$ and $a(n) < b(1)$
  (c) $m = n$ and $a(int(n/2)) < b(1) < b(m) < a(int(n/2)+1)$
  (d) $n = 2*m$ and $a(i) < b(i) < a(i+1)$ for all i between 1 and m
  (e) $n = 2*m$ and $a(m+i) < b(i) < a(m+i+1)$ for all i between 1 and m
  (f) $n = 2*m$ and $a(2*i) < b(i) < a(2*i+1)$ for all i between 1 and m
  (g) $m = 1$ and $b(1) = a(int(n/2))$
  (h) $m = 1$ and $b(1) < a(1)$
  (i) $m = 1$ and $a(n) < b(1)$

7. Generate two randomly sorted files of size 100 and merge them by each of the methods of Exercise 6, keeping track of the number of comparisons made. Do the same for two files of size 10 and two files of size 1000. Repeat the experiment 10 times. What do the results indicate about the average efficiency of the merge methods?

8. Write a routine that sorts a file by first applying the radix sort to the most significant r digits (where r is a given constant) and then uses straight insertion to sort the entire file. This eliminates excessive passes on low-order digits, which may not be necessary.

9. Write a program that prints all sets of six positive integers $a1$, $a2$, $a3$, $a4$, $a5$, and $a6$ such that

$$a1 \leq a2 \leq a3 \leq 20$$
$$a1 < a4 \leq a5 \leq a6 \leq 20$$

and the sum of the squares of $a1$, $a2$, and $a3$ equals the sum of the squares of $a4$, $a5$, and $a6$. (*Hint*: Generate all possible sums of three squares, and use a sorting procedure to find duplicates.)

9

Searching

In this chapter we consider the problem of searching through large amounts of data to find one particular piece of information. As we shall see, certain methods of organizing data make the search process more efficient. Since searching is such a common task in computing, a knowledge of these methods goes a long way toward making a good programmer.

1. BASIC SEARCH TECHNIQUES

Before we consider specific search techniques, let us define some terms. A *table* or a *file* is a group of elements, each of which is called a *record*. (We are using the terms "file" and "record" here in their general sense. They should not be confused with the same terms as they refer to specific BASIC constructs.) Associated with each record is a key which is used to differentiate among different records. The association between a record and its key may be simple or complex. In the simplest form, the key is a field within the record contained at a specific offset from the start of the record. Such a key is called an *internal key* or an *embedded key*. In other cases, the key is the relative position of the record within a file or there is a separate table of keys which includes pointers to the records. Such keys are called *external keys*. For each file there is at least one set of keys (possibly more) that is unique (i.e., no two records in the file have the same key value). Such a key is called a *primary key*. For example, if the file is stored as an array, the index within the array of an element is a unique external key for that element. However, since any field of a record can serve as the key in a particular application, keys need not always be unique. For example, in a file of names and addresses, if the state is used as the key for a particular search, it will probably not be unique, since there may be two records with the same state in the file. Such a key is called a *secondary key*. Some of the algorithms we present assume unique keys, while others allow for multiple keys. When adopting an algorithm for a particular application the programmer should know whether the keys are unique and make sure that the algorithm is appropriate.

A *search algorithm* is an algorithm that accepts an argument *a* and tries to locate a record whose key is *a*. The algorithm may return the entire record or, more commonly, it may return a pointer to that record. A successful search is often called a *retrieval*. However, it is possible that the search for a particular argument in a table is unsuccessful; that is, there is no record in the table with that argument as its key. In such a case, the algorithm may return a special "null record" or a null pointer. More commonly, such a condition causes an error or sets a flag to a particular value which indicates that the record is missing. Very often, if a search is unsuccessful it may be desirable to add a new record with the argument as its key. An algorithm that does this is called a *search and insertion algorithm*.

In some cases it is desirable to insert a record with primary key *key* into a file without first searching for another record with the same key. Such a situation could arise if it had already been determined that no such record already exists in the file. In subsequent discussions we investigate and comment upon the relative efficiency of various algorithms. In such cases, the reader should note whether the comments refer to a search, to an insertion, or to a search and insertion.

Note that we have said nothing about the manner in which the table or file is organized. It may be an array of records, a linked list, a tree, or even a graph. Because different search techniques may be suitable for different table organizations, a table is often designed with a specific search technique in mind. The table may be contained completely in memory, completely in auxiliary storage, or it may be divided between the two. Clearly, different search techniques are necessary under these different assumptions. Searches in which the entire table is constantly in main memory are called *internal searches*, while those in which most of the table is kept in auxiliary storage (such as disk or tape) are called *external searches*. As with sorting, we discuss only internal searching, and leave it to the reader to investigate the extremely important topic of external searching.

Sequential Searching

The simplest form of a search is the *sequential search*. This search is applicable to a table that is organized as either an array or a linked list. Let us assume that *k* is an array of *n* keys and *r* an array of records such that $k(i)$ is the key of $r(i)$. Let us also assume that *key* is a search argument. We wish to set the variable *search* to the smallest integer i such that $k(i) = key$, if such an i exists, and 0 otherwise. The algorithm for doing this is as follows:

$$
\begin{aligned}
&\textit{for } i = 1 \textit{ to } n \\
&\quad \textit{if } key = k(i) \\
&\qquad \textit{then } search = i \\
&\qquad\quad \textit{return} \\
&\quad \textit{endif} \\
&\textit{next } i \\
&search = 0 \\
&\textit{return}
\end{aligned}
$$

The algorithm examines each key in turn. Upon finding one that matches the search argument, its index (which acts as a pointer to its record) is returned. If no match is found, 0 is returned.

This algorithm can easily be modified to add a record *rec* with key *key* to the table, if *key* is not already in the table. The following statements replace the last two statements above.

$$
\begin{aligned}
&n = n + 1 &&\text{'increase the table size} \\
&k(n) = key &&\text{'insert the new key and} \\
&r(n) = rec &&\text{'record} \\
&search = n \\
&\textit{return}
\end{aligned}
$$

Note that if insertions are made using only the revised algorithm, then no two records can have the same key. When this algorithm is implemented in BASIC, we must ensure that increasing n by 1 does not make its value go beyond the upper bound of the array. To use a sequential insertion search on an array, sufficient storage must have been previously allocated for the array.

Storing a table as a linked list has the advantage that the size of the table can be increased dynamically as needed. Let us assume that the table is organized as a linear linked list pointed to by *table* and linked by a pointer field *nxt*. Then assuming that k, r, key, and rec as before, the sequential insertion search for a linked list may be written as follows:

$$
\begin{aligned}
&q = null \\
&p = table \\
&\textit{while } (p <> null) \textit{ do} \\
&\quad \textit{if } k(p) = key \\
&\qquad \textit{then } search = p \\
&\qquad\quad \textit{return} \\
&\quad \textit{endif} \\
&\quad q = p \\
&\quad p = nxt(p) \\
&\textit{endwhile}
\end{aligned}
$$

'*record must be inserted*
$s =$ *getnode*
$k(s) =$ *key*
$r(s) =$ *rec*
$nxt(s) =$ *null*
if $q =$ *null*
  then *table* $= s$
  else $nxt(q) = s$
endif
search $= s$
return

· Another advantage of storing a table as a linked list rather than an array is
that it is easier to delete a record from a linked list. Deleting an element from an
array requires moving half the elements in the array on the average. (Why?)

One method of improving the efficiency of deleting a record from an array
is to add a field *flag(i)* to each record. Initially, when there is no record in position *i*, *flag(i)* is off. When a record is inserted at position *i*, the flag is turned on.
When the record at position *i* is deleted, its flag is turned off. New records are
inserted at the end of the array. If there are a substantial number of insertions, all
the space in the array is soon exhausted. If an attempt is made to insert a new
record when there is no more room in the array, the array is condensed by overwriting all records whose flags are off. This yields an array that contains all valid
records at the beginning, and room for new records at the end. The new record
may then be inserted. (Of course, one must be certain that no other programs
depend on the locations of the records, as their locations have now been
changed.) If the records do not have to be maintained in the order in which they
were inserted, deletion can be accomplished simply by replacing the record to be
deleted with the last record in the array and reducing by one the number of sequential positions currently occupied by the file.

There is another method that avoids the necessity of periodically condens-
ing the array but also entails lowered efficiency in individual insertions. In this
method an insertion involves traversing the array sequentially, looking for a record that has been flagged as deleted. The new record is inserted over the first
record whose flag is off. Yet another method is to link together all flagged records. This does not require any extra space since the information content of a
deleted record is irrelevant and can therefore be overwritten by a pointer to the
next deleted record. This available list of records can be maintained as a stack to
make insertion into the list more efficient. However, these methods are not possible if the records must be maintained in order of insertion. Further, if an insertion
is performed only after a search, no efficiency gains result from these methods
since the entire table must be searched for an existing record with the same key.
We leave the development of these ideas into algorithms and programs as exercises for the reader.

Efficiency of Sequential Searching

How efficient is a sequential search? Let us examine the number of comparisons that must be made by a sequential search in searching for a given key. If we assume no insertions or deletions, so that we are searching through a table of constant size n, the number of comparisons depends on where the record with the argument key appears in the table. If the record is the first one in the table, only one comparison is performed; if the record is the last one in the table, n comparisons are necessary. If it is equally likely for the argument to appear at any given table position, a successful search will take (on the average) $(n+1)/2$ comparisons, and an unsuccessful search will take n comparisons. In any case, the number of comparisons is $O(n)$.

However, it is usually the case that some arguments are presented to the search algorithm more often than others. For example, in the files of a college registrar, the records of a senior who is applying for transcripts for graduate school, or of a freshman whose high school average is being updated, are more likely to be called for than are those of the average sophomore and junior. Similarly, the records of scofflaws and tax cheats are more likely to be retrieved from the files of a motor vehicles bureau or the Internal Revenue Service than are those of a law-abiding citizen. (As we shall see later in this chapter, these examples are unrealistic because it is unlikely that a sequential search would be used for such large files; but for the moment, let us assume that a sequential search is being used.) Then, if frequently accessed records are placed at the beginning of the file, the average number of comparisons is sharply reduced since the most commonly accessed records take the least amount of time to retrieve.

Let us assume that $p(i)$ is the probability that record i is retrieved. [$p(i)$ is a number between 0 and 1 such that if m retrievals are made from the file, $m*p(i)$ of them will be for record i.] Let us also assume that $p(1) + p(2) + \ldots + p(n) = 1$, so that there is no possibility that an argument key is missing from the table. Then the average number of comparisons that are made in searching for a record is

$$p(1) + 2*p(2) + 3*p(3) + \ldots + n*p(n)$$

Clearly, this number is minimized if

$$p(1) \geq p(2) \geq p(3) \geq \ldots \geq p(n)$$

(Why?). Thus, given a large stable file, reordering the file in order of decreasing probability of retrieval achieves a greater degree of efficiency each time that the file is searched. Of course, this method implies that an extra field p is kept with each record, which gives the probability of accessing that record, or that p can be computed based on some other information in each record.

Reordering a List for Maximum Search Efficiency

If many insertions and deletions are to be performed on a table, a list structure is preferable to an array. However, even in a list it would be better to maintain the relationship

$$p(1) \geqslant p(2) \geqslant p(3) \geqslant \ldots \geqslant p(n)$$

to provide for efficient sequential searching. This can be done most easily if a new item is inserted into the list at its proper place. This means that if *prob* is the probability that a record with a given key will be the search argument, that record should be inserted between records $r(i)$ and $r(i+1)$, where i is such that

$$p(i) \geqslant prob \geqslant p(i+1)$$

Unfortunately, the probabilities $p(i)$ are rarely known in advance. Although it is quite common for certain records to be retrieved more often than others, it is almost impossible to identify those records in advance. Also, the probability that a given record will be retrieved may change over time. To use the example of the college registrar given earlier, a student begins as a freshman (high probability of retrieval) and then becomes a sophomore and a junior (low probability) before becoming a senior (high probability). Thus it would be helpful to have an algorithm which would continually reorder the table so that more frequently accessed records would drift to the front, while less frequently accessed records would drift to the back.

Several methods can be used to accomplish this. One of these is known as the ***move-to-front*** method and is efficient only for a table that is organized as a list. In this method, whenever a search is successful (i.e., when the argument is found to match the key of a record in the list), the retrieved record is removed from its current location in the list and is placed at the head of the list. Another method is the ***transposition*** method, in which a successfully retrieved record is interchanged with the record that immediately precedes it. We present an algorithm to implement the transposition method on a table stored as a linked list. The algorithm sets the variable *search* to point to the retrieved record, or the null pointer if the record is not found. As before, *key* is the search argument, k and r are the tables of keys and records. *table* is a pointer to the first node of the list.

```
p = table
q = null    'q is one step behind p
s = null    's is two steps behind p
while (p <> null) do
      if k(p) = key
          then 'We have found the record. Transpose
               'the records pointed to by p and q.
               if q = null
                   then 'We have found the key at the first position
                        'in the table so that no transposition is necessary
                        search = p
                        return
               endif
```

$$nxt(q) \ = \ nxt(p)$$
$$nxt(p) \ = \ q$$
if $s \ = \ null$
   then $table \ = \ p$
   else $nxt(s) \ = \ p$
endif
$search \ = \ p$
return
endif
$s \ = \ q$
$q \ = \ p$
$p \ = \ nxt(p)$
endwhile
$search \ = \ null$
return

We leave the implementation of the transposition method for an array and the move-to-front method for both an array and a list as exercises for the reader.

Both of these methods are based on the observed phenomenon that a record that has been retrieved is likely to be retrieved again. By advancing such records toward the front of the table, subsequent retrievals are more efficient. The rationale behind the move-to-front method is that since the record is likely to be retrieved again, it should be placed at the position within the table at which such retrieval will be most efficient. However, the counterargument for the transposition method is that a single retrieval does not yet imply that the record will be retrieved frequently. Placing it at the front of the table reduces search efficiency for all the other records that formerly preceded it. By advancing a record only one position each time that it is retrieved, we ensure that it will advance to the front of the list only if it is retrieved frequently. Indeed, it has been shown that, in general, the transposition method eventually yields more efficient searches than the move-to-front method for lists in which the probability of accessing a particular element remains constant over time. However, the transposition method takes longer than the move-to-front method to achieve its maximum efficiency. Thus a mixed strategy, in which move-to-front is used initially to reorder the list rapidly, and then transposition is used to maintain the list in nearly optimal order, may be recommended.

Another advantage of the transposition method over the move-to-front method is that it can be applied efficiently to tables stored in array form as well as to list-structured tables. Transposing two elements in an array is a rather efficient operation, while moving an element from the middle of an array to its front involves (on the average) moving half the array. (However, in this case the average number of moves is not so large since the element to be moved most often comes from the first portion of the array.)

Searching an Ordered Table

If a table is stored in ascending or descending order of the record keys, there are several techniques that can be used to improve the efficiency of searching. This is especially true if the table is of fixed size. One immediately obvious advantage in searching a sorted file over searching an unsorted file is in the case where a record with the argument key is absent from the file. In the case of an unsorted file, n comparisons are needed to detect this fact. In the case of a sorted file, assuming that the argument keys are uniformly distributed over the range of keys in the file, only $(n+1)/2$ comparisons (on the average) are needed. This is because we know that a record with a given key is missing from a file that is sorted in ascending order of keys as soon as we encounter a key in the file which is greater than the argument.

Suppose that it is possible to collect a large number of retrieval requests before any of them are processed. For example, in many applications a response to a request for information may be deferred to the next day. In such a case, all requests in a specific day may be collected and the actual searching may be done overnight, when no new requests are coming in. If both the table and the list of requests are sorted, the sequential search can proceed through both concurrently beginning the search for each additional requested element at the point where the last search ended. Thus it is not necessary to search through the entire table for each retrieval request. In fact, if there are many such requests uniformly distributed over the entire table, each request will require only a few lookups (if the number of requests is less than the number of table entries) or perhaps only a single comparison (if the number of requests is greater than the number of table entries). In such situations sequential searching is probably the best method to use.

Because of the simplicity and efficiency of sequential processing on sorted files, it may be worthwhile to sort a file before searching for keys in it. This is especially true in the situation described in the preceding paragraph, where we are dealing with a ''master'' file and a large ''transaction'' file of requests.

The Indexed Sequential Search

There is another technique to improve search efficiency for a sorted file, but it involves an increase in the amount of space required. This method is called the *indexed sequential* search method. An auxiliary table, called an *index*, is set aside in addition to the sorted file itself. Each element in the index consists of a key *kindex* and a pointer to the record in the file that corresponds to *kindex*. The elements in the index, as well as the elements in the file, must be sorted on the key. If the index is one-eighth the size of the file, then every eighth record of the file is represented initially in the index. This is illustrated by Figure 9.1.1.

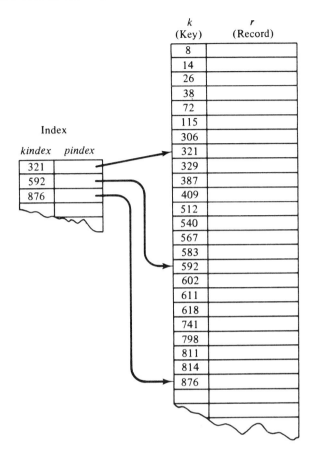

Figure 9.1.1 An indexed sequential file.

The algorithm used for searching an indexed sequential file is straightforward. Let *r, k,* and *key* be defined as before, let *kindex* be the array of the keys in the index and let *pindex* be the array of pointers within the index to the actual records in the file. We assume that the file is stored as an array, that *n* is the size of the file, and that *indxsze* is the size of the index.

```
i = 1
while (i <= indxsze) and (kindex(i) <= key) do
        i = i + 1
endwhile
'set lowlim to the lowest possible position of the item in the table
if i = 1
   then lowlim = 1
   else lowlim = pindex(i − 1)
endif
```

```
    'set hilim to the highest possible position of the item in the table
  if i = indxsze + 1
    then hilim = n
    else hilim = pindex(i) − 1
  endif
    'search the table between positions lowlim and hilim
  for j = lowlim to hilim
      if k(j) = key
        then search = j
              return
      endif
  next j
  search = 0
  return
```

Note that in the case of multiple records with the same key, the algorithm above does not necessarily return a pointer to the first such record in the table.

The real advantage of the indexed sequential method is that the items in the table can be examined sequentially if all the records in the file must be accessed, yet the search time for a particular item is sharply reduced. A sequential search is performed on the smaller index rather than on the larger table. Once the correct index has been found, a second sequential search is performed on a small portion of the record table itself.

The use of an index is applicable to a sorted table stored as a linked list, as well as to one stored as an array. Use of a linked list implies a larger space overhead for pointers, although insertions and deletions can be performed much more readily. A mixed implementation, in which all records between two adjacent index entries are maintained in a separate small table which also contains a pointer to the next such small table, can also be used.

If the table is so large that even the use of an index does not achieve sufficient efficiency (either because the index is large in order to reduce sequential searching in the table, or because the index is small so that adjacent keys in the index are far from each other in the table), a second-level index can be used. The second-level index acts as an index to the primary index which points to entries in the sequential table. This is illustrated in Figure 9.1.2.

Deletions from an indexed sequential table can be made most easily by flagging deleted entries. In sequential searching through the table, deleted entries are ignored. Note that if an element is deleted, then even if its key is in the index, nothing need be done to the index; only the original table entry is flagged.

Insertion into an indexed sequential table is more difficult since there may not be room between two already existing table entries, thus necessitating a shift

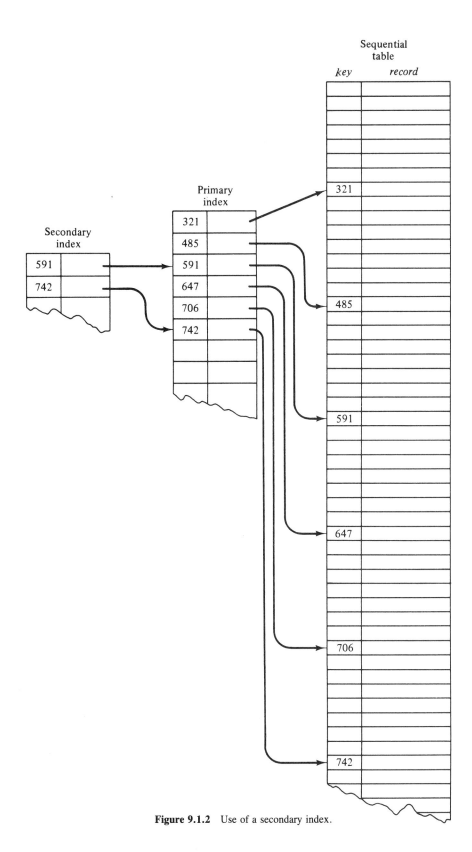

Figure 9.1.2 Use of a secondary index.

in a large number of table elements. However, if a nearby item has been flagged in the table as deleted, then only a few items need be shifted and the deleted item can be overwritten. This may in turn necessitate alteration of the index, if an item pointed to by an index element is shifted. Generally, when a table is initialized, empty records are dispersed through the table to leave room for insertion. An alternative method is to keep an overflow area at some other location and link together any inserted records. However, this would require an extra pointer field in each record of the original table. A possible remedy to this problem is to include only a single pointer after each group of records, insert the new record in its proper place, and shift any records past the inserted record forward one position. If the last record in the group is shifted, it is placed in the overflow area pointed to by the single pointer in the group. You are asked to explore these possibilities as an exercise.

The Binary Search

The most efficient method of searching an ordered array without the use of auxiliary indices or tables is the binary search. You should be familiar with this search technique from Sections 5.1 and 5.2. Basically, the argument is compared with the key of the middle element of the table. If they are equal, the search ends successfully; otherwise, either the upper or lower half of the table must be searched in a similar manner.

In Chapter 5 it was noted that the binary search can best be defined recursively. As a result, a recursive definition, a recursive algorithm, and a simulated recursive program were presented for the binary search. However, the large overhead that is associated with recursion makes it inappropriate for use in practical situations in which efficiency is a prime consideration. We therefore present the following nonrecursive version of the binary search algorithm:

$$low = 1$$
$$hi = n$$
while ($low <= hi$) **do**
$\qquad mid = int ((low + hi)/2)$
$\qquad$**if** $key = k(mid)$
$\qquad\quad$**then** $search = mid$
$\qquad\qquad\quad$**return**
$\qquad$**endif**
$\qquad$**if** $key < k(mid)$
$\qquad\quad$**then** $hi = mid - 1$
$\qquad\quad$**else** $low = mid + 1$
$\qquad$**endif**
endwhile
$search = 0$
return

Each comparison in the binary search reduces the number of possible candidates by a factor of 2. Thus the maximum number of key comparisons that will be made is approximately $\log_2 n$. [Actually, it is $2\log_2 n$ since in BASIC two key comparisons are made each time through the loop: $key = k(mid)$ and $key < k(mid)$. However, in assembly language or in FORTRAN using an arithmetic IF statement, only one comparison is made.] Thus we may say that the binary search algorithm is $O(\log n)$.

Note that the binary search may be used in conjunction with the indexed sequential table organization mentioned earlier. Instead of searching the index sequentially, a binary search can be used. The binary search can also be used in searching the main table once two boundary records are identified. However, the size of this table segment is likely to be small enough so that a binary search is not more advantageous than a sequential search.

Unfortunately, the binary search algorithm can be used only if the table is stored as an ordered array. This is because it makes use of the fact that the indices of array elements are consecutive integers. For this reason the binary search is practically useless in situations where there are many insertions or deletions, so that an array structure is inappropriate.

EXERCISES

1. Modify the search and insertion algorithms of this section so that they become update algorithms. If an algorithm finds an i such that $key = k(i)$, then change the value of $r(i)$ to rec.
2. Implement the sequential search and the sequential search and insertion algorithms in BASIC for both arrays and linked lists.
3. Compare the efficiency of searching an ordered sequential table of size n and searching an unordered table of the same size for the key key:
   (a) If no record with key is present.
   (b) If one record with key key is present and only one is sought.
   (c) If more than one record with key key is present and it is desired to find only the first one.
   (d) If more than one record with key key is present and it is desired to find them all.
4. Assume that an ordered table is stored as a circular list with two external pointers: *table* and *other*. *table* always points to the node containing the record with the smallest key. *other* is initially equal to *table*, but is reset each time a search is performed to point to the record that is retrieved. If a search is unsuccessful, *other* is reset to *table*. Write a BASIC routine that accepts TABLE, OTHER, and KEY, implements this method, resets the variable OTHER as described, and sets the variable SEARCH to point to a retrieved record or a null pointer if the search is unsuccessful. Explain how keeping the pointer OTHER can reduce the average number of comparisons in a search.

5. Consider an ordered table implemented as an array or as a doubly linked list so that the table can be searched sequentially either backward or forward. Assume that a single pointer *p* points to the last record successfully retrieved. The search always begins at the record pointed to by *p* but may proceed in either direction. Write routines for an array and a doubly linked list to retrieve a record with key *key* and to modify *p* accordingly. Compare the numbers of key comparisons in both the successful and unsuccessful cases with those of the method of Exercise 4, where the table may be scanned in only one direction but the scanning process may start at one of two points.

6. Modify the indexed sequential search so that in the case of multiple records with the same key, it returns the first such record in the table.

7. Consider the following BASIC implementation of an indexed sequential file:

```
10   DIM INDX (100,2)
20   KINDEX = 1
30   PINDEX = 2
40   DIM TABLE (1000,3)
50   K = 1
60   R = 2
70   FLAG = 3
```

Write a BASIC routine *create* that initializes such a file from input data. Each input line contains a key and a record. The input is sorted in ascending key order. Each index entry corresponds to 10 table entries. FLAG is set to TRUE in an occupied table entry and to FALSE in an unoccupied entry. Two of every 10 table entries are left unoccupied, to allow for future growth.

8. Given an indexed sequential file as in Exercise 7, write a BASIC routine *search* to print the record in the file with key KEY if it is present and an indication that the record is missing if no record with that key exists. (How can you ensure that an unsuccessful search is as efficient as possible?) Also, write routines *insert* to insert a record REC with key KEY and *delete* to delete the record with key KEY.

9. Consider the following version of the binary search, which assumes a special element $k(0)$ which is smaller than every possible key:

$$mid = int((n + 1)/2)$$
$$len = int(n/2)$$
$$finish = false$$
while $(key <> k(mid))$ **and** $(finish = false)$ **do**
    if $key < k(mid)$
        then $mid = int(mid - (len + 1)/2)$
        else $mid = int(mid + (len + 1)/2)$
    endif

$$if\ len\ =\ 1$$
$$then\ finish\ =\ true$$
$$else\ len\ =\ int(len/2)$$
$$endif$$
$$endwhile$$
$$if\ key\ =\ k(mid)$$
$$then\ search\ =\ mid$$
$$else\ search\ =\ 0$$
$$endif$$
$$return$$

Prove that this algorithm is correct. What are the advantages and/or disadvantages of this method over the method presented in the text?

10. The following search algorithm on a sorted array is known as the *Fibonaccian search* because of its use of Fibonacci numbers. (For a definition of Fibonacci numbers and the *fib* function, see Section 5.1.)

$$j\ =\ 1$$
$$while\ fib(j)\ <\ n\ +\ 1\ do$$
$$j\ =\ j\ +\ 1$$
$$endwhile$$
$$mid\ =\ n\ -\ fib(j\ -\ 2)\ +\ 1$$
$$f1\ =\ fib(j\ -\ 2)$$
$$f2\ =\ fib(j\ -\ 3)$$
$$finish\ =\ false$$
$$while\ (key\ <>\ k(mid))\ and\ (finish\ =\ false)\ do$$
$$if\ (mid\ <=\ 0)\ or\ (key\ >\ k(mid))$$
$$then\ if\ f1\ =\ 1$$
$$then\ finish\ =\ true$$
$$else\ mid\ =\ mid\ +\ f2$$
$$f1\ =\ f1\ -\ f2$$
$$f2\ =\ f2\ -\ f1$$
$$endif$$
$$else\ if\ f2\ =\ 0$$
$$then\ finish\ =\ true$$
$$else\ mid\ =\ mid\ -\ f2$$
$$t\ =\ f1\ -\ f2$$
$$f1\ =\ f2$$
$$f2\ =\ t$$
$$endif$$
$$endif$$
$$endwhile$$
$$if\ finish$$
$$then\ search\ =\ 0$$
$$else\ search\ =\ mid$$
$$endif$$

Explain how this algorithm works. Compare the number of key comparisons with the number used by the binary search.

11. Modify the binary search of the text so that in the case of an unsuccessful search, it returns the index i such that $k(i) < key < k(i+1)$. If $key < k(1)$, then it returns 0, and if $key > k(n)$, then it returns n. Do the same for the searches of Exercises 9 and 10.

2. TREE SEARCHING

In the preceding section we discussed search operations on a file that is organized either as an array or as a list. In this section we consider several ways of organizing files as trees and some associated searching algorithms.

In Sections 6.1 and 8.3 we presented a method of using a binary tree to store a file in order to make sorting the file more efficient. In that method, all the left descendants of a node with key key have keys that are less than key and all the right descendants have keys that are greater than or equal to key. The inorder traversal of such a binary tree yields the file in ascending key order.

Such a tree may also be used as a binary search tree. Using binary tree notation, the algorithm for searching for the key key in such a tree is as follows. (We assume that each node contains four fields: k, which holds the record's key value; r, which holds the record itself; and $left$ and $right$, which are pointers to the subtrees.)

```
p = tree
while p <> null do
    if key = k(p)
        then search = p
            return
    endif
    if key < k(p)
        then p = left(p)
        else p = right(p)
    endif
endwhile
search = null
return
```

Note that the binary search of Section 1 actually uses a sorted array as an implicit binary search tree. The middle element of the array can be thought of as the root of the tree, the lower half of the array (all of whose elements are less than the middle element) can be considered the left subtree, and the upper half (all of whose elements are greater than the middle element) can be considered the right subtree.

A sorted array can be produced from a binary search tree by traversing the tree in inorder and inserting each element sequentially into the array as it is visited. On the other hand, there are many binary search trees that correspond to a given sorted array. Viewing the middle element of the array as the root of a tree and viewing the remaining elements recursively as left and right subtrees produces a relatively balanced binary search tree [Figure 9.2.1(a)]. Viewing the first element of the array as the root of a tree and each successive element as the right son of its predecessor produces a very unbalanced binary tree [Figure 9.2.1(b)].

The advantage of using a binary search tree over a sorted array is that a tree enables search, insertion and deletion operations to be performed efficiently. If an array is used, an insertion or deletion requires that approximately half of the elements of the array be moved (Why?). Insertion or deletion in a search tree, on the other hand, requires that only a few pointers must be adjusted.

Inserting into a Binary Search Tree

The following algorithm searches a binary tree and inserts a new record into the tree if the search is unsuccessful. (We assume the existence of a routine *maketree,* which accepts a value and constructs and returns a pointer to a binary tree consisting of a single node whose information field contains that value. This routine is described in Section 6.1. However, in our particular version, we assume that *maketree* inputs two values, a record and a key.)

```
q = null
p = tree
while p <> null do
        if key = k(p)
            then search = p
                    return
        endif
        q = p
        if key < k(p)
            then p = left(p)
            else p = right(p)
        endif
endwhile
v = maketree(rec,key)
if q = null
    then tree = v
    else if key < k(q)
            then left(q) = v
            else right(q) = v
        endif
endif
search = v
return
```

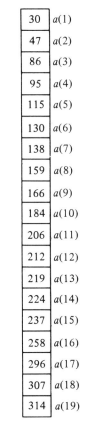

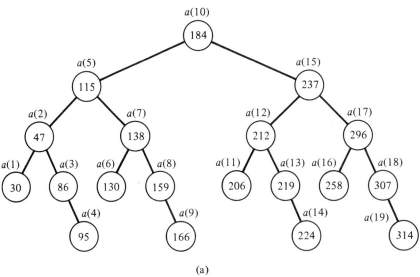

(a)

Figure 9.2.1 A sorted array and two of its binary tree representations.

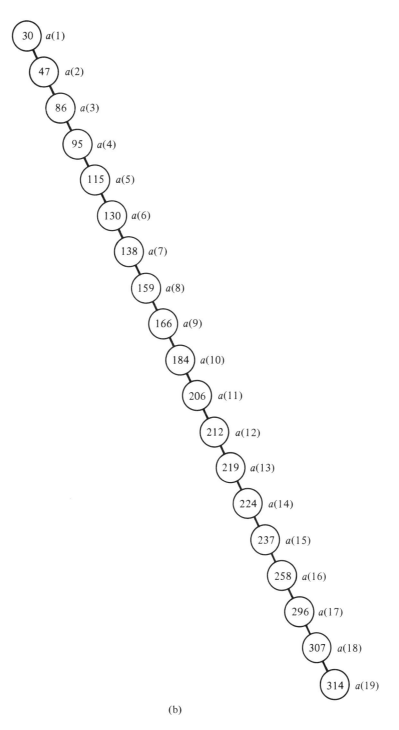

(b)

Figure 9.2.1 (*continued*).

Note that after a new record is inserted, the tree retains the property of being sorted in an inorder traversal.

Deleting from a Binary Search Tree

We now present an algorithm that deletes a node with key *key* from a binary search tree and leaves the tree as a binary search tree. There are three cases to consider. If the node to be deleted has no sons, it may be deleted without further adjustment to the tree. This is illustrated in Figure 9.2.2(a). If the node to be deleted has only one subtree, its only son can be moved up to take its place. This is illustrated in Figure 9.2.2(b). If, however, the node *p* to be deleted has two subtrees, its inorder successor *s* (or its inorder predecessor) must take its place. The inorder successor cannot have a left subtree (since if it did, a left descendant would be the inorder successor of *p*). Thus the right son of *s* can be moved up to take the place of *s*. This is illustrated in Figure 9.2.2.(c), where the node with key 12 replaces the node with key 11 and is replaced, in turn, by the node with key 13.

In the following algorithm, if no node with key *key* exists in the tree, the tree is left unchanged.

```
p = tree
q = null                              ← DITEM
'Search for the node with key key. Set p to point to
'the node and q to its father, if any.
while (p <> null) and (k(p) <> key) do
      q = p
      if key < k(p)
         then p = left(p)
         else p = right(p)
      endif
endwhile
if p = null
   then 'the key does not exist in the tree.
        'leave the tree unchanged.
        return
endif
'Set the variable v to the node that will replace node(p).
'First two cases: the node to be deleted has at most one son.
if left(p) = null
   then v = right(p)
   else if right(p) = null
           then v = left(p)
           else 'Third case: node(p) has two sons. Set v to the
                'inorder successor of p and t to the father of v.
```

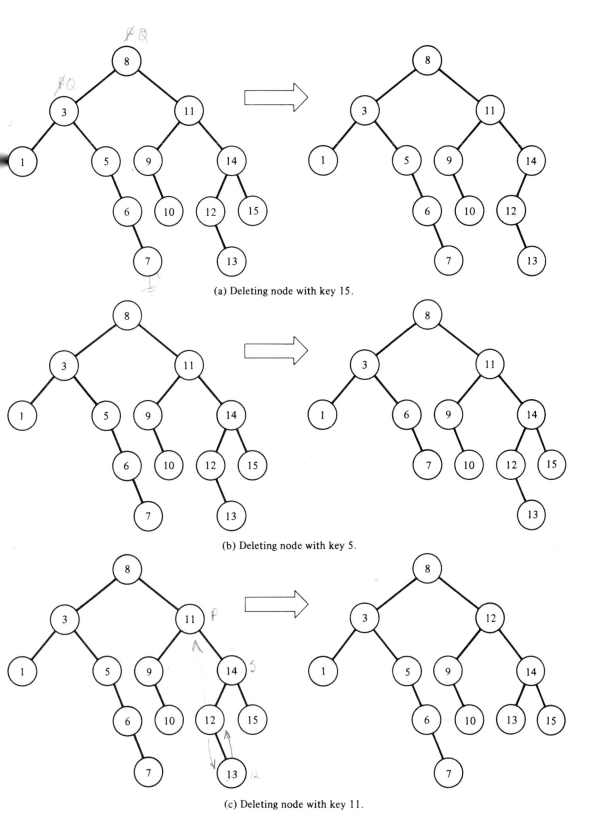

(a) Deleting node with key 15.

(b) Deleting node with key 5.

(c) Deleting node with key 11.

Figure 9.2.2   Deleting nodes from a binary search tree.

```
              t = p
              v = right(p)
              s = left(v)        's is the left son of v
              while s <> null do
                      t = v
                      v = s
                      s = left(v)
              endwhile
              'At this point, v is the inorder successor of p
              if t <> p
                then 'p is not the father of v and v = left(t)
                      'Remove node(v) from its current position and
                      'replace it with the right son of node(v).
                      left(t) = right(v)
                      'Adjust the sons of v to be the sons of p
                      right(v) = right(p)
              endif
              left(v) = left(p)
          endif
      endif
      'Insert node(v) into the position formerly occupied by node(p)
      if q = null
        then 'node(p) was the root of the tree
              tree = v
        else if p = left(q)
                then left(q) = v
                else right(q) = v
              endif
      endif
      freenode(p)
      return
```

Efficiency of Binary Tree Search

As we have already seen in Section 8.3 (see Figures 8.3.1 and 8.3.2), the time required to search a binary search tree varies between $O(\log n)$ and $O(n)$, depending on the structure of the tree. If elements are inserted into the tree by the insertion algorithm presented above, the structure of the tree depends on the order in which the records are inserted. If the records are inserted in sorted (or reverse) order, the resulting tree will contain all null left (or right) links, so that the tree search reduces to a sequential search. If, however, the records are inserted so that half the records inserted after any given record r with key k have keys smaller than k and half have keys greater than k, a balanced tree is achieved in which approximately $\log_2 n$ key comparisons are sufficient to retrieve an element. (Again, it should be noted that examining a node in our insertion algorithm requires two comparisons: one for equality and the other for less than. However, in machine language and in some compilers, these can be combined into a single comparison.)

If the records are presented in random order (i.e., any permutation of the n elements is equally likely), balanced trees will result more often than not, so that on the average, the search time remains $O(\log n)$. However, the constant of proportionality will be greater on the average than in the specific case of an evenly balanced tree.

All of the preceding assumes that it is equally likely for the search argument to equal any key in the table. However, in actual practice it is usually the case that some records are retrieved very often, some moderately often, and some are almost never retrieved. Suppose that records are inserted into the tree so that a more commonly accessed record precedes one that is not so frequently accessed. Then the most frequently retrieved records will be nearer the root of the tree, so that the average successful search time will be reduced. (Of course, this assumes that reordering the keys in order of reduced frequency of access does not seriously unbalance the binary tree, since if it did, the reduced number of comparisons for the most frequently accessed records might be offset by the increased number of comparisons for the vast majority of records.)

If the elements to be retrieved form a constant set, with no insertions or deletions, it may pay to set up a binary search tree which makes subsequent searches more efficient. For example, consider the binary search trees of Figure 9.2.3. Both the trees of Figure 9.2.3(a) and (b) contain three elements, $K1$, $K2$, and $K3$, where $K1 < K2 < K3$, and are valid binary search trees for that set. However, a retrieval of $K3$ requires two comparisons in Figure 9.2.3(a) but requires only one comparison in Figure 9.2.3(b). Of course, there are still other valid binary search trees for this set of keys.

The number of key comparisons necessary to retrieve a record is equal to the level of that record in the binary search tree plus 1. Thus a retrieval of $K2$ requires one comparison in the tree of Figure 9.2.3(a) but requires three comparisons in the tree of Figure 9.2.3(b). An unsuccessful search for an argument lying immediately between two keys a and b requires as many key comparisons as the maximum number of comparisons required by successful searches for either a or b. (Why?) This is equal to 1 plus the maximum of the levels of a or b. For example, a search for a key lying between $K2$ and $K3$ requires two key comparisons in Figure 9.2.3(a) and three comparisons in Figure 9.2.3(b), while a search for a key greater than $K3$ requires two comparisons in Figure 9.2.3(a), but only one comparison in Figure 9.2.3(b).

Suppose that $p1$, $p2$, and $p3$ are the probabilities that the search argument equals $K1$, $K2$, and $K3$, respectively. Suppose also that $q0$ is the probability that

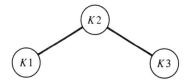

(a) Expected number of comparisons:

$2p1 + p2 + 2p3 + 2q0 + 2q1 + 2q2 + 2q3$

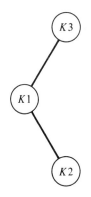

(b) Expected number of comparisons:

$2p1 + 3p2 + p3 + 2q0 + 3q1 + 3q2 + q3$ **Figure 9.2.3**   Two binary search trees.

the search argument is less than $K1$, $q1$ is the probability that it is between $K1$ and $K2$, $q2$ is the probability that it is between $K2$ and $K3$, and $q3$ is the probability that it is greater than $K3$. Then $p1 + p2 + p3 + q0 + q1 + q2 + q3 = 1$. The **expected number** of comparisons in a search is the sum of the products of the probability that the argument has a given value times the number of comparisons required to retrieve that value, where the sum is taken over all possible search argument values. For example, the expected number of comparisons in searching the tree of Figure 9.2.3(a) is

$$2p1 + p2 + 2p3 + 2q0 + 2q1 + 2q2 + 2q3$$

while the expected number of comparisons in searching the tree of Figure 9.2.3(b) is

$$2p1 + 3p2 + p3 + 2q0 + 3q1 + 3q2 + q3$$

This expected number of comparisons can be used as a measure of how "good" a particular binary search tree is for a given set of keys and a given set of probabilities. Thus, for the probabilities listed below on the left, the tree of Figure 9.2.3(a) is more efficient; for the probabilities listed on the right, the tree of Figure 9.2.3(b) is more efficient.

$$p1 = .1 \qquad\qquad\qquad\qquad p1 = .1$$
$$p2 = .3 \qquad\qquad\qquad\qquad p2 = .1$$
$$p3 = .1 \qquad\qquad\qquad\qquad p3 = .3$$
$$q0 = .1 \qquad\qquad\qquad\qquad q0 = .1$$
$$q1 = .2 \qquad\qquad\qquad\qquad q1 = .1$$
$$q2 = .1 \qquad\qquad\qquad\qquad q2 = .1$$
$$q3 = .1 \qquad\qquad\qquad\qquad q3 = .2$$

Expected number for 9.2.3(a) = 1.7   Expected number for 9.2.3(a) = 1.9

Expected number for 9.2.3(b) = 2.4   Expected number for 9.2.3(b) = 1.8

A binary search tree that minimizes the expected number of comparisons for a given set of keys and probabilities is called ***optimum***. Although an algorithm to produce such a tree may be very expensive, the tree that it produces yields efficiencies in all subsequent searches. Unfortunately, however, it is rare that the probabilities of the search arguments are known in advance.

Balanced Trees

As noted above, if the probability of searching for a key in a table is the same for all keys, a balanced binary tree yields the most efficient search. Unfortunately, the search and insertion algorithm presented above does not ensure that the tree remains balanced—the degree of balance is dependent on the sequence in which keys are inserted into the tree. We would like to have an efficient search and insertion algorithm which maintains the search tree as a balanced binary tree.

Let us first define more precisely the notion of a "balanced" tree. The ***height*** of a binary tree is the maximum level of its leafs (this is also sometimes known as the ***depth*** of the tree). For convenience, the height of a null tree is defined as -1. The ***balance*** of a node in a binary tree is defined as the height of its left subtree minus the height of its right subtree. A ***balanced binary tree*** (sometimes called an ***AVL tree***) is a binary tree in which the absolute value of the balance of each node is less than or equal to 1. Figure 9.2.4(a) illustrates a balanced binary tree. Each node in a balanced binary tree has a balance of 1, -1, or 0, depending on whether the height of its left subtree is greater than, less than, or equal to the height of its right subtree. The balance of each node is indicated in Figure 9.2.4(a).

Suppose that we are given a balanced binary tree and use the search and insertion algorithm above to insert a new node p into the tree. Then the resulting tree may or may not remain balanced. Figure 9.2.4(b) illustrates all possible insertions that may be made to the tree of Figure 9.2.4(a). Each insertion that yields a balanced tree is indicated by a B. The unbalanced insertions are indicated by a U and are numbered from 1 to 12. It is easy to see that the tree becomes unbalanced only if the newly inserted node is a left descendant of a node that previously had a balance of 1 [this occurs in cases $U1$ through $U8$ in Figure

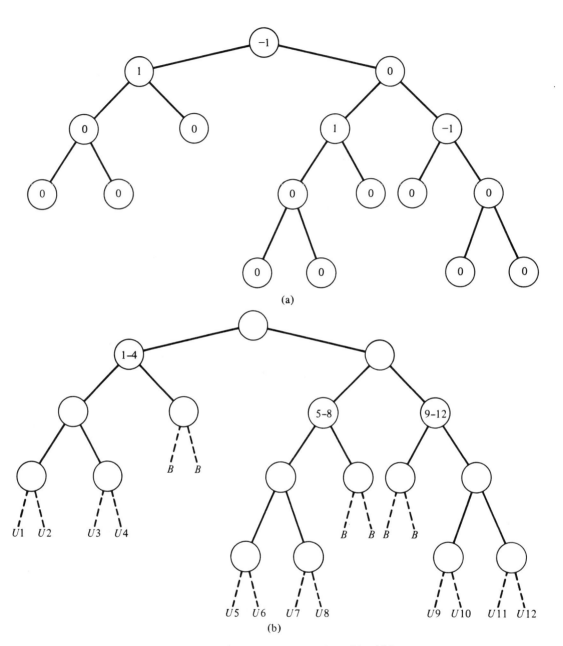

Figure 9.2.4 A balanced binary tree and possible additions.

9.2.4(b)] or if it is a right descendant of a node that previously had a balance of
−1 (cases *U*9 through *U*12). In Figure 9.2.4(b), the youngest ancestor that becomes unbalanced in each insertion is indicated by the numbers contained in
three of the nodes.

Let us examine further the subtree rooted at the youngest ancestor to become unbalanced as a result of an insertion. We illustrate the case where the balance of this subtree was previously 1, leaving the other case to the reader. Figure
9.2.5 illustrates this case. Let us call the unbalanced node *A*. Since *A* had a balance of 1, its left subtree was nonnull; we may therefore designate its left son as
B. Since *A* is the youngest ancestor of the new node to become unbalanced, node
B must have had a balance of 0. (You are asked to prove this fact as an exercise.)
Thus node *B* must have had (before the insertion) left and right subtrees of equal
height *n* (where possibly $n = -1$). Since the balance of *A* was 1, the right subtree of *A* must also have been of height *n*.

There are now two cases to consider, illustrated by Figure 9.2.5(a) and (b).
In Figure 9.2.5(a) the newly created node is inserted into the left subtree of *B*,
changing the balance of *B* to 1 and the balance of *A* to 2. In Figure 9.2.5(b) the
newly created node is inserted into the right subtree of *B*, changing the balance of
B to −1 and the balance of *A* to 2. To maintain a balanced tree, it is necessary to
perform a transformation on the tree so that

1. The inorder traversal of the transformed tree is the same as for the original
   tree (i.e., the transformed tree remains a binary search tree).

2. The transformed tree is balanced.

Consider the trees of Figure 9.2.6. The tree of Figure 9.2.6(b) is said to be
a ***right rotation*** of the tree rooted at *A* of Figure 9.2.6(a). Similarly, the tree of
Figure 9.2.6(c) is said to be a ***left rotation*** of the tree rooted at *A* of Figure
9.2.6(a).

An algorithm to implement a left rotation of a subtree rooted at *p* is as follows:

$$q = right(p)$$
$$hold = left(q)$$
$$left(q) = p$$
$$right\ (p) = hold$$

Let us call this operation *leftrotation(p)*. *rightrotation(p)* may be defined
similarly. Of course, in any rotation the value of the pointer to the root of the
subtree being rotated must also be changed to point to the new root. [In the case
of the left rotation above, this new root is *node(q)*.] Note that the order of the
nodes in an inorder traversal is preserved under both right and left rotation. It
therefore follows that any number of rotations (left or right) can be performed on
an unbalanced tree in order to obtain a balanced tree, without disturbing the order
of the nodes in an inorder traversal.

Let us now return to the trees of Figure 9.2.5. Suppose that a right rotation

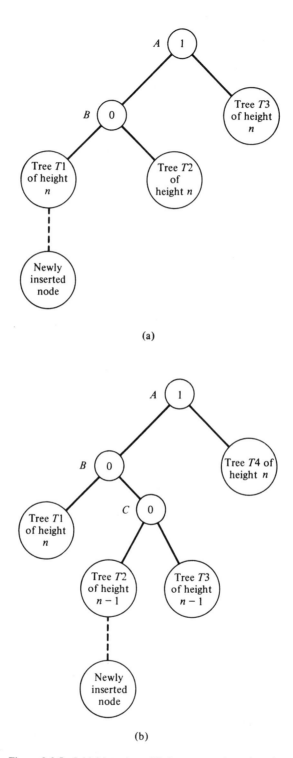

(a)

(b)

Figure 9.2.5 Initial insertion; all balances are prior to insertion.

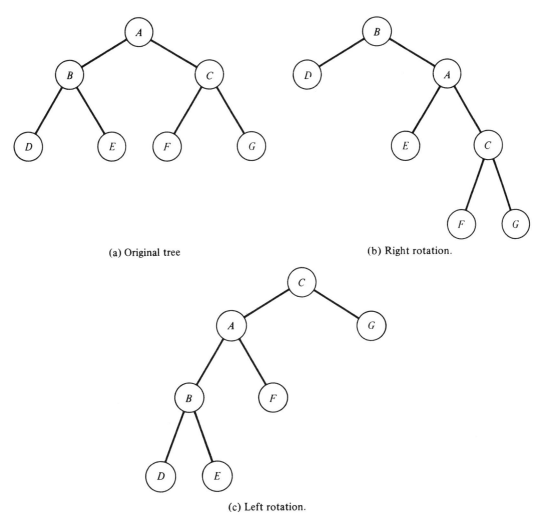

(a) Original tree   (b) Right rotation.

(c) Left rotation.

Figure 9.2.6 Simple rotation on a tree.

is performed on the subtree rooted at A in Figure 9.2.5(a). The resulting tree is shown in Figure 9.2.7(a). Note that the tree of Figure 9.2.7(a) yields the same inorder traversal as that of Figure 9.2.5(a) and is also balanced. Also, since the height of the subtree of Figure 9.2.5(a) was $n+2$ before the insertion and the height of the subtree of Figure 9.2.7(a) is $n+2$ after the insertion and rebalancing, the balance of each ancestor of node A in the original tree remains undisturbed. Thus, replacing the subtree of Figure 9.2.5(a) with its right rotation of Figure 9.2.7(a) guarantees that a balanced binary search tree is maintained.

Let us now turn to the tree of Figure 9.2.5(b), where the newly created node is inserted into the right subtree of B. Let C be the right son of B. (There are three

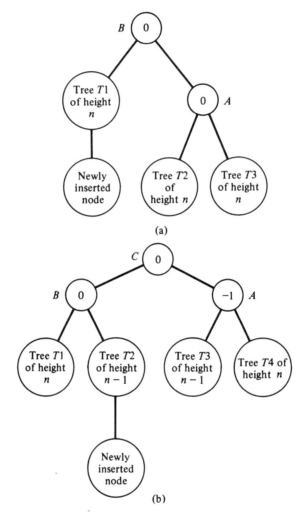

(a)

(b)

Figure 9.2.7   After rebalancing; all balances are after insertion.

cases: C may be the newly inserted node, in which case $n = -1$, or the newly inserted node may be in the left or right subtree of C. Figure 9.2.5(b) illustrates the case where it is in the left subtree; the analysis of the other cases is analogous.) Suppose that a left rotation on the subtree rooted at B is followed by a right rotation on the subtree rooted at A. Figure 9.2.7(b) illustrates the resulting tree. Verify that the inorder traversals of the two trees are the same and that the tree of Figure 9.2.7(b) is balanced. The height of the tree in Figure 9.2.7(b) is $n+2$, which is the same as the height of the tree in Figure 9.2.5(b) before the insertion and rebalancing, so that the balance in all ancestors of A is unchanged.

Therefore, by replacing the tree of Figure 9.2.5(b) with that of Figure 9.2.7(b) whenever it occurs after insertion, a balanced search tree is maintained.

Let us now present an algorithm to search and insert into a nonempty balanced binary tree. Each node of the tree contains five fields: *k* and *r,* which hold the key and record, respectively; *left* and *right,* which are pointers to the left and right subtrees, respectively; and *bal,* whose value is 1, −1, or 0, depending on the node's balance. In the first part of the algorithm, if the desired key is not found in the tree, a new node is inserted into the binary search tree without regard to balance. This first phase also keeps track of the youngest ancestor, *ya,* which may become unbalanced upon insertion. The algorithm makes use of the function *maketree* described above and routines *rightrotation* and *leftrotation,* each of which accept a pointer to the root of a subtree and perform the desired rotation.

```
'part i: search and insert into the binary tree
s = null
p = tree
v = null
ya = p
      'ya points to the youngest ancestor that may become unbalanced.
      'v points to the father of ya, and s points to the father of p.
while p <> null do
      if key = k(p)
        then search = p
               return
      endif
      if key < k(p)
        then q = left(p)
        else q = right(p)
      endif
      if q <> null
        then if bal(q) <> 0
               then v = p
                    ya = q
             endif
      endif
      s = p
      p = q
endwhile
'insert a new record
q = maketree (rec,key)
bal(q) = 0
if key < k(s)
   then left(s) = q
   else right(s) = q
endif
```

'the balance on all nodes between *node(ya)* and *node(q)* must be changed from 0
if *key* < *k(ya)*
  then *s = left(ya)*
  else *s = right(ya)*
endif
p = s
while *p* <> *q* **do**
    if *key* < *k(p)*
      then *bal(p) = 1*
          p = left(p)
      else *bal(p) = −1*
          p = right(p)
    endif
endwhile

'*part ii:* ascertain whether or not the tree is unbalanced.
'If it is, *q* is the newly inserted node, *ya* is its youngest
'unbalanced ancestor, *v* is the father of *ya,* and *s* is the
'son of *ya* in the direction of the imbalance.
if *key* < *k(ya)*
  then *imbal = 1*
  else *imbal = −1*
endif
if *bal(ya) = 0*
  then 'Another level has been added to the tree.
      'The tree remains balanced.
      bal(ya) = imbal
      search = q
      return
endif
if *bal(ya)* <> *imbal*
  then 'The added node has been placed in the opposite direction of the imbalance.
      'The tree remains balanced.
      bal(ya) = 0
      search = q
      return
endif

'*part iii*: the additional node has unbalanced the tree.
'Rebalance it by performing the required rotations
'and then adjust the balances of the nodes involved.

if *bal(s)* = *imbal*
  then '*ya* and *s* have been unbalanced in the same direction;
    'see Figure 9.2.5(a), where *ya* = *A* and *s* = *B*
    p = *s*
    if *imbal* = 1
      then *rightrotation(ya)*
      else *leftrotation(ya)*
    endif
    bal(ya) = 0
    bal(s) = 0
  else '*ya* and *s* are unbalanced in opposite directions;
    'see Figure 9.2.5(b) where *ya* = *A* and *s* = *B*
    if *imbal* = 1
      then *p* = *right(s)*
        leftrotation(s)
        left(ya) = *p*
        rightrotation(ya)
      else *p* = *left(s)*
        rightrotation(s)
        right(ya) = *p*
        leftrotation(ya)
  endif
  'Adjust *bal* field for involved nodes
  if *bal(p)* = 0
    then '*p* was the inserted node
      bal(ya) = 0
      bal(s) = 0
    else if *bal(p)* = *imbal*
      then 'See Figure 9.2.5(b) and 9.2.7(b)
        bal(ya) = − *imbal*
        bal(s) = 0
      else 'See Figures 9.2.5(b) and 9.2.7(b)
        'but assume that the new node was inserted into *T*3
        bal(ya) = 0
        bal(s) = *imbal*
      endif
    endif
    bal(p) = 0
endif
'Adjust the pointer to the rotated subtree; *v* is the father of *ya*
if *v* = *null*
  then *tree* = *p*
  else if *ya* = *right(v)*
    then *right(v)* = *p*
    else *left(v)* = *p*
  endif
endif

$search = q$
return

The algorithm to delete a node from a balanced binary search tree while maintaining its balance is even more complex and is left as an exercise.

Digital Search Trees

Another method of using trees to expedite searching is to form a general tree based on the symbols of which the keys are comprised. For example, if the keys are integers, each digit position determines one of 10 possible sons of a given node. A forest representing one such set of keys is illustrated in Figure 9.2.8. If the keys consist of alphabetic characters, each letter of the alphabet determines a branch in the tree. Note that every leaf node contains the special symbol *eok*, which represents the end of a key. Such a leaf node must also contain a pointer to the record that is being stored.

If a forest is represented by a binary tree, as in Section 6.5, each node of the binary tree contains three fields: *symbol,* which contains a symbol of the key; *son,* which is a pointer to the node's oldest son in the original tree; and *brother,* which is a pointer to the node's next younger brother in the original tree. The first tree in the forest is pointed to by an external pointer *tree* and the roots of the other trees in the forest are linked together in a linear list by the *brother* field. The *son* field of a leaf in the original forest points to a record; the concatenation of all the *symbol*s in the path of nodes from the root to the leaf in the original forest is the key of the record. We make two further stipulations which will speed up the search and insertion process for such a tree. Each list of brothers is arranged in the binary tree in ascending order of the *symbol* field. The symbol *eok* is considered to be larger than any other.

Using this binary tree representation, we may present an algorithm to search and insert into such a nonempty *digital tree*. *key* is the key for which we are searching and *arec* is a pointer to record that we wish to insert if *key* is not found. We also let *key(i)* be the *i*th symbol of the key. If the key has n symbols, we also assume that $key(n+1)$ equals *eok*. The algorithm uses the *getnode* operation to allocate a new tree node when necessary. The algorithm sets *search* to the pointer to the record that is being sought.

```
p = tree
father = null      'father is the father of p
for i = 1 to n+1
    q = null      'q points to the older brother of p
    while (p <> null) and (symbol(p) < key(i)) do
        q = p
        p = brother(p)
    endwhile
```

Keys
180
185
1867
195
207
217
2174
21749
217493
226
27
274
278
279
2796
281
284
285
286
287
288
294
307
768

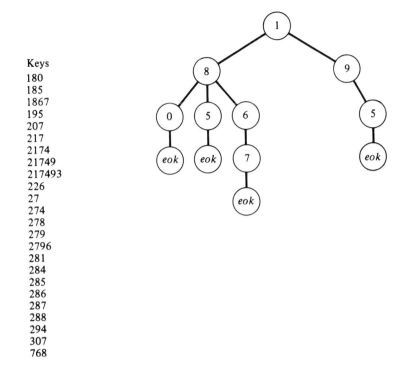

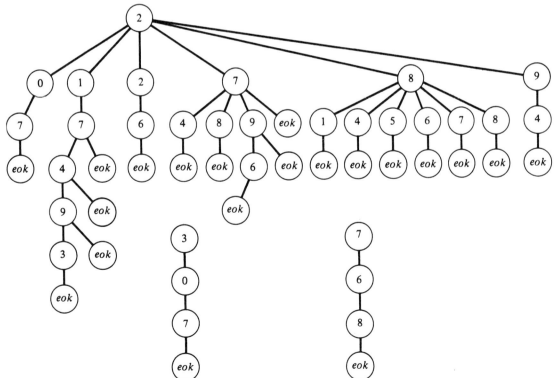

Figure 9.2.8 A forest representing a table of keys.

if $(p = null)$ *or* $(symbol(p) > key\ (i))$
    then 'insert the *i*th symbol of the key
        $s = getnode$
        $symbol(s) = key(i)$
        $brother(s) = p$
        if tree $= null$
          then tree $= s$
          else if $q <> null$
                then $brother(q) = s$
                else if father $= null$
                    then tree $= s$
                    else $son(father) = s$
                  endif
              endif
        endif
        'insert the remaining symbols of the key
        for $j = i$ *to* $n+1$
          if $key(j) = eok$
            then $son(s) = arec$
               $search = son(s)$
               return
          endif
          $father = s$
          $s = getnode$
          $symbol(s) = key(j+1)$
          $son(father) = s$
          $brother(s) = null$
        next j
    endif
    'at this point $symbol(p)$ equals $key(i)$
    if $key(i) = eok$
      then $search = son(p)$
        return
      else father $= p$
        $p = son(p)$
    endif
next i

Note that by keeping the table of keys as a general tree, we need search only a small list of sons to find whether a given symbol appears at a given position within the keys of the table. However, it is possible to make the tree even smaller by eliminating those nodes from which only a single leaf can be reached. For example, in the keys of Figure 9.2.8, once the symbol "7" is recognized, the only key that can possibly match is 768. Similarly, upon recognizing the two symbols "1" and "9", the only matching symbol is 195. Thus the forest of Figure 9.2.8 can be abbreviated to the one of Figure 9.2.9. In that figure, a box indicates a key, while a circle indicates a tree node. A dashed line is used to indicate a pointer from a tree node to a key.

There are some significant differences between the trees of Figures 9.2.8 and 9.2.9. In Figure 9.2.8, a path from a root to a leaf represents an entire key, so there is no need to repeat the key itself. In Figure 9.2.9, however, a key may be recognized only by its first few symbols. In those cases where the search is made for a key that is known to be in the table, then upon finding a leaf, the record corresponding to that key can be accessed. If, however, as is more likely, it is not known whether the key is present in the table, it must be confirmed that the key is indeed correct. Thus the entire key must be kept in the record as well. Furthermore, a leaf node in the tree of Figure 9.2.8 can be recognized because it contains *eok*. Thus its *son* pointer need not be null but can be used instead to point to the record which that leaf represents. However, a leaf node of Figure 9.2.9 may contain any symbol. Thus in order to use the *son* pointer of a leaf to point to the record, an extra flag is required in each node to indicate whether or not the node is a leaf. We leave the representation of the forest of Figure 9.2.9 and the implementation of a search-and-insert algorithm for it as an exercise for the reader.

The tree representation of a table of keys is efficient when each node has relatively few sons. For example, in Figure 9.2.9 only one node has as many as six (out of a possible 10) sons, while most nodes have only one, two, or three sons. Thus the process of searching through the list of sons to match the next symbol in the key is relatively efficient. However, if the set of keys is *dense* within the set of all possible keys (i.e., if almost any possible combination of symbols actually appears as a key), then most nodes will have a large number of sons and the cost of the search process becomes prohibitive. For example, if the files of the Internal Revenue Service were keyed by social security number, the cost of a digital tree search would be prohibitive.

Tries

A modification of the digital tree proves to be quite efficient when the set of keys in the table is dense. Instead of storing the table as a tree, the table is stored as a two-dimensional array. Each row of the array represents one of the possible symbols that may appear in the key and each column represents a node in a digital tree. Each entry in the array is a pointer to either another column in the array or to a key and its record. In searching for a key *key*, *key*(1) is used to index the first column of the array. The entry that is found at row *key*(1) and column 1 is either a pointer to a key and record, in which case there is only one key in the table that begins with the symbol *key*(1) or it is a pointer to another column of the array, say column *j*. Column *j* represents all keys in the table that begin with *key*(1).

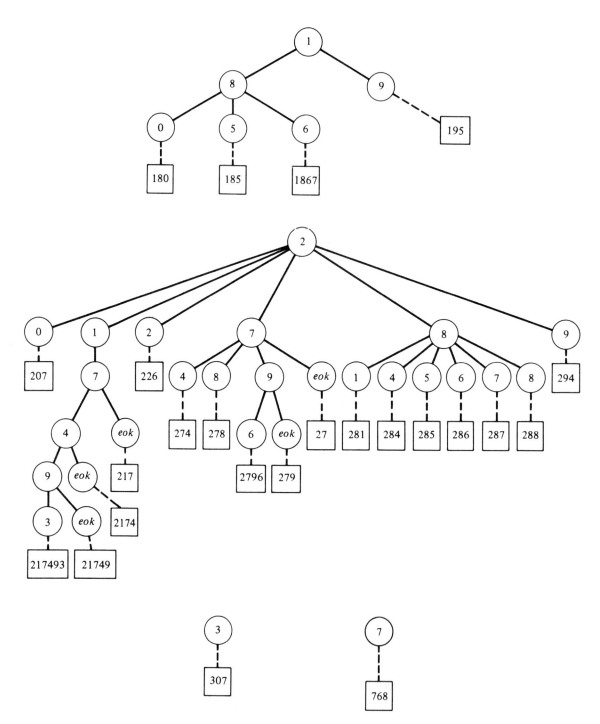

Figure 9.2.9 A condensed forest representing a table of keys.

$key(2)$ is used as a row number to index column j to determine either the only key in the table beginning with $key(1)$ and $key(2)$, or the column representing all keys in the table beginning with those two symbols. Similarly, each column in the array represents the set of all keys that begin with the same initial symbols. Such an array is called a **trie** (from the word re*trie*val).

Figure 9.2.10 illustrates a trie containing the keys of Figures 9.2.8 and 9.2.9. A pointer to a key and its corresponding record is indicated by an unparenthesized number which is the actual key, while a pointer to a column is indicated by a parenthesized number. In an actual implementation, an extra flag would be required to differentiate between these two types of pointers.

For example, suppose that a search is to be made for a record whose key is 274, in the trie of Figure 9.2.10. In this case, $key(1) = 2$, $key(2) = 7$, and $key(3) = 4$. $key(1)$ is used to index column 1. Row 2 of column 1 points to column 4; thus column 4 represents all keys whose first character is 2. $key(2)$ is then used to index column 4. Row 7 of column 4 points to column 9; thus column 9 represents all keys whose first two characters are 2 and 7, respectively. $key(3)$ is then used to index column 9, in which row 4 contains the key 274. At this point the search is successful. Actually, since the array that forms the trie is dynamic (columns must be added as new records are inserted), a trie is best implemented as a general tree in which each node has a fixed number of sons. Each node of the general tree represents a column of the trie.

You will note that the trie of Figure 9.2.10 contains a large amount of unused space. This is because the set of keys in this example is not dense, so that there are many digits at many positions which do not appear in a key. If the set of keys is dense, most of the entries in the trie will be filled. The reason that a trie is

	1	2	3	4	5	6	7	8	9	10	11	12	13	14
0			180	207										
1	(2)			(5)							281			
2	(4)			226										
3	307							217493						
4						(7)			274		284			
5			185								285			
6			1867							2796	286			
7	768			(9)	(6)						287			
8		(3)		(11)					278		288			
9		195		294			(8)		(10)					
eok						217	2174	21749	27	279				

Figure 9.2.10   A trie.

so efficient is that for each symbol of the key, only a single table lookup rather than a list traversal need be performed.

EXERCISES

1. Write an efficient insertion algorithm for a binary search tree to insert a new record whose key is known not to exist in the tree.

2. Show that it is possible to obtain a binary search tree in which only a single leaf exists, even if the elements of the tree are not inserted in strictly ascending or descending order.

3. Verify by simulation that if records are presented to the binary tree search and insertion algorithm in random order, the number of key comparisons will be $O(\log n)$.

4. Prove that every n-node binary search tree is not equally likely (assuming that items are inserted in random order), and that balanced trees are more probable than straight-line trees.

5. Write an algorithm to delete a node from a binary tree which replaces the node with its inorder predecessor rather than its inorder successor.

6. Suppose that the nodes of a binary search tree are defined as follows:

```
10   DIM INFO (100,2)
20       K = 1
30       R = 2
40   DIM PTR (100,2)
50       LEFT = 1
60       RIGHT = 2
```

INFO (I,K) and INFO (I,R) contain the key and record of node I, and PTR (I,LEFT) and PTR (I,RIGHT) are pointers to the node's left and right sons, respectively. Write a BASIC routine *sinsert* to search and insert a record REC with key KEY into a binary search tree pointed to by TREE.

7. Write a BASIC routine *sdelete* to search and delete a record with key KEY from a binary search tree pointed to by TREE implemented as in Exercise 6. If such a record is found, the routine returns the value of its R field; if it is not found, the routine returns 0.

8. Write a BASIC routine *delete* to delete all records with keys between KEY1 and KEY2 (inclusive) from a binary search tree whose nodes are declared as in Exercises 6 and 7.

9. Consider the search trees of Figure 9.2.11.
   (a) How many permutations of the integers 1 through 7 would produce the binary search trees of Figure 9.2.11(a), (b), and (c), respectively? The tree is constructed by inserting each element of the permutation in turn into a tree that is initially null.

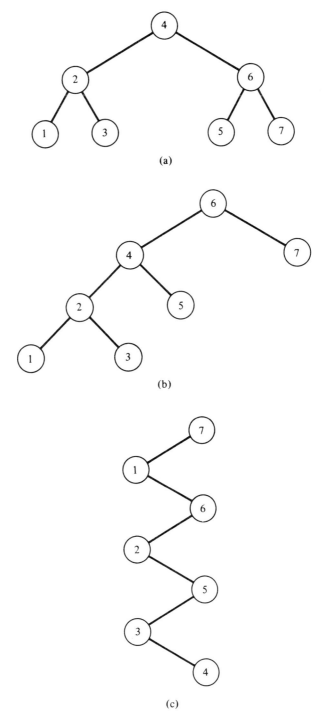

(a)

(b)

(c)

Figure 9.2.11

(b) How many permutations of the integers 1 through 7 would produce binary search trees that are similar to the trees of Figure 9.2.11 (a), (b), and (c), respectively? (See Exercise 6.1.6.)

(c) How many permutations of the integers 1 through 7 would produce binary search trees with the same number of nodes at each level as the trees of Figure 9.2.11(a), (b), and (c), respectively?

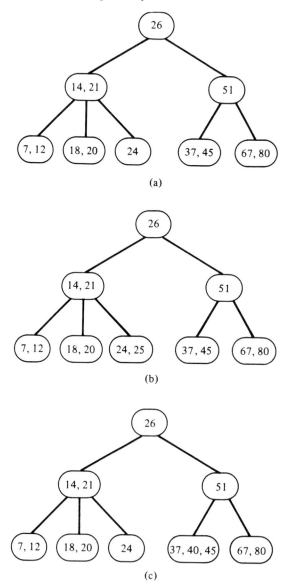

Figure 9.2.12 A 3-2 tree.

(**d**) Find an assignment of probabilities to the first seven positive integers as search arguments which makes each of the trees of Figure 9.2.11(a), (b), and (c) optimum.

10. A **3-2** *tree* is one in which each node has two or three sons and contains either one or two keys. If a node has two sons, it contains one key. All keys in the left subtree are less than that key, and all keys in the right subtree are greater than that key. If a node has three sons, it contains two keys. All keys in the left subtree are less than the left key, which is less than all keys in the middle subtree. All keys in the middle subtree are less than the right key, which is less than all keys in the right subtree. Figure 9.2.12(a) illustrates such a tree. (The 2 or 3 subtrees of a leaf are all null.)

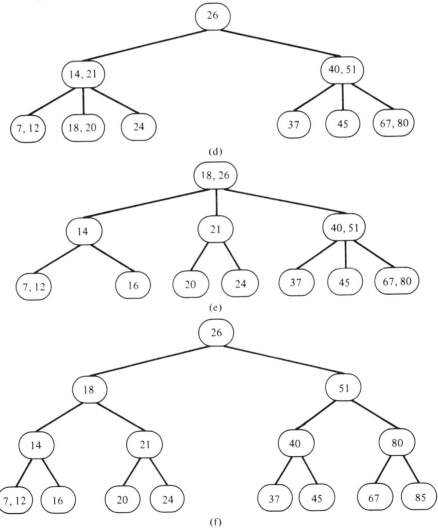

(d)

(e)

(f)

Figure 9.2.12 *(continued)*.

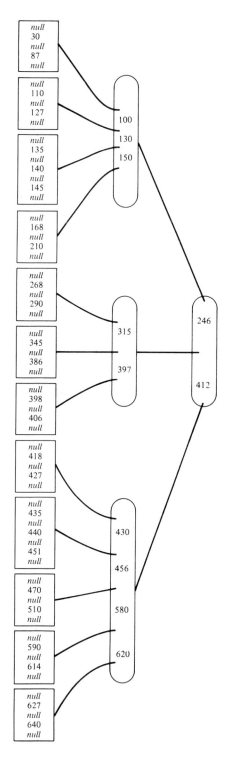

Figure 9.2.13 A *B*-tree of order 5.

A key is inserted into such a tree as follows. First, find the leaf into which the key would be inserted if there were no limit to the number of keys to a node. For example, Figure 9.2.12(b) illustrates the key 25 inserted into a leaf, while Figure 9.2.12(c) illustrates the key 40 inserted into a leaf. The tree of Figure 9.3.12(b) is a valid 3-2 tree, so that the key 25 has been properly inserted. Figure 9.2.12(c) is not a valid 3-2 tree, since one node contains 3 keys. In this case, the insertion process continues by moving the middle one of the 3 keys into the father node and splitting the other two keys into two separate nodes, as shown in Figure 9.2.12(d). Since the resulting tree is a 3-2 tree, the insertion process terminates. Figure 9.2.12(e) illustrates the 3-2 tree that finally results from an insertion of the key 16 into the tree of Figure 9.2.12(d), and Figure 9.2.12(f) illustrates the tree that results from an insertion of the key 85 into the tree of Figure 9.2.12(e). Develop a BASIC implementation of 3-2 trees and write search and insertion and deletion algorithms for them.

11. A **B-tree of order m** is a generalization of the 3-2 tree of Exercise 10. Such a tree is defined as a general tree that satisfies the following properties:

   (1) Each node contains at most $m - 1$ keys.
   (2) Each node except for the root contains at least $int((m - 1)/2)$ keys.
   (3) The root has at least two sons, unless it is a leaf.
   (4) All leafs are on the same level.
   (5) A nonleaf node with n keys has $n + 1$ sons.

   Figure 9.2.13 illustrates a B-tree of order 5. Note that each node may be thought of as an ordered set

$$(p_1, k_1, p_2, k_2, \ldots, k_{n-1}, p_n)$$

where p_i is a pointer (possibly null, if the node is a leaf) and k_i is a key. All keys in the node pointed to by p_i are between k_{i-1} and k_i and $k_1 < k_2 < \ldots < k_{n-1}$ within each node.

   (a) Develop an algorithm to search and insert into a B-tree of order m.
   (b) Convert your algorithm in part (a) into a BASIC program.
   (c) Why are B-trees particularly useful in external searching?

3. HASHING

In the preceding two sections, we assumed that the record being sought was stored in a table and that it was necessary to pass through some number of keys before finding the desired one. The organization of the file (sequential, indexed sequential, binary tree, etc.) and the order in which the keys are inserted determine the number of keys that must be inspected before obtaining the desired one. Obviously, the efficient search techniques are those which minimize the number of these comparisons. Optimally, we would like to have a table organization in which there are no unnecessary comparisons. Let us see if such a table organization is feasible.

If each key is to be retrieved in a single access, the location of the record within the table can depend only on the key; it may not depend on the locations of other keys as in a tree. The most efficient way to organize such a table is as an array; that is, each record is stored at a specific offset from the base address of the table. If the record keys are integers, the keys themselves can be used as indices to the array.

Let us consider an example of such a system. Suppose that a manufacturing company has an inventory file consisting of 100 parts, each part having a unique two-digit part number. Then the obvious way to store this file is to declare an array:

$$10 \quad \text{DIM PART (99)}$$

where PART (I) (and possibly additional fields indexed by I) represents the record whose part number is I. (Here, and in the remainder of this section, we are assuming that the lower bound of the array is 0.) In this situation, the part numbers are keys which are used as indices to the array. Even if the company stocks fewer than 1000 parts, the same structure can be used to maintain the inventory file (provided that the keys are still two digits). Although many locations in PART would then correspond to nonexistent keys, this waste is offset by the advantage of direct access to each of the existent parts.

Unfortunately, however, such a system is not always practical. For example, suppose that the company has an inventory file of more than 100 items and the key to each record is a seven-digit part number. To use direct indexing using the entire seven-digit key, an array of 100 million elements would be required. This clearly wastes an unacceptably large amount of space, since it is extremely unlikely that a company stocks more than a few thousand parts.

What is necessary is some method of converting a key into an integer within a limited range. Ideally, no two keys should be converted into the same integer. Unfortunately, such an ideal method usually does not exist. Let us attempt to develop methods that come close to the ideal and determine what action to take when the ideal is not achieved.

Let us reconsider the example of a company with an inventory file in which each record is keyed by a seven-digit part number. Suppose that the company has fewer than 1000 parts and that there is only a single record for each part. Then an array of 1000 elements is sufficient to contain the entire file. The array is indexed by an integer between 0 and 999 inclusive. The last three digits of the part number are used as the index for that part's record in the array. This is illustrated in Figure 9.3.1. Note that two keys which are relatively close to each other numerically, such as 4618396 and 4618996, may be farther from each other in the table than two keys which are widely separated numerically, such as 0000991 and 9846995. This is because only the last three digits of the key are used in determining the position of a record.

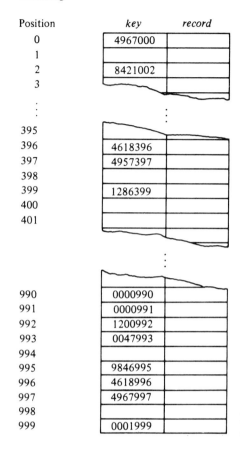

Figure 9.3.1 Part records stored in an array.

A function that transforms a key into a table index is called a **hash function**. If h is a hash function and *key* is a key, then $h(key)$ is called the **hash** of *key* and is the index at which a record with key *key* should be placed. If we let $mod(x,y)$ represent the remainder obtained on dividing x by y, the hash function in the example above is $h(key) = mod(key, 1000)$. The values that h produces should cover the entire set of indices in the table. For example, the function $mod(x, 1000)$ can produce any integer between 0 and 999, depending on the value of x. As we shall see shortly, it is a good idea for the table size to be somewhat larger than the number of records that are to be inserted. This is illustrated in Figure 9.3.1, where several positions in the table are unused.

The method above has one flaw. Suppose that two keys $k1$ and $k2$ are such that $h(k1) = h(k2)$. Then when a record with key $k1$ is entered into the table, it is inserted at position $h(k1)$. But when $k2$ is hashed, the position obtained is the position at which the record with key $k1$ is stored. Clearly, two records cannot occupy the same position. Such a situation called a **hash collision** or a **hash clash**. A hash clash occurs in the inventory example of Figure 9.3.1 if a record with key 0596397 is added to the table. We will explore shortly how to resolve such a situation. However, it should be noted that a good hash function is one that minimizes collisions and spreads the records uniformly throughout the table. That is why it is desirable to have the array size larger than the number of actual records. The larger the range of the hash function, the less likely it is that two keys will yield the same hash value. Of course, this involves a space/time trade-off. Leaving empty spaces in the array is space inefficient but it reduces the necessity of resolving hash clashes and is therefore more time efficient.

Resolving Hash Clashes by Open Addressing

Let us consider what would happen if we wanted to enter a new part number 0596397 into the table of Figure 9.3.1. Using the hash function $mod(key, 1000)$, we find that $h(0596397) = 397$ and that the record for that part belongs in position 397 of the array. However, position 397 is already occupied since the record with key 4957397 is in that position. Therefore, the record with key 0596397 must be inserted elsewhere in the table.

The simplest method of resolving hash clashes is to place the record in the next available position in the array. In Figure 9.3.1, for example, since position 397 is already occupied, the record with key 0596397 is placed in location 398, which is still open. Once that record has been inserted, another record, which hashes to either 397 (such as 8764397) or 398 (such as 2194398), is inserted at the next available position, which is 400.

This technique is called *linear probing* and is an example of a general method for resolving hash clashes called *rehashing* or *open addressing*. In general, a *rehash function*, *rh*, accepts one array index and produces another. If array location $h(key)$ is already occupied by a record with a different key, *rh* is applied to the value of $h(key)$ to find another location where the record may be placed. If position $rh(h(key))$ is also occupied, it, too, is rehashed to see if $rh(rh(h(key)))$ is available. This process continues until an empty location is found. Thus we may write a search and insertion algorithm using hashing as follows. We assume a hash function h and a rehash function rh. The special value *nullkey* is used to indicate an empty record, and *index* is used to indicate the index of the inserted record.

$i = h(key)$ 'hash the key
while $(k(i) <> key)$ **and** $(k(i) <> nullkey)$ **do**
　　$i = rh(i)$ 'we must rehash
endwhile
if $k(i) = nullkey$
　　then 'insert the record into the empty position
　　　　$k(i) = key$
　　　　$r(i) = rec$
endif
$index = i$
return

In the example of Figure 9.3.1, $h(key)$ is the function $mod(key,1000)$ and $rh(i)$ is the function $mod(i+1,1000)$ (i.e., the rehash of any index is the next sequential position in the array, except that the rehash of 999 is 0).

Let us examine the algorithm more closely to see if we can determine the properties of a "good" rehash function. In particular, we focus our attention on the loop, since the number of iterations determines the efficiency of the search. The loop can be exited in one of two ways: Either i is set to a value such that $k(i)$ equals *key* (in which case the record is found) or i is set to a value such that $k(i)$ equals *nullkey* (in which case an empty position is found and the record may be inserted).

It may happen, however, that the loop may execute forever. There are two possible reasons for this. First, the table may be full, so that it is impossible to insert any new records. This situation can be detected by keeping a count of the number of records in the table. When the count is equal to the table size, no additional positions are examined.

However, it is possible for the algorithm to loop infinitely even if there are some (or even many) empty positions. Suppose, for example, that the function $rh(i) = mod(i+2,1000)$ is used as a rehash function. Then any key that hashes into an odd integer rehashes into successive odd integers, and any key that hashes into an even integer rehashes into successive even integers. Consider the situation in which all odd positions of the table are occupied and all the even ones are empty. Despite the fact that half the positions of the array are empty, it is impossible to insert a new record whose key hashes into an odd integer. Of course, it is unlikely that all the odd positions are occupied while none of the even positions are. However, if the rehash function $rh(i) = mod(i+200,1000)$ is used, each key can be placed in only one of five places [since $mod(x, 1000) = mod(x+1000,1000)$] and it is quite possible for these five places to be full while much of the table is empty.

One property of a good rehash function is that for any index i, the successive rehashes $rh(i)$, $rh(rh(i))$, . . . cover as many of the integers between 0 and $m-1$ (where m is the number of elements in the table) as possible (ideally, all of them). The rehash function $rh(i) = mod(i+1,1000)$ has this property. In fact, any function $rh(i) = mod(i+c,m)$ where c is a constant value such that c and m are relatively prime (i.e., they cannot both be divided evenly by a single integer other than 1) produce successive values that cover the entire table. You are invited to confirm this fact by choosing some examples; the proof is left as an exercise.

There is another measure of the suitability of a rehash function. Consider the case of the rehash function $mod(i+1,m)$. Assuming that the hash function produces indices which are uniformly distributed over the interval 0 through $m-1$ [i.e., it is equally likely that $h(key)$ is any particular integer in that range], then initially, when the entire array is empty, it is equally likely that a random record will be placed at any given empty position within the array. However, once entries have been inserted and several hash clashes have been resolved, this is no longer true. For example, in Figure 9.3.1 it is five times as likely for a record to be inserted at position 994 than at position 401. This is because any record whose key hashes into 990, 991, 992, 993, or 994 will be placed in 994, while only a record whose key hashes into 401 will be placed in that location. This phenomenon, where two keys that hash into different values compete with each other in successive rehashes, is called *clustering*.

The same phenomenon occurs in the case of the rehash function $rh(i) = mod(i+c,m)$. For example, if $m = 1000$, $c = 21$, and positions 10, 31, 52, 73, and 94 are all occupied, any record whose key is any one of these five integers will be placed at location 115. In fact, any rehash function that depends solely on the index to be rehashed causes clustering.

One way to eliminate clustering is to use *double hashing*, which involves the use of two hash functions, $h1(key)$ and $h2(key)$. $h1$, which is known as the *primary* hash function, is used first to determine the position at which the record should be placed. If that position is occupied, the rehash function $rh(i) = mod(i+h2(key),m)$ is used successively until an empty location is found. As long as $h2(key1)$ does not equal $h2(key2)$, records with keys $key1$ and $key2$ do not compete for the same set of locations. This is true despite the possibility that $h1(key1)$ may indeed equal $h1(key2)$. The rehash function depends not only on the index to be rehashed but also on the original key. Note that the value $h2(key)$ does not have to be recomputed for each rehash—it need be computed only once for each key that must be rehashed. Optimally, therefore, one should choose functions $h1$ and $h2$ which distribute the hashes and rehashes uniformly over the interval 0 to $m-1$ and also minimize clustering. Such functions are not always easy to find.

Another approach is to allow the rehash function to depend on the number of times that the function is applied to a particular hash value. In this approach, rh is a function of two arguments. $rh(i,j)$ yields the rehash of the integer i if the key is being rehashed for the jth time. One example is $rh(i,j) = mod(i+j,m)$. The first rehash yields $rh1 = rh(h(key),1) = mod(h(key) + 1,m)$, the second yields $rh2 = mod(rh1+2,m)$, the third yields $rh3 = mod(rh2+3,m)$, and so on.

Resolving Hash Clashes by Chaining

There are several reasons why rehashing may not be an adequate method to deal with hash clashes. First, it assumes a fixed table size. If the number of records grows beyond that size, it is impossible to insert them without allocating a larger table and recomputing the hash values of the keys of all records already in the table using a new hash function. Furthermore, it is difficult to delete a record from such a table. For example, suppose that record $r1$ is at position p. To add a record $r2$ whose key $k2$ hashes into p, it must be inserted into the first free position from among $rh(p)$, $rh(rh(p))$, . . . Suppose that $r1$ is then deleted so that position p becomes empty. A subsequent search for record $r2$ begins at position

$h(k2)$, which is p. But since that position is now empty, the search process may erroneously conclude that record $r2$ is absent from the table.

One possible solution to this problem is to mark a deleted record as "deleted" rather than "empty" and to continue searching whenever a "deleted" position is encountered in the course of a search. But this is feasible only if there are a small number of deletions; otherwise, an unsuccessful search would require a search through the entire table because most positions will be marked "deleted" rather than "empty."

Another method of resolving hash clashes is called ***chaining*** and involves keeping a linked list of all records whose keys hash into the same value. Suppose that the hash function produces values between 0 and $m-1$. Then an array of header nodes of size m, called ***buckets***, is declared. *bucket(i)* points to the list of all records whose keys hash into i. In searching for a record, the list head that occupies position i in the bucket array is accessed and the list that it initiates is traversed. If the record is not found, it is inserted at the end of the list. Figure 9.3.2 illustrates chaining. We assume a 10-element array and that the hash function is *mod(key,10)*. The keys in that figure are presented in the order

$$75 \quad 66 \quad 42 \quad 192 \quad 91 \quad 40 \quad 49 \quad 87 \quad 67 \quad 16 \quad 417 \quad 130 \quad 372 \quad 227$$

We may write a search and insertion algorithm using chaining with a hash function h and a bucket array *bucket* and nodes that contain three fields: k for the key, r for the record, and *nxt* as a pointer to the next node in the list.

```
i = h(key)
q = null
p = bucket(i)
while p <> null do
        if k(p) = key
          then search = p
                return
        endif
        q = p
        p = nxt(p)
endwhile
'the key has not been found, insert a new record
s = getnode
k(s) = key
r(s) = rec
nxt(s) = null
if q = null
  then bucket(i) = s
  else nxt(q) = s
endif
search = s
return
```

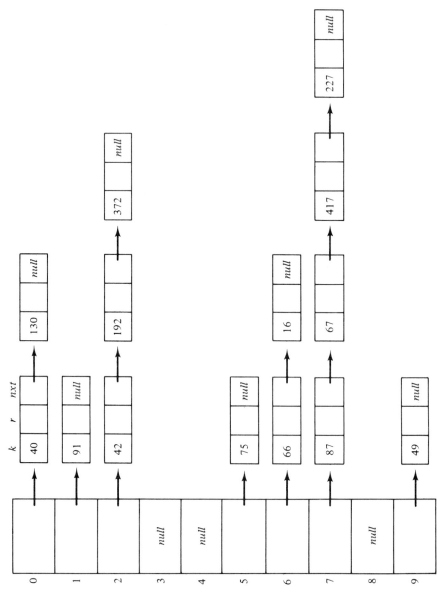

Figure 9.3.2 Resolving hash clashes by chaining.

Deleting a node from a table that is constructed by hashing and chaining involves simply removing a node from a linked list. A deleted node has no effect on the efficiency of the search algorithm; the algorithm continues as though the node had never been inserted. Note that the lists may be reordered dynamically for more efficient searching by the methods of Section 1.

The primary disadvantage of chaining is the extra space that is required for buckets and pointers. However, the initial array is usually smaller in schemes that use chaining than in those that use rehashing. This is because under chaining it is less catastrophic if the entire array becomes full—it is always possible to allocate more nodes and add them to the various lists. Of course, if the lists become very long, the whole purpose of hashing—direct addressing and resultant search efficiency—is defeated.

Choosing a Hash Function

Let us now turn to the question of how to choose a good hash function. Clearly, the function should produce as few hash clashes as possible; that is, it should spread the keys uniformly over the possible array indices. Of course, unless the keys are known in advance, it cannot be determined whether a particular hash function will disperse them properly. However, although it is rare to know the keys before selecting a hash function, it is fairly common to know some properties of the keys which will affect their dispersal.

For example, the most common hash function (which we have used in the examples of this section) uses the *division method*, in which an integer key is divided by the table size and the remainder is taken as the hash value. This is the hash function $h(key) = mod(key,m)$. Suppose, however, that m equals 1000 and that all the keys end in the same three digits (e.g., the last three digits of a part number might represent a plant number, and the program is being written for that plant). Then the remainder on dividing by 1000 will yield the same value for all the keys, so that a hash clash will occur for each record except the first. Clearly, given such a collection of keys, a different hash function should be used. It has been found that the best results with the division method are achieved when the table size m is prime (i.e., m is not divisible by any positive integer other than 1 and m.)

In another hash function, known as the *midsquare method*, the key is multiplied by itself and the middle few digits (the exact number depends on the number of digits allowed in the index) of the square are used as the index. If the square is considered as a decimal number, the table size must be a power of 10, while if it is considered as a binary number, the table size must be a power of 2.

(The reason the number is squared before extracting middle digits is that all digits in the original number contribute in determining the middle digits of the square.) The *folding method* breaks up a key into several segments which are added or exclusive *or*ed together to form a hash value. For example, suppose that the internal bit-string representation of a key is 010111001010110 and 5 bits are allowed in the index. The three bit strings 01011, 10010, and 10110 are exclusive *or*ed to produce 01111, which is 15 as a binary integer. (The *exclusive or* of two bits is 1 if the two bits are different, and 0 if they are the same.)

There are many other hash functions, each with its own advantages and disadvantages, depending on the set of keys to be hashed. One consideration in choosing a hash function is efficiency of calculation; it does no good to be able to find an object on the first try if that try takes longer than several tries in an alternative method.

If the keys are not integers, they must be converted into integers before applying one of the hash functions described above. There are several ways to do this. For example, for a character string the internal bit representation of each character can be interpreted as a binary number. One disadvantage of this is that the bit representations of all the letters or digits tend to be very similar on most computers. If the keys consist of letters alone, the index of each letter in the alphabet can be used to create an integer. Thus the first letter of the alphabet (A) is represented by the digits 01, while the fourteenth (N) is represented by the digits 14. The key "HELLO" is represented by the integer 0805121215. Once an integer representation of a character string exists, the folding or midsquare method can be used to reduce it to manageable size.

EXERCISES

1. Implement the function *mod(x,y)* in BASIC.

2. Write a BASIC routine *search* that searches a hash table, TBLE, for a record with key KEY. The routine inputs an integer key and a table declared by

```
10   MAXTBLE = 99
20   DIM TBLE(MAXTBLE,3)
30      K = 1
40      R = 2
50      F = 3
```

TBLE(I,K) and TBLE(I,R) are the Ith key and record, respectively. TBLE(I,F) equals FALSE if the Ith table position is empty and TRUE if it is occupied. The routine returns a number in the range 0 to MAXTBLE if a record with key KEY is present in the table. If no such record exists, the function returns −1. Assume the existence of a hashing routine *h* and a rehashing routine *rh* both of which produce integers in the range 0 to MAXTBLE.

3. Write a BASIC routine *sinsert* to search and insert into a hash table as in Exercise 2.

4. Develop a mechanism for detecting when all possible rehash positions of a given key have been searched. Incorporate this method into the routines *search* and *sinsert* of Exercises 2 and 3.

5. Suppose that a key is equally likely to be any integer between a and b. Suppose that the midsquare hash method is used to produce a binary integer between 0 and $2^k - 1$. Is the result equally likely to be any integer within that range? Why?

6. Given a BASIC routine that implements a hash function, $h(key)$, for a table of size m:
   (**a**) Write a BASIC simulation program to determine each of the following quantities after $.8m$ random keys have been generated. The keys should be random six-digit integers.

   (1) The precentage of integers between 0 and $m-1$ that do not equal $h(key)$ for some generated key
   (2) The percentage of integers between 0 and $m-1$ that equal $h(key)$ for more than one generated key
   (3) The maximum number of keys that hash into a single value between 0 and $m-1$
   (4) The average number of keys that hash into values between 0 and $m-1$, not including those values into which no key hashes

   (**b**) Run the program to test the uniformity of each of the following hash functions:

   (1) $h(key) = mod(key,m)$ for m a prime
   (2) $h(key) = mod(key,m)$ for m a power of 2
   (3) The folding method using exclusive *or* to produce 5-bit indices, where $m = 32$
   (4) The midsquare method using decimal arithmetic to produce four-digit indices, where $m = 10000$

7. If a hash table contains m positions, and n records currently occupy the table, then the *load factor* is defined as n/m. Show that if a hash function uniformly distributes keys over the m positions of the table and if lf is the load factor of the table, then $(n-1)*lf/2$ of the n keys in the table collided upon insertion with a previously entered key.

8. Assume that n random positions of an m-element hash table are occupied, using hash and rehash functions that are equally likely to produce any index in the table. What is the average number of comparisons needed to insert a new element in terms of m and n? Explain why linear probing does not satisfy this condition.

4. EXAMPLES AND APPLICATIONS

In this section we examine several problems, some of which were discussed in previous chapters, to see how the search techniques of this chapter can be applied to make the solutions more efficient. We examine some trade-offs in time and space among various solutions and show how searching plays an important role in problem solving.

Example 9.4.1: The Huffman Algorithm

Our first example is the Huffman algorithm of Section 6.3. Readers are asked to reread that section to refamiliarize themselves with the problem and the solution presented therein.

We focus our attention on the program *findcode,* especially on the loop that searches for the nodes with smallest FREQ value, controlled by the code FOR I $=$ N $+$ 1 TO 2*N $-$ 1. The nodes of a strictly binary tree with N leafs are represented by the integers between 1 and 2*N $-$ 1. The array FTHER contains pointers to the fathers of the nodes in the tree, and the array INFO contains the information associated with the nodes.

We begin with INFO(I) defined for I between 1 and N and with FTHER(I) equal to 0 for all I. That is, we are given frequencies for the original symbols, each of which is a root of its own single-element binary tree. These nodes are to be combined into a single binary tree. The unoccupied nodes (from N $+$ 1 through 2*N $-$ 1) are thought of as an available list of nodes. The algorithm proceeds through this available list in sequence, setting each node as the father of two previously allocated nodes.

In choosing two previously allocated nodes to set as the sons of a newly allocated node, the program searches the set of nodes without fathers for the two nodes with the smallest FREQ values. We reproduce the section of code that accomplishes this. I is the index of the newly allocated node, P1 and P2 are set to point to the two nodes that are found by the search process, and J1 and J2 are the relative frequencies of *node*(P1) and *node*(P2), respectively.

```
240   J1 = 9999
250   J2 = 9999
260   P1 = 0
270   P2 = 0
280   FOR Q = 1 TO I − 1
290   IF FTHER(Q) = 0
         THEN IF INFO(Q) < J1
               THEN P2 = P1: J2 = J1: P1 = Q: J1 = INFO(Q)
               ELSE IF INFO(Q) < J2 THEN P2 = Q:J2 = INFO(Q)
300   NEXT Q
```

Once the two nodes P1 and P2 are identified, they are set as the sons of node I by the code

```
310   P = I: 'allocate node(P)
320   INFO(P) = J1 + J2: 'compute the frequency of the new node
330   'set P1 to the left subtree of P and P2 to the right subtree
340   FTHER(P1) = − P
350   FTHER(P2) = P
```

The search process is inefficient because each time a new node is allocated, all the previous nodes must be examined in searching for the two root nodes with the smallest frequency.

The first improvement that can be made is to keep a separate list of root nodes [i.e., nodes Q such that FTHER(Q) = 0]. If this is done, we need not search through all allocated nodes—only through those which have no father. Also, the test for whether FTHER(Q) equals 0 can be eliminated from the loop. These benefits are not without disadvantages: extra space is required for the pointers that link together the list of root nodes, and extra time is required to add or delete an element from this list. These are the general disadvantages that must be faced in moving from an array to a list representation: in an array, elements are ordered implicitly, whereas in a list they must be linked explicitly. (However, in this case it is possible to use the FTHER field of all root nodes to link together the list. In the interest of clarity, we do not pursue this possibility here but leave it as an exercise for the reader.)

Thus we may add a variable FIRSTROOT and an array NXTROOT defined by

$$10 \text{ DIM NXTROOT}(2*N-1)$$

NXTROOT(I) is undefined if I is not a root node. If I is a root node, NXTROOT(I) is the next root node after I on the list of root nodes. If I is the last root node on the list, NXTROOT(I) equals 0. FIRSTROOT is the index of the first root node on the list. These variables are initialized as follows:

```
100   FIRSTROOT = 1
110   FOR I = 1 TO N−1
120       NXTROOT(I) = I+1
130   NEXT I
140   NXTROOT(N) = 0
```

The search may then be rewritten as follows. K remains one step behind P in traversing the list of root nodes. K1 and K2 are set to the nodes immediately preceding P1 and P2, respectively, on the list of root nodes. Their values will be used when we remove the nodes P1 and P2 from the list.

```
300   J1 = 9999
310   J2 = 9999
320   P1 = 0
330   P2 = 0
340   K1 = 0
350   K2 = 0
360   K = 0
370   P = FIRSTROOT
380   IF P = 0 THEN GOTO 440
```

```
390   'else traverse the list of root nodes
400      IF INFO(P) < J1
            THEN P2 = P1: J2 = J1: P1 = P: J1 = INFO(P): K2 = K1: K1 = K
            ELSE IF INFO(P) < J2 THEN P2 = P: J2 = INFO(P): K2 = K
410      K = P
420      P = NXTROOT(P)
430   GOTO 380
440   . . .
```

The code to remove nodes P1 and P2 from the list of root nodes, insert them into the binary tree, and insert the new root node I into the list of root nodes becomes more complex. The following code performs these tasks, inserting I in place of P2 and removing P1 from the list entirely.

```
440   'insert I into the binary tree
450   FTHER(P1) = −I
460   FTHER(P2) = I
470   INFO(I) = J1 + J2
480   'replace node (P2) in the list of root nodes by I
490   NXTROOT(I) = NXTROOT(P2)
500   IF K2 = 0 THEN FIRSTROOT = I
                ELSE NXTROOT (K2) = I
510   IF NXTROOT(I) = P1 THEN K1 = I
520   'remove node(P1) from the list of root nodes
530   IF K1 = 0 THEN FIRSTROOT = NXTROOT(P1)
                ELSE NXTROOT (K1) = NXTROOT(P1)
```

This code can be simplified somewhat and made more efficient if the list of root nodes is maintained as a circular list. We leave this implementation as an exercise for the reader.

Further efficiency will be realized if the list of root nodes is kept sorted, ordered by increasing values of the INFO field. Then the search for the two nodes of smallest frequency is eliminated—they are the first two nodes on the list. Thus the entire search loop can be replaced by the two statements

```
300   P1 = FIRSTROOT
310   P2 = NXTROOT(P1)
```

However, to keep the list sorted, the N original symbols must first be sorted using one of the sorting techniques of Chapter 8. Also, each time a new node I is inserted into the list of root nodes, it must be inserted into its proper position. The code to insert I into the binary tree and the ordered root node list therefore becomes

```
320   'insert node(I) into the binary tree
330   FTHER(P1) = −I
340   FTHER(P2) = I
350   INFO(I) = INFO(P1) + INFO(P2)
360   'remove node(P1) and node(P2) from the root
      'node list and insert into that list
370   FIRSTROOT = NXTROOT(P2)
380   K = 0
390   P = FIRSTROOT
400   IF P = 0 THEN GOTO 450
410      IF INFO(P) >= INFO(I) THEN GOTO 450
420      K = P
430      P = NXTROOT(P)
440   GOTO 400
450   IF K = 0 THEN FIRSTROOT = I
               ELSE NXTROOT(K) = I
460   NXTROOT(I) = P
```

Thus the search process has been moved from the first step (finding the two nodes with lowest frequency) to the second (inserting a new node into its proper place). However, in the second step it is not necessary to search through the entire list of root nodes, but rather only until the proper position for the new node is found. Whether or not this is appreciably faster depends on the initial distribution of frequencies. For example, if the initial frequencies are successive integers starting at N, every new root node allocated will have to be placed at the end of the list. In most cases, however, the search time is reduced by a factor of 2.

This saving must be weighed against the cost of initially sorting the N original symbols, which may be quite expensive. As N becomes larger and the saving in search time becomes more worthwhile, the cost of sorting increases. We leave it to the reader to determine which method is more efficient for various values of N.

EXERCISES

1. Rewrite the program implementing the Huffman algorithm with the list of root nodes kept as an unordered circular list.
2. Implement the Huffman algorithm using an ordered list of root nodes using various sort techniques of Chapter 8 to create initially the ordered list.
3. How does the efficiency of the implementations in Exercise 2 vary depending on the distribution of initial frequencies? Can you find a distribution of initial frequencies such that a newly allocated node is always placed at the end of the root node list? Can you find a distribution such that a newly allocated node is always placed at the front of the list? Explain.

4. Modify the Huffman program so that the FTHER field is used to link together all root nodes. The NXTROOT field is no longer necessary.

Example 9.4.2: A Scheduling Problem

Our next example of the application of search techniques is the scheduling problem of Section 7.3. Again, you should reread that section to refamiliarize yourself with the problems and the solutions presented therein.

The primary search problem of the scheduling algorithm is to search through the nodes of a graph represented by a linked data structure. This search takes place at two distinct points in the solution presented in Section 7.3. (We are now focusing our attention on the first solution presented in Section 7.3, in which a singly linked list is used for the graph nodes. This solution is presented in that section as the first BASIC program named *schedule*.)

1. When a precedence relationship is input, indicating that task S1TASK must be performed before task S2TASK, an arc must be drawn from S1TASK to S2TASK. All the nodes in the graph must be searched for nodes with contents S1TASK and S2TASK, respectively. If no nodes with contents S1TASK or S2TASK exist, they must be allocated and added to the list of graph nodes. This search and insertion is performed by the routine *find,* which is called twice from within the loop consisting of statements 250–370. (Actually an immediate saving in efficiency would result if the list of graph nodes were traversed only once for each pair of input tasks to search for both S1TASK and S2TASK simultaneously.)

2. In the output phase of the program (the loop consisting of statements 400–770), the entire list of graph nodes must be searched during each time period to find those nodes whose COUNT field is 0. These nodes are removed from the graph and placed on another list from which they are subsequently printed. As noted in Section 7.3, the only reason that this search is necessary is because a node cannot be removed from a singly linked list without a pointer to its predecessor. This prevents us from placing a node on the output list at the time that its count is reduced to 0, because at that time, we have a pointer only to the node itself and not to its predecessor. One way to eliminate this search, as noted in Section 7.3, is to keep the list of graph nodes as a doubly linked list so that a node contains a pointer to its predecessor as well as to its successor.

A careful analysis of the program *schedule* yields the interesting observation that there is no reason whatever to keep the graph nodes in a list except to perform the two searches noted above. The list of graph nodes is never traversed for any reason other than to search for particular nodes at one of the two points. But since searching an unordered linear list is very inefficient, another way of organizing the graph nodes should improve the search efficiency significantly with no adverse effect on the remainder of the program.

What data structure shall we use to represent the graph nodes? In adding new nodes to the graph (point 1 above), it must be possible to access a graph node from the string which names the task that it represents. Thus the SUBTASK field of the graph node acts as the key to the record, which is the node itself. The most direct way to access a node from its key is by using a hash function. If a hashing method is to be used, we must determine how to handle hash clashes. This consideration leads directly into the issue of the number of graph nodes that are to be allowed. If hash clashes are resolved by rehashing, the number of graph nodes is limited to the number of positions in the hash table. On the other hand, if collisions are resolved by chaining, an unlimited number of graph nodes is permitted.

Since an array implementation was used in Section 7.3, we will adhere to that implementation and use rehashing to resolve collisions. The set of graph nodes is declared by

```
30   DEFSTR S
40   NMAX = 100
50   DIM SUBTASK (NMAX)
60   DIM COUNT(NMAX)
70   DIM ARCPTR(NMAX)
80   DIM NXTNODE(NMAX)
```

The graph nodes are no longer linked together on a list; the pointer NXTNODE in each node is not used until the node is placed into an output list.

We assume the existence of a hash function *hash* which transforms a character string into an integer between 1 and 100 and a rehash function *rehash* which accepts an integer in the same range and returns an integer in that range. Then the routine *find*, to search and insert a node into the graph, can be written as follows:

```
1000   'subroutine find
1010   'inputs: STASK
1020   'outputs: FIND
1030   'locals: CNT, HASH, I, INDEX, J, REHASH
1040   GOSUB 8000: 'subroutine hash accepts STASK and sets the variable HASH
1050   I = HASH
1060   IF SUBTASK(I) = " " THEN SUBTASK(I) = STASK: COUNT(I) = 0:
                                   FIND = I: RETURN
1070   IF SUBTASK(I) = STASK THEN FIND = I: RETURN
1080   CNT = 0
1090   INDEX = I
1100   GOSUB 9000:'subroutine rehash accepts INDEX and sets the variable REHASH
1110   J = REHASH
1120   IF J = I OR CNT = NMAX THEN GOTO 1180
1130      IF SUBTASK(J) = " " THEN SUBTASK(J) = STASK: COUNT(J) = 0:
                                   FIND = J: RETURN
1140      IF SUBTASK(J) = STASK THEN FIND = J: RETURN
1150      INDEX = J
```

```
1160     CNT = CNT + 1
1170   GOTO 1100
1180   PRINT "ERROR- "; STASK;
                          " CANNOT BE INSERTED INTO THE GRAPH"
1190   STOP
1200   'endsub
```

By using this *find* function the input loop can be rewritten with very few changes
from the way it appears in Section 7.3.

By representing a graph using a hash table, the first search problem has
been solved. Let us see how we can solve the second. We first note that when a
node is identified as a candidate for output (i.e., when its COUNT field becomes
0), it can be placed on the output list. However, it is no longer necessary to remove it from the list of graph nodes since there is no list of graph nodes. Since
the input phase and the output phase of the program are separate and no new
nodes are added in the course of processing, it is unnecessary to delete any nodes
from the hash table. (If it were necessary to delete nodes, chaining would be preferable to rehashing as the method for resolving hash clashes.) Thus our second
problem, which was the necessity to traverse the entire set of graph nodes in order to remove a particular node, does not exist.

We may therefore write a revised version of the scheduling program as follows:

```
 10   'program schedule (revised)
 20   DEFSTR S
 30   NMAX = 100
 40   DIM SUBTASK(NMAX)
 50   DIM COUNT(NMAX)
 60   DIM ARCPTR (NMAX)
 70   DIM NXTNODE(NMAX)
 80   AMAX = 200
 90   DIM NDPTR(AMAX)
100   DIM NEXARC(AMAX)
110   AAVAIL = 1
120   FOR I = 1 TO AMAX - 1
130      NEXARC(I) = I + 1
140   NEXT I
150   NEXARC(AMAX) = 0
160   'construct the graph
170   READ S1TASK, S2TASK
180   IF S1TASK = "FINISH" THEN GOTO 280
190      STASK = S1TASK
200      GOSUB 1000: 'subroutine find sets the variable FIND
210      P = FIND
```

```
220    STASK = S2TASK
230    GOSUB 1000:'subroutine find
240    Q = FIND
250    GOSUB 1500: 'subroutine join accepts P and Q
260    COUNT(Q) = COUNT(Q) + 1
270  GOTO 170
280  'the graph has been constructed
     'traverse the hash table and place all graph nodes
     'with zero count on the output list
290  OTPT = 0: 'OTPT points to the output list
300  FOR P = 1 TO NMAX
310      IF SUBTASK(P) = '' '' THEN GOTO 330
320      IF COUNT(P) = 0 THEN NXTNODE(P) = OTPT: OTPT = P
330  NEXT P
340  'simulate the time periods
350  PERIOD = 1
360  IF OTPT = 0 THEN GOTO 630
370     PRINT ''PERIOD'', PERIOD
380     'initialize output list for next period
390     OPNX = 0
400     'traverse the output list
410     P = OTPT
420     IF P = 0 THEN GOTO 590
430       PRINT SUBTASK(P)
440       'traverse arcs emanating from graphnode(P)
450       R = ARCPTR(P)
460       IF R = 0 THEN GOTO 570
470          RR = NEXARC(R)
480          'reduce count in terminating node
490          T = NDPTR(R)
500          COUNT(T) = COUNT(T) − 1
510          'if the count of node(T) is 0, place it on next period's output list
520          IF COUNT(T) = 0 THEN NXTNODE(T) = OPNX: OPNX = T
530          FRARC = R
540          GOSUB 2000: 'subroutine freearc accepts the variable FRARC
550          R = RR
560       GOTO 460
570       P = NXTNODE(P)
580     GOTO 420
590     'reset output list for the next period
600     OTPT = OPNX
610     PERIOD = PERIOD + 1
620  GOTO 360
630  END
700  DATA . . .
```

```
               . . .
1000   'subroutine find

               . . .
1500   'subroutine join

               . . .
2000   'subroutine freearc

               . . .
```

Two points should be noted in passing. Because the list of graph nodes has been eliminated, it is no longer possible to test for cycles. Further, if chaining is used to resolve hash clashes, the list of all graph nodes whose contents hash into the same value must be linked together by their NXTNODE field. Thus we again have the problem of removing a graph node from a list before inserting it into the output list. This can be solved by using doubly linked lists, as indicated in Section 7.3, or by adding another field to each node, as in Exercise 2. An alternative method is to traverse the list of all nodes hashing to the same value from the initial hash bucket. This list should be relatively short and therefore would not involve the same overhead as would a search through the entire list of graph nodes.

EXERCISES

1. Rewrite the program *schedule* of Section 7.3 so that the two list traversals represented by calls to the subroutine *find* in the input loop are combined into a single traversal represented by in-line code.

2. One possible solution to the problem of traversing the list of graph nodes to find those whose COUNT field is 0 is to add another field OUNXT to each graph node, and use it to to link together nodes on the output list. This makes it unnecessary to remove a node from the graph list in order to place it on the output list. Implement this solution as a BASIC program.

3. Modify the program *schedule* in this section so that it detects cycles in the original graph.

Example 9.4.3: An Airline Reservation System

Our next example is the application of search techniques to an airline reservation system. Consider the problem of programming an airline reservation system. The input consists of a control group containing flight data used to initialize the system, followed by a passenger group containing data on passenger reservations. The control group consists of one input line containing a single number (representing the number of flights available that day) followed by a set of input lines (one for each flight) each of which contains a flight number and the seating capacity for that flight. A sample control group is illustrated in Figure 9.4.1(a).

Once this control group has been read, a separate line is read for each passenger request for service. The requests may be of three types: reservation, cancellation, or inquiry. The type of each request is indicated by the word *RESERVE, CANCEL,* or *INQUIRE.* A request for a reservation or a cancellation is accompanied by a passenger name and a flight number. An inquiry is accompanied by a passenger name only. (We assume that a passenger inquires about all the flights on a particular journey, but may cancel one particular leg of the journey.) A sample set of data for a passenger request group is shown in Figure 9.4.1(b).

We are to write a program that processes these two groups of inputs. For each passenger service request, a message describing the action taken is to be printed. Before we proceed with the example, a word of caution is necessary. Because a real-world reservation system must store huge quantities of information, the data are usually kept in an external file system. Thus such a system must be programmed using external search techniques which are not discussed in this text. Furthermore, a large portion of such a system consists of systems programs to handle remote terminals accessing the common data base. That type of programming is also beyond the scope of this text.

Before designing a program, the requirements of the problem must be defined more precisely. In particular, it must be determined what action is to be taken for each of the possible passenger requests. In the case of a reservation, the passenger is to be placed on a flight list for the flight if the flight is not full. If the

DATA	4	
DATA	153	10
DATA	097	50
DATA	860	175
DATA	214	95

(a) Flight control group for airline problem

DATA	"RESERVE"	"JOAN DOE"	097
DATA	"RESERVE"	"JOE JACKSON"	153
DATA	"INQUIRE"	"JOE JACKSON"	
DATA	"CANCEL"	"JOAN DOE"	097

(b) Passenger request group for airline problem

Figure 9.4.1

flight is full, the passenger is to be placed on a waiting list so that he or she will
be placed on the flight if there are any cancellations. In the case of a cancellation,
the passenger is to be deleted from the flight list if he or she is currently booked
on the flight, and the first passenger from the waiting list (if any) is to be placed
on the flight list. If the canceled passenger is on the waiting list, he or she must
be removed from it. Finally, in the case of an inquiry, a list of all flights on
which the passenger is either booked or waiting is to be printed.

Now that we have defined the actions to be taken for the various requests,
we may consider the data organizations that will be necessary. Because the number of flights is fixed, the basic flight data will be maintained in a set of arrays.
Such basic information includes the flight number, the flight capacity, and other
items that do not relate to the reservations of specific passengers. In addition, two
lists are required for each flight: a list of passengers currently booked on the
flight, and a waiting list for the flight. The passenger list has no restrictions as to
where a passenger may be inserted or deleted. The waiting list, however, should
be a queue, so that if a cancellation occurs, the first person on the waiting list will
be the first to be given a seat on the flight. However, we must also have the
capability of deleting a passenger from the middle of the waiting list (in case of a
cancellation). For each flight in the system, it will be necessary to retain pointers
to each of the two lists. Let us see what searches are required by this data organization to service our requests.

For a reservation request, a sequential search must be performed on the array of flight numbers and then the name must be added to a passenger list or a
waiting queue. The sequential array search (which is performed by locating the
index of the flight within the array of flight numbers) is inefficient but not overly
so if the number of flights is small. To improve the speed of the search, the
flights could be stored in an array sorted by flight number, allowing the use of a
binary search. The insertion into the appropriate list is a single operation that involves no searching. Thus the reservation operation can be said to be moderately
efficient under this organization.

For a cancellation request, a sequential search must be performed on the
array of flight numbers and then one or two sequential searches must be performed through the passenger list and the waiting list. These sequential searches
are fairly inefficient.

An inquiry is the least efficient operation under the organization described
above. A sequential search through every single passenger list and many waiting
lists must be performed in searching for a particular name.

To print the passenger list and waiting list for a particular flight, the array of
flight numbers must be searched sequentially to locate the flight. Then the two
lists for the flight must be traversed. Any implementation of this operation is fairly efficient, since the list traversals are part of the problem specification. We
leave the coding of the airline reservation system using the list structures described above as an exercise for the reader.

We would like to develop data structures that will improve the efficiency of a cancellation and an inquiry. To eliminate the sequential array search for a flight number, the table of flights may be kept as a binary search tree as described in Section 2. Whether or not the tree should be balanced depends on the number of flights, the order in which they appear in the input, and the frequency with which searches are made for a particular flight. The question here is whether the efficiency of searching a balanced tree is worth the extra work involved in inserting elements into such a tree. If there are n flights, keeping them as a tree rather than as an array reduces the search time from $O(n)$ to $O(\log n)$. We leave the coding of the main program (which inserts the flights into the tree) and a subroutine *treesearch* (which returns a pointer to the node which represents flight with flight number F in the tree pointed to by TREE) as exercises for the reader.

What information should each flight node contain? In addition to the two list pointers mentioned above, it is also necessary to include left and right tree pointers. (If a balanced binary tree is used, a field containing the balance is also needed.) It is still necessary to have a passenger list emanating from each flight node so that the list may be traversed in constructing a passenger roster. However, since cancellations involve accessing a passenger node through the passenger name, the passenger list must be doubly linked to make it possible to delete a passenger node given only a pointer to that node. Similarly, it is necessary to have doubly linked waiting lists, which must be organized as queues so that the first passenger placed on the waiting list will be the first to get a seat in case of a cancellation. An indication of the capacity and current passenger count on each flight is also needed. Thus we may declare a flight node by

```
30   MAX = 100
40   DIM NUMFLT(MAX): 'flight number
50   DIM FLIGHT(MAX,2): CAPACITY = 1: COUNT = 2: 'info on each flight
60   DIM PSLST(MAX): 'pointer to passenger list
70   DIM WAITLST(MAX,2): FRNT = 1: REAR = 2: 'pointers to waiting list
80   DIM PTRTREE (MAX,2): LFT = 1: RGHT = 2: 'tree pointers
```

In order to make cancellations and inquiries more efficient, it must be possible to access a passenger node directly from the passenger name rather than by traversing a passenger list. In order to do this, the entire passenger list is kept as a hash table. Since it must be possible to remove passengers from a passenger list in case of a cancellation, and since it is not known how many passengers there will be, hash clashes are resolved by chaining rather than by rehashing.

Each passenger node contains the passenger name as well as three pointers: one to the next node on the same passenger list, one to the previous node on the same passenger list, and one to the next node which hashes into the same value. One of these pointer fields doubles as a pointer to the next available free node (if the passenger node is on the available list). It is also necessary to keep an indication in the passenger node of which flight list a particular passenger is associated with and whether he or she is booked or waiting for that flight. This is necessary so that when making an inquiry of the flights that a particular passenger is on, the appropriate messages can be printed directly from the passenger node. Note that this information is unnecessary if a passenger node is accessed only through a flight node rather then directly through its hash. We may therefore declare a passenger node by

```
 70   MPASS = 1000:        'maximum number of passenger nodes
 80   DIM ZPASS(MPASS):    'passenger name
 90   DIM PFLT(MPASS):     'flight number of passenger
100   DIM BOOK(MPASS):     'TRUE if booked, FALSE if waiting
110   DIM PASSPTR(MPASS,3): NXTPASS = 1: PREVPASS = 2: HASHNXT = 3
```

Actually, there is much more information associated with each passenger, such as address, phone number, special meal information, and so on, but we ignore these details here.

Our next decision is one that is crucial in many searching applications—choosing a key for our records. We use the passenger name as the key. Applying a hash function *hash* to a passenger name yields an index of a bucket array. The entry at that index is a pointer to a list of passenger nodes (linked together by the HASHNXT field) all of whose passenger names hashed into the same index. When a search is made for a specific passenger name on a specific flight (as in a cancellation), the passenger name is hashed and this list is traversed searching for the entry for that particular name. All reservations for a given passenger are on the same list. This means that there may be multiple records with the same key, which almost guarantees that hash clashes will occur. Thus the cancellation operation is somewhat inefficient since the chain must be searched sequentially. (The same inefficiency occurs when information is requested about a specific passenger on a specific flight.)

A possible solution to this inefficiency is to combine the passenger name field and the flight number as a single key. Then, when searching for a specific passenger on a specific flight, the combination can be hashed directly. However, in the present situation, such an extended key is impractical. In processing an inquiry for the list of all flights for a given passenger, it would be highly inefficient to combine the given passenger name with every possible flight number to produce a set of keys for hashing. Rather, the passenger name alone is hashed to access to list of all the flights on which the name appears (this list might also contain extraneous nodes representing other passengers whose names happen to hash into the same value, but these nodes can be skipped). The number of flights on which an average passenger is booked is small enough so that in the case of a cancellation, it does not present an overhead significant enough to outweigh the alternative overhead in case of inquiry. This illustrates a general phenomenon in choosing a search key: Placing more information in a key makes it easier to find a very specific item but more difficult to satisfy a general query.

Let us now examine the bucket table. The number of entries in this table should be slightly larger (about 10%) than the number of passenger names kept at any one time. This avoids long lists of names hashing into the same index. The size of the table should also be a prime number since it has been found that taking a remainder upon division by a prime number yields a good distribution of hash values. We arbitrarily assume approximately 900 different passenger names and 1000 passenger nodes to allow for a passenger booked or waiting on several flights (this is very small for a real system) and declare the bucket table by

120   DIM TBLE(1009): *'hash table*

We now present two of the routines that satisfy service requests, leaving the main program and the other routines for the reader as exercises. The first routine, *cancel*, accepts a passenger name and a flight number and removes the passenger's reservation from that flight. We assume the following declarations:

```
 20   DEFSTR Z
 30   MAX = 100
 40   DIM NUMFLT(MAX): 'flight numbers
 50   DIM FLIGHT(MAX,2): CAPACITY = 1: COUNT = 2: 'info on each flight
 60   DIM PSLST(MAX): 'pointer to passenger list
 70   DIM WAITLST(MAX,2): FRNT = 1: REAR = 2: 'pointers to waiting list
 80   DIM PTRTREE(MAX,2): LFT = 1: RGHT = 2: 'tree pointers
 90   MPASS = 1000: 'maximum number of passenger nodes
100   DIM ZPASS(MPASS): 'passenger name
110   DIM PFLT(MPASS): 'flight number of passenger
120   DIM BOOK (MPASS): 'TRUE if booked, FALSE if waiting
130   DIM PASSPTR(MPASS,3): NXTPASS = 1: PREVPASS = 2: HASHNXT = 3:
                                          'pointers between passenger nodes
140   DIM TBLE(1009): 'hash table
150   NULL = 0
160   TRUE = 1
170   FALSE = 0
```

We also assume the routines *hash* and *treesearch* described above, and the existence of an auxiliary list manipulation routine at line 7000 called *delete*, which accepts two pointers XPTR and Y, the first to a flight node and the second to a passenger node and deletes *node*(Y) from either the passenger list or waiting queue [depending on the value of BOOK (Y)] emanating from the *node*(XPTR) without freeing *node*(Y). In addition, we use the routine *freenode*, which accepts a pointer, FRNODE, to a passenger node and returns the node to the available list.

```
3000   'subroutine cancel
3010   'inputs: F, ZNAM: 'flight number and passenger name
3020   'outputs: none
3030   'locals: FPTR, FRNODE, R, S, T, V, XPTR, Y
3040   'find the flight node
3050   GOSUB 5000: 'subroutine treesearch sets the variable FPTR
3060   IF FPTR = 0 THEN PRINT "ILLEGAL FLIGHT NUMBER": RETURN
```

```
3070   'hash the passenger name and search the hash list
3080   GOSUB 6000: 'subroutine hash accepts ZNAM and sets the variable H
3090   R = 0
3100   S = TBLE(H)
3110   'search the passenger list of flights using the hash list
3120   IF S = 0 THEN GOTO 3170
3130      IF ZPASS (S) = ZNAM AND PFLT(S) = F
               THEN GOTO 3180
3140      R = S
3150      S = PASSPTR(S,HASHNXT)
3160   GOTO 3120
3170   PRINT "NO SUCH PASSENGER FOR THAT FLIGHT": RETURN
3180   'at this point, S points to the passenger node.
       'remove the passenger node pointed to by S from the hash table
3190   IF R = 0 THEN TBLE(H) = PASSPTR(S,HASHNXT)
               ELSE PASSPTR(R,HASHNXT) = PASSPTR(S,HASHNXT)
3200   'remove the passenger node from the passenger or waiting list
3210   XPTR = FPTR
3220   Y = S
3230   GOSUB 7000: 'subroutine delete deletes passenger node pointed to
                     'by Y from flight pointed to by XPTR
3240   'the passenger node was on the waiting list
3250   IF BOOK(S) = FALSE
          THEN PRINT ZNAM: "DELETED FROM WAITING LIST OF FLIGHT"; F:
               GOTO 3420
3260   'else do stmts 3270-3410
3270   'node was on the passenger list
3280   PRINT ZNAM; "DELETED FROM FLIGHT"; F
3290   T = WAITLST(FPTR,FRNT)
3300   IF T = 0 THEN FLIGHT (FPTR,COUNT) = FLIGHT(FPTR,COUNT) - 1:
               GOTO 3420
3310   'remove first passenger from waiting list and insert into 'passenger list
3320   XPTR = FPTR
3330   Y = T
3340   GOSUB 7000: 'subroutine delete
3350   BOOK(T) = TRUE
3360   V = PSLST(FPTR)
3370   PSLST(FPTR) = T
3380   PASSPTR(T,PREVPASS) = 0
3390   PASSPTR(T,NXTPASS) = V
3400   IF V <> 0 THEN PASSPTR(V,PREVPASS) = T
3410   PRINT ZPASS(T); "NOW BOOKED ON FLIGHT"; F
3420   'free passenger node and return to the available list
3430   FRNODE = S
```

3440   GOSUB 1000: *'subroutine* freenode *accepts FRNODE*
3450   RETURN
3460   *'endsub*

The next routine we present is for an inquiry. We wish to list all flights on which a given passenger name appears. It is straightforward.

4000   *'subroutine* inquire
4010   *'inputs*: *ZNAM*
4020   *'outputs*: *none*
4030   *'locals*: *H, S*
4040   PRINT ZNAM; "FOUND ON FOLLOWING FLIGHTS":
4050   GOSUB 6000: *'subroutine* hash *accepts ZNAM and sets the variable H*
4060   S = TBLE(H)
4070   *'search through the flights using pointers in hash table*
4080   IF S = 0 THEN GOTO 4130
4090   IF ZNAM <> ZPASS(S) THEN GOTO 4110
4100   IF BOOK(S) = TRUE
                THEN PRINT "BOOKED ON"; PFLT(S)
                ELSE PRINT "WAITING FOR"; PFLT(S)
4110   S = PASSPTR(S,HASHNXT)
4120   GOTO 4080
4130   PRINT "END OF LIST"
4140   RETURN
4150   *'endsub*

EXERCISES

1. Write a BASIC program that implements the airline reservation system in which the passenger lists and the waiting lists are maintained as linear lists.

2. Write a BASIC program that reads a flight control group as described in the text and builds a binary search tree of flight nodes. Modify your routine to build a balanced binary tree.

3. Write a BASIC routine *treesearch* as described in the text.

4. Write the routine *delete* described in the text.

5. Write a BASIC program that accepts a passenger name and cancels all reservations and waiting-list entries for that passenger. What field would you change in the passenger node to make this operation more efficient? Rewrite the routines of this section under the modified representation.

6. Write a BASIC routine that accepts a passenger name and flight number and reserves a seat for the passenger on the flight or puts him or her on the waiting list if the flight is full.

Bibliography

The following bibliography contains books in two subject areas: algorithms and data structures, and introductory BASIC programming. Of course, the BASIC language manual of the microcomputer that you are using is essential in determining the dialect of BASIC available to you and the language features included in that dialect.

1. ALGORITHMS AND DATA STRUCTURES

AHO, A., J. HOPCROFT, AND J. ULLMAN: *Data Structures and Algorithms,* Addison-Wesley, Reading, Mass., 1982.

AHO, A., J. HOPCROFT, AND J. ULLMAN: *The Design and Analysis of Computer Algorithms,* Addison-Wesley, Reading, Mass., 1974.

AUGENSTEIN, M. J., AND A. M. TENENBAUM: *Data Structures and PL/1 Programming,* Prentice-Hall, Englewood Cliffs, N.J., 1979.

BAASE, S.: *Computer Algorithms: Introduction to Design and Analysis,* Addison-Wesley, Reading, Mass., 1978.

BAILEY, T. E., AND K. LUNDGAARD: *Programming Design with Pseudocode,* Brooks/Cole, Monterey, Calif. 1983.

BARON, B. J., AND L. G. SHAPIRO: *Data Structures and Their Implementation,* Prindle, Weber & Schmidt, Boston, 1980.

BEIDLER, J.: *An Introduction to Data Structures,* Allyn and Bacon, Boston, 1982.

BERZTISS, A. T.: *Data Structures, Theory and Practice,* 2nd ed., Academic Press, New York, 1977.

BRILLINGER, P. C., AND D. J. COHEN: *Introduction to Data Structures and Non-numeric Computation*, Prentice-Hall, Englewood Cliffs, N.J., 1972.

COLEMAN, D.: *A Structured Programming Approach to Data*, Macmillan, London, 1978.

DEO, N.: *Graph Theory with Applications to Engineering and Computer Science*, Prentice-Hall, Englewood Cliffs, N.J., 1974.

ELLZEY, R. S.: *Data Structures for Computer Information Systems*, Science Research Associates, Palo Alto, Calif., 1982.

ELSON, M.: *Data Structures*, Science Research Associates, Palo Alto, Calif., 1975.

EVEN, S.: *Graph Algorithms*, Computer Science Press, Rockville, Md., 1978.

FLORES, I.: *Data Structure and Management*, Prentice-Hall, Englewood Cliffs, N.J., 1970.

GOODMAN, S. F., AND S. T. HEDETNIEMI: *Introduction to the Design and Analysis of Algorithms*, McGraw-Hill, New York, 1977.

GOTLIEB, C. C., AND L. B. GOTLIEB: *Data Types and Structures*, Prentice-Hall, Englewood Cliffs., N.J. 1978.

GRILLO, J. P., AND J. D. ROBERTSON: *Data Management Techniques*, Wm. C. Brown, Dubuque, Iowa, 1982.

HARRISON, M. C.: *Data Structures and Programming*, Scott, Foresman, Glenville, Ill., 1973.

HOROWITZ, F., AND S. SAHNI: *Algorithms: Design and Analysis*, Computer Science Press, Rockville, Md., 1977.

HOROWITZ, F., AND S. SAHNI: *Fundamentals of Data Structures*, Computer Science Press, Rockville, Md., 1975.

KERNIGHAN, E., AND P. J. PLAUGER: *Software Tools*, Addison-Wesley, Reading, Mass., 1976.

KNUTH, D. E.: *Fundamental Algorithms*, 2nd ed., Addison-Wesley, Reading, Mass., 1973.

KNUTH, D. E.: *Sorting and Searching*, Addison-Wesley, Reading, Mass., 1973.

LEWIS, T. G., AND M. Z. SMITH: *Applying Data Structures*, Houghton Mifflin, Boston, 1976.

MAURER, H. A.: *Data Structures and Programming Techniques*, Prentice-Hall, Englewood Cliffs, N.J., 1977.

NIJENHUIS, A., AND H. S. WILF: *Combinatorial Algorithms*, Academic Press, New York, 1975.

PAGE, E. S., AND L. B. WILSON: *Information Representation and Manipulation in a Computer*, Cambridge University Press, Cambridge, 1973.

PFALTZ, J. L.: *Computer Data Structures*, McGraw-Hill, New York, 1977.

POLYA, G.: *How to Solve it*, Doubleday, New York, 1957.

REINGOLD, E. M., AND W. J. HANSEN: *Data Structures*, Little, Brown, Boston, 1983.

REINGOLD, E. M., J. NIEVERGELT, AND N. DEO: *Combinatorial Algorithms: Theory and Practice*, Prentice-Hall, Englewood Cliffs, N.J., 1977.

REYNOLDS, J. C.: *The Craft of Programming*, Prentice-Hall, Englewood Cliffs, N.J., 1981.

RICH, R. P.: *Internal Sorting Methods Illustrated with PL/I Programs*, Prentice-Hall, Englewood Cliffs, N.J., 1972.

SEDGEWICK, B.: *Algorithms*, Addison-Wesley, Reading, Mass., 1983.

STANDISH, T. A.: *Data Structure Techniques*, Addison-Wesley, Reading, Mass., 1980.

STONE, H.: *Introduction to Computer Organization and Data Structures*, McGraw-Hill, New York, 1972.

TENENBAUM, A. M., AND M. J. AUGENSTEIN: *Data Structures Using Pascal,* Prentice-Hall, Englewood Cliffs, N.J., 1981.

TREMBLAY, J. P., AND P. G. SORENSON: *An Introduction to Data Structures with Applications,* McGraw-Hill, New York, 1976.

WAITE, W. M.: *Implementing Software for Non-numeric Applications,* Prentice-Hall, Englewood Cliffs, N.J., 1973.

WIRTH, N.: *Algorithms + Data Structures = Programs,* Prentice-Hall, Englewood Cliffs, N.J., 1976.

WIRTH, N.: *Systematic Programming: An Introduction,* Prentice-Hall, Englewood Cliffs, N.J., 1973.

2. BASIC

ALBRECHT, B., L. FINKEL, AND J. R. BROWN: *BASIC for Home Computers: A Self-teaching Guide,* Wiley, New York, 1978.

AMSBURY, W.: *Structured BASIC and Beyond,* Computer Science Press, Rockville, Md., 1980.

CLARK, J. F., AND W. O. DRUM: *BASIC Programming: A Structured Approach,* South-Western, Cincinnati, Ohio, 1983.

GRILLO, J. P., AND J. D. ROBERTSON: *Techniques of BASIC,* Wm. C. Brown, Dubuque, Iowa, 1982.

HENNEFELD, J.: *Using BASIC: An Introduction to Computer Programming,* 2nd ed., Prindle, Weber & Schmidt, Boston, 1981.

KOFFMAN, E. B., AND F. L. FRIEDMAN: *Problem Solving and Structured Programming in BASIC,* Addison-Wesley, Reading, Mass., 1979.

LEDGARD, H. F.: *Programming Proverbs,* Hayden, Rochelle Park, N.J., 1975.

LIEN, D. A.: *The BASIC Handbook: An Encyclopedia of the BASIC Computer Language,* Compusoft Publishing, San Diego, Calif., 1978.

MARATECK, S.: *BASIC,* 2nd ed., Academic Press, New York, 1982.

NEVISON, J. M.: *The Little Book of BASIC Style,* Addison-Wesley, Reading, Mass., 1978.

SHELLY, G. B., AND T. J. CASHMAN: *Introduction to BASIC Programming,* Anaheim Publishing, Brea, Calif., 1982.

Index